Fodor's Japan

Fodor's Travel Publications, Inc.
New York • London • Toronto • Sydney • Auckland

ISBN 0-679-02523-5

Fodor's Japan

Editor: Paula Consolo
Contributors: Hannah Borgeson, Diane Durston, Nigel Fisher, Amy Hunter, Kiko Itasaka, Caroline Liou, Jared Lubarsky, Marcy Pritchard, Linda K. Schmidt, Oliver Statler, Jon Spayde
Creative Director: Fabrizio La Rocca
Cartographer: David Lindroth
Illustrator: Karl Tanner
Cover Photograph: Brian Lovell/Nawrocki Stock Photo

Design: Vignelli Associates

Special Sales

Fodor's Travel Publications are available at special discounts for bulk purchases for sales promotions or premiums. Special editions, including personalized covers, excerpts of existing guides, and corporate imprints, can be created in large quantities for special needs. For more information, contact your local bookseller or write to Special Markets, Fodor's Travel Publications, 201 East 50th Street, New York, NY 10022. Inquiries from Canada should be directed to your local Canadian bookseller or sent to Random House of Canada, Ltd., Marketing Department, 1265 Aerowood Drive, Mississauga, Ontario L4W 1B9. Inquiries from the United Kingdom should be sent to Fodor's Travel Publications, 20 Vauxhall Bridge Road, London, England SW1V 2SA.

MANUFACTURED IN THE UNITED STATES OF AMERICA
10 9 8 7 6 5 4 3 2 1

Contents

Foreword *vi*

Highlights *viii*

Fodor's Choice *x*

Introduction *xxiv*
by Oliver Statler

1 **Essential Information** *1*

Before You Go *2*

Government Information Offices *2*
Tours and Packages *2*
When to Go *4*
National Holidays *5*
Festivals and Seasonal Events *6*
What to Pack *6*
Taking Money Abroad *8*
Getting Money from Home *8*
Currency *9*
What It Will Cost *9*
Passports and Visas *10*
Customs and Duties *11*
Traveling with Cameras *12*
Staying Healthy *12*
Insurance *13*
Car Rentals *15*
Rail Passes *16*
Student and Youth Travel *17*
Traveling with Children *18*
Hints for Travelers with Disabilities *18*
Hints for Older Travelers *20*
Further Reading *21*

Arriving and Departing *22*

From North America by Plane *22*
From the United Kingdom by Plane *25*

Getting Around Japan *25*

By Train *25*
By Plane *26*
By Bus *26*
By Ferry *26*
By Taxi *27*
By Car *27*

Staying in Japan *27*

Tourist Information *27*
Language *28*

Addresses *30*
Telephones *30*
Mail *31*
Dining *31*
Lodging *32*
Credit Cards *36*
Tipping *36*
Shopping *36*
Opening and Closing Times *37*
Sports *37*
Bathhouses *39*
Hot Springs *39*
Customs, Manners, and Etiquette *40*
Doing Business *40*

Great Itineraries *42*

2 Portraits of Japan *47*

Japan at a Glance: A Chronology *48*

"The Discreet Charm of Japanese Cuisine," by Diane Durston *51*

"The Springs of Ecstasy," by Simon Winchester *64*

3 Tokyo *70*

4 Tokyo Excursions *208*

Nikko *209*
Kamakura *220*
Yokohama *231*
Fuji-Hakone-Izu National Park *240*

5 Nagoya, Ise-Shima, and the Kii Peninsula *258*

6 The Japan Alps *284*

7 Kyoto *321*

8 Nara *385*

9 Osaka *401*

10 Kobe *428*

11 Western Honshu *441*

12 Shikoku *479*

13 Kyushu *495*

14 Tohoku *524*

15 Hokkaido *560*

Japanese Vocabulary *601*

Index *612*

Maps

Japan *xvi–xvii*
Tokyo *xviii–xix*
Kansai *xx–xxi*
World Time Zones *xxii–xxiii*
Tokyo Overview *72–73*
Tokyo Subways *80–81*
Imperial Palace *90–91*
Akihabara and Jimbocho *99*
Ueno *104*
Asakusa *114*
Tsukiji and Shimbashi *123*
Nihombashi, Ginza, and Yurakucho *129*
Roppongi, Akasaka, and Aoyama *136–137*
Shibuya and Harajuku *143*
Shinjuku *149*
Tokyo Shopping *158*
Tokyo Dining *170–171*
Tokyo Lodging *184–185*
Nikko Area *212*
Kamakura *223*
Yokohama *236*
Fuji-Hakone-Izu National Park *243*
Nagoya *262*
Nagoya Excursions *266*
Japan Alps *290–291*
Takayama *297*
Kanazawa *300*
Kyoto *324–325*
Eastern Kyoto *330*
Western Kyoto *341*
Central Kyoto *348*
Kyoto Dining *366–367*
Kyoto Lodging *377*
Nara *390*
Western Nara Temples *395*
Osaka *408*
Kobe *432*
Western Honshu *445*
Hiroshima *452*
Shikoku *484*
Kyushu *498*
Nagasaki *504*
Tohoku *529*
Sapporo *569*
Hokkaido *576–577*

Foreword

We wish to express our gratitude to those who helped prepare this guide: Maria Heffner and the New York staff of the Japan National Tourist Organization (JNTO); the JNTO Tokyo staff, especially Mihoko Suzuki; and Morris Simoncelli of Japan Airlines.

While every care has been taken to ensure the accuracy of the information in this guide, the passage of time will always bring change, and consequently, the publisher cannot accept responsibility for errors that may occur.

All prices and opening times quoted here are based on information supplied to us at press time. Hours and admission fees may change, however, and the prudent traveler will avoid inconvenience by calling ahead.

Fodor's wants to hear about your travel experiences, both pleasant and unpleasant. When a hotel or restaurant fails to live up to its billing, let us know and we will investigate the complaint and revise our entries where the facts warrant it.

Send your letters to the editors of Fodor's Travel Publications, 201 East 50th Street, New York, NY 10022.

Highlights and Fodor's Choice

Highlights

A lot has changed since 1992, when the bubble burst on Japan's runaway speculative economy. The Japanese are more thoughtful now about what they spend on travel and entertainment, and while prices remain high, the slowdown offers other benefits for the foreign visitor. Hotels have more vacancies; trains and domestic flights are less crowded; taxis in the nightlife and restaurant quarters are easier to wave down.

Transportation

Japan spread its welcome mat a bit wider in December 1992, with the opening of a second terminal building at Tokyo's **Narita International Airport.** The new terminal is home to Japan Airlines (JAL) and All-Nippon Airways (ANA), the carriers of choice for most Japanese travelers. The new terminal is conveniently located above a new train station where the superfast Narita Express and other trains pull in. Meanwhile, the construction of two new runways, held up for years by land acquisition problems, is still being delayed; these will open in 1995 at the very earliest.

Tokyo's **Haneda Airport,** which handles more than 41 million passengers a year, has also been expanded to ease congestion. This expansion includes the new West Terminal, which at press time was scheduled to open by October 1993. It will be accessed via an underground walkway from the main terminal and by the monorail from downtown Tokyo.

Some of the congestion in Tokyo's airports may be relieved with the completion of Osaka's new **Kansai International Airport,** but at press time this project was beset by cost overruns and technical problems and was still behind schedule. It is now expected to open for business in late summer of 1994.

New on the rails is the ***Nozomi,*** the fastest of the Shinkansen trains. It speeds at 280 kph (175 mph) along the Tokyo–Hakata corridor. Tickets for the *Nozomi* cost about 17% more than tickets for the regular Shinkansen trains, and the *Nozomi* is not covered by the JR Rail Pass.

It may become less expensive, however, to travel between the railway stations and your hotel. The Japanese government is considering a move to deregulate **taxi fares,** which would create competition among taxi companies. Tokyo is likely to be the first area where deregulation is instituted.

Accommodations

To meet the travel passion of the Japanese as well as overseas visitors, some 50 major hotels have opened around Japan in the past three years. The hotel that made the biggest headlines in Tokyo is the **Four Seasons Chinzan-so,** which poses a serious challenge for the capital's older top hotels. In Sapporo, the **Ramada Renaissance** is a recent welcome addition, and in Osaka, the 500-room **Hyatt Regency** is scheduled to open in mid-1994 as part of Cosmo Square, a newly reclaimed commercial district close to the World Trade Center.

Sights Sporting enthusiasts should check out the new **Fukuoka Dome,** Japan's first dome with a retractable roof. Located in the Seaside Momochi District of Fukuoka, it can hold a crowd of 52,000 fans.

New sights in Tokyo include the **Tokyo-Edo Museum,** which holds exhibits that highlight the history, culture, and evolution of the capital of Japan. The main part of the museum is in Ryugoku, but it also has a branch in Koganei, where you'll find reproductions of 13 historical buildings, including a farmhouse from the Edo period.

In keeping with Japanese tradition, every 20 years the **Ise Jingu Shrines** in Ise-shi are rebuilt, and in 1993 the reconstruction was once again completed.

Plans are underway for a new museum in Osaka that will bring visitors to the city's Ebie Sewage Treatment Plant, west of Umeda. Called the **Sewage Science Museum,** the five-story building will include a labyrinth of mock sewers for visitors to crawl through and a rooftop greenhouse with fish living in purified sewage water. The 1995 opening date is set to commemorate the centennial of Osaka's modern waste removal system.

Lifestyles Entrepreneur of the year award goes to Ms. Yuko Sawada, whose company, **Home-A-Loan,** offers Japanese "wanna be" travelers the experience of living abroad without the hassle, danger, and expense (?) of actually going anywhere. The Home-A-Loan Company rents Tokyo-area apartments previously tenanted by foreigners, adds a few more touches of verisimilitude, and then provides clients with a month-long living experience "overseas." Residents of the Beverly Hills Bungalow, for example, arrive to find *People* magazine on the coffee table, Pepto-Bismol in the medicine chest, and Jell-O and Hungry-Man dinners in the refrigerator. Kensington Mews tenants will find Olde English props—pipe racks and wall-to-wall leather-bound Dickens volumes—and can dine on steak and kidney pie from the freezer. At Calcutta Condo the thermostat is pushed to the max, TV Bombay is piped in, and the closets are filled with saris. Sawada has even rigged apartment telephones so that local calls are charged at overseas rates, helping authenticate the experience by discouraging "travelers" from calling neighbors to chat. So far, 350 clients have purchased Home-A-Loan experiences, shelling out almost as much money as a real overseas holiday would have cost. But then they don't get jet lag. Unless of course, they follow her "jet-lag guidelines," designed to ensure clients arrive at their destinations appropriately desiccated, weary, and addled. The jet-lag feature is optional, and there is no extra charge.

Fodor's Choice

No two people will agree on what makes a perfect vacation, but it's fun, and it can be helpful, to know what others think. We hope you'll have a chance to experience some of Fodor's Choices yourself while visiting Japan. We have tried to offer something for everyone and from every price category. For more information about each entry, refer to the appropriate chapters (listed in the margin) within this guidebook.

Sights

Tokyo	Noh by Torchlight
	Omotesando District
	Tsukiji Fish Market
Kamakura	Daibutsu (Great Buddha)
Yokohama	Bay Bridge by night
Fuji-Hakone-Izu	Dogashima, Izu Peninsula
	Mt. Fuji reflected in Lake Kawaguchi
	Togendai Gondola, Hakone
Nagoya	Dorokyo Gorge, Kii Peninsula
	Cherry Blossoms at Mt. Yoshino
	Ukai Fishing, Gifu and Kiso River
Japan Alps	Chubu-Sangaku National Park, Kamikochi
	Kiso Valley Old Post Villages
	Sado Skyline Drive, Sado Island
	Shirakawa Gassho-mura, Ogimachi
	Takayama
Kyoto	Gion Corner
	Arashiyama
	Nishiki-koji Food Market
Osaka	National Bunraku Theater
	Cherry Blossoms at the Mint Garden
Kobe	Kitano
	Portliner Monorail to Port Island
Western Honshu	Carp in the Tsuwanogawa River
	Torii Gate, Itsukushima Jinja Shrine, Miyajima
	Hagi Pottery Town

	Kurashiki
Kyushu	Mt. Aso
Tohoku	Matsushima Bay
	Tono Basin (old farmhouses)
Hokkaido	Akan Traverse, Akan National Park
	Ice Floes in the Sea of Ohkutsk
	Mating Dance of the Red-crested Crane (Tancho), Kushiro Great Marsh
	Orofure Pass, Skikotsu-Toya National Park
	Sounkyo Gorge, Daisetsuzan National Park

Temples and Shrines

Tokyo	Hie Jinja Shrine
	Sengakuji Temple
	Sensoji Temple
	Yasukuni Jinja Shrine
Nikko	Toshogu Shrine
	Futaarasan Shrine
	Rinnoji Temple
Kamakura	Engakuji Temple
	Hasedera Temple
	Kenchoji Temple
	Tsurugaoka Hachimangu Shrine
Nagoya	Grand Shrines at Ise (Ise Jingu Shrine), Ise
	Mt. Koya Temples
	Tagata Jinga Shrine, Tagata
Japan Alps	Myoryuji Temple (Ninjadera), Kanazawa
	Zenkoji Temple, Nagano
Kyoto	Ginkakuji Temple (Silver Pavilion)
	Jakko-in Temple
	Kinkakuji Temple (Gold Pavilion)
	Kiyomizudera Temple
Nara	Horyuji Temple
	Kasuga Taisha Shrine
	Todaiji Temple
Osaka	Shintennoji Shrine
Western Honshu	Dashoin Temple, Hagi

	Itsukushima Jinja Shrine, Miyajima
	Izumo Taisha Shrine
	Taikodani-Inari Jinja Shrine, Tsuwano
Shikoku	Kotohiragu Shrine, Kotohira
Tohoku	Hojusan Risshakuji Temple, Yamagata

Buildings and Monuments

Tokyo	Imperial Palace
	Kabuki-za Theater
Nagoya	Inuyamajo Castle, Inuyama
Japan Alps	Matsumotojo Castle, Matsumoto
	Samurai Houses, Kanazawa
Kyoto	Katsura Detached Villa
	Kawai Kanjiro Memorial House
	Nijojo Castle
Osaka	Osakajo Castle
Western Honshu	A-Bomb Dome, Hiroshima
	Himejijo Castle, Himeji
	Matsuejo Castle, Matsue
	Meimei-an Tea House, Matsue
Shikoku	Kochijo Castle, Kochi
	Kompira O-Shibai Kabuki Theater, Kotohira
Kyushu	Glover Mansion, Nagasaki
	Kumamotojo Castle, Kumamoto
Tohoku	Hirosakijo Castle, Hirosaki
	Samurai Houses, Kakunodate
	Storehouses, Kitakaka

Museums

Tokyo	Tokyo National Museum
	Nezu Institute of Fine Arts
	Yamatane Museum of Art
Fuji-Hakone-Izu	Hakone Open-Air Museum, Chokoku-no-mori
	MOA Art Museum, Atami
Japan Alps	Hida Minzoku-mura (Folk Village), Takayama
	Japan Ukiyo-e Museum, Matsumoto
	Seisonkaku Villa, Kanazawa

Kyoto	Kyoto Museum of Traditional Industry
	Kyoto National Museum
Western Honshu	Kurashiki Folkcraft Museum, Kurashiki
	Ohara Art Museum, Kurashiki
	Peace Memorial Museum, Hiroshima
Hokkaido	Ainu Folklore Museum, Shiraoi

Parks and Gardens

Tokyo	Garden of Denbo-in Temple
	Nezu Institute of Fine Arts Garden
	New Otani Hotel
	Shinjuku Gyoen Garden
Kamakura	Hokokuji Temple Gardens
Yokohama	Sankeien Garden
Japan Alps	Gyokusenen Garden, Kanazawa
	Kenrokuen Garden, Kanazawa
Kyoto	Heian Jingu Shrine Garden
	Ryoanji Temple Garden
Nara	Nara-Koen Park
Western Honshu	Korakuen Garden, Okayama
	Shizuki-Koen Park, Hagi
Shikoku	Ritsurin-Koen Garden, Takamatsu
Kyushu	Suizenji Gardens, Kumamoto

Dining

Tokyo	Attore *(Very Expensive)*
	Inakaya *(Very Expensive)*
	Heichinrou *(Expensive)*
	Sasashu *(Expensive)*
Kamakura	Tori-ichi *(Moderate–Expensive)*
Nagoya	Koraku *(Very Expensive)*
	Yaegaki *(Expensive)*
Japan Alps	Tsubajin, Kanazawa *(Very Expensive)*
	Suzaki, Takayama *(Expensive)*
	Miyoshian, Kanazawa *(Moderate)*
Kyoto	Heihachi-Jaya *(Moderate–Expensive)*
	Ogawa *(Moderate–Expensive)*

	Yagenbori *(Moderate–Expensive)*
	Nishiki *(Moderate)*
	Sagano *(Moderate)*
	divo-diva *(Inexpensive–Moderate)*
Nara	Onjaku *(Very Expensive)*
	Yanagi-chaya *(Moderate)*
Osaka	Rose Room *(Very Expensive)*
	The Seasons *(Very Expensive)*
	Tako-ume *(Moderate)*
Kobe	Aragawa *(Very Expensive)*
	Salaam *(Moderate)*
	Wang Thai *(Inexpensive)*
Western Honshu	Mitakiso Ryokan, Hiroshima *(Expensive)*
	Kanawa Restaurant, Hiroshima *(Moderate)*
Kyushu	Togasaku Honten, Kumamoto *(Very Expensive)*
	Shikairo, Nagasaki *(Inexpensive–Moderate)*
Hokkaido	Izakaya Karumaya, Sapporo *(Moderate)*

Lodging

Tokyo	Four Seasons Hotel Chinzan-so *(Very Expensive)*
	Hotel Okura *(Very Expensive)*
	Palace Hotel *(Very Expensive)*
	Hotel Ginza Ocean *(Moderate)*
Fuji-Hakone-Izu	Ryokan Naraya, Miyanoshita *(Very Expensive)*
	Ryokan Sanyoso, Izu-Nagaoka *(Very Expensive)*
	Taikanso Ryokan, Atami *(Very Expensive)*
	Fujiya Hotel, Miyanoshita *(Very Expensive)*
Nagoya	Nagoya Castle Hotel *(Expensive–Very Expensive)*
	Rengejoin Temple, Koyasan *(Moderate)*
	Asanaro Minshuku, Kashikojma *(Inexpensive)*
Japan Alps	Ryokan Asadaya, Kanazawa *(Very Expensive)*
	Ryokan Kinkikan, Takayama *(Very Expensive)*
	Hotel Fujiya, Nagano *(Moderate–Very Expensive)*
Kyoto	Tawaraya *(Very Expensive)*
	Hotel Fujita Kyoto *(Expensive)*
	Kyoto Brighton Hotel *(Expensive)*

Hirota Guest House *(Inexpensive)*

Nara Edo-San *(Expensive)*

Kankaso *(Expensive)*

Nara Hotel *(Expensive)*

Osaka Hotel New Otani Osaka *(Very Expensive)*

Osaka Hilton International *(Very Expensive)*

Kobe Hotel Okura Kobe *(Very Expensive)*

Oriental Hotel *(Expensive)*

Western Honshu Iwaso Ryokan, Miyajima *(Expensive–Very Expensive)*

Ryokan Kurashiki, Kurashiki *(Expensive)*

Marusei Ryokan, Kasumi *(Moderate)*

Minshuku Susa, Susa *(Inexpensive–Moderate)*

Minshuku Genroku Bekkan, Kundani *(Inexpensive)*

Kyushu Sakamoto-ya, Nagasaki *(Very Expensive)*

Clio Court Hotel, Fukuoka *(Moderate)*

Sakaeya, Beppu *(Inexpensive)*

Tohoku Ryokan Matsushimajo, Matsushima *(Moderate–Expensive)*

Sukayu Onsen, Hachimantai *(Moderate–Expensive)*

Fukuzanso Inn, Tono *(Moderate)*

Hokkaido Grand Hotel, Sapporo *(Very Expensive)*

Harbor View Hotel, Mombetsu *(Moderate)*

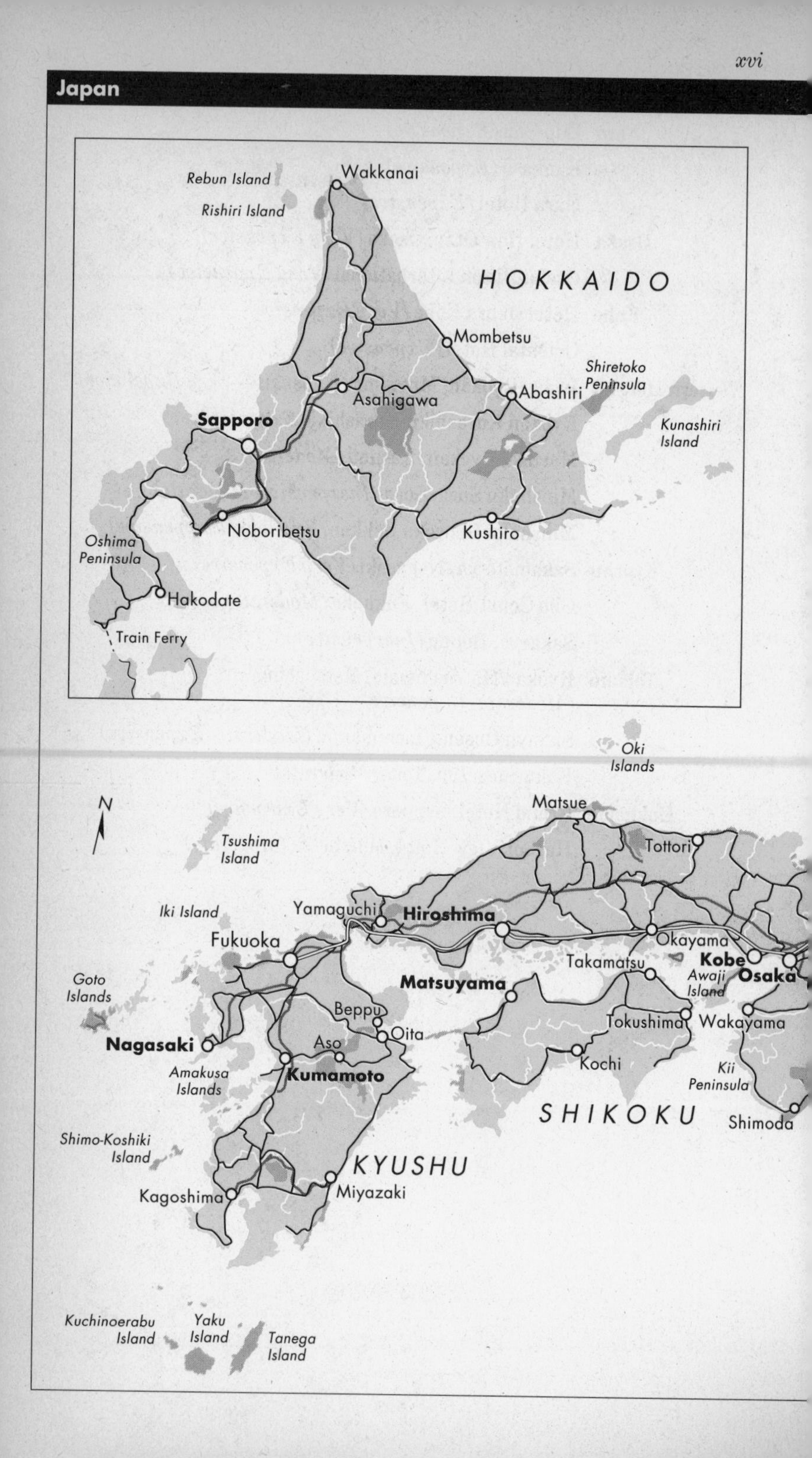
Japan
Rebun Island
Wakkanai
Rishiri Island
HOKKAIDO
Mombetsu
Shiretoko Peninsula
Abashiri
Asahigawa
Kunashiri Island
Sapporo
Noboribetsu
Kushiro
Oshima Peninsula
Hakodate
Train Ferry
Oki Islands
N
Matsue
Tsushima Island
Tottori
Iki Island
Yamaguchi
Hiroshima
Fukuoka
Okayama
Takamatsu
Kobe
Goto Islands
Matsuyama
Awaji Island
Osaka
Beppu
Tokushima
Wakayama
Nagasaki
Oita
Aso
Kochi
Amakusa Islands
Kumamoto
Kii Peninsula
SHIKOKU
Shimoda
Shimo-Koshiki Island
KYUSHU
Kagoshima
Miyazaki
Kuchinoerabu Island
Yaku Island
Tanega Island

HOKKAIDO
(see inset)
Hakodate
Tsugaru Peninsula
Shimokita Peninsula
Sea of Japan
Aomori
Akita
Morioka
Sado Island
Niigata
Yamagata
Sendai
Noto Peninsula
Fukushima
Kanazawa
Toyama
Nikko
Nagano
Utsunomiya
Fukui
Matsumoto
Takayama
Maebashi
Oyama
Mito
Gifu
Kofu
Kyoto
Tokyo
Nagoya
Mt. Fuji
Chiba
Yokohama
Nara
Tsu
Shizuoka
Izu Peninsula
Oshima Island
HONSHU
PACIFIC OCEAN
KEY
JR Trains
Shinkansen (Bullet Train)
Roads
0
50 miles
0
75 km

Tokyo
0
1 mile
0
1 km
N
Mejiro-dori Ave.
Mejiro
Takadanobaba
Waseda-dori Ave.
Okubo
Shin-Okubo
Seibu-Shinjuku
Ome-kaido Ave.
SHINJUKU
Shinjuku
Yashuku
Ichigaya
Shinjuku-dori Ave.
ICHIBAN-CHO
Yoyogi
Shinjuku Gyoen Garden
Yotsuya
Sendagaya
Shinanomachi
Akasaka Palace
Meiji Shrine Inner Garden
Meiji-dori Ave.
Meiji Shrine Outer Garden
Aoyama-dori Ave.
Sotobori-dori Ave.
Akasaka-mitsuke
Yoyogi Park
Aoyama-Itchome
AKASAKA
Harajuku
HARAJUKU
Meiji-Jingu-mae
Gaien-Higashi-dori Ave.
AOYAMA
Omotesando
SHIBUYA
Shibuya
Roppongi
ROPPONGI
HIROO
KEY
JR Trains
Shinkansen (Bullet Train)
Subway
Private rail line
Daikanyama

ASAKUSA
Koishikawa Botanical Gardens
Hongo-dori Ave.
Uguisudani
Showa-dori Ave.
Kappabashi-dori Ave.
Hakusan-dori Ave.
Ueno Park
UENO
Ueno
Kiyosubashi-dori Ave.
Asakusa-dori Ave.
Kasuga-dori Ave.
Korakuen Garden
YUSHIMA
Okachi-machi
Suidobashi
Kuramae-dori Ave.
Iidabashi
Ochanomizu
AKIHABARA
Jimbocho
JIMBOCHO
Akihabara
Asakusa bashi
Kanda
HAMA-CHO
IMPERIAL PALACE
Tokyo
Nihombashi
NIHOMBASHI
Uchibori-dori Ave.
Chuo-dori Ave.
Showa-dori Ave.
Hibiya
YURAKUCHO
Yurakucho
EITAI
Sumidagawa River
Eitai-dori Ave.
Hibiya Park
Ave.
GINZA
Ave.
Tsukiji
Ohashi-dori
SHIMBASHI
Shimbashi
ETCHUJIMA
TSUKIJI
Shin
Kiyosumi-dori Ave.
Hibiya-dori
Hama Rikyu Garden
Hamamatsucho
Shiba Rikyu Garden
HARUMI
TOYOSU

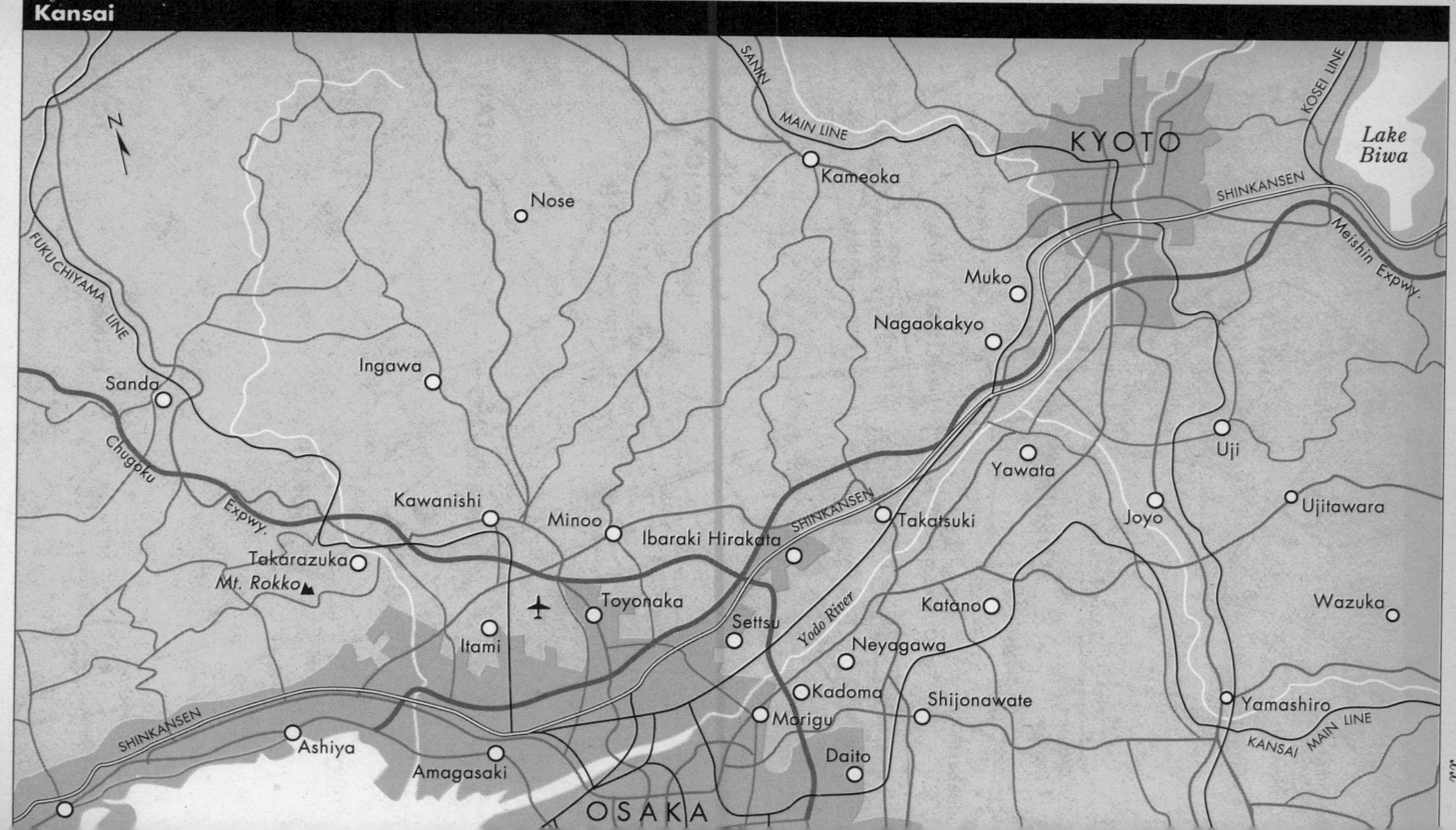

Kansai
N
KYOTO
Lake Biwa
KOSEI LINE
SANIN MAIN LINE
SHINKANSEN
Meishin Expwy.
Kameoka
Nose
Muko
Nagaokakyo
FUKUCHIYAMA LINE
Ingawa
Sanda
Uji
Yawata
Chugoku Expwy.
Kawanishi
Minoo
Ibaraki
Hirakata
Takatsuki
Joyo
Ujitawara
Takarazuka
Mt. Rokko
Toyonaka
Itami
Settsu
Yodo River
Katano
Wazuka
Neyagawa
Kadoma
Shijonawate
Yamashiro
KANSAI MAIN LINE
Morigu
Ashiya
Amagasaki
Daito
OSAKA

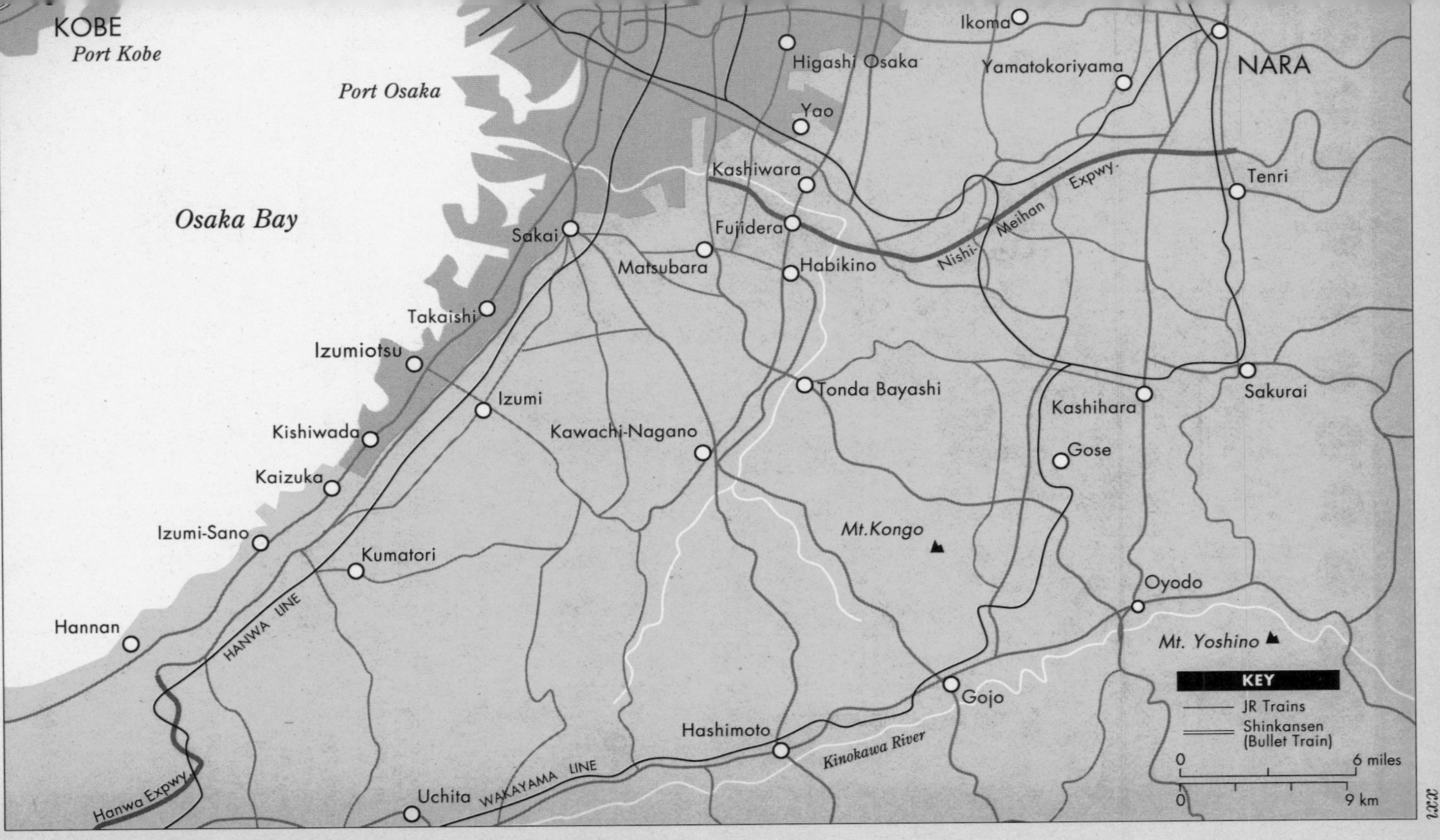
KOBE
Port Kobe
Port Osaka
Osaka Bay
Ikoma
Higashi Osaka
Yamatokoriyama
NARA
Yao
Kashiwara
Tenri
Nishi-Meihan Expwy.
Sakai
Fujidera
Matsubara
Habikino
Takaishi
Izumiotsu
Izumi
Tonda Bayashi
Kashihara
Sakurai
Kishiwada
Kawachi-Nagano
Gose
Kaizuka
Mt.Kongo
Izumi-Sano
Kumatori
Oyodo
Hannan
HANWA LINE
Mt. Yoshino
KEY
JR Trains
Shinkansen (Bullet Train)
Gojo
Hashimoto
Kinokawa River
Hanwa Expwy.
Uchita
WAKAYAMA LINE
0
6 miles
0
9 km

World Time Zones

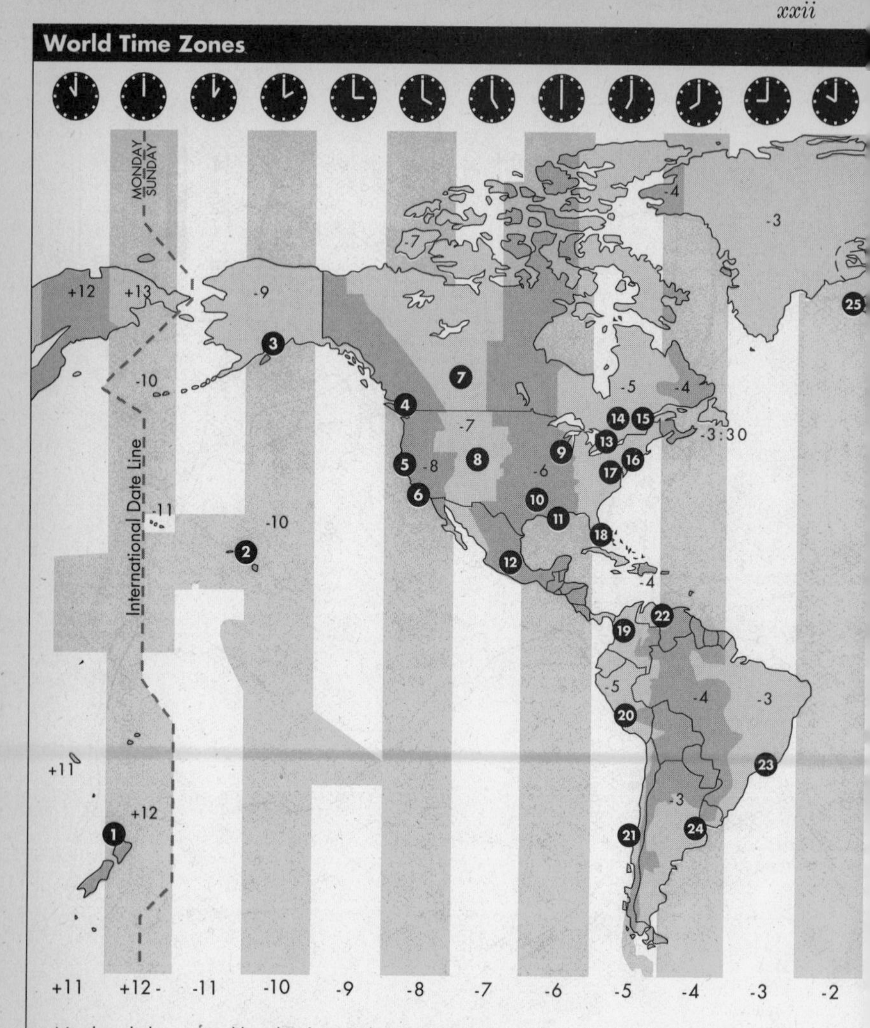

Numbers below vertical bands relate each zone to Greenwich Mean Time (0 hrs.). Local times frequently differ from these general indications, as indicated by light-face numbers on map.

Algiers, **29**
Anchorage, **3**
Athens, **41**
Auckland, **1**
Baghdad, **46**
Bangkok, **50**
Beijing, **54**
Berlin, **34**
Bogotá, **19**
Budapest, **37**
Buenos Aires, **24**
Caracas, **22**
Chicago, **9**
Copenhagen, **33**
Dallas, **10**
Delhi, **48**
Denver, **8**
Djakarta, **53**
Dublin, **26**
Edmonton, **7**
Hong Kong, **56**
Honolulu, **2**
Istanbul, **40**
Jerusalem, **42**
Johannesburg, **44**
Lima, **20**
Lisbon, **28**
London (Greenwich), **27**
Los Angeles, **6**
Madrid, **38**
Manila, **57**

Mecca, **47**
Mexico City, **12**
Miami, **18**
Montréal, **15**
Moscow, **45**
Nairobi, **43**
New Orleans, **11**
New York City, **16**
Ottawa, **14**
Paris, **30**
Perth, **58**
Reykjavík, **25**
Rio de Janeiro, **23**
Rome, **39**
Saigon (Ho Chi Minh City), **51**
San Francisco, **5**
Santiago, **21**
Seoul, **59**
Shanghai, **55**
Singapore, **52**
Stockholm, **32**
Sydney, **61**
Tokyo, **60**
Toronto, **13**
Vancouver, **4**
Vienna, **35**
Warsaw, **36**
Washington, D.C., **17**
Yangon, **49**
Zürich, **31**

Introduction

By Oliver Statler

Currently a resident of Honolulu, Oliver Statler has lived in Japan, off and on, for more than 18 years. His several books include Japanese Inn, Shimoda Story, *and* Japanese Pilgrimage.

I first came to Japan after World War II, when it was an occupied country. My most vivid memory is of the industrial area between Yokohama and Tokyo. As far as the eye could see on both sides of the highway, the flat earth was black. The only structures standing were the chimneys of factories the firebombs had consumed.

Like everyone else in the occupying force, I was comfortably housed and amply fed. But for the Japanese, food and clothing were scarce, and housing was at a premium. Faces were gray, and foreign correspondents reported an air of hopelessness. Those close to Prime Minister Shigeru Yoshida have told how, after a day of coping with Japan's problems and occupation officials, he sometimes smoked his postprandial cigar while pacing the garden of his official residence, looking out over ruined Tokyo, and muttering, "Will it ever be rebuilt? Will it ever be rebuilt?"

I came with curiosity about the nation I had been fighting against, but with precious little knowledge of it. I intended to stay only the two years called for by my contract. The two years stretched to 11. My involvement with Japan became lifelong.

Looking back, I can trace three paths that drew me into this fascinating, beautiful, and exasperating country. The first was Japan's contemporary prints. The moment I saw a small exhibition, I fell in love with them. I began collecting, I was able to meet many of the artists, and I formed bonds of friendship that endure to this day. My first book, *Modern Japanese Prints*, grew out of this enthusiasm.

The second path led to the Minaguchi-ya, a *ryokan*, the Japanese inn whose story I eventually set down. Frustrated because I never could get a reservation at any of the Western-style resort hotels the occupation authorities had taken over (they had overlooked none and had declared every other hostelry in the country off-limits to us), I found, one lucky day, a small advertisement announcing that the Minaguchi-ya had been placed "on-limits" (by the small detachment of American military police stationed in the nearby city, I learned later; they wanted to use the inn). The Minaguchi-ya was a considerable distance from Yokohama, where I was based, and the red tape encountered in getting there was formidable, but I made it, and another love affair began. That was my introduction to the ryokan, and I remain addicted to the special delights of those uniquely Japanese retreats: the quiet elegance of traditional Japanese architecture; the personal service that eschews lobbies and restaurants to coddle you in your rooms, where all attention is focused on you; and the fine food, beautifully served.

The third path took me to the Kabuki theater, which, not at first but at second or third sight, enthralled me and still does. There I found glorious stagecraft put to dramatizing the long and engrossing history of Japan. I had been lured into that history by the story of the Minaguchi-ya; Kabuki quickened my interest by showing me, in action, the princely feudal lords called *daimyo*, their samurai, and commoners of every calling—merchants, farmers, artisans, gamblers, ruffians, and acquiescent waitresses.

I mention my own experiences because I am convinced that pursuing one's personal interests is the best way of meeting Japan. Few of us share with Japan the kind of cultural linkage that bonds us to Europe and the Middle East. For most of us, our ancestors, our language, our heroes, our folklore, and our way of thinking are Western, and it takes some effort to appreciate the equally great civilizations of the East. The handiest bridge is an interest already formed. Whatever it may be—pottery, food, religion, railroads, music, gardens, or marketing—pursuing it can add depth and zest to travel.

The Japanese themselves have always been avid tourists: you must not be surprised to find yourself vastly outnumbered at any popular spot. The Japanese think of travel as education. "If you love your son, let him travel," says one of their proverbs, and there is a corollary: "A traveler is without shame." Travel offers a release from the inhibitions and restraints at home; it's a license to misbehave that is sometimes exercised.

In days past, when travel was difficult—almost entirely on foot and sometimes sharply restricted by feudal regulation—most literate travelers kept a diary (a practice I suggest to you). Most, of course, were personal efforts to waken memories later or to share with family or friends. But some were "public diaries" meant to be published, like the diaries of Samuel Pepys and Daniel Defoe. Among these are some of the masterpieces of Japanese literature. Two favorites of mine are *The Tosa Diary*, about a journey in 935, and *The Narrow Road to the Deep North* (as the title is commonly translated), written 754 years later, in 1689.

The first is by a nobleman and distinguished poet named Tsurayuki, about his journey home to the capital after serving for five years as the governor of the distant province of Tosa (now Kochi Prefecture) on the Pacific side of the island of Shikoku. The second was written by Japan's most famous haiku poet, Basho, the man who raised the 17-syllable verse into art.

Basho shaped and even fictionalized his diary to reflect the landscape of his mind as well as the landscape he journeyed through. Tsurayuki, too, used fictional techniques; he pretended that his diary was written by a woman, perhaps because he considered that a central theme—sorrow over the loss of a little daughter who had died in Tosa—could best be expressed by a mother, and perhaps because he chose to write in colloquial Japanese instead of the elevated style expected of an educated man.

Both are poetic diaries. Both men turned to poetry when their feelings were too intense to be expressed in prose. This was not unusual, for in their times any cultured man was supposed to be able to toss off a poem when the occasion called for it. Even today a great deal of poetry is written by amateurs—shopkeepers, politicians, housewives, businessmen—just for the love of it.

I do not put much faith in analyses that attempt to explain the Japanese character and personality. Of course, in some ways the Japanese are different from us because their history and their culture are different, but human beings are human beings, and we have much more in common than we have differences.

Still, the Japanese do have their particular hang-ups and idiosyncrasies. They explain many of these by the fact that they are a homogeneous people. Certainly just about everybody has black hair (unless henna or age has intervened), which, as a friend has remarked, makes for a neat-looking crowd. Because of their homogeneity and because they have lived so closely together for so long, they maintain that they are so attuned to each other that much need not be said: nuance in tone or phrase conveys unspoken meaning. There is truth in this, but if it were totally true there would be no misunderstandings between the Japanese, which is not the case. It is also true that in the West what is unspoken is often more meaningful than what is said, and we, too, have our formulas for avoiding the overt. When casual acquaintances part by saying, "Let's get together sometime," they both understand that they have no intention of planning another meeting.

Because the Japanese have their own nuances, the foreigner would do well to listen carefully; if there is a shadow of a doubt, it's best to probe a bit for the real meaning. The Japanese may consider this gauche, but it is preferable to a misunderstanding. As has been pointed out, the Japanese often say yes to mean that they understand you, not that they agree with you.

Japan is all islands—more than 3,300 of them, of which about 440 are inhabited. The four biggest are Hokkaido, in the north; Honshu, curving south and west; Kyushu, in the west; and Shikoku, smallest of the four, cradled between Honshu and Kyushu across the Inland Sea. The mountaintops that are these islands are themselves very mountainous. Plains are few: The Japanese can cultivate only about 16% of the land they live on. Today that 16% is crowded, but in early centuries it was more than adequate and very attractive to immigrants. And so, long after the land bridge had disappeared, people kept coming in boats. A hundred miles of dangerous sea divide southern Korea and northern Kyushu, but that is the part of Japan closest to the Asian continent, and it was the gateway for both people and culture entering from the continent. Its ports were busy with a continuing flow of settlers and innovations. In that area, metals first replaced stone for making tools and weapons, and hunting and foraging gave way to the cultivation of rice in wet fields. Farming made people stop roaming and settle down in communities—little "kingdoms"—which promptly started to fight each other. As the strong conquered the weak, a few powerful fiefdoms emerged. For a long time, northern Kyushu was the most advanced area of Japan. It is where Japan began.

Legends tell us that the group of clans that produced the imperial family originated in Kyushu and fought their way eastward along the Inland Sea to the inviting plain where eventually rose the cities of Nara, Osaka, and Kyoto. In an area called Yamato, they dug in and asserted their right to rule all Japan.

The early history of Japan is still shrouded in mist that archaeologists and historians are patiently working to disperse, but we know that the Yamato group was not unchallenged. There were other centers of power. Separately, they gave way, some to force of arms, some to persuasion and concession.

What remains for all to see are two great Shinto shrines, which symbolize forces once surely locked in conflict. The Ise Shrine on the Pacific coast is the shrine of the imperial family; one complex of the shrine is dedicated to the family's legendary ancestress, the Sun Goddess, and is the shrine of the victors. The Izumo Shrine on the Sea of Japan, the opposite side of Honshu, is dedicated to the legendary adversary of the Sun Goddess, her unruly brother; it is usually considered the shrine of a people who yielded politically but held on to their gods and their identity. Both shrines are magnificent, but they are different. Ise celebrates light, while Izumo embodies brooding power. Ise and Izumo are high on my list of important places.

Today, politically, economically, socially, everything in Japan heads up in Tokyo. There is much talk of decentralization and of invigorating the provincial cities, but decentralization seems mostly to end with extending Tokyo's sprawl by pushing some government installations to satellite cities.

Today, Tokyo is more than ever the heart of things; it's the site of government, the financial center, the preeminent headquarters for business, the magnet for intellectuals, the focus of the arts. It is Washington, New York, and Boston rolled into one. It pulses with energy and runs on split-second schedules, yet turn a corner and you find a neighborhood where housewives trade gossip as they shop for the day's groceries in mom-and-pop stores that spill into the street. The city has been called ugly, but I do not agree. It has grand vistas, spacious parks, inviting residential areas, and a giddy mix of architecture that ranges from the cheerfully vulgar and outrageously fantastic to the strong and innovative. It offers more to do than any resident can possibly keep up with, much less a visitor. Above all, Tokyo is exciting; it is never dull.

When people ask me, "Where can I find the *real* Japan?" they usually have in mind the idyllic: thatch-roofed farmhouses set in verdant paddy fields. My answer probably surprises them. "Tokyo," I say. "Today, Tokyo is the real Japan."

1 Essential Information

Before You Go

Government Information Offices

Tourist Information Contact the **Japan National Tourist Organization** (JNTO) for information on travel to and in Japan.

In the U.S. 630 Fifth Ave., Suite 2101, New York, NY 10111, tel. 212/757–5640; 401 North Michigan Ave., Chicago, IL 60601, tel. 312/222–0874; 2121 San Jacinto St., Suite 980, Dallas, TX 75201, tel. 214/754–1820; 360 Post St., Suite 401, San Francisco, CA 94108, tel. 415/989–7140; 624 South Grand Ave., Suite 2640, Los Angeles, CA 90017, tel. 213/623–1952.

In Canada 165 University Ave., Toronto M5H 3B8, Ontario, tel. 416/366–7140.

In the U.K. 167 Regent St., London W1R 7FD England, tel. 071/734–9638.

U.S. Government Travel Briefings The U.S. Department of State's **Citizens Emergency Center** issues Consular Information Sheets, which cover crime, security, and health risks as well as embassy locations, entry requirements, currency regulations, and other routine matters. For the latest information, stop in at any U.S. passport office, consulate, or embassy; call the interactive hotline (tel. 202/647–5225); or, with your PC's modem, tap into the Bureau of Consular Affairs's computer bulletin board (tel. 202/647–9225).

Tours and Packages

Should you buy your travel arrangements to Japan packaged or do it yourself? There are advantages either way. Buying packaged arrangements saves you money, particularly if you can find a program that includes exactly the features you want. You also get a pretty good idea of what your trip will cost from the outset. Generally, you have two options: fully escorted tours and independent packages. Escorted tours are most often via motorcoach, with a tour director in charge. They're ideal if you don't mind having limited free time and traveling with strangers. Your baggage is handled, your time rigorously scheduled, and most meals planned. Such tours are therefore the most hassle-free way to see a destination, as well as generally the least expensive. Independent packages allow plenty of flexibility. They generally include airline travel and hotels, with certain options available, such as sightseeing, car rental, and excursions. Such packages are usually more expensive than escorted tours, but your time is your own.

While you can book directly through tour operators, you will pay no more to go through a travel agent, who will be able to tell you about tours and packages from a number of operators. Whatever program you ultimately choose, be sure to find out exactly what is included: taxes, tips, transfers, meals, baggage handling, ground transportation, entertainment, excursions, sports or recreation (and rental equipment if necessary). Ask about the level of hotel used, its location, the size of its rooms, the kind of beds, and its amenities, such as pool, room service, or programs for children, if they're important to you. Find out the operator's cancellation penalties. Nearly everyone charges them, and the only way to avoid them is to buy trip-cancellation insurance (*see* Trip Insurance, *below*). Also ask about the single supplement, a surcharge assessed to solo travelers. Some operators do not make you pay it if you agree to be matched up with a roommate of the same sex, even if one is not found by departure time. Remember that a program that has features you won't use, whether for rental sporting equipment or discounted museum admissions, may not be the most cost-wise choice for you. Don't buy a Rolls-Royce, even at a reduced price, if all you want is a Chevy.

Fully Escorted Tours

Escorted tours are usually sold in three categories: deluxe, first-class, and tourist or budget class. The most important differences are the price, of course, and the level of accommodations. Some operators specialize in one category, while others offer a range. Many escorted tours visit Japan as part of a larger Asia/Orient package.

Contact **Abercrombie & Kent** (1520 Kensington Rd., Oak Brook, IL 60521, tel. 800/323-7308 or 708/954-2944) and **Maupintour** (Box 807, Lawrence, KS 66044, tel. 800/255-4266 or 913/843-1211) in the deluxe category; **American Express Vacations** (300 Pinnacle Way, Norcross, GA 30071, tel. 800/241-1700), **Globus-Gateway** (95-25 Queens Blvd., Rego Park, NY 11374, tel. 800/221-0090 or 718/268-7000), **InterPacific Tours** (111 E. 15th St., New York, NY 10003, tel. 800/221-3594 or 212/953-6010), **Nawas International** (formerly Pacific Orient Tours, 777 Post Rd., Darien CT 06820, tel. 800/221-4984 or 203/656-3033), and **Pacific Delight Tours** (132 Madison Ave., New York, NY 10016, tel. 800/221-7179 or 212/684-7707) in the first-class category; and **Cosmos,** a sister company of Globus (*see above*), in the budget category.

For U.K. Residents

Among the many companies offering packages to Japan and the Orient from Great Britain are: **Japan Travel Bureau** (10 Maltravers St., London WC2R 3EE, tel. 071/836-9367), **Kuoni Travel Ltd.** (Kuoni House, Dorking, Surrey RH5 4AZ, tel. 0306/740888), **British Airways Holidays** (Atlantic House, Hazelwick Ave., Three Bridges, Crawley, W. Sussex RH10 1NP, tel. 0293/611611), and **Travelsphere Ltd.** (Compass House, Rockingham Road, Market Harborough, Leicestershire LE16 7QD, tel. 0858/410818).

Independent Packages

Independent packages, which travel agents call FITs (for foreign independent travel), are offered by airlines, tour operators who may also do escorted programs, and any number of other companies from large, established firms to small, new entrepreneurs.

Contact **Delta Dream Vacations** (tel. 800/872-7786), **Fair Town Tours** (17 Elizabeth St., Room 608, New York, NY 10013, tel. 800/882-6868 or 212/226-2007), **InterPacific** (111 E. 15th St., New York, NY 10003, tel. 800/221-3594 or 212/953-6010), **Japan & Orient Tours** (2131 Camino del Rio N., Suite 1080, San Diego, CA 92108, tel. 800/377-1080 or 619/282-3131), **Pacific Delight Tours** (*see above*), **Pacific Select** (120 W. 45th St., 9th floor, New York, NY 10036, tel. 800/722-4349 or 212/575-2460), **TBI Tours** (787 Seventh Ave., New York, NY 10019, tel. 800/223-0266 or 212/489-1919), and **Visitours** (tour division of Japan Airlines, tel. 800/367-4368).

Special-Interest Travel

Special-interest programs may be fully escorted or independent. Some require a certain amount of expertise, but most are for the average traveler with an interest and are usually hosted by experts in the subject matter. When the program is escorted, it enjoys the advantages and disadvantages of all escorted programs; because your fellow travelers are apt to be passionate or knowledgeable about the subject, they can prove as enjoyable a part of your travel experience as the destination itself. The price range is wide, but the cost is usually higher—sometimes a lot higher—than for ordinary escorted tours and packages, because of the expert guiding and special activities.

Cultural **Journeys East** (2443 Fillmore St., #289, San Francisco, CA 94115, tel. 510/601–1677 or 415/647–9565) offers tours of Japan covering everything from museum visits to soaking in hot springs.

Journeys (4011 Jackson, Ann Arbor, MI 48103, tel. 800/255–8735 or 313/665–4407) offers cultural and adventure programs to Japan.

Music **Dailey-Thorp** (330 W. 58th St., New York, NY 10019, tel. 212/307–1555) offers music tours, usually opera, to Japan.

Golf **InterPacific** (*see above*) does golf programs that combine Japan and Hong Kong.

Trekking **Mountain Travel/Sobek Expeditions** (6420 Fairmount Ave., El Cerrito, CA 94530, tel. 800/227–2384 or 510/527–8100) offers treks through the Northern Alps region that often include visits to hot springs resorts.

When to Go

The best seasons to travel to Japan are spring and fall, when the weather is at its best. In the spring, the country is warm, with only occasional showers, and flowers grace landscapes in both rural and urban areas. The first harbingers of spring are plum blossoms in early March; cherry blossoms follow, beginning in Kyushu and usually arriving in Tokyo by mid-April. Summer brings on the rainy season, with particularly heavy rains and mugginess in July. Fall is a welcome relief, with clear blue skies and beautiful foliage. Occasionally a few surprise typhoons occur in early fall, but the storms are usually as quick to leave as they are to arrive. Winter is gray and chilly, with little snow in most areas. Temperatures rarely fall below freezing.

For the most part, the climate of Japan is temperate and resembles the East Coast of the United States. The exceptions are the subtropical southern islands of Okinawa, located south of Kyushu, and the northern island of Hokkaido, where it snows for several months in the winter and is pleasantly cool in the summer.

It is best not to travel at times when most Japanese are vacationing. For the most part, Japanese cannot select when they want to take their vacations; they tend to do so on the same holiday dates. As a result, airports, planes, trains, and hotels are booked far in advance and are extremely crowded. Many businesses, shops, and restaurants are closed during these holidays. Holiday periods include the few days before and after New Year's; Golden Week, which follows Greenery Day (April 29); and mid-August at the time of the Obon festivals, when many Japanese return to their hometowns. Travel at these times should be avoided as much as possible.

Climate What follows are the average daily maximum and minimum temperatures for major cities in Japan.

Tokyo									
	Jan.	46F	8C	**May**	72F	22C	**Sept.**	78F	26C
		29	-2		53	12		66	19
	Feb.	48F	9C	**June**	75F	24C	**Oct.**	70F	21C
		30	-1		62	17		56	13
	Mar.	53F	12C	**July**	82F	28C	**Nov.**	60F	16C
		35	2		70	21		42	6
	Apr.	62F	17C	**Aug.**	86F	30C	**Dec.**	51F	11C
		46	8		72	22		33	1

Kyoto									
	Jan.	48F	9C	**May**	75F	24C	**Sept.**	82F	28C
		35	2		56	13		68	20
	Feb.	53F	12C	**June**	82F	28C	**Oct.**	74F	23C
		32	0		66	19		53	12
	Mar.	59F	15C	**July**	93F	34C	**Nov.**	62F	17C
		40	4		72	22		46	8
	Apr.	65F	18C	**Aug.**	89F	32C	**Dec.**	53F	12C
		44	7		74	23		33	1

Fukuoka									
	Jan.	53F	12C	**May**	74F	23C	**Sept.**	80F	27C
		35	2		57	14		68	20
	Feb.	58F	14C	**June**	80F	27C	**Oct.**	74F	23C
		37	3		68	20		53	12
	Mar.	60F	16C	**July**	89F	32C	**Nov.**	65F	18C
		42	6		75	24		48	9
	Apr.	62F	17C	**Aug.**	89F	32C	**Dec.**	53F	12C
		48	9		75	24		37	3

Sapporo									
	Jan.	29F	-2C	**May**	60F	16C	**Sept.**	72F	22C
		10	-12		40	4		51	11
	Feb.	30F	-1C	**June**	70F	21C	**Oct.**	60F	16C
		13	11		50	10		40	4
	Mar.	35F	2C	**July**	75F	24C	**Nov.**	46F	8C
		20	-7		57	14		29	-2
	Apr.	51F	11C	**Aug.**	78F	26C	**Dec.**	33F	1C
		32	0		60	16		18	-8

Information Sources For current weather conditions for cities in the United States and abroad, plus the local time and helpful travel tips, call the **Weather Channel Connection** (tel. 900/932–8437; 95¢ per minute) from a touch-tone phone.

National Holidays

When a holiday falls on a Sunday, it is celebrated on the following Monday.

Jan. 1. New Year's Day is the "festival of festivals" for the Japanese. Some women dress in traditional kimonos, and many people visit shrines and hold family reunions. Although the day is solemn, streets are often decorated with pine twigs, plum branches, and bamboo stalks.

Jan. 15. Adults' Day honors those who have reached the voting age of 20.

Feb. 11. National Foundation Day celebrates accession to the throne by the first emperor.
Mar. 21 (or 20). Vernal Equinox Day celebrates the start of spring.
Apr. 29. Greenery Day. The first day of **Golden Week,** when many people are taking vacation and hotels, trains, and attractions are crowded. Not a good week to visit Japan.
May 3. Constitution Memorial Day. This day commemorates the adoption of the Japanese constitution.
May 5. Children's Day. Families with little boys display paper or cloth carp on bamboo poles outside the house or a set of warrior dolls inside the home.
Aug. 13–16. The Obon Festival, a time of Buddhist ceremonies in honor of ancestors. Many Japanese take off the entire week to travel to their home towns. Tourists should avoid this time.
Sept. 15. Respect for the Aged Day.
Sept. 23 (or 24). Autumnal Equinox Day.
Oct. 10. Health-Sports Day commemorates the Tokyo Olympics of 1964.
Nov. 3. Culture Day, a fairly new holiday, encourages the Japanese to cherish peace, freedom, and culture, both old and new.
Nov. 23. Labor Thanksgiving Day is recognized by harvest celebrations in some parts of the country.
Dec. 23. The Emperor's Birthday.
Dec. 27. Osho-Gatsu, the first day of the week-long New Year celebrations. Travel not recommended.

Festivals and Seasonal Events

Festivals are very important to the Japanese, and a large number are held throughout the year. Many of these festivals originated in folk and religious rituals and date back hundreds of years. Gala festivals take place annually at Buddhist temples and Shinto shrines. Because festivals offer a unique glimpse into Japanese culture and traditions, you should consider dates and places for festivals when you are planning your trip. Contact the nearest branch of the Japan National Tourist Organization (*see* Tourist Information, *above*) for further information.

What to Pack

Clothing Pack light, because porters can be hard to find and baggage restrictions on international flights are tight. What you pack depends more on the time of year than on any dress code. For travel in the cities, pack as you would for an American or European city. At more expensive restaurants and nightclubs, men will usually need to wear a jacket and tie, and women will need a dress or skirt. Conservative-colored clothing is recommended for both men and women to wear at business meetings. Casual clothes are fine for sightseeing. Jeans are as popular in Japan as they are in the United States and are perfectly acceptable for informal dining and sightseeing. Although there are no strict dress codes for visiting temples and shrines, you will be out of place in shorts or immodest outfits. For sightseeing, leave sandals and open-toe shoes behind; you'll need sturdy walking shoes for the gravel pathways that surround the temples and fill the parks. Make sure to bring comfortable clothing that isn't too tight to wear in traditional Japanese restaurants, where you may need to sit on tatami-matted floors. For beach and mountain resorts, pack informal clothes for both day and evening wear.

Japanese do not wear shoes in private homes or in many of the temples and traditional inns. Having shoes you can quickly slip in and out of is a decided advantage. For winter visits, take some wool socks along to help you through those shoeless occasions.

Miscellaneous If you're a morning coffee addict, take along packets of instant coffee. Hotels often provide a thermos of hot water and bags of green tea in every room, but for coffee you'll have to either call room service (which can be expensive) or buy very sweet coffee in a can from a vending machine. If you're staying in a Japanese inn, they probably won't have coffee, and it may be hard to find in rural areas.

Although sunglasses, sunscreen lotions, and hats are readily available, you're better off buying them at home, because they're much more expensive in Japan. It's a good idea to carry a couple of plastic bags to protect your camera and clothes during sudden cloudbursts.

It is not customary to tip in Japan, but it is a good idea to take along small gift items, such as scarves or perfume sachets, to reward someone who has been attentive to you.

Bring an extra pair of eyeglasses or contact lenses. If you have a health problem that may require you to purchase a prescription drug, pack enough to last the duration of the trip, or have your doctor write a prescription using the drug's generic name, since brand names vary from country to country. And don't forget to pack a list of the addresses of offices that supply refunds for lost or stolen traveler's checks.

Electricity The electrical current is 100 volts, 50 cycles alternating current (AC) in eastern Japan, and 100 volts, 60 cycles in western Japan; the United States runs on 110-volt, 60-cycle AC current. Wall outlets in Japan accept plugs with two flat prongs, like in the United States, but do not accept U.S. three-prong plugs.

Luggage *Regulations* Free baggage allowances on an airline depend on the airline, the route, and the class of your ticket. In general, on domestic flights and on international flights to and from the United States, you are entitled to check two bags—neither exceeding 62 inches, or 158 centimeters (length + width + height), or weighing more than 70 pounds (32 kilograms). A third piece may be brought aboard as a carryon; its total dimensions are generally limited to less than 45 inches (114 centimeters), so it will fit easily under the seat in front of you or in the overhead compartment. There are variations, so ask in advance. The single rule, a Federal Aviation Administration safety regulation that pertains to carry-on baggage on U.S. airlines, requires that carryons be properly stowed and allows the airline to limit allowances and tailor them to different aircraft and operational conditions. Charges for excess, oversize, or overweight pieces vary, so inquire before you pack.

If you are flying between two foreign destinations, note that baggage allowances may be determined not by piece but by weight, which generally allows 88 pounds (40 kilograms) of luggage in first class, 66 pounds (30 kilograms) in business class, and 44 pounds (20 kilograms) in economy. If your flight between two cities abroad *connects* with your transatlantic or transpacific flight, the piece method still applies.

Taking Money Abroad

Traveler's Checks Although you will want plenty of cash when visiting small cities or rural areas, traveler's checks are usually preferable. The most widely recognized are **American Express, Barclay's, Thomas Cook,** and those issued by major commercial banks such as **Citibank** and **Bank of America.** American Express also issues *Traveler's Cheques for Two*, which can be countersigned and used by you or your traveling companion. Some checks are free; usually the issuing company or the bank at which you make your purchase charges 1% of the checks' face value as a fee. Be sure to buy a few checks in small denominations to cash toward the end of your trip, when you don't want to be left with more foreign currency than you can spend. Always record the numbers of checks as you spend them, and keep this list separate from the checks.

Currency Exchange Banks and bank-operated exchange booths at airports and railroad stations are usually the best places to change money. Hotels, stores, and privately run exchange firms typically offer less favorable rates.

Before your trip, pay attention to how the dollar is doing vis-à-vis Japan's currency. If the dollar is losing strength, try to pay as many travel bills as possible in advance, especially the big ones. If it is getting stronger, pay for costly items overseas, and use your credit card whenever possible—you'll come out ahead, whether the exchange rate at which your purchase is calculated is the one in effect the day the vendor's bank abroad processes the charge, or the one prevailing on the day the charge company's service center processes it at home.

To avoid lines at airport currency-exchange booths, arrive in a foreign country with a small amount of the local currency already in your pocket—a so-called tip pack. **Thomas Cook Currency Services** (630 Fifth Ave., New York, NY 10111, tel. 212/757-6915) supplies foreign currency by mail.

Getting Money from Home

Cash Machines Automated-teller machines (ATMs) are proliferating; many are tied to international networks such as **Cirrus** and **Plus.** You can use your bank card at ATMs away from home to withdraw money from an account and get cash advances on a credit-card account (providing your card has been programmed with a personal identification number, or PIN). Check in advance on limits on withdrawals and cash advances within specified periods. Ask whether your bank-card or credit-card PIN number will need to be reprogrammed for use in the area you'll be visiting—a possibility if the number has more than four digits. Remember that on cash advances you are charged interest from the day you get the money from ATMs as well as from tellers. And note that, although transaction fees for ATM withdrawals abroad will probably be higher than fees for withdrawals at home, Cirrus and Plus exchange rates tend to be good.

Be sure to plan ahead: Obtain ATM locations and the names of affiliated cash-machine networks before departure. For specific foreign Cirrus locations, call 800/424–7787; for foreign Plus locations, consult the Plus directory at your local bank.

American Express Cardholder Services The company's **Express Cash** system lets you withdraw cash and/or traveler's checks from a worldwide network of 57,000 American Express dispensers and participating bank ATMs. You must *enroll first* (call 800/227–4669 for a form and allow two weeks for processing). Withdrawals are charged not to your card but to a designated bank account. You can withdraw up to $1,000 per seven-day period on the basic card, more if your card is gold or platinum. There is a 2% fee (minimum $2.50, maximum $10) for each cash transaction, and a 1% fee for traveler's checks (except for the platinum card), which are available only from American Express dispensers.

At AmEx offices, cardholders can also cash personal checks for up to $1,000 in any seven-day period (21 days abroad); of this $200 can be in cash, more if available, with the balance paid in traveler's checks, for which all but platinum cardholders pay a 1% fee. Higher limits apply to the gold and platinum cards.

Wiring Money You don't have to be a cardholder to send or receive an **American Express MoneyGram** for up to $10,000. To send one, go to an American Express MoneyGram agent, pay up to $1,000 with a credit card and anything over that in cash, and phone a transaction reference number to your intended recipient, who needs only to present identification and the reference number to the nearest MoneyGram agent to pick up the cash. There are MoneyGram agents in more than 60 countries (call 800/543–4080 for locations). Fees range from 5% to 10%, depending on the amount and how you pay. You can't use American Express, which is really a convenience card—only Discover, MasterCard, and Visa credit cards.

You can also use **Western Union.** To wire money, take either cash or a check to the nearest office. (Or you can call and use a credit card.) Fees are roughly 5%–10%. Money sent from the United States or Canada will be available for pick up at agent locations in Japan within minutes. (Note that once the money is in the system it can be picked up at *any* location. You don't have to miss your train waiting for it to arrive in City A, because if there's an agent in City B, where you're headed, you can pick it up there, too.) There are approximately 20,000 agents worldwide (call 800/325–6000 for locations).

Currency

The unit of currency in Japan is the yen (¥). There are bills of ¥10,000, ¥5,000, and ¥1,000. Coins are ¥500, ¥100, ¥50, ¥10, ¥5, and ¥1. Japanese currency floats on the international monetary exchange, so changes can be dramatic. At press time the exchange rate was about ¥100 to to the U.S. dollar, ¥75 to the Canadian dollar, and ¥150 to the pound sterling.

What It Will Cost

You may have heard horror stories about exorbitant prices in Japan. An American freelance writer, upon arriving in Tokyo, said, "I feel as though I am from a Third World country. I can't afford anything. Everything seems so expensive and inaccessible." This is, of course, an exaggeration, and while a melon can cost the equivalent of U.S. $100, this is because melons are imported luxury goods or specially cultivated on the island of Kochi.

It is undeniable that Japan is expensive, but there are ways to cut costs. This requires, to some extent, an adventurous spirit and the courage to stray from the standard tourist paths. Avoid taxis (they tend to get stuck in traffic anyway) and try the inexpensive, efficient subway and bus systems; instead of going to a restaurant with menus in English and Western-style food, go to places where you can rely on your good old index finger to point at the dish you want and try food that the Japanese eat.

Taxes There is an across-the-board, nonrefundable 3% consumer tax levied on all sales. Since the tax was introduced in April 1989, vendors have either been absorbing the tax in their quoted retail prices or adding it on to the sale. Always inquire which is the case if you are planning a major purchase.

Sample Prices A cup of coffee: ¥350–¥600; a bottle of beer: ¥350–¥1,000; a 2-km taxi ride: ¥540 (¥600 in Tokyo); a McDonald's hamburger: ¥270; a bowl of noodles: ¥700; an average dinner: ¥2,500; a double room in Tokyo: ¥9,000–¥34,000.

Passports and Visas

If your passport is lost or stolen abroad, report it immediately to the nearest embassy or consulate and to the local police. If you can provide the consular officer with the information contained in the passport, he or she will usually be able to issue you a new passport. For this reason, it is a good idea to keep a copy of the data page of your passport in a separate place, or to leave the passport number, date, and place of issuance with a relative or friend at home.

U.S. Citizens All U.S. citizens, even infants, need a valid passport to enter Japan for stays of up to 90 days. You can pick up new and renewal application forms at any of the 13 U.S. Passport Agency offices and at some post offices and courthouses. Although passports are usually mailed within two weeks of your application's receipt, it's best to allow three weeks for delivery in low season, five weeks or more from April through summer. Call the Department of State Office of Passport Services' information line (1425 K St. NW, Washington, DC 20522, tel. 202/647–0518) for fees, documentation requirements, and other details.

Canadian Citizens Canadian citizens need a valid passport to enter Japan for stays of up to 90 days. Application forms are available at 23 regional passport offices as well as post offices and travel agencies. Whether applying for a first or subsequent passport, you must apply in person. Children under 16 may be included on a parent's passport but must have their own passport to travel alone. Passports are valid for five years and are usually mailed within two weeks of an application's receipt. For fees, documentation requirements, and other information in English or French, call the passport office (tel. 514/283–2152).

U.K. Citizens Citizens of the United Kingdom need a valid passport to enter Japan for stays of up to six months. Applications for new and renewal passports are available from main post offices as well as at the six passport offices, located in Belfast, Glasgow, Liverpool, London, Newport, and Peterborough. You may apply in person at all passport offices, or by mail to all except the London office. Children under 16 may travel on a parent's passport when accompanying them. All passports are valid for 10 years. Allow a month for processing.

Customs and Duties

On Arrival Japan is strict about bringing firearms, pornography, and narcotics into the country. Anyone caught with drugs is liable to be detained, deported, and refused re-entry into Japan. Certain fresh fruits, vegetables, plants, and animals are also illegal. Nonresidents are allowed to bring in duty-free: (1) 400 cigarettes or 100 cigars or 500 grams of tobacco; (2) three bottles of alcohol; (3) 2 ounces of perfume; (4) other goods up to ¥200,000 value.

Returning Home
U.S. Customs Provided you've been out of the country for at least 48 hours and haven't already used the exemption, or any part of it, in the past 30 days, you may bring home $400 worth of foreign goods duty-free. So can each member of your family, regardless of age; and your exemptions may be pooled, so one of you can bring in more if another brings in less. A flat 10% duty applies to the next $1,000 of goods; above $1,400, the rate varies with the merchandise. (If the 48-hour or 30-day limits apply, your duty-free allowance drops to $25, which may not be pooled.) Please note that these are the *general* rules, applicable to most countries, including Japan.

Travelers 21 or older may bring back 1 liter of alcohol duty-free, provided the beverage laws of the state through which they reenter the United States allow it. In addition, 100 non-Cuban cigars and 200 cigarettes are allowed, regardless of your age. Antiques and works of art more than 100 years old are duty-free.

Gifts valued at less than $50 may be mailed duty-free to stateside friends and relatives, with a limit of one package per day per addressee (do not send alcohol or tobacco products, nor perfume valued at more than $5). These gifts do not count as part of your exemption, unless you bring them home with you. Mark the package "Unsolicited Gift" and include the nature of the gift and its retail value.

For a copy of "Know Before You Go," a free brochure detailing what you may and may not bring back to the United States, rates of duty, and other pointers, contact the **U.S. Customs Service** (Box 7407, Washington, DC 20044, tel. 202/927–6724).

Canadian Customs Once per calendar year, when you've been out of Canada for at least seven days, you may bring in $300 worth of goods duty-free. If you've been away less than seven days but more than 48 hours, the duty-free exemption drops to $100 but can be claimed any number of times (as can a $20 duty-free exemption for absences of 24 hours or more). You cannot combine the yearly and 48-hour exemptions, use the $300 exemption only partially (to save the balance for a later trip), or pool exemptions with family members. Goods claimed under the $300 exemption may follow you by mail; those claimed under the lesser exemptions must accompany you on your return.

Alcohol and tobacco products may be included in the yearly and 48-hour exemptions but not in the 24-hour exemption. If you meet the age requirements of the province through which you reenter Canada, you may bring in, duty-free, 1.14 liters (40 imperial ounces) of wine or liquor *or* two dozen 12-ounce cans or bottles of beer or ale. If you are 16 or older, you may bring in, duty-free, 200 cigarettes, 50 cigars or cigarillos, and 400 tobacco sticks or 400 grams of manufactured tobacco. Alcohol and tobacco must accompany you on your return.

Gifts may be mailed to friends in Canada duty-free. These do not count as part of your exemption. Each gift may be worth up to $60; label the package "Unsolicited Gift—Value under $60." There are no limits on the number of gifts that may be sent per day or per addressee, but you can't mail alcohol or tobacco.

For more information, including details of duties on items that exceed your duty-free limit, ask the Revenue Canada Customs and Excise Department (Connaught Bldg., MacKenzie Ave., Ottawa, Ont., K1A OL5, tel. 613/957–0275) for a copy of the free brochure "I Declare/Je Déclare."

U.K. Customs From countries outside the EC such as Japan, you may import duty-free 200 cigarettes, 100 cigarillos, 50 cigars or 250 grams of tobacco; 1 liter of spirits or 2 liters of fortified or sparkling wine; 2 liters of still table wine; 60 millileters of perfume; 250 millileters of toilet water; plus £36 worth of other goods, including gifts and souvenirs.

For further information or a copy of "A Guide for Travellers," which details standard customs procedures as well as what you may bring into the United Kingdom from abroad, contact HM Customs and Excise (New King's Beam House, 22 Upper Ground, London SE1 9PJ, tel. 071/620–1313).

Traveling with Cameras

About Film and Cameras If your camera is new or if you haven't used it for a while, shoot and develop a few rolls of film before leaving home. Pack some lens tissue and an extra battery for your built-in light meter, and invest in an inexpensive skylight filter, to both protect your lens and provide some definition in hazy shots. Store film in a cool, dry place—never in the car's glove compartment or on the shelf under the rear window.

Fluorescent lighting, which is used a lot in Japan, will give photographs a greenish tint. You can counteract this discoloration with a FL filter.

Films above ISO 400 are more sensitive to damage from airport security X-rays than others; very high speed films, ISO 1,000 and above, are exceedingly vulnerable. To protect your film, don't put it in checked luggage; carry it with you in a plastic bag and ask for a hand inspection. Such requests are honored at American airports but are up to the inspector abroad. Don't depend on a lead-lined bag to protect film in checked luggage—the airline may very well turn up the dosage of radiation to see what you've got in there. Airport metal detectors do not harm film, although you'll set off the alarm if you walk through one with a roll in your pocket. Call the Kodak Information Center (tel. 800/242–2424) for details.

Staying Healthy

Finding a Doctor The **International Association for Medical Assistance to Travellers** (IAMAT, 417 Center St., Lewiston, NY 14092, tel. 716/754–4883; 40 Regal Rd., Guelph, Ontario N1K 1B5; 57 Voirets, 1212 Grand-Lancy, Geneva, Switzerland) publishes a worldwide directory of English-speaking physicians whose qualifications meet IAMAT standards and who have agreed to treat members for a set fee. Membership is free.

Assistance Companies Pretrip medical referrals, emergency evacuation or repatriation, 24-hour telephone hot lines for medical consultation, dispatch of medical personnel, relay of medical records, up-front cash for emergencies, and other personal and legal assistance are among the services provided by several membership organizations specializing in medical assistance to travelers. Among them are **International SOS Assistance** (Box 11568, Philadelphia, PA 19116, tel. 215/244–1500 or 800/523–8930; Box 466, Pl. Bonaventure, Montréal, Québec H5A 1C1, tel. 514/874–7674 or 800/363–0263), **Near Services** (450 Prairie Ave., Suite 101, Calumet City, IL 60409, tel. 708/868–6700 or 800/654–6700), and **Travel Assistance International** (1133 15th St. NW, Suite 400, Washington, DC 20005, tel. 202/331–1609 or 800/821–2828), part of Europ Assistance Worldwide Services, Inc.

Insurance

For U.S. Residents Most tour operators, travel agents, and insurance agents sell specialized health-and-accident, flight, trip-cancellation, and luggage insurance as well as comprehensive policies with some or all of these features. But before you make any purchase, review your existing health and homeowner policies to find out whether they cover expenses incurred while travelling.

Health-and-Accident Insurance Supplemental health-and-accident insurance for travelers is usually a part of comprehensive policies. Specific policy provisions vary, but they tend to address three general areas, beginning with reimbursement for medical expenses caused by illness or an accident during a trip. Such policies may reimburse anywhere from $1,000 to $150,000 worth of medical expenses; dental benefits may also be included. A second common feature is the personal-accident, or death-and-dismemberment, provision, which pays a lump sum to your beneficiaries if you die, or to you for loss of one or both limbs or your eyesight. This is similar to the flight insurance described below, although it is not necessarily limited to accidents involving airplanes or even other "common carriers" (buses, trains, and ships) and can be in effect 24 hours a day. The lump sum awarded can range from $15,000 to $500,000. A third area generally addressed by these policies is medical assistance (referrals, evacuation, or repatriation and other services). Some policies reimburse travelers for the cost of such services; others may automatically enroll you as a member of a particular medical-assistance company.

Flight Insurance This insurance, often bought as a last-minute impulse at the airport, pays a lump sum to a beneficiary when a plane crashes and the insured dies (and sometimes to a surviving passenger who loses eyesight or a limb); thus it supplements the airlines' own coverage as described in the limits-of-liability paragraphs on your ticket (up to $75,000 on international flights, $20,000 on domestic ones—and that is generally subject to litigation). Charging an airline ticket to a major credit card often automatically signs you up for flight insurance; in this case, the coverage may also embrace travel by bus, train, and ship.

Baggage Insurance In the event of loss, damage, or theft on international flights, airlines limit their liability to $20 per kilogram for checked baggage (roughly about $640 per 70-pound bag) and $400 per passenger for unchecked baggage. On domestic flights, the ceiling is $1,250 per passenger. Excess-valuation insurance can be bought directly from the airline at check-in but leaves your bags vulnerable on the ground.

Trip Insurance There are two sides to this coin. **Trip-cancellation-and-interruption insurance** protects you in the event you are unable to undertake or finish your trip. **Default** or **bankruptcy insurance** protects you against a supplier's failure to deliver. Consider the former if your airline ticket, cruise, or package tour does not allow changes or cancellations. The amount of coverage to buy should equal the cost of your trip should you, a traveling companion, or a family member get sick, forcing you to stay home, plus the nondiscounted one-way airline ticket you would need to buy if you had to return home early. Read the fine print carefully; pay attention to sections defining "family member" and "preexisting medical conditions." A characteristic quirk of default policies is that they often do not cover default by travel agencies or default by a tour operator, airline, or cruise line if you bought your tour and the coverage directly from the firm in question. To reduce your need for default insurance, give preference to tours packaged by members of the United States Tour Operators Association (USTOA), which maintains a fund to reimburse clients in the event of member defaults. Even better, pay for travel arrangements with a major credit card, so that you can refuse to pay the bill if services have not been rendered—and let the card company fight your battles.

Comprehensive Policies Companies supplying comprehensive policies with some or all of the above features include **Access America, Inc.**, underwritten by BCS Insurance Company (Box 11188, Richmond, VA 23230, tel. 800/284-8300); **Carefree Travel Insurance**, underwritten by The Hartford (Box 310, 120 Mineola Blvd., Mineola, NY 11501, tel. 516/294-0220 or 800/323-3149); **Tele-Trip** (Mutual of Omaha Plaza, Box 31762, Omaha, NE 68131, tel. 800/228-9792), a subsidiary of Mutual of Omaha; **The Travelers Companies** (1 Tower Sq., Hartford, CT 06183, tel. 203/277-0111 or 800/243-3174); **Travel Guard International**, underwritten by Transamerica Occidental Life Companies (1145 Clark St., Stevens Point, WI 54481, tel. 715/345-0505 or 800/782-5151); and **Wallach and Company, Inc.** (107 W. Federal St., Box 480, Middleburg, VA 22117, tel. 703/687-3166 or 800/237-6615), underwritten by Lloyds, London. These companies may also offer the above types of insurance separately.

U.K. Residents Most tour operators, travel agents, and insurance agents sell specialized policies covering accident, medical expenses, personal liability, trip cancellation, and loss or theft of personal property. Some policies include coverage for delayed departure and legal expenses, winter-sports, accidents, or motoring abroad. You can also purchase an annual travel-insurance policy valid for every trip you make during the year in which it's purchased (usually only trips of less than 90 days). Before you leave, make sure you will be covered if you have a preexisting medical condition or are pregnant; your insurers may not pay for routine or continuing treatment, or may require a note from your doctor certifying your fitness to travel.

For advice by phone or to receive a free booklet, "Holiday Insurance," that sets out what to expect from a holiday-insurance policy and gives price guidelines, contact the **Association of British Insurers** (51 Gresham St., London EC2V 7HQ, tel. 071/600–3333; 30 Gordon St., Glasgow G1 3PU, tel. 041/226–3905; Scottish Provincial Bldg., Donegall Sq. W, Belfast BT1 6JE, tel. 0232/249176; call for other locations).

Car Rentals

Driving along the Tokyo-Kyoto-Hiroshima corridor and in other built-up areas of Japan is not advisable. Trains and subways will get you to your destinations faster and more comfortably. The roads are congested, gas is expensive (about ¥132 per liter or $4.80 per gallon), and highway tolls are exorbitant (tolls between Tokyo and Kyoto cost ¥9,250). In major cities, parking is a nightmare.

Even though public transport is far more efficient and comprehensive in Japan than in the U.S., a car can be the best means for exploring the rural parts of Japan. Major roads are sufficiently marked in the Roman alphabet, and on country roads there is usually someone to ask for help. However, it's a good idea to have a detailed map with towns written in *kanji* (Japanese characters) and the Roman alphabet. As in the United Kingdom, driving in Japan is on the left side.

Some major car-rental companies are represented in Japan, including **Budget** (tel. 800/527–0700), **Hertz** (tel. 800/654–3131, 800/263-0600 in Canada), and **National** (tel. 800/227–7368), known internationally as InterRent and Europcar. In cities, unlimited-mileage rates range from about $47 per day for an economy car to about $168 for a full-size car; weekly unlimited-mileage rates range from about $283 to $1,084. This does not include VAT tax, which in Japan is 3% on car rentals.

In most cities it is possible to make arrangements for a hired car and guide. Cars with drivers cost around ¥8,500 per hour. The cost of an English-speaking guide is approximately ¥20,000–¥30,000 a day, plus expenses. Arrangements can be made through major hotels, or by calling the **Japan Guide Association** (tel. 03/213–2706) for a list of guides. Prices are negotiated directly with the guides.

Requirements An International Driver's Permit, available from the American or Canadian Automobile Association, is necessary.

Extra Charges Picking up the car in one city and leaving it in another may entail drop-off charges or one-way service fees that can be substantial. The cost of a collision- or loss-damage waiver (*see below*) can be high, also. Automatic transmissions and air-conditioning are not universally available abroad; ask for them when you book if you want them, and check the cost before you commit yourself to the rental.

Cutting Costs If you know you will want a car for more than a day or two, you can save by planning ahead. Major international companies have programs that discount their standard rates by 15%–30% if you make the reservation before departure (anywhere from two to 14 days), rent for a minimum number of days (typically three or four), and prepay the rental. Ask about these advance-purchase schemes when you call for information. More economical rentals may be available as part of fly/drive or other packages, even those as bare-bones as the rental plus an airline ticket (*see* Tours and Packages, *above*).

One last tip: Remember to fill the tank when you turn in the vehicle to avoid being charged for refueling at what you'll swear is the most expensive pump in town.

Insurance and Collision Damage Waiver The standard rental contract includes liability coverage (for damage to public property, injury to pedestrians, etc.) and coverage for the car against fire, theft (not included in certain countries), and collision damage with a deductible—most commonly $2,000–$3,000, occasionally more. In the case of an accident, you are responsible for the deductible amount unless you've purchased the collision damage waiver (CDW), which costs an average $12 a day, although this varies depending on what you've rented, where, and from whom.

Because this adds up quickly, you may be inclined to say "no thanks"—and that's certainly your option, although the rental agent may not tell you so. Note before you decline that deductibles are occasionally high enough that totaling a car would make you responsible for its full value. Planning ahead will help you make the right decision. By all means, find out if your own insurance covers damage to a rental car while traveling (not simply a car to drive when yours is in for repairs). And check whether charging car rentals to any of your credit cards will get you a CDW at no charge.

Rail Passes

The **Japan Rail Pass** is recommended for anyone who plans to travel extensively by rail. This pass offers unlimited travel on Japan Railways (JR) trains. It is possible to purchase one-, two-, or three-week passes. A one-week pass is less expensive than a regular round-trip ticket from Tokyo to Kyoto.

Japan Rail Passes are available in coach class and first class (Green Car), but most people find that coach class is more than adequate. A one-week adult pass costs ¥27,800 coach class, ¥37,000 first-class; a two-week pass costs ¥44,200 coach class, ¥60,000 first-class; and a three-week pass costs ¥56,600 coach class, ¥78,000 first-class. Travelers under 18 pay lower rates.

A voucher for the Japan Rail Pass must be bought prior to departure for Japan and must be used within three months of purchase. The pass is available only to people with tourist visas, as opposed to business, student, and diplomatic visas. It can be purchased through travel agents or any of the following: **Japan Airlines** (JAL, 655 Fifth Ave., New York, NY 10022, tel. 212/838–4400), **Japan Travel Bureau** (JTB, 787 Seventh Ave., New York, NY 10019, tel. 212/246–8030), or **Nippon Travel Agency** (NTA, 120 W. 45th St., New York, NY 10036, tel. 212/944–8660). JAL, JTB, and NTA also have bureaus in other major U.S. cities.

When you arrive in Japan, you must exchange your voucher for the Japan Rail Pass. You can do this at the Japan Railways (JR) desk in the Arrivals Hall at Narita Airport or at the JR stations of major cities. When you make this exchange, you determine the day that you want the rail pass to begin—and, by definition, when it ends. You do not have to begin travel on the day that you make the exchange. Pick the starting date to maximize the pass's use. The Japan Rail Pass allows you to travel on all

JR operated trains (which cover most destinations in Japan), but not lines owned by other companies. It also allows you to use buses operated by Japan Railways. You can make seat reservations without paying a fee on all trains that have reserved-seat coaches, usually the long-distance trains. The Japan Rail Pass does not cover the cost of sleeping compartments on overnight trains (called Blue trains).

Student and Youth Travel

Travel Agencies The foremost U.S. student travel agency is **Council Travel,** a subsidiary of the nonprofit Council on International Educational Exchange. It specializes in low-cost travel arrangements, is the exclusive U.S. agent for several discount cards, and, with its sister CIEE subsidiary, **Council Charter,** is a source of airfare bargains. The Council Charter brochure and CIEE's twice-yearly *Student Travels* magazine, which details its programs, are available at the Council Travel office at CIEE headquarters (205 E. 42nd Street, New York, NY 10017, tel. 212/661–1450) and at 37 branches in college towns nationwide (free in person, $1 by mail). The **Educational Travel Center** (ETC, 438 N. Francis St., Madison, WI 53703, tel. 608/256–5551) also offers low-cost rail passes, domestic and international airline tickets (mostly for flights departing from Chicago), and other budgetwise travel arrangements. Other travel agencies catering to students include **Travel Management International** (TMI, 18 Prescott St., Suite 4, Cambridge, MA 02138, tel. 617/661–8187) and **Travel Cuts** (187 College St., Toronto, Ontario M5T 1P7, tel. 416/979–2406).

Discount Cards For discounts on transportation and on museum and attractions admissions, buy the **International Student Identity Card** (ISIC) if you're a bona fide student, or the **International Youth Card** (IYC) if you're under 26. In the United States the ISIC and IYC cards cost $15 each and include basic travel accident and sickness coverage. Apply to **CIEE** (*see* address *above*, tel. 212/661–1414; the application is in *Student Travels*). In Canada the cards are available for $15 each from **Travel Cuts** (*see above*). In the United Kingdom they cost £5 and £4 respectively at student unions and student travel companies, including Council Travel's London office (28A Poland St., London W1V 3DB, tel. 071/437–7767).

Hosteling An **International Youth Hostel Federation** (IYHF) membership card is the key to more than 5,300 hostel locations in 59 countries; the sex-segregated, dormitory-style sleeping quarters, including some for families, go for $7–$20 a night per person. Membership is available in the United States through **American Youth Hostels** (AYH, 733 15th St. NW, Washington, DC 20005, tel. 202/783–6161), the American link in the worldwide chain, and costs $25 for adults 18–54, $10 for those under 18, $15 for those 55 and over, and $35 for families. Volume 2 of the two-volume *Guide to Budget Accommodation* lists hostels in Asia and Australia as well as in Canada and the United States ($13.95 including postage). IYHF membership is available in Canada through the **Canadian Hostelling Association** (1600 James Naismith Dr., Suite 608, Gloucester, Ontario K1B 5N4, tel. 613/748–5638) for $26.75, and in the United Kingdom through the **Youth Hostel Association of England and Wales** (8 St. Stephen's Hill, St. Albans, Herts. AL1 2DY, tel. 0727/55215) for £9.

Traveling with Children

Publications
Newsletter
Family Travel Times, published 10 times a year by Travel With Your Children (TWYCH, 45 W. 18th St., 7th Floor Tower, New York, NY 10011, tel. 212/206–0688; annual subscription $55), covers destinations, types of vacations, and modes of travel.

Books
Great Vacations with Your Kids, by Dorothy Jordan and Marjorie Cohen ($13; Penguin USA, 120 Woodbine St., Bergenfield, NJ 07621, tel. 800/253–6476) and *Traveling with Children—And Enjoying It,* by Arlene K. Butler ($11.95 plus $3 shipping per book; Globe Pequot Press, Box 833, Old Saybrook, CT 06475, tel. 800/243–0495, or 800/962–0973 in CT), both help plan your trip with children, from toddlers to teens.

Tour Operators
GrandTravel (6900 Wisconsin Ave., Suite 706, Chevy Chase, MD 20815, tel. 301/986–0790 or 800/247–7651) offers international and domestic tours for grandparents traveling with their grandchildren. The catalogue, as charmingly written and illustrated as a children's book, positively invites armchair traveling with lap-sitters aboard. **Rascals in Paradise** (650 Fifth St., Suite 505, San Francisco, CA 94107, tel. 415/978–9800, or 800/872–7225) specializes in programs for families.

Getting There
Air Fares
On international flights, the fare for infants under two not occupying a seat is generally 10% of the accompanying adult's fare; children ages 2–11 usually pay half to two-thirds of the adult fare. On domestic flights, children under two not occupying a seat travel free, and older children currently travel on the "lowest applicable" adult fare.

Baggage
In general, infants paying 10% of the adult fare are allowed one carry-on bag, not to exceed 70 pounds or 45 inches (length + width + height). The adult baggage allowance applies for children paying half or more of the adult fare. Check with the airline for particulars, especially regarding flights between two foreign destinations where allowances for infants may be less generous than those above.

Safety Seats
The FAA recommends the use of safety seats aloft and details approved models in the free leaflet **"Child/Infant Safety Seats Recommended for Use in Aircraft"** (available from the Federal Aviation Administration, APA-200, 800 Independence Ave. SW, Washington, DC 20591, tel. 202/267–3479). Airline policy varies. U.S. carriers must allow FAA-approved models, but because these seats are strapped into a regular passenger seat, they may require that parents buy a ticket even for an infant under two who would otherwise ride free. Foreign carriers may not allow infant seats, may charge the child's rather than the infant's fare for their use, or may require you to hold your baby during takeoff and landing, thus defeating the seat's purpose.

Baby-Sitting Services
Some very expensive Western-style hotels and resort hotels have supervised playrooms where you can drop children off. The baby-sitters, however, are unlikely to speak English. Child-care arrangements can be made through the concierge, but some properties require up to a week's notice.

Hints for Travelers with Disabilities

Organizations
Several organizations provide travel information for people with disabilities, usually for a membership fee, and some pub-

lish newsletters and bulletins. Among them are the **Information Center for Individuals with Disabilities** (Fort Point Pl., 27–43 Wormwood St., Boston, MA 02210, tel. 617/727–5540 or 800/462–5015 in MA between 11 and 4, or leave message; TDD/TTY tel. 617/345–9743); **Mobility International USA** (Box 3551, Eugene, OR 97403, voice and TDD tel. 503/343–1284), the U.S. branch of an international organization based in Britain (*see below*) and present in 30 countries; **MossRehab Hospital Travel Information Service** (1200 W. Tabor Rd., Philadelphia, PA 19141, tel. 215/456–9603, TDD tel. 215/456–9602); the **Society for the Advancement of Travel for the Handicapped** (SATH, 347 Fifth Ave., Suite 610, New York, NY 10016, tel. 212/447–7284, fax 212/725–8253); the **Travel Industry and Disabled Exchange** (TIDE, 5435 Donna Ave., Tarzana, CA 91356, tel. 818/368–5648); and **Travelin' Talk** (Box 3534, Clarksville, TN 37043, tel. 615/552–6670).

In the United Kingdom

Main information sources include the **Royal Association for Disability and Rehabilitation** (RADAR, 25 Mortimer St., London W1N 8AB, tel. 071/637–5400), which publishes travel information for the disabled in Britain, and **Mobility International** (228 Borough High St., London SE1 1JX, tel. 071/403–5688), the headquarters of an international membership organization that serves as a clearinghouse of travel information for people with disabilities.

Travel Agencies and Tour Operators

Directions Unlimited (720 N. Bedford Rd., Bedford Hills, NY 10507, tel. 914/241–1700), a travel agency, has expertise in tours and cruises for the disabled. **Evergreen Travel Service** (4114 198th St. SW, Suite 13, Lynnwood, WA 98036, tel. 206/776–1184 or 800/435–2288) operates Wings on Wheels Tours for those in wheelchairs, White Cane Tours for the blind, and tours for the deaf, and makes group and independent arrangements for travelers with any disability. **Flying Wheels Travel** (143 W. Bridge St., Box 382, Owatonna, MN 55060, tel. 800/535–6790 or 800/722–9351 in MN), a tour operator and travel agency, arranges international tours, cruises, and independent travel itineraries for people with mobility disabilities. **Nautilus,** at the same address as TIDE (*see above*), packages tours for the disabled internationally.

Publications

In addition to the fact sheets and newsletters mentioned above are several free publications available from the Consumer Information Center (Pueblo, CO 81009): "**New Horizons for the Air Traveler with a Disability,**" a U.S. Department of Transportation booklet describing changes resulting from the 1986 Air Carrier Access Act and those still to come from the 1990 Americans with Disabilities Act (include Department 608Y in the address), and the Airport Operators Council's ***Access Travel: Airports*** (Dept. 5804), which describes facilities and services for the disabled at more than 500 airports worldwide.

Twin Peaks Press (Box 129, Vancouver, WA 98666, tel. 206/694–2462 or 800/637–2256) publishes the ***Directory of Travel Agencies for the Disabled*** ($19.95), listing more than 370 agencies worldwide; ***Travel for the Disabled*** ($19.95), listing some 500 access guides and accessible places worldwide; the ***Directory of Accessible Van Rentals*** ($9.95) for campers and RV travelers worldwide; and ***Wheelchair Vagabond*** ($14.95), a collection of personal travel tips. Add $2 per book for shipping.

Hints for Older Travelers

Organizations The **American Association of Retired Persons** (AARP, 601 E St. NW, Washington, DC 20049, tel. 202/434-2277) provides independent travelers with the Purchase Privilege Program, which offers discounts on hotels, car rentals, and sightseeing, and arranges group tours, cruises, and apartment living through AARP Travel Experience from American Express (400 Pinnacle Way, Suite 450, Norcross, GA 30071, tel. 800/927-0111); these can be booked through travel agents, except for the cruises, which must be booked directly (tel. 800/745-4567). AARP membership is open to those 50 and over; annual dues are $8 per person or couple.

Two other membership organizations offer discounts on lodgings, car rentals, and other travel products, along with such nontravel perks as magazines and newsletters. The **National Council of Senior Citizens** (1331 F St. NW, Washington, DC 20004, tel. 202/347-8800) is a nonprofit advocacy group with some 5,000 local clubs across the United States; membership costs $12 per person or couple annually. **Mature Outlook** (6001 N. Clark St., Chicago, IL 60660, tel. 800/336-6330), a Sears Roebuck & Co. subsidiary with 800,000 members, charges $9.95 for an annual membership.

Note: When using any senior-citizen identification card for reduced hotel rates, mention it when booking, not when checking out. At restaurants, show your card before you're seated; discounts may be limited to certain menus, days, or hours. If you are renting a car, ask about promotional rates that might improve on your senior-citizen discount.

Educational Travel **Elderhostel** (75 Federal St., 3rd floor, Boston, MA 02110, tel. 617/426-7788) is a nonprofit organization that has offered inexpensive study programs for people 60 and older since 1975. Programs take place at more than 1,800 educational institutions in the United States, Canada, and 45 other countries; courses cover everything from marine science to Greek myths to cowboy poetry. Participants generally attend lectures in the morning and spend the afternoon sightseeing or on field trips; they live in dorms on the host campuses. Fees for two- to three-week international trips—including room, board, and transportation from the United States—range from $1,800 to $4,500.

Interhostel (University of New Hampshire, 6 Garrison Ave., Durham, NH 03824, tel. 800/733-9753), a newer enterprise than Elderhostel, caters to a slightly younger clientele—that is, 50 and over—and runs programs in some 25 countries. But the idea is similar: Lectures and field trips mix with sightseeing, and participants stay in dormitories at cooperating educational institutions or in modest hotels. Programs are usually two weeks in length and cost $1,500-$2,100, not including airfare from the United States.

Tour Operators **Saga International Holidays** (222 Berkeley St., Boston, MA 02116, tel. 800/343-0273), which specializes in group travel for people over 60, offers a selection of variously priced tours and cruises covering five continents. If you want to take your grandchildren, look into **GrandTravel** (*see* Traveling with Children, *above*).

Further Reading

History Fourteen hundred years of history is rather a lot to take in when going on a holiday, but two good surveys make the task much easier: Richard Storry's *A History of Modern Japan* (by modern, he means everything post-prehistoric) and George Sansom's *Japan: A Short Cultural History*. Sansom's three-volume *History of Japan* is a more exhaustive treatment.

For those interested in earlier times, Ivan Morris's *The World of the Shining Prince*, uses diaries and literature of the time to reconstruct life in the ancient city of Heian (Kyoto) from 794 to 1192. It should be required reading for anyone wishing to tour old Kyoto. *The Culture of the Meiji Period*, by Irokawa Daikichi, covers Japan's 19th century encounters with the West. Oliver Statler's *Japanese Inn* deals with 400 years of Japanese social history.

Religion Anyone wanting to read a Zen Buddhist text should try *The Platform Sutra of the Sixth Patriarch*, one of the Zen classics, written by an ancient Chinese head of the sect and translated by Philip B. Yampolsky. Another Zen text of high importance is the Lotus Sutra; it has been translated by Leon Hurvitz as *The Scripture of the Lotus Blossom of the Fine Dharma: The Lotus Sutra*. Stuart D. Picken has written books on both major Japanese religions: *Shinto: Japan's Spiritual Roots* and *Buddhism: Japan's Cultural Identity*. William R. LaFleur's recommended *Karma of Words: Buddhism and the Literary Arts in Medieval Japan* traces how Buddhism affected medieval Japanese mentality and behavior.

Literature The great classic of all Japanese fiction is the *Tale of Genji;* Genji or the Shining Prince has long been taken as the archetype of ideal male behavior. The novel was written by a woman of the court, Murasaki Shikibu, around the year 1000; two translations are available, one by Arthur Waley and another by Edward Seidensticker. Of the same period, Japan's "Golden Age," is *The Pillow Book of Sei Shonagon*, the diary of a woman's courtly life, eloquently translated by Ivan Morris.

The Edo period is well covered by literary translations. Howard Hibbett's *Floating World in Japanese Fiction* gives an excellent selection with commentaries. The racy prose of Saikaku Ihara, who lived at the end of the 17th century and embodied the rough bravura of the growing merchant class, is translated in various books, including *Some Final Words of Advice*, *Life of an Amorous Man*, and *Five Women Who Loved Love*. More serious literature of the same period are *haikai* poems. Basho produced great examples of these 17-syllable verses; his *Narrow Road to the Deep North and Other Travel Sketches* is available in translation. A general overview of Japanese poetry may be found in the *Penguin Book of Japanese Verse*.

Several modern Japanese novelists have been translated into English. One of the best-known writers among Westerners is Yukio Mishima, author of *The Sea of Fertility* trilogy, among many other works. His books often deal with the effects of post-war Westernization on Japanese culture. Two superb prose stylists are Junchiro Tanizaki, author of *The Makioka Sisters*, *Some Prefer Nettles*, and *Seven Japanese Tales*, and Nobel Prize winner Yasunari Kawabata, whose novels include *Snow*

Country, Beauty and Sadness, and *The Sound of the Mountain.*

Sociology The Japanese have a genre they refer to as *nihonjin-ron,* or studies of "Japaneseness." Western-style studies of the Japanese way of life in relation to the West also abound. Perhaps the best is Ezra Vogel's *Japan As Number One: Lessons for America.* A fine study of the Japanese mind is found in Takeo Doi's *The Anatomy of Dependence* and Chie Nakane's *Japanese Society.* Edwin O. Reischauer's *The Japanese* and his more recent *The Japanese Today* are general overviews of Japanese society.

An exceptionally enlightening book on the Japanese socio-political system, especially for diplomats and business people intending to work with the Japanese, is *The Enigma of Japanese Power* by Harel van Wolferen.

Art/Architecture A wealth of literature exists on Japanese art. Much of the early writing has not withstood the test of time, but R. Paine and Alexander Soper's *Art and Architecture of Japan* remains a good place to start. A more recent survey, though narrower in scope, is Joan Stanley-Smith's *Japanese Art.*

The *Japan Arts Library,* a multivolume survey published by Kodansha, covers most of the styles and personalities of Japanese art, including architecture. The series has volumes on castles, teahouses, screen painting, and wood-block prints. A more detailed look at the architecture of Tokyo is Edward Seidensticker's *Low City, High City. What is Japanese Architecture?,* by Kazuo Nishi and Kazuo Hozumi, is full of information on the history of Japanese architecture, with examples of buildings you will actually see on your travels.

Arriving and Departing

From North America by Plane

Flights are either nonstop, direct, or connecting. A **nonstop** flight requires no change of plane and makes no stops. A **direct** flight stops at least once and can involve a change of plane, although the flight number remains the same; if the first leg is late, the second waits. This is not the case with a **connecting** flight, which involves a different plane and a different flight number.

Airports and Airlines More than 40 international carriers offer regular flights to Tokyo. Fares vary with the airline, season, and type of ticket. **Japan Airlines** (JAL; tel. 800/525–3663) offers nonstop service to seven American cities, as well as flying to Toronto and Vancouver. JAL covers 14 cities within Japan, making it easy for a visitor to travel throughout the country with just one airline ticket. **All Nippon Airways** (tel. 800/235–9262) is the other major Japanese international carrier with nonstop flights to Tokyo from Los Angeles, New York, and Washington, D.C.

Northwest Airlines (tel. 800/447–4747) has become the leading airline servicing the Pacific Rim countries, and Tokyo's Narita airport is Northwest's Far East hub. **United Airlines** (tel. 800/538–2929) is the other major U.S. carrier, with nonstop flights to Tokyo from both coasts.

Other major airlines with regular routes to Japan include **Canadian Airlines International** (tel. 800/426–7000), **Korean Air** (tel. 800/223–1155), **American Airlines** (tel. 800/433–7300), and **Continental Airlines** (tel. 800/231–0856). **Thai Airways International** (tel. 800/426–5204) also flies nonstop to Tokyo from Los Angeles en route to Bangkok.

Flying Time Typical flight times are: from New York, 13¾ hours; from Chicago, 12¾ hours; from Los Angeles, 9½ hours.

Cutting Flight Costs The Sunday travel section of most newspapers is a good source of deals. When booking, particularly through an unfamiliar company, call the Better Business Bureau to find out whether any complaints have been registered against the company, pay with a credit card if you can, and consider trip-cancellation and default insurance (*see* Insurance, *above*).

Promotional Airfares All the less expensive fares, called promotional or discount fares, are round-trip and involve restrictions. The exact nature of the restrictions depends on the airline, the route, and the season and on whether travel is domestic or international, but you must usually buy the ticket—commonly called an APEX (advance purchase excursion) when it's for international travel—in advance (seven, 14, or 21 days are usual). You must also respect certain minimum- and maximum-stay requirements (for instance, over a Saturday night or at least seven and no more than 30, 45, or 90 days), and you must be willing to pay penalties for changes. Airlines generally allow some changes for a fee. But the cheaper the fare, the more likely the ticket is to be nonrefundable; it would take a death in the family for the airline to give you any of your money back if you had to cancel. The lowest fares are also subject to availability; because only a certain percentage of the plane's total seats will be sold at that price, they may go quickly.

Consolidators Consolidators or bulk-fare operators—also known as bucket shops—buy blocks of seats on scheduled flights that airlines anticipate they won't be able to sell. They pay wholesale prices, add a markup, and resell the seats to travel agents or directly to the public at prices that still undercut the airline's promotional or discount fares. You pay more than on a charter but ordinarily less than for an APEX ticket, and, even when there is not much of a price difference, the ticket usually comes without the advance-purchase restriction.

The biggest U.S. consolidator, C.L. Thomson Express, sells only to travel agents. Well-established consolidators selling to the public include **UniTravel** (Box 12485, St. Louis, MO 63132, tel. 314/569–0900 or 800/325–2222); **Council Charter** (205 E. 42nd St., New York, NY 10017, tel. 212/661–0311 or 800/800–8222), a division of the Council on International Educational Exchange and a longtime charter operator now functioning more as a consolidator; and **Travac** (989 Sixth Ave., New York, NY 10018, tel. 212/563–3303 or 800/872–8800), also a former charterer.

Charter Flights Charters usually have the lowest fares and the most restrictions. Departures are limited and seldom on time, and you can lose all or most of your money if you cancel. (Generally, the closer to departure you cancel, the more you lose, although sometimes you will be charged only a small fee if you supply a substitute passenger.) The charterer, on the other hand, may legally cancel the flight for any reason up to 10 days before departure; within 10 days of departure, the flight may be canceled only if it becomes physically impossible to operate it. The charterer may also revise the itinerary or increase the price after you have bought the ticket, but if the new arrangement constitutes a "major change," you have the right to a refund. Before buying a charter ticket, read the fine print for the company's refund policy and details on major changes. Money for charter flights is usually paid into a bank escrow account, the name of which should be on the contract. If you don't pay by credit card, make your check payable to the escrow account (unless you're dealing with a travel agent, in which case, his or her check should be payable to the escrow account). The Department of Transportation's Consumer Affairs Office (I–25, Washington, DC 20590, tel. 202/366–2220) can answer questions on charters and send you its "Plane Talk: Public Charter Flights" information sheet.

Charter operators may offer flights alone or with ground arrangements that constitute a charter package. Well-established charter operators include **Council Charter** (205 E. 42nd St., New York, NY 10017, tel. 212/661–0311 or 800/800–8222), now largely a consolidator, despite its name, and **Travel Charter** (1120 E. Long Lake Rd., Troy, MI 48098, tel. 313/528–3570 or 800/521–5267), with Midwestern departures. **DER Tours** (Box 1606, Des Plains, IL 60017, tel. 800/782–2424), a charterer and consolidator, sells through travel agents.

Discount Travel Clubs

Travel clubs offer their members unsold space on airplanes, cruise ships, and package tours at nearly the last minute and at well below the original cost. Suppliers thus receive some revenue for their "leftovers," and members get a bargain. Membership generally includes a regular bulletin or access to a toll-free telephone hot line giving details of available trips departing anywhere from three or four days to several months in the future. Packages tend to be more common than flights alone, so if airfares are your only interest, read the literature before joining. Reductions on hotels are also available. Clubs include **Discount Travel International** (114 Forrest Ave., Suite 203, Narberth, PA 19072, tel. 215/668–7184; $45 annually, single or family), **Moment's Notice** (425 Madison Ave., New York, NY 10017, tel. 212/486–0503; $45 annually, single or family), **Travelers Advantage** (CUC Travel Service, 49 Music Sq. W, Nashville, TN 37203, tel. 800/548–1116; $49 annually, single or family), and **Worldwide Discount Travel Club** (1674 Meridian Ave., Miami Beach, FL 33139, tel. 305/534–2082; $50 annually for family, $40 single).

Enjoying the Flight

Flights to Japan are long and trying. Fly at night if you're able to sleep on a plane. Because the air aloft is dry, drink plenty of beverages while on board; remember that drinking alcohol contributes to jet lag, as do heavy meals. Sleepers usually prefer window seats to curl up against; restless passengers ask to be on the aisle. Bulkhead seats, in the front row of each cabin, have more legroom, but since there's no seat ahead, trays attach awkwardly to the arms of your seat, and you must stow all possessions overhead. Bulkhead seats are usually reserved for the disabled, the elderly, and people traveling with infants.

Smoking

Since February 1990, smoking has been banned on all domestic flights of less than six hours duration; the ban also applies to domestic segments of international flights aboard U.S. and foreign carriers. On U.S. carriers flying to Japan and other destinations abroad, a seat in a no-smoking section must be provided for every passenger who requests one, and the section must be enlarged to accommodate such passengers if necessary as long as they have complied with the airline's deadline for check-in and seat assignment. If smoking bothers you, request a seat far from the smoking section.

Foreign airlines are exempt from these rules but do provide no-smoking sections, and some nations, including Japan, have gone as far as to ban smoking on all domestic flights; other countries may ban smoking on flights of less than a specified duration. The International Civil Aviation Organization has set July 1, 1996, as the date to ban smoking aboard airlines worldwide, but the body has no power to enforce its decisions.

From the United Kingdom by Plane

By Plane **British Airways** (Box 10, London-Heathrow Airport, Hounslow, Middlesex TW6 2JA, tel. 081/897–4000) and **Japan Airlines** (5 Hanover Sq., London W1R ODR, tel. 071/629–9244) are the major operators serving Japan. They have daily flights to Tokyo's Narita Airport, some nonstop (flight time 11½ hrs.), others stopping at Anchorage (flight time 17½ hrs.). Other airlines serving Japan include **All Nippon Airways** (tel. 071/355–1155); **Korean Air** (tel. 071/930–6513); **Lufthansa** (tel. 071/408–0442); **Swissair** (tel. 071/439–4144); and **Thai Airways International** (tel. 071/499–9113), with one or more transfers.

Getting Around Japan

By Train

Japanese trains are efficient and convenient, running frequently and on time. The Shinkansen (bullet train), one of the fastest trains in the world, connects major cities north and south of Tokyo. It is only slightly less expensive than flying but is in many ways more convenient because train stations are more centrally located than airports.

Other trains, though not as fast as the Shinkansen, are just as convenient and substantially cheaper. There are three types of train services: *futsu* (local service), *tokkyu* (limited express service), and *kyuko* (express service). Both the tokkyu and the kyuko offer a first-class compartment known as the Green Car.

Note: When getting around by rail it is a good idea to travel light. There are no porters or carts at train stations, and the flights of stairs connecting train platforms can turn even the lightest bag into a heavy burden. Savvy travelers often have their main luggage sent ahead to a hotel that they plan to reach later in their wanderings.

Purchasing Tickets If you are using a rail pass, there is no need to buy individual tickets, but it is advisable to make reservations for long trips and during peak travel times. This guarantees you a seat and is also a useful reference for the times of train departures and arrivals. You can reserve up to two weeks in advance or just minutes before the train departs. If you fail to make a train, there is no penalty and you can reserve again. Seat reservations for any JR route may be made at any JR Station except those in the tiniest villages. The reservation windows or offices, *Midori-no-*

madoguchi, have green signs in English and green-striped windows. For those traveling without a Japan Rail Pass, there is a surcharge of approximately ¥500 (depending upon distance traveled) for seat reservations, and if you miss the train you'll have to pay for another reservation. When making your seat reservation, you may request a nonsmoking or smoking car. Your reservation ticket will show the date and departure time of your train as well as your car and seat number. On the platform, you can figure out where to wait for a particular train car. Notice the markings painted on the platform or on little signs above the platform; ask someone which markings correspond to car numbers. If you don't have a reservation, ask which cars are unreserved. Sleeping berths, even with a rail pass, are additional. Nonreserved tickets can be bought at regular ticket windows. There are no reservations made on local service trains. For traveling short distances, tickets are usually sold at vending machines.

Most clerks at train stations know a few basic words of English and can read Roman script. Moreover, they are invariably helpful in plotting your route. The complete railway timetable is a mammoth book written only in Japanese; however, the Japan National Tourist Organization (JNTO) distributes a limited schedule in English that covers the Shinkansen and a few of the major JR Limited Express trains. JNTO's booklet, *The Tourist's Handbook*, provides helpful information about purchasing tickets in Japan.

By Plane

All major Japanese cities have airports connected by domestic flights. The two major services are **All Nippon Airways** (3-6-3 Irifunecho, Chuo-ku, Tokyo, tel. 03/3552–6311) and **Japan Airlines** (5-37-8 Shiba, Minato-ku, Tokyo, tel. 03/3456–2111).

By Bus

Japan Railways offers a number of overnight long-distance buses that are not very comfortable but are inexpensive. Japan Rail Passes may be used on these buses. City buses are quite convenient, but be sure of your route and destination, because the bus driver will probably not speak English. Some buses have a set cost from ¥120 to ¥180, depending on the route and municipality, in which case you board at the front of the bus and pay as you get on. On other buses, cost is determined by the distance you travel. You take a ticket when you board at the rear door of the bus; it will bear the number of the stop at which you boarded. Your fare is indicated by a board with rotating numbers at the front of the bus. Under each boarding point, indicated by a number, the fare will increase the farther the bus travels.

By Ferry

Ferries connect most of the islands of Japan. Some of the more popular routes are from Tokyo to Tomakomai or Kushiro in Hokkaido; from Tokyo to Shikoku; and from Tokyo or Osaka to Kyushu. You can purchase tickets in advance from travel agencies or before boarding. The ferries are inexpensive and are a pleasant if slow way of traveling. Private cabins are available, but it is more fun to travel in the economy class, where everyone sleeps in one large room. Passengers eat, drink, and enjoy themselves, creating a convivial atmosphere.

By Taxi

Taxis are an expensive way of getting around cities in Japan. The first 2 kilometers cost about ¥520 (¥600 in Tokyo), and it is ¥90 for every additional 370 meters (400 yards). If possible, avoid use of taxis during rush hours (8 AM–9 AM and 5:30 PM–6:30 PM).

In general, it is easy to hail a cab. Do not shout or wave wildly; simply raise your hand. Do not try to open the taxi door, because all taxis have an automatic door-opening function, and the door will slam into you if you are too close to it. When you leave the cab, do not try to close the door; the driver will use the automatic system. Only the curbside rear door opens. A red light on the dashboard indicates an available taxi, and a green light indicates an occupied taxi.

Drivers are for the most part courteous, although sometimes they will balk at the idea of a foreign passenger because they do not speak English. Unless you are going to a well-known destination such as a major hotel, it is advisable to have a Japanese person write out your destination in Japanese. Remember, there is no need to tip.

By Car

It is possible for foreigners to drive in Japan with an international driver's license, and though few select this option, it is becoming more popular. Many highways have transliterated signs, though the smaller roads do not. A good map really helps. Except in Tokyo and a few other major cities, exploring in a rented car can be rewarding. However, long-distance traveling by car is ill-advised. Except for the expensive toll roads, highways tend to be congested, making driving frustrating and considerably slower than taking the train. Consider renting a car locally for a day or even half a day in those areas where exploring the countryside will be the most interesting. Gas costs about ¥132 per liter (about $4.80 a gallon).

Rules. Driving is on the left side of the street, as in the United Kingdom. Speed limits vary, but generally the limit is 80 kilometers per hour (50 mph) on highways, 40 (25 mph) in cities.

Staying in Japan

Tourist Information

Tourist Information Centers

The Japan National Tourist Organization (JNTO) operates **Tourist Information Centers** (TIC) which offer travel information, pamphlets, and suggestions for tour itineraries. Reservations are not handled here. You can either visit or call the TIC offices; all offices are closed on Sundays and national holidays.

Tokyo Office. Kotani Building, 1-6-6 Yurakucho, Chiyoda-ku, tel. 03/3502–1461. Open weekdays 9–5, Saturday 9–noon.

Tokyo International Airport Office, Airport Terminal Building, Narita Airport, Chiba Prefecture, tel. 0476/32–8711. Open weekdays 9–8, Saturday 9–noon.

Kyoto Office. Kyoto Tower Building, Higashi-Shiokojicho, Shimogyo-ku, tel. 075/371–5549. Open weekdays 9–5, Saturday 9–noon.

Japan Travel-Phone If you have travel-related questions or need help in communicating, call the TIC's Travel-Phone service, daily 9–5. In Tokyo and Kyoto, call the TIC offices listed above. Elsewhere, dial toll-free 0120/222–800 for information on eastern Japan and 0120/444–800 for western Japan. The Travel-Phone service is available through yellow, blue, or green public telephones (not red ones), and through private phones. When using a public telephone, insert a ¥10 piece, which will be returned.

Teletourist Service A tape-recorded listing in English of cultural events going on in Tokyo is available by calling tel. 03/3503–2911; in Kyoto, call tel. 075/361–2911.

Good-Will Guides JNTO sponsors a Good-Will Guide program in which local citizens volunteer to show visitors around their home towns. These are not professional guides; they usually volunteer both because they enjoy welcoming foreigners to their town and because they want to practice their English. The services of Good-Will Guides are free, but you should pay for their travel costs, their admission fees, and any meals they eat while with you. Make arrangements for a Good-Will Guide in advance through JNTO in the United States or through the tourist office in the area where you want the guide to meet you. The program operates in many areas, including Tokyo, Kyoto, Nara, Nagoya, Osaka, and Hiroshima.

Home Visit System Through the Home Visit System, travelers can get a sense of domestic life in Japan by visiting a local family in their home. The program is voluntary on the homeowner's part, and there is no charge for a visit. It is active in many cities throughout the country, including Tokyo, Yokohama, Nagoya, Kyoto, Osaka, Hiroshima, Nagasaki, Sapporo, and others. An application in writing to make a home visit should be submitted at least a day in advance to the local tourist information office of the place you are visiting. Contact the Japan National Tourist Organization before leaving for Japan for more information on the program.

Language

Communicating in Japan can be a challenge. This is not because the Japanese don't speak English but because most of us know little, if any, Japanese. It is worthwhile to take some time before you leave home to learn a few basic words, such as where (*doko*), what time (*nanji*), bathroom (*benjo*), thanks (*arigato*), excuse me (*sumimasen*), and please (*onegai shimas*).

English is a required subject in Japanese schools, so most Japanese study English for nearly a decade. This does not mean, however, that everyone speaks English. Schools emphasize reading, writing, and grammar; less time is spent on spoken English. As a result, many Japanese can read English but can speak only a few basic phrases. Furthermore, when asked "Do you speak English?" many Japanese will, out of modesty, say no, even if they do understand and speak a fair amount of it. It is usually best to ask what you really want to know slowly, clearly, and as simply as possible. If the person you ask understands, he or she will answer or perhaps take you where you need to go; if that person does not understand, try someone else.

Although a local may understand your simple question, he or she cannot always give you an answer that requires complicated instructions. For example, you may ask someone on the subway how to get to a particular stop, and he may direct you to the train across the platform and then say something in Japanese that you do not understand. You may discover too late that the train runs express to the suburbs after the third stop; the person who gave you directions was trying to tell you to switch trains at the third stop. To avoid this kind of trouble, ask more than one person for directions every step of the way. You could have avoided that trip to the suburbs if you had asked someone *on* the train how to get to your desired destination. Remember that you are communicating on a very basic level, and it is easy to misunderstand. The Japanese are generally very polite and willing to help, but you must ask for assistance.

One of the biggest problems for travelers is that they can't read Japanese. Buy a phrase book that shows English, English transliterations of Japanese, and Japanese. You can use the English transliterations to speak Japanese, and you can match the Japanese writing in the phrase book with characters on signs and menus. And if all else fails, you can ask for help by pointing to the Japanese words in your book.

Japanese is not an easy language to learn. Japanese writing consists of three character systems: Kanji, or Chinese characters, which represent ideas, and two forms of kana—hiragana and katakana—which represent sounds. Hiragana is used to write Japanese words, verb inflections, and adjectives; katakana is used to represent such things as foreign words, slang expressions, and technical terms. There are 47 kana and more than 6,000 Kanji characters, although most Japanese use less than 1,000 Kanji. This is more than a tourist can learn in a short stay, so you will find yourself scanning your surroundings for Romanized Japanese, which is easier to interpret.

The most common system of writing Japanese words in Roman letters is the Hepburn system, which spells out Japanese words phonetically and is followed in this book. Note that there is no stress on any one syllable in Japanese. For example, most English speakers pronounce the Japanese word for good-bye *sa-yo-NAH-ra*, placing the stress on the second to last syllable as is done in many English words. But the correct pronunciation of this word is *sa-yo-na-ra*, with each syllable getting equal stress.

The vowels of Romanized Japanese words are pronounced the same way in every word and sound a lot like Italian vowels. *A* is pronounced like the "ah" in *father*. *E* is pronounced like the "eh" sound in *men*. *I* is pronounced like the "e" in *eat*. *O* is pronounced like the "oh" sound in *only*. *U* is pronounced like the "oo" sound in *boot*. When you see the "ei" combination in a word, pronounce both vowels, *eh-i*. Also, when a word contains a double consonant, break the word between the consonants and say it as if it were two separate words, hesitating slightly between the syllables. Thus, *Nippon* is pronounced *Nip-pon*.

(*Also see* Vocabulary, at end of this book.)

Addresses

Broken down into single elements, Japanese addresses are very simple. The following is an example of a typical Japanese address: 6-chome 8–19, Chuo-ku, Fukuoka-shi, Fukuoka-ken. In this address the "chome" indicates a precise area, and the numbers following "chome" indicate the location within the area, not necessarily in sequential order—numbers may have been assigned when a building was erected. However, only the postmen in Japan seem to be familiar with the area defined by the chome. Sometimes, instead of a "chome," a "machi" is used. "Ku" refers to a ward, or in other words, a district of a city. "Shi" refers to a city name, and "ken" indicates a prefecture, which is roughly equivalent to a state in America. It is not unusual for the prefecture and the city to have the same name, as in the above address. There are a few geographic areas in Japan that are not called ken. One is Hokkaido. The other exceptions are greater Tokyo, which is called Tokyo-to, and Kyoto and Osaka, which are followed by the suffix "-fu"—Kyoto-fu, Osaka-fu.

Not all addresses will conform exactly to the above format. Rural addresses, for example, do not have "ku," because only urban areas are divided into wards.

It is important to note that often even Japanese people cannot find a building based on the address alone. Do not assume if you get in a taxi with an address written down, the driver will be able to find your destination. Usually, people provide very detailed instructions or maps to explain their exact locations. A common method is to give the location of your destination in relation to a major building or department store.

Telephones

The country code for Japan is 81.

Pay phones are one of the great delights of Japan. Not only are they conveniently located in hotels, restaurants, and on street corners, but pay phones, at ¥10 for three minutes, have to be one of the few remaining bargains in Japan. Telephones come in three styles: pink, red, and green. Pink phones, for local calls, accept only ¥10 coins. Most red phones are only for local use, but some accept ¥100 coins and can be used for long-distance domestic calls. Domestic long distance rates are reduced as much as 50% after 9 PM (40% after 7 PM). Green phones take coins and often accept what are known as telephone cards—disposable cards of fixed value that you use up in increments of ¥10. Telephone cards, sold in vending machines, hotels, and a variety of stores, are tremendously convenient, because you will not have to search for the correct change. International calls can be made from the many green phones that have gold plates indicating, in English, that the telephone can be used for these calls. There are three Japanese companies that provide international service: KDD (001), ITJ (0041), and IDC (0061). Dial: company code + country code + city/area code and number of your party. KDD offers the clearest connection, but is also the most expensive. Telephone credit cards are especially convenient for international calls. For operator assistance in English on long-distance calls, dial 0051.

AT&T's **USADirect** program allows callers to take advantage of AT&T rates; to reach the service in Japan dial 0039–111. You can then either dial direct (1 + area code + number), billing the call to an AT&T credit card or your local calling card, or make a collect call. It costs $3.36 for the first minute and $1.24 for additional minutes. In addition to per-minute charges, there is a $2.50 service charge for each call billed to a calling card and a $5.75 charge for collect calls. For more information call 800/874–4000 or 412/553–7458, ext. 314 collect from outside the United States. You can also use MCI from Japan; for the United States, dial 0039–121. MCI charges $3.15 for the first minute and $1.17 for each additional minute, and adds a $2 fee for calling card calls and $5 for collect calls. For more information call 800/950–5555 or, in Japan, 0031–12–1022.

Mail

The Japanese postal service is very efficient. Although numerous post offices exist in any given city, it is probably best to use central post offices located near the main train station in a city, because the workers speak English and can handle foreign mail. Some of the smaller post offices are not equipped to send packages. Post offices are open weekdays 8–5 and Saturday 8–noon. Some of the central post offices have longer hours, such as the one in Tokyo, located near Tokyo Station, which is open 24 hours, year-round.

It costs ¥100 to send a letter by air to the United States or Canada; ¥120 to Europe. An airmail postcard costs ¥70 to North America; ¥70 to Europe. Aerograms cost ¥100.

It is possible to receive mail sent *poste restante* at the central post office in major cities; unclaimed mail is returned after 30 days. American Express offices, located in all major Japanese cities, are other good places to have mail sent. The address of the main office in Tokyo is American Express, Halifax Building, 16-26 Roppongi 3-chome, Minato-ku, Tokyo.

Dining

Japanese food is not only delicious and healthy but also aesthetically pleasing. Even the most humble *bento* lunch box procured at a stand in a train station will be created with careful attention paid to the color combination and general presentation. Be warned that portions may be small, so you may feel that the price of beauty is a less-than-full stomach.

Food, like many things in Japan, is expensive. Eating at hotels and famous restaurants is costly, but by looking for standard restaurants that may not have signs in English, you can eat well at reasonable prices. Many less-expensive restaurants have plastic replicas of the dishes they serve displayed in their front windows, so you can always point to what you want to eat. A good place to look for moderately priced dining spots is in the restaurant concourse of department stores, usually on the bottom floor.

In general, Japanese restaurants are very clean. The water is safe, even when drawn from a tap. Most hotels have Western-style rest rooms, but restaurants may have Japanese-style toilets, with bowls recessed into the floor, over which you must squat.

There are many types of restaurants in Japan. **Sushiya** usually offer only sushi. Places that do not list their prices can be extremely expensive. Some sushi places have revolving counters, where you pick dishes off a conveyor belt and are charged according to the number of empty plates. These automatic sushi places are inexpensive and fun, but be cautious in the summer months, when the fish might not be fresh.

Noodle fans can go to a **ramenya,** for an inexpensive but filling bowl of *ramen* (Japanese noodles). Ramenya also serve beer and *gyoza* (fried dumplings). **Sobaya** are close relatives of ramenya and serve buckwheat noodles hot or cold; they are a refreshing light meal or snack.

Nomiya are bars, but in addition to beer, sake, and whiskey, they often serve simple, tasty food. Many nomiya have a red lantern hanging outside. These places are not sophisticated and fancy, but they can provide a glimpse of the life of the working person.

Outdoor food stalls are located on many urban street corners and offer a variety of food, including yakitori (chicken on skewers), noodles, or simple roast chestnuts. This food is safe to eat and inexpensive.

Japanese coffee shops, known as **kissaten,** are always good places for weary tourists. Although you may be astonished by the high price of a cup of coffee (there are no refills), you can sit as long as you like, long after you have finished your coffee. Some coffee shops offer "morning set" breakfasts consisting of a hard-boiled egg, toast, and a small salad. Priced at only a few hundred yen, they are one of the few really inexpensive meals in Japan.

For those who tire of Japanese food, Western, Chinese, and other types of food are available, particularly in urban areas. In recent years, ethnic food has become popular, so those in need of a taco or a spicy Thai curry can fulfill their desires.

Tipping, Tax, and Service Charge

A 3% federal consumer tax is added to all restaurant bills. Another 3% local tax is added to the bill if it exceeds ¥7,500. At the more expensive restaurants, a 10%–15% service charge is added to the bill. Tipping is not the custom.

Lodging

Overnight accommodations in Japan run from luxury hotels to traditional inns to youth hostels and even capsules. Western-style rooms with Western-style bathrooms are widely available in large cities, but in smaller, out-of-the-way towns it may be necessary to stay in a Japanese-style room.

Hotels

Full-service, first-class hotels in Japan are similar to their counterparts all over the world, and because many of the staff speak English these are the easiest places for foreigners to stay. They are also among the most expensive.

Business hotels are a reasonable alternative. These are clean and comfortable, though the Western-style rooms vary from tiny to minuscule and the services are limited. Business hotels are often conveniently located near the railway station. The staff may not speak English, and there is usually no room service.

Designed to accommodate the modern Japanese urbanite, the capsule hotel is a novel idea. The rooms are a mere 3½ feet in width, 3½ feet in height, and 7¼ feet in length. They have an alarm clock, television, and phone, and little else. Capsules are often used by commuters who have had an evening of excess and cannot make the long journey home. Although you may want to try sleeping in a capsule, you probably won't want to spend a week in one.

Ryokan Those who want to sample the Japanese way should spend at least one night in a *ryokan*, or Japanese-style inn. Usually one- or two-story small wood structures with a garden or scenic view, they provide traditional Japanese accommodations: simple tatami rooms in which the bedding is rolled out onto the floor at night.

Ryokan vary in price and quality. Some long-established older inns cost as much as ¥80,000 per person, whereas humbler places that are more like bed-and-breakfasts are as low as ¥5,000. Unlike hotels, prices are per person and include the cost of breakfast, dinner, and tax. Some inns allow guests to stay without having dinner and lower the cost accordingly. However, this is not recommended, because the service and meals are part of the ryokan experience. Not all inns are willing to accept foreign guests because of language and cultural barriers, so it is important to make reservations in advance. To find the inn that best suits your needs, contact the **Japan Ryokan Association** (1-8-3 Marunouchi, Chiyoda-ku, Tokyo, tel. 03/231–5310) or JNTO.

It is important to follow Japanese customs in all ryokan. Upon entering take off your shoes, as you would do in a Japanese household, and put on the slippers that are provided in the entryway. A maid, after bowing to welcome you, will escort you to your room, which will have tatami (straw mats) on the floor and will probably be partitioned off with *shoji* (sliding paper-paneled walls). Remove your slippers before entering your room; you should not step on the tatami with either shoes or slippers. The room will have little furniture or decoration—perhaps one small low table and cushions on the tatami, with a long simple scroll on the wall. Often the rooms overlook a garden.

Most guests arrive in the late afternoon. After relaxing in their room with a cup of green tea, they have a long hot bath. In ryokan with thermal pools, you can take to the waters anytime, although the doors to the pool are usually locked from 11 PM to 6 AM. In ryokan without thermal baths or private baths in guest rooms, guests must stagger their visit to the one or two public baths. Typically the maid will ask what time you would like your bath and fit you into a schedule. In Japanese baths, you wash and rinse off entirely before entering the tub. Because other guests will be using the same bathwater after you, it is important to observe these customs. After your bath, change into a *yukata*, a simple cotton kimono, provided in your room. Do not feel abashed at walking around in what is essentially a robe—all the guests will be doing the same.

Dinner, included in the price of the room, is served in the room. After you are finished, a maid will discreetly come in, clear away the dishes, and lay out your futon. In Japan *futon* means bedding, and this consists of a thin cotton mattress and a heavy, thick comforter. In summer, the comforter is replaced with a thinner quilt. The small, hard pillow is filled with grain. The less expensive ryokan (under ¥7,000 for one) have become slightly lackadaisical in changing the sheet cover over the quilt with each new guest; feel free to complain. In the morning, a maid will gently wake you, clear away the futon, and bring in your Japanese-style breakfast. If you are not fond of Japanese breakfasts, often consisting of fish, raw egg, and rice, the staff will usually be able to rustle up some coffee and toast.

Because the staffs of most ryokan are small and dedicated, it is important to be considerate and understanding of their somewhat rigid schedules. Guests are expected to arrive in the late afternoon and eat around 6. Usually the doors to the inn are locked at 10, so plan for early evenings. Breakfast is served around 8, and checkout is at 10.

Part of the charm of a ryokan is its simplicity. To the unaccustomed eye, the rooms may seem barren and the bedding rather Spartan. Ryokan are not for those who cannot stand the thought of sleeping on the floor with simple bedding, sharing a bath with others, or eating rice and fish for breakfast. But those who are willing to try an evening in the Japanese spirit will find solace in the simple elegance of the inn.

A genuine traditional ryokan with exemplary service is exorbitantly expensive—more than ¥30,000 a night with two meals. Many modern hotels with Japanese-style rooms are now referring to themselves as ryokan, and though meals may be served in the guests' rooms, they are a far cry from the traditional ryokan. There are also small inns claiming the status of ryokan, but they are really nothing more than bed-and-breakfast establishments where meals are taken in a communal dining room and service is minimal. Prices are around ¥5,000 for a single room, ¥7,000 for a double. JNTO offers a publication listing some of these.

Minshukus Minshukus are private homes that accept guests. Usually they cost about ¥5,000 per person, including two meals. Unlike in a ryokan, where you need not lift a finger, in a minshuku you are expected to lay out and put away your own bedding and bring your own towels. Meals are often served in communal dining rooms. Minshukus vary in size and atmosphere; some are literally private homes that take on only a few guests, while others are more like no-frill inns. For more information, contact the **Japan Minshuku Association** (1-29-5 Takadanobaba, Shinjuku-ku, Tokyo, tel. 03/3232–6561).

Youth Hostels Youth hostels cost approximately ¥2,500–¥3,000 per day, including two meals. Hostels provide little more than a bunk bed or a futon and have strictly enforced curfew hours. Some require a membership card from a youth-hostel association. Memberships and further information are available at the **Japan Youth Hostel Association,** Hoken Kaikan, 1-1, Ichigaya-Sadohara-cho, Shinjuku-ku, Tokyo, tel. 03/3269–5831. JNTO has a free pamphlet and map listing every hostel in Japan.

Temples It is possible to arrange for accommodations in Buddhist temples. JNTO has lists of temples that accept guests. A stay at a temple generally costs ¥3,000–¥9,000 a night, including two meals. Some temples offer instruction in meditation or allow the guests to observe the temple religious practices, while others simply offer a room. The Japanese-style rooms are very simple and range from beautiful, quiet havens to not-so-comfortable, basic cubicles. Still, temples provide a taste of traditional Japan.

Inexpensive Accommodations JNTO publishes a listing of some 200 accommodations that are reasonably priced. To be listed, properties must meet Japanese fire codes and charge less than ¥8,000 per person without meals. For the most part, the properties charge ¥5,000–¥6,000. These properties welcome foreigners (many Japanese hotels and ryokan do not like to have foreign guests). Properties include business hotels, ryokan of very rudimentary nature, minshukus, and pensions. It's the luck of the draw whether you choose a good or less than good property. In most cases, the rooms are clean, but very small. Except in business hotels, private baths are not common, and you will be expected to have your room lights out by 10 PM.

Many accommodations on the JNTO's list can be reserved through the nonprofit organization **Welcome Inn Reservation Center** (International Tourism Center of Japan, 2nd. Floor, Kotani Bldg., 1-6-6 Yurakucho, Chiyoda-ku, Tokyo 100, tel. 03/3580–8353, fax 03/3580–8256). Reservations forms are available from your nearest JNTO office. You will need to have your reservation requests received by the Center at least two weeks before your departure to allow processing time. If you are already in Japan, JNTO's Tourist Information Centers (TICs) at Narita Airport, downtown Tokyo, and Kyoto can make immediate reservations for you at these Welcome Inns.

Home Exchange This is obviously an inexpensive solution to the lodging problem, because house-swapping means living rent-free. You find a house, apartment, or other vacation property to exchange for your own by becoming a member of a home-exchange organization, which then sends you its annual directories listing available exchanges and includes your own listing in at least one of them. Arrangements for the actual exchange are made by the two parties to it, not by the organization. Principal clearinghouses include **Intervac U.S./International Home Exchange** (Box 590504, San Francisco, CA 94159, tel. 415/435–3497), the oldest, with thousands of foreign and domestic homes for exchange in its three annual directories; membership is $62, or $72 if you want to receive the directories but remain unlisted. The **Vacation Exchange Club** (Box 650, Key West, FL 33041, tel. 800/638–3841), also with thousands of foreign and domestic listings, publishes four annual directories plus updates; the $50 membership includes your listing in one book. **Loan-a-Home** (2 Park La., Apt. 6E, Mount Vernon, NY 10552, tel. 914/664–7640) specializes in long-term exchanges; there is no charge to list your home, but the directories cost $35 or $45 depending on the number you receive.

Tax and Service Charge A 3% federal consumer tax is added to all hotel bills. Another 3% local tax is added to the bill if it exceeds ¥15,000. You may save money if you pay for your hotel meals separately rather than charge them to your bill.

At first-class, full-service, and luxury hotels, a 10% service charge will be added to the bill in place of individual tipping. At the more expensive ryokan, where individualized maid service is offered, the service charge will usually be 15%. At business hotels, minshukus, youth hostels, and economy inns, no service charge will be added to the bill.

Credit Cards

The following credit card abbreviations are used: AE, American Express; DC, Diners Club; D, Discover; MC, MasterCard; and V, Visa.

Tipping

Tipping is not common in Japan. It is not necessary to tip taxi drivers, or at beauty parlors, barber shops, bars, and nightclubs. A chauffeur for a hired car will usually receive a tip of ¥500 for a ½-day excursion and ¥1,000 for a full-day trip. Porters charge fees of ¥250–¥300 per bag at railroad stations and ¥200 per piece at airports. It is not customary to tip employees of hotels, even porters, unless a special service has been rendered. In such cases, a gratuity of ¥2,000 or ¥3,000 should be placed in an envelope and handed to the staff member discreetly.

Shopping

Despite the high value of the yen and the high price of many goods, shopping is one of the great pleasures of a trip to Japan. You may not find terrific bargains here, but if you know where to go and what to look for, you can purchase unusual gifts and souvenirs at reasonable prices. Don't shop for items that are cheaper at home; Japan is not the place to buy a Gucci bag. Look for things that are Japanese-made for Japanese people and sold in stores that do not cater primarily to tourists.

Don't pass up your chance to purchase Japanese handicrafts. Color, balance of form, and superb craftsmanship make these items exquisite and well worth the price you'll pay. That doesn't mean they're all cheap; in fact, some handicrafts are quite expensive. For example, Japanese **lacquerware** carries a hefty price. But if you like the shiny boxes, bowls, cups, and trays and consider that quality lacquerware is made to last a lifetime, the cost is justified. Be careful, though: Some lacquer items are made from a pressed-wood product rather than solid wood, and only experts can tell the difference. If the price seems low, it probably means the quality is low, too.

Handmade paper—in the form of stationery, cards, moneyholders, gift wrapping, and more—is one of the best buys in Japan. Delicate sheets of almost-transparent writing paper, blank cards tied with gold ribbons, and colorful folded-paper dolls in traditional wedding garb can all be bought for the price of a Hallmark card. In addition, there are small rectangular boxes (suitable for jewelry) covered with finely printed paper and hexagonal pencil boxes pretty enough to hold the paper-covered pencils sold in the same stationery stores.

At first look, the **ceramics** displayed in Japan seem priced for a prince's table. But if you keep shopping, you can find both functional and decorative ceramics at prices comparable to what you'd expect to pay at home. And since presentation of food and flowers is so important in Japanese culture, the vessels produced here tend to be of higher quality for the money. The best places to shop for ceramics are department stores, where the selection is vast and prices range from outrageously costly to moderate, with sale items sold at bargain prices. Covered rice bowls, sake jars and cups, and chopstick holders make great inexpensive gifts.

Department stores are also good places to look for **woodblock prints.** One floor of these stores often is devoted to traditional arts and crafts. Clear, bright copies of prints made by famous Japanese woodblock artists, such as Hiroshige, can be bought for about $10.

Another item worth purchasing is **printed fabric,** whether in yardage or in the form of finished scarves, napkins, tablecloths, or pillows. The complexity of the designs and the quality of the printing make these items special. Again, try the department stores, where you are most likely to find salespeople who speak English. Large fabric stores are great for browsing, but you may have trouble finding out if a given fabric is pure silk or a blend.

When you need to buy a gift for someone who has everything, head to the basement level of a department store, where **food products** are presented in lovely gift boxes. Japanese snacks make interesting presents, as do the beautifully packaged (although overpriced) sweets. These can also be bought at kiosks at train stations.

Packaging is a high art in Japan. Everything from tea cups to pearl necklaces is wrapped as if it were a wedding present, so even the smallest gift can be presented to your friends and family back home with style.

To get an idea of how the middle class manages its daily life, head to one of the shopping arcades, often located below train or subway stations. Everything is sold in these arcades: clothes, stationery, records, toiletries, food, and so on. You may find some bargains here, but you will probably notice that the quality of goods is reflected in the prices.

Opening and Closing Times

General business hours in Japan are 9–5. Many offices are also open at least half of the day on Saturday but are generally closed on Sunday.

Banks are open 9–3 weekdays and 9–noon on the first and last Saturday of the month. They are closed on Sunday.

Department stores are usually open 10–7 but are closed one day a week, which varies with each department store. Other stores are open 10 or 11 to 7 or 8.

Sports

Participant Sports

Beaches

For a country that consists entirely of islands, Japan has surprisingly few good beaches. Those just outside of Tokyo, in areas such as Kamakura and the Izu Peninsula, are absolutely mobbed with high-school and college students during the summer. The beaches of Kyushu and Shikoku are less crowded, more pleasant, and have clear blue water. The best beaches in Japan are in the subtropical Ryukyu Islands. Keep in mind, however, that many Japanese find it less expensive to fly to Hawaii than to go to the Ryukyus.

Bicycling

In most of Japan the conditions for biking are not ideal. The roads are narrow and much of the terrain is mountainous. The best cycling is on some of the remote islands, such as Sado, on the Sea of Japan, or Iki, a small island off the coast of Kyushu. For exploring a more rural area or provincial towns such as Takayama or Hagi, bicycles can be an inexpensive way to travel. In such places a store that rents bikes can usually be found close to the bus or railway station. The approximate charge for rental is ¥300 per hour. Cyclists should bear in mind that cars drive on the left side of the road in Japan.

Fitness Although health clubs and aerobic studios abound in most major Japanese cities, memberships are usually long-term and expensive. Many of the major hotels in Tokyo have excellent fitness facilities that are open to their guests.

Joggers will probably find Japanese streets too narrow and crowded. Many runners in Tokyo enjoy the jogging course around the Imperial Palace.

Skiing Japan's mountains are beautiful and snowy in the winter season, with very good skiing conditions. Many ski areas are located near natural hot springs, so it is possible to combine a day of skiing with a long, restful soak. Japan's most popular ski areas are around Nagano (where the 1998 Winter Olympics are to be held); at Jozankei, near Sapporo, and on the western slopes of Daisetsuzan National Park on Hokkaido; and on northern Honshu at Mt. Zao, near Yamagata.

The major drawback of skiing in Japan is the crowds, particularly on weekends and holidays. Not only are the slopes crowded, but the trains and highways heading toward ski areas are also congested, and accommodations are nearly always full. Those determined to ski in Japan should try to go on weekdays, or else head for Hokkaido.

Spectator Sports

Baseball Baseball is so near and dear to the hearts of most Japanese that they probably do not even remember that it is American in origin. A baseball game in Japan is not all that different from one in the United States. The field is slightly smaller and crowds are a bit more orderly, with cheering done in unison. Do not be surprised to see a few non-Japanese on the fields, as two foreign players are allowed per team. American baseball notables such as Reggie Smith and Bob Horner have played in Japan. In Tokyo, the place to see pro baseball is the Korakuen, a new dome-shaped indoor stadium. Bleacher seats are approximately ¥700.

Sumo The earliest recorded sumo matches were held around AD 200, and it is a sport that is deeply steeped in tradition. A Shinto-style roof is hung from the ceiling over a clay circular ring; two wrestlers face each other in the ring and toss salt into the ring as a purification ritual. The match is concluded when any part of the sumo wrestler's body touches the ground or he is pushed out of the ring.

Sumo wrestlers are of enormous girth, usually weighing 90–165 kilograms (200–365 pounds). During the match they are clad in loincloths that cover little of the massive bodies that push and shove during the match. Yet there is a certain elegance in their movements that is enhanced by their top-knot hairstyles slicked down with linseed oil.

Although inexpensive seats can be purchased for ¥500, it is worthwhile to buy the more expensive seats (¥5,000–¥6,500) because you get a carrier bag full of refreshments and souvenirs. The food is a tasty meal of generous portions, with sushi, yakitori chicken sticks, and other Japanese foods, along with bottles of beer. Souvenirs include ceramic items or small lamps with sumo-related patterns.

Bathhouses

The art of bathing has been part of Japanese culture for centuries. Baths are for washing and cleansing, but for many they are also for relaxation and pleasure. Traditionally, Japanese went to communal bathhouses that served as centers for social gatherings. Although most Japanese houses and apartments in modern times have bathtubs, many Japanese still prefer the pleasures of communal bathing—either in hot springs on vacations or in public bathhouses. Baths are places where confidences are exchanged and many a joke is retold.

Private or communal, Japanese baths are meant for soaking and not for washing. The water in the bath is drawn only once and discarded only after everyone has finished; bathers must wash and rinse before getting into the bath to keep the water clean. Because the water is used by more than one person, it is a cardinal rule that no soap gets into the bathwater. Unlike Western bathtubs, in which the bather reclines, Japanese tubs are deep enough for bathers to sit upright with water up to their necks. The water is as hot as the body can endure, but the reward for a moment of unease upon entry is the pleasure of soaking in water that does not get tepid.

The procedures for taking a Japanese bath are simple. First you sit on a stool outside the bathtub and, using a pail with a long handle, dip water (either from the bath or from faucets), cleanse yourself with soap, and then rinse thoroughly. Do not worry about spilling the water, because there is a drain outside the tub. In public baths it is common for one bather to wash other people's backs and to help them rinse off. If you are in a private home, remember to place the lid on top of the tub so that the water remains as hot as possible for the next bather.

Because most major hotels in cities only offer Western-style reclining bathtubs, those in search of the Japanese bathing experience should either stay in a Japanese-style inn or go to a public bathhouse. Public baths are both clean and hygienic, and are not hard to find; there is at least one in nearly every neighborhood. Although small towels are available for a small fee, it is best to bring your own. The bathhouses are divided into male and female areas. Do as the other bathers do: Undress in the front room, leave your clothes in small lockers or baskets, venture into the washing area, and from there into the bath. Be prepared to see another side of Japanese life. The retiring women, for example, that you encounter on the streets will be far more forward, far more ribald than they would be in other situations. If you are more interested in a peaceful soak than in experiencing the hubbub of bathhouse life, go in the middle of the afternoon, when you will probably encounter only a few subdued elderly folk.

Hot Springs

It is fortuitous for the Japanese, who are great aficionados of bathing, that natural hot springs, known as *onsen*, dot the Japanese archipelago. Many onsen are surrounded by resorts ranging from large Western-style hotels to small, humble inns.

For the most part, onsen water is piped into hotel rooms or large communal baths, but some onsen are located outdoors. Onsen areas are usually open year-round, so it is possible to soak while surrounded by a snowy winter landscape.

For years, going to onsen was considered to be for old men and women who wanted to rest their weary bones, but in the past few years there has been a great resurgence in their popularity. Some of the more well-known spas near Tokyo are Atami, Hakone, Ito, and Nikko. Some of the more famous resorts in other parts of Japan are Beppu and Unzen in Kyushu; Arima, near Kobe, in Gunma Prefecture of Honshu; and Noboribetsu in Hokkaido.

Customs, Manners, and Etiquette

Propriety is an important part of Japanese society. Many Japanese expect foreigners to behave differently and are tolerant of faux pas, but are pleasantly surprised when people acknowledge and observe their customs. The easiest way to ingratiate yourself with the Japanese is by taking the time to learn and respect their ways.

It is customary upon meeting someone to bow. The art of bowing is not simple; the depth of your bow depends on your social position in respect to that of the other person. Younger people, or those of lesser status, must bow deeper in order to indicate their respect and acknowledge their position. Foreigners are not expected to understand the complexity of these rules, and a basic nod of the head will suffice. Many Japanese are familiar with Western customs and will offer their hand for a handshake.

Do not be offended if you are not invited to someone's home. In general, most entertaining is done in restaurants or bars. It is an honor when you are invited to a home; this means that your host feels comfortable and close with you. If you do receive an invitation, bring along a small gift—a souvenir from your country is always the best present, but food and liquor are also appreciated. Upon entering a home, remove your shoes in the foyer and put on the slippers that are provided. It is important to have socks or stockings that are in good condition.

Japanese restaurants often provide a small hot towel called an *oshibori*. This is to wipe your hands but not your face. You may see some Japanese wiping their faces with their oshibori, but generally this is considered to be bad form. When you are finished with your oshibori, do not just toss it back onto the table, but fold or roll it up. Those who are not accustomed to eating with chopsticks may ask for a fork instead. When eating from a shared dish, do not use the part of the chopsticks that have entered your mouth; instead, use the end that you have been holding in your hand.

Doing Business

As Japan's role in the global economy expands, the number of business travelers to Japan increases. Although many business practices are universal, certain customs remain unique to Japan. It is not necessary to observe these precepts, but Japanese will always appreciate their observance.

Business cards are mandatory in Japan. Upon meeting someone for the first time, it is common to bow and to proffer your business card simultaneously. Do not worry about getting your cards printed in Japanese—English will do. In a sense, the cards are simply a convenience. Japanese sometimes have difficulty with Western names, and they like to refer to the cards. Also, in a society where hierarchy matters, Japanese like to know job titles and rank, so it is useful if your card indicates your position in your company. Japanese often place the business cards they have received in front of them on a table or desk as they conduct their meetings. Follow suit, and do not simply shove the card in your pocket.

The concept of being fashionably late does not exist in Japan; it is extremely important to be prompt for both social and business occasions. Japanese addresses tend to be complicated, and traffic is often heavy, so allow for adequate travel time.

Most Japanese are not accustomed to using first names in business circumstances. Even workmates of 20 years' standing use surnames. Unless you are sure that the Japanese person is extremely comfortable with Western customs, it is probably better to stick to last names. Also, respect the hierarchy, and as much as possible address yourself to the most senior person in the room.

Don't be frustrated if decisions are not made instantly. Individual businesspeople are rarely empowered to make decisions, and must confer with their colleagues and superiors. Even if you are annoyed, don't express anger or aggression. Losing one's temper is equated with losing face in Japan.

A separation of business and private lives remains sacrosanct in Japan, and it is best not to ask about personal matters. Rather than asking about a person's family, it is better to stick to neutral subjects. This does not mean that you can only comment on the weather, but rather that you should be careful not to be nosy. Because of cramped housing, many Japanese entertain in restaurants or bars. It is not customary for Japanese to bring wives along. If you are traveling with your spouse, do not assume that an invitation includes both of you. You may ask if it is acceptable to bring your spouse along, but remember that it is awkward for a Japanese person to say no. You should pose the question carefully, or not at all.

Usually, entertaining is done over dinner, followed by an evening on the town. Drinking is something of a national pastime in Japan. If you would rather not suffer from a hangover the next day, do not refuse your drink—sip, but keep your glass at least half full. An empty glass is nearly the equivalent of requesting another drink. You should never pour your own drink or let your companions pour theirs.

A special note to women traveling on business in Japan: Remember that although the situation is gradually changing, most Japanese women do not have careers. Many Japanese businessmen do not yet know how to interact with Western businesswomen. They may be uncomfortable, aloof, or patronizing. Be patient and, if the need arises, gently remind them that, professionally, you expect to be treated as any man would be.

Great Itineraries

Each chapter in *Fodor's Japan* is described as an itinerary through a particular city or region of Japan. The following are suggestions for other itineraries that cross from one area to another and combine parts of the exploring sections of the various chapters. Keep in mind that if you are planning to do a lot of train travel, it is best to get a Japan Rail Pass, which must be purchased outside of Japan (*see* Japan Rail Pass, *above*).

Introduction to Traditional Japan (One Week)

Like every nation, Japan has some sights that are more famous than others. These sights tend to be in the major cities. The following itinerary covers the barest minimum, but it does include modern Tokyo; the splendor of Nikko; the temples and shrines of Kamakura, the power center of Japan's first shogunate; the temples of classical Kyoto; and Nara, Japan's first permanent capital. Be warned that this itinerary barely scratches the surface of Japan's heritage.

Day 1: Arrive in Tokyo. Flights from the United States tend to arrive in the late afternoon, which means that by the time you reach your hotel in downtown Tokyo, it is early evening.

Day 2: Visit the major Tokyo sites that appeal to you (*see* Chapter 3). Arrange it so that your evening is spent in one or two of the nighttime districts, such as Roppongi or Shinjuku.

Day 3: Visit Nikko either on your own or with a tour (*see* Chapter 4). Return to Tokyo for evening pleasures.

Day 4: Visit Kamakura on your own, traveling from Tokyo by train (*see* Chapter 4). If there is time left in the day, stop on the way back to Tokyo to visit Yokohama (*see* Chapter 4).

Day 5: Take one of the morning Shinkansen trains from Tokyo to Kyoto (*see* Chapter 7). Visit the sights in the Eastern District (Higashiyama) in the afternoon and enjoy the Gion District in the evening.

Day 6: In the morning visit more of the Eastern District sights and in the afternoon visit the Western District sights.

Day 7: Cover Central Kyoto in the morning and travel to Nara in the afternoon (*see* Chapter 8).

Day 8: Return to Tokyo via Kyoto and go straight to the airport.

An Extended Introduction to Japan (Two Weeks)

Two weeks is obviously better than one week in Japan. Covering the same ground as the one-week itinerary of Japan, this itinerary also includes some of the Japan Alps, Hiroshima, and the Seto Inland Sea.

Day 1–4: Same as above.

Day 5: Take the train to Nagano and visit Zenkoji Temple. Continue by train to Matsumoto and visit Karasujo Castle, the Japan Folklore Museum, and the Japan Ukiyo-e Museum (*see* Chapter 6).

Day 6: Travel via Kamikochi to Takayama (*see* Chapter 6).

Day 7: Visit Takayama sights and in the late afternoon travel by train via Toyama to Kanazawa (*see* Chapter 6).

Day 8: Visit the sights of Kanazawa (*see* Chapter 6) and catch the late-afternoon train to Kyoto (*see* Chapter 7).

Day 9: Visit Kyoto's Eastern District (Higashiyama) in the afternoon and enjoy the Gion District in the evening.

Day 10: In the morning visit more of the Eastern District sights and in the afternoon visit the Western District sights.

Day 11: Cover Central Kyoto in the morning and Northern Kyoto in the afternoon.

Day 12: Travel to Nara in the afternoon to see the sights there (*see* Chapter 8).

Day 13: Travel by train to Himeji to visit the castle (*see* Chapter 11). Continue on to Okayama and reach Kurashiki by early afternoon.

Day 14: Leave Kurashiki by train in time to be in Hiroshima for lunch. Visit the Peace Memorial Park and Museum and then take the train and ferry to Miyajima Island and spend the night there (*see* Chapter 11).

Day 15: Return to Tokyo in the morning and go straight to the airport.

Scenic Japan

Tohoku, in northern Honshu, is a mixture of modern cities and small villages, rustic farmhouses and glorious temples, and high mountain ranges and indented shorelines. Tohoku has yet to be commercialized; there is still the feeling that one is traveling in another era. The chapter on Tohoku (Chapter 14) is an itinerary in itself. Here we have shortened the itinerary so that it can easily be managed in a week and also include a visit to Nikko.

Day 1: Take the Shinkansen train from Tokyo to Sendai. See the sights in Sendai and then take the train to Matsushima.

Day 2: Spend most of the day exploring Matsushima and return to Sendai for the night.

Day 3: Take the train to Hiraizumi and visit the sights. Reboard the train to Morioka.

Day 4: Take the train north as far as Obuke and transfer to a bus to cross the Hachimantai Plateau. At the end of the Aspite Skyline Drive, change buses and head south to Tozawako.

Day 5: Take the train to Kakunodate to visit the samurai houses. Reboard the train to travel to Yamegata to visit Yamadera.

Day 6: Take the train south to Yamagata and on to Fukushima, where you can board the Shinkansen train for Utsonomiya. Here, rather than return to Tokyo, you can take a local train up to Nikko (*see* Chapter 4).

Day 7: Return to Tokyo.

Into the Northern Frontier

Northern Japan is rural Japan, steeped in folklore and natural beauty. Though tourist facilities are available throughout the area of northern Honshu and Hokkaido, the number of tourists is fewer. This itinerary gives the traveler the chance to see the other side of Japan—not the industry that has spawned the country's economic miracle or the aristocratic temples of Imperial Japan—but rustic Japan, with more of what the country looked like before it was swept into 20th-century Western technology.

The itinerary starts in Sapporo in Hokkaido, on the assumption that one arrives there by plane.

Day 1: Explore Sapporo (*see* Chapter 15).

Day 2: Visit the Shakotan Peninsula by rented car, or by a bus/train combination. Return to Sapporo in the evening, perhaps dining at Otaru on the way back (*see* Chapter 15).

Day 3: Take the train to Asahigawa and rent a car for the drive to Sounkyo in the Daisetsuzan National Park. You can also travel by bus (*see* Chapter 15).

Day 4–5: Travel by car or bus to Akan National Park. You may want to spend two nights here exploring (*see* Chapter 15).

Day 6: Travel by car or by bus and train to Abashiri and go north to Mombetsu (*see* Chapter 15).

Day 7: Travel back to Ashigawa, return the car and take the train back to Sapporo. There is the option of traveling north from Mombetsu to Wakkanai and visiting Rebun and Rishiri islands (*see* Chapter 15).

Day 8: Travel by bus to Lake Toya and on to Noboribetsu Onsen (*see* Chapter 15).

Day 9: By train travel to Hakodate, visit the town (*see* Chapter 15) and then reboard the train for Aomori. Change trains and go on to Hirosaki (*see* Chapter 14).

Day 10: Travel south to Akita by train and then change for a train to Kakunodate to visit the samurai houses. Reboard the train and continue on to Tozawako (*see* Chapter 14).

Day 11: Travel by train to Morioka and farther west to Miyako, with a visit to Jodogahama Beach (*see* Chapter 14).

Day 12: By train travel to Kamaishi and then east to Tono (*see* Chapter 14).

Day 13: Continue by train to Hanamaki and change for the train going to Hiraizumi. Visit the temples and before nightfall catch the train on to Sendai (*see* Chapter 14).

Day 14: Visit Matsushima and spend the day exploring. You can either spend the night or return to Tokyo via Sendai (*see* Chapter 14).

Castles

Only 12 donjons from the feudal period have survived intact. The following is a tour designed to cover the best of them, though we have had to omit the one in Hirosaki since it is off by itself in northern Tohoku (northern Honshu). While this six-day tour travels from castle town to castle town, there are plenty of other sights to see in the vicinity of each castle. At certain places you will probably wish to stay longer than the itinerary below suggests, and make it a 10-day trip.

Day 1: Leaving Tokyo or Kyoto by Shinkansen train, the first stop is Himeji and its magnificent castle. Then continue on to Okayama to visit its castle, which is the only one on this tour that is a replica. Rather than spend the night at Okayama, take the train to Kurashiki and stay there (*see* Chapter 11).

Day 2: Cross over to Shikoku either by train or ferry, and continue by bus to Kochi and its castle (*see* Chapter 12).

Day 3: Using a combination of train and bus, head for Uwajima and its castle before continuing by train to Matsuyama and its castle (*see* Chapter 12).

Day 4: By ferry, cross over the Inland Sea to Hiroshima and take the train north to Matsue and its castle (*see* Chapter 11).

Day 5: Take the train to Hikone in the direction of Kyoto, visit the castle, and then continue by train via Gifu to Inuyama (*see* Chapter 5).

Day 6: From Inuyama, return to Gifu and then take the train to Matsumoto to visit one of the most attractive feudal castles. From Matsumoto, return to Tokyo (*see* Chapter 6).

In the Shadow of the Mountains

Old traditional Japan is fast disappearing, but the north coast of Western Honshu has largely avoided the eyesore of modern industrialism. This area is ideal for anyone willing to go off the beaten track and take a leisurely trip through small villages, rustic countryside, and medieval castle towns. Minimally this itinerary will take five or six days, but it could easily be extended to a leisurely 10-day exploration (*see* Chapter 11).

Day 1: Head west from Kyoto on the Shinkansen to Ogori. From Ogori (west of Hiroshima) cross from the south coast of Western Honshu to Hagi on the north coast by bus. See Hagi's sights.

Day 2: Travel by bus to Tsuwano and spend the rest of the day here.

Day 3: Take the train to Masuda and begin heading northeast along the coast. If you have the time, you may want to make Matsue your first stop.

Day 4: Make sure that you visit the Izumo Taisha Shrine.

Day 5: Continue northwest along the coast to Tottori and the Tottori Sand Dunes, then on to Kasumi and Kirosaki for the night.

Day 6: The last major sight on the coast is Amanohashidate, one of the Big Three Scenic Wonders in Japan. From here Kyoto is less than three hours away by train.

2 Portraits of Japan

Japan at a Glance: A Chronology

10,000–300 BC Neolithic Jomon hunting and fishing culture leaves richly decorated pottery.

300 AD Yayoi culture displays knowledge of farming and metallurgy imported from Korea.

After 300 The Yamato tribe consolidates power in the rich Kansai plain and expands westward, forming the kind of military aristocratic society that was to dominate Japan's history.

c. 500 Yamato leaders, claiming to be descended from the sun goddess, Amaterasu, take the title of emperor.

552 Buddhism, introduced to the Yamato court from China by way of Korea, complements rather than replaces the indigenous Shinto religion. Horyuji, a Buddhist temple built at Nara in 607, includes the oldest surviving wooden building in the world.

593–622 Prince Shotoku encourages the Japanese to embrace Chinese culture.

Nara Period

710–784 Japan has first permanent capital (at Nara); great age of Buddhist sculpture, piety, and poetry.

The Fujiwara or Heian Period

794–1160 The capital is moved from Nara to Heiankyo (Kyoto), where the imperial court is dominated by the Fujiwara family. Lady Murasaki's novel *The Tale of Genji*, written c. 1020, describes the elegant, ceremonious court life.

The Kamakura Period

1185–1335 Feudalism enters, with military and economic power in the provinces and the emperor a powerless, ceremonial figurehead in Kyoto. Samurai warriors welcome Zen, a new sect of Buddhism from China.

1192 After a war with the Taira family, Yoritomo of the Minamoto family becomes the first shogun; he places his capital in Kamakura.

1274, 1281 The fleets sent by Chinese emperor Kublai Khan to invade Japan are destroyed by typhoons, praised in Japanese history as *kamikaze*, or divine wind.

Ashikaga Period

1336–1568 The Ashikaga family assumes the title of shogun and settles in Kyoto. The Zen aesthetic flourishes in painting, landscape gardening, and tea ceremony. The Silver Pavilion on Ginkaku-ji in

Kyoto, built in 1483, is the quintessential example of Zen-inspired architecture. The period is marked by constant warfare but also by increased trade with the mainland. Osaka develops into an important commercial city, and trade guilds appear.

1543 Portuguese sailors, the first Europeans to reach Japan, initiate trade relations with the lords of western Japan and introduce the musket, which changes Japanese warfare.

1549–1551 St. Francis Xavier, the first Jesuit missionary, introduces Christianity.

The Momoyama Period of National Unification

1568–1600 Two generals, Nobunga Oda and Hideyoshi Toyotomi, are the central figures of this period.

1592, 1597 Hideyoshi invades Korea. He brings back Korean potters, who rapidly develop a Japanese ceramic industry.

The Tokugawa Period

1600–1868 Ieyasu Tokugawa becomes shogun after the battle of Sekigahara. The military capital is established at Edo (Tokyo), which shows phenomenal economic and cultural growth. A hierarchy of four social classes—warriors, farmers, artisans, and merchants—is rigorously enforced. The merchant class, however, is increasingly prosperous and effects a transition from a rice to a money economy. Also, merchants patronize new, popular forms of art: kabuki, haiku, and the ukiyo-e school of painting. The life of the latter part of this era is beautifully illustrated in the wood block prints of the artist Hokusai (1760–1849).

1618 Persecution of Christians who refuse to recant.

1637–1638 Japanese Christians massacred in the Shimabara uprising. Japan is closed to the outside world except for a Dutch trading post in Nagasaki harbor.

1853 The American Commodore Perry reopens Japan to foreign trade.

The Meiji Restoration

1868–1912 Supporters of Emperor Meiji, calling for direct imperial rule, depose the shogun and move the capital to Edo, renaming it Tokyo. Japan is modernized along Western lines with a constitution proclaimed in 1889; a system of compulsory education and a surge of industrialization follow.

1902–1905 Japan defeats Russia in the Russo–Japanese War and achieves world-power status.

1910 Japan annexes Korea.

1914–1918 Japan joins the Allies in World War I.

1923 A catastrophic earthquake shakes Tokyo and Yokohama.

1931 Japan seizes the Chinese province of Manchuria.

1937 Following years of increasing military and diplomatic activity in northern China, open warfare breaks out (until 1945); it is resisted by both Nationalists and Communists.

1939–1945 Japan, having signed anti-Communist treaties with Nazi Germany and Italy (1936 and 1937), invades and occupies French Indochina.

1941 The Japanese attack on Pearl Harbor on December 7 brings the United States into war against Japan in the Pacific.

1942 Japan's empire extends to Indo-China, Burma, Malaya, the Philippines, and Indonesia. Defeat by U.S. forces at Midway in June turns the tide of Japanese military success.

1945 Tokyo and 50 other Japanese cities are devastated by U.S. bombing raids. The United States drops atomic bombs on Hiroshima and Nagasaki, precipitating Japanese surrender.

1945–1952 The American occupation under General Douglas MacArthur disarms Japan and encourages the establishment of a democratic government. Emperor Hirohito retains his position.

1953 After the Korean War, Japan begins a period of great economic growth.

1964 Tokyo hosts the Summer Olympic games.

Late 1960s Japan develops into one of the major industrial nations in the world.

Mid-1970s Japanese production of electronics, cars, cameras, and computers places her at the heart of the emerging "Pacific Rim" economic sphere and threatens to spark a trade war with the industrial nations of Europe and the United States.

1989 Emperor Hirohito dies.

1990 Coronation of Emperor Akihito. Prince Fumihito marries Kiko Kawashima.

1991 The Diet approves use of Japanese Military forces under United Nations auspices.

The Discreet Charm of Japanese Cuisine

By Diane Durston

A resident of Kyoto for more than 10 years, Diane Durston is the author of Old Kyoto: A Guide to Traditional Shops, Restaurants and Inns *and* Kyoto: Seven Paths to the Heart of the City.

Leave behind the humidity of Japan in summer and part the crisp linen curtain of the neighborhood *sushi-ya* some hot night in mid-July. Enter a world of white cypress and chilled sea urchin, where a welcome *oshibori* (hot towel) awaits your damp forehead, and a master chef stands at your beck and call. A cup of tea to begin. A tiny mound of ginger to freshen the palate, and you're ready to choose from the colorful array of fresh seafood on ice inside a glass case before you. Bite-size morsels arrive in friendly pairs. A glass of ice-cold beer. The young apprentice runs up and down making sure everyone has tea—and anything else that might be needed. The chef has trained for years in his art, and he's proud, in his stoic way, to demonstrate it. The *o-tsukuri* (sashimi) you've ordered arrives; today the thinly sliced raw tuna comes in the shape of a rose (Is it really your birthday?). The fourth round you order brings with it an unexpected ribbon of cucumber, sliced with a razor-sharp sushi knife into sections that expand like an accordion. The chef's made your day. . . .

Red paper lanterns dangling in the dark above a thousand tiny food stalls on the back streets of Tokyo. To the weary Japanese salaried man on his way home from the office, these *akachochin* lanterns are a prescription for the best kind of therapy known for the "subterranean homesick blues," Japanese style: one last belly-warming bottle of sake, a nerve-soothing platter of grilled chicken wings, and perhaps a few words of wisdom for the road. Without these comforting nocturnal way stations, many a fuzzy-eyed urban refugee would never survive that rumbling, fluorescent nightmare known as the last train home.

And where would half of Japan's night-owl college students be, if not for the local *shokudo*, as the neighborhood not-so-greasy spoon is known? Separated at last from mother's protective guidance (and therefore without a clue as to how an egg is boiled or a bowl of soup is heated), the male contingent of young lodging-house boarders put their lives in the hands of the old couple who runs the neighborhood café. Bent furtively over a platter of *kare-raisu* (curry and rice) or *tonkatsu teishoku* (pork cutlet set meal), these ravenous young men thumb through their baseball comics each night, still on the road to recovery from a childhood spent memorizing mathematical formulas and English phrases they hope they'll never have to use.

Down a dimly lit back street not two blocks away, a geisha in all her elaborate finery walks her last silk-suited customer out to his chauffeur-driven limousine. He has spent the evening being pampered, feasted, and fan-danced in the rarefied air of one of Tokyo's finest *ryotei.* (You must be invited to these exclusive eateries—or be a regular patron, introduced years earlier by another regular patron who vouched for your reputation with his own.) There has been the most restrained of traditional dances, some samisen playing—an oh-so-tastefully suggestive tête-à-tête. The customer has been drinking the very finest sake, accompanied by a succession of exquisitely presented hors d'oeuvres—what amounts to a seven-course meal in the end is the formal Japanese *haute cuisine* known as *kaiseki.* His grapes have all been peeled. If it were not for his company's expense account, by now he would have spent the average man's monthly salary. Lucky for him, he's not the average man.

On a stool, now, under the flimsy awning of a street stall, shielded from the wind and rain by flapping tarps, heated only by a portable kerosene stove and the steam from a vat of boiling noodles, you'll find neither tourist nor ptomaine. Here sits the everyday workingman, glass of *shochu* (a strong liquor made from sweet potatoes) in sunbaked hand, arguing over the Tigers' chances of winning the Japan Series, as he zealously slurps down a bowl of hot noodle soup sprinkled with red-pepper sauce—more atmosphere, and livelier company than you're likely to find anywhere else in Japan. The *yatai-san,* as these inimitable street vendors are known, are an amiable, if disappearing, breed.

Somewhere between the street stalls and the exclusive ryotei, a vast culinary world exists in Japan. Tiny, over-the-counter restaurants, each with its own specialty—from familiar favorites, such as tempura, sukiyaki, or sushi, to exotic delicacies like *unagi* (eel), or *fugu* (blowfish)—inhabit every city side street. Comfortable, country-style restaurants abound, serving a variety of different *nabemono,* the one-pot stew dishes cooked right at your table. There are also lively neighborhood *robatayaki* grills, where cooks in *happi* coats wield skewered bits of meat, seafood, and vegetables over a hot charcoal grill as you watch.

Ten years ago, sukiyaki and tempura were exotic enough for most Western travelers. Those were the days when raw fish was still something a traveler needed fortitude to try. But, with *soba* (noodle) shops and sushi bars popping up everywhere from Los Angeles to Paris, it seems that—at long last—the joy of Japanese cooking has found its way westward . . . and it's about time.

There *is* something special, however, about visiting the tiger in his lair. Something no tame circus cat could ever match. Although tours to famous temples and scenic places can provide important historical and cultural background material, there is nothing like a meal in a local restaurant—be it under the tarps of the liveliest street stall, or within the quiet recesses of an elegant Japanese inn—for a taste of the real Japan. Approaching a platter of fresh sashimi in Tokyo is like devouring a hot dog smothered in mustard and onions in Yankee Stadium. There's nothing like it in the world.

The Essentials of a Japanese Meal

As exotic as it might seem, the basic formula for a traditional Japanese meal is simple. It starts with soup, followed by raw fish, then the entrée (grilled, steamed, simmered or fried fish, chicken, or vegetables), and ends with rice and pickles, with perhaps some fresh fruit for dessert, and a cup of green tea. As simple as that, almost.

An exploration of any cuisine should begin at the beginning, with a basic knowledge of what it is you're eating. Rice, of course, the traditional staple. And seafood—grilled, steamed, fried, stewed, or raw. Chicken, pork, or beef, at times—in that order of frequency. A wide variety of vegetables (wild and cultivated), steamed, sautéed, blanched, or pickled, perhaps—but never overcooked. Soybeans in every form imaginable, from tofu to soy sauce. Seaweed, in and around lots of things.

The basics are just that. But there are, admittedly, a few twists to the story, as could be expected. Beyond the raw fish, it's the incredible variety of vegetation used in Japanese cooking that still surprises the Western palate: *take-no-ko* (bamboo shoots); *renkon* (lotus root); and the treasured *matsutake* mushrooms (which grow wild in jealously guarded forest hideaways and sometimes sell for over $60 apiece), to name but a few.

Tangy garnishes, both wild and domestic, such as *kinome* (leaves of the Japanese prickly ash pepper tree), *mitsuba* (trefoil, of the parsley family), and *shiso* (a member of the mint family) are used as a foil for oily foods. The more familiar sounding ingredients, such as sesame and ginger, appear in abundance, as do the unfamiliar—*wasabi* (Japanese horseradish), *uri-ne* (lily bulbs), *ginnan* (ginko nuts), and *daikon* (gigantic white radishes). Exotic? Perhaps, but delicious, and nothing here bites back. Simple? Yes, if you understand a few of the ground rules.

Absolute freshness is first. According to world-renowned Japanese chef Shizuo Tsuji, soup and raw fish are the two test pieces of Japanese cuisine. Freshness is the criterion for both: "I can tell at a glance by the texture of their skins—like the bloom of youth on a young girl—whether the fish is really fresh," Tsuji says in *The Art of Japanese Cooking*. A comparison as startling, perhaps, as it is revealing. To a Japanese chef, freshness is an unparalleled virtue, and much of his reputation relies on his ability to obtain the finest ingredients at the peak of season: fish brought in from the sea this morning (not yesterday), and vegetables from the earth (not the hothouse), if at all possible.

Simplicity is next. Rather than embellishing foods with heavy spices and rich sauces, the Japanese chef prefers his flavors *au naturel*. Flavors are enhanced, not elaborated; accented rather than concealed. Without a heavy dill sauce, fish is permitted a degree of natural fishiness—a garnish of fresh red ginger will be provided to offset the flavor rather than to disguise it.

The third prerequisite is beauty. Simple, natural foods must appeal to the eye as well as to the palate. Green peppers on a vermilion dish, perhaps, or an egg custard in a blue bowl. Rectangular dishes for a round eggplant. So important is the seasonal element in Japanese cooking that maple leaves and pine needles will be used to accent an autumn dish. Or two small summer delicacies, a pair of freshwater *ayu* fish, will be grilled with a purposeful twist to their tails to make them "swim" across a crystal platter to suggest the coolness of a mountain stream on a hot August night.

That's next: the mood. It can make or break the entire meal, and the Japanese connoisseur will go to great lengths to find the perfect yakitori stand—a smoky, lively place—an environment appropriate to the occasion, offering a night of grilled chicken, cold beer, and camaraderie. To a place like this, he'll take only friends he knows will appreciate the gesture.

Atmosphere depends as much on the company as it does on the lighting or the color of the drapes. In Japan, this seems to hold particularly true. The popularity of a particular *nomiya*, or bar, depends entirely on the affability of the *mama-san*, that long-suffering lady who's been listening to your troubles for years. In fancier places, mood becomes a fancier problem, to the point of quibbling over the proper amount of "water music" trickling in the basin outside your private room.

Culture: The Main Course

Sipping coffee at a sidewalk café on the Left Bank, you begin to feel what it means to be a Parisian. Slurping noodles on tatami in a neighborhood soba shop overlooking a tiny interior garden, you start to understand what it's like to live in Japan. Food, no matter which country you're in, has much to say about the culture as a whole.

Beyond the natural dictates of climate and geography, Japanese food has its roots in the centuries-old cuisine of the Imperial Court, which was imported from China—a religiously formal style of meal called *yusoku ryori*. It was prepared only by specially appointed chefs, who had the status of priests in the service of the emperor, in a culinary ritual that is now nearly a lost art. Although it was never popularly served in centuries past (a modified version can still be found in Kyoto), much of the ceremony and careful attention to detail of yusoku ryori is reflected today in the formal kaiseki meal.

Kaiseki Ryori: Japanese Haute Cuisine

Kaiseki refers to the most elegant of all styles of Japanese food available today, and *ryori* means cuisine. With its roots in the banquet feasts of the aristocracy, by the late 16th century it had developed into a meal to accompany ceremonial tea. The word kaiseki refers to a heated stone *(seki)* that Buddhist monks placed inside the folds *(kai)* of their kimonos to keep off the biting cold in the unheated temple halls where they slept and meditated.

Cha-kaiseki, as the formal meal served with tea *(cha)* is called, is intended to take the edge off your hunger at the beginning of a formal tea ceremony and to counterbalance the astringent character of the thick green tea. In the tea ceremony, balance—and the sense of calmness and well-being it inspires—is the keynote.

The formula for the basic Japanese meal derived originally from the rules governing formal kaiseki—not too large a portion, just enough; not too spicy, but perhaps with a savory sprig of trefoil to offset the bland tofu. A grilled dish is served before a steamed one, a steamed dish before a simmered one; a square plate is used for a round food; a bright green maple leaf is placed to one side to herald the arrival of spring.

Kaiseki ryori appeals to all the senses at once. An atmosphere is created in which the meal is to be experienced. The poem in calligraphy on a hanging scroll and the flowers in the alcove set the seasonal theme, a motif picked up in the pattern of the dishware chosen for the evening. The colors and shapes of the vessels complement the foods served on them. The visual harmony presented is as vital as the balance and variety of flavors of the foods themselves, for which the ultimate criterion is freshness. The finest ryotei will never serve a fish or vegetable out of its proper season—no matter how marvelous a winter melon today's modern greenhouses can guarantee. Melons are for rejoicing in the summer's bounty . . . period.

Kaiseki ryori found its way out of the formal tearooms and into a much earthier realm of the senses when it became the fashionable snack with sake in the teahouses of the geisha quarters during the 17th and 18th centuries. Not only the atmosphere, but the Chinese characters used to write the word *kaiseki* are different in this context; they refer to aristocratic "banquet seats." And banquets they are. To partake in the most exclusive of these evenings in a teahouse in Kyoto still requires a personal introduction and a great deal of money, though these days many traditional restaurants offer elegant kaiseki meals (without the geisha) at much more reasonable prices.

One excellent way to experience this incomparable cuisine on a budget is to visit a kaiseki restaurant at lunchtime. Many of them offer *kaiseki bento* lunches at a fraction of the dinner price, exquisitely presented in lacquered boxes, as a sampler of their full-course evening meal.

Shojin Ryori: Zen-Style Vegetarian Cuisine

Like an overnight stay in a Buddhist temple, *shojin ryori*, the Zen-style vegetarian cuisine, is another experience you shouldn't pass up. In traditional Japanese cuisine, the emphasis is on the natural flavor of the freshest ingredients in season, without the embellishment of heavy spices and rich sauces. This probably developed out of the Zen belief in the importance of simplicity and austerity as paths to enlightenment. Protein is provided by an almost limitless number of dishes made from soybeans—such as *yudofu*, or boiled bean curd, and *yuba*, sheets of pure protein skimmed from vats of steaming soy milk. The variety and visual beauty of a full-course shojin ryori meal offers new dimensions in dining to the vegetarian gourmet. *Gomadofu*, or sesame-flavored bean curd, for example, is a delicious taste treat, as is *nasu-dengaku*, grilled eggplant covered with a sweet *miso* sauce.

There are many fine restaurants (particularly in the Kyoto area) that specialize in shojin ryori, but it's best to seek out one of the many temples throughout Japan that open their doors to visitors; here you can try these special meals within the actual temple halls, which often overlook a traditional garden.

Sushi, Sukiyaki, Tempura, and Nabemono: A Comfortable Middle Ground

Leaving the rarefied atmosphere of teahouses and temples behind, an entire realm of more down-to-earth gastronomic pleasures waits to be explored.

Sushi, sukiyaki, and tempura are probably the three most commonly known Japanese dishes in the Western world. Restaurants serving these dishes are to be found in abundance in every major hotel in Japan. It is best, however, to try each of these in a place that specializes in just one.

An old Japanese proverb says "*Mochi wa mochi-ya e*"—if you want rice cakes, go to a rice-cake shop. The same goes for sushi. Sushi chefs undergo a lengthy apprenticeship, and the trade is considered an art form. Possessing the discipline of a judo player, the *itamae-san* (or "man before . . . or behind . . . the counter," depending on your point of view) at a sushi-ya is a real master. Every neighborhood has its own sushi shop, and everyone you meet has his own secret little place to go for sushi.

The Tsukiji Fish Market district in Tokyo is so popular for its sushi shops that you usually have to wait in line for a seat at the counter. Some are quite expensive, some are relatively cheap. "Know before you go" is the best policy; "ask before you eat" is next.

Among the dozens of kinds of sushi available, some of the most popular are *maguro* (tuna), *ebi* (shrimp), *hamachi* (yellowtail), *uni* (sea urchin), *anago* (conger eel), *tako* (octopus), and *awabi* (abalone). The day's selection is usually displayed in a glass case at the counter, which enables you to point at whatever catches your eye. (Try the *akagai*, or red shellfish. The word is a euphemistic expression for the female organ, for reasons blushingly recognizable.)

Tempura, the battered and deep-fried fish and vegetable dish, is almost certain to taste better at a small shop that serves nothing else. The difficulties of preparing this seemingly simple dish lie in achieving the proper consistency of the batter and the right temperature and freshness of the oil in which it is fried.

Sukiyaki is the popular beef dish that is sautéed with vegetables in an iron skillet at the table. The tenderness of the beef is the determining factor here, and many of the best sukiyaki houses also run their own butcher shops so that they can control the quality of the beef they serve. Although beef did not become a part of the Japanese diet until the turn of the century, the Japanese are justifiably proud of their notorious beer-fed and hand-massaged beef (e.g., the famous Matsuzaka beef from Kobe, and the equally delicious Omi beef from Shiga Prefecture). Though certainly a splurge, no one should pass up an opportunity to try a beef dinner in Japan.

Apart from sukiyaki and beef, *shabu-shabu* is another possibility, though this dish has become more popular with tourists than with the Japanese. It is similar to sukiyaki in that it is prepared at the table with a combination of vegetables, but it differs in that shabu-shabu is swished briefly in boiling water, while sukiyaki is sautéed in oil and, usually, a slightly sweetened soy sauce. The word *shabu-shabu* actually refers to this swishing sound.

Nabemono, or one-pot dishes, are not as familiar to Westerners as the three mentioned above, but the variety of possibilities is endless, and nothing tastes better on a cold winter's night. Simmered in a light, fish-base broth, these stews can be made of almost anything: chicken *(tori-nabe)*, oysters *(kaki-nabe)*, or the sumo wrestler's favorite, the hearty *chanko-nabe* . . . with something in it for everyone. Nabemono is a popular family or party dish. The restaurants specializing in nabemono often have a casual, country atmosphere.

Bento, Soba, Udon, and Robatayaki: Feasting on a Budget

Tales of unsuspecting tourists swallowed up by money-gobbling monsters disguised as quaint little restaurants on the back streets of Japan's major cities abound in these days of the high yen. There are, however, many wonderful little places that offer excellent meals and thoughtful service—and have no intention of straining anyone's budget. To find them, you must not be afraid to venture outside your hotel lobby or worry about the fact that the dining spot has no menu in English. Many restaurants have menus posted out front that clearly state the full price you can expect to pay. (Some do add on a 10% tax, and possibly a service charge, so ask in advance.)

Here are a few suggestions for Japanese meals that do not cost a fortune and are usually a lot more fun than relying on the familiar but unexciting international fast-food chains for quick meals on a budget: *bento* lunches, *soba* or *udon* noodle dishes, and the faithful neighborhood *robatayaki* grills, ad infinitum.

The Bento. This is the traditional Japanese box lunch, available for take-out everywhere, and usually comparatively inexpensive. It can be purchased in the morning to be taken along and eaten later, either outdoors or on the train as you travel between cities. The bento consists of rice, pickles, grilled fish or meat, and vegetables, in an almost limitless variety of combinations to suit the season.

The basement level of most major department stores sell beautifully prepared bento lunches to go. In fact, a department store basement is a great place to sample and purchase the whole range of foods offered in Japan: among the things available are French bread, imported cheeses, traditional bean cakes, chocolate bonbons, barbecued chicken, grilled eel, roasted peanuts, fresh vegetables, potato salads, pickled bamboo shoots, and smoked salmon.

The *o-bento* (the "o" is honorific) in its most elaborate incarnation is served in gorgeous multilayered lacquered boxes as an accompaniment to outdoor tea ceremonies or for flower-viewing parties held in spring. Exquisite *bento-bako* (lunch boxes) made in the Edo period (1603–1868) can be found in museums and antiques shops. They are inlaid with mother-of-pearl and delicately hand-painted in gold. A wide variety of sizes and shapes of bento boxes are still handmade in major cities and small villages throughout Japan in both formal and informal styles. They make excellent souvenirs.

A major benefit to the bento lunch is its portability. Sightseeing can take you down many an unexpected path, and you need not worry about finding an appropriate place to stop for a bite to eat—if you bring your own bento. No Japanese family would ever be without one tucked carefully inside their rucksacks right beside the thermos bottle of tea on a cross-country train trip. If they do somehow run out of time to prepare one in advance—no problem—there are hundreds of wonderful options in the form of the beloved *eki-ben* ("train-station box lunch").

Each whistle-stop in Japan takes great pride in the uniqueness and flavor of the special box lunches, featuring the local delicacy, sold right at the station or from vendors inside the trains. The pursuit of the eki-ben has become a national pastime in this nation in love with its trains. Entire books have been written in Japanese explaining the features of every different eki-ben available along the 16,120 miles (26,000 kilometers) of railways in the country. This is one of the best ways to sample the different styles of regional cooking in Japan, and is highly recommended to any traveler who plans to spend time on the Japan Railway trains *(see* Regional Differences, *below)*.

Soba and Udon Noodles. Soba and udon noodle dishes are another life-saving treat for stomachs (and wallets) unaccustomed to exotic flavors (and prices). Small shops serving soba (thin, brown, buckwheat noodle) and udon (thick, white, wheat noodle) dishes in a variety of combinations can be found in every neighborhood in the country. Both can be ordered plain (ask for *o-soba* or *o-udon)*, in a lightly seasoned broth flavored with bonito and soy sauce, or in combination with things like tempura shrimp (*tempura soba* or *udon*), or chicken (*tori-namba soba* or *udon*). For a refreshing change in summer, try *zaru soba*, cold noodles to be dipped in a tangy soy sauce. *Nabeyaki-udon* is a hearty winter dish of udon noodles, assorted vegetables, and egg served in the pot in which it was cooked.

Robatayaki Grill. Perhaps the most exuberant of inexpensive options is the robatayaki. Beer mug in hand, elbow-to-elbow at the counter of one of these popular neighborhood grills—that is the best way to relax and join in with the local fun. You'll find no pretenses here, just a wide variety of plain good food (as much or as little as you want) with the proper amount of alcohol to get things rolling.

Robata means fireside, and the style of cooking is reminiscent of old-fashioned Japanese farmhouse meals cooked over a charcoal fire in an open hearth. It's easy to order at a robatayaki shop, because the selection of food to be grilled is lined up behind glass at the counter. Fish, meat, vegetables, tofu—take your pick. Some popular choices are *yaki-zakana* (grilled fish), particularly *kare-shio-yaki* (salted and grilled flounder) and *asari saka-mushi* (clams simmered in sake, Japanese rice wine). Try the grilled Japanese *shiitake* (mushrooms), *ao-to* (green peppers), and the *hiyayakko* (chilled tofu sprinkled with bonito flakes, diced green onions, and soy sauce). Yakitori can be ordered in most robatayaki shops, though many inexpensive drinking places specialize in this popular barbecued chicken dish.

The budget dining possibilities in Japan don't stop there. **Okonomiyaki** is another choice. Somewhat misleadingly called the Japanese pancake, it is actually a mixture of vegetables, meat, and seafood in an egg-and-flour batter grilled at your table, much better with beer than with butter. It's most popular for lunch or as an after-movie snack.

Another is **kushi-age,** skewered bits of meat, seafood, and vegetables battered, dipped in bread crumbs, and deep-fried. There are many small restaurants serving only kushi-age at a counter, and many of the robatayaki grills serve it as a sideline. It's also a popular drinking snack.

Oden, a winter favorite, is another inexpensive meal. A variety of meats and vegetables slowly simmered in vats, it goes well with beer or sake. This, too, you may order piece by piece *(ippin)* from the assortment you see steaming away behind the counter, or *moriawase*, in which case the cook will serve you up an assortment.

Sake: The Samurai Beverage

With all this talk about eating and drinking, it would be an unforgivable transgression to overlook Japan's number one alcoholic beverage, sake (pronounced *sa-kay*), the "beverage of the samurai," as one brewery puts it. The ancient myths call this rice wine the "drink of the gods," and there are over 2,000 different brands produced throughout Japan. A lifetime of serious scene-of-the-crime research would be necessary to explore all the possibilities and complexities of this interesting drink.

Like other kinds of wine, sake comes in sweet *(amakuchi)* and dry *(karakuchi)* varieties; these are graded *tokkyu* (superior class), *ikkyu* (first class), and *nikkyu* (second class) and are priced accordingly. (Connoisseurs say this ranking is for tax purposes and is not necessarily a true indication of quality.)

Best drunk at room temperature *(nurukan)* so as not to alter the flavor, sake is also served heated *(atsukan)* or with ice *(rokku de)*. It is poured from *tokkuri* (small ceramic vessels) into tiny cups called *choko*. The diminutive size of these cups shouldn't mislead you into thinking you can't drink too much. The custom of making sure that your drinking companion's cup never runs dry often leads the novice astray.

Junmaishu is the term for pure rice wine, a blend of rice, yeast, and water to which no extra alcohol has been added. Junmaishu has the strongest and most distinctive flavor, compared with various other methods of brewing, and is preferred by the sake *tsu*, as connoisseurs are known.

Apart from the *nomiya* (bars) and restaurants, the place to sample sake is the *izakaya*, a drinking establishment that serves only sake, usually dozens of different kinds, including a selection of *jizake*, the kind produced in limited quantities by small regional breweries throughout the country.

In the words of Ikkyu, one of Japan's most revered and notorious 15th-century imbibers (and one of its "highest" Buddhist priests):

I have been ten days in this temple
and my heart is restless.
The scarlet thread of lust at my feet
has reached up long.
If someday you come looking for me,
I will be in a shop that sells fine seafood,
a good drinking place,
or a brothel.

Regional Differences

Tokyo people are known for their candor and vigor, as compared with the refined restraint of people in the older, more provincial Kyoto. This applies as much to food as it does to language, art, and fashion. Foods in the Kansai district (including Kyoto, Nara, Osaka, and Kobe) tend to be lighter, the sauces less spicy, the soups not as hardy as those of the Kanto district, of which Tokyo is the center. How many Tokyoites have been heard to grumble about the "weak" soba broth on their visits to Kyoto? You go to Kyoto for the delicate and formal kaiseki; to Tokyo for sushi.

Nigiri-sushi, with pieces of raw fish on bite-size balls of rice (the form with which most Westerners are familiar), originated in the Kanto district, where there is a bounty of fresh fish. *Saba-sushi* is the specialty of landlocked Kyoto. Actually the forerunner of nigiri-sushi, it is made by pressing salt-preserved mackerel onto a bed of rice in a mold.

Every island in the Japanese archipelago has its specialty, and, within each island, every province has its own *meibutsu ryori*, or specialty dish. In Kyushu, try *shippoku-ryori*, a banquet-style feast of different dishes in which you eat your way up to a large fish mousse topped with shrimp. This dish is the local specialty in Nagasaki, for centuries the only port through which Japan had contact with the West.

On the island of Shikoku, try *sawachi-ryori*, an extravaganza of elaborately prepared platters of fresh fish dishes, the specialty of Kochi, the main city on the Pacific Ocean side of the island. In Hokkaido, where salmon dishes are the local specialty, try *ishikari-nabe*, a hearty salmon-and-vegetable stew.

The Bottom Line

There are a couple of things that take some getting used to. Things will be easier for you in Japan if you've had some experience with chopsticks. Some of the tourist-oriented restaurants (and of course all those serving Western food) provide silverware, but most traditional restaurants in Japan offer only chopsticks. It's a good idea to practice. The secret is to learn to move only the chopstick on top, rather than to try to move both chopsticks at once.

Sitting on the floor is another obstacle for many, including the younger generation of Japanese to whom the prospect of sitting on a cushion on tatami mats for an hour or so means nothing but stiff knees and numb feet. Because of this, many restaurants now have rooms with tables and chairs. The most traditional restaurants, however, have kept to the customary style of dining in tatami rooms. Give it a try. Nothing can compare with a full-course kaiseki meal brought to your room at a traditional inn. Fresh from the bath, robed in a cotton kimono, you are free to relax and enjoy it all, including the view. After all, the carefully landscaped garden outside your door was designed specifically to be seen from this position.

The service in Japan is usually superb, particularly at a *ryori-ryokan*, as restaurant/inns are called. A maid is assigned to anticipate your every need (even a few you didn't know you had). *"O-kyakusan wa kamisama desu"* (the customer is god), as the old Japanese proverb goes. People who prefer to dine in privacy have been known to say the service is too much.

Other problems? "The portions are too small" is a common complaint. The solution is an adjustment in perspective. In the world of Japanese cuisine, there are colors to delight in and shapes, textures, and flavors are balanced for your pleasure. Naturally, the aroma, flavor, and freshness of the foods have importance, but so do the dishware, the design of the room, the sound of water in a stone basin outside. You are meant to leave the table delighted—not stuffed. An appeal is made to all the senses through the food itself, the atmosphere, and appreciation for a carefully orchestrated feast in every sense of the word—these, and the luxury of time spent in the company of friends.

This is not to say that every Japanese restaurant offers aesthetic perfection. Your basic train-platform, stand-up, gulp-it-down noodle stall ("eat-and-out" in under six minutes) should leave no doubts as to the truth of the old saying that "all feet tread not in one shoe."

In the end, you'll discover that the joy of eating in Japan lies in the adventure of exploring the possibilities. Along every city street, you'll find countless little eateries specializing in anything you can name—and some you can't. In the major cities, you'll find French restaurants, British pubs, and little places serving Italian, Chinese, Indian, and American food, if you need a change of pace. In country towns, you can explore a world of regional delicacies found nowhere else.

There is something for everyone and every budget—from the most exquisitely prepared and presented formal kaiseki meal to a delicately sculpted salmon mousse à la nouvelle cuisine, from skewers of grilled chicken in barbecue sauce to a steaming bowl of noodle soup at an outdoor stall. And much to the chagrin of culinary purists, Japan has no dearth of international fast-food chains—from burgers to spareribs to fried chicken to doughnuts to 31 flavors of American ice cream.

Sometimes the contradictions of this intriguing culture—as seen in the startling contrast between ancient traditions and modern industrial life—seem almost overwhelming. Who would ever have thought you could face salad with lettuce, tomatoes, and seaweed . . . or green-tea ice cream? As the famous potter, Kawai Kanjiro, once said, "Sometimes it's better if you don't understand everything. . . . It makes life so much more exciting."

Manners

1) Don't point or gesture with chopsticks. Licking the ends of your chopsticks is rude, as is taking food from a common serving plate with the end of the chopstick you've had in your mouth.

2) There is no taboo against slurping your noodle soup, though women are generally less boisterous about it than men.

3) Pick up the soup bowl and drink directly from it, rather than lean over the table to sip it. Take the fish or vegetables from it with your chopsticks. Return the lid to the soup bowl when you are finished. The rice bowl, too, is to be picked up and held in one hand while you eat from it.

4) When drinking with a friend, don't pour your own. Take the bottle and pour for the other person. He will in turn reach for the bottle and pour for you. Japanese will attempt to top your drink off after every few sips.

5) Japanese don't pour sauces on their rice in a traditional meal. Sauces are intended for dipping foods lightly, not for dunking or soaking.

6) Among faux pas that are considered nearly unpardonable, the worst perhaps is blowing your nose. Excuse yourself and leave the room if this becomes necessary.

7) Although McDonald's and Hâagen-Dazs have made great inroads on the custom of never eating in public, it is still considered gauche to munch on a hamburger (or an ice-cream cone) as you walk along a public street.

The Springs of Ecstasy

By Simon Winchester

Asia-Pacific editor of Condé Nast Traveler *and Pacific region correspondent of* The Guardian *of London, Simon Winchester has reached* yudedako *more than once.*

Of all the many and varied degrees of the sublime to which the modern Japanese may aspire, none quite compares with that known as *yudedako*. The word means, quite simply, boiled octopus, and Japanese of all ages and both sexes will journey for miles and search for days for the perfect place to become one.

They do so for the simple reason that the attainment of *yudedako* is, so everyone from Hokkaido to Okinawa is led to believe from birth, a triumphal final step on the road to perfect physical health. It is an absolute essential for anyone ever hoping to achieve personal sobriety and mental serenity. It helps if you want marital harmony, to enjoy lifelong freedom from constipation and boils, to secure happiness, a clear skin, the faultless functioning of your sexual equipment, and to be rewarded with whatever else constitutes the Shinto equivalent of earthly Nirvana.

And the best, indeed the only place in which to become like a boiled octopus, where *yudedako* is to be found (in exchange for a paltry sum in folding money), is that most hallowed of Japanese institutions, the hot spring, the *onsen*. Of which, a cursory look at a good Japanese map will display, there are very, very many. The country, fissured from end to end with the cracks and crannies that are the geophysical consequence of being sited on a line of volcanoes, positively wheezes with steam and water. It gushes and sprays almost everywhere, in forest and glade, on meadowland and mountaintop. There are hot springs up in the snowfields. There are others on which float bananas and melon-size oranges. A mad-Ludwig look-alike has channeled one into a mountainside cable car, so you can steam as you fly. Monkeys will chatter and steal your towel from springs down south, while melting icicles will drip into boiling waterfalls up in Hokkaido. Some waters are naturally bloodred and scented with hibiscus, others are milky white with suspended sulfur—and smell understandably vile.

There are hundreds of them, in every prefecture, on every offshore island, even (hidden in office buildings and beside cinemas) in cities that have been built, incautiously, above the very fault lines themselves. And to all these superheated hollows flock the inhabitants of the empire in a ceaseless stream of enthusiasm. Small industries—in some towns, very large industries indeed—have sprung up around the *onsen* to cater to the needs of those who would plunge and soak and steam themselves in the *ofuro*, the baths. Some bath lovers confess to being *ofuro*holics, and it's said that there are clinics set up to cater to their excess. "Their passion for hot bathing is proverbial, and no other people in the world take such pride in their sanitary arrangements," as a Government Railway Guide put it, 50 years ago.

Modern lyricists go further. To understand the Japanese, they chorus, there is only one True Way: You must bathe with them. Go on in, they urge—the water's fine. Become a boiled octopus, and discern in your personal conversion alongside them their true nature, their inner soul—the *kokoro*, as the language has it, of the mysterious people of Nippon.

Why not indeed? Well, one reason many Westerners—*gaijin*, as the Japanese rather smoothly call everyone who is not one of them—prefer not to take time out to go bathing in Japan is the understanding that you have to, er, take all your clothes off. *In front of them.* And you *know* they will stare at your body, quite probably finding it a good deal less lovely than their own. They may even laugh or snigger behind their hands.

Furthermore, there are stories of terrible Asian protocols involved in bathing—a series of unwritten and unspoken rules known by every Japanese from conception, the careless breaking of any of which would result in the most frightful retribution. *What if I drop the soap in the ofuro?* is a typical fear. And so most innocent wanderers through Japan, invited to go bathing, prefer to stay snug inside their Hiltons and their Tokyus, mumbling excuses about the nearest *onsen* being too far, their schedule being too tight, or that they are quite clean enough anyway, and thanks very much for asking.

I am not an *ofuro*holic, nor do I entirely hold to the view that the Japanese are an enigmatic master race knowable only by those who watch them wash. But on the other hand, hot-spring bathing, I have discovered, is enormous fun, and in certain places at certain times it can be truly memorable, the stuff that dreams are made on. So, in the fond hope that others may share the enthusiasm, what follows is a brief illustration of what to do and how to do it and, to a very limited extent, where.

In my case, my first bath was taken at a place in eastern Kyushu called Yufu-in; and while there are scores of other springs well within the purview of Tokyo and Osaka and Kyoto, readily accessible to the timorous or the city-bound, it is to Yufu-in I will journey, since its memory lingers most poignant.

It was an autumn morning. I caught the *Shinkansen* from Tokyo westward to Hakata and was thus hurled in hyperdrive between Honshu and Kyushu, arriving at the vast station of Shin-Hakata at the predicted split second. A quick scurry along platforms, down flights of granite stairs, along passageways bright with colored neon and robotic salesgirls and the *Blade Runner* twitterings of computer-generated messages, then up more granite stairways to where, slightly dusty and forlorn, stood a country train!

This was an antique that had old leather and fur where the *Shinkansen* had polished steel and ripstop nylon, and it creaked and swayed as it moved out over the switches. And while the bullet train had vanished bloodlessly into tunnels and darted through arrow-straight cuttings, this old dear rumbled arthritically around curves and over trestle bridges, up and ever upward until it was in the heart of the hills, where the maple trees brushed the windows and the waterfalls splashed the carriage walls. The divine wind—the infamous kamikaze that had once scattered Kubla Khan's fleet in Hakata Bay—may have blown stiffly down at sea level: Up here it was still, and clouds stood unmoving by the mountaintops.

The stations slipped by. Moderate-size cities such as Futsukaichi and Kurume, where they make patterned cloths and rubberware. Small towns beside river crossings, with pottery factories and paper mills. And then little clusters of houses—Era and Bungomori and Bungo-Nakamura—where I first spied the telltale signs of seismic waters. In the pine forests behind each hamlet there were wisps of steam rising into the still air, like New York avenues at night and when Con Edison is at work, so rural Japan is a place of steam, hissing and bubbling out of the very earth.

And then the train eased into Yufu-in and creaked to a halt on a curve. It was warm, and there was a smell of creosote and pine tar, and a hint of sulfur in the air. After a few moments the train pulled away, and the station yard fell silent but for the cawing of a pair of crows high up in a tree. An old lady stepped from the shade, nudged me, and pointed to a crowd of bicycles for rent; 500 yen until nightfall, she suggested. I handed over the notes, she handed me a map, and on a cycle frame 10 sizes too small I wobbled off into town.

The woman had drawn crosses on the chart to indicate the best baths, but I had a guide with me, a young secretary from Fukuoka who hadn't been to an *onsen* for weeks and had said she was happy to swap her linguistic expertise for an hour or two of soaking. And so the pair of us headed south along a country lane, bound for a *ryokan*—a Japanese inn—called Kozenin.

There seemed to be no one about. The small dining room stood quite empty except for a stuffed boar standing by a table. But a wood fire smoldered quietly in an open grate, and a discreet cough brought an ancient attendant from behind a screen. She bowed low many times, and there was some conversation from which I caught only the word *furo*, then many *dōmo arigato gozaimashita* and much more low bowing and smiling. Then the two of us were handed *yukata*—cotton dressing gowns—and a pair of tiny squares of tie-dyed cloth called *furoshiki*. We walked outside again, down a graveled path through a small grove of pines, before coming to a pair of doors set in a plane-tree palisade. "A *rotemburo*," Yoko whispered. "Open-air pool. We're lucky."

My *kanji* is poor at the best of times, but I have become accustomed to the fact that the ideograph of "men" looks a sight more complicated than that for "women." So I pointed at what I thought was my door, Yoko grinned her assent, and we went our separate ways.

Inside was a changing room: flagstones worn smooth by centuries of use, stripped-oak walls, a few old iron hooks, a hand pump, some bamboo hand-dippers, half a dozen tiny stools with commodelike openings on top, and a wooden box filled with bars of industrial-strength soap. Beyond, all I could see was steam rising from the surface of what seemed a long and pretty lake that reached deep into the forest. This was the *rotemburo* itself; other springs at Yufu-in might be indoors, but this one was in as natural a setting as its Shinto gods had decreed. I could hear the gurgling of water running into it along bamboo gutters. It was all very peaceful and—mercifully—there seemed to be no one around.

I slipped off my *yukata* and put it on a hook. For a few seconds, and lest anyone should be lurking, I held my *furoshiki*, with studied casualness, in the approximate area that is always fuzzed-out in Japanese sex films. Then I pumped water into the hand-dipper, took a bar of Lifebuoy, carried my stool down to the edge of the lake, and began to scrub.

This, I had been told, was crucial. Wash and scrub and soap and scrape every square millimeter of your body until not one molecule of grubbiness remains. And this I did, pummeling myself ruthlessly, determined to get it right. "How you doing?" shouted Yoko from behind her bamboo curtain. I replied, breathlessly, that I was doing all I should be doing, and it seemed to be going well.

"Not a drop of soapy water in the bath!" she warned, and I baled and sluiced frantically as one small trickle of foaming liquid seemed to course its errant way toward the steam. But most *onsen* seem to have been designed by hydraulic architects of some skill: It would take a clumsy fellow indeed to get soapy water into the *ofuro*, so many and so effective are the little dams of stone erected everywhere as a precaution. The only way to pollute the bath is to get into it unbathed, unrinsed, or, heaven forfend, while holding and planning to use the soap itself. And that you never, never do. As Yoko, in one final reminder, called out.

"Ready?" she then asked. And I heard a splash and a sudden gasp of pleasure. She was in.

Now came the difficult bit. I was clean as a new pin, my skin tingled from the springwater, every atom of saponified glycerin long gone. I dropped my *furoshiki* completely and walked across smooth humps of granite to the edge. I dipped my toe into the steaming bath. The water was hot, indeed, but at the same time so extraordinarily soft that there seemed no pain in going farther. I stepped onto a rock slab, gasped at the slight shock, then walked forward to a deeper slab. The water rose steadily about me until it was waist-deep.

"Come on!" urged Yoko, who was, quite unashamedly, watching the entire performance. I could see her now through the mist, her head and shoulders just above the water that beached and lapped against the swell of her breasts. The outline of her body below was refracted out of any recognition too precise for decency.

The only way to retain my own dignity as she watched was to submerge, and so I pitched forward and down and sat as gently as I could on a convenient boulder. Yoko was a few feet away. I smiled at her and she smiled back. She touched my toe with one of hers, then moved toward me slightly and began to massage my foot with both of her naked legs. I closed my eyes and, content and warm and blanketed in the pleasing softness of the water, began to think of paradise.

When I opened my eyes—perhaps five or 10 minutes later—I was looking up at the deep blue sky. It was framed by dozens of maple trees, their leaves brilliant red and yellow after the first frosts of autumn. Once in a while one would dislodge, then drop and float, curling in the heat, on the surface of the bath. The air above the pool was cooler now—it was late afternoon, the sun was dipping behind Mount Yufu, and flocks of birds were flying back to their nests.

The bath steamed even more vigorously in the cool of the gloaming, and the bamboo runnels carrying the source water from the springs seemed to froth with new energy. Sitting beneath one of these proved a scalding reminder of what high temperature is all about: Yoko sat gaily beneath one for a good minute and then shouted triumphantly: "*Yudedako!*" I looked over at her; she had turned a bright red, like—well, just like a boiled octopus, though minus half a dozen arms. And as I looked down I seemed to be going the same way.

So out we climbed, she careless of the looks, me still taking care to avoid the gazes of the few children who had come in while I dozed. But none of them seemed more than mildly curious; no one seemed to mind, let alone to giggle. "*Hadaka to hadaka no tsukiai,*" ("Relationships between naked people are honest relationships") they say—bathing friends are the best of friends, the bath becomes a great equalizer, no one is more curious than he should be, no one ever behaves such as to spoil the enjoyment of any other bather, no one is embarrassed nor causes embarrassment.

And in that particular sense the bath *is* Japan, and the lyricists are right. For the manners of the Japanese, lately so corrupted in the cities and by the boardrooms, seem to revert to their impeccable type in the unalloyed egalitarianism of the *onsen*. Here, rank and title, riches and power, are stripped away with the clothes: There is no way to tell if the body lolling beside you belongs to the boss of Mitsubishi, to an ambassador, to a pauper, to a mendicant priest. With rank neither claimed nor recognized, each bather offers to the other an equal degree of respect and regard.

Then again, a man is well aware in a mixed-sex bath—like this one in Yufu-in—that naked women are all about him, yet the eroticism this induces is only of the mildest form, and all is diminished by the perfect decorum. For above all, decorum and studied delight rule the protocols of bathing—you seek pleasure from the waters, and you ensure that those about you are allowed to seek it too. Small wonder so few psychiatrists find employment in Japan. The *onsen* to which the Japanese repair each week or each month or every six months seem marvelous devices for purging the soul of envy and anxiety and stress, as well (it is claimed) as for curing all known ills, cleansing the liver and the brain, ensuring potency and attractiveness, long life—and wealth of spirit, if not necessarily of pocket.

And thus we spent the remainder of that autumn evening. We emerged from the first bath, toweled ourselves briskly dry, and cycled to another, and another, until it got too dark to see and we feared we might miss the last train. We sampled iron springs with red water; we found silky-smooth alkali springs that gushed forth *unagi*, or "eel water"; and Yoko knew of a tiny *harinoyu*, or "needle bath," which felt like immersing into a tub filled with small and very hot hedgehogs, and yet was much more pleasant than it sounds.

But in Yufu-in there were no mud baths nor radioactive sand baths, no seaside baths, not a single bath in a cable car, nor any of the astonishingly hot *atsu-yu*, where men with paddles slap at the water to try to keep it from boiling, and where there are Bath Masters to make sure you stay only for the three minutes needed to attain *yudedako*, and not a fatal second longer. For all these delights I had to wait for other places, other springs.

We caught the train at 10, having dined before a log fire and drunk deep of hot sake and Sapporo beer. The cycle lady was still there, waiting in the starlight, and she smiled as we climbed aboard the old train. She said something to Yoko as we left, and both women laughed. I asked what it was. "The *gaijin* looks younger," said Yoko. "A very young boiled octopus. Very good, don't you think? Very good."

3 Tokyo

By Jared Lubarsky and Nigel Fisher

A resident of Tokyo, Jared Lubarsky has lived in Japan since 1973. His articles have appeared in The New York Times, Travel & Leisure, Travel-Holiday, *and major in-flight magazines.*

Nigel Fisher is the editor of Voyager International; *he has traveled extensively in Japan for more than 20 years.*

Tokyo: Of all the major cities in the world, it is perhaps the hardest to understand, to feel comfortable in, and to see in any single perspective. To begin with, consider the sheer, outrageous size of it. Tokyo incorporates 23 wards, 26 smaller cities, seven towns, and eight villages, together sprawling 55 miles east to west and 15 miles north to south. The wards alone enclose an area of 227 square miles—home to some 8.5 million people. More than 2 million of these residents pass through Shinjuku Station, one of the major hubs in the transportation network, every day.

It's staggering to think what the population density would be if Tokyo went up as well as out. Mile after mile, the houses rise only one or two stories above the ground, that low uniformity broken here and there by the sore thumb of an apartment building. Space, that most precious of commodities, is so scarce that pedestrians have to weave in and out around the utility poles as they walk along the narrow sidewalks—and everywhere, space is wasted. Begin with that observation, and you discover that the very fabric of life in this city is woven of countless, unfathomable contradictions.

Tokyo is a state-of-the-art financial marketplace, where billions of dollars are whisked electronically around the globe every day, in the blink of an eye—and where automatic cash dispensers shut down at 7 PM. (The machines levy a service charge of ¥103 for withdrawals after 6 PM.) It's a metropolis of exquisite politenesses, where the taxi drivers open the door for you when you get in and out—and where the man in the subway will push an old woman out of the way to get a seat. A city of astonishing beauty in its small details, Tokyo also has some of the ugliest buildings on the planet and generates 20,000 tons of garbage a day. It installed its first electric light in 1833, yet still has hundreds of thousands of households without a bathtub.

Life was simpler here in the 12th century, when Tokyo was a little fishing village called Edo, near the mouth of the Sumida River on the Kanto Plain. The Kanto was a strategic granary, large and fertile; over the next 400 years it was governed by a succession of warlords and other rulers. One of them, named Dokan Ota, built the first castle in Edo in 1457. That deed is still officially regarded as the founding of the city, but the honor really belongs to Ieyasu, the first Tokugawa shogun, who arrived in 1590. When the civil wars of the 16th century came to an end, Ieyasu was the vassal of Generalissimo Hideyoshi Toyotomi, who gave him the eight provinces of Kanto and eastern Japan in exchange for three provinces closer to Kyoto—the imperial capital and ostensibly the seat of power. Ieyasu was a farsighted soldier; the swap was fine with him. In place of Ota's stronghold, he built a mighty fortress of his own—from which, 10 years later, he was ruling the whole country.

By 1680, there were over a million people here, and a great city had grown up out of the reeds in the marshy lowlands of Edo Bay. Tokyo can only really be understood as a *joka-machi*—a castle town. Ieyasu had fought his way to the shogunate, and he had a warrior's concern for the geography of his capital. Edo Castle had the high ground, but that wasn't enough; all around it, at strategic points, he gave large estates to allies and trusted retainers. These lesser lords' villas would also be garrisons, outposts on a perimeter of defense.

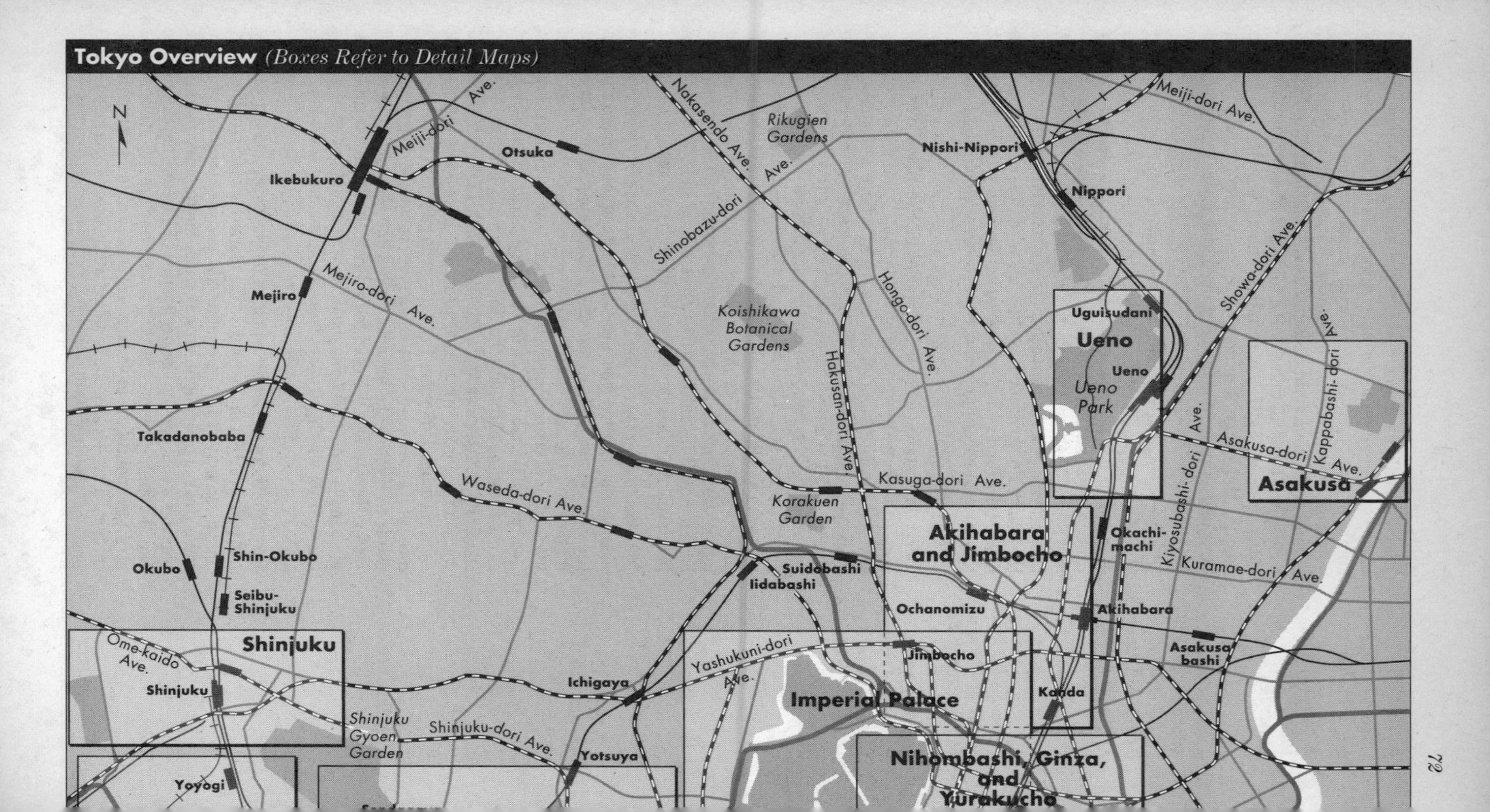
Tokyo Overview (Boxes Refer to Detail Maps)
N
Ikebukuro
Otsuka
Meiji-dori Ave.
Nakasendo Ave.
Rikugien Gardens
Shinobazu-dori Ave.
Nishi-Nippori
Nippori
Meiji-dori Ave.
Showa-dori Ave.
Mejiro
Mejiro-dori Ave.
Koishikawa Botanical Gardens
Hongo-dori Ave.
Hakusan-dori Ave.
Uguisudani
Ueno
Ueno
Ueno Park
Kappabashi-dori Ave.
Asakusa-dori Ave.
Asakusa
Takadanobaba
Waseda-dori Ave.
Kasuga-dori Ave.
Korakuen Garden
Kiyosubashi-dori Ave.
Akihabara and Jimbocho
Okachi-machi
Kuramae-dori Ave.
Okubo
Shin-Okubo
Seibu-Shinjuku
Suidobashi
Iidabashi
Ochanomizu
Akihabara
Asakusa bashi
Shinjuku
Ome-kaido Ave.
Shinjuku
Yashukuni-dori Ave.
Jimbocho
Ichigaya
Imperial Palace
Kanda
Shinjuku Gyoen Garden
Shinjuku-dori Ave.
Yotsuya
Yoyogi
Nihombashi, Ginza, and Yurakucho

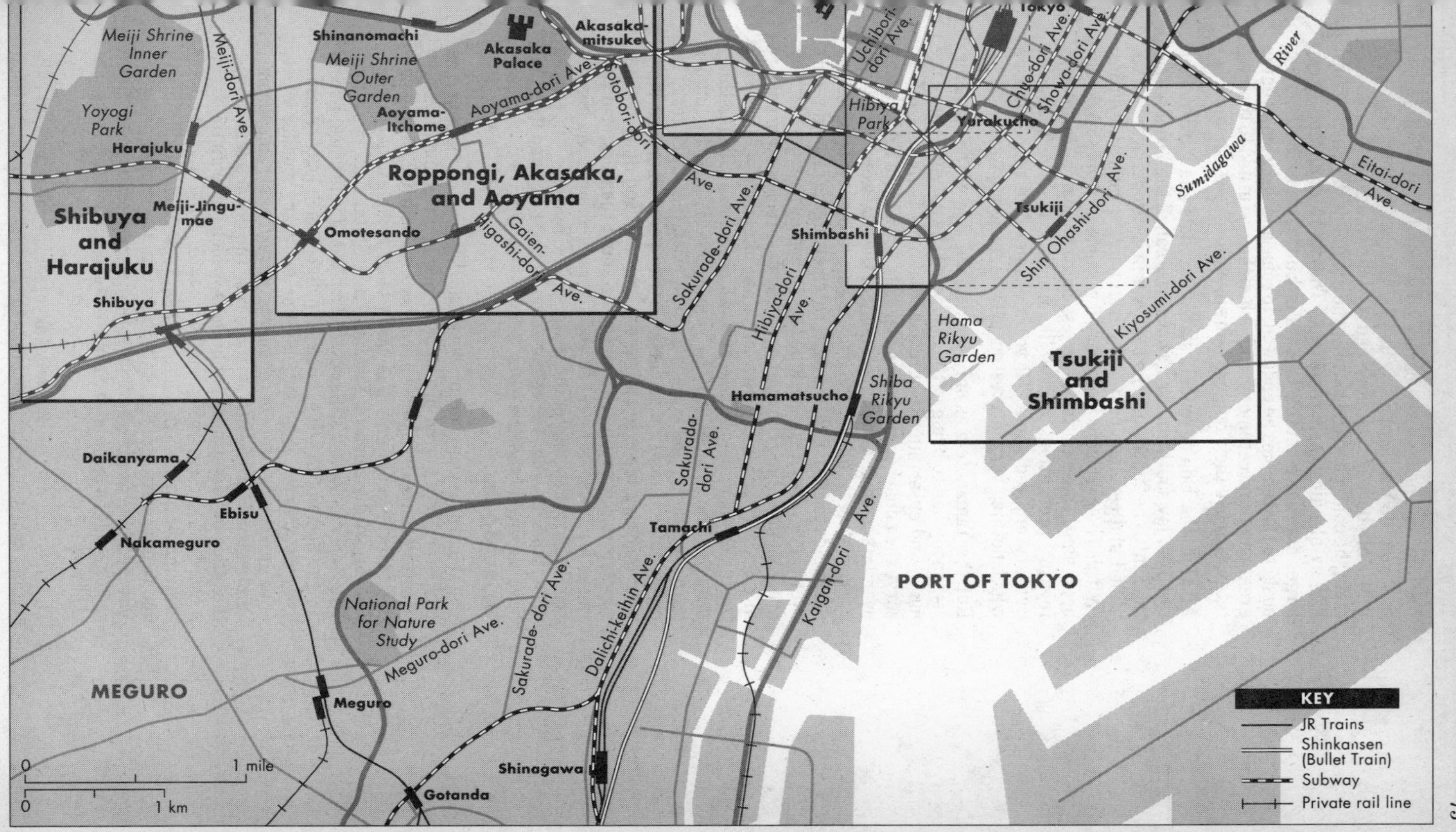
Shibuya and Harajuku
Roppongi, Akasaka, and Aoyama
Tsukiji and Shimbashi
Meiji Shrine Inner Garden
Yoyogi Park
Harajuku
Meiji-dori Ave.
Meiji-Jingu-mae
Shibuya
Shinanomachi
Meiji Shrine Outer Garden
Aoyama-Itchome
Akasaka Palace
Akasaka-mitsuke
Aoyama-dori Ave.
Sotobori-dori Ave.
Omotesando
Gaien-Higashi-dori Ave.
Uchibori-dori Ave.
Hibiya Park
Yurakucho
Chuo-dori Ave.
Showa-dori Ave.
Tokyo
Tsukiji
Shin Ohashi-dori Ave.
Sumidagawa
River
Eitai-dori Ave.
Kiyosumi-dori Ave.
Shimbashi
Sakurade-dori Ave.
Hibiya-dori Ave.
Hama Rikyu Garden
Shiba Rikyu Garden
Hamamatsucho
Sakurada-dori Ave.
Tamachi
Kaigan-dori Ave.
PORT OF TOKYO
Daikanyama
Ebisu
Nakameguro
National Park for Nature Study
Meguro-dori Ave.
Sakurade-dori Ave.
Dalichi-keihin Ave.
MEGURO
Meguro
Shinagawa
Gotanda
0 1 mile
0 1 km
KEY
JR Trains
Shinkansen (Bullet Train)
Subway
Private rail line

Farther out, he kept the barons he trusted least of all. Ieyasu had won the Battle of Sekigahara (1600), which made him shogun, only because someone had switched sides at the last moment; he controlled the barons who might one day turn against him by bleeding their treasuries. They were required to keep large, expensive establishments in Edo; to contribute generously to the temples he endowed; to come and go twice a year in great pomp and ceremony; and, when they returned to their estates, to leave their families—in effect, hostages—behind.

All this, the Edo of feudal estates, of villas and gardens and temples, lay south and west, but it was called the *Yamanote*—the Bluff, the "uptown." Here, all was in its proper order, disciplined and ceremonious; every man had his rank and duties. (Within the garrisons were very few women.) Almost from the beginning, those duties were less military than bureaucratic; Ieyasu's precautions worked like a charm, and the Tokugawa dynasty enjoyed some 250 years of unbroken peace, during which nothing very interesting ever happened uptown.

But the Yamanote was only the demand side of the economy: somebody had to bring in the fish, weed the garden, weave the mats, and entertain the bureaucrats during their time off. To serve the noble houses, common people flowed into Edo from all over Japan; their allotted quarters of the city were jumbles of narrow streets, alleys, and culs-de-sac, in the low-lying estuarine lands to the north and east. Often enough, the land wasn't even there when it was assigned to them; they had to *make* it by draining and filling the marshes. (The first reclamation project in Edo dates to 1457.) The result was Shitamachi—the "downtown," the part below the castle, which sat on a hill. Bustling, brawling Shitamachi was the supply side: it had the lumber yards, markets, and workshops; the wood-block printers, kimono makers, and moneylenders. The people here gossiped over the back fence in the earthy, colorful Edo dialect. They supported the bathhouses and the Kabuki theaters, had fireworks festivals, and went to Yoshiwara, making it the biggest licensed brothel quarter in the world. The Edokko—the people of Shitamachi—haven't changed much; their city and its spirit have survived, and the great estates uptown are now mostly parks and hotels.

The shogunate was overthrown in 1867. The following year, the Emperor Meiji moved his court to Edo and renamed it Tokyo (Eastern Capital). By now it was home to nearly 2 million people, and the geography was vastly more complex than before. The broad divisions of Yamanote and Shitamachi remained. The Imperial Palace still provided a point of reference, a locus for the heart of the city, but Tokyo defied such easy organization. As it grew, it became not one but many smaller cities, with different centers of commerce, government, amusement, and transportation. In Yamanote rose the department stores, the office buildings, and public halls, which made up the architecture of an emerging modern state. The workshops of Shitamachi multiplied, some of them to become small jobbers and family-run factories. Still, there was no planning, no grid. The neighborhoods and subcenters were worlds unto themselves, and the traveler from one was soon hopelessly lost in another.

The firebombings of 1945 left Tokyo, for the most part, in rubble and ashes. Here was an opportunity to start again: to build a planned city, like Kyoto, Barcelona, or Washington, with a rational shape. It never happened. Tokyo reverted to type; it became once again an aggregation of small towns and villages. Author Donald Richie once described them as "separate, yet welded to the texture of the metropolis itself." One village was much like any other; the nucleus was always the *shoten-gai* (shopping arcade). Every arcade had a butcher, a grocer, a rice dealer, a mat maker, a barber, and a pinball parlor; every arcade also had a florist and a bookstore—sometimes two of each. You could live your whole life in the neighborhood of the shotengai; it was sufficient to your needs.

People seldom moved out of these villages; the vast waves of new residents who arrived after World War II (about three-quarters of the people in the Tokyo metropolitan area today were born elsewhere) just created more villages. Everybody who lived in one knew his way around; there was no particular need to name the streets. Houses were numbered, not in sequence, but in the order in which they were built; #3 might well share a mailbox with #12. People still take their local geography for granted; the closer you get to the place you're looking for, the harder it is to get coherent directions. Away from main streets and landmarks, a stranger, or even a taxi driver, can get hopelessly lost.

Fortunately, there are the *kobans:* small police boxes, or substations, usually with two or three officers assigned to each of them full time, to look after the affairs of the neighborhood. These kobans are one important reason for the legendary safety of Tokyo: On foot or on white bicycles, the police are a visible presence, covering the beat. (Burglaries are not unknown, but street crime is very rare.) You can't go far in any direction without finding a koban. The officer on duty knows where everything is, and is glad to point the way; like the samurai-bureaucrats of Edo, he seldom has anything more pressing to do.

Outsiders, however, seldom venture very far into the labyrinths of residential Tokyo. For the tourist, especially, the city is the sum of its districts and neighborhoods, such as Ueno, Asakusa, Ginza, Roppongi, Shibuya, and Shinjuku. Harajuku is a more recent addition to that list, and soon the waterfront will add another; the *attention* of Tokyo shifts constantly, seeking new patches of astronomically expensive land on which to realize its enormous commercial energy. (Even with the collapse of the speculative bubble in 1992, you can't buy a square yard anywhere in the city's central wards for much under $35,000.)

Tokyo is still really two areas, Shitamachi and Yamanote. The heart of Shitamachi, proud and stubborn in its Edo ways, is Asakusa; the dividing line is Ginza; to the west lie the boutiques and department stores, the banks and engines of government, the pleasure domes and swell cafés. Today there are 10 subway lines weaving the two areas together. Another special feature of Tokyo's geography is found where the lines intersect: vast underground malls, with miles of shops in fluorescent-lit, air-conditioned corridors. These stores sell anything you might want to buy between subway rides.

Up on the surface, confusion reigns, or seems to. Tokyo is the most impermanent of cities, constantly tearing itself down and building over. Whole blocks disappear overnight; the next day, a framework of girders is already rising on the empty lot. It's no longer possible to put up a single-family house in the eight central wards of the city; the plot to put it on costs more than the average person will earn in several lifetimes. Home owners live in the suburbs, an hour or more by train from their jobs. Only developers can afford the land closer in; they build office buildings, condominiums, and commercial complexes. Tokyo has no skyline, no prevailing style of architecture, nothing for a new building to measure itself against. Every new project is an environment unto itself. World-famous architects like Arata Isozaki, Fumihiko Maki, and Kisho Kurokawa revel in this anarchy; so do the designers of neon signs, show windows, and interior spaces. The kind of creative energy you find in Tokyo could flower only in an atmosphere where there are virtually no rules to break.

Not all of that is for the best. Many of the buildings in Tokyo are merely grotesque, and most of them are supremely ugly. In the large scale, Tokyo is not an *attractive* city; neither is it gracious, and it is certainly not serene. The pace of life is wedded to the one stupefying fact of population: Within a 20-mile radius of the Imperial Palace live almost 30 million souls, all of them in a hurry, and all of them ferocious consumers. They live in a city that went from rubble to dazzling affluence in a generation; they are very sure of what they have accomplished, but they are terribly uncertain about who they are. They consume to identify themselves—by what they wear, where they eat, and how they use their leisure time.

Tokyo is a magnet. Its attractive power, of course, is money—enormous amounts of it, looking for new ways of turning itself over. The economy, despite recent setbacks, is still strong, and the Japanese remain among the world's foremost consumers—not merely of things, but of culture and leisure. Everything shows up here, sooner or later: van Gogh's *Sunflowers*, the Berlin Philharmonic, Chinese pandas, Mexican food. Even the Coney Island carousel is here—lovingly restored to the last gilded curlicue on the last prancing unicorn, brought to life again at an amusement park called Toshima-en. And now, because you are reading this guide, the magnet is drawing you. What follows is an attempt to chart a few paths for you through this exasperating, exciting, movable feast of a city.

Essential Information

Arriving and Departing

By Plane Tokyo has two airports, Narita and Haneda. Narita Airport is 50 miles (80 kilometers) northeast of Tokyo and serves all international flights, except for those operated by (Taiwan's) China Airways, which uses Haneda Airport. Ten miles (16 kilometers) southwest of Tokyo, Haneda Airport serves all domestic flights. Narita added a new terminal building in 1992, which has somewhat eased the burden on it, but it can still be bottlenecked. Narita is the only Japanese airport that imposes a departure tax (¥2,000, ¥1,000 for children 2–11 years old; no tax for children under 2 or for transit passengers flying out the same day as their arrival).

Narita has more direct flights arriving from around the world than any other Japanese airport. Japan Airlines (JAL) and United Airlines are the major carriers between North America and Narita; Northwest, American Airlines, and All Nippon Airways (ANA) also link North American cities with Tokyo. Japan Airlines, Cathay Pacific, Virgin Atlantic Airways, and British Airways fly between Narita and Great Britain; Japan Airlines, United Airlines, and Qantas fly between Narita and Australia; and Japan Airlines and Air New Zealand fly between Narita and New Zealand. An extensive network of domestic flights in and out of Haneda is operated by JAL, ANA, and Japan Air System. For information on arrival and departure times, call the individual airlines.

Narita Terminal #2 has two wings, north and south, that adjoin each other. When you arrive, your first task should be to convert your money into yen; you'll need it for transport into Tokyo. In both wings, money exchange counters are located in the wall between the customs inspection area and the arrival lobby. Directly across from the customs area exit are the ticket counters for Airport Limousine Buses to Tokyo. (*See* By Bus, *below.*) In between the two wings is the Japan National Tourist Organization's Tourist Information Center, where maps, brochures, and information can be obtained free of charge. It is well worth visiting this center if you have extra time before your bus departs.

Between Narita Airport and Center City

By Bus. Two services, the **Airport Limousine Bus** and the **Airport Express Bus,** run from Narita to many of Tokyo's major hotels located in the city's different areas, such as Akasaka, Ginza, Ikebukuro, Shiba, and Shinagawa (cost: ¥2,200–¥2,900, depending on your destination). These buses are the best method of reaching your destination; even if you are not staying at one of the hotel drop-off points, take the bus going closest to your hotel, and then use a taxi for the remaining distance. Most of the hotels in the Very Expensive category (*see* Lodging, *below*) serve as drop-off points. However, these buses only run every hour, and they do not run after 11 PM. The trip usually takes two hours because of traffic congestion, though the scheduled time is 90 minutes. Tickets for these buses are sold at the large ticket counter in the arrival lobby, directly across from the customs area exit. The buses depart right outside the terminal exit. They leave exactly on time; the departure time is stated on the ticket.

A regularly scheduled bus to the Tokyo City Air Terminal (TCAT) leaves approximately every 20 minutes from 6:40 AM to 11:30 PM (cost: ¥2,700). The problem is that TCAT is located in Nihombashi in north-central Tokyo, which is far from most convenient destinations. From TCAT you can connect directly with the Suitengu station on the Hanzomon subway line, and then to anywhere in the subway network; if you take a taxi from TCAT, it will cost about ¥3,000 to reach most of the major hotels.

By Train. Trains run every 30–40 minutes between Narita Airport Train Station and the Keisei-Ueno Station on the privately owned Keisei Line; the ride takes approximately an hour. (Cost: ¥1,740 on the Keisei Skyliner, taking 57 minutes; ¥940 on the Keisei limited express, taking 72 minutes). Trains start at 7:48 AM (7:13 AM on weekends and holidays). It only makes sense to take the Keisei, however, if your final destination is around Ueno; otherwise, you must change to the Tokyo subway system or the Japan Railways loop line at Ueno (the station is adjacent to the Keisei-Ueno Station) or take a cab to your hotel.

Japan Railways (JR East Infoline, tel. 03/3423–0111) has greatly improved its airport service, with trains that stop at both terminals. The fastest and most comfortable is the **Narita Limited Express**—N'EX—which makes 23 runs a day in each direction. Trains from the airport go directly to Tokyo Station, in just under an hour, then continue on to Yokohama and Ofuna; daily departures begin at 7:43 AM; the last train is at 9:43 PM. The one-way fare is ¥2,890 (¥4,890 for the 1st-class "Green Car" and ¥5,280 per person for a private compartment that seats four). All seats are reserved; make reservations in advance, as this train fills quickly. The less-elegant Rapid Train *(kaisoku)* on JR's Narita Line also runs from the airport to Tokyo Station, by way of Chiba; there are 16 departures daily, starting at 7 AM. The fare to Tokyo is ¥1,260 (¥930 more for the Green Car); the ride takes 1 hour and 27 minutes. JR also runs one Limited Express, called the Wing Azusa, daily at 2:27 PM from Narita to Shinjuku Station in Tokyo (¥2,850), but on a very irregular schedule; call the JR English-language phone service (tel. 03/3423–0111) for details.

By Taxi. Taxis are rarely used between Narita Airport and central Tokyo, because the cost of approximately ¥20,000 is prohibitive. Also, because taxis have small trunks, your luggage may have to be placed in the front passenger seat, thus causing cramped conditions if there are three or more passengers. Station wagon taxis do exist, and the meter rates are the same as for the standard sedans, but they are not always available. Limousines are also very expensive; for example, a limousine ride from Narita Airport to the Imperial Hotel costs approximately ¥60,000.

Between Haneda Airport and Center City

By Monorail. The monorail train from Haneda Airport to Hamamatsucho Station in Tokyo is the best and most frequently used method; the journey takes about 17 minutes and operates approximately every 10 minutes (cost: ¥300). From Hamamatsucho Station, change to the subway or take a taxi.

By Taxi. A taxi to the center of Tokyo takes about 40 minutes (cost: approximately ¥6,000).

By Train

The JR Shinkansen (bullet train) and JR express trains on the Tokaido Line (to Nagoya, Kyoto, Kobe, Osaka, Hiroshima, and the island of Kyushu) use Tokyo Station in central Tokyo. The JR Shinkansen and express trains on the Tohoku Line (to Sendai and Morioka) use Ueno Station, just north of Tokyo Station. The JR Shinkansen and express trains on the Joetsu Line (to Niigata) also use Ueno Station. JR trains to the Japan Alps (Matsumoto) use Shinjuku Station.

By Bus

Most bus arrivals and departures are at Tokyo Train Station or Shinjuku Bus Station.

Getting Around

Daunting in its sheer size, Tokyo is, in fact, an extremely easy city to negotiate. If you have any anxieties about getting from place to place, remind yourself first that a transportation system obliged to cope with 4 or 5 million commuters a day simply *has* to be efficient, extensive, and reasonably easy to understand. Remind yourself also that virtually anyplace you're likely to go as a visitor is within a five-minute walk of a train or subway station—and that station stops are always marked in English. Of course, exceptions to the rule exist; the system has its flaws. In the outline here you'll find a few things to avoid, and also a few pointers that will save you time—and money—as you go.

By Train **Japan Railways (JR).** Trains are color-coded, making it easy to identify the different lines. The **Yamanote Line** (green or silver, with green stripes) makes a 22-mile (35-kilometer) loop around the central wards of the city in about an hour. The 29 stops include the major hub stations of Tokyo, Yurakucho, Shimbashi, Shinagawa, Shibuya, Shinjuku, and Ueno. The **Chuo Line** (orange) runs east to west through the loop from Tokyo to the distant suburb of Takao. During the day, however, these are limited express trains that don't stop at most of the stations inside the loop; for local crosstown service, which also extends west to neighboring Chiba Prefecture, you have to take the **Sobu Line** (yellow). The **Keihin Tohoku Line** (blue) goes north to Omiya in Saitama Prefecture and south to Ofuna in Kanagawa, running parallel to the Yamanote Line between Tabata and Shinagawa. Where they share the loop, the two lines usually use the same platform—Yamanote trains on one side, and Keihin Tohoku trains headed in the same direction on the other. This requires a little care. Suppose, for example, you want to take the loop line from Yurakucho around to Shibuya, and you board a blue train instead of a green one; four stops later, where the lines branch, you'll find yourself on an unexpected trip to Yokohama.

JR fares start at ¥120; you can get anywhere on the loop for ¥190 or less. Most stations have a chart in English somewhere above the row of ticket vending machines, so you can check the fare to your destination; if not, you can simply buy the cheapest ticket and pay the difference at the other end. In any case, hold on to your ticket: you'll have to turn it in at the exit. Tickets are valid only on the day you buy them, but if you plan to use the JR a lot, you can save time and trouble with an Orange Card, available at any station office. The card is electronically coded; at vending machines with orange panels, you insert the card, punch the cost of the ticket, and that amount is automatically deducted. ¥1,000 and ¥3,000 Orange Cards are worth their face values; ¥5,000 Cards are coded for ¥5,300 and ¥10,000 for ¥10,700 worth of fares. Your Japan Rail Pass can be used on all JR trains.

Shinjuku, Harajuku, and Shibuya are notorious for the long lines that form at ticket dispensers. If you're using a card, make sure you've lined up at a machine with an orange panel; if you're paying cash, and have no change, make sure you've lined up at a machine that will change a ¥1,000 note—not all of them do!

Yamanote and Sobu trains begin running about 4:30 AM and stop around 12:30 at night. The last departures are indicated at each station—but only in Japanese. Bear in mind that 7–9:30 AM and 5–7 PM trains are packed to bursting with commuters; avoid the trains at these times, if possible. During these hours, smoking is not allowed in JR stations or on platforms.

By Subway Tokyo is served by 10 subway lines, seven of them operated by the Rapid Transportation Authority (Eidan) and three by the Tokyo Municipal Authority (Toei). Maps, bilingual signs at en-

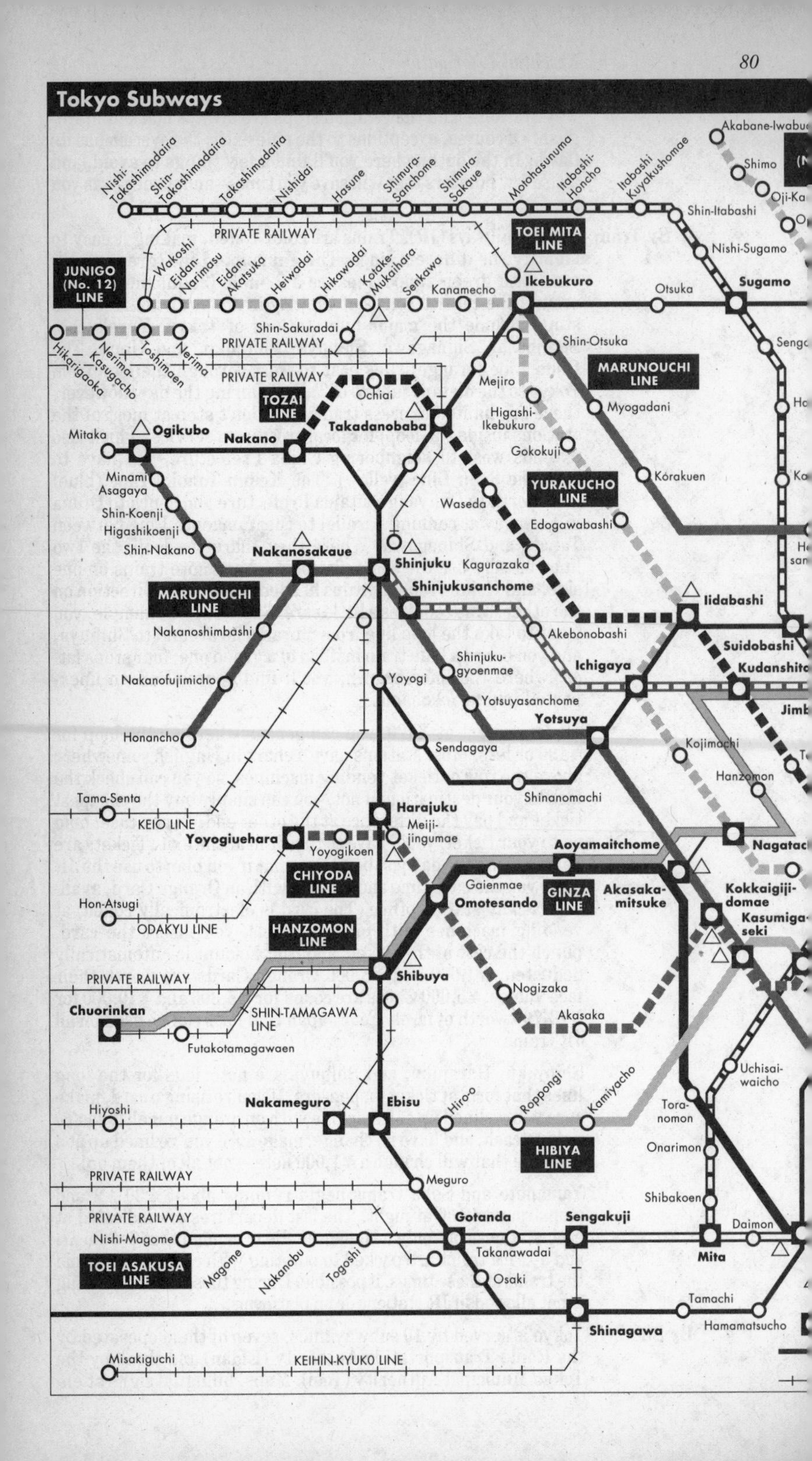
Tokyo Subways
Nishi-Takashimadaira
Shin-Takashimadaira
Takashimadaira
Nishidai
Hasune
Shimura-Sanchome
Shimura-Sakaue
Motohasunuma
Itabashi-Honcho
Itabashi Kuyakushomae
Shin-Itabashi
Nishi-Sugamo
Sugamo
Akabane-Iwabuc
Shimo
Oji-Ka
TOEI MITA LINE
PRIVATE RAILWAY
JUNIGO (No. 12) LINE
Wakoshi
Eidan-Narimasu
Eidan-Akatsuka
Heiwadai
Hikawadai
Kotake-Mukaihara
Senkawa
Kanamecho
Ikebukuro
Otsuka
Hikarigaoka
Nerima-Kasugacho
Toshimaen
Nerima
Shin-Sakuradai
PRIVATE RAILWAY
Shin-Otsuka
Sengo
MARUNOUCHI LINE
PRIVATE RAILWAY
Ochiai
Mejiro
TOZAI LINE
Higashi-Ikebukuro
Myogadani
Mitaka
Ogikubo
Nakano
Takadanobaba
Gokokuji
Minami Asagaya
Korakuen
Shin-Koenji
Higashikoenji
Shin-Nakano
Waseda
YURAKUCHO LINE
Edogawabashi
Nakanosakaue
Shinjuku
Kagurazaka
Shinjukusanchome
MARUNOUCHI LINE
Iidabashi
Nakanoshimbashi
Akebonobashi
Suidobashi
Shinjuku-gyoenmae
Ichigaya
Kudanshita
Nakanofujimicho
Yoyogi
Yotsuyasanchome
Yotsuya
Jimb
Honancho
Sendagaya
Kojimachi
Hanzomon
Shinanomachi
Tama-Senta
KEIO LINE
Harajuku
Meiji-jingumae
Yoyogiuehara
Yoyogikoen
Aoyamaitchome
Nagata
CHIYODA LINE
Gaienmae
Omotesando
GINZA LINE
Akasaka-mitsuke
Kokkaigijidomae
Kasumigaseki
Hon-Atsugi
ODAKYU LINE
HANZOMON LINE
PRIVATE RAILWAY
Shibuya
Nogizaka
Chuorinkan
SHIN-TAMAGAWA LINE
Akasaka
Futakotamagawaen
Uchisaiwaicho
Hiyoshi
Nakameguro
Ebisu
Hiro-o
Roppongi
Kamiyacho
Toranomon
HIBIYA LINE
Onarimon
PRIVATE RAILWAY
Meguro
PRIVATE RAILWAY
Shibakoen
Gotanda
Sengakuji
Nishi-Magome
Daimon
Takanawadai
Mita
TOEI ASAKUSA LINE
Magome
Nakanobu
Togoshi
Osaki
Tamachi
Hamamatsucho
Shinagawa
Misakiguchi
KEIHIN-KYUKO LINE

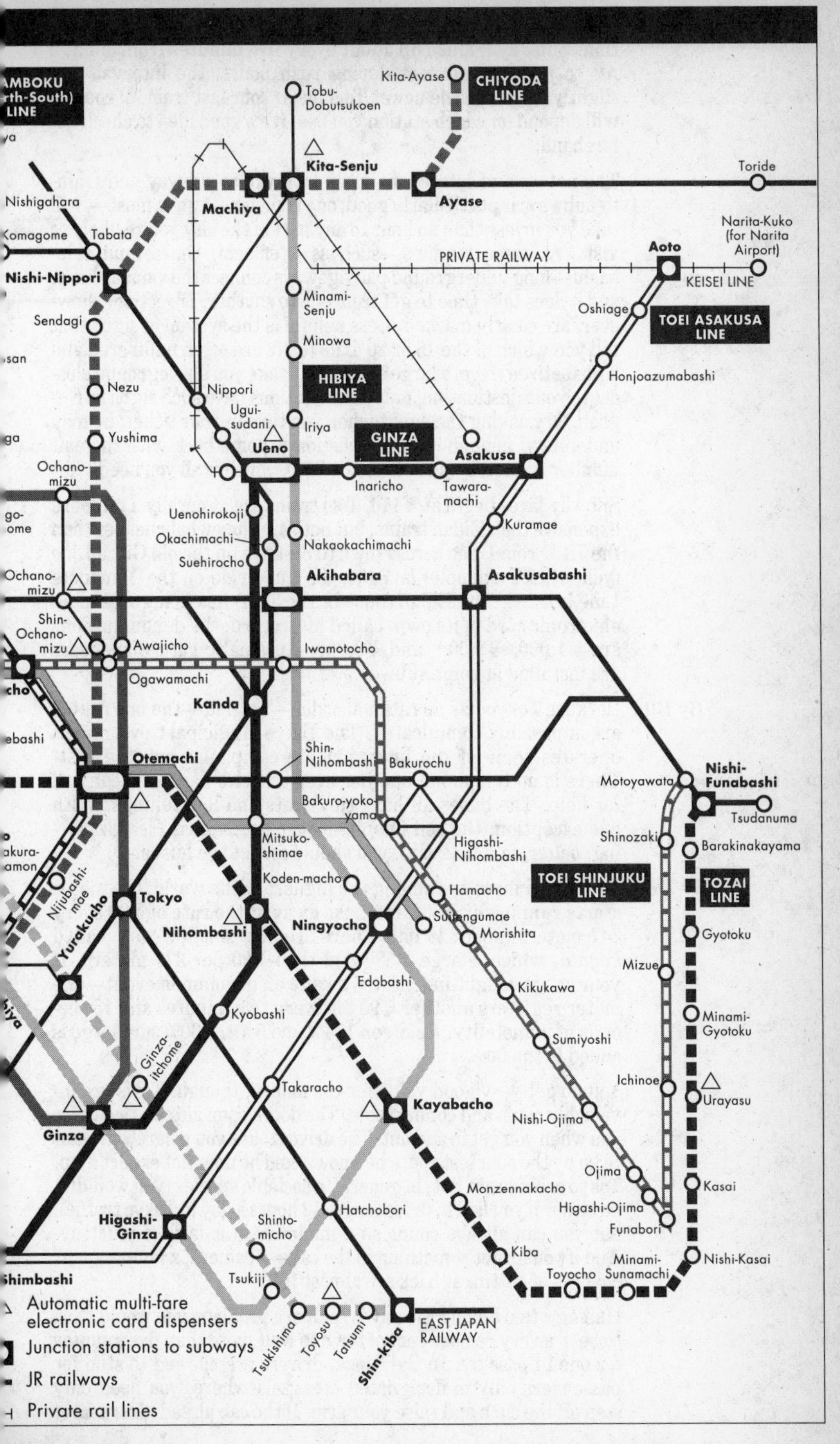
CHIYODA LINE
HIBIYA LINE
GINZA LINE
TOEI ASAKUSA LINE
TOEI SHINJUKU LINE
TOZAI LINE
PRIVATE RAILWAY
KEISEI LINE
EAST JAPAN RAILWAY
Kita-Ayase
Tobu-Dobutsukoen
Kita-Senju
Machiya
Ayase
Toride
Nishigahara
Komagome
Tabata
Nishi-Nippori
Narita-Kuko (for Narita Airport)
Aoto
Minami-Senju
Oshiage
Sendagi
Minowa
Honjoazumabashi
Nezu
Nippori
Ugui-sudani
Iriya
Yushima
Ueno
Asakusa
Ochano-mizu
Inaricho
Tawara-machi
Uenohirokoji
Kuramae
Okachimachi
Nakaokachimachi
Suehirocho
Akihabara
Asakusabashi
Shin-Ochano-mizu
Awajicho
Iwamotocho
Ogawamachi
Kanda
Shin-Nihombashi
Bakurochu
Otemachi
Motoyawata
Nishi-Funabashi
Tsudanuma
Bakuro-yoko-yama
Mitsuko-shimae
Higashi-Nihombashi
Shinozaki
Barakinakayama
Koden-macho
Hamacho
Nijubashi-mae
Tokyo
Nihombashi
Suitengumae
Ningyocho
Morishita
Gyotoku
Yurakucho
Mizue
Edobashi
Kikukawa
Minami-Gyotoku
Kyobashi
Sumiyoshi
Ginza-itchome
Ichinoe
Urayasu
Takaracho
Kayabacho
Nishi-Ojima
Ginza
Ojima
Monzennakacho
Kasai
Higashi-Ojima
Funabori
Higashi-Ginza
Hatchobori
Shinto-micho
Kiba
Nishi-Kasai
Toyocho
Minami-Sunamachi
Shimbashi
Tsukiji
Tsukishima
Toyosu
Tatsumi
Shin-kiba
Automatic multi-fare electronic card dispensers
Junction stations to subways
JR railways
Private rail lines

trances, and even the trains are color-coded for easy identification. Subway trains run about every five minutes from about 5 AM to midnight; except during rush hours, the intervals are slightly longer on the newer Toei lines. Your last train, of course, will depend on which station you use: It's a good idea to check beforehand.

The network of interconnections (subway-to-subway and train-to-subway) is particularly good; one transfer—two at most—will take you in less than an hour to any part of the city you're likely to visit. At some stations—such as Otemachi, Ginza, and Iidabashi—long underground passageways connect the various lines, and it does take time to get from one to another. Directions, however, are clearly marked. Less helpful is the system of signs that tell you which of the 15 or 20 exits (exits are often numbered and alphabetized) from a large station will take you aboveground closest to your destination; only a few stations have such signs in English. Try asking the agent when you turn in your ticket; he may understand enough of your question to come back with the exit number and letter (such as A3 or B12), which is all you need.

Subway fares begin at ¥140. Toei trains are generally a bit more expensive than Eidan trains, but both are somewhat cheaper than the JR. From Ueno across town to Shibuya on the old Ginza Line (yellow), for example, is ¥160; the same ride on the Yamanote Line is ¥190. The Eidan (but *not* the Toei) has inaugurated an electronic card of its own, called Metrocard; the denominations are ¥1,000, ¥2,000, and ¥3,000. Automatic card dispensers are installed at some subway stations.

By Bus Because Tokyo has no rational order—no grid—the bus routes are impossibly complicated. The Tokyo Municipal Government operates some of the lines; private companies run the rest. There is no telephone number even a native Japanese can call for help. The buses all have tiny seats and low ceilings. With one exception, the red double-decker in Asakusa (*see* Exploring, *below*, for Asakusa), you should forget the buses.

By Taxi Tokyo taxi fares are among the highest in the world; the meter starts running at ¥600 and ticks away at the rate of ¥90 every 347 meters (about ⅕ mi). There are also smaller cabs, called *kogata*, which charge ¥580 and then ¥90 per 371 meters. If your cab is caught in traffic—hardly an uncommon event—the meter registers another ¥90 for every two minutes and 15 seconds of immobility. Between 11 PM and 5 AM, a 30% surcharge is added to the fare.

You do get very good value for the money, though. Taxis are invariably clean and comfortable. The doors open automatically for you when you get in and out. The driver takes you where you want to go by the shortest route he knows, and he does not expect a tip. Tokyo cabbies are not, in general, a sociable species (you wouldn't be either if you had to drive for 10–12 hours a day in Tokyo traffic), but you can always count on a minimum standard of courtesy. And if you forget something in the cab—a camera, a purse—your chances of getting it back are almost 100%.

Hailing a taxi during the day is seldom a problem; you would have to be in a very remote part of town to wait more than five minutes for one to pass by. In the Ginza, drivers are allowed to stop for passengers only in designated areas; elsewhere, you need only step off the curb and raise your arm. If the cab already has a fare, there will be a green light on the dashboard, visible through the windshield; if not, the light will be red.

Night changes the rules a bit, when everyone's been out drinking and wants a ride home. Don't be astonished if a cab with a red light doesn't stop for you: The driver may have had a radio call, or he may be heading for an area where he can pick up a long, profitable fare to the suburbs. (Or he may simply not feel like coping with a passenger in a foreign language. Refusing a fare is against the law—but it's done all the time.) Between 11 PM and 2 AM on Friday and Saturday nights, you have to be very lucky to get a cab in any of the major entertainment districts; in Ginza, it is almost impossible.

By Ferry The best ride in Tokyo, hands down, is the "river bus," operated by the Tokyo Cruise Ship Company from **Hinode Pier** (2-7-104 Kaigan, Minato-ku, tel. 03/3457–7830), at the mouth of the Sumida River, upstream to Asakusa. The pier is a seven-minute walk from the JR Hamamatsucho Station on the Yamanote Line; the glassed-in double-decker boats depart roughly every 30 minutes, 9:50 AM–6:30 PM, daily; extended weekday service to 7:35 PM July–Aug.). The trip takes 35 minutes, and costs ¥560; children ride at half-fare.

The Sumida River was once Tokyo's lifeline, a busy highway for travelers and freight alike; the ferry service dates back to 1885. Some people still take it to work, but today the passengers are primarily tourists, most of them Japanese. On its way to Asakusa, the boat passes under 11 bridges; though they are all of modern construction, the guided tour (a recording on the boat's loudspeaker) deems it worthy to comment upon them at length. There are far more interesting things to see: **Tsukiji Market,** the largest wholesale fish and produce market in the world (*see* Exploring, *below,* for Tsukiji); the vast reclamation/construction projects meant to sate the city's insatiable need for high-tech office space; the old lumberyards and warehouses upstream; and the Kokugikan (*see* Off the Beaten Track, *below*), with its distinctive green roof, which is the new arena and headquarters of sumo wrestling.

Another place to catch the ferry is at the **Hamarikyu Gardens,** a 15-minute walk from Ginza. Once part of the Imperial Detached Palace, the gardens are open to the public, although you will have to pay a separate ¥200 entrance fee; the ferry landing is inside, a short walk to the left as you enter the main gate. Boats depart at 45-minute intervals every weekday 10:15–4:05; the adult fare to Asakusa is ¥520; from Asakusa to Hamarikyu, the fare is ¥560.

By Hired Car Large and comfortable cars may be hired (the Japanese call them *haiya*) for about ¥6,000 per hour for a midsize car, up to ¥14,000 per hour for a Cadillac limousine. Call **Hinomaru** (tel. 03/3505–0707). The Imperial, Okura, and Palace hotels also offer limousine services.

By Rental Car Congestion, lack of road signs in English, and the difficulty of parking make driving in Tokyo impractical for the foreign visitor. However, should you wish to rent a car, **Avis International** (Landic No. 3 Akasaka Bldg. 2F, 2-3-2 Akasaka, Minato-Ku, tel 03/3583–0911), **Nippon Interrent** (2-1 Yaesu, Chou-ku, tel. 03/3271–6643), and **Toyota Rent-a-Car** (2-3-18 Kudan Minami, Chiyoda-Ku, tel. 03/3263–6321) are national car-rental companies with offices all around Tokyo and Japan. The cost is approximately ¥15,000 per day. An international driving license is required.

Maps Excellent maps of the subway system, with the major JR lines included, are available at any station office, free of charge; you'll find the same map in the monthly *Tour Companion* magazine. Hotel kiosks and English-language bookstores stock a wide variety of pocket maps, some of which have suggested walking tours that also mark the locations of JR and subway stations along the way. A bit bulkier to carry around, but by far the best and most detailed resource, is *Tokyo: A Bilingual Atlas* (Kodansha Publishing, ¥1,850; $14.95 in the United States), which contains subway and rail-system guides and area maps. Because all notations are in both English and Japanese, you can always get help on the street, even from people who do not speak your language, just by pointing at your destination.

Important Addresses and Numbers

Tourist Information The **Tourist Information Center** (TIC) (1-6-6 Yurakucho, Chiyoda-ku, tel. 03/3502–1461) is an extremely useful office for free maps and brochures, as well as for planning any trip in Japan. It is definitely worth visiting this office early in your stay in Tokyo. The closest subway stations to the TIC are Hibiya and Yurakucho. The Hibiya station is on the same avenue, Harumi-dori, as the TIC (take exit A4, walk toward the railway bridge, and the TIC is on the right hand side of the street); Yurakucho Station is just to the north of the TIC; if you follow the overhead train tracks south one block, the TIC office is across the street. *Open weekdays 9–5, Sat. 9–noon.*

Travel Information Information in English on all domestic travel, buses, and trains can be acquired by phoning the TIC (tel. 03/3502–1461). You may also call Japan Railways (tel. 03/3423–0111) or the toll-free **Japan Travel Phone** (0120/222–800 for eastern Japan; 0120/444–800 for western Japan) for information in English.

Current Events/ Exhibitions A taped recording in English (tel. 03/3503–2911) gives information on current events in Tokyo and vicinity. ***The Tour Companion,*** a free weekly newspaper available at hotels, provides some information on events, exhibitions, festivals, plays, etc. ***The Tokyo Journal,*** however, has a more comprehensive monthly listing of what's happening in Tokyo. It also lists services and stores that may have special interest for foreigners (cost: ¥600). ***The Japan Times,*** the country's daily English-language newspaper, is good for national and international news coverage, as well as for entertainment reviews and listings.

Embassies and Consulates **U.S. Embassy and Consulate,** 1-10-5 Akasaka, Minato-ku, tel. 03/3224–5000. Consulate open 8:30–12:30 and 2–4:30; closed Sat., Sun., and U.S./Japanese national holidays.

Australian Embassy, 2-1-14 Mita, Minato-ku, tel. 03/5232–4111. Open 9 AM–noon and 1:30–5.

British Embassy and Consulate, 1 Ichiban-cho, Chiyoda-ku, tel. 03/3265–5511. Consulate open 9–noon and 2–4; closed Sat. and holidays.

Canadian Embassy, 7-3-38 Akasaka, Minato-ku, tel. 03/3408–2101. Open weekdays 9–12:30 and 1:30–5:30.

New Zealand Embassy, 20-40 Kamiyama-cho, Shibuya-ku, tel. 03/3467–2271. Open weekdays 9–12:30 and 1:30–5:30.

Telephone Directory For Tokyo numbers, dial 104; for elsewhere in Japan, dial 105.

General Information NTT (Japanese Telephone Corporation, tel. 03/3277–1010) will help find information (in English), such as telephone numbers, museum openings, and various other facts that it has in its data bases.

Emergencies **Ambulance** and **Fire,** tel. 119; **Police,** tel. 110; **Tokyo English Life Line** (TELL; tel. 03/5481–4347) is a telephone service available 9 AM–4 PM and 9–11 PM for anyone in distress who cannot communicate in Japanese. The service will relay your emergency to the appropriate Japanese authorities and/or will serve as a counselor. Assistance in English is available 24 hrs. a day on the toll-free **Japan Helpline** (tel. 0120/461–997).

Doctors **International Catholic Hospital** (Seibo Byoin), 2-5-1 Naka Ochiai, Shinjuku-ku, tel. 03/3951–1111. Open Mon.–Sat. 8–11 AM.
International Clinic, 1-5-9 Azabudai, Roppongi, Minato-ku, tel. 03/3582–2646 or 03/3583–7831. Accepts emergencies. Open weekdays 9 AM–noon and 2:30–5 PM, Sat. 9 AM–noon.
St. Luke's International Hospital (Member of American Hospital Association), 10-1 Akashi-cho, Chuo-ku, tel. 03/3541–5151. Accepts emergencies. Open Mon.–Sat. 8:30–11 AM.
Tokyo Medical and Surgical Clinic, 32 Mori Building, 3-4-30 Shiba-Koen, Minato-ku, tel. 03/3436–3028. Open weekdays 9–5:30, Sat. 9AM–1PM.

Dentists **Yamauchi Dental Clinic** (member of American Dental Association), Shiroganedai Gloria Heights 1F, 3-16-10 Shiroganedai, Minato-ku, tel. 03/3441–6377. Open weekdays 9–1 and 3–6; Sat. 9 AM–noon.

Pharmacies No drugstores in Tokyo are open 24 hours a day, but grocery stores carry basics such as aspirin. The **American Pharmacy** (Hibiya Park Building, 1-8-1 Yurakucho, Chiyoda-ku, tel. 03/3271–4034) and **Hill Pharmacy** (4-1-6 Roppongi, Minato-ku, tel. 03/3583–5044) both stock American products. The American Pharmacy is conveniently located near the Tourist Information Center (*see above*) and is open Mon.–Sat. 9–7 and Sun. 11–7; Hill Pharmacy is open Mon.–Sat. 8–7 but is closed on Sunday. **Nagai Yakkyoku** (1-8-10 Azabu-Juban, Minato-ku, tel. 03/3583–3889) will mix a Chinese and/or Japanese herbal medicine for you after a consultation. A little English is spoken.

English-Language Bookstores Most of the top hotels have a bookstore with a modest selection of English-language books. However, for a wide selection of English and other non-Japanese-language books, the **Kinokuniya Bookstore** (17-7 Shinjuku 3-chome, Shinjuku-ku, tel. 03/3354–0131) has some 40,000 books and magazine titles (closed 3rd Wed. of each month, except Apr. and Dec.). Kinokuniya also has a branch store in the Tokyu Plaza Building (1-2-2 Dogenzaka, Shibuya-ku, tel. 03/3463–3241) across from the Shibuya Station. The **Jena Bookstore** (5-6-1 Ginza, Chuo-ku, tel. 03/3571–2980) also carries a wide range of books and is located near the Ginza and Marunouchi subway line exits in Ginza. **Yaesu Book Center** (2-5-1 Yaesu, Chuo-ku, tel. 03/3281–1811) is located near the Tokyo Train Station.

Travel Agencies **Japan Travel Bureau** (1-13-1 Nihombashi, Chuo-ku, tel. 03/3276–7777) has the most extensive network of agencies throughout Tokyo and Japan. This bureau organizes various tours conducted in English, in and around Tokyo; it will make arrangements for your travels throughout Japan and overseas, if you wish.

Other travel agencies include **American Express International** (4-3-13 Toranomon, Minato-ku, tel. 03/3504–3004) and **Japan Amenity Travel** (2-3-5 Yuraku-cho, Chiyoda-Ku, tel. 03/3573–1417).

Lost and Found **The Central Lost and Found Office** of the Metropolitan Police is located at 1-9-11, Koraku, Bunkyo-ku, Tokyo, tel. 03/3814–4151. Open weekdays 8:30–5:15, Sat. 8:30–12:30; closed Sun., the second and fourth Sat. of every month, and holidays. If you have lost something on the train, report it to the lost and found office at any station. However, the main lost and found offices for Japan Railways are at the JR Tokyo Station Lost Properties Office (tel. 03/3231–1880) and at Ueno Station (tel. 03/3841–8069).

If you leave something on the subways, contact **Teito Rapid Transit Authority** (TRTA) at its Ueno Lost Properties Office (tel. 03/3834–5577).

If you leave something in a taxi, contact the **Tokyo Taxi Kindaika Center** (7-3-3 Minami-Suna, Koto-Ku, tel. 03/3648–0300). Only Japanese is spoken here.

Currency Exchange and Banks Most hotels will change both traveler's checks and notes into yen. However, their rates are always lower than banks. Because Japan is so safe and virtually free from street crime, one may consider exchanging large sums of money into yen at banks at any time. Most of the larger banks have a foreign exchange counter. Banking hours: weekdays 9–3; closed Sat., Sun., and national holidays.

The major banks can transfer funds to and from overseas. Two banks that may be familiar to you are **Bank of America** (Arc Mori Building, 1-12-32 Akasaka, Minato-ku, tel. 03/3587–3111) and **Chase Manhattan Bank** (1-24-1 Minami-Aoyama, Minato-ku, tel. 03/3470–8261). **American Express** has a banking office in the Toranomon Mitsui Building, 3-8-1 Kasumigaseki, Chiyoda-ku, tel. 03/3595–4571 (open weekdays 9:30–5:30) and new headquarters in the American Express Tower (4-30-16 Ogikubo, Suginami-ku, tel. 03/3220–6000).

Post and Telegraph Offices Most hotels have stamps and will mail your letters and postcards; they will also give you directions to the nearest post office. The main **International Post Office** is on the Imperial Palace side of the JR Tokyo Station (2-3-3 Otemachi, Chiyoda-Ku, tel. 03/3241–4891). For cables, contact the KDD International Telegraph Office (2–3–2 Nishi-Shinjuku, Shinjuku-ku, tel. 03/3344–5151).

Guided Tours

Orientation Tours Organized by the Japan Travel Bureau, **Sunrise Tours** (tel. 03/3276–7777) offers guided tours in English around Tokyo. The sights on tours vary according to current popularity, but some recently offered tours are as follows: A morning tour (4 hours) includes the Tokyo Tower Observatory, Asakusa, the Imperial East Garden, flower arrangement at the Tasaki Pearl Gallery (cost: ¥4,420 adults; ¥3,460 children age 6–11). Incorporating a Sumida river cruise, the afternoon tour includes the Imperial

Palace Plaza, the Asakusa Kannon Temple, the Ginza and Kasumigaseki districts, and the Tokyo Tower Observatory (cost: ¥4,850/¥3,720). A full-day tour (7 hours) combines most of what is covered in the morning and afternoon tours, with a tea ceremony at the Happosen gardens and lunch at the traditional Chinzan-so inn (cost: ¥10,920/¥8,620, lunch included). Tours are conducted in large, air-conditioned buses that set out from Hamamatsucho Bus Terminal, but there is also free pickup and return from the major hotels. (If one travels independently and uses the subway, we estimate that the full-day tour's itinerary can be accomplished for about ¥2,250, including lunch.) **The Japan Gray Line** (tel. 03/3433–5745) offers tours similar to Sunrise's.

Special-Interest Tours **Sunrise Tours** (tel. 03/3276–7777) has two, popular "Industrial Tours". One includes the Tokyo Stock Exchange and Isuzu Motors; the other tour includes a monorail trip to Haneda Airport to visit the Japan Air Lines Maintenance Base, and a tour of Isuzu Motors. These tours offered only on Tuesdays and Thursdays, cost ¥10,560. Other tours include a full-day in Tokyo Disneyland (cost: ¥9,820 adults; ¥9,240 children 12–17, ¥5,990 children 4–11) and a trip to several craft centers (cost: ¥11,170/¥8,890).

Nightlife Tours **Sunrise Tours** (tel. 03/3276–7777) offers night tours (6–11 PM) of Tokyo, which, depending on the one selected, include Kabuki drama at the Kabuki-za theater, a geisha show at Matsubaya, or a cabaret/floor show at the Shogun in Roppongi (cost: ¥9,560–¥13,480, depending on which portions of the tour you include). **The Japan Gray Line** (tel. 03/3433–5745) has similar programs.

Tours from Tokyo To Nikko, **Sunrise Tours** (tel. 03/3276–7777) offers one-day tours (cost: ¥19,000 adults; ¥14,300 children under 12; lunch included) and two-day tours (cost: ¥29,300 adults, ¥24,600 children under 12. One lunch and overnight accommodation included). **Tobu Travel** (tel. 03/3281–6622, a division of Tobu Railways) offers full-day trips to Nikko 9–6:45 (with pickup and return to major hotels) with an English-speaking guide, reserved train travel, lunch, and admission fees (cost: ¥19,000 adults; ¥14,300 children 6–11). **Sunrise Tours** (tel. 03/3276–7771), **Japan Amenity Travel** (tel. 03/3573–1417), and **The Japan Gray Line** (tel. 03/3433–5745) offer tours to Mt. Fuji and Hakone; one-day tours cost ¥19,000 adults, ¥14,300 children under 12 (lunch included), and two-day tours cost ¥42,200 adults, ¥37,500 children under 12 (meals and accommodation included). Some of these tours include a quick visit to Kamakura. There are also excursions to Kyoto via the Shinkansen that cost from ¥46,500 to ¥76,400.

Personal Guides **The Japan Guide Association** (tel. 03/3213–2706) will introduce you to English-speaking guides. However, you will need to establish an itinerary and price with the guide. Assume that the fee will be ¥20,000 to ¥30,000 for a full eight-hour day.

Exploring

Orientation

The distinctions of "downtown" (Shitamachi: north and east) and "uptown" (Yamanote: south and west) have shaped the character of Tokyo since the 17th century and will be your guide, too, as you explore the city. At the risk of an easy generalization, it might be said that downtown offers the visitor more to *see*, and uptown more things to *do;* another way of putting it is that Tokyo north and east of the Imperial Palace embodies more of the city's history, its traditional way of life, whereas the fruit of modernity—the glitzy, ritzy side of Tokyo as an international city—lies generally south and west.

The following exploring section has been divided into 10 tours of major areas of Tokyo. The first six tours follow a downtown loop that starts in central Tokyo at the Imperial Palace District and proceeds north to Akihabara and Jimbocho, and from there to Ueno. From Ueno, the tours turn east to Asakusa, then south to Tsukiji and Shimbashi, returning to the center of the city by way of Nihombashi, Ginza, and Yurakucho.

The four tours of Tokyo's uptown take you south to Roppongi and then north to Akasaka (which is west of the Imperial Palace district). The tours continue from Akasaka to the western part of Tokyo, through Aoyama, Shibuya, Harajuku, and finally Shinjuku.

Fortunately, no point on any of these 10 itineraries is very far from a subway station; you can use Tokyo's efficient subway system to hop from one area to another, to cut a tour short, or to return to a tour the next day. The areas in the 10 tours are not always contiguous—Tokyo is too spread out for that—but they generally border on each other to a useful degree. You will probably want to improvise; you can skip segments of tours according to your fancy, or combine parts of one tour with another in order to end your day exploring the area of your choice.

Let's begin, then, in central Tokyo, with the Imperial Palace District.

Imperial Palace District

Numbers in the margin correspond to points of interest on the Imperial Palace map.

The **Imperial Palace** occupies what were once the grounds of Edojo Castle. The first feudal lord here, a local chieftain named Dokan Ota, was assassinated in 1486, and the castle he built was abandoned for more than 100 years. When Ieyasu Tokugawa chose the site for his castle in 1590, he had two goals in mind: first, it would have to be impregnable; second, it would have to reflect the power and glory of his position. He was lord of the Kanto, the richest fief in Japan, and would soon be shogun, the military head of state. The fortifications he devised called for a triple system of moats and canals, incorporating the bay and the Sumida River into a huge network of waterways that enclosed both the castle keep (the stronghold or tower) and the palaces and villas of his court—in all, an area of about 450 acres. The castle had 99 gates (36 in the outer wall), 21 watchtowers (of which three are still standing), and 28 armories. The outer defenses stretched from present-day Shimbashi Station to Kanda. Completed in 1640 and later expanded, it was at the time the largest castle in the world.

The walls of Edojo Castle and its moats were made of stone from the Izu Peninsula, about 60 miles (96 kilometers) to the southwest. The great slabs were brought by barge—each of the largest was a cargo in itself—to the port of Edo (then much closer to the castle than the present port of Tokyo is now), and hauled through the streets on sledges by teams of 100 men or more. Thousands of stonemasons were brought from all over the country to finish the work; under the gates and castle buildings, the blocks of stone are said to have been shaped and fitted so precisely that a knife blade could not be slipped between them.

The inner walls divided the castle into four main areas, called *maru*. The innermost (Hon Maru) area contained the shogun's audience halls, his private residence, and, for want of a better word, his seraglio: the O-oku, where the shogun kept his wife and concubines, with their ladies-in-waiting, attendants, cooks, and servants. (Concubines came and went; at any given time, as many as 1,000 women might be living in the O-oku. Intrigue, more than sex, was its principal concern, and tales of the seraglio provided a rich source of material for the Japanese literary imagination.) Below the Hon Maru was the second fortress (Ni-no-Maru), where the shogun lived when he transferred his power to an heir and retired. Behind it, to the north, was the Kita-no-maru, now a public park; south and west was the Nishi-no-maru, a subsidiary fortress.

Not much of the Tokugawa glory remains. The shogunate was abolished in 1868; the Emperor Meiji (1868–1912), restored to power, moved his court from Kyoto to Edo—renaming it Tokyo—and Edojo Castle was chosen for the site of the Imperial Palace. Many of the buildings had been destroyed in the turmoil of the Meiji Restoration (1868); others fell victim to fire in 1872; still others were simply torn down. Of the 28 original *tamon* (armories), only two survived. The present-day Imperial Palace is open to the public only twice a year: on January 2 (New Year's) and December 23 (Emperor's Birthday), when many thousands of people assemble under the balcony to offer their good wishes to the imperial family. In 1968, to mark the completion of the current palace, the area that once encompassed the Hon Maru and Ni-no-Maru were opened to the public as the East Imperial Garden. There are three entrance gates—Otemon, Hira-kawamon, and Kita Hanebashimon. Each can easily be reached from the Otemachi or Takebashi subway stations.

A good place to start this exploration of the Imperial Palace area is **Tokyo Station.** ❶ The Otemachi subway stop (Chiyoda, Marunouchi, Tozai, and Toei Mita lines) is a closer and handier connection, but the old redbrick Tokyo Station building is a more compelling place. The work of Kingo Tatsuno, one of Japan's first modern architects, it was completed in 1914; Tatsuno modeled his creation on the railway station of Amsterdam. The building lost its original top story in the air raids of 1945, but it was promptly repaired; more recent plans to tear it down entirely were scotched by a protest movement, and the idea now is to have it "remodeled"—which, to judge by the prevailing standards of architecture in Tokyo, can do it very little good. The best thing about the building is the **Tokyo Station Hotel,** which wanders along the west side on the second and third floors; the windows along the corridor look out over the station rotunda. The hotel's frosted glass, flocked wallpaper, and heavy red drapes have seen better days, but it still has enough pride of place—you couldn't ask for a more central location—to charge ¥20,000 to ¥25,000 for a double room. The din-

British Embassy, **15**
Budokan, **20**
Chidori-ga-fuji-Koen Park, **17**
Crafts Gallery, **21**
Fushimi Yagura, **8**
Hanzomon, **14**
Hirakawamon, **26**
Imperial Palace Outer Garden, **6**
Inuimon, **22**
Kikyomon, **4**
Kita Hanebashi Gate, **23**
Kitanomaru-Koen Park, **19**
Metropolitan Police Department, **10**
National Diet Building, **11**
National Museum of Modern Art, **25**
National Theater, **13**
Nijubashi, **7**
Otemon, **2**
Sakashitamon, **5**
Sakuradamon, **9**
Supreme Court, **12**
Takebashi, **24**
Tatsumi Yagura, **3**
Tayasumon, **18**
Tokyo Station, **1**
Yasukuni Jinja, **16**

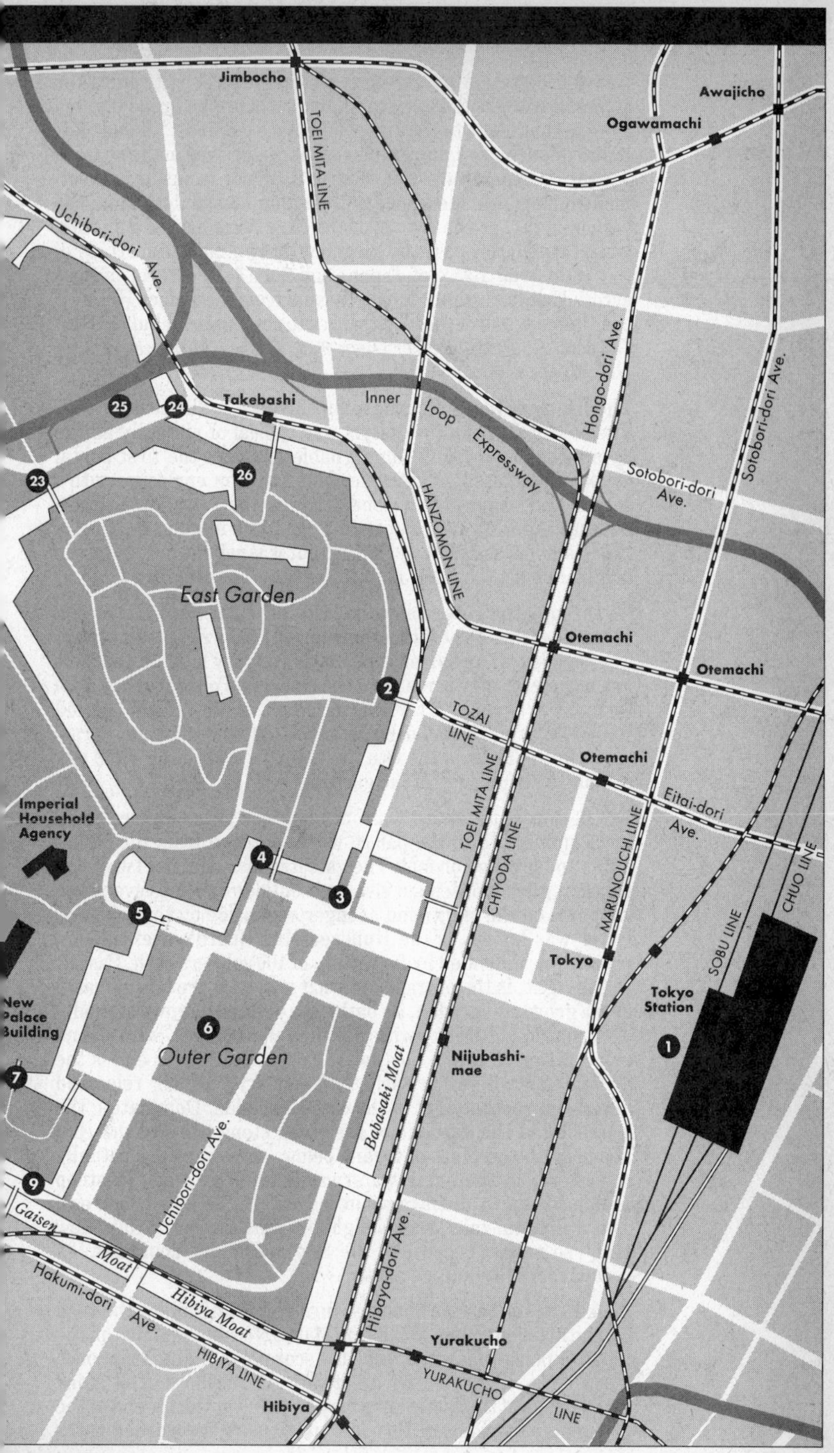

Jimbocho
Awajicho
Ogawamachi
TOEI MITA LINE
Uchibori-dori Ave.
Hongo-dori Ave.
Sotobori-dori Ave.
Takebashi
Inner Loop Expressway
Sotobori-dori Ave.
HANZOMON LINE
East Garden
Otemachi
Otemachi
TOZAI LINE
Otemachi
Eitai-dori Ave.
TOEI MITA LINE
CHIYODA LINE
MARUNOUCHI LINE
CHUO LINE
SOBU LINE
Imperial Household Agency
Tokyo
Tokyo Station
New Palace Building
Outer Garden
Babasaki Moat
Nijubashi-mae
Uchibori-dori Ave.
Gaisen Moat
Hibiya Moat
Hakumi-dori Ave.
Hibaya-dori Ave.
Yurakucho
YURAKUCHO LINE
HIBIYA LINE
Hibiya

ing room serves a fairly decent breakfast for ¥1,500. *1-9-1 Marunouchi, Chiyoda-ku, tel. 03/3231–2511.*

Leave the station by the Marunouchi Central exit, cross the street in front at the taxi stand, and walk up the broad divided avenue that leads to the Imperial Palace grounds. To your left is Marunouchi, to your right is Otemachi: you are in the heart of Japan, Incorporated—the home of its major banks and investment houses, its insurance and trading companies. Take the second right, at the corner of the New Marunouchi Building; walk two blocks, past the gleaming brown marble fortress of the Industrial Bank of Japan, and turn left. Ahead of you, across Uchibori (Inner Moat) Avenue from the Palace Hotel, is (2) the **Otemon,** one of three entrances to the Imperial Palace **East Garden.** *Admission free. Open 9–3. Closed Mon., Fri., and Dec. 25–Jan. 5.*

The Otemon was in fact the main entrance to the castle itself. The so-called *masu* (box) style was typical of virtually all the approaches to Ieyasu's impregnable fortress: the first portal (*mon* is Japanese for "gate") leads to a narrow enclosure with a second and larger gate beyond, offering the defenders inside a devastating field of fire upon any would-be intruders. Most of the Otemon was destroyed in 1945 but was rebuilt in 1967 on the original plans; the outer part of the gate, however, survived.

Go through the gate, collect a plastic token at the office on the other side (there's no admission fee), and walk up the driveway. The bloodcurdling shrieks and howls you may hear on your left are harmless; they come from the National Police Agency *dojo* (martial arts hall). The hall was built in the Taisho period (1912–1925) and is still used for *kendo* (Japanese fencing) practice. On the right is the Ote Rest House, where for ¥100 you can buy a simple map of the garden.

At the top of the drive was once another gate, where feudal lords summoned to the palace would descend from the palanquins and proceed on foot. The gate itself is gone, but two 19th-century guardhouses survive; one outside the massive stone supports on the right, and a longer one inside on the left. The latter was known as the Hundred-Man Guardhouse; this approach was defended by four shifts of 100 soldiers each. Past it, to the right, is the entrance to what was once the Ni-no-maru, now a grove and garden, its pathways defined by rows of rhododendrons manicured to within an inch of their lives, with a pond and a waterfall in the northwest corner. At the far end is the **Suwa Tea Pavilion,** an early 19th-century building relocated here from another part of the castle grounds. Dominating the west side of the garden are the steep stone walls of the Hon Maru, with the Moat of Swans below (the swans are actually elsewhere, in the outer waterways); halfway along, a steep path leads up to an entrance in the wall to the upper fortress. This is **Shio-mi-zaka,** which might be translated as "Briny View Hill," so named because in the Edo period one could see the ocean from this vantage point.

Walk back to the guardhouses, turn right, and follow the road for the main entrance to the Hon Maru. Nothing remains on the broad expanse of lawn to recall the scores of buildings that once stood here, connected by a network of corridors. The stone foundations of the castle keep may be found at the far end of the grounds. As you enter, turn left and explore the wooded paths that skirt the perimeter. There is shade and quiet and benches are available where you can sit, rest your weary feet, and listen to bird song. In the southwest corner, through the trees, you can see the back of the **Fujimi Yagura,** the only surviving watchtower of the Hon Maru; farther along the path, on the west side, is the **Fujimi Tamon,** one of the two remaining armories.

The foundations of the keep make a platform with a fine view of **Kitanomaru-Koen Park** and the city to the north. The view must have been even finer from the keep itself; built and rebuilt three times, it soared more than 250 feet over Edo, five stories high. The other castle buildings were all plastered white; the keep was black, unadorned but for a golden roof. In 1657, a fire destroyed most of the city. Strong winds carried the flames across the moat, where it consumed the keep in a heat so fierce that it melted the gold in the vaults underneath. The keep was never rebuilt.

Now it's time to review your priorities. You can abbreviate your tour of the palace area from here in one of two ways. To the left of the keep, there is an exit from the Hon Maru that leads to the **Kita Hanebashi Gate;** to the right, another road leads past the **Toka Music Hall** (an octagonal tower faced in mosaic tile, built in honor of the empress in 1966) down to the Ni-no-Maru and out of the gardens by way of the **Harakawa Gate.** Both these exits will bring you to **Takebashi** (Bamboo Bridge), which you encounter much later in the day on the longer course of this excursion.

To take a longer course, leave the Hon Maru the way you came in. Stop for a moment at the rest house on the west side of the park, and look at the pairs of before-and-after photographs along the wall; these are the same views of the castle, taken about 100 years apart. In the 1870s, much of the castle was in astonishing disrepair, and the warriors of the Hundred-Man Guardhouse were a trifle ragtag. Turn in your plastic token, turn to the right as you leave the Otemon, and walk along the moat.

Where the wall makes a right angle, you will see the second of ❸ the three surviving watchtowers, the **Tatsumi,** or **Niju** (Double-Tiered), **Yagura.** Here the sidewalk opens out to a parking lot for tour buses and the beginning of a broad promenade. In the far corner to your right, where the angle of the wall turns ❹ again, is the **Kikyomon,** a gate used primarily for deliveries to the palace. (Short and prestigious indeed is the roster of *Goyotashi*—Purveyors to the Imperial Household.) At the far end ❺ of the parking lot is **Sakashitamon,** the gate used by the officials of the Imperial Household Agency itself.

From here to **Hibiya-Koen Park,** along both sides of Uchibori- ❻ dori Avenue, stretches the concourse of the **Imperial Palace Outer Garden.** This whole area once lay along the edge of Tokyo Bay. Later, the shogun had his most trusted retainers build their estates here; these in turn gave way to the office buildings of the Meiji government. In 1899, the buildings were relocated; the promenade was planted with the wonderful stands of pine trees you see today. Walk along the broad gravel path to ❼ **Nijubashi** (Two-Tiered Bridge) and the **Seimon** (Main Gate).

This is surely the most photogenic spot on your tour of the Castle, though you can approach it no closer than the head of the short stone bridge called the **Seimon Sekkyo.** Cordoned off on the other side is the gate through which ordinary mortals may pass only on January 2 and December 23; the guards in front of their little copper-roof octagon sentry boxes change every hour on the hour—alas, with nothing like the pomp and ceremony of Buckingham Palace. Nijubashi makes its graceful arch over the moat here from the area inside the gate; the building in the background, completing the picture, is the **Fushimi Yagura,** built in the 17th century and the last of the three surviving original watchtowers.

Continue on the gravel walk past the Seimon, turn right, and pass through the **Sakuradamon** (Gate of the Field of Cherry Trees). (Before you do, turn and look back down the concourse: you will not see another expanse of open space like this anywhere else in Tokyo.) Sakuradamon is another masu gate; by hallowed use and custom, the little courtyard between the portals is where joggers warm up for their 3-mile run around the palace. Many of them will already have passed you on your exploration; jogging around the palace is a ritual that begins as early as 6 AM and goes on all through the day, no matter what the weather. Almost everybody runs the course counterclockwise; now and then you may spot someone going the opposite way, but rebellious behavior of this sort is frowned upon in Japan.

Across the street as you pass through the gate is the beginning of Sakurada-dori Avenue, with the **Metropolitan Police Department** building on the north corner, by world-renowned architect Kenzô Tange; the older brick buildings on the south corner belong to the **Ministry of Justice.** Sakurada-dori runs through the heart of official Japan; between here and Kasumigaseki are the ministries—from Foreign Affairs and Education to International Trade and Industry—that comprise the central government. They inhabit, however, what are surely the most uninteresting buildings, architecturally, of any government center in the world; they should not tempt you from your course. Turn right, and follow the moat as you walk up the hill.

Ahead of you, where the road branches to the left, you will see the squat pyramid of the **National Diet Building,** which houses the Japanese Parliament. Completed in 1936 after 17 years of work, it is a building best contemplated from a distance; on a gloomy day, it might well have sprung from the screen of a German Expressionist movie. Bear right as you follow the moat, to the five-point intersection where it curves again to the north. Across the street are the gray stone slabs of the

Supreme Court; this, and the **National Theater** next door, are worth a short detour.

The Supreme Court building, by architect Shinichi Okada, was the last in a series of open design competitions sponsored by the various agencies charged with the reconstruction of Tokyo after World War II. Completed in 1968, its fortresslike planes and angles speak volumes for the role of the law in Japanese society; here is the very bastion of the established order. Okada's winning design was one of 217 submitted; before it was finished, the open competition had generated so much controversy that the government did not hold another one for almost 20 years. *4-2 Hayabusa-cho, Chiyoda-ku (nearest subway station: Hanzomon). Call the Public Relations Office (Kohoka) at 03/3264–8111 for permission to visit inside. Guided tours are normally offered only to Japanese student groups, but can sometimes be arranged for others in May and Oct.*

Like the Supreme Court, Hiroyuki Iwamoto's National Theater (1966) was also a design-competition winner; the result was a rendition in concrete of the ancient *azekura* (storehouse) style, best exemplified by the 8th-century Shosoin Imperial Repository in Nara. The large hall seats 1,746 and features primarily Kabuki theater, ancient court music, and dance; the small hall seats 630 and is used primarily for Bunraku puppet theater and traditional music. *4-1 Hayabusa-cho, Chiyoda-ku (nearest subway station: Hanzomon), tel. 03/3265-7411. Ticket prices vary considerably depending on the performance.*

Cross back to the palace side of the street. At the top of the hill, on your right, a police contingent guards the road to the

14 **Hanzomon**—and beyond it, to the new Imperial Palace. At the foot of this small wooden gate was once the house of the legendary Hattori Hanzo, leader of the shogun's private corps of spies and infiltrators (and assassins, if need be)—the black-clad *ninja,* perennial material for historical adventure films and television dramas.

North from here, along the Hanzo-bori Moat, is a narrow strip

15 of park; facing it, across the street, is the **British Embassy.** Along this western edge of his fortress, the shogun kept his personal retainers, called *hatamoto,* divided by district (*bancho*) into six regiments. Today these six bancho comprise one of the most sought-after residential areas in Tokyo, where high-rise apartments commonly fetch $1 million or more.

At the next intersection, review your priorities again. You can turn right, and complete your circuit of the palace grounds by way of the **Inuimon,** or you can continue straight north on

16 Uchibori-dori Avenue to Kudanzaka and **Yasukuni Jinja** (Shrine of Peace for the Nation).

Time Out A good, moderately priced place for lunch, if you choose the latter course, is **Tony Roma's**—just past the intersection on the west side of the street. The specialty here, as it is in this chain's umpteen locations, from London to Okinawa, is charcoal-broiled spare ribs. *1 Sambancho, Chiyoda-ku, tel. 03/3239-0273. Open noon–3 PM for lunch, 5–11 PM for dinner.*

Where Uchibori-dori Avenue comes to an end, cross the street to the grounds of the Yasukuni Jinja Shrine. Founded in 1869, Yasukuni enshrines the souls—worshiped as deities—of some 2.5 million people who gave their lives in the defense of the Japanese Empire. Since most of that "defense" took place in the course of what others regard as opportunistic wars abroad, Yasukuni is a very controversial place. It is a memorial out of keeping with the postwar constitution, which commits Japan to the renunciation of militarism forever; on the other hand, hundreds of thousands of Japanese visit the shrine every year, simply to pray for the repose of friends and relatives they have lost. Prime ministers and other high officials try to skirt this controversy, with no great success, by making their visits as private individuals, not in their official capacities.

Pick up a pamphlet and simplified map of the shrine in English from the guard station on the right as you enter. Just ahead of you, in a circle on the main avenue, is a statue of Masujiro

Omura, commander of the imperial forces that subdued the Tokugawa loyalist resistance to the new Meiji government in 1868. From here, as you look down the avenue to your right, you see the enormous steel outer *torii* (arch) of the main entrance to the shrine at Kudan-shita; to the left, you see the bronze inner torii, erected in 1887. (The arches of Shinto shrines are normally made of wood and are painted red.) Beyond the inner torii is the gate to the shrine itself, with its 12 pillars and chrysanthemums—the imperial crest—embossed on the doors.

The shrine is not one structure but a complex of buildings that includes the **Main Hall** and the **Hall of Worship,** both built in the simple, unadorned style of the ancient shrines at Ise. In the complex are various reception halls, a museum, a Noh theater, and, in the far western corner, a sumo-wrestling ring. Both Noh and sumo have their origins in religious ritual, as performances offered to please and divert the gods; sumo matches are held at Yasukuni April 23, during the first of its three festivals.

Turn right in front of the Hall of Worship, and cross the grounds to the museum, called the **Yushukan.** None of the documents and memorabilia on display here are identified in English, although in some cases the meanings are clear enough; the rooms on the second floor house an especially fine collection of medieval swords and armor. Perhaps the most bizarre exhibit is the *Kaiten* (Human Torpedo) in the main hall on the first floor; this is the submarine equivalent of a kamikaze plane. The Kaiten was a black cylinder about 50 feet long and 3 feet in diameter, with 3,400 pounds of high explosives in the nose and a man in the center, squeezed into a seat, who peered into a periscope and worked the directional vanes with his feet. It was carried into battle on the deck of a ship and launched against the enemy; on its one-way journey, it had a maximum range of about 5 miles (8 kilometers). *3-1-1 Kudan-kita, Chiyoda-ku, tel. 03/3261–8326. Admission: ¥200 adults, ¥50 children under 12. Museum open Mar.–Sept., 9–5; Oct.–Feb., 9–4:30. Closed June 22–23, Dec. 28–31. Grounds of the shrine open generally sunrise to sunset.*

If time permits, turn right as you leave the Yushukan and walk past the other implements of war (cannons, ancient and modern; a tank, incongruously bright and gay in its green-and-yellow camouflage paint) arrayed out front of the pond at the rear of the shrine. There is, unfortunately, no admittance to the teahouses on the far side, but the pond is among the most serene and beautiful in Tokyo, especially in spring, when the irises are in bloom. If you are pressed, leave Yasukuni Jinja the way you came in, cross the street, turn left, and walk down the hill. About 50 yards from the intersection, on the right, is the

⑰ entrance to **Chidori-ga-fuji-Koen Park.** The park is a pleasant green strip of promenade, high on the edge of the moat, lined with cherry trees. It leads back in the direction of the Imperial Palace; halfway along, it widens, and opposite the **Fairmont Hotel** a path leads down to the **Chidori-ga-fuji Boathouse.** Long before Edojo Castle, there was a lovely little lake here, which Ieyasu Tokugawa incorporated into his system of defenses; now it's possible to rent a rowboat and explore it at your leisure. *Tel. 03/3234–1948. Boat rentals: ¥200 for 30 min. Open 9:30–4:30 (July and Aug. to 5:30). Closed Mon. in Mar. and Dec. 16–Feb. 28.*

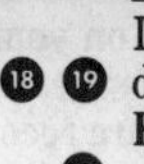

Leave the park the way you came in, turn right, and continue down the hill to the **Tayasumon**, the entrance to **Kitanomaru-Koen Park.** This is one of the largest and finest of the surviving masu gates to the castle; inside, you come first to the **Budokan** (2-3 Kitanomaru Koen, Chiyoda-ku, tel. 03/3216–5100), built as a martial arts arena for the Tokyo Olympics of 1964. The octagonal design was based on the Hall of Dreams of the Horyuji Temple in Nara. Apart from hosting tournaments and exhibitions of judo, karate, and kendo (fencing), this arena also serves as a concert hall, especially for visiting superstars. Tokyo rock promoters are fortunate in their audiences, who don't seem to mind that the ticket prices are exorbitant, the acoustics are unforgivable, and the overselling is downright hazardous.

Just opposite the main entrance to the Budokan, past the parking lot, a pedestrian walkway leads off through the park, back in the direction of the palace. Cross the bridge at the other end of the walk, turn right, and right again before you leave the park, on the driveway that leads to the Kogeikan, the **Crafts Gallery** of the National Museum of Modern Art. Built in 1910, the Kogeikan was once the headquarters of the Imperial Guard; it is a rambling redbrick building, neo-Gothic in style, with exhibition halls on the second floor. The gallery features work of traditional craftsmanship—primarily lacquerware, textiles, pottery, and metalworking—by the modern masters. The exhibits are all too few, but many of the craftspeople represented here have been designated by the government as Living National Treasures—a recognition given only to lifetimes of the finest work in each of these fields. *1-1 Kitanomaru Koen, Chiyoda-ku, tel. 03/3211–7781. Admission: ¥400 adults, ¥70 children under 12; this ticket includes admission to the National Museum. Additional fee for special exhibitions. Open 10–4:30. Closed Mon.*

Return to the park exit, and cross the street to the palace side. Ahead of you is the **Inuimon** (Northwest Gate); a driveway here leads to the Imperial Household Agency and the palace. This gate is used primarily by members of the imperial family and by the fortunate few who have managed to obtain special permission to visit the palace itself. A bit farther down the hill is the **Kita Hanebashi** (North Drawbridge) **Gate,** mentioned earlier as one of the entrances to the Imperial Palace East Garden.

At the foot of the hill is **Takebashi** (Bamboo Bridge); the original bridge material has long since given way to reinforced concrete. Here, depending on how you have organized your tour, you might want to cross the street and walk the short distance uphill to the **National Museum of Modern Art.** Founded in 1952 and moved to its present site in 1969, the museum mounts a number of major exhibitions of 20th-century Japanese and Western art throughout the year. The second through fourth floors house the permanent collection (painting, prints, and sculpture), which includes works by Rousseau, Picasso, Foujita, Ryuzaburo Umehara, and Taikan Yokoyama. *3 Kitanomaru Koen, Chiyoda-ku, tel. 03/3214–2561. Admission: ¥400 for adults, ¥70 children under 12; this ticket includes admission to the Crafts Gallery. Additional fee for special exhibitions. Open 10–4:30. Closed Mon.*

Cross back to the palace side of the street. A short walk from Takebashi is **Hirakawamon,** the third entrance to the Imperial

(Palace East) Garden and the last stop on your tour. The approach to this gate, recently restored, is the only wood bridge that spans the moat; the gate itself is also a reconstruction, but an especially beautiful one—it looks much as it must have when the Hirakawamon was used by the shogun's ladies, on their rare excursions from the seraglio. From here, follow the moat as it turns south again; in a few minutes you will find yourself back at Otemon, tired but triumphant.

Akihabara and Jimbocho

Numbers in the margin correspond to points of interest on the Akihabara and Jimbocho map.

This is it: the greatest sound-and-light show on earth. **Akihabara** is a merchandise mart for anything—and everything—that runs on electricity, block after block of it, with a combined annual turnover well in excess of ¥30 trillion. Here you'll find microprocessors, washing machines, stereo systems, blenders, television sets, and gadgets that beep when your bathwater is hot. Wherever you go in the world, if people know nothing else about Japan, they recognize the country as a cornucopia of electronics equipment and household appliances; about 10% of what Japan's electronics industry makes for the domestic market passes through Akihabara.

Just after World War II there was a black market here, around the railroad station, where the Yamanote Loop Line and the crosstown Sobu Line intersect. In time, most of the stalls were doing a legitimate business in radio parts, and in 1951 they were all relocated in one dense clump under the tracks. Retail and wholesale suppliers prospered there in less-than-peaceful coexistence, as they spread out into the adjacent blocks and made the area famous for cut-rate prices.

No visitor to Tokyo neglects this district; the mistake is to come here merely for shopping. Akihabara may be consumer heaven, but it is also the first stop on a walking tour through the general area known as Kanda (where the true Edokko, the born-and-bred Tokyoite of the old town, claimed his roots) to the bookstalls of Jimbocho. In a sense, this tour is a journey through time: it's a morning's walk from satellite-broadcast antennas to the sacred precincts of the printed word.

Start at the west exit of JR Akihabara Station. (There's also a stop nearby on the Hibiya subway line, but the JR provides much easier access.) Come out to the left into the station square, turn right, and walk to the main thoroughfare; ahead of ❶ you on the other side of the street you'll see the **LAOX** building, one of the district's major discount stores. *1-2-9 Soto Kanda, Chiyoda-ku, tel. 03/3255-9041. Open daily 10–7:45, Sun. 10–7:15.*

Before you get to the corner, on the right, is a little warren of stalls and tiny shops that cannot have changed an iota since the days of the black market—except for their merchandise. Wander through the narrow passageways and see an astonishing array of switches, transformers, resistors, semiconductors, printed circuit cards, plugs, wires, connectors, and tools; this corner of Akihabara is for people who know—or want to know—what the latest in Japanese electronic technology looks

Bookstores of Jimbocho, **6**
Kanda Myojin Shrine, **3**
LAOX, **1**
Nikolai Cathedral, **5**
Yamagiwa, **2**
Yushima Seido, **4**

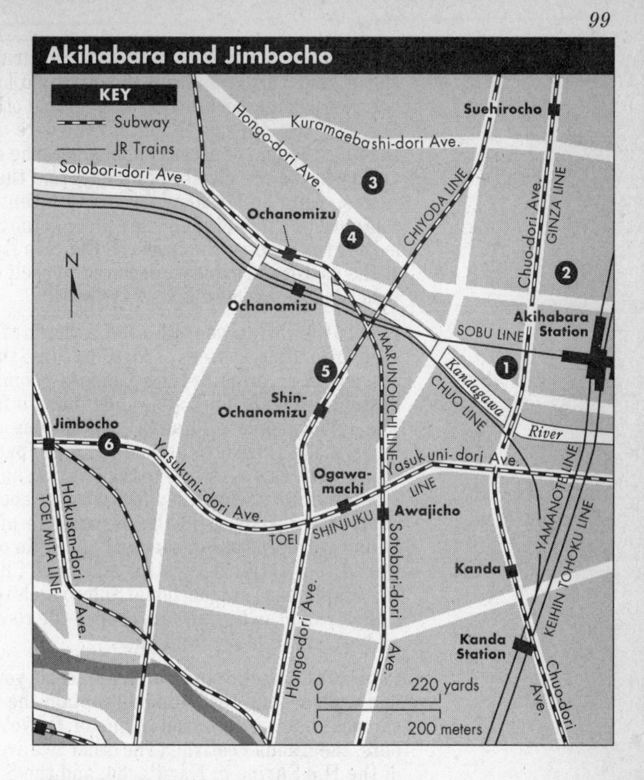

like from the inside. (A lot of the foreign browsers here seem to confer in Eastern European languages.)

Turn right at the corner, and walk north on Chuo-dori Avenue. Music blares at you from hundreds of storefronts as you walk along; this is the heart of the district.

❷ Just past the second intersection, on the right, is **Yamagiwa,** a store that stocks simply everything, from computer software to chandeliers to hearing aids, including a considerable selection of imported goods. There's also an annex for duty-free shopping (bring your passport). *4-1-1 Soto Kanda, Chiyoda-ku, tel. 03/3253–2111. Open Sun.–Thurs. 10–5:30, Fri.–Sat. 10–8. Closed second Wed. of the month, except July and Dec.)*

Rival **Minami,** at the far end of the block, offers a similar variety of goods, plus an entire sixth floor devoted to European antiques. *4-3-3 Soto Kanda, Chiyoda-ku, tel. 03/3255–3173. Open daily 9–5:30.*

Cross the street, continue northward to the Soto Kanda 5-chome intersection (there's an entrance to the Suehiro-cho subway station on the corner), and turn left on Kuramaebashi-dori Avenue. Walk about five minutes—you will cross one more intersection with a traffic light—and in the middle of the next block you will see a flight of steps on the left, between two new brick buildings. Red, green, and blue pennants flutter from the
❸ handrails; this is the back entrance to the **Kanda Myojin Shrine.**

Kanda Myojin is said to have been founded in 730 in a village called Shibasaki, where the Otemachi financial district stands today. Three principle deities are enshrined here: Daikoku, Ebisu, and Taira no Masakado. Daikoku looks after the well-being of farming and fishing villages and other small communities; one also appeals to him for the cure of various diseases. Ebisu is the god of success in business; he concerns himself as well with the prosperity of families and the happiness of marriages. Taira no Masakado was a 10th-century warrior whose contentious spirit earned him a place in the Shinto pantheon: he led a revolt against the Imperial Court in Kyoto, seized control of the eastern provinces, declared himself emperor—and was beheaded for his rebellious ways in 940.

In 1616 the shrine was relocated, a victim of Ieyasu Tokugawa's ever-expanding system of fortifications; the present site was chosen, in accordance with Chinese geomancy, to afford the best view from Edojo Castle and protect it from evil influences. The townspeople of Kanda, contentious souls in their own right, made Taira no Masakado a kind of patron saint, and even today (oblivious somehow to the fact that he lost) they appeal to him for victory when they face a tough encounter. The shrine itself was destroyed in the earthquake of 1923; the present buildings reproduce in concrete the style of 1616. Ieyasu preferred the jazzier decorative effects of Chinese Buddhism to the simple lines of traditional Shinto architecture; this is especially evident in the curved, copper-tile roof of the main shrine and in the two-story front gate.

Some of the smaller buildings you see as you come up the steps and walk around the main hall contain the *mikoshi*—portable shrines that are featured in one of Tokyo's three great blowouts, the Kanda Festival. (The other two are the Sanno Festival of the Hie Shrine in Nagatacho, and the Sanja Festival of the Asakusa Shrine.) The essential shrine festival is a procession in which the gods, housed for the occasion in their mikoshi, pass through the streets and get a breath of fresh air. The Kanda Festival began in the early Edo period; heading the procession then were 36 magnificent floats, most of which were destroyed in the fires that raged through the city after the earthquake of 1923. The floats that lead the procession today move in stately measure on wheeled carts, attended by the priests and officials of the shrine in Heian-period (794–1185) costume; behind them come the mikoshi, some 70 of them, bobbing and weaving, carried on the shoulders of the townspeople. The spirit of Taira no Masakado is channeled on this day into a determination to shout the loudest, drink the most beer, and have the best time. *2-16-2 Soto Kanda, Chiyoda-ku, tel. 03/3254–0753. The Kanda Festival takes place in odd-numbered years; it is next scheduled for May 1995.*

Leave the shrine by the main gate. The seated figures in the alcoves on either side are its guardian gods; carved in camphor wood, they are depicted in Heian costume, holding long bows. From the gate down to the copper-clad torii (arch) on Hongodori Avenue is a walk of a few yards; on either side are shops that sell the specialties famous in this neighborhood: pickles, miso (fermented bean paste), and sweet sake (rice wine) laced with ground ginger. On the other side of the avenue you will see the wall and wooded grounds of the **Yushima Seido.**

4

This, too, is a shrine, but one of a very different sort: It was founded in 1632 as a hall for the study of the Chinese Confucian classics. The original building was in Ueno; its headmaster was

Razan Hayashi, the official Confucian scholar to the Tokugawa government. The Tokugawas found these Chinese teachings, with their emphasis on obedience and hierarchy, particularly attractive. Confucianism became a kind of state ideology, and the hall (moved to its present site in 1691) turned into an academy for the ruling elite. In a sense, nothing has changed: In 1872, the new Meiji government established the country's first teacher training institute here, and that, in turn, evolved into Tokyo University—the graduates of which still make up much of the ruling elite.

To get to Yushima Seido, cross Hongo-dori Avenue and turn left, following the wall downhill. Turn right at the first narrow side street, and right again at the bottom; the entrance to Yushima Seido is a few steps from the corner. Japan's first museum and its first national library were built on these grounds; both were soon relocated. As you walk up the path, you will see a statue of Confucius on your right; where the path ends, a flight of stone steps leads up to the main hall of the shrine—destroyed six times by fire, and each time rebuilt. The last repairs date to 1954. The hall could almost be in China; painted black, weathered and somber, it looks like nothing else you are likely to see in Japan. Confucian scholarship, it seems, did not lend itself to ornamentation. In May of odd-numbered years, when the Kanda Festival passes by, the spirit enshrined here must take a dim view of the frivolities on the other side of the wall. *1-4-25 Yushima, Bunkyo-ku, tel. 03/3251-4606. Admission free. Open daily 9:30-5.*

Retrace your steps, turn right as you leave the shrine, and walk along the continuation of the wall on the side street leading up to **Hijiribashi** (Bridge of Sages), which spans the Kandagawa River at Ochanomizu Station on the JR Sobu Line. Cross the bridge (you're now back on Hongo-dori); ahead of you, just beyond the station on the right, you'll see the dome of **Nikolai Cathedral**, center of the Orthodox Church in Japan. Formally, this is the Holy Resurrection Cathedral; the more familiar name derives from its founder, St. Nikolai Kassatkin (1836–1912), a Russian missionary who came to Japan in 1861 and spent the rest of his life here propagating the Orthodox faith. The building, planned by a Russian engineer and executed by a British architect, was completed in 1891. Heavily damaged in the earthquake of 1923, the cathedral was restored with a dome much more modest than the original. Even so, it endows this otherwise featureless part of the city with the charm of the unexpected. *4-1 Surugadai, Kanda, Chiyoda-ku, tel. 03/3295-6879. Admission free. Open Tues.-Sat. 1-4.*

Continue south on Hongo-dori Avenue to the major intersection at Yasukuni-dori Avenue. Surugadai, the area to your right as you walk down the hill, is a kind of fountainhead of Japanese higher education: Two of the city's major private universities—Meiji and Nihon—occupy a good part of the hill. Not far from these is a score of elite high schools, public and private. In the 1880s, several other universities were founded in this area. They have since moved away, but the student population here is still enormous; Nihon University alone accepted some 15,000 freshmen this year to its four-year program.

Students are not as serious as they used to be. So saith every generation, but as you turn right on Yasukuni-dori Avenue, you encounter palpable proof. Between you and your objec-

6 tive—the **bookstores of Jimbocho**—are three blocks of stores devoted almost exclusively to electric guitars, records, travel bags, skis, and skiwear. The bookstores begin at the intersection called Surugadai-shita, and continue along Yasukuni-dori Avenue for about a ¼-mile, most of them on the south (left) side of the street. This area is to print what Akihabara is to electronics; browse here for art books, catalogs, scholarly monographs, secondhand paperbacks, and dictionaries in most known languages. Jimbocho is home as well to wholesalers, distributors, and many of Japan's most prestigious publishing houses.

A number of the antiquarian booksellers here carry not only rare typeset editions but also wood-block–printed books of the Edo period and individual prints. At shops like **Isseido** (1-7 Kanda Jimbocho, Chiyoda-ku, tel. 03/3292–0071) and **Ohya Shobo** (1-1 Kanda Jimbocho, Chiyoda-ku, tel. 03/3291–0062), it is still possible to find a genuine Hiroshige or Toyokuni print (granted, not in the best condition) at an affordable price.

What about that word processor or CD player you didn't buy at the beginning of your walk because you didn't want to carry it all this way? No problem. There's a subway station (Toei Mita Line) right on the Jimbocho main intersection; ride one stop north to Suidobashi, transfer to the JR Sobu Line, and five minutes later you're back in Akihabara.

Ueno

Numbers in the margin correspond to points of interest on the Ueno map.

The JR station at **Ueno** is Tokyo's Gare du Nord: the gateway to (and from) the provinces. The single most important fact of Japanese life since the 17th century has been the pull of the cities, the great migration from the villages in pursuit of a better life; since 1883, when the station was completed, the people of Tohoku—the northeast—have begun that pursuit here.

Ueno was a place of prominence, however, long before the coming of the railroad. When Ieyasu Tokugawa established his capital here in 1603, it was merely a wooded promontory, called Shinobugaoka (The Hill of Endurance), overlooking the bay. The view was a pleasant one, and Ieyasu gave a large tract of land on the hill to one of his most important vassals, Todo Takatora, who designed and built Edojo Castle. Ieyasu's heir, Hidetada, later commanded the founding of a temple on the hill. Shinobugaoka was in the northeast corner of the capital; in Chinese geomancy, the northeast approach required a particularly strong defense against evil influences.

That defense was entrusted to Tenkai (1536–1643), a priest of the Tendai sect of Buddhism and an adviser of great influence to the first three Tokugawa shoguns. Tenkai turned for his model to Kyoto, guarded on the northeast by Mt. Hiei and the great temple complex of Enryakuji. The temple he built on Shinobugaoka was called Kaneiji, and he became the first abbot. Mt. Hiei was loftier, but the patronage of the Tokugawas and their vassal barons made Kaneiji Temple a seat of power and glory. By the end of the 17th century, it occupied most of the hill. To the magnificent Main Hall were added scores of other buildings—including a pagoda and a shrine to Ieyasu—and

36 subsidiary temples. The city of Edo itself expanded to the foot of the hill; most of present-day Ueno was once called Monzen-machi (the town in front of the gate).

The power and glory of Kaneiji came to an end in one day: April 11, 1868. An army of clan forces from the western part of Japan, bearing a mandate from Emperor Meiji, had marched on Edo and demanded the surrender of the castle. The shogunate was by then a tottering regime; it capitulated, and with it went everything that had depended on the favor of the Tokugawas. The Meiji Restoration began with a bloodless coup.

A band of some 2,000 Tokugawa loyalists then assembled on Ueno Hill and defied the new government. On May 15, the imperial army attacked; outnumbered and surrounded, the loyalists, known as the Shogitai, soon discovered that right was on the side of modern artillery. A few survivors fled; the rest committed ritual suicide—and took the Kaneiji with them; they put the temple and most of its outbuildings to the torch.

The new Meiji government turned Ueno Hill into one of the nation's first public parks. The intention was not merely to provide a bit of greenery, but to make the park an instrument of civic improvement and a showcase for the achievements of an emerging modern state. It would serve as the site of trade and industrial expositions; it would have a national museum, a library, a university of fine arts, and a zoo. That policy continued well into the present era, with the building of further galleries and concert halls, but Ueno is more than its museums. The Shogitai failed to take everything with them; some of the most important buildings in the temple complex have survived or been restored. The "town in front of the gate" is gone, but here and there, in the narrow streets below the hill, the way of life is much the way it was 100 years ago. Exploring Ueno can be one excursion, or two: It can be an afternoon of culture-browsing, or it can be a full day of discoveries in one of the great centers of the city.

The best way to begin, in either case, is to come to Ueno on the JR, and leave the station by the Park Exit (Koenguchi) on the ❶ upper level. Directly across from the exit is the **Tokyo Metropolitan Festival Hall** (Tokyo Bunka Kaikan), designed by architect Kunio Maekawa and completed in 1961. This is the city's largest and finest facility for classical music, the one most often booked for visiting orchestras and concert soloists. The large auditorium seats 2,327; the smaller one seats 661. *5-45 Ueno Koen, Taito-ku, tel. 03/3828–2111.*

❷ Opposite the Festival Hall on the right is the **National Museum of Western Art.** The building was designed by Le Corbusier and houses what was once the private collection of a wealthy businessman named Kojiro Matsukata. The Rodins in the courtyard—*The Gate of Hell, The Thinker,* and the magnificent *Burghers of Calais*—are genuine; an admirer of French impressionism, Matsukata somehow acquired castings from Rodin's original molds, along with some 850 paintings, sketches, and prints by masters like Renoir, Monet, and Cézanne. He kept the collection in Europe; it was returned by the French government after World War II, left to the country in Matsukata's will, and opened to the public in 1959. Since then, the museum has diversified a bit; more recent acquisitions include works by Reubens, Tintoretto, El Greco, Max Ernst, and

Ameya Yokocho Market, **23**
Jigendo, **5**
Jusanya, **19**
Kaneiji Temple, **6**
Kiyomizu Kannon Hall, **14**
Kuromon Gate, **13**
National Museum of Western Art, **2**
National Science Museum, **3**
Pagoda of the Kaneiji Temple, **11**
Shinobazu Pond, **10**
Shitamachi Museum, **20**
Shogitai Memorial, **16**
Shrine to Benten, **21**
Statue of Takamori Saigo, **17**
Suzumoto, **18**
Tokudaiji Temple, **22**
Tokyo Metropolitan Art Museum, **8**
Tokyo Metropolitan Festival Hall, **1**
Tokyo National Museum, **4**
Tokyo University of Arts Exhibition Hall, **7**
Toshogu Shrine, **12**
Ueno no Mori Royal Museum, **15**
Ueno Zoo, **9**

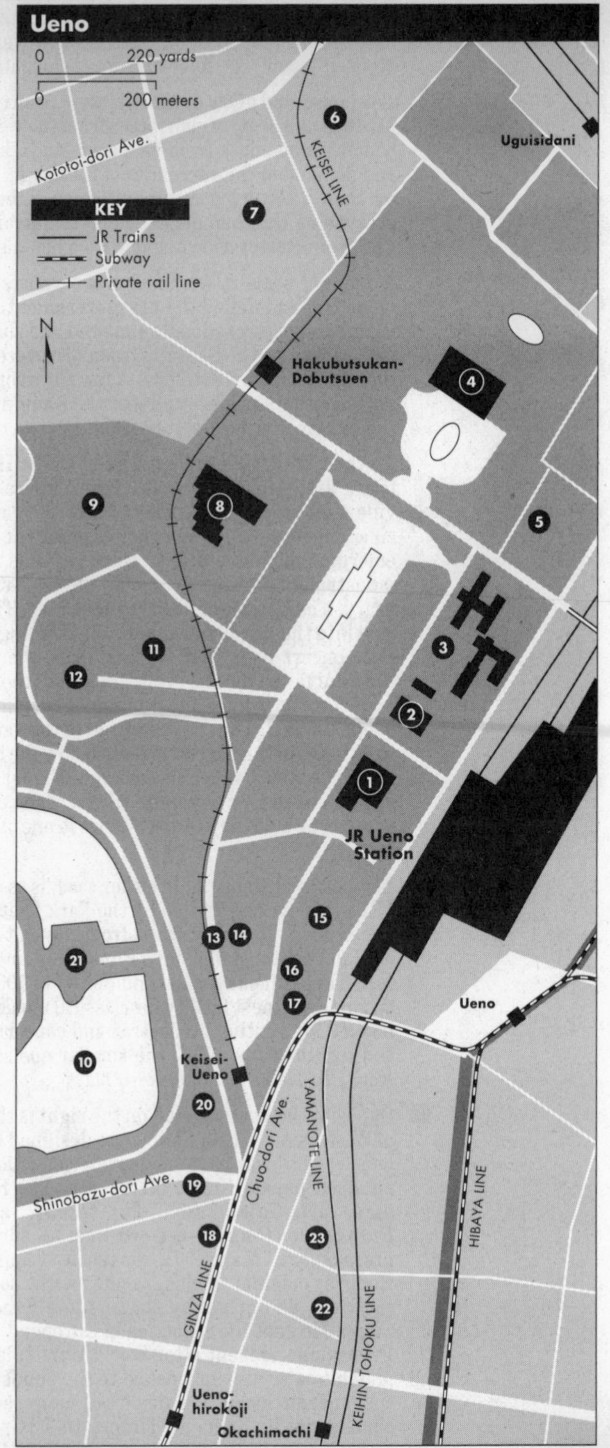

Jackson Pollock. *7-7 Ueno Koen, Taito-ku, tel. 03/3828-5131. Admission: ¥400 adults, ¥70 children under 12. Additional fee for special exhibitions. Open 9:30-4:30. Closed Mon.*

Just behind the National Museum of Western Art, to the right, ❸ is the **National Science Museum**—a natural-history museum very much in the conventional mode. That is, it has everything from dinosaurs to moon rocks on display, but it offers relatively little in the way of hands-on learning experiences. This is not a place to linger if your time is short. *7-20 Ueno Koen, Taito-ku, tel. 03/3822-0111. Admission: ¥400 adults, ¥70 children under 12. Open 9-4. Closed Mon.*

Beyond the National Science Museum, you will come to a broad street that cuts through the park; turn left, and you come almost immediately to the ❹ **Tokyo National Museum.** Here, you should plan to spend some time, even if you are not overly fond of museums: The Tokyo Kokuritsu Hakubutsukan, as it is called in Japanese, is one of the world's great repositories of oriental art and archaeology.

The museum consists of four buildings grouped around a courtyard; on this site once stood the temple-residence of the abbot of Kaneiji Temple. The building on the left is the **Hyokeikan,** the oldest and smallest of the three; completed in 1909, it has only nine exhibition rooms, all devoted to archaeological objects. Look especially for the flamelike sculptured rims and elaborate markings of Middle Jomon-period pottery (c. 3500-2000 BC), so different from anything produced in Japan before or since. Look also for the terra-cotta figures called *haniwa,* unearthed at burial sites dating from the 4th to the 7th century; these figures are deceptively simple in shape, and mysterious and comical at the same time in their effects.

Behind the Hyokeikan is a two-story building clled the **Horyuji Treasure Hall** (Horyuji Homotsukan), which is open only on Thursdays. In 1878, the 7th-century Horyuji Temple in Nara presented 319 works of art in its possession—sculpture, scrolls, masks, and other objects—to the Imperial Household; these were later transferred to the National Museum, and in 1964 the Horyuji Treasure Hall was built to house them. If at all possible, schedule your visit to the museum on Thursday, but bear in mind that these works of wood and paper are more than 1,000 years old; if the weather is too hot or wet, the hall may not be open.

The central building in the complex, the **Honkan,** was built in 1937 and houses Japanese art exclusively: paintings, calligraphy, sculpture, textiles, ceramics, swords, and armor. The more attractive **Toyokan,** on the right, completed in 1968, is devoted to the art of other Asian cultures. Altogether, the museum has some 87,000 objects in its permanent collection, with several thousand more on loan from shrines, temples, and private owners. Among these are 84 objects designated by the government as National Treasures. The Honkan rotates the works on display several times during the year; it also hosts two special exhibitions a year, April-May and October-November, featuring important collections from foreign museums. These, unfortunately, can be an ordeal: The lighting in the Honkan is not particularly good, the explanations in English are sketchy at best, and the hordes of visitors make it impossible to linger over a work you especially want to study. *13-9 Ueno Koen,*

Taito-ku, tel. 03/3822–1111. Admission: ¥400 adults, ¥70 children under 12. Open 9–4. Closed Mon.

Turn to the left as you leave the museum, walk east, and turn left again at the first corner. The building across the road on 5 your right is the **Jigendo,** a memorial hall to Abbot Tenkai, who was given the posthumous title of Jigen Daishi (Great Master of the Merciful Eye). The six bronze lanterns in front, with their dragon faces, are especially fine. At the end of the road that passes the Jigendo, turn left again and walk along the back of the museum; to your right is the **cemetery** of the Kaneiji Temple. Several of the Tokugawa shoguns had their mausoleums here; these were destroyed in the air raids of 1945, but you will see the gate that once led to the tomb of the fourth shogun, Ietsuna. At the end of the road, in the far northwest corner of 6 the park, is the **Kaneiji Temple** itself.

The main hall of the Kaneiji, built in 1638, has covered a lot of territory in its day. Abbot Tenkai had it moved to Ueno from a temple in the town of Kawagoe, about 25 miles (40 kilometers) from Tokyo, where he had once been a priest; it was moved again, to its present site, in 1879, and looks a bit weary of its travels. Behind the temple is the ornately carved gate to what was once the mausoleum of Tsunayoshi, the fifth shogun. Tsunayoshi is famous in the annals of Tokugawa history first for his disastrous fiscal mismanagement, and second for his *Shorui Awaremi no Rei (Edicts on Compassion for Living Things)*, which, among other things, made it a capital offense for a human being to kill a dog. *1-14-11 Ueno Sakuragi, Taito-ku. Admission free, but contributions welcomed. Open 9–5.*

Turn right as you leave the temple, and walk south until you come again to the main road around the park. If you turn right 7 off this road, you will soon come to the **Tokyo University of Arts Exhibition Hall** on the left side of the road. The collection here has some interesting works, some of which are designated National Treasures, but it is not actually a museum. The exhibitions on display are intended primarily as teaching materials for courses in the school curriculum. *12-8 Ueno Koen, Taito-ku, tel. 03/3828–6111. Admission free. Open to the public 10–4 weekdays during the school year, mid-Apr.–mid-July and Sept.–mid-Dec.*

You may skip the Exhibition Hall and instead turn left when you reach the main road through the park. Return to the entrance of the National Museum, and cross the street to the long esplanade with its reflecting pool. At the opposite end, turn 8 right and walk down the path to the **Tokyo Metropolitan Art Museum.**

There are three floors of galleries in the Tokyo Metropolitan; the museum displays its own collection of modern Japanese art on the lower level, and rents out the remaining spaces to various organizations. At any given time, there will be at least five different exhibitions in the building: work by promising young painters, for example, or new forms and materials in sculpture, or modern calligraphy. Completed in 1975, the museum was designed by Kunio Maekawa, who also did the nearby Metropolitan Festival Hall. *8-36 Ueno Koen, Taito-ku, tel. 03/3823–6921. Admission free to the permanent collection; varying fees (usually ¥300 to ¥800) for other exhibitions. Open 9–4. Closed 3rd Mon. of each month.*

Return to the south end of the esplanade, and you will see a ❾ sign for the entrance to the **Ueno Zoo.** Opened in 1882, the zoo gradually expanded to its present 35 acres; the original section on the hill was connected to the one below, along the edge of ❿ **Shinobazu Pond,** by a bridge and a monorail. The zoo houses some 900 different species, most of which look less than enthusiastic about being there. Ueno is not among the most attractive zoos in the world. On the other hand, it does have a pair of giant pandas whose union gave birth to Yuyu in June 1988 (their quarters are near the main entrance). You might decide it's worth a visit on that score alone. On a pleasant Sunday afternoon, however, upwards of 20,000 Japanese are likely to share your opinion; don't expect to have a leisurely view. *9-83 Ueno Koen, Taito-ku, tel. 03/3828–5171. Admission: ¥400 adults, children under 12 free. Open 9:30–4. Closed Mon.*

The zoo has one other attraction that makes it unusual: the process of expansion somehow left within the zoo's confines the ⓫ five-story **Pagoda of the Kaneiji Temple.** Built in 1631 and rebuilt after a fire in 1639, the 120-foot pagoda is painted vermilion and has a copper roof on the top level; most visitors find it a bit out of keeping with the bison cages next door.

A much better view of the pagoda is from the path that leads to ⓬ the **Toshogu Shrine.** Return to the esplanade, and follow the sign to the shrine until you see a small police substation; just beyond it, on a narrow path, the entrance to the shrine is marked by a stone torii (arch), built in 1633. Ieyasu, the first Tokugawa shogun, died in 1616, and the following year was given the posthumous name Tosho-Daigongen (The Great Incarnation Who Illuminates the East). He was declared by the Imperial Court a divinity of the first rank, thenceforth to be worshiped at Nikko, in the mountains north of his city, at a shrine he had commissioned before his death. That shrine is the first and foremost Toshogu Shrine. The one here in Ueno dates to 1627; miraculously, it has survived the disasters that destroyed most of the other original buildings on the hill—the fires, the revolt of 1868, the earthquake of 1923, the bombings of 1945—and is thus one of the very few early Edo-period buildings left in Tokyo.

The path from the torii to the shrine is lined with 200 stone lanterns; another stone lantern *(obaketoro)*, inside the grounds, is more than 18 feet high—one of the three largest in Japan. Beyond these is a double row of bronze lanterns, presented by the feudal lords of the 17th century as expressions of their piety and loyalty to the regime; the lanterns themselves were arrayed in the order of the wealth and ranking of their donors. On the left, before you reach the shrine itself, is the **Peony Garden** (for which you must pay a separate entrance fee), where some 200 varieties are on display. *Tel. 03/3822–3575. Admission: ¥800 adults, ¥400 children under 12. Open 9:30–4:30 Jan.–Feb. and Apr.–May.*

At the end of the path, pay your admission fee and walk around the shrine to the entrance. You'll notice, on the left, a graceful little tea-ceremony pavilion, where Ieyasu Tokugawa's vassal Todo Takatora (who built the shrine itself) is said to have entertained the second and third shoguns. The Toshogu, like its namesake in Nikko, is built in the ornate style called *gongen-zukuri;* it is gilded, painted, and carved with motifs of plants and animals. The carpentry of roof supports and ceilings is especially intricate. The shrine and most of the works of art in it have been designated National Treasures.

The first room inside is the Hall of Worship; the four paintings in gold on wood panels are by Tan'yu, one of the famous Kano family of artists who enjoyed the patronage of emperors and shoguns from the late 15th century to the end of the Edo period. Tan'yu was appointed *goyo eshi* (official court painter) in 1617; his commissions included the Tokugawa castles at Edo and Nagoya, and the Nikko Toshogu Shrine. The framed tablet between the walls, with the name of the shrine in gold, is in the calligraphy of Emperor Go-Mizunoo (1596–1680); other works of calligraphy are by the abbots of the Kaneiji Temple. Behind the Hall of Worship, connected by a passage called the *haiden*, is the Sanctuary, where the spirit of Ieyasu is enshrined.

The real glories of the Toshogu are its so-called Chinese Gate, which you reach at the end of your tour of the building, and the fence on either side. Like its counterpart at Nikko, the fence is a kind of natural-history lesson, with carvings of birds, animals, fish, and shells of every description; unlike the one at Nikko, however, this fence was left unpainted. The two long panels of the gate, with their dragons carved in relief, are attributed to Jingoro Hidari—a brilliant sculptor of the early Edo period whose real name is unknown (*hidari* means "left"; Jingoro was reportedly left-handed). The lifelike appearance of his dragons have inspired a legend. Every morning they were found mysteriously dripping with water; finally it was discovered that they were sneaking out at night to drink from the nearby Shinobazu Pond, and wire cages were put up around them to curtail this disquieting habit. *9-88 Ueno Koen, Taito-ku, tel. 03/3822–3455. Admission: ¥200 adults, ¥100 children under 12. Open 9–5.*

Retrace your steps to the police substation, turn right, and follow the avenue south. Shortly you will see a kind of tunnel of red-lacquer torii, in front of a small shrine to Inari, a Shinto deity of harvests and family prosperity. Shrines of this kind are to be found all over the downtown part of Tokyo, tucked away in alleys and odd corners, always with their guardian statues of foxes—the mischievous creatures with which the god is associated. A few steps farther, down a small road that branches to the right, is a shrine to Michizane Sugawara (854–903), a Heian-period nobleman and poet worshiped as the Shinto deity Tenjin. Because he is associated with scholarship and literary achievement, Japanese students visit his various shrines by the hundreds of thousands in February and March to pray for success on their entrance exams.

Return to the main road and continue south. You will see on ⓭ your left a black gate called the **Kuromon,** a replica of one that once stood at the entrance to the entire Kaneiji Temple complex. The Kuromon, built in the early 17th century, was the main gate of the National Museum until it was moved to this site in 1937; the numerous bullet holes in it were made during the battle for Ueno Hill in 1868. Go through the gate and up the ⓮ stone steps to the **Kiyomizu Kannon Hall.**

Kiyomizu was a part of Abbot Tenkai's grand attempt to echo the holiness of Kyoto; the model for it was the magnificent Kiyomizudera Temple in that city. The echo is a little weak. Where the original rests on enormous wood pillars over a gorge, the Kiyomizu Hall in Ueno merely perches on the lip of a little hill. The hall is known to afford a grand view of Shinobazu Pond—which itself was landscaped to recall Lake Biwa, near Kyoto—but in fact the trees in front of the terrace are too high and full most of the year to afford any view at all. The Kyoto original is maintained in perfect condition; the copy, much smaller, is a little down-at-the-heels. Another of the few buildings that survived the battle of 1868, Kiyomizu is designated a National Treasure.

The principal Buddhist image of worship here is the Senju Kannon (Thousand-Armed Goddess of Mercy). Another figure, however, receives greater homage; this is the Kosodate Kannon, who is believed to answer the prayers of women having difficulty conceiving children. If their prayers are answered, they return to Kiyomizu and leave a doll, as both an offering of thanks and a prayer for the child's health. In a ceremony held every September 25, the dolls that have accumulated during the year are burned in a bonfire. *1-29 Ueno Koen, Taito-ku. Admission free. Open 9–5.*

Leave the hall by the front gate, on the south side. As you look to your left, you will see a new two-story brick services/administration building; on the other side of this is the **Ueno no Mori Royal Museum.** This museum has no permanent collection of its own, but makes its galleries available to various groups, primarily for exhibitions of painting and calligraphy. A more professional museum staff could do some good things here; the Royal Museum has two floors of prime space, but accomplishes very little with it. *1-2 Ueno Koen, Taito-ku, tel. 03/3833–4191. Admission varies, but often free. Open 10–5.*

If you continue south from the Kiyomizu Kannon Hall, you soon come to where the park narrows to a point, and two flights of steps lead down to the main entrance, on Chuo-dori Avenue. Before you reach the steps, on the left, is the **Shogitai Memorial.** Time seems to heal wounds very quickly in Japan; only six years after they had destroyed most of Ueno Hill, the Meiji government permitted the Shogitai to be honored with a gravestone, erected on the spot where their bodies had been cremated. Descendants of one of the survivors still tend the memorial. A few steps away, with its back to the stone, stands the **statue of Takamori Saigo** (1827–1877), chief of staff of the imperial army that took the surrender of Edo and overthrew the shogunate—the army that the Shogitai had died defying. Ironically, Saigo himself fell out with the other leaders of the new Meiji government and was killed in an unsuccessful rebellion of his own. The sculptor Koun Takamura's bronze, made in 1893, sensibly avoids presenting him in uniform.

Time Out Walk down the two flights of steps, leave the park, turn right on Chuo-dori Avenue, and right again at the second corner. One block in from the avenue brings you to the authentic part of Shitamachi; off the beaten tourist path here is **Futaba,** an inexpensive *tonkatsu* (fried pork cutlet) restaurant. If you get lost in the narrow streets here, just ask for it by name; this part of Ueno is considered the original home of tonkatsu restaurants, and Futaba is one of the oldest and best. Anyone you stop will know it. Try the *teishoku* (set menu). *2-8-11 Ueno, Taito-ku, tel. 03/3831–6483. Open 11:30–2:30 and 5–7:30.*

Retrace your steps, keeping on the west side of Chuo-dori Avenue, to where Shinobazu-dori Avenue comes in on the left. About a block before this corner, you'll see a building hung with banners; this is **Suzumoto,** a theater specializing in a traditional narrative comedy called *rakugo.* In Japan, a monologue comedian does not stand up to ply his trade: He sits on a purple cushion, dressed in a kimono, and tells stories that have been handed down for centuries. The rakugo storyteller has only a fan for a prop; he plays a whole cast of characters, with their different voices and facial expressions, by himself. The audience may have heard his stories 20 times already, and they still laugh in all the right places. Suzumoto dates back to about 1857, making it the oldest theater of its kind in Tokyo. The present building, however (in front of which, incidentally, is a stop on the red double-decker bus for Asakusa), is new. *2-7-12 Ueno, Taito-ku, tel. 03/3834–5906. Admission: ¥2,200. Continual performances daily 12–4:30 and 5–8:50.*

Turn left at the intersection, and walk west on Shinobazu-dori Avenue. A few doors from the corner is **Jusanya** (2-12-21 Ueno, Taiko-ku, tel. 03/3831–3238), a shop selling handmade boxwood combs. The business was started in 1736 by a samurai who couldn't support himself in the martial arts, and it has been in the same family ever since. Directly across the avenue is an entrance to the grounds of Shinobazu Pond; just inside, on the right, is the small black and white building that houses the **Shitamachi Museum.**

Shitamachi (Town Below the Castle) lay originally between Ieyasu's fortifications on the west and the Sumida River on the east. As it expanded, it came to include what today constitute the Chuo, Taito, Sumida, and Koto wards. During the Edo period, some 80% of the city was allotted to the warrior class, the temples, and the shrines; in the remaining 20% lived the common people, who made up more than half the population. Well into the modern period, the typical residential units in this part of the city were the *nagaya*, long, single-story tenements, one jammed up against the next along narrow alleys and unplanned streets. The density of Shitamachi shaped the character of the people who lived there: They were gossipy, short-tempered, quick to help a neighbor in trouble, hardworking, and not overly inclined to save for a rainy day. Their way of life will soon be gone completely; the Shitamachi Museum was created to preserve and exhibit what it was still like as late as 1940.

The two main displays on the first floor are a merchant house and a tenement, intact with all their furnishings. Visitors can take their shoes off and step up into the rooms; this is a hands-on museum. On the second floor are displays of toys, tools, and utensils, which were donated, in most cases, by people who had grown up with them and used them all their lives. Photographs of Shitamachi and video documentaries of craftspeople at work may be seen. Occasionally there are demonstrations of various traditional skills, and visitors are welcome to take part. The space in this museum is used with great skill, and there's even a passable brochure in English. Don't miss it. *2-1 Ueno Koen, Taito-ku, tel. 03/3823–7451. Admission: ¥200 adults, ¥100 children under 12. Open 9:30–4:30; closed Mon.*

In front of the museum, take the path that follows the western shore of Shinobazu Pond. During the first week of June, the path is lined on both sides with the stalls of the annual All-

Japan Azalea Fair, a spectacular display of *bonsai* (miniature) flowering shrubs and trees; nurserymen in *happi* (workmen's) coats sell a variety of plants, seedlings, bonsai vessels, and ornamental stones.

Shinobazu was once an inlet of Tokyo Bay; reclamation turned it into a freshwater pond, and Abbot Tenkai had an island made (21) in the middle of it, on which he built the **Shrine to Benten,** a patron goddess of the arts. Later improvements included a causeway to the island, embankments, and even (1884–1893) a race course. Today the pond is in three sections. The first, with its famous lotus plants, is a sanctuary for about 15 species of birds, including pintail ducks, cormorants, great egrets, and grebes. Some 5,000 wild ducks migrate here from as far away as Siberia, remaining September–April. The second section, to the north, belongs to the Ueno Zoo; the third, to the west, is a small lake for boating.

Walk up the east side of the embankment to the causeway, and cross to the shrine. The goddess Benten is one of the Seven Gods of Good Luck, a pantheon that emerged sometime in the medieval period from a jumble of Indian, Chinese, and Japanese mythology; she is depicted holding a musical instrument called a *biwa*, and is thus associated with the lake of the same name, near Kyoto—which Abbot Tenkai wanted to recall in his landscaping of Shinobazu Pond. The shrine, with its distinctive octagonal roof, was destroyed in the bombings of 1945; the present version is a faithful copy.

Cross to the other side of the pond, turn left in front of the boat house (open 9–4:30; cycle boats: ¥500 for 30 min., rowboats ¥500 for 1 hr.), and follow the embankment back to Shinobazu-dori Avenue. Off to your right as you walk, a few blocks away and out of sight, begin the precincts of Tokyo University, the nation's most prestigious seat of higher learning, alma mater to generations of bureaucrats. Turn left as you leave the park, and walk back in the direction of the Shitamachi Museum. When you reach the intersection, cross Chuo-dori and turn right; walk past the ABAB clothing store and turn left at the second (22) corner: at the end of this street is the **Tokudaiji Temple** and the (23) heart of **Ameya Yokocho Market.**

The Tokudaiji (4-6-2 Ueno, Taito-ku) is a curiosity in a neighborhood of curiosities: a temple on the second floor of a supermarket. The principal image of worship is the Indian goddess Marishi, a daughter of Brahma, usually depicted with three faces and four arms; she is believed to help worshipers overcome various sorts of difficulties and to prosper in business. The other image is that of the bodhisattva Jizo; the act of washing this statue is believed to help safeguard one's health. Among the faithful visitors to the Tokudaiji are the merchants of Ameya Yokocho.

The history of Ameya Yokocho (often shortened to Ameyoko) begins in the desperate days immediately after World War II. Ueno Station had survived; virtually everything around it was rubble; and anyone who could make his way here from the countryside with rice and other small supplies of food could sell them at exorbitant black-market prices. One thing not to be had in postwar Tokyo at any price was sugar; before long, there were hundreds of stalls in the black market selling various kinds of *ame* (confections), most of them made from sweet potatoes. These stalls gave the market its name: Ameya Yokocho means "Confectioners' Alley."

Shortly before the Korean War, the market was legalized, and soon the stalls were carrying a full array of watches, chocolate, ballpoint pens, blue jeans, and T-shirts that had somehow been "liberated" from American PXs. In the years to follow, the merchants of Ameyoko diversified still further—to fine Swiss timepieces and French designer luggage of dubious authenticity, cosmetics, jewelry, fresh fruit, and fish. The market became especially famous for the traditional prepared foods of the New Year, and during the last few days of December, as many as half a million people crowd into the narrow alleys under the railroad tracks to stock up for the holiday.

There are over 500 little shops and stalls in the market, stretching from Okachimachi at the south end (the *o-kachi*—"honorable infantry"—were the samurai of lowest rank in the shogun's service; this part of the city was allotted to them for their homes) to the beginning of Showa-dori Avenue at the north. Follow the JR tracks as you wander north; in a few minutes, you will find yourself in front of Ueno Station, your exploring done for the day.

Asakusa

Numbers in the margin correspond to points of interest on the Asakusa map.

In the year 628, so the legend goes, two brothers named Hamanari and Takenari Hinokuma were fishing on the lower reaches of the Sumida River when they dragged up a small gilded statue of Kannon—an aspect of the Buddha worshiped as the Goddess of Mercy. They took the statue to their master, Naji no Nakamoto, who enshrined it in his house. Later, a temple was built for it in nearby **Asakusa.** Now called **Sensoji,** the temple was rebuilt and enlarged several times over the next 10 centuries—but Asakusa itself remained just a village on a river crossing a few hours' walk from Edo. Then Ieyasu Tokugawa made Edo his capital, and Asakusa blossomed. Suddenly, it was the party that never ended, the place where the free-spending townspeople of the new capital came to empty their pockets. Also, for the next 300 years it was the wellspring of almost everything we associate with Japanese popular culture.

The first step in that transformation came in 1657, when Yoshiwara—the licensed brothel quarter not far from Nihombashi—was moved to the countryside farther north: Asakusa found itself square in the road, more or less halfway between the city and its only nightlife. The village became a suburb and a pleasure quarter in its own right. In the narrow streets and alleys around Sensoji Temple, stalls sold toys, souvenirs, and sweets; there were acrobats, jugglers, and strolling musicians; there were sake shops and teahouses—where the waitresses often provided more than tea. (The Japanese have never worried much about the impropriety of such things; the approach to a temple is still a venue for very secular enterprises of all sorts.) Then, in 1841, the Kabuki theaters—which the government looked upon as a source of dissipation second only to Yoshiwara—were also moved to Asakusa.

Highborn and lowborn, the people of Edo flocked to Kabuki. They loved its extravagant spectacle, its bravado and brilliant language; they cheered its heroes and hissed its villains. They bought wood-block prints, called *ukiyo-e*, of their favorite actors. Asakusa was home to the Kabuki theaters for only a short time, but that was enough to establish it as *the* entertainment quarter of the city—a reputation it held unchallenged until World War II.

When Japan ended its long, self-imposed isolation in 1868, where else would the novelties and amusements of the outside world first take root but in Asakusa? The country's first photography studios appeared here in 1875. Japan's first skyscraper, a 12-story mart called the Junikai, filled with shops selling imported goods, was built in Asakusa in 1890. The area around Sensoji Temple had by this time been designated a public park and was divided into seven sections; the sixth section, called Rokku, was Tokyo's equivalent of 42nd Street and Times Square. The nation's first movie theater opened here in 1903—to be joined by dozens more, and these in turn were followed by music halls, cabarets, and revues. The first drinking establishment in Japan to call itself a "bar" was started in Asakusa in 1880; it still exists.

Most of this area was destroyed in 1945. As an entertainment district, it never really recovered, but Sensoji Temple was rebuilt almost immediately. The people here would never dream of living without it—just as they would never dream of living anywhere else. This is the heart and soul of *Shitamachi* (downtown), where you can still hear the rich, breezy Tokyo accent of the 17th and 18th centuries. Where if you sneeze in the middle of the night, your neighbor will demand to know the next morning why you aren't taking better care of yourself. Where a carpenter will refuse a well-paid job if he doesn't think the client has the mother wit to appreciate good work when he sees it. Where you can still go out for a good meal and not have to pay through the nose for a lot of uptown pretensions. Even today, the temple precinct embraces an area of narrow streets, arcades, restaurants, shops, stalls, playgrounds, and gardens; it is home to a population of artisans and small entrepreneurs, neighborhood children and their grandmothers, hipsters and hucksters and mendicant priests. In short, if you have any time at all to spend in Tokyo, you really have to devote at least a day of it to Asakusa.

Start your exploration from Asakusa Station, at the end of the Ginza Line. (This was in fact Tokyo's first subway, opened from Asakusa to Ueno in 1927; it became known as the Ginza Line when it was later extended through Ginza to Shimbashi and Shibuya.) Follow the signs (clearly marked in English) to Exit #1; when you come up to the street level, turn right and walk west along the broad street called Kaminarimon-dori. In a few steps you will come to **Kaminarimon** (Thunder God Gate), with its huge, red paper lantern hanging in the center. This is the main entrance to the grounds of Sensoji Temple. *Admission free. Temple grounds open 6 AM–sundown.*

Two other means of transportation can take you to Kaminarimon. The "river bus ferry" from Hinode Pier stops in Asakusa at the south corner of **Sumida Park.** Walk out to the three-way intersection, cross two sides of the triangle, and turn right. Kaminarimon is in the middle of the second block.

Asakusa Jinja, **6**
Bentenyama, **8**
Denbo-in Temple, **9**
Five-story Pagoda, **4**
Hozomon, **3**
Kaminarimon, **1**
Kappabashi, **11**
Main Hall of Sensoji Temple, **5**
Nakamise-dori, **2**
Niimi Building, **10**
Nitenmon, **7**
Sogenji Temple, **12**

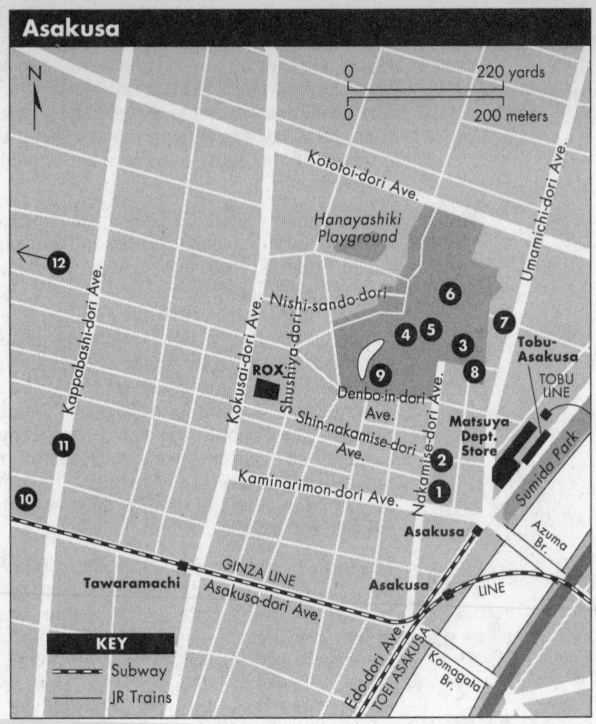

Another way to get here is on the red double-decker bus that runs between Kaminarimon and the Suzumoto Theater in Ueno. The service began in 1981, when the Merchants' Association in Asakusa borrowed a London double-decker for a month to move the overflow crowds they expected for a street fair. The idea proved so popular that it was decided to inaugurate a regular service—but there was an unexpected hitch: by law, a commercial bus could be no higher than 3.8 meters (12½ feet), and the English double-decker was 70 centimeters (28 inches) over the limit. The solution was to order three custom vehicles from a German company; a fourth was added later. The bus runs every ½-hour (every 20 minutes on weekends), 10–7, from Ueno, and 10:25–7:25 from Asakusa. The fare is ¥200 for adults, ¥100 for children under 12.

Take note of the Asakusa Tourist Information Center, just opposite Kaminarimon (2-18-9 Kaminarimon, Taito-ku, tel. 03/3842–5566); a volunteer staff with some English is on duty here 10–5 daily and will happily load you down with maps and brochures.

Traditionally, two fearsome guardian gods are installed in the alcoves of a temple gate, to protect the temple from evil spirits. The Thunder God (*Kaminari no Kami*) of the Sensoji gate is on the left; he shares his duties with the Wind God (*Kaze no Kami*) on the right. Few Japanese visitors neglect to stop at **Tokiwado** (1-3 Asakusa), the shop on the west side of the gate, to buy some of Tokyo's most famous souvenirs: *kaminari okoshi* (thunder crackers), made of rice, millet, sugar, and beans. The

original gate itself was destroyed by fire in 1865; the replica that stands here now was built after World War II.

From Kaminarimon to the inner gate of the temple runs a long, ❷ narrow avenue called **Nakamise-dori** (The Street of Inside Shops), once composed of stalls that were leased out to the townspeople who cleaned and swept the temple grounds. The rows of redbrick buildings now belong to the municipal government, but the leases are, in effect, hereditary: some of the shops have been in the same families since the Edo period. One worth stopping at is **Ichiban-ya,** about 100 yards down on the right, for its handmade toasted *sembei* (rice crackers) and its seven-pepper spices in gourd-shape bottles of zelkova wood. Another recommended shop, on the left, is **Hyotanya,** which carries ivory carvings and utensils. At the end of the street, on the right, is **Sukeroku,** specializing in traditional handmade dolls and models clothed in the costumes of the Edo period.

From here, you enter the courtyard of Sensoji Temple through ❸ a two-story gate called the **Hozomon,** which serves as a repository for sutras (Buddhist texts) and other treasures of the temple. This gate, too, has its guardian gods; if either of them should decide to leave his post for a stroll, an enormous pair of sandals is hanging on the back wall—the gift of a village famous for its straw-weaving, in Yamagata Prefecture.

At this point, you must take an important detour. To the left of the gate is a two-story modern building that houses the temple's administrative offices: walk in, go down the corridor on the right to the third door on the left, and ask for permission to see the **Garden of Denbo-in Temple.** There is no charge; you simply enter your name and address in a register and receive a ticket. Hold on to the ticket; you'll get to the Denbo-in later on your excursion.

Two of the three most important buildings in the compound are ❹ ❺ the **Five-story Pagoda,** on the left side, and the **Main Hall of Sensoji Temple** (2-3-1 Asakusa, Taito-ku); both are faithful copies in concrete of originals that burned down in 1945. Most visitors stop at the huge bronze incense burner, in front of the Main Hall, to bathe their hands and faces in the smoke—it's a charm to ward off illnesses—before climbing the stairs to offer a prayer to Kannon.

The Main Hall, about 115 feet long and 108 feet wide, is not an especially impressive piece of architecture. Unlike in many temples, however, part of the inside has a concrete floor, so visitors come and go without removing their shoes. In this area hang the Sensoji's chief claims to artistic importance: a collection of votive paintings on wood, from the 18th and 19th centuries. Plaques of this kind, called *ema,* are still offered to the gods at shrines and temples, but they are commonly simpler and smaller; the worshiper buys a little tablet of wood with the picture already painted on one side, and inscribes his prayer on the other. The temple owns over 50 of these works, which were removed to safety in 1945 and so escaped the air raids; only eight of them, depicting various scenes from Japanese history and mythology, are on display. A catalogue of the collection is on sale in the hall, but the text is in Japanese only. The lighting is poor in the hall, and the actual works are difficult to see. This is also true of the ceiling, done by two contemporary masters of Nihonga (traditional Japanese-style painting): the dragon is by

Ryushi Kawabata, and the motif of angels and lotus blossoms is by Insho Domoto. One thing that visitors cannot see at all is the holy image of Kannon itself, which supposedly lies buried somewhere deep under the temple. Not even the priests of Sensoji have ever seen it, and in fact there is no conclusive evidence that it really exists!

That doesn't seem to matter to the people of Shitamachi. It took 13 years, when most of them were still rebuilding their own bombed-out lives, to raise the money for the restoration of their beloved Sensoji. To them—and especially to those involved in the world of entertainment—it is far more than a tourist attraction. Kabuki actors still come here before a new season of performances, and sumo wrestlers come before a tournament, to pay their respects. The large lanterns in the Main Hall were donated by the geisha associations of Asakusa and nearby Yanagibashi.

Several structures in the temple complex survived the bombings of 1945. The largest, to the right of the Main Hall, is ❻ **Asakusa Jinja** (2-3-1 Asakusa, Taito-ku)—a Shinto shrine to the Hikonuma brothers and their master Naji no Nakatomo. (In Japan, Buddhism and Shintoism have enjoyed a comfortable coexistence since the former arrived from China in the 6th century; it's the rule, rather than the exception, to find a Shinto shrine on the same grounds as a Buddhist temple.) The shrine, built in 1649, is also known as Sanja Samma (Shrine of the Three Guardians). The Sanja Festival, held every year on the third weekend in May, is the biggest, loudest, wildest party in Tokyo. Each of the neighborhoods under Sanja Samma's protection has its own *mikoshi* (portable shrine); on the second day of the festival, these palanquins are paraded through the streets of Asakusa, bouncing and swaying on the shoulders of the participants, to the shrine itself. Many of the "parishioners" take part naked to the waist, or with the sleeves of their tunics rolled up, to expose fantastic red-and-black tattoo patterns that sometimes cover their entire backs and shoulders. These are the tribal markings of the Japanese underworld.

Near the entrance to the shrine is another survivor of World War II: the east gate to the temple grounds, called the ❼ **Nitenmon,** built in 1618 and designated by the government as an Important Cultural Property. It was made originally for a shrine to Ieyasu Tokugawa, which was also part of Sensoji in the early 17th century.

From the Nitenmon, walk back in the direction of the Kaminarimon to the southeast corner of the grounds. On a small plot of ground stands the shrine to Kume no Heinai, a 17th-century outlaw who repented and became a priest of one of the subsidiary temples of Sensoji. Late in life he carved a stone statue of himself and buried it where many people would walk over it; in his will, he expressed the hope that his image would be trampled upon forever. Somehow, Heinai came to be worshiped as the patron god of lovers—as mystifying an apotheosis as you will ever find in Japanese religion.

Just beyond this shrine is the entrance to a narrow street that runs back to Asakusa-dori Avenue, parallel to Nakamise-dori ❽ Avenue. On the left as you enter this street is **Bentenyama** (2-3 Asakusa, Taito-ku), a tiny hillock with a shrine to the Goddess of Good Fortune perched on top. Next to it is the **Toki-no-kane**

Belfry, built in the 17th century; the bell used to toll the hours, and it was said that you could hear it anywhere in Shitamachi—a radius of about 4 miles. The bell still sounds at 6 AM every day, when the temple grounds are opened to the faithful, and on New Year's Eve—108 strokes in all, beginning just before midnight, to "ring out" the 108 sins and frailties of mankind and make a clean start for the coming year.

Opposite Bentenyama is a shop called **Nakaya** (2-2-12 Asakusa, Taito-ku, tel. 03/3841–7877), where they sell all manner of regalia for the Sanja Festival. Best buys at Nakaya are the thick woven firemen's jackets, called *sashiko hanten,* and *happi* coats (cotton tunics printed in bright colors with Japanese characters or *ukiyo-e* wood-block pictures), available in children's sizes.

Next door is **Kuremutsu** (2-2-13 Asakusa, Taito-ku, tel. 03/3842–0906; open 4–10 PM), a tiny old teahouse now turned into a fairly expensive *nomiya* (literally, "drinking place," the drink of choice in this case being sake), and next to Kuremutsu is **Hyakusuke** (2-2-14 Asakusa, Taito-ku, tel. 03/3841–7058), the last place in Tokyo to carry government-approved skin cleanser made from powdered nightingale droppings. Ladies of the Edo period—especially the geisha—swore by it; they mixed the powder with water and patted it on gently, as a boon to their complexions. There's only one source left in Japan for this powder—a fellow in the mountains of Aichi Prefecture who collects and dries the droppings from about 2,000 birds. (Nightingale ranching! Japan is a land of many vocations.) Hyakusuke is over 100 years old and has been in the same family for three generations; it sells relatively little nightingale powder now, but it still does a steady trade in cosmetics and theatrical makeup for Kabuki actors, geisha, and traditional weddings. Interesting things to fetch home from here are seaweed shampoo and camellia oil, as well as handmade wool brushes, bound with cherry wood, for applying cosmetics.

Three doors up, on the same side of the street, is **Fujiya** (2-2-15 Asakusa, Taito-ku, tel. 03/3841–2283), a shop that deals exclusively in printed cotton hand towels called *tenugui.* Owner Keiji Kawakami literally wrote the book on this subject. His *Tenugui fuzoku emaki* (roughly, The Scroll Book of Hand Towel Customs and Usages) is the definitive work on the hundreds of traditional towel motifs that have come down from the Edo period: geometric patterns; scenes from Bunraku puppet theater, Kabuki, and festivals; artifacts from folklore and everyday life; plants and animals. The tenugui in the shop were all designed and dyed by Kawakami himself. They unfold to about 3 feet, and many people buy them to frame. Kawakami towels are in fact collector's items; when he feels that he has made enough of one, he destroys the stencil.

Turn right at the corner past Fujiya and walk west, until you cross Nakamise-dori Avenue. On the other side of the intersection, on the left, is **Yonoya** (1-37-10 Asakusa, Taito-ku, tel. 03/3844–1755), purveyors of very pricey handmade boxwood combs. The shop itself is postwar, but the family business goes back about 300 years. The present owner/master craftsman is Mitsumasa Minekawa; his grandfather, he observes, was still making combs when he retired at 85. Traditional Japanese coiffures and wigs are very complicated, and they need a lot of different tools; Yonoya sells combs in all sizes, shapes, and serrations, some of them carved with auspicious motifs (peonies, hollyhocks, cranes) and all engraved with the family benchmark.

Now it's time to cash in the ticket you've been carrying around. Walk west another 50 feet or so, and on the right you will see an ❾ old black wood gate; it's the side entrance to **Denbo-in Temple.** The Abbot of Sensoji has his living quarters here. The only part of the grounds you can visit is the garden, believed to have been made in the 17th century by Enshu Kobori, the genius of Zen landscape design. Go through the small door in the gate, across the courtyard and through another door, and present your ticket to the caretaker in the house at the end of the alley; the entrance to the garden is down a short flight of stone steps to the left.

This is the best-kept secret in Asakusa. The front entrance to Denbo-in Temple can be seen from Nakamise-dori Avenue, behind an iron fence in the last block of shops, but the thousands of Japanese visitors passing by seem to have no idea what it is; if they do, it somehow never occurs to them to apply for an admission ticket. The garden of Denbo-in is usually empty and always utterly serene—an island of privacy in a sea of pilgrims. As you walk along the path that circles the pond, a different vista presents itself at every turn. The only sounds are the cries of birds and the splashing of carp. Spring is the ideal time to be here; in the best of all possible worlds, you come on a Monday when the wisteria is in bloom, and there's a tea ceremony in the pavilion at the far end of the pond.

Retrace your steps, and turn to the right as you leave the black gate; next door is a small Shinto shrine to the *tanuki* (raccoons) who were displaced when Denbo-in was built. Japanese visitors come here more often, however, to leave an offering at the statue of the bodhisattva Jizo, who looks after the well-being of children.

Farther on, in the row of knockdown clothing stalls along the right side of the street, is the booth of calligrapher Koji Matsumaru, who makes *hyosatsu,* the Japanese equivalent of doorplates. A hyosatsu is a block of wood (preferably cypress) hung on a gatepost or an entranceway, with the family name on it in India ink. Enormous reverence still attaches in Japan to penmanship; opinions are drawn about you from the way you write. The hyosatsu is, after all, the first thing people will learn about a home; the characters on it must be well- and felicitously formed, so one comes to Matsumaru. Famous in Asakusa for his fine hand, he also does lanterns, temple signboards, certificates, and other weighty documents. Western names, too, can be rendered in the *katakana* syllabic alphabet, should you decide to take home a hyosatsu of your own.

Time Out Opposite the row of clothing stalls mentioned above, on the corner of Orange Street, is the redbrick Asakusa Public Hall; performances of Kabuki and traditional dance are sometimes held here, as well as exhibitions of life in Asakusa before World War II. Across the street is **Nakase,** one of the best of Asakusa's many fine tempura restaurants. Founded about 120 years ago, it was destroyed in the war and rebuilt in the same style. The tatami-mat rooms look out on a perfect little interior garden—hung, in May, with great fragrant bunches of white wisteria. The pond is stocked with carp and goldfish; you can almost lean out from your room and trail your fingers in the water as you listen to the fountain. Nakase is a bit steep: lunches at the tables inside are ¥2,800; more elaborate meals by the garden start at ¥7,000. *1-39-13 Asakusa, Taito-ku, tel. 03/3841-4015. Open noon–8. Closed Tues.*

Now review your options. If you have the time and energy, you may want to explore the streets and covered arcades on the south and west sides of Denbo-in. Where Denbo-in-dori (the avenue you have been following along the south side of the garden) meets Sushiya-dori (the main avenue of Rokku, the entertainment district), there is a small flea market; turn right here, and you are in what remains—alas!—of the old movie-theater district. East of the movie theaters, between Rokku and Sensoji, runs Nishi-sando-dori Avenue, an arcade where you can find kimonos and yukata fabrics, traditional accessories, fans, and festival costumes at very reasonable prices. If you turn to the left at the flea market, you soon come to the **ROX Building,** a misplaced attempt to endow Asakusa with a glitzy vertical mall. Just beyond it, you can turn left again and stroll along Shin-nakamise-dori Avenue (New Street of Inside Shops). This arcade and the streets that cross it north–south are lined with stores selling clothing and accessories, restaurants and coffee shops, and purveyors of crackers, seaweed, and tea. This area is Asakusa's answer to the suburban shopping center.

When you have browsed to saturation, turn south, away from Denbo-in Temple on any of these side streets, return to Kaminarimon-dori Avenue, turn right, and walk to the end. Cross Kokusai-dori Avenue, turn left, and then right at the next major intersection; on the corner is the entrance to Tawaramachi Station on the Ginza Subway Line. At the second traffic light, you will see the **Niimi Building** across the street, and atop the Niimi Building is the guardian god of Kappabashi: an enormous chef's head in plastic, 30 feet high, beaming, mustachioed, and crowned (as every chef in Japan is crowned) with a tall white hat. Turn right.

10

11 **Kappabashi** is Tokyo's wholesale restaurant supply street: ½-mile of shops—more than 200 of them—selling everything the city's purveyors of food and drink could possibly need to do business, from paper supplies to bar stools, from signs to soup tureens. In their wildest dreams, the Japanese themselves would never have cast Kappabashi as a tourist attraction, but indeed it is.

For one thing, it is *the* place to buy plastic food. From the humblest noodle shop or sushi bar to neighborhood restaurants of middling price and pretension, it's customary in Japan to stock a window with models of what is to be had inside. The custom began, according to one version of the story, in the early days of the Meiji Restoration, when anatomical models made of wax first came to Japan as teaching aids in the new schools of Western medicine. A businessman from Nara decided that wax models would also make good point-of-purchase advertising for restaurants. He was right: the industry grew in a modest way at first, making models mostly of Japanese food, but in the boom years after 1960, restaurants began to serve all sorts of cookery ordinary people had never seen before, and the models offered much-needed reassurance. ("So *that's* a cheeseburger.

It doesn't look as bad as it sounds; let's go in and try one.") By the mid-1970s, the makers of plastic food were turning out creations of astonishing virtuosity and realism, and foreigners had discovered them as pop art.

In the first two blocks of Kappabashi, at least a dozen shops sell plastic food; at the second intersection, on the right, is the main showroom of the **Maizuru Company**, one of the oldest and largest firms in the industry. They are virtuosos in the art of counterfeit cuisine. In 1960, models by Maizuru were included in the "Japan Style" Exhibition at London's Victoria and Albert Museum. Here, one can buy individual pieces of plastic sushi, or splurge on a whole Pacific lobster, perfect in coloration and detail down to the tiniest spines on its legs. *1-5-17 Nishi Asakusa, Taito-ku, tel. 03/3843–1686. Open 9–6.*

Across the street from Maizuru is **Nishimura**, a shop specializing in *noren*—the short divided curtains that hang from a bamboo rod over the door of a shop or restaurant to announce that it is open for business. The curtain is made of cotton, linen, or silk, and it is usually dyed to order with the name and logo of the shop or what it has for sale. Nishimura also carries ready-made noren with motifs of all sorts, from landscapes in white-on-blue to geisha and sumo wrestlers in polychromatic splendor. Use your imagination; they make wonderful wall hangings and dividers. *1-10-10 Matsugaya, Taito-ku, tel. 03/3844–9954. Open 9:30–5:30. Closed Sun.*

In the next block is **Kondo Shoten**, which specializes in all sorts of bamboo trays, baskets, scoops, and containers. *3-1-13 Matsugaya, Taito-ku, tel. 03/3841–3372. Open 9–5:30. Closed Sun.*

Generally, however, the exploring is better on the Maizuru side of the street. A few doors down, for example, is **Biken Kogei**, a general supplier of signs, waterwheels, and assorted shop displays; this is a good place to look for the folding red paper lanterns (*aka-chochin*) that grace the front of inexpensive bars and restaurants. *1-5-16 Nishi Asakusa, Taito-ku, tel. 03/3842–1646. Open Mon.–Sat. 9–6, Sun. 11–4.*

In the middle of the next block is **Iida Shoten**, which stocks a good selection of embossed cast-iron kettles and casseroles, called *nambu* ware—craftwork certified by the Association for the Promotion of Traditional Craft Products. *2-21-6 Nishi Asakusa, Taito-ku, tel. 03/3842–3757. Open Mon.–Sat. 9:30–5:30, Sun. 10–5.*

On the next corner is the **Union Company**, which sells everything one needs to run a coffee shop: roasters, grinders, beans, flasks and filters of every description, cups, mugs, demitasse, sugar bowls, and creamers. Coffee lovers pronounce the coffee shops of Japan among the best in the world; here's where the professionals come for their apparatus. *2-22-6 Nishi Asakusa, Taito-ku, tel. 03/3842–4041. Open Mon.–Sat. 9–6, Sun. 10–5.*

The intersection here is about in the middle of Kappabashi; turn left, and just past the next traffic light, on the right, you (12) come to **Sogenji Temple** (3-7-2 Matsugaya, Taito-ku, tel. 03/3841–2035)—better known as the Kappa Temple, with its shrine to the imaginary creature that gives this district its name. In the 19th century, so the story goes, there was a river here (and a bridge, back at the intersection where you took the left turn); the surrounding area was poorly drained and was often flooded. A local shopkeeper began a project to improve the drainage, investing all his own money, but met with little success until a troupe of *kappa*—mischievous green water sprites—emerged from the river to help him. The local people still come to the shrine at Sogenji to leave offerings of cucumber and sake—the kappa's favorite food and drink. (A more prosaic explanation for the name of the district points out that the lower-ranking retainers of the local lord used to earn money on the side by making straw raincoats, also called kappa, that they spread to dry on the bridge.)

Retrace your steps to the intersection; there is more of Kappabashi to the left, but you can safely ignore it and continue east, straight past Union Company down the narrow side street. In the next block, on the left, is **Tsubaya Hochoten.** A *hocho* is a knife; Tsubaya Hochoten sells cutlery for professionals—knives of every length and weight and balance, for every imaginable use, from slicing sashimi to making decorative cuts in fruit. The best of these, too, carry the Traditional Craft Association seal: hand-forged tools of tempered blue steel, set in handles banded with deer horn to keep the wood from splitting. *3-7-2 Nishi Asakusa, Taito-ku, tel. 03/3845-2005. Open Mon.-Sat. 9-6, Sun. 9-5.*

Continue on this street east to Kokusai-dori Avenue, and turn left; as you walk you will see several shops selling Buddhist household altars (*butsudan*). The most elaborate of these, hand-carved in ebony and covered with gold leaf, are made in Toyama Prefecture and can cost as much as ¥1 million. No proper Japanese household is without a butsudan, even if it is somewhat more modest; it is the spiritual center of the family, where reverence for one's ancestors and continuity of the family traditions are expressed. In a few moments, you will be back at Tawaramachi Station—the end of your excursion.

Tsukiji and Shimbashi

Numbers in the margin correspond to the points of interest on the Tsukiji and Shimbashi map.

Tsukiji reminds us of the awesome disaster of the great fire of 1657. In the space of two days, it leveled almost 70% of Ieyasu Tokugawa's new capital and killed more than 100,000 people. Ieyasu was not a man to be discouraged by mere catastrophe, however; he took it as an opportunity to plan an even bigger and better city, one that would incorporate the marshes east of his castle. Tsukiji, in fact, means "reclaimed land," and it was a substantial block of land, laboriously drained and filled, from present-day Ginza to the bay.

The common people in tenements and alleys, who had suffered most in the great fire, benefited not at all from this project; the land was first allotted to feudal lords and to temples. After 1853, when Japan opened its doors to the outside world, Tsukiji became Tokyo's first Foreign Settlement—the site of the American legation and an elegant two-story brick hotel, and home to a heroic group of missionaries, teachers, and doctors. Today, this area is best known for its astonishing fish market, the largest in Asia. This is where, if you are prepared to get up early enough, you should begin your exploration.

Take the Hibiya subway line to Tsukiji and exit by the stairs closest to the back of the train. Cross Shin-Ohashi-dori Avenue to the Tsukiji Honganji Temple (which looks like a transplant from India), turn right, and walk west on Shin-Ohashi-dori (you'll return to the temple later). Cross Harumi-dori Avenue, go over the bridge, and take the first left; walk to the end of the road, and turn right. If you reach this point at precisely 5 AM, you will hear a signal for the start of Tokyo's greatest ongoing open-air spectacle: the fish auction at the **Central Wholesale Market.**

The city's fish market used to be farther uptown, in Nihombashi; it was moved to Tsukiji after the Great Kanto Earthquake of 1923, and it occupies the site of what was once Japan's first naval training academy. Today the market sprawls over some 54 acres of reclaimed land. Its warren of buildings houses about 1,200 wholesale shops, supplying 90% of the fish consumed in Tokyo every day and employing some 15,000 people. One would expect to see docks here, and unending streams of fish spilling from the holds of ships, but, in fact, most of the seafood sold in Tsukiji comes in by truck, arriving through the night from fishing ports all over the country.

What makes Tsukiji a great show is the auction system. The catch—over 100 varieties in all, including whole frozen tuna, Styrofoam cases of shrimp and squid, and crates of crabs—is laid out in the long covered area between the river and the main building; then the bidding begins. Only members of the wholesalers' association may take part. Wearing license numbers fastened to the front of their caps, they register their bids in a kind of sign language, shouting to draw the attention of the auctioneer and making furious combinations in the air with their fingers. The auctioneer keeps the action moving in a hoarse croak that sounds like no known language; spot quotations change too fast for ordinary mortals to follow.

Different fish are auctioned off at different times and locations, but by 6:30 AM or so, this part of the day's business is over, and the wholesalers fetch their purchases back into the market in barrows. The restaurant owners and retailers arrive about 7, making the rounds of favorite suppliers for their requirements. Chaos seems to reign, but everybody here knows everybody else, and they all have it down to a system.

A word to the wise: these people are not running a tourist attraction. They're in the fish business, and this is their busiest time of day. The cheerful banter they use with each other can turn snappish if you get in their way. Also bear in mind that you are not allowed to take photographs while the auctions are underway (flashes are a distraction). The market is kept spotlessly clean, which means the water hoses are running all the time. Boots are helpful, but if you don't want to carry them, bring a pair of heavy-duty trash bags to slip over your shoes and secure them above your ankles with rubberbands.

If you come after 9 AM, there is still plenty to do and see. You'll have missed the auctions, but you may want to explore the maze of alleys between the market and Harumi-dori Avenue; there are fishmongers here by the score, of course, but also sushi bars, restaurants, and stores for pickles, tea, crackers, kitchen knives, baskets, and crockery. Markets like these are a vital counterpoint to the museums and monuments of conventional sightseeing; they

Central Wholesale Market, **1**
Hama Rikyu Detached Palace Garden, **9**
International Trade Center, **2**
Kabuki-za Theater, **11**
Monument to Ryotaku Maeno and Genpaku Sugita, **4**
St. Luke's International Hospital, **5**
Shimbashi Embujo Theater, **10**
Sumiyoshi Myojin Shrine, **8**
Tsukiji Honganji Temple, **3**
Tsukudajima, **6**
Tsukugen, **7**

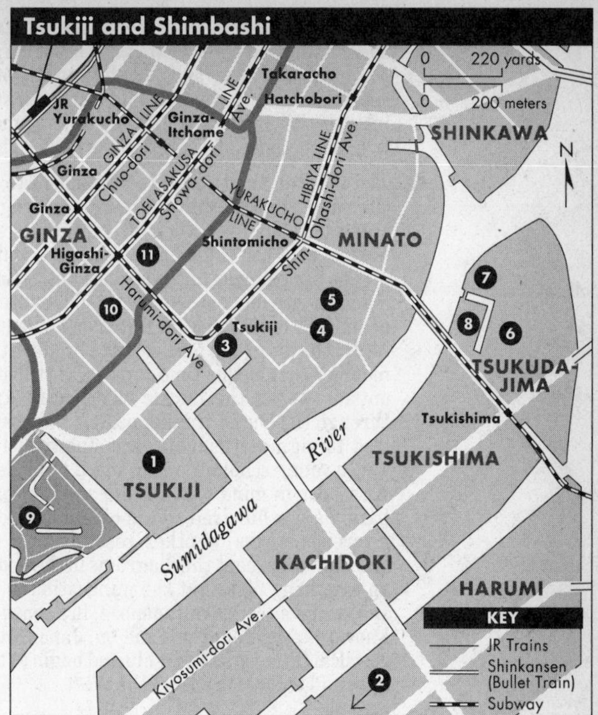

bring you up close to the way people really live in the cities you visit. If you have time on your itinerary for just one market, this is the one to see.

Return to Shin-Ohashi-dori Avenue, and walk back in the direction of Honganji Temple. When you reach Harumi-dori Avenue, you may want to make a detour. If you walk to the right, cross two bridges, and take the second right, you will eventually (it's a longish walk) reach the **International Trade Center** (5-3-53 Harumi, Chuo-ku, tel. 03/3533–5314). The expositions presented here during the year—electronics and information systems, imported foods, toys, automobiles, recreation equipment—attract huge throngs of visitors; check the publication *Tour Companion* to see if there's a show running you'll want to catch.

If not, return to **Tsukiji Honganji Temple.** This is the main branch temple in Tokyo of the Nishi Honganji Temple in Kyoto. It was located here after the fire of 1657, but disaster seemed to follow it—the temple was destroyed again at least five times, and reconstruction in wood was finally abandoned after the Great Kanto Earthquake. The present stone building dates from 1935. It was designed by Chuta Ito, a pupil of Kingo Tatsuno, who built Tokyo Station. Ito's other credits include the Meiji Jingu Shrine in Harajuku; he also lobbied for Japan's first law for the preservation of historic buildings. Ito traveled extensively in the Orient. The evocations of classical Hindu architecture in the domes and ornaments of Honganji were his homage to India for being the cradle of Buddhism.

Turn right on Shin-Ohashi-dori as you leave the main gate of the temple, and right again at the first corner; walk south until you cross a bridge, and turn left on the other side. When you cross another bridge, turn right: in the traffic island at the next intersection, you will see two stone memorials that mark the true importance of Tsukiji in the modern history of Japan.

4 The taller of the two is the **Monument to Ryotaku Maeno and Genpaku Sugita.** With a group of colleagues, these two men translated the first work of European science into Japanese. Maeno and his collaborators were samurai and physicians. Maeno himself was in the service of the Lord Okudaira, whose mansion was one of the most prominent in Tsukiji. In 1770, he acquired a book, a text in Dutch on human anatomy, in Nagasaki. It took his group four years to produce their translation. Remember that at this time Japan was still officially closed to the outside world; the trickle of scientific knowledge accessible through the Dutch trading post at Nagasaki—the only authorized foreign settlement—was enormously frustrating to the eager young scholars who wanted to modernize their country. Also bear in mind that Maeno and his colleagues began with barely a few hundred words of Dutch among them and had no reference works or other resources on which to base their translation, except the diagrams in the book. It must have been an agonizing task, but the publication in 1774 of *Kaitai shinsho*, as it was called in Japanese, in a sense shaped the world we know today. From this time on, Japan would turn away from classical Chinese scholarship and begin to take its lessons in science and technology from the West.

The other stone memorial commemorates the founding of Keio University by Yukichi Fukuzawa (1835–1901), the most influencial educator and social thinker of the Meiji period. Fukuzawa was the son of a low-ranking samurai in the same clan as Maeno. Sent by his lord to start a school of Western learning, he began teaching classes at the Matsudaira residence in Tsukiji in 1858. Later the school was moved west to Mita, where the university is today. Engraved on the stone is Fukuzawa's famous statement: "Heaven created no man above another, nor below." Uttered when the Tokugawa feudal regime was still in power, this was an enormously daring and disturbing thought. It took Japan almost a century to catch up with Fukuzawa's liberal and egalitarian vision.

5 Across the street to the left is **St. Luke's International Hospital,** founded in 1900 by Dr. Rudolf Teusler, an American medical missionary; the present building dates to 1933. In the several square blocks north of the hospital was the foreign settlement created after the signing of the U.S.–Japan Treaty of Commerce in 1858. (Among the residents here in the latter part of the 19th century was a Scottish surgeon and missionary named Henry Faulds. Intrigued by the Japanese custom of putting their thumbprints on documents for authentication, he began the research that established for the first time that no two person's fingerprints were alike. In 1880, he wrote a paper for *Nature* magazine, suggesting that this fact might be of some use in criminal investigation.)

Review your priorities. From here, you can retrace your steps to the subway, moving on to Higashi-Ginza and Shimbashi, or 6 you can take a longish but rewarding detour to **Tsukudajima.** If you choose the latter, walk west from the monuments to the

next corner, turn right, and walk north for two blocks. Cross the main intersection here, and turn right; the street rises to become the Tsukuda-Ohashi Bridge, and just before it crosses the river you'll find a flight of steps leading up to the pedestrian walkway.

Built up from mud flats at the mouth of the Sumida River, Tsukudajima was first created in the early 17th century. Over the years, more and more land has been reclaimed from the bay, more than doubling the size of the island and adding other areas to the south and west. The part to explore is the original section: a few square blocks on your left as you cross the bridge. This neighborhood—its maze of narrow alleys, its profusion of potted plants and bonsai, its old houses with tile roofs—almost could have come straight out of the Edo period.

In 1613, the shogunate ordered a group of fishermen from Tsukuda (a village, now part of Osaka) to relocate on these flats. Officially, they were brought here to provide the castle with whitebait; unofficially, their role was to keep watch and report on any suspicious maritime traffic in the bay. They also developed a method of preserving the fish they caught, by boiling it in soy sauce and salt; this delicacy, called *tsukudani*, is 7 still the island's most famous product. **Tsukugen** (1-3-13 Tsukuda, Chuo-ku, tel. 03/3531–2649), a shop on the first street along the breakwater as you leave the bridge, has been making tsukudani since the 17th century. *Open daily 9:30–5:30.*

Go to the end of the breakwater, and turn right; from here it's a 8 short walk to the torii of the **Sumiyoshi Myojin Shrine** (1-1 Tsukuda, Chuo-ku), established by the fishermen from Osaka when they first settled on the island. The god enshrined here is the protector of those who make their livelihoods from the sea; once every three years (next is in 1996), the shrine celebrates its main festival. On the first weekend in August, the god is brought out for his procession in an unusual eight-side palanquin, preceded by huge golden lion heads carried high in the air, their mouths snapping in mock ferocity to drive any evil influences out of the path. As the palanquin passes, the people of the island douse it with water, recalling the custom, before the breakwater was built, of carrying it to the river for a high-spirited ducking.

If you have time, wander through the area bounded by the breakwater and the L-shape canal. It's ramshackle in places (even a little scruffy), but this is an authentic corner of Shitamachi that cannot last much longer. Having survived most of the natural disasters of the past three centuries, it faces a new threat—the huge development project on the north end of the island—that will eventually doom the village to modernity.

Time Out Retrace your steps to the Tsukiji subway station, and continue along Shin-Ohashi-dori Avenue in the direction of the fish market. On the right side of the avenue is **Edo-Gin,** a sushi bar founded in 1924 that is legendary for its generous portions—slices of raw fish that almost hide the balls of rice underneath. Pricey for dinner; ¥1,000 set menu for lunch. *4-5-1 Tsukiji, Chuo-ku, tel. 03/3543–4401. Open Mon.–Sat. 11–9:30.*

Pass the market on your left and the Asahi Newspapers Building on your right. The avenue curves and brings you to an ele-

9 vated walkway; on the left is the entrance to the **Hama Rikyu Detached Palace Garden.** The land here was originally owned by the Owari branch of the Tokugawa family from Nagoya, and it extended to part of what is now the fish market. When one of this family became shogun, in 1709, his residence was turned into a shogunal palace—complete with pavilions, ornamental gardens, groves of pine and cherry trees, and duck ponds. The garden became a public park in 1945, although a good portion of it (including the two smaller ponds) is fenced off as a nature preserve. None of the original buildings survives, but on the island in the large pond is a reproduction of the pavilion where former U.S. President Ulysses S. Grant and Mrs. Grant had an audience with the Emperor Meiji in 1879. The building can be rented for parties. (The path to the left as you enter the garden leads to the "river bus" ferry landing, from which you can leave this excursion and begin another: up the Sumida to Asakusa.) *Hama Rikyu Teien, Chuo-ku, tel. 03/3541–0200. Admission: ¥200; children under 6 free. Open 9–4. Closed Mon.*

Retrace your steps, cross the overhead pedestrian bridge, and continue north on the street that brought you from Tsukiji. The next major intersection is Showa-dori Avenue; if you turned left here, across another elevated walkway, your route would take you past the huge JR Shiodome railroad yards (an "O" marker here and a section of the original tracks commemorate the starting point of Japan's first railway service, between Shimbashi and Yokohama, in 1872) and on to Shimbashi Station.

Almost nothing remains in **Shimbashi** to recall its golden age—the period after the Meiji Restoration, when this was one of the most famous geisha districts of the new capital. Its reputation as a pleasure quarter is even older. In the Edo period, when there was a network of canals and waterways here, it was the height of luxury to charter a covered boat (called a *yakata-bune*) from one of the Shimbashi boathouses for a cruise on the river; a local restaurant would cater the excursion, and a local geisha house would provide the companionship. After 1868, the geisha moved indoors. There were many more of them, and the pleasure quarter became much larger and more sophisticated—a reputation it still enjoys among the older (and wealthier) generation of Japanese men. There are perhaps 150 geisha still working in Shimbashi; they entertain at some 30 or 40 *ryotei* (traditional restaurants) tucked away on the back streets of the district, but you are unlikely to encounter any on your exploration. From time to time, the newspapers still delight in the account of some distinguished widower, a politician or captain of industry, who marries a Shimbashi geisha—in the vain expectation that he will be treated at home the way he was treated in the restaurant.

Turn right instead on Showa-dori Avenue, away from Shimbashi Station. At the next major intersection, turn right again, and left at the third corner; walk northeast in the direction of Higashi-Ginza Station. In the second block, on your right, is 10 the **Shimbashi Embujo Theater** (*see* The Arts, *below*). On the left is the Nissan Motor Company headquarters. A brisk minute's walk from here will bring you to the intersection of Harumi-dori Avenue; turn left, and on the next block, on the 11 right, you will see the **Kabuki-za Theater.**

Soon after the Meiji Restoration, Kabuki began to reestablish itself in this part of the city, from its enforced exile in Asakusa. The first Kabuki-za was built in 1889, with a European facade. Here, two of the hereditary theater families, Ichikawa and Onoe, developed a brilliant new repertoire that brought Kabuki into the modern era. In 1912, the Kabuki-za was taken over by the Shochiku theatrical management company, and in 1925 the old theater building was replaced. Designed by architect Shin'ichiro Okada, it was damaged during World War II but was soon restored. (For information on performances, *see* The Arts, below). *4-12-15 Ginza, Chuo-ku, tel. 03/3541–8597.*

Just in front of the Kabuki-za is the Higashi-Ginza Station of the Hibiya subway line, where you can bring your exploration to a close.

Nihombashi, Ginza, and Yurakucho

Numbers in the margin correspond to points of interest on the Nihombashi, Ginza, and Yurakucho map.

Tokyo is a city of many centers. Now that the new City Hall is completed, the administrative center has shifted from Marunouchi to Shinjuku. For almost 350 years, the center of power was Edo Castle, and the great stone ramparts still define—for the visitor, at least—the heart of the city. History, politics, entertainment, fashion, traditional culture: Every tail we want to pin on the donkey goes in a different spot. Geographically speaking, however, there is one and only one center of Tokyo: a tall, black iron pole on the north side of **Nihombashi Bridge**—and if the tail you were pinning represented high finance, you would also have to pin it right here.

When Ieyasu Tokugawa had the first bridge constructed at Nihombashi (Bridge of Japan), he designated it the starting point for the five great roads leading out of his city, the point from which all distances were to be measured. His decree is still in force: The black pole on the present bridge, erected in 1911, is the "Zero Kilometer" marker for all the national highways.

In the early days of the Tokugawa Shogunate, Edo had no port. As the city grew, almost everything it needed was shipped from the western part of the country, which was economically more developed. Because the bay shore was marshy and full of tidal flats, the ships would come only as far as Shinagawa, a few miles down the coast, and unload to smaller vessels. These in turn would take the cargo into the city through a network of canals to wharves and warehouses at Nihombashi. The bridge and the area south and east became a wholesale distribution center, not only for manufactured goods but also for foodstuffs. The city's first fish market, in fact, was established at Nihombashi in 1628 and remained here until the great earthquake of 1923.

All through the Edo period, this was part of Shitamachi (downtown). Except for a few blocks between Nihombashi and Kyobashi, where the deputy magistrates of the city had their villas, it belonged to the common people—not all of whom lived elbow-to-elbow in poverty. There were huge fortunes to be made in the markets, and the early millionaires of Edo built their homes in the Nihombashi area. Some, like the legendary timber magnate Bunzaemon Kinokuniya, spent everything they made in the pleasure quarters of Yoshiwara and died penniless; others founded great trading houses—Mitsui, Mitsubishi, Sumitomo—that exist today and still have warehouses not far from Nihombashi.

It was appropriate, then, that when Japan's first corporations were created and the Meiji government developed a modern system of capital formation, the **Tokyo Stock Exchange** (Shoken Torihikijo) would be built on the west bank of the Nihombashi River. Next to the exchange now are most of the country's major securities companies, which move billions of yen around the world electronically—a far cry from the early years of high finance, when they burned a length of rope on the floor of the exchange; trading was over for the day when it had smoldered down to the end.

A little farther west, money—the problems of making it and moving it around—shaped the area in a somewhat different way. In the Edo period, there were three types of currency in circulation: gold, silver, and copper, each with its various denominations. Determined to unify the system, Ieyasu Tokugawa started minting his own silver coins in 1598, in his home province of Suruga, even before he became shogun. In 1601, he established a gold mint; the building was only a few hundred yards from Nihombashi, on the site of what is now the Bank of Japan. In 1612, he relocated the Suruga plant to a patch of reclaimed land to the west of his castle; the area soon came to be known informally as the Ginza (Silver Mint).

The value of these various currencies fluctuated. There were profits to be made in the changing of money, and this business eventually came under the control of a few large merchant houses. One of the most successful of these merchants was a man named Takatoshi Mitsui, who had a dry-goods shop in Kyoto and opened a branch in Edo in 1673. The shop, called Echigoya, was just north of Nihombashi; by the end of the 17th century, it was the base of a commercial empire—in retailing, banking, and trading—known today as the Mitsui Group. Not far from the site of Echigoya stands its direct descendant: the Mitsukoshi Department Store.

Rui wa tomo wo yobu, goes the Japanese expression: "Like calls to like." From Nihombashi through Ginza to Shimbashi is the domain of all the Noble Houses that trace their ancestry back to the dry-goods and kimono shops of the Edo period: Mitsukoshi, Takashimaya, Matsuzakaya, Matsuya. All are intensely proud of their places at the upper end of the retail business, as purveyors of an astonishing range of goods and services. Together, they are but the latest expression of this area's abiding concern with money. Take some of it with you on your exploration: you may find an opportunity here and there to spend it.

Begin at Tokyo Station. Take the Yaesu Central exit, cross the main avenue in front of you (Sotobori-dori), and turn left. Walk north until you cross a bridge under the Shuto Expressway, and turn right at the second corner, between the Bank of Tokyo (1) and the **Bank of Japan** (2-2 Nihombashi Hongokucho, Chuoku). The older part of the Bank of Japan is the work of Tatsuno Kingo, who also designed Tokyo Station; completed in 1896, the bank is one of the very few surviving Meiji-era Western buildings in the city.

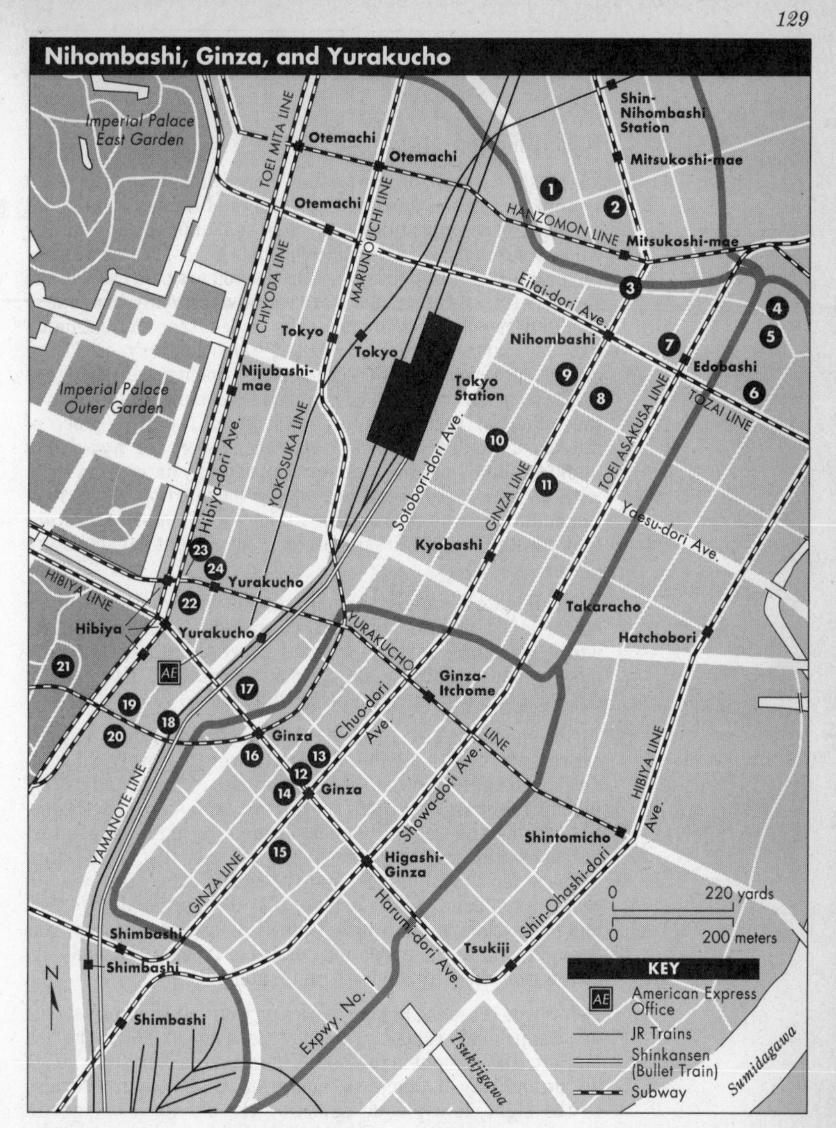

Nihombashi, Ginza, and Yurakucho

Bank of Japan, **1**
Bridgestone Museum of Art, **11**
Dai-ichi Mutual Life Insurance Company Building, **22**
Hibiya-Koen Park, **21**
Idemitsu Museum of Arts, **24**
Imperial Hotel, **20**
Imperial Theater, **23**
International Shopping Arcade, **18**
Kabuto Jinja Shrine, **4**
Kite Museum, **7**
Kyukyodo, **14**
Maruzen, **9**
Matsuzakaya Department Store, **15**
Mikimoto, **13**
Mitsukoshi Department Store, **2**
Mullion Building, **17**
Nihombashi Bridge, **3**
Sukiyabashi, **16**
Takarazuka Theater, **19**
Takashimaya Department Store, **8**
Tokyo Stock Exchange, **5**
Wako, **12**
Yaesu Underground Arcade, **10**
Yamatane Museum of Art, **6**

Walk east two blocks to the main intersection at Chuo-dori Avenue. To your left is the Mitsui Bank, to your right is **Mitsukoshi Department Store** (1-41 Nihombashi). The small area around the store, formerly called Surugacho, is the birthplace of the Mitsui conglomerate.

Takatoshi Mitsui made his fortune by revolutionizing the retail system for kimono fabrics. The drapers of his day usually did business on account, taking payment semiannually and adding various surcharges to the price of their goods. Mitsui started the practice of unit pricing, and his customers paid cash on the spot. As time went on, the store was always ready to adapt to changing needs and merchandising styles; these adjustments included garments made to order, home delivery, imported goods, and even—as the 20th century opened and Echigoya had grown, diversified, and changed its name to Mitsukoshi—the hiring of women to the sales force. The emergence of Mitsukoshi as Tokyo's first department store, or *hyakkaten* (hundred-kinds-of-goods emporium), actually dates from 1908, with a three-story Western building modeled on Harrods of London. This was replaced in 1914 by a five-story structure that boasted Japan's first escalator. The present flagship store is vintage 1935.

Turn right on Chuo-dori Avenue. As you walk south, you'll see on the left a shop founded in 1849, called **Yamamoto Noriten,** which specializes in *nori*, or dried seaweed, once the most famous product of Tokyo Bay. *1-6-3 Nihombashi Muromachi, Chuo-ku, tel. 03/3241-0261. Open 9–6:30.*

At the end of the next block is the **Nihombashi Bridge.** Why the expressway *had* to be routed directly over this lovely old landmark, back in 1962, is one of the mysteries of Tokyo and its city planning—or lack thereof. There were protests and petitions, but they had no effect. Planners argued the high cost of alternative locations; at that time Tokyo had only two years left to prepare for the Olympics, and the traffic congestion was already out of hand. So the bridge, with its graceful double arch and ornate lamps, its bronze Chinese lions and unicorns, was doomed to bear the perpetual rumble of trucks overhead—its claims overruled by concrete ramps and pillars.

Before you cross the bridge, notice on your left the small statue of a sea princess seated by a pine tree: a monument to the fish market. To the right is the Zero Kilometer marker, from which all the highway distances are measured. On the other side, also to the right, is a plaque depicting the old wood bridge. In the Edo period, the south end of the bridge was set aside for the posting of public announcements—and for displaying the heads of criminals.

Turn left as soon as you cross the bridge, and walk past the Nomura Securities building to where the expressway loops overhead and turns south. This area is called Kabuto-cho, after the small **Kabuto Jinja Shrine** here on the left, under the loop. Legend has it that a noble warrior of the 11th century, sent by the Imperial Court in Kyoto to subdue the barbarians of the north, stopped here and prayed for assistance. His expedition was successful, and on the way back he buried a golden helmet (*kabuto*) on this spot as an offering of thanks. Few Japanese are aware of this legend; "Kabuto-cho" invokes instead the world of brokers and securities. With good reason: Just across the

5 street from the shrine is the **Tokyo Stock Exchange.** At the exchange's new Exhibition Plaza and Gallery, visitors may watch the fast and furious action on the trading floor. A robot, which resembles a character from *Star Wars*, demonstrates hand signals at the touch of a button. The robot also lectures on the daily trading of securities at the Tokyo Stock Exchange. An array of video exhibits introduces companies and offers worldwide stock news and trading terms. *2-1 Nihombashi Kabuto-cho, Chuo-ku, tel. 03/3666–0141. Admission: free. Open weekdays 9–4. Trading hours: weekdays 9–11 and 12:30–3.*

From the main entrance of the exchange, turn right; walk south two blocks to the intersection at Eitai-dori Avenue and turn right again. The black building on the corner is Yamatane Securities Building; on the eighth and ninth floors is the

6 **Yamatane Museum of Art.** The museum specializes in *nihonga*, or painting in the traditional Japanese style, from the Meiji period and later; it was designed with an interior garden by architect Yoshiro Taniguchi, who also did the National Museum of Modern Art in Takebashi. The museum's own private collection includes masterpieces by such painters as Taikan Yokoyama, Gyoshu Hayami, Kokei Kobayashi, and Gyokudo Kawai. The exhibitions, which sometimes include works borrowed from other collections, change every two months. The decor and display at the Yamatane make it an oasis of quiet and elegance in the world of high finance; the chance to buy the lavish catalogue of the collection would be well worth the visit. *7-12 Nihombashi Kabutocho, Chuo-ku, tel. 03/3669–4056. Admission: ¥600–800 adults, ¥200–300 children under 12. Open 10–5. Closed Mon.*

Time Out Turn right as you leave the Yamatane Building, and continue west on Eitai-dori Avenue across the intersection with Showa-dori Avenue. Turn right onto Showa-dori Avenue, and left on the first small street behind the Bank of Hiroshima; just off the next corner is **Taimeiken,** a restaurant serving Western food at very reasonable prices. (A portion of cabbage salad and vegetable soup, for example, is only ¥50—the same price it was when the restaurant first opened, some 40 years ago.) At lunch, Taimeiken is packed with people from the nearby banks and securities companies; you buy a ticket for the meal you want at the counter to the left of the entrance, and then look for a table to share. *1-12-10 Nihombashi, Chuo-ku, tel. 03/3271–2463. Open 11–8. Closed Sun.*

After lunch, take the elevator from the Taimeiken restaurant to the fifth floor, where the late Shingo Motegi, who founded

7 the restaurant, established a wonderful **Kite Museum.** Kite flying is an old tradition in Japan; the Motegi collection includes examples of every shape and variety, from all over the country, hand-painted in brilliant colors with figures of birds, geometric patterns, and motifs from Chinese and Japanese mythology. Call ahead, and the museum will arrange a kite-making workshop for groups of children. *1-12-10 Nihombashi, Chuo-ku, tel. 03/3275–2704. Admission: ¥200 adults, ¥100 children under 12. Open 11–5. Closed Sun.*

Retrace your steps to Eitai-dori Avenue, continue west to Chuo-dori Avenue, and turn left. One block south, on the left,

8 is the **Takashimaya Department Store** (2-4-1 Nihombashi); on

9 the right is **Maruzen,** one of Japan's largest booksellers (2-3-10

Nihombashi, Chuo-ku, tel. 03/3272–7211; open 10–7; closed Sun.). Maruzen prospers in large part on its imports—at grossly inflated rates of exchange. On the second floor, you can find books in Western languages on any subject from Romanesque art to embryology. There's an extensive collection here of books about Japan, and also a small crafts center.

If you look to your right at the next intersection, you will see that you have come back almost to Tokyo Station; below the avenue from here to the station runs the **Yaesu Underground Arcade,** with hundreds of shops and restaurants. The whole area here, west of Chuo-dori Avenue, was named after Jan Joosten, a Dutch sailor who was shipwrecked on the coast of Kyushu with William Adams—hero of the recent novel *Shogun*—in 1600. Like Adams, Joosten became an adviser to Ieyasu Tokugawa, took a Japanese wife, and was given a villa not far from the castle. "Yaesu" (originally Yayosu) was as close as the Japanese could come to the pronunciation of his name. Adams, an Englishman, lived out his life in Japan; Joosten died at sea, off the coast of Indonesia, in an attempt to return home.

On the southeast corner of the intersection is the **Bridgestone Museum of Art,** one of Japan's best private collections of French impressionist art and sculpture and also of post-Meiji Japanese painting in Western styles, by such artists as Shigeru Aoki and Tsuguji Foujita. The collection, assembled by Bridgestone Tire Company founder Shojiro Ishibashi, also includes work by Rembrandt, Picasso, Utrillo, and Modigliani. In addition, the Bridgestone often organizes or co-organizes major exhibitions from private collections and museums abroad. *1-10-1 Kyobashi, Chuo-ku, tel. 03/3563–0241. Admission: ¥500 adults, ¥200 children under 12. Open 10–5:30. Closed Mon.*

Consider your feet. By now, they may be telling you that you would really rather not walk to the next point on your exploration; if so, get on the Ginza Line (there's a subway entrance right in front of the Bridgestone Museum) and ride one stop to **Ginza.** Take any exit for the *4-chome* intersection; when you come up to the surface, you can orient yourself by the Ginza branch of the **Mitsukoshi Department Store** (4-6-16 Ginza) on the northeast corner and the round **Sanai Building** (5-7-2 Ginza) on the southwest.

Ieyasu's silver mint moved out of this area in 1800. The name *Ginza* remained, but it was not until much later that it began to acquire any cachet for wealth and style. The turning point was 1872, when a fire destroyed most of the old houses here. In the same year, the country's first railway line was completed, from nearby Shimbashi to Yokohama. This prompted the city to one of its periodic attempts at large-scale planning: the main street of Ginza, together with a grid of cross streets and parallels, was rebuilt as a Western *quartier*. It had two-story brick houses with balconies; it had the nation's first sidewalks and horse-drawn streetcars; and it had gas lights and, later, telephone poles. Before the turn of the century, Ginza had attracted the great mercantile establishments that still define its character. The **Wako** (4-5-11 Ginza) department store, for example, on the northwest corner of the 4-chome intersection, established itself here as Hattori, purveyors of clocks and watches; the clock on the present building was first installed in the Hattori clock tower, a Ginza landmark, in 1894.

Many of the shops nearby have lineages almost as old, or older. A few steps north of the intersection, on Chuo-dori Avenue, is ⓭ **Mikimoto** (4-5-5 Ginza), selling the famous cultured pearls first developed by Kokichi Mikimoto in 1883; his first shop in Tokyo dates to 1899. South of the intersection, next door to the Sanai ⓮ Building, is **Kyukyodo** (5-7-4 Ginza), with its wonderful variety of handmade Japanese papers, paper products, incense, brushes, and other materials for calligraphy; Kyukyodo has been in business since 1663, and on the Ginza since 1880. Across ⓯ the street and one block south is **Matsuzakaya Department Store** (6-10-1 Ginza), which began as a kimono shop in Nagoya in 1611. Exploring this area (there's even a name for browsing: *Gin-bura*, or "Ginza-wandering") is best on Sundays, noon–6 or 7 (depending on the season), when Chuo-dori Avenue is closed to traffic, from Shimbashi all the way to Ueno, and becomes one long pedestrian mall. On Saturday afternoons, 3–6 or 7, the avenue is closed to traffic between Shimbashi and Kyobashi.

Backtrack and walk west on Harumi-dori Avenue in the direction of the Imperial Palace. From Chuo-dori Avenue to the in- ⓰ tersection called **Sukiyabashi** (named for a bridge that once stood here), your exploration should be free-form: the side streets and parallels north–south are ideal for wandering, particularly if you are interested in art galleries—of which there are 300 or more in this part of the Ginza. The art world works a bit differently here: a few of these establishments, like the venerable **Nichido** (7-4-12 Ginza), **Gekkoso** (6-3-17 Ginza), **Yoseido** (5-5-15 Ginza), **Yayoi** (7-6-61 Ginza), and **Kabutoya** (8-8-7 Ginza), actually function as dealers, representing particular artists, as well as acquiring and selling art. The vast majority, however, are nothing more than rental spaces. The artists or groups pay for the gallery by the week, publicize the show themselves, and in some cases even hang their own work. Not unreasonably, one suspects that a lot of these shows, even in so prestigious a venue as the Ginza, are "vanity" exhibitions by amateurs with money to spare—but that's not always the case. The rental spaces are also the only way for serious professionals, independent of the various art organizations that might otherwise sponsor their work, to get any critical attention; if they're lucky, they can at least recoup their expenses with an occasional sale.

West of Sukiyabashi, from Sotobori-dori Avenue to Hibiya-Koen Park and the Outer Gardens of the Imperial Palace, is the district called **Yurakucho.** The name derives from one Urakusai Oda, younger brother of the warlord who had once been Ieyasu Tokugawa's commander. Urakusai, a Tea Master of some note (he was a student of Sen no Rikyu, who developed the Tea Ceremony), had a town house here, beneath the castle ramparts, on land reclaimed from the tidal flats of the bay. He soon left Edo for the more refined comforts of Kyoto, but his name stayed behind, becoming Yurakucho—the *Quarter (cho)* where one can *Have (yu) Pleasures (raku)*—in the process. Sukiyabashi was the name of the bridge near Urakusai's villa that led over the moat—long gone in the course of modernization—to the Silver Mint.

The "pleasures" associated with this district in the early postwar period stemmed from the fact that a number of the buildings here survived the air raids of 1945 and were requisitioned by the Allied forces. Yurakucho quickly became the haunt of the so-called *pan-pan* girls, who provided the GIs with female company. Because it was so close to the military Post Exchange in Ginza, the area under the railroad tracks became one of the city's largest black markets. Later, the black market gave way to clusters of cheap restaurants, most of them little more than counters and a few stools, serving yakitori (bits of grilled chicken on bamboo skewers) and beer. Office workers on meager budgets, and journalists from the nearby *Mainichi*, *Asahi*, and *Yomiuri* newspaper headquarters, would gather here at night; Yurakucho-under-the-tracks was smoky, loud, and friendly, a kind of open-air substitute for the local taproom. Alas, the area has long since moved upscale, and no more than a handful of the yakitori stalls survive.

From Sukiyabashi, keep on the left side of the avenue as you cross the intersection; on the opposite side, you will see the 17 curved facade of the **Mullion Building**, a new shopping and entertainment complex of the sort that is rapidly turning Yurakucho into a high-fashion extension of the Ginza. (The Seibu Department Store, which occupies half the building, is a leader in marketing the fusion of modern and traditional Japanese design.) Take your first left down the narrow side street that runs along the west side of the Hankyu Department Store (the horned monstrosity in the pocket park on your right is by sculptor Taro Okamoto), cross at the corner, take the street that goes under the JR tracks and walk west. On both sides of the street, just under the bridge, you will see entrances for the 18 **International Shopping Arcade**, a collection of stores that feature kimonos and happi coats, pearls and cloisonné, prints, cameras, and consumer electronics—one-stop shopping for presents and souvenirs. In the next block, on the right, you will 19 20 see the **Takarazuka Theater**, and on the left the **Imperial Hotel**; walk to the end of the street, where it runs into Hibiya-dori Avenue, and turn right.

21 Across the avenue is **Hibiya-Koen Park.** This was Japan's first Western-style public park and dates to 1903. With its lawns and fountains, it makes a pretty place for office workers in the nearby buildings to take their lunches on a warm spring afternoon, but there's nothing here to detain you on your exploration. Press on—across the Harumi-dori Avenue intersection, past 22 the Marunouchi Police Station, to the **Dai-ichi Mutual Life Insurance Company Building.** Built like a fortress, it survived World War II virtually intact and was taken over by the Supreme Command of the Allied Powers. From his office here, General Douglas MacArthur directed the affairs of Japan for six years (1945–1951). The room is kept exactly as it was then; it can be visited on appointment. *1-1-13 Yurakucho, Chiyoda-ku, tel. 03/3216–1211. Admission free, by appointment, Mon.–Sat. 9–4:30.*

On the next corner is the International Building, with the 23 **Imperial Theater** on the first floor. The original Imperial, built in 1911, was Japan's first purely Western-style theater; the present version, by architect Yoshiro Taniguchi, is the venue of choice for big-budget musicals, such as the Japanese productions of *Man of La Mancha* and *Fiddler on the Roof.* Turn right here, and walk halfway down the block to the main entrance of 24 this building; on the ninth floor is the **Idemitsu Museum of Arts.**

With its four spacious rooms, the Idemitsu is one of the largest private museums in Tokyo, and it is one of the best designed. The strength of the collection is in its Chinese porcelain of the Tang and Song dynasties, and in Japanese ceramics—including works by Ninsei Nonomura and Kenzan Ogata, and masterpieces of Old Seto, Oribe, Old Kutani, Karatsu, and Kakiemon ware. There are also outstanding examples of Zen painting and calligraphy, wood-block prints, and genre paintings of the Edo period. Of special interest to scholars is the resource collection of shards from virtually every pottery-making culture of the ancient world. *3-1-1 Marunouchi, Chiyoda-ku, tel. 03/3213-9404. Admission: ¥500 adults, children under 12 free. Open 10–5. Closed Mon.*

Turn left as you leave the International Building, and right at the second corner. A minute's walk will bring you to the JR Yurakucho Station, the end of your exploration.

Roppongi

Numbers in the margin correspond to points of interest on the Roppongi, Akasaka, and Aoyama map.

The best way to arrive in **Roppongi,** in southern Tokyo, is to surface from the subway at Roppongi Station on the Hibiya Line. Street traffic, especially from the late afternoon through the evening, can be horrendously congested. Roppongi has two personalities. By day, the area is relatively quiet, with housewives doing their shopping and delivery trucks restocking the bars and restaurants for another evening of revelry. By night, the neighborhood hums with people from all over Tokyo who come to enjoy the local discos, restaurants, and bars.

Once a sleepy suburban area, Roppongi has become a fashionable high-rent district. Many of the embassies that did not locate in Akasaka have settled here, and executives from overseas corporations often select the area for their Tokyo bases. Consequently, Roppongi is Tokyo's international and cosmopolitan neighborhood for both living and partying. Indeed, the district claims to have the best bars and nightclubs at affordable prices, compared with the exceedingly high cost of Ginza's nightlife. As a result, the area appeals to affluent university graduates working their way up the corporate ladder. Roppongi is Yuppieland, with entertainment considerably more sophisticated than that of raunchy Shinjuku and more polished than that of Shibuya.

❶ The first stop on this tour is **Almond** (the Japanese omit the "l" in their pronunciation), just across from the Roppongi Station on the southwest corner of Roppongi-dori Avenue and Imoarai-zaka Slope. This multistory pink café is used by many as a meeting place, and that habit has not died, despite the inferior coffee and cakes served. Farther down (southwest) Roppongi-dori Avenue, on the left-hand side, is a huge outdoor video screen. ❷ That belongs to **Wave** (6-2-27 Roppongi, Minato-ku), one of the best places in Tokyo to shop for music. The first four floors sell tapes and CDs from a stock that exceeds 60,000; through a computer linkup, information on any recorded music is retrieved instantaneously. Downstairs in the basement of the building is an avant-garde movie theater.

Akasaka Prince Hotel, **10**
Almond, **1**
Asahi Kogaku, **3**
Axis Building, **6**
Brooks Brothers, **20**
Canadian Embassy, **13**
Capitol Tokyu Hotel, **7**
Geihinkan, **12**
Hie Jinja Shrine, **8**
Japan Traditional Craft Center, **19**
Jingu Baseball Stadium, **15**
Kaigakan Museum, **18**
Meiji Jingu Shrine Outer Garden, **16**
National Children's Castle, **22**
National Stadium, **17**
New Otani Hotel, **11**
Nezu Institute of Fine Arts, **21**
Roppongi Prince Hotel, **5**
Sogetsu Kaikan, **14**
Square Building, **4**
Suntory Museum, **9**
Wave, **2**

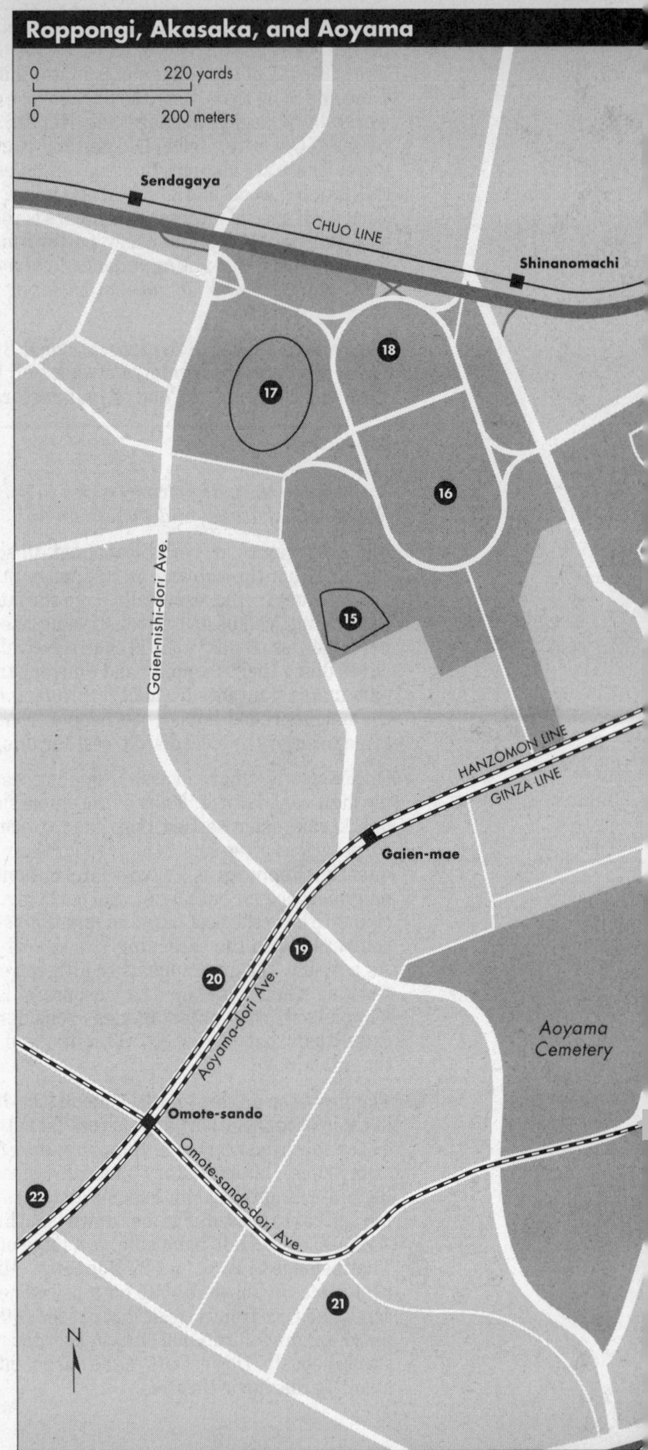

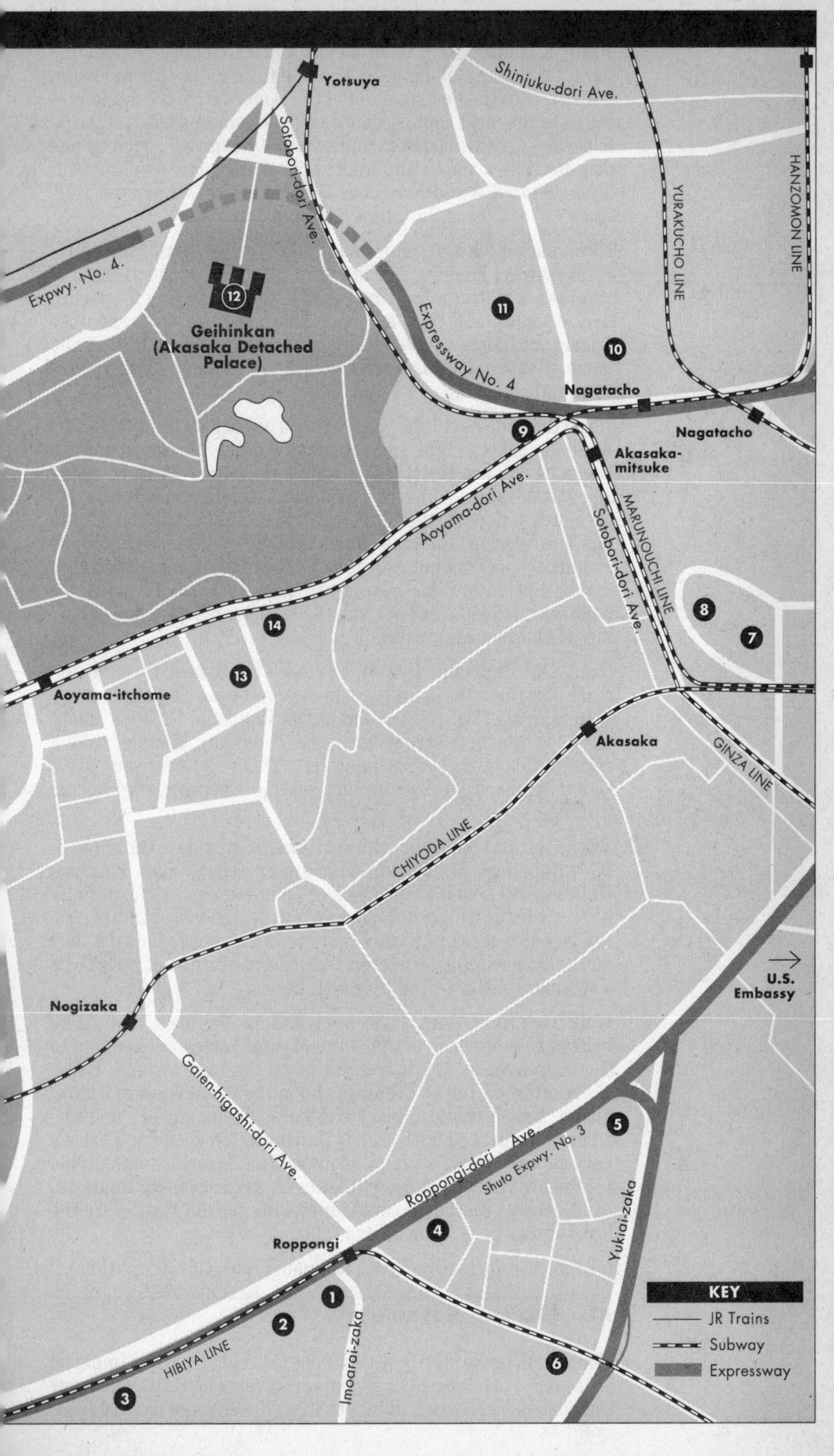

Yotsuya
Shinjuku-dori Ave.
Sotobori-dori Ave.
YURAKUCHO LINE
HANZOMON LINE
Expwy. No. 4.
Geihinkan
(Akasaka Detached Palace)
Expressway No. 4
Nagatacho
Nagatacho
Akasaka-mitsuke
Aoyama-dori Ave.
MARUNOUCHI LINE
Sotobori-dori Ave.
Aoyama-itchome
Akasaka
GINZA LINE
CHIYODA LINE
U.S. Embassy
Nogizaka
Gaien-higashi-dori Ave.
Roppongi-dori Ave.
Shuto Expwy. No. 3
Yukiai-zaka
Roppongi
Imoarai-zaka
HIBIYA LINE
KEY
JR Trains
Subway
Expressway

A block farther down (southwest) Roppongi-dori Avenue is the ❸ **Asahi Kogaku,** also known as the Pentax Gallery. Asahi, the parent company of Pentax, has 3,400 items in this museum, which traces the development of the camera from the daguerreotype to the most sophisticated modern cameras with electronic eyes. This exhibition includes novelty cameras, such as one disguised as a watch and another as a ballpoint pen. *3-21-20, Nishi-Azabu, Minato-ku, tel. 03/3401–2186. Admission free. Open 10–5. Closed Sun. and national holidays.*

Next, backtrack along Roppongi-dori Avenue, under the Shuto Expressway, keeping to the right-hand side of the avenue. If you take a right on the first small street after Gaien-higashi-dori Avenue, and then an immediate left, you will reach the ❹ **Square Building,** (3-10-3 Roppongi, Minato-ku), which is the home of seven discos. Keep the location in mind when you return in the evening.

If you take the next left, you will soon be back on Roppongi-dori Avenue. Take a right and continue walking northeast for the ❺ **Roppongi Prince Hotel** (3-2-7 Roppongi, Minato-ku). In about 200 yards, take a right up a small street, and immediately left up a steep slope is the hotel's entrance. Especially on a summer's afternoon, the café tables around the hotel's courtyard swimming pool are much in demand, perhaps not for refreshing drinks but rather for people-watching. The pool's sides are built with transparent acrylic; the swimmers look like wallowing whales in an aquarium.

From the Roppongi Prince, cut back southwest through the maze of streets to Gaien-higashi-dori Avenue. The easiest way is to take a left at the bottom of the Roppongi Prince's ramp. Then, at the first street after the Zengakuji Temple, take a right for 50 yards before going left. This will bring you out on Gaien-higashi-dori Avenue just south of the Roppongi Forum Building.

❻ Take a left on Gaien-higashi-dori Avenue; the **Axis Building** (5-17-1, Roppongi, Minato-ku) will be across the avenue. The Axis Building has a well-known collection of stores, with especially fine textiles and high-quality interior-design merchandise. Actually, the wares in Axis are more than just goods for sale; they make up an exhibition of creative design. You do not have to be a shopper to be inspired by a visit here.

Walk back (north) up Gaien-higashi-dori Avenue and you'll be back at the entrance of the Almond café. Instead of keeping to the main avenue, try to wander down the back streets. Especially after six in the evening, the party mood is everywhere; discos, restaurants, clubs, and bars vie for space, and the streets are packed with trendy Japanese fun-seekers. This is a very safe area and, with its cosmopolitan flavor, is comfortable for the foreigner to explore. However, as the evening wears on, taxis become scarce, so consider leaving the district before the last subway does (soon after 11:30).

(For more information about Roppongi, *see* Nightlife, *below*).

Akasaka and Aoyama

Though **Akasaka** is only a 15-minute taxi ride from the Imperial Palace, not much more than a hundred years ago Akasaka grew tea bushes and *akane,* plants that produced a red dye. Indeed, that is how Akasaka, which means "red slope," received its name. Then, in 1936, when the mammoth granite Diet building, which houses the national government, moved to Nagatacho (the area north of Akasaka), the neighborhood became an important pleasure quarter for politicos and their lobbyists. Accordingly, the geishas were upgraded, and so was the neighborhood. The geisha houses and *ryotei* (expensive traditional restaurants) with their unobtrusive signs are still to be found—a Mercedes or BMW in the courtyard will help spot them. As the neighborhood improved, it developed an international flair. Many foreign countries, including the United States, established their embassies here to be close to the National Diet. To service those visiting the area, new deluxe hotels sprang up, including the prestigious Hotel Okura. When TBS Television moved to Akasaka in 1960, it brought screen personalities of national fame to the district. In their wake came shops, cabarets, bars, and nightclubs.

Begin your visit to Akasaka at Kokkai Gijido-mae Subway Station (you'll have arrived on either the Chiyoda Line or the Marunouchi Line). If you started from Tokyo Station, you'll be on the Marunouchi Line and will need to walk through the passageways of Kokkai Gijido-mae Station to leave from the Chiyoda exit. When you reach the street, you'll be opposite the
7 rear entrance of the **Capitol Tokyu Hotel** (2-10-3 Nagatacho, Chiyoda-ku). To save yourself a climb up the hill and around the hotel, enter the building through this rear entrance and take the elevator to the main lobby. The Capitol Tokyu is a good place to start the day with breakfast, either Western or Japanese. In the breakfast room you can look on to a garden surrounding a pond. Then, leave the hotel by the main entrance,
8 and the **Hie Jinja Shrine** will be before you.

As in so much of Tokyo, traditional Japan is hidden among the modern concrete structures. The Hie Jinja is an example of this old Japan. The entrance to the shrine is easily spotted by the large torii in front of the steps leading up to the shrine complex. Notice the archway before the shrine; it is distinctive for its unusual triangular roof. The present building was rebuilt in 1959, and the gates in 1962, but its inspiration is from the late 15th century, when a military commander dedicated the building to Oyamakuni-no-Kami, a tutelary deity of Edo. Later, the shrine became a favorite of the Tokugawa Shogunate, and some of the best festivals during the Edo period were held here. Several festivals a year still take place here, but by far the most important is Sanno Matsuri, held June 11–16, with processions of palanquins and marchers that recall the days of the Tokugawa Shogunate, when the event was known as the "Festival Without Equal." For the rest of the year, the shrine has a special appeal to those seeking protection against miscarriages; note the statue in the main courtyard of the female monkey holding her offspring. Recently, people have visited the shrine to protect themselves against traffic accidents; it is not unusual to see a Shinto priest blessing a new car. *2-10-5 Nagatacho, Chiyoda-ku. Admission free. Open sunrise–sunset.*

To the right of the Hie Jinja on Kasumigaseki Hill is the National Diet Building (*see* Imperial Palace District tour, *above*). Instead of climbing up the hill to the Diet, walk back down past the Capitol Tokyu to Akasaka's main avenue, Sotobori-dori, and turn right. Here is Akasaka's shopping area, with stores above and below ground flanking both sides of the street. On the left, running parallel to Sotobori-dori, are two smaller avenues, Tamachi-dori and Hitotsugi-dori. On these two streets, and their cross streets and alleys, are housed Akasaka's evening pleasures: lots of small bars, restaurants, and cafés. Nearby is the Cordon Bleu, a popular cabaret. The few remaining geisha houses are at the southern end of this area. However, unless you have affluent Japanese friends to invite you to a geisha party, you will only be able to note the houses' traditional architecture from the street, or perhaps spot a geisha, dressed in her elaborate kimono as she leaves for an assignment.

At the top end of Sotobori-dori Avenue is the Akasaka-mitsuke Station and the intersection with Aoyama-dori Avenue. Across the intersection on the left, on the other side of the overpass, is the Suntory Building. On its 11th floor is the **Suntory Museum,** which rotates in exhibition its own substantial collection of traditional art objects, which includes paintings, prints, lacquerware, glassware, and costumes; it also holds special loan exhibitions throughout the year. For the size of the museum, the admission charge is high; but the exhibits are carefully selected, extremely well displayed, and often are the finest of their kind. To one side of the museum is a teahouse. *1-2-3 Moto-Akasaka, Minato-ku, tel. 03/3470–1073. Admission: ¥500 adults, ¥200 children under 12 (Sun. and holidays ¥300/¥100). Tea and traditional Japanese sweets are served for an additional ¥300. Open Tues.–Thurs. and weekends; 10–4:30; Fri. 10–7. Closed Mon.*

For those wanting something more than tea, Suntory opens a beer garden on its building's rooftop during the summertime (open 5–9). However, the beer garden's views are only of Akasaka-mitsuke's busy intersection, while from across the road, at the **Akasaka Prince Hotel** (1-2 Kioicho, Chiyoda-ku), the views include all of Tokyo.

You can't miss the Akasaka Prince Hotel. It's on the other side of Aoyama-dori Avenue from the Suntory Building. The 40-story half-moon structure stands on top of a small hill and dominates the landscape. Designed by Kenzo Tange, the building meets either with acclaim for its contemporary architecture or with criticism for being cold and sterile. Certainly the building's starkness, with nothing but the sky for its backdrop, stands out as a bold example of 20th-century architecture. Whatever your reaction to the building's design, you will not dispute the views from the hotel's upper floors. It's hard to surpass the view of Tokyo from its penthouse Gardenia Lounge (open 7–10 for dinner) or from the cocktail lounge, the Top of Akasaka (open 5 PM–2 AM). Indeed, it is worth making a special effort to come here just before twilight to see the sprawl of Tokyo turn into flickering lights against the night's darkening sky.

Across the street from the Akasaka Prince is the **New Otani Hotel** (4-1 Kioicho, Chiyoda-ku), the largest hotel in Asia. Even if you abhor huge hotels, the New Otani holds a certain futuristic fascination as a minicity. Not only does it have 2,100 guest rooms, but there are also banquet facilities for any event, arcades of shops, a minisupermarket in its basement, and numerous bars and restaurants. At times, the New Otani seems more like a crowded subway at rush hour than a hotel, but it does have one area of tranquillity. The hotel's Garden Lounge looks on to a 400-year-old Japanese garden with vermilion bridges

over ponds and winding paths—a little of traditional Japan, amid the endless stream of people pacing the hallways of the hotel and browsing through its high-fashion shops. Across the expressway and to the west of the New Otani are the gardens
12 and fountains of **Geihinkan** (also known as the Akasaka Detached Palace; 2-1-1 Moto-Akasaka, Minato-ku). The palace was formerly the home of the crown prince, who was later to become the Taisho emperor (1912–1926); it is now an official state-guest house. The palace is a copy of Buckingham Palace, and the interior, which is not open to the public, imitates the style of Versailles.

Running along the south side of the Geihinkan gardens is Aoyama-dori Avenue, which goes all the way through the area to Shibuya. The distance is about 3 miles, or four subway stops on the Ginza Line if you use the Akasaka-mitsuke Station (opposite the Suntory Building and at the top end of Sotobori-dori Ave.). To give your feet a rest, we suggest taking the subway for two stops to Gaienmae Station. You'll miss walking past the
13 14 **Canadian Embassy** and **Sogetsu Kaikan,** a famous Ikebana flower school where lessons are given in English on Tuesdays 10–noon. *7-2-21 Akasaka, Minato-ku, tel. 03/3408–1126. Cost: ¥4,690 for 1st lesson, ¥3,390 thereafter. Reservations must be made a day in advance.*

The Gaienmae Station on Aoyama-dori Avenue takes you to the neighborhood of **Aoyama.** This is also the subway stop for the
15 **Jingu Baseball Stadium** (13 Kasumigaoka, Shinjuku-ku tel. 03/3404–8999), home field of the Yakult Swallows. You'll see it across the street from the Chichibunomiya Rugby and Football
16 Ground. Actually, the stadium is in the **Meiji Jingu Shrine Outer Garden** (Jingu Gaien Park); on the other side of this park is
17 the **National Stadium** (10 Kasumigaoka, Shinjuku-ku), the main venue of the 1964 Summer Olympics and Japan's largest stadium, with seating for 75,000 people. Across Gaien-nishi-
18 dori Avenue from the stadium is the **Kaigakan Museum** (the Meiji Memorial Picture Gallery), which exhibits approximately 80 paintings depicting events in the life of Emperor Meiji. *9 Kasumigaoka, Shinjuku-ku, tel. 03/3401–5179. Admission: ¥300 adults, ¥100 children under 15. Open 9–4.*

Now you come to the real reason for getting off the subway at Gaienmae. If you walk about five minutes along Aoyama-dori
19 Avenue toward Shibuya district (west), you'll spot the **Japan Traditional Craft Center** (Zenkoku Dentoteki Kogeihin Senta). Located on the second floor of the Plaza 246 Building, the Center exhibits and sells a wide range of traditional craft products from all over Japan, including lacquerware, ceramics, paper products, dolls, and metalwork. Some of the exhibits have English descriptions, others do not, but someone is usually available to ask a question if a particular item takes your fancy. A visit to this center provides a head start to understanding different regional crafts and techniques before one leaves Tokyo to travel Japan's hinterland. *3-1-1 Minami Aoyama, Minato-ku, tel. 03/3403–2460. Admission free. Open 10–6. Closed Thurs.*

If you continue walking down (south) Aoyama-dori Avenue
20 toward Shibuya, past a branch of America's **Brooks Brothers** on the right, you'll reach the Omotesando Subway Station. If you take a left at the crossroads on to Omotesando-dori Avenue and
21 walk another 10 minutes, you'll find the **Nezu Institute of Fine**

Arts. The museum has a priceless collection of oriental art that includes superb examples of Japanese paintings and scrolls. An extremely attractive aspect of this museum is its extensive garden, with a traditional pond and five tea-ceremony houses. *6-5-1 Minami Aoyama, Minato-ku, tel. 03/3400–2536. Admission: ¥1,000 adults, ¥700 students. Open 9:30–4:30. Closed Mon. and the day after national holidays.*

The Nezu Institute of Fine Arts is about halfway between Roppongi and Shibuya. If it is still daytime, you might proceed to Shibuya, or even over to the area of Harajuku and the Meiji Shrine. If you do go directly to Shibuya from the Nezu Institute, it's about a 20-minute walk. Return first to Aoyama-dori Avenue and take a left. It will lead straight to Shibuya, first passing the **National Children's Castle** (5-53-1 Jingumae, Shibuya-ku, tel. 03/3797–5666), an emporium designed to constructively entertain the young with its swimming pool, gym, concerts, theater, and audiovisual library.

Shibuya and Harajuku

Numbers in the margin correspond to points of interest on the Shibuya and Harajuku map.

Traffic in Shibuya hardly compares to that in Shinjuku, but it is still a major city center. Two subways, three private railways, the JR Yamanote Line, and the bus terminal move about a million people a day through Shibuya. The commercial character of this hub is shaped by the fierce battle for supremacy between the Seibu and Tokyo department store chains. As fast as one of them puts up a new branch building, vertical mall, or specialty store, its rival counters with another; every new venture incorporates a trendy restaurant or a concert hall or a flashy gallery—something to draw a bigger share of Shibuya's predominately younger crowd of students and office workers. The result: a consumer paradise, busy, noisy, confusing—and fun.

The flagship store of the Tokyu Department Store, **Tokyu Plaza** (1-2-2 Dogenzaka, Shibuya-ku), dominates the Shibuya Station neighborhood. If you select a window table at one of the two dozen restaurants on the top two floors of the building, you will find yourself gazing in awe at the seething flow of commuters around the station. On the fifth floor of Tokyu Plaza is a branch of **Kinokuniya Bookstore** (tel. 03/3463–3241), with a large selection of books written in English. The selection, however, is not as large as that of the Kinokuniya store in Shinjuku.

Unfortunately, from the restaurants' windows you cannot see the **Statue of Hachiko.** For that, you must return to the station plaza and go to the north exit. You'll spot the statue by the number of people who are standing around it waiting for someone. "Meet you by Hachiko" is an arrangement frequently made by Tokyoites. Hachiko was an Akita, a Japanese breed of dog. Every day he walked his master, a professor at Tokyo University, to Shibuya Station. In the evening, he would return to the station and greet his master off the train. One day in 1925, while at the university, the professor died of a stroke. Every evening for the next seven years, the dog went to the station and waited until the last train had pulled out of the station. Crestfallen, the dog would return to his home to try again the next evening. Then the dog died, too, and his story made the national newspa-

Furusato, **3**
Iris Garden, **15**
Japanese Sword Museum, **17**
La Foret, **11**
Meiji Jingu Shrine, **14**
Meiji Jingu Shrine Inner Garden, **13**
National Yoyogi Sports Center, **9**
NHK Broadcasting Center, **7**
NHK Hall, **8**
Oriental Bazaar, **12**
Ota Memorial Museum of Art, **10**
Parco, **5**
Seibu Department Store, **4**
Statue of Hachiko, **2**
Tobacco and Salt Museum, **6**
Tokyu Plaza, **1**
Treasure House, **16**

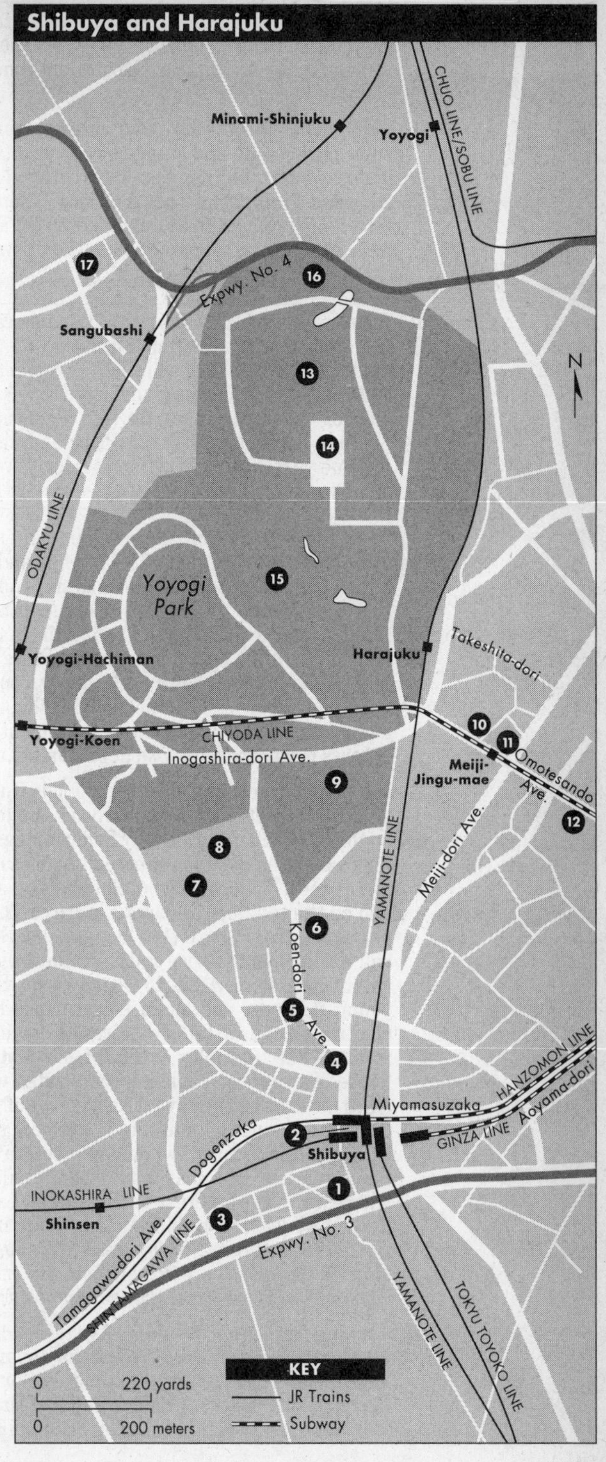

pers. Gifts flooded in. A bronze statue was built, and the dog was stuffed to keep vigil in the Tokyo Museum of Art. The statue seen today is a replica; the original was melted down for its metal in World War II.

Shibuya has become a popular area for evening entertainment, such as shopping and going to restaurants and *nomiya* (inexpensive bars). It is not as international or cosmopolitan as Akasaka or Roppongi, but it is less expensive than those districts. Most places in Shibuya, however, are unaccustomed to foreigners, so be prepared to use one or two words of Japanese if you enter a small restaurant.

Time Out ❸ Those who want a taste off traditional rural Japan should visit the well-known restaurant **Furusato** (3-4-1 Aobadai, Meguro-ku, tel. 03/3463–2310), which offers regional foods in a restored 300-year-old farmhouse transferred to Tokyo from the Hida region of the Japan Alps. To find Furusato, walk west from Shibuya Station past Tokyu Plaza and along Tamagawa-dori Avenue. After you cross Yamate-dori Avenue, Furusato will be on your left.

From Shibuya Station, plaza department stores and shops are spread out along Aoyoma-dori Avenue and Meiji-dori Avenue. Tokyu has seven stores, Seibu has six, and Marui has two. For this tour, leave the station plaza in the direction that the Hachiko statue is facing, and cross the major intersection. On ❹ your left will be **Seibu Department Store** (21-1 Udagawacho, Shibuya-ku), which has a particularly good selection of European and Japanese designer-label fashions. Equally fascinating is a walk through Seibu's basement, which has one of Tokyo's most extensive food departments.

The street branching left after Seibu is Koen-dori Avenue, the smartest street in the neighborhood. A short way uphill, again ❺ on the left, is **Parco,** owned by Seibu and said to be Tokyo's leading fashion complex. Parco actually comes in four parts. Parco 1 and Parco 2 (3 Udagawacho, Shibuya-ku) specialize in fashion, and on the top floor of Parco 1 is Parco Theater, for plays and performances. Parco 3 (14 Udagawacho, Shibuya-ku) has interior design merchandise and a floor devoted to visiting cultural exhibitions. Parco 4 (32–13 Udagawacho, Shibuya-ku) features young fashions, and has a performance hall called the Club Quattro on the fifth floor. Across Koen-dori Avenue, not far ❻ from the Parco complex, is the **Tobacco and Salt Museum,** which houses every conceivable item associated with tobacco and salt since the days of the Maya. The displays of smoking utensils are fascinating, but the museum is perhaps more interesting for the Japanese, many of whom are inveterate smokers, than for the foreigner who may have seen similar exhibitions elsewhere. Of more interest is the special exhibit on the fourth floor of *ukiyo-e*, wood-block prints depicting smokers' necessities. *1-16-8 Jinnan, Shibuya-ku, tel. 03/3476–2041. Admission: ¥100 adults, ¥50 children under 12. Open 10–5:30. Closed Mon., 2nd Tues. of June, and New Year's.*

❼ Walking farther up Koen-dori Avenue leads to **NHK Broadcasting Center** (Nippon Hoso Kyokai) for Japanese National Public Television. This 23-story building was originally built as the Olympic Information Center. Parts of the broadcasting complex are open to visitors. In the main building, a tour route is offered, and techniques for sound effects and film are shown. Explanations are given only in Japanese, so foreign tourists may be a little baffled. Perhaps the most exciting part of the tour permits you to watch an actual filming of a television scene and some of the stage sets. *2-2-1 Jinnan, Shibuya-ku, tel. 03/3465–1111. Admission free. Open 9:30–5. Closed 4th Mon. of each month.*

❽ The building next to the NHK Broadcast Center is the **NHK Hall,** which serves as a multipurpose auditorium designed for opera and concert performances. It is quite large, with a seating capacity of 4,000, but its pièce de résistance is its 7,640-piece pipe organ, foremost of its kind in the world (*see* The Arts, *below*).

❾ Across the street from NHK Hall is the **National Yoyogi Sports Center** (2-1-1 Jinnan, Shibuya-ku), consisting of two ultramodern structures designed by Kenzo Tange. His ability to work with ferro-concrete to evoke a templelike simplicity is impressive. The center was built for the 1964 Olympics, and both the stadium, which can accommodate 15,000 spectators for swimming and diving events, and the annex, which houses a basketball court with a seating capacity of 4,000, are open to visitors when there are no competitions (admission free; open 10–4). The bronze bust in the center of the Sports Center is of Yoshitoshi Tokugawa. In 1910, he became Japan's pioneer aviator by staying aloft for four minutes and traveling 230 feet. (His plane is on display at the Transportation Museum in the Koto ward.)

Across from the Sports Center are the green lawns of **Yoyogi-Koen Park.** It was once the barracks for the Japanese Army; then, after World War II, the U.S. Army took it over, and the area became known as Washington Heights. In 1964 it was used as the Olympic Village. Now it is public parkland lined with paths and, on Sundays, is often the venue for groups of young people to dance, mime, or play their music to the amusement of spectators. This is **Harajuku,** a mini-downtown that attracts the youth of Tokyo.

Perhaps the presence of the U.S. occupation forces stationed in this area after World War II has caused Harajuku to permit a more liberal, Western-type behavior. In the late 1970s and early 1980s, the youth of Tokyo seemed to congregate every Sunday on the wide street between NHK and Harajuku Subway Station. The more exhibitionist youths formed groups that acted out their fantasies in dance, break dancing, skateboard antics, bands, or pantomime. The more inhibited would only watch. The youth were named the "bamboo-shoot children," Japan's counterpart to the flower children of America. Their numbers have since declined, but on Sundays, a variety of amusing performances is still offered.

Today's Japanese youth are the product of a new consumerism that is sweeping through the nation after decades of austerity. The young come here on Sundays to be anticorporate and to rebel against the pressure to succeed. They also come to consume. Dressed in the latest fashion fads, they seek out the bargains from the stalls and shops that remain open all day on Sunday.

The JR Harajuku Station is easy to recognize. The 1924 building looks more like an English village station than a metropolitan subway stop. Directly across the road from the station is **Omotesando Avenue,** bustling with pedestrians and shoppers. And, on Sundays, it seems that all the trendy Japanese young people are here, dressed in their finery. Up a small street, on ⑩ the left-hand side before Meiji-dori Avenue, is the **Ota Memorial Museum of Art.** On two floors, you'll find a rotating exhibit of *ukiyo-e* (wood-block prints) from the private collection of Seizo Ota. For anyone interested in ukiyo-e, some of Japan's best-known artists are represented here, including Hiroshige, Sharaku, and Utamaro. *1-10-10 Jingumae, Shibuya-ku, tel. 03/3403-0880. Admission: ¥500/¥800 adults, ¥100/¥250 children under 12. Open 10:30-5. Closed Mon., New Year's, and from the 28th to the end of each month for new installations.*

Across the road from the Ota Memorial Museum, on the corner ⑪ of Omotesando Avenue and Meiji-dori Avenue, is **La Foret** (1-11-6 Jingumae, Shibuya-ku). This is the main fashion building in Harajuku. Inside La Foret are about 110 shops, most of them high-price boutiques. You can rest at one of the coffee shops in the building if you need time to decide on a purchase.

Lined with ginkgo trees, Omotesando Avenue is rich with boutiques and shops, including Paul Stewart from the United States. However, the one store that is really worth looking at ⑫ for Japanese antiques is the **Oriental Bazaar** (next to Shakey's Pizza). Downstairs in the basement, salesmen set up their stalls and offer a range of old Japanese items, such as kimonos, jewelry, dolls, and wood-block prints. It's like a hands-on museum. *5-9-13 Jingumae, Shibuya-ku, tel. 03/3400-3933. Open 9:30-6:30. Closed Thurs.*

Backtrack about 100 yards to Meiji-dori Avenue, take a right, and more boutique and fashion stalls will greet you. If you are still not overwhelmed by the mass consumerism, walk a little farther along Meiji-dori Avenue and take a left onto **Takeshita-dori,** a 300-yard street that is crammed with fashion vendors, with names such as Rap City and Octopus Army, and youthful buyers. Takeshita-dori leads back to Harajuku Station, and on ⑬ the other side of the train tracks is the **Meiji Jingu Shrine Inner** ⑭ **Garden,** the grounds for the **Meiji Jingu Shrine.**

The Meiji Jingu Shrine is a welcome contrast of serene solemnity to the youthful consumerism exhibited on the shop-filled streets around Harajuku. The two torii gates, made from 1,700-year-old cypress trees from Mt. Ari in Taiwan, each tower 40 feet high. Indeed, they are the largest (but not the tallest) gates in Japan; here, more than ever, they fulfill their role of symbolizing the separation between the mundane, everyday world and the spiritual world of the Shinto shrine. Legend has it that the shape of the torii gates derives from the shape of a rooster's perch, and that it was the rooster whose crowing awoke the sun goddess, who thus brought light to the world. (The Meiji Jingu Shrine's two gates have perches spanning 56 feet.) The shrine was built in memory of Emperor Meiji, who died in 1912, and his wife, Empress Dowager Shoken, who died two years later. He was the emperor who brought Japan out from the isolationist policies of the Tokugawa Shogunate and opened the country's doors to the West. (Incidentally, Emperor Meiji would not be surprised by the behavior of the youth of Harajuku. In 1881, concerned about the influence of Western civilization, he issued a book on public morality.)

Even though the shrine is new (completed in 1920 and rebuilt in 1958 after being badly damaged by fire in 1945), it evokes the traditional asceticism of Japan's past. The buildings (the main hall forms a quadrangle with the outlying structures) are made with Japanese cypress, and the curving green copper roofs seem to symbolize the eternal sweep of time. The shrine—and its surrounding garden, which has some 100,000 shrubs, many of which were donated by the Japanese people—is one of the most popular with the Japanese. At New Year's, about 2½ million people come to pay their ancestral respects. *1-1 Kamizonocho, Yoyogi, Shibuya-ku. Admission free. Open sunrise–sunset.*

Before you reach the shrine, on the left when you walk from ⓯ Harajuku Station, is the **Iris Garden.** In late June the garden is worth visiting, when the flowers are in bloom. Beyond the ⓰ shrine is the **Treasure House,** a repository for the personal effects and clothes of Emperor and Empress Meiji—perhaps of less interest to the foreign visitor than to the Japanese. *1-1 Kamizonocho, Yoyogi, Shibuya-ku, tel. 03/3379–5511. Admission: ¥200 adults, ¥100 children under 12. Open Mar. 1–Oct. 30, 9–4:30 (9–4 in winter). Closed 3rd Fri. of each month.*

If you have walked as far as the Treasure House, consider exiting the Inner Garden on the northeast side, and walk beyond ⓱ Sangubashi Subway Station to the **Japanese Sword Museum,** which exhibits the works of noted swordsmiths, both ancient and modern. Sword making is a complex and intricate art in Japan and was perfected during the shogun period. Swords still hold an aura of dignity and honor. Only a few swordsmiths are left in modern Japan; many live and work in the small town of Seki, north of Nagoya. *4-25-10, Yoyogi, Shibuya-ku, tel. 03/3379–1386. Admission: ¥515 adults, ¥310 children under 12. Open 9–4. Closed Mon.*

From the Sword Museum, if you retrace your steps to Sangubashi Subway Station, it is two stops north on the Odayku Line to Shinjuku, the antithesis of the serenity of the Meiji Jingu Shrine. If you did not make it to either the Treasure House or the Sword Museum, then walk back to Harajuku Station and take the JR Yamanote Line two stops north to Shinjuku.

Shinjuku

Numbers in the margin correspond to points of interest on the Shinjuku map.

To experience **Shinjuku,** one should arrive by subway, though we would not recommend using the subway during the morning or evening rush hour. More than 2 million commuters pass through Shinjuku Station twice a day. Nine trains and subway lines converge in Shinjuku to transport human cargo. Broad-shouldered men in white gloves ease commuters into packed trains with a determined shove. The sight of the endless ebb and flow of humanity is worth seeing, but not experiencing.

Shinjuku is a microcosm of Japan, where the ultramodern confronts the past: high-tech industries work alongside the oldest professions; modern, slick, deluxe hotels look down on pink motels, where rooms rent by the hour; and 50-story buildings, complete with plazas and underground parking, tower over one- or two-level buildings crammed into twisting alleys. Shinjuku is a fascinating nightmare, which is alternately off-putting and exciting.

When Ieyasu Tokugawa became shogun and made Edo his capital, Shinjuku was at the junction of two important arteries leading into the city from the west. Here, travelers could rest their horses and freshen up or dally with ladies of pleasure before entering Edo. When the Tokugawa Dynasty collapsed in 1868, the 16-year-old Emperor Meiji moved his capital to Edo, renaming it Tokyo (Eastern Capital). Shinjuku in this modern age was destined to become the connecting railhead to Japan's western provinces. As a playground, its reputation was maintained with its artists, writers, and students, and it became the bohemian section of Tokyo in the 1930s. After the war, Tokyo spread west rather than east; Shinjuku has now developed into Tokyo's high-tech center. By the 1970s, the property values of the district were the nation's most expensive, far outstripping the Ginza area.

The heart of Shinjuku is still a commuting junction. In the maze of passageways leading to the trains, a vast underground shopping center of more than 130 shops is located. The large department stores near Shinjuku Station offer everything from bargain basements to museums to restaurants on their upper floors, while the station itself is a bewildering city. One week in the station would not be sufficient time to know half of it, especially with 60 exits from which to choose.

Shinjuku is divided by its train station into its two very different areas, western Shinjuku and eastern Shinjuku.

Western Shinjuku

The New Metropolitan Center is on the west side (Nishi-Shinjuku) of Shinjuku Station. This is Tokyo's 21st-century model city, with modern high rises separated by concrete plazas. All of Tokyo is subject to serious earthquakes, except, apparently, Shinjuku. In the 1923 quake that virtually paralyzed Japan's capital, Shinjuku was the only suburb left vertical. On that basis, and because of some sounder scientific evidence, a virtual forest of skyscrapers has been built here in the past two decades, including the new City Hall.

Three of the skyscrapers here are hotels. The first to be built (1) was the **Keio Plaza Inter-Continental Hotel** (2-2-1 Nishi-(2) Shinjuku, Shinjuku-ku). The **Century Hyatt** (2-7-2 Nishi-Shin-(3) juku, Shinjuku-ku) and the **Tokyo Hilton** (6-6-2 Nishi-Shinjuku, Shinjuku-ku) followed. The other skyscrapers contain banks, government offices, and showrooms for Japanese computer, optical, and electronics companies.

(4) The skyscraper closest to the railway tracks is the **Yasuda Kasai Kaijo Building** (Yasuda Fire and Marine Insurance Building). On the 42nd floor is the **Togo Seiji Museum.** Seiji Togo was a master of putting to canvas the grace and charm of young maidens; more than a hundred of his works are on display at any time. This is also the museum that bought the painting *Sunflowers* by Vincent van Gogh for more than ¥5 billion. The museum's gallery has an obstructed view of the old part of Shinjuku, where clubs and pink hotels abound. *1-26-1 Nishi-Shinjuku, Shinjuku-ku, tel. 03/3349–3081. Admission: ¥500 adults, ¥200 children under 12. Open 9:30–4:30. Closed Mon.*

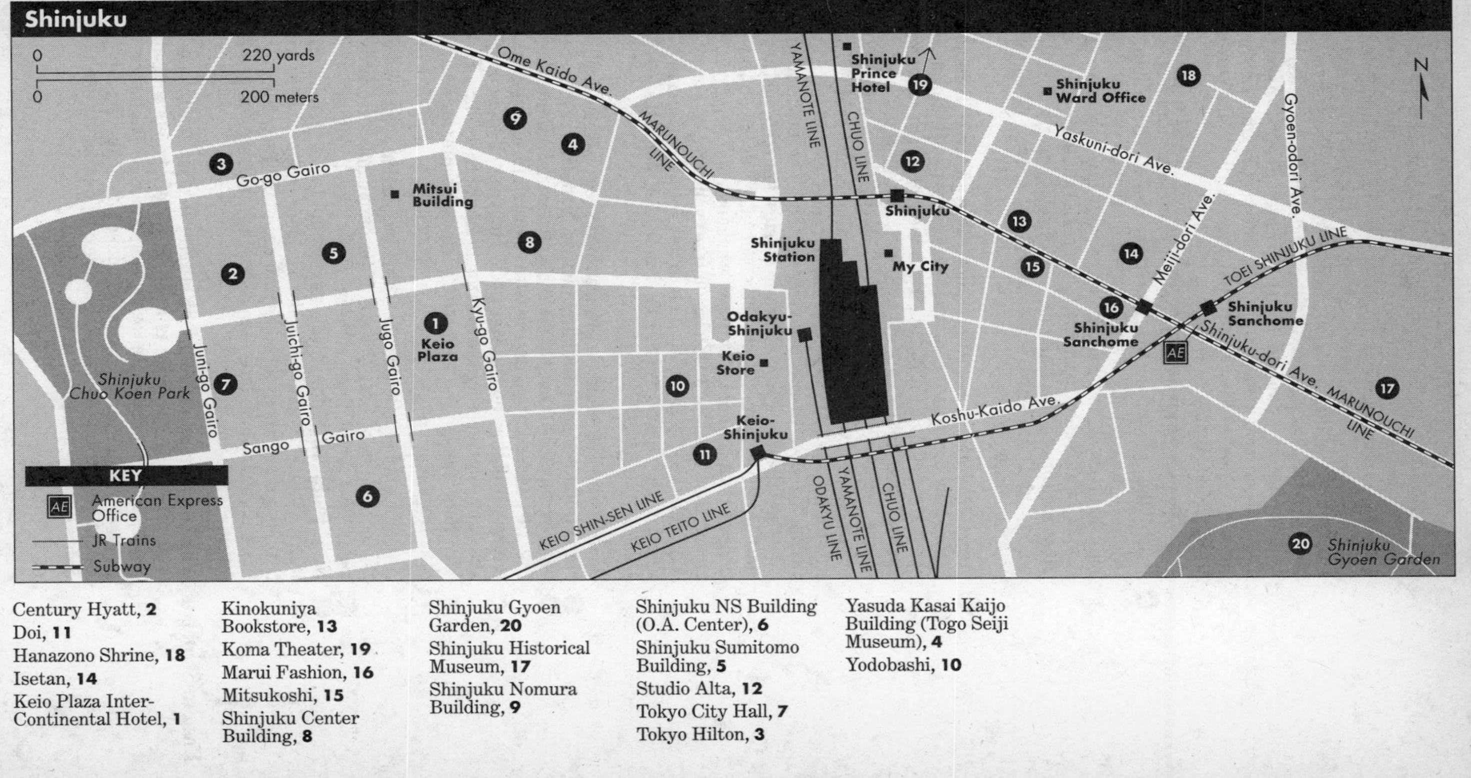

Century Hyatt, **2**
Doi, **11**
Hanazono Shrine, **18**
Isetan, **14**
Keio Plaza Inter-Continental Hotel, **1**
Kinokuniya Bookstore, **13**
Koma Theater, **19**
Marui Fashion, **16**
Mitsukoshi, **15**
Shinjuku Center Building, **8**
Shinjuku Gyoen Garden, **20**
Shinjuku Historical Museum, **17**
Shinjuku Nomura Building, **9**
Shinjuku NS Building (O.A. Center), **6**
Shinjuku Sumitomo Building, **5**
Studio Alta, **12**
Tokyo City Hall, **7**
Tokyo Hilton, **3**
Yasuda Kasai Kaijo Building (Togo Seiji Museum), **4**
Yodobashi, **10**

5 A few blocks from the Yasuda Building, the **Shinjuku Sumitomo Building** (2-6-1 Nishi-Shinjuku, Shinjuku-ku) stands across from the Century Hyatt. Notable for its futuristic architecture, this is actually a 52-story, six-sided building, but because three of its sides are wider, it appears triangular. The center of the building is a long hollow well, and from the ground floor you can look up to see light reflected in by its glass roof. If you are hungry, ride up to the top three floors, where you'll find several restaurants catering to the people who work in the building. Most of the restaurants open at 10 AM and stay open through the evening.

If you walk two blocks south of the Sumitomo Building, you'll 6 reach the **Shinjuku NS Building** (2-4-1 Nishi-Shinjuku, Shinjuku-ku), a little dwarfed by the other skyscrapers with only 30 floors; it, too, has a hollow core that allows one's attention to be directed to the 24-foot clock standing in the lobby. Most visitors to this building head directly to the fifth floor, where the **O.A. Center** is located. Here, around 20 computer companies display their latest wares.

7 Architect Kenzo Tange's grandiose **Tokyo City Hall** complex, which now dominates this whole area, opened in March 1991. Built at a cost of ¥157 billion, it was clearly meant to celebrate the fact that Tokyo's annual budget is bigger than that of the entire People's Republic of China. Is the intricate lattice facade supposed to invoke a Gothic cathedral or a microchip? Tokyoites either love it or hate it; it's been called everything from "a fitting tribute" to a "forbidding castle." The main building, now the tallest in Tokyo, soars 48 stories, splitting on the 33rd floor into two towers; from the observation decks on the 45th floor of both towers (open 10–6, weekends and holidays 10–8, closed Dec. 29–Jan. 3; admission free) you can see—on a clear day—all the way from Mt. Fuji to the Boso Peninsula in Chiba Prefecture. *Open 10–5:30, weekends and holidays 10–7:30. Closed Mon.*

Several other buildings in the area have free observation floors: 8 the **Shinjuku Center Building** (across from the Yasuda Build- 9 ing), on the 53rd floor; the **Shinjuku Nomura Building** (next to the Yasuda Building), on the 50th floor; and the **Shinjuku Sumitomo Building,** on the 51st floor. However, a more comfortable way of inspecting the horizon is on the Keio Plaza Hotel's 47th floor; take in the view with some refreshment at the Pole Star Lounge.

As you walk back toward the Shinjuku Station, you may want to stop at a few of Tokyo's leading discount camera stores in the 10 area. Two well-known camera shops are **Yodobashi** (1-11-1 11 Nishi-Shinjuku, Shinjuku-ku, near Chuo-dori Ave.) and **Doi** (1-18-27 Nishi-Shinjuku, Shinjuku-ku, near Kokusai-dori Ave.); both shops are about a block from Keio Mall near the station. Even if you have no intention of buying, the array of goods on display is a vision in itself.

Eastern Shinjuku

While the west side of Shinjuku is a sterile wasteland of modern high rises, the east side is a labyrinth of streets and alleys packed with department stores, shops, bars, restaurants, theaters, strip shows, and hotels for temporary stays. It starts out as a jumbled mass of shopping stores; as one walks north, the sights become more and more tawdry.

As you leave the station by the east exit (*higashi-guchi*), a huge video screen marks **Studio Alta** (3-24-3 Shinjuku, Shinjuku-ku). It's a well-known landmark, with a crowd usually gathered to look at its flickering images. The building houses a television studio, and beneath it is the largest subterranean plaza in Japan. Full of shops and restaurants, this is a good place to come during the winter months for something to eat and to watch the melee of people walking around.

Studio Alta is on one end of **Shinjuku-dori Avenue,** a street full of shops. Here you'll find **Kinokuniya Bookstore** (3-17-7 Shinjuku, Shinjuku-ku), with its sixth floor devoted to foreign-language books, including 40,000 English titles. Right near Kinokuniya is **Camera no Sakuraya** (3-26-10 Shinjuku, Shinjuku-ku), a discount store for cameras and electronics goods. Farther up on the same side of the street as Kinokuniya is **Isetan** (3-14-1 Shinjuku, Shinjuku-ku), the trendiest of the fashion stores in the neighborhood, with a foreign customer-service counter on the fifth floor. On the opposite side of the street are the two big stores, **Mitsukoshi** (3-29-1 Shinjuku, Shinjuku-ku) and **Marui Fashion** (3-30-16 Shinjuku, Shinjuku-ku). On Sundays, Shinjuku-dori Avenue and its side streets are closed to traffic; the area becomes a sea of shoppers.

You may want to visit the **Shinjuku Historical Museum,** which opened in March 1989. It displays, through historical documents, artifacts, and models, Shinjuku's growth during the Edo and Showa periods. Shinjuku was virtually leveled during the firebombing of Tokyo at the end of World War II. The museum offers a glimpse of city life in old traditional Japan. *22 San-ei-cho, Shinjuku-ku, tel. 03/3359–2131. Admission: ¥200 adults, ¥100 children under 18. Open 9–4:30. Closed Mon.*

If you retrace your steps, a few blocks north of Isetan department store and Yasukuni-dori is **Hanazono Shrine.** It is far from being one of Tokyo's major shrines, but in the hub of bacchanalian pleasure palaces, this is a tranquil oasis tucked between shops and tall office buildings. The shrine, constructed before the Edojo Castle, is believed to aid a businessman's commercial prosperity. *Admission free. Open sunrise–sunset.*

To the north of Yasukuni-dori Avenue and west of Hanazono Shrine is **Kabukicho.** After the courtesans were liberated in 1872 and the formalities governing geisha entertainment were dissolved, this area became Japan's largest center of prostitution until laws against the practice became more strict. In an attempt to change the neighborhood's image after World War II, plans were made to replace the fire-gutted Ginza **Kabuki-za Theater** with a new one in Shinjuku. The plans never came to fruition (the old theater was resurrected), but the area got its name. Today, however, Kabukicho has the **Koma Theater** (1-19-1 Kabuki-cho, Shinjuku-ku), which houses several discos and bars, as well as a theater with a revolving stage and more than 2,000 seats. The theater serves as a useful central landmark in the district.

Bewildering as it is, Kabukicho is a maze of bars, discos, strip joints, and theaters. It is unrefined nightlife at its best, and raunchy seediness at its worst. Neon signs flash the world of various pleasures, and, at the places not to visit, touts try to lure their customers into bars where the ¥18,000 bottle of beer has been made famous. However, if you do not follow these touts, and instead choose a place that looks respectable, there is rarely any problem. Perhaps stay away from the cheap *nomiya* (bars) under the railway tracks in Shomben-yokocho. For the Ni-chome area beyond the Koma Theater—where many of the bars are decidedly gay—you might want a knowledgeable guide. But do not be intimidated by the area. It is fun and one of the least expensive areas of Tokyo in which to engage in nighttime pleasures.

If one visits Shinjuku during the day and is anxious for some 20 peace of mind, the **Shinjuku Gyoen Garden** is the place to head for. It's a stiff 20–30 minute walk from Shinjuku Station, so you may prefer to hop on the subway (the Marunouchi Line for one stop, to Shinjuku-Gyoenmae Station, which brings you close to the north end of the park). Shinjuku Gyoen was once the estate of the powerful *daimyo* (feudal lord) Naito, but became part of the imperial household after the Meiji Restoration. After World War II, it was opened to the public as a national park. A place for discovery, the park is perfect for leisurely walks; it has 150 acres of gardens, landscaped with artificial hills, ponds with bridges, and thoughtfully placed stone lanterns. The paths wind their way through more than 3,000 different kinds of plants, shrubs, and trees and lead to Japanese-, French-, and English-style gardens, as well as a greenhouse filled with tropical plants. However, the most noted times to visit are during cherry blossom time (early April), when 1,900 trees of 65 different species flower, and in the fall, during the chrysanthemum exhibition. *11 Naitocho, Shinjuku-ku. Admission: ¥160 adults, ¥50 children. Open 9–4:30. Closed Mon., except in cherry-blossom season.*

What to See and Do with Children

Amusement Centers

Korakuen. A small amusement center is situated near the Korakuen baseball stadium and Korakuen Garden. The major attraction is the giant roller coaster and the "circus train" that does a loop. *1-3-61 Koraku, Bunkyo-ku, tel. 03/3811–2111. Admission: ¥1,400 adults, ¥700 children under 12. Open 9:30–6.*

Tokyo Disneyland. Ever since Tokyo Disneyland opened in April 1983, some 10 million visitors a year have been coming to this amusement park, where Mickey-san and his coterie of Disney characters entertain just the way they do in the California and Florida Disney parks.

The easiest way to reach Tokyo Disneyland is by the shuttle bus, which leaves Tokyo Station's Yaesu North exit every 30 minutes 7:30 AM to 7:10 PM (cost: ¥600; ¥300 children under 18). You may also go by subway; from Nihombashi, take the Tozai Line to Urayasu Station and walk over to the Tokyo Disneyland Bus Terminal for the 15-minute ride (cost: ¥200 adults, ¥100 children). *1-1 Maihama, Urayasu-shi, tel. 0473/54–0001. There are several types of admission tickets. For example, one can purchase the entrance admission for ¥3,400 (¥3,100 juniors, ¥2,300 children), then buy individual tickets. However, if you plan to see most of the attractions, the Tokyo Disneyland Pass-*

port at ¥4,800 (¥4,400 juniors, ¥3,300 children) is the most economical buy. Tickets can be purchased in advance in Tokyo Station, near the Yaesu-guchi exit (you'll notice red-jacketed attendants standing outside the booth), or from any travel agent, such as the Japan Travel Bureau. Tokyo Disneyland is open every day 9–7 (Fri. 9–8), except for 6 days in Dec., 6 days in Jan., and 3 days in Feb.

Toshima-en Amusement Park. This is a large, well-equipped amusement park located in the northwest corner of Tokyo. There are four roller coasters, a German carousel, haunted houses, and seven swimming pools. To reach it, take a subway from Tokyo Station to Ikebukuro and change to a special train that runs frequently from Seibu-Ikebukuro Station to Toshima-en. *3-25-1 Koyama, Nerima-ku, tel. 03/3990–3131. Admission: ¥1,000 adults, ¥500 children under 12. Admission plus amusement tickets are ¥3,000 adults, ¥2,000 children. Open 9:30–4:30.*

Museums

Goto Planetarium. This planetarium, located on Aoyama-dori Avenue, near Shibuya Station, has daily shows displaying the seasonal movements of the constellations, the moons of the universe, and other heavenly bodies projected onto a dome 65 feet in diameter. A special Saturday evening show adds music to the stars. Be warned that the narrative is only in Japanese. *Tokyu Bunkakaikan, 2-21-12 Shibuya, Shibuya-ku, tel. 03/3407–7409. Admission: ¥700 adults, ¥400 children 6–15, ¥300 children under 6. Shows run about an hour continuously from 11:10 AM; the last show begins at 6 PM. No seating after the show begins. Closed Mon.*

NHK Broadcasting Center (Nippon Hoso Kyokai). The Japanese National Public Television offers tours around the broadcasting complex where techniques for sound effects and film are displayed. Explanations are given only in Japanese, although there is a pamphlet available in English. Perhaps the most exciting part of the tour is when one is permitted to watch an actual filming of a scene and some of the stage sets. An Edo mansion fit for a samurai, for example, seems more authentic than the real thing. *2-2-1 Jinnan, Shibuya-ku, tel. 03/3465–1111. Admission free. Open 9:30–4. Closed 4th Mon. of each month.*

Transportation Museum. This is a fun place to take children. Displays include the early development of the railway system and a miniature layout of the rail services, as well as Japan's first airplane, which lifted off in 1903. *1-25 Kanda Sudacho, Chiyoda-ku, tel. 03/3251–8481. Admission: ¥300 adults, ¥150 children 4–15. Open 9:30–4:30. Closed Mon.*

Shops

Kiddyland. All the toys and playthings here will surely keep children and teenagers busy. *6-1-9 Jingu-mae, Shibuya-ku, tel. 03/3409–3431. Open 10–8.*

Toy Park. This is reputedly the largest toy shop in Japan. *Hakuhinkan 2F-4F, 8-8-11 Ginza, Chuo-ku, tel. 03/3571–8008. Open 11–8.*

Zoos

Shinagawa Suizokukan. The best feature of Tokyo's small but well-stocked aquarium is a glass tunnel that you walk through while dozens of species of fish swim around and above you. Alas, there are no guidebooks or explanation panels in English. The aquarium grounds include a park with a salt-water pond and lots of rocks for kids to climb on. Avoid Sundays, when crowds are impossible. Take the local train from Shinagawa to Omorikaigan Station on the Keihin-Kyuko Line. Turn left as you exit the station and follow the ceramic fish on the sidewalk to the first traffic light, then turn right. *Katsushima 3-2-1, Shinagawa-ku, tel. 03/3762–3431. Admission: ¥800 adults, ¥300 children 6–18, ¥300 pre-schoolers. Open 10–5. Dolphin shows four times daily, on a varying schedule. Closed Tues. and Dec. 29–Jan. 1.*

Tama Dobutsu Koen. At least here animals have space to roam, usually with moats to keep them separated from the visitors. In the Lions Park, visitors ride through in a minibus. To reach this zoo, take the Keio Line from Shinjuku and transfer at Takata Fudo Station for the train going to Dobutsu Koen Station. *7-1-1 Hodokubo, Hino-shi, tel. 0425/91–1611. Admission: ¥400 adults, ¥100 children 12–15. Open 9:30–5. Closed Mon.*

Ueno Dobutsuen. The Ueno Zoo's major attraction is the pair of pandas and their child. However, the zoo is terribly crowded on weekends, and the animals are penned in such small cages it is almost criminal. *9-83 Ueno-koen, Taito-ku, tel. 03/3828–5171. Admission: ¥400 adults, ¥100 children 12–15. Open 9:30–4:30 (enter by 4). Closed Mon.*

Off the Beaten Track

The Arakawa Line. Feeling nostalgic? Take the JR Yamanote Line to Otsuka, cross the street in front of the station, and change to the Arakawa Line—Tokyo's last surviving trolley. West, the line goes to Higashi-Ikebukuro (site of the Sunshine City skyscraper complex, billed as a "complete city within a city" and remarkable only as a complete flop) and Zoshigaya, before turning south to the terminus at Waseda, not far from Waseda University. East, the trolley takes you through the back gardens of old neighborhoods to Oji—once the site of Japan's first Western-style paper mill, built in 1875 by the Oji Paper Manufacturing Company. The mill is long gone, but the memory lingers on at the **Oji Paper Museum,** the only one of its kind in Japan. Some of the exhibits here show the process of milling paper from pulp; others illustrate the astonishing variety of things that can be made from paper itself. *1-1-8 Horifune, Kita-ku, tel. 03/3911–3545. Walk south from the trolley stop about 100 yards; the museum is between the Arakawa tracks and those of the JR. Admission: ¥200 adults, ¥100 children under 12. Open 9:30–4:30. Closed Mon. and national holidays.*

Asakura Sculpture Gallery. In the past two or three years, tourists have begun to "discover" the Nezu and Yanaka areas of Shitamachi (downtown)—much to the dismay of the handful of foreigners who have lived for years in this inexpensive, charming part of the city. To some, the appeal lies in its narrow streets, with their old shops and houses; others are drawn to the fact that many of the greatest figures in the world of modern Japanese culture lived and died in this same area, including novelists Ogai Mori, Soseki Natsume, and Ryunosuke Akutagawa; scholar Tenshin Okakura, who founded the Japan Art Institute; painter Taikan Yokoyama; and sculptors Koun Takamura and Fumio Asakura. If there's one single attraction here, it is probably Asakura's home and studio, converted into a gallery after his death in 1964.

Asakura's work was deeply influenced by Confucian thought, which is expressed symbolically by the arrangement of stones in the extraordinary little pond and rock garden in the central courtyard of the house. The studio is filled with Asakura's works, among them many of his most famous pieces. The tearoom on the opposite side of the courtyard is a haven of quietude from which to contemplate his garden. *7-18-10 Yanaka, Taito-ku, tel. 03/3821-4549. From the south end of the JR Nippori Station, walk west (the Tennoji Temple will be on the left side of the street) until you reach a police box. Turn right, then right again at the end of the street; the museum is a 3-story black building on the right, a few hundred yards down. Admission: ¥200 adults, ¥100 children 6-15. Open 9:30-4. Closed Mon. and Fri.*

Asakusabashi and Ryogoku. Sumo, the centuries-old national sport of Japan, is not to be taken lightly—as anyone who has ever seen a sumo wrestler will testify. Indeed, sheer weight is almost a prerequisite to success; one of the current champions tips the scales at a touch under 570 pounds. There are various techniques of pushing, grappling, and throwing in sumo, but the basic rules are exquisitely simple: except for hitting below the belt (which is all a sumo wrestler wears) and striking with the closed fist, almost anything goes. The contestants square off in a dirt ring about 15 feet in diameter and charge; the first one to step out of the ring, or touch the ground with anything but the soles of his feet, loses.

There are no free agents in sumo. To compete, you must belong to a *heya* (stable) run by a retired wrestler who has purchased that right from the Sumo Association. Sumo is very much a closed world, hierarchical and formal. Youngsters recruited into the sport live in the stable dormitory, doing all the community chores and waiting on their seniors while they learn; when they rise high enough in the tournament rankings, they acquire servant-apprentices of their own.

While tournaments and exhibitions are held in different parts of the country at different times, all the stables in the Sumo Association—now some 30 in number—are in Tokyo. Most of them are clustered on both sides of the Sumida River near the new Kokugikan (National Sumo Arena), with its distinctive green roof, in the areas called Asakusabashi and Ryogoku. One of the easiest to find is the Tatsunami Stable (3-26-2 Ryogoku), only a few steps from the west end of the JR Sobu Line Ryogoku Station (turn left when you come through the turnstile and left again as you come out on the street; then walk along the station building to the second street on the right). Another, a few blocks farther south, where the Shuto Expressway passes overhead, is the Izutsu Stable (Ryogoku 2-2-7). Wander this area when the wrestlers are in town (Jan., May, and Sept. are best bets), and you are more than likely to see some of them on the streets, cleaving the air like leviathans in their wood clogs and kimonos; come 7–11 AM, and you can peer through the doors and windows of the stable to watch them in practice sessions.

Sengakuji Temple. One day in the year 1701, a young provincial baron named Asano Takumi no kami, serving an official term of duty at the shogun's court, attacked and seriously wounded a courtier named Kira Yoshinaka. Kira had demanded the usual tokens of esteem that someone in his high position would expect for his goodwill; Asano refused, and Kira had humiliated him in public to the point where he could no longer contain his rage.

Kira survived the attack. Asano, for daring to draw his sword in the confines of Edojo Castle, was ordered to commit suicide; his family line was abolished and his fief confiscated. Headed by Oishi Kuranosuke, the clan steward, 47 of Asano's loyal retainers vowed revenge. Kira was rich and well protected; Asano's retainers were *ronin*—masterless samurai. It took them almost two years of planning, subterfuge, and hardship, but on the night of December 14, 1702, they stormed Kira's villa in Edo, cut off his head, and brought it in triumph to Asano's tomb at Sengakuji, the family temple. Oishi and his followers were also sentenced to commit suicide—which they accepted as the reward not the price, of their honorable vendetta—and were buried in the temple graveyard with their lord.

The event captured the imagination of the Japanese like nothing else in their history; through the centuries it has become the national epic, the last word on the subject of loyalty and sacrifice, celebrated in every medium from Kabuki to film. The temple still stands; the graves are still there, the air around them filled with the smoke from bundles of incense that visitors still lay reverently on the tombstones.

The story gets even better. There's a small museum on the temple grounds with a collection of weapons and other memorabilia of the event; one of these items dispels forever the myth of Japanese vagueness and indirection in the matter of contracts and formal documents. Kira's family, naturally, also wanted to give him a proper burial, but the law insisted that this could not be done without his head. They asked for it back, and Oishi—mirror of chivalry that he was—agreed. He entrusted it to the temple, and the priests wrote him a receipt, which survives even now in the corner of a dusty glass case. "Item," it begins, "One head." *2-11-1 Takanawa, Minato-ku, tel. 03/3441–2208. Take the Toei Asakusa subway line to the Sengakuji stop, turn right as you exit and walk up the hill. The temple is just past the first traffic light, on the left. Admission to the museum: ¥200 adults, ¥100 children under 12. Open 9–4.*

Shopping

By Kiko Itasaka

You have all heard horror stories about prices in Japan. Many of them are true. Yes, a cup of coffee can cost U.S. $10, a melon can cost U.S. $100, and a taxi ride from the airport to central Tokyo costs about U.S. $250. The yen has appreciated drastically over the past few years, making the U.S. dollar in Japan seem to have the power of a peso. This does not mean that potential shoppers should get discouraged; shopping in Japan isn't always impossibly expensive, and bargains can still be found. If you need gifts and souvenirs you will still be able to find them, though shopping in Tokyo requires a certain amount of ingenuity and effort.

Some items are better bought at home, such as European designer clothing or imported fruit, but why would anyone go all the way to Tokyo to buy these items? The best shoppers in Japan know that they should concentrate on Japanese goods that are hard to find in America, such as crafts, toys, and kimonos. These are all items that can be found in areas that are easy to reach by public transportation. Try to avoid taxis and instead use Tokyo's convenient subways and trains. Traffic and the Byzantine mazes of streets make travel by taxi time-consuming and inordinately expensive. The shopper with only limited time should stick to hotel arcades, department stores, and stores that specifically cater to foreigners. For those with more time and a sense of adventure, Tokyo shopping can be fascinating.

Remember that in some cases, prices in smaller stores and markets might be listed with *kanji* (Japanese pictographs derived from Chinese written characters) instead of Arabic numbers. In such cases, just ask, "How much?" It's a phrase that all Japanese will recognize, because it is the name of a popular TV game show in Japan, and someone will either tell you or write down the price for you.

Shopping in Tokyo is generally an extremely pleasant experience, because salespeople are often helpful and polite. In major stores, many people speak at least enough English for you to complete your transactions. There is a saying in Japan that the customer equals God. Upon entering a store, you will be greeted with a bow and the word *Iraashaimase* (welcome). The salespeople are definitely there to serve you.

On April 1, 1989, Japan instituted an across-the-board 3% value added tax (VAT) in place of past taxes imposed on luxury goods, as well as on restaurant and hotel bills. This tax can be avoided at the duty-free airport shops and at **Amita** in the Tokyo Hilton Hotel (6–6–2 Nishi-Shinjuku, Shinjuku-ku, tel. 03/3348–3887; open 10–8). However, because these places tend to have higher profit margins, any tax savings is often offset by the higher cost of goods.

Stores in Tokyo generally open around 10–11 and close around 7–8. The stores mentioned in this section are open daily, except where noted.

Other shopping options may be found in the Exploring section earlier in this chapter.

Shopping Districts

Ginza Ginza was the first entertainment and shopping district in Tokyo, dating back to the Edo period (1603–1868). Tokyo's first department store, Mitsukoshi, was founded in this area, which once consisted of long, willow-lined avenues. The willows have long since gone, and the streets are now lined with department stores and boutiques. The exclusive stores in this area feature quality and selective merchandise at higher prices. Here it is not unusual to see a well-turned out Japanese woman in a kimono on a shopping spree, accompanied by her daughter, who is exquisitely dressed in a Chanel suit. *Nearest train: Yurakucho (Yamanote Line); nearest subway stations: Ginza (Marunou-*

Akihabara, **2**
Aoyama, **7**
Asakusa, **1**
Ginza, **8**
Harajuku, **4**
Omotesando, **5**
Shibuya, **6**
Shinjuku, **3**

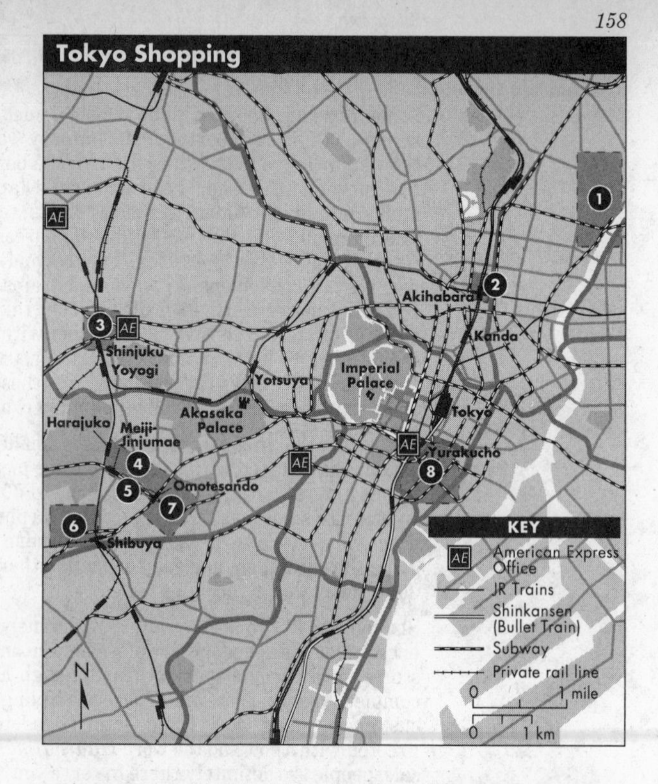

chi, Ginza, and Hibiya lines), Ginza Itchome (Yurakucho Line).

Shibuya This area is primarily an entertainment district filled with movie theaters, restaurants, and bars, mostly geared toward teenagers and young adults. The shopping is also catered toward these groups, with many reasonably priced smaller shops, and a few department stores that are casual yet chic. *Nearest train station: Harajuku (Yamanote Line); nearest subway station: Hanzomon (Ginza Line).*

Shinjuku Amid the honky-tonk atmosphere of this bustling area, which includes the red-light and gay districts of Tokyo, are some of the city's most fashionable department stores. Shinjuku's merchandise reflects the crowds—young, stylish, and slightly flashy. In addition to clothing, this area features a cluster of electronic goods stores. *Nearest train station: Shinjuku (Yamanote Line); nearest subway stations: Shinjuku (Marunouchi and Toei Shinjuku Lines).*

Harajuku Teenagers all seem to congregate in Harajuku, particularly on the main avenue known as Takeshita-dori. A wild sense of fashion prevails, from '50s greaser looks to '60s mod styles to a variety of assorted looks that are perhaps indicative of what will be the rage in the year 2000. The average age on this street is clearly under 20, and maybe even under 16. Teens all over the world are strapped for cash, so, not surprisingly, everything in this area is moderately priced. The multitude of tiny stores offer not only clothing and accessories but also a lot of kitsch.

Nearest train station: Harajuku (Yamanote Line); nearest subway station: Meiji Jingumae (Chiyoda Line).

Omotesando Known as the Champs-Elysées of Tokyo, this long, wide avenue is lined with cafés and designer boutiques. Paradoxically, it is nearly parallel to the neighboring Takeshita-dori of Harajuku, but it couldn't be more different in atmosphere. Boutiques and cafés, however, are not the only attractions. You'll find a number of antiques and print shops, as well as one of the best toy shops in Tokyo—Kiddyland. Closed to traffic on Sundays, this is a street for browsers, strollers, and those who like to languish over café au lait before sauntering into the next store. *Nearest subway station: Omotesando (Chiyoda and Hanzomon lines).*

Aoyama Shopping in Aoyama is an aesthetically pleasing experience, but it can empty your wallet in no time. For those interested in fashion, this is where many of the leading Japanese and Western designers have boutiques. Although the prices of most European and American designers will be high, Japanese designer clothes are 30%–40% lower than they are in the United States. Even if you do not want to buy anything, you'll have fun simply observing the sense of display: Aoyama tends to be a showcase, not merely of couture, but of the latest concepts in commercial architecture and interior design. In fact, shopping here is similar to walking through an art gallery—enjoying the masterpieces, reveling in the atmosphere, and not bothering with the price tags. *Nearest subway station: Omotesando (Chiyoda and Hanzomon lines).*

Akihabara For the camera and electronic-goods buff who wants to see everything available on the market, Akihabara is high-tech heaven, with its endless multistory buildings. Walkman and portable CD players were on sale here long before they made it across the ocean. The best deals in Japan may be found here, but in general, prices are lower in the United States. *Nearest train station: Akihabara (Yamanote Line); nearest subway station: Akihabara (Hibiya Line).*

Asakusa While sightseeing in this area, take the time to stroll through its arcades. Many of the wares are the kind of souvenirs that you would expect to find on sale at any tourist stop, but if you look a little harder, you will find shops that have tortoiseshell accessories, beautiful wood combs, delicate fans, and other gift items. Venture to some of the back streets, where the small shops have been in business for many generations and offer fine traditional goods. *Nearest subway station: Asakusa (Toei Asakusa and Ginza lines).*

Gifts

The best presents and gifts from Japan are those that are uniquely Japanese. Obviously you do not want to buy a Gucci bag that would cost far less at home. For reasonable prices, you can find a wide range of interesting things, from traditional crafts to kitsch examples of popular culture.

Ceramics Ceramics and pottery in Japan are fragile and cumbersome, but they make wonderful gifts if you are willing to take the trouble of bringing the packages home. In the 16th century, the art of making pottery flourished with the popularity and demand for tea-ceremony utensils. Feudal lords from all over Japan competed to have the finest wares, and as a result, distinctive styles of pottery developed in various regions. Some of the more prominent pottery centers are Arita in Kyushu, where the ceramic ware often features patterns with flowers and birds; Mashiko, outside of Tokyo in the Tochigi Prefecture, with pottery having a simple and rough dark-brown glaze; and Kasama, in Ibaraki Prefecture, with its unique pottery glaze made from ash and ground rocks.

Those who cannot take the time to travel all over Japan can try Tokyo's specialty shops or department stores, which tend to have fairly complete selections of wares.

Tachikichi. This shop has a selection of pottery from different localities. *5-5-8 Ginza, Chuo-ku, tel. 03/3571–2924. Open 11–6:30. Closed Sun.*

Kisso. This store offers an excellent variety of ceramics in modern design, using traditional glazes, as well as a restaurant and a gift shop. *Axis Bldg. B1, 5-17-1 Roppongi, Minato-ku, tel. 03/3582–4191. Open 11:30–2 and 5:30–9. Closed Sun.*

Dolls

Many types of traditional dolls are available in Japan, each with its own charm. **Kokeshi** dolls are long, cylindrical, painted, and made of wood, with no arms or legs. Fine examples of Japanese folk art, they date back to the Edo period (1603–1868). **Daruma** are papier-mâché dolls, having rounded bottoms and faces that are often painted with amusing expressions. They are constructed so that no matter how you push them, they roll and remain upright. Legend has it that they are modeled after a Buddhist priest who maintained his seated lotus position for long periods of time. **Hakata** dolls, made in Hakata City of Kyushu, are clay dolls of traditional Japanese figures, such as geisha or samurai.

Kyugetsu. This shop has been in business for over a century and offers every kind of doll imaginable. *1-20-4 Yanagibashi, Taito-ku, tel. 03/3861–5511. Open daily 9:15–6.*

Electronics Goods

The best bargains for electronics goods are found at home and not in Japan. If you are curious to see what is available you should go to the area surrounding Akihabara Station, where you will find over 200 stores full of stereos, refrigerators, CD players, and anything else you can plug in. If you must buy something, look for shops that sell products that are made for export. These will come with instructions written in English rather than Japanese, and if you have a tourist visa in your passport, you can purchase these export models duty free. One such store is **Yamagiwa** (4-1-1 Soto Randa, Chiyoda-ku).

Folk Crafts

Japanese folk crafts, called *mingei*, are simple and sturdy, yet imbued with Japanese aesthetics. They are unique, durable, and reasonably priced. While folk crafts may lack the sophistication of a delicately painted scroll, they do have a basic beauty that speaks for itself. Many objects fall into this category, such as bamboo wares, fabrics, paper boxes, dolls, and toys.

Bingo-ya. A complete selection of crafts from all over Japan can be found here. *10-6 Wakamatsucho, Shinjuku, tel. 03/3202–8778. Open 10–7. Closed Mon.*

Japan Traditional Craft Center. This gallery is a good place to familiarize yourself with the wonders of Japanese folk crafts. Their creation is demonstrated in videos, and many of the folkcraft items are for sale. *Plaza 246, 2F: 3-1-1 Minami Aoya. Minato-ku, tel. 03/3403–2460. Open 10–6. Closed Thurs.*

Oriental Bazaar. Here are floors of just about everything you want in a traditional Japanese (or Chinese or Korean) handicraft souvenir, from painted screens to pottery to antique chests, at fairly reasonable prices. Kimonos are one flight down. *5-9-13 Jingu-mae, Shibuya-ku, tel. 03/3400–3933. Open 9:30–6:30. Closed Thurs.*

Kimonos Kimonos in Japan are usually only worn on special occasions, such as weddings or graduations, and, like tuxedos in the United States, are often rented instead of purchased. They are extremely expensive and difficult to maintain. A wedding kimono, for example, can cost as much as ¥1 million.

In general, most foreigners, who are unwilling to pay this much for a garment that they probably want to use as a bathrobe, settle for a secondhand or antique silk kimono. These vary in price and quality. You can get one for as low as ¥1,000, but to find one in decent condition, you should expect to pay about ¥5,000. If you are willing to forgo silk, new cotton kimonos, known as *yukata*, with attractive geometric blue-and-white designs, are about ¥5,000. Department stores usually have good selections of new silk kimonos, but some smaller stores feature less expensive or secondhand goods.

Hayashi. This store specializes in ready-made kimonos, sashes, and dyed *yukata* (cotton summer robes). *1-7-23 Uchisaiwaicho, Chiyoda-ku, tel. 03/3501–4014. Open Mon.–Sat. 10–7, Sun. 10–6.*

Lacquerware For its history, diversity, and fine workmanship, lacquerware rivals ceramics as the traditional Japanese craft nonpareil. One warning: lacquerware thrives on humidity. Cheaper pieces usually have plastic rather than wood underneath; since they won't shrink and crack in dry climates, they make safer—but no less attractive—buys.

Inachu. Specializing in the lacquerware of the Wajima, this is one of the most elegant (and expensive) craft shops in Tokyo. *1-5-2 Akasaka, Minato-ku, tel. 03/3582–4451. Open 10–6. Closed Sun.*

Tokyo Lacquerware. A good place to browse for less expensive pieces in a variety of styles. *2-11-13 Minami-Aoyama, Minato-ku, tel. 03/3401–5118. Open Mon.–Fri. 11–6:30, Sat. 11–5. Closed Sun.*

Paper What packs light and flat in your suitcase, won't break, doesn't cost much, and makes great gifts? The answer is traditional handmade paper, called *washi*, which the Japanese make in thousands of colors, textures, and designs, and fashion into an astonishing array of useful and decorative objects.

Ozu Gallery. In business since the 17th century, this shop has one of the largest washi showrooms in the city and its own gallery of antique papers. *2-6-3 Nihonbashi Honcho, Chuo-ku, tel. 03/3663–8788. Open 10–6. Closed Sun.*

Yushima no Kobayashi. Here you can also tour a papermaking workshop, and learn the art of paper-folding, or *origami*. *1-7-14 Yushima, Bunkyo-ku, tel. 03/3811–4025. Open 9–5. Closed Sun.*

Pearls Japan remains one of the best places in the world to buy pearls. They will not be inexpensive, but pearls of the same quality cost considerably more in the United States. It is best to go to a reputable dealer where you know that you will be guaranteed the best in pearls and will not be misled.

Mikimoto. Kokichi Mikimoto created his technique for cultured pearls in 1893. Since then, the name Mikimoto has become associated with the highest quality in pearls. Although the prices at Mikimoto are high, you would pay more for pearls of this quality in the United States. *4-5-5 Ginza, Chuo-ku, tel. 03/3535-4611. Open 10:30–6. Closed Wed.*

Tasaki Pearl Gallery. Tasaki offers pearls at slightly lower prices than does Mikimoto. The store has several showrooms and offers tours that demonstrate the technique of culturing pearls and explain the maintenance and care of these gems. *1-3-3 Akasaka, Minato-ku, tel. 03/5561–8881. Open 9–6:30.*

Arcades and Shopping Centers

For shoppers who do not have the time or energy to dash about Tokyo in search of the perfect gifts, there are arcades and shopping centers that carry a wide selection of merchandise. Many of these establishments are used to dealing with foreigners.

Axis. On the first floor of this complex is **Living Motif,** a home furnishings shop with high-tech foreign and Japanese goods of exquisite design. On the basement floor is **Nuno,** a fabric shop that sells traditional Japanese materials with modern touches. The fabrics are all creations of Junichi Arai, who once designed fabrics for such famous Japanese designers as Rei Kawakubo of Comme des Garçons and Issey Miyake. Be sure to look at **Kisso.** Although this is a restaurant, in the front and back, along with lacquered chopsticks and fine baskets, is an extraordinary selection of unique, modern handmade ceramics in contemporary designs, shapes, and colors. *5-17-1 Roppongi, Minato-ku.*

International Arcade. This selection of shops has a range of goods (including cameras, electronics goods, pearls, and kimonos) all sold by sales help using excellent English. Not only is the arcade conveniently located near the Imperial Hotel and TIC (Tourist Information Center), but the shops are all tax-free. *1-7-3 Uchisaiwaicho, Chiyoda-ku.*

Boutiques

Japanese boutiques can often make you forget you are shopping. Of course, the function of these boutiques is to sell clothes, but in many cases you will not be aware that crass materialism is at work. As much attention is paid to the interior decoration and the lighting as to the clothing, so you have a sense that you are viewing works of art. Although many Japanese designers are represented in department stores for convenient shopping, you'll get a sense of Japanese aesthetics by visiting the simple and elegant boutiques in Aoyama and Omotesando; the stores are conveniently located within walking distance of one another. Even if you don't buy anything, you will be sure to enjoy yourself.

Comme Des Garçons. This is one of the earliest and still most popular "minimalist" design houses, where you can get almost any kind of $70 tank top you want, as long as it's black. *5-11-5 Minami-Aoyama, Minato-ku, tel. 03/3407–2480. Open 11–8.*

From 1st Building (5-3-10 Minami-Aoyama, Minato-ku). This building houses the boutiques of several of Japan's leading designers, including **Issey Miyake** and Alpha Cubic, as well as several smart restaurants. "Produced" by Yasuhiro Hamano, whose atelier designs many of Tokyo's trendiest commercial spaces, From 1st is one of the earliest and best examples of the city's upmarket vertical malls.

Hanae Mori Building. In this glass-mirrored structure, designed by the famous Japanese architect Kenzo Tange, you can see the designs of the doyenne of Japanese fashion, Hanae Mori. Mori's clothing has a classic look with a European influence. On the first floor, there is a café where you can observe Japan's beautiful people walking along the street or sitting next to you. *3-6-1 Kita-Aoyama, Minato-ku, tel. 03/3406-1021. Open 10:30-7.*

Koshino Junko. Available here are upmarket clothes and accessories with a European accent, for the sophisticated shopper. *6-5-36 Minami-Aoyama, Minato-ku, tel. 03/3406-7370. Open 11-7. Closed Sat.*

Department Stores

Today, most Japanese department stores are part of conglomerates that own railways, real estate, and even baseball teams. These stores often include travel agencies, theaters, and art galleries. A shopper can easily spend an afternoon or even an entire day shopping, especially because a cluster of reasonably priced restaurants is usually located on the top or basement floor. Many floors have coffee shops for lighter meals.

Major department stores accept credit cards and provide shipping services. Some staff will speak English. If you are having communication difficulties, someone will eventually come to the rescue. On the first floor of most stores is a general-information booth that has maps of the store in English. Because many of the stores are confusing, these guides are useful.

A trip to a Japanese department store is not merely a shopping excursion; it will also provide insights into Japanese culture.

Arrive just before opening hours, and you will witness a ceremony with all of the pomp of the changing of the guard at Buckingham Palace. At 10 AM sharp, two immaculately groomed young women will face the customers from behind the doors and bow ceremoniously, after which they open the doors. As you walk through the store, you will find that everyone is standing at attention, bowing and welcoming you. Notice the uniformity of the angle of the bows—many stores have training sessions in which new employees are taught this art.

For yet another look at Japanese culture, head for the basement floor, which usually houses food halls. Here you will see more clearly than anywhere else just what the average Japanese person eats. Needless to say, the fish section is large, and the meat prices are exorbitant. Many counters have small samples of food for the customers' benefit. If you can be discreet, or give the impression that you are planning on making a purchase, you can try some of these samples.

Ginza/Nihombashi

Matsuya. In contrast to all the refined shopping in the Ginza/Nihombashi area, this slightly disorganized department store is a welcome change. The merchandise here is geared toward a younger crowd. The shopper with the patience to comb through the offerings will be rewarded with many good finds, particularly in the sections for young women's clothing. *3-6-1 Ginza, Chuo-ku, tel. 03/3567–1211. Open 10–7. Closed Tues.*

Matsuzakaya. Not quite as old as the nearby Mitsukoshi, this store is a mere 350 years old. It offers both Western and Japanese traditional goods. *6-10-1 Ginza, Chuo-ku, tel. 03/3572–1111. Open 10–7. Closed Wed.*

Mitsukoshi was founded in 1673 as a dry-goods store. In later years, it became one of the first stores to introduce Western merchandise to Japan. Through the years it has retained its image of quality and excellence, with a particularly strong representation of Western fashion designers, such as Chanel, Lanvin, and Givenchy. Mitsukoshi also has a fine selection of traditional Japanese goods. Catering to a distinguished clientele, it is one of Japan's most prestigious department stores. *1-4-1 Nihombashi Muromachi, Chuo-ku, tel. 03/3241–3311. Open 10–6:30. Closed Mon.; 4-6-16 Ginza, Chuo-ku, tel. 03/3562–1111. Open 10–7.*

Takashimaya. This store has a broad and upscale appeal, with both Japanese and Western designer goods. This is where many brides-to-be shop for their weddings, because the kimono department is one of the best in Tokyo. This store also features a complete selection of traditional crafts, antiques, and curios. *2-4-1 Nihombashi, Chuo-ku, tel. 03/3211–4111. Open 10–7. Closed Wed.*

Wako. This is a specialty store that borders on being a department store. With a reputation for quality at high prices, Wako is particularly known for its glassware. It is also known for its very pretty saleswomen, who tend to marry well-to-do customers. *4-5-11 Ginza, Chuo-ku, tel. 03/3562–2111. Open weekdays and Sun. 10–5:30, Sat. 10–6.*

Shibuya

Parco. This is actually not one store but four, all located near one another. Not surprisingly, they are owned by Seibu (*see below*). Actually, more than being department stores, Parco Part 1, Part 2, Part 3, and Part 4, as they are called, are malls that extend upward—filled with small retail stores and boutiques. Parts 1 and 4 are for a very young crowd, Part 2 is mainly designer fashions, and Part 3 is a mixture of men's and women's fashions and household goods. *15-1 Udagawacho, Shibuya-ku, tel. 03/3464–5111. Open daily 10–8:30.*

Seibu. The main branch of this store is rather out of the main shopping course, in Ikebukuro. The Shibuya branch, while smaller, is more manageable than the Ikebukuro branch, where even many Japanese customers get lost. The department store is a leading member of a group of stores that owns a railway line and even a baseball team, the Seibu Lions. If you follow Japanese baseball, when the Lions win the pennant, prepare to go shopping—all of the Seibu stores have major sales on all merchandise the following day. This store has an excellent selection of household goods, from furniture to chinaware and lacquer. *21-1 Udagawa-cho, Shibuya-ku, tel. 03/3462–0111. Open 10–7. Closed Wed.*

Tokyu. This standard department store offers a good selection of imported clothing, accessories, and home furnishings. *2-24-1 Dogenzaka, Shibuya-ku, tel. 03/3477–3111. Open 10–7. Closed Tues.*

Tokyu Hands. Known commonly as just "Hands," this specialty-hobby store is crowded any day, any time. It offers an excellent selection of carpentry tools, sewing accessories, kitchen goods, plants, and an impressive assortment of other related do-it-yourself merchandise. The toys department is chock-full of kitsch, such as plastic foods, and the stationery department has a very complete selection of Japanese papers. *12-18 Udagawa-cho, Shibuya-ku, tel. 03/5489-5111. Open 10-8. Closed 2nd and 3rd Wed. of each month.*

Shinjuku **Isetan.** Often called the Bloomingdale's of Japan, a description that does not quite do this store justice, Isetan has become a favorite with shoppers of all ages. It features one of the most complete selections of Japanese designers in one place. For those who want distinctive designer looks but not the high prices, the store includes many spin-offs. In addition to European designers, a number of Americans are represented, such as Calvin Klein and Norma Kamali. Don't be surprised if the fit is a little different from that in America—these clothes are made specifically for the Japanese. Chinaware, stationery, furniture, you name it—all reflect the general tone of Isetan: high quality and interesting design. Look at the folk-crafts department for a small but good selection of fans, table mats, and other gifts. *3-14-1 Shinjuku, Shinjuku-ku, tel. 03/3352-1111. Open 10-7. Closed Wed., except in Mar.*

Keio. This no-nonsense department store has a standard but complete selection of merchandise. *1-1-4 Nishi-Shinjuku, Shinjuku-ku, tel. 03/3342-2111. Open 10-7. Closed Thurs.*

Marui. More than a department store, Marui is a group of specialty stores that seem to be spawning all over Shinjuku. Of the most interest are the fashion stores—Young Fashion and Men's. Marui has been wildly successful for its easy credit policies. Many young people shop here simply because it is the only place where they can get credit. The merchandise is for the young and carefree. Twice a year, in February and July, prices are slashed dramatically in major clearance sales. At these times, incredible bargains can be found. If you are in the neighborhood, you will know exactly when the sales are taking place: The lines will extend into the street and around the block. (Let it not be said that Japanese men do not care about fashion. The most enthusiastic customers line up from 6AM for the men's sales.) *3-30-16 Shinjuku, Shinjuku-ku, tel. 03/3354-0101. Open 11-8. Closed Wed.*

Odakyu. Slightly snazzier than its neighboring Keio, this is a very family-oriented store. It is particularly good for children's clothing. Across the street from the main building is Odakyu Halc, which has a varied selection of home furnishings and interior goods on its upper floors. *1-1-3 Nishi-Shinjuku, Shinjuku-ku, tel. 03/3342-1111. Open 10-7. Closed Tues.*

Fitness Centers

The only health club in the city that offers short-term temporary memberships is the **Clark Hatch Fitness Center** (Azabu Towers, 2-1-3 Azabudai, Minato-ku, tel. 03/3584-4092; 1-week membership ¥9,270). Tokyo does have, however, an abundance of good hotels with fine fitness facilities, important for a traveler in a city with limited greenery, much traffic, and a difficult language. These are some of the hotels:

Century Hyatt (2-7-2 Nishi-Shinjuku, Shinjuku-ku, tel. 03/3349-0111), on the edge of Shinjuku Chuo Koen (Shinjuku Central Park), has exercise rooms for men and women, provides jogging maps in each room, and has an Olympic-size pool on the hotel's 28th floor.

Hotel New Otani and Tower (4-1 Kioi-cho, Chiyoda-ku, tel. 03/3265–1111), not far from the Imperial Gardens, provides jogging route maps in each room. It also boasts four tennis courts, an outdoor Olympic-size pool, and a golf driving range. Its private health club is open to hotel guests when not being used by members.

Hotel Okura (10-4 Toranomon 2-chome Minato-ku, tel. 03/3582–0111) is across from the U.S. Embassy and a perennial favorite with foreign business travelers. It has both indoor and outdoor six-lane 25-meter pools, a modern fitness room with an instructor, and a health-food restaurant prepares special meals. The hotel is a 15-minute jog from the Imperial Gardens.

Imperial Hotel (1-1-1 Uchisaiwaicho, Chiyoda-ku, tel. 03/3504–1111) overlooks the Imperial Gardens and provides complimentary jogging gear to guests. It also has a glass-enclosed pool, sauna, and massage room.

Miyako Hotel Tokyo (1-1-50 Shiroganedai, Minato-ku, tel. 03/3447–3111) has a 25-meter four-lane indoor pool and, for a fee, fitness rooms for men and women.

Tokyo Hilton International (6-2 Nishi-Shinjuku 6-chome, Shinjuku-ku, tel. 03/3344–5111) has tennis courts, a large indoor pool, and modern exercise equipment.

Dining

By Jared Lubarsky

A resident of Tokyo, Jared Lubarsky has reviewed restaurants for the Mainichi Daily News.

At last count, there were over 187,000 bars and restaurants in Tokyo; wining and dining is a major component in the local way of life. Japanese companies nationwide spend about $65 million a day (that, at least, is what they report to the tax authorities) on business entertainment, and a good slice of that is spent in Tokyo.

That gives you your first caveat: all that spending on company tabs tends to drive up the bill, and dining out can be hideously expensive. The other side of that coin, of course, is that Tokyo's 187,000 choices also include a fair number of bargains—good cooking of all sorts, at prices the traveler on a budget can handle. The options, in fact, go all the way down to street food and yakitori joints under railroad trestles, where the Japanese go when they have to spend their own money. Food and drink, incidentally, are safe wherever you go.

Tokyo is not really an international city yet; in many ways, it is still stubbornly provincial. Whatever the rest of the world has pronounced good, however, eventually makes its way here—sometimes in astonishing variety. (The Highlander Bar in the Hotel Okura, for example, stocks 224 different brands of Scotch whisky, 48 of them single malts.) French, Italian, Chinese, Indian, Middle Eastern, Latin, East European: it's hard to think of a national cuisine of any prominence that goes unrepresented, as Japanese chefs by the thousands go abroad, learn their craft at great restaurants, and bring it home to this city.

Restaurants in Japan naturally expect most of their clients to be Japanese, and the Japanese are the world's champion modifiers. Only the most serious restaurateurs refrain from editing out some of the authenticity of foreign cuisines; in areas like Shibuya, Harajuku, and Shinjuku, all too many of the foreign restaurants cater to students and young office workers, who come for the *fuinki* (the atmosphere) but can't make much of an informed judgment about the food. Choose your bistro or trattoria carefully, and expect to pay dearly for the real thing—but count also on the fact that Tokyo's best is world-class.

Here are a few general hints and observations. Tokyo's finest hotels also have some of the city's first-rate places to eat and drink. (Alas, this is not always the case elsewhere.) A good number of France's two- and three-star restaurants have established branches and joint ventures in Tokyo, and they regularly send their chefs over to supervise. Some of them stay, find backers, and open restaurants of their own. The style almost everywhere is *nouvelle cuisine:* small portions, with picture-perfect garnishes and light sauces. More and more, you find interesting fusions of French and Japanese culinary traditions. Meals are served in poetically beautiful presentations, in bowls and dishes of different shapes and patterns; fresh Japanese ingredients, like *shimeji* mushrooms and local wild vegetables, are often used.

Tokyoites know and like French food. They have less of a chance, unfortunately, to experience the real range and virtuosity of Italian cuisine; only a small handful of the city's Italian restaurants would measure up to Italian standards. Indian food here, however, is consistently good and relatively inexpensive. Chinese food is the most consistently modified; it can be quite appetizing, but for repertoire and richness of taste, travelers coming here through Hong Kong will be disappointed. Significantly, Tokyo has no Chinatown.

A few pointers are in order on the geography of food and drink. The farther "downtown" you go—into Shitamachi—the less likely you are to find the real thing in foreign cuisines. There is superb Japanese food all over the city, but aficionados of sushi swear (with excellent reason) by Tsukiji; the sushi bars in the area around the central fish market tend to have the best ingredients, serve the biggest portions, and charge the most reasonable prices. Asakusa takes pride in its tempura restaurants, but tempura is reliable almost everywhere, especially at branches of the well-established, citywide chains. Every department store and skyscraper office building in Tokyo has at least one whole floor devoted to restaurants; none of them have any great distinction, but they are all inexpensive and are quite passable places for lunch.

The quintessential Japanese restaurant is the *ryotei*, a large, villalike establishment, usually walled off from the bustle of the outside world and containing a number of small, private dining rooms. The rooms are all in traditional style, with tatami-mat floors, low tables, and a hanging scroll or a flower arrangement in the alcove. One or more of the staff is assigned to each room to serve the many dishes that comprise the meal, pour your sake, and provide light conversation. ("Waitress" is the wrong word; "attendant" is closer, but there really isn't a suitable term in English.) A ryotei is an adventure, an encounter with foods you've never seen before, and with a graceful, almost ritualized style of service that is unique to Japan and centuries old. Many parts of the city are proverbial for their ryotei; the top houses tend to be in Akasaka, Tsukiji, Asakusa and nearby Yanagibashi, and Shimbashi.

Price-category estimates for the restaurants below are based on the cost of an average meal (three courses, if Western style) per person, exclusive of drinks, taxes, and service charges; thus, a restaurant listed as **Moderate** can easily slide up a category to **Expensive** when it comes time to pay the bill.

A 3% national consumer tax is added to all restaurant bills. Another 3% local tax is added to the bill if it exceeds ¥7,500. At more expensive restaurants, a 10%–15% service charge is also added to the bill. Tipping is not necessary.

Note that business hours indicate when the last order of the evening is accepted, not when the restaurant actually closes.

The most highly recommended restaurants are indicated by a star ★.

Category	Cost*
Very Expensive	over ¥10,000
Expensive	¥6,000–¥10,000
Moderate	¥3,000–¥6,000
Inexpensive	under ¥3,000

**Cost is per person without tax, service, or drinks*

Japanese

Aoyama **Higo Batten.** This restaurant specializes in a style called *kushi-yaki,* which refers simply to a variety of ingredients—meat, fish, vegetables—cut into bits and grilled on bamboo skewers. There's nothing ceremonious or elegant about *kushi-yaki;* it resembles the more familiar *yaki-tori* (Japanese-style chicken kebabs), except there's more variety to it. At Higo Batten you can feast on such dishes as shiitake mushrooms stuffed with minced chicken; scallops wrapped in bacon; and bonito, shimp, and eggplant with ginger. The decor here is sort of postmodern traditional, with wooden beams painted black, paper lanterns, and sliding paper screens. There's tatami, table, and counter seating. This spot draws a young crowd, among them a lot of the fancy-free Westerners who like the scene in Aoyama—which probably accounts for the helpful English menu. *AG Bldg. 1F, 3-18-17 Minami-Aoyama, Minato-ku (nearest subway: Omotesando), tel. 03/3423–4462. Reservations not necessary. Dress: informal. AE, V. Open 5–11:15 PM. Inexpensive–Moderate.*

Asakusa **Tatsumiya.** This is a *ryotei* (a traditional Japanese restaurant) with at least two delightfully untraditional features: It is neither inaccessible nor outrageously expensive. Most ryotei tend to oppress the first-time visitor a little with the weight of their antiquity and the ceremonious formality of their service. Tatsumiya opened in 1980, and it takes a different attitude to the past: The rooms are almost cluttered—with antique chests, braziers, clocks, lanterns, bowls, utensils, and craftwork (some of which are even for sale). The cuisine itself follows the *kaiseki* repertoire, derived from the tradition of the tea-ceremony meal. Seven courses are offered: something raw, something boiled, something vinegared, something grilled. The atmosphere is relaxed and friendly, in the *Shitamachi* (downtown) style. *1–33–5 Asakusa, Taito-ku (nearest subway station: Asakusa), tel. 03/3842–7373. Reservations advised. Jacket and tie advised. No credit cards. Open noon–2 and 5–9:30 (enter by 8:30). Closed Mon. Very Expensive.*

Ginza **Hakkaku.** On the second floor of the Yuraku Food Center building, crammed between other restaurants, this small bar can easily be recognized by its big red lantern hanging outside. At lunchtime, good tempura dishes are offered at very reasonable prices. There is table seating or a counter/bar; you'll be rubbing elbows with local businessmen. *Ginza Ins 2, 2-2 Nishi-Ginza, Chuo-ku (nearest subway station: Yurakucho), tel. 03/3561–0539. No reservations. Dress: casual. AE, DC, MC, V. Open 11–9:30. Closed Sun. Moderate.*

Ikebukuro ★ **Sasashu.** Strictly speaking, Sasashu is not a restaurant but an *izakaya*—a drinkery that specializes in sake. It's included here for two reasons. First, it stocks only the finest and rarest, the Latours and Mouton-Rothschilds, of sake: these are wines that take gold medals in the annual sake concours year after year. Second, the restaurant serves the best food of any izakaya in town—the Japanese wouldn't dream of drinking well without eating well. Sasashu is a rambling, two-story building in traditional style, with thick beams and step-up tatami floors. The specialty of the house is salmon steak, brushed with sake and soy sauce and broiled over a charcoal hibachi. *2-2-6 Ikebukuro, Toshima-ku (nearest subway station: Ikebukuro), tel. 03/3971–6796. Reservations advised, especially Jan.–Feb. Dress: informal. AE, DC, MC, V. Open 5–9:30. Closed Sun. and holidays. Expensive.*

Meguro ★ **Tonki.** Meguro, distinguished for almost nothing else culinary, has the numero uno *tonkatsu* (deep-fried pork cutlet) restaurant in Tokyo. It's a family joint, with Formica-top tables and a fellow who comes around to take your order ahead while you're waiting in line. And people do wait in line, every night. Tonki is one of those successful places that never went conglomerate; it kept getting more popular and never got around to putting frills on what it does best: pork cutlets, soup, raw cabbage salad, rice, pickles, and tea. That's the standard course, and almost everybody orders it, with good reason. *1-1-2 Shimo-Meguro, Meguro-ku (nearest JR station: Meguro), tel. 03/3491–9928. No reservations; expect a 10-min. wait. Dress: informal. DC, MC, V. Open 4–10:45. Closed Tues. and every third Mon. Inexpensive.*

Roppongi ★ **Inakaya.** The style here is *robatayaki* (charcoal grill cookery), while the ambience is pure theater. The centerpiece is a large U-shape counter. Inside, two cooks in traditional garb sit on cushions behind the grill, with a wonderful cornucopia of food spread out in front of them: fresh vegetables, fish and seafood, skewers of beef and chicken. Point to what you want, or tell your waiter (they all speak a little English); the cook will bring it up out of the pit, prepare it, and hand it across on an 8-foot wooden paddle. *Reine Bldg. 1F, 5-3-4 Roppongi, Minatoku (nearest subway station: Roppongi), tel. 03/3408–5040. No reservations; expect a ½-hour wait any evening after 7. Dress: informal. AE, DC, MC, V. Open 5 PM–5 AM. Closed New Year's Day. Very Expensive.*

Ganchan. While the Japanese prefer their sushi bars to be immaculately clean and light, they expect yakitori joints to be smoky, noisy, and cluttered—like Ganchan. There's counter

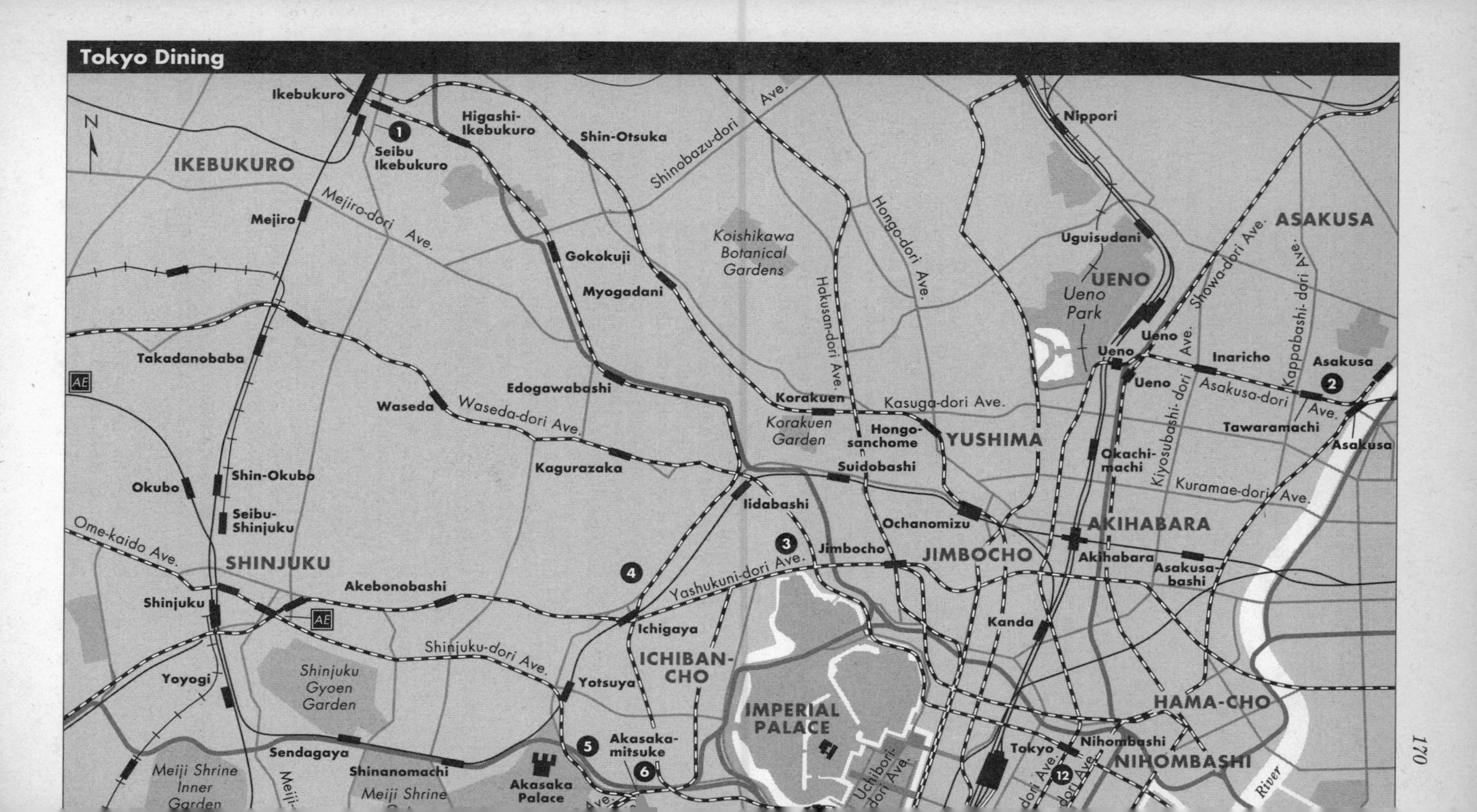
Tokyo Dining
N
IKEBUKURO
Ikebukuro
Seibu Ikebukuro
Higashi-Ikebukuro
Shin-Otsuka
Shinobazu-dori Ave.
Mejiro
Mejiro-dori Ave.
Gokokuji
Myogadani
Koishikawa Botanical Gardens
Hongo-dori Ave.
Hakusan-dori Ave.
Nippori
Uguisudani
UENO
Ueno Park
Ueno
ASAKUSA
Showa-dori Ave.
Kappabashi-dori Ave.
Inaricho
Asakusa
Asakusa-dori Ave.
Tawaramachi
Takadanobaba
AE
Edogawabashi
Waseda
Waseda-dori Ave.
Korakuen
Korakuen Garden
Kasuga-dori Ave.
Hongo-sanchome
YUSHIMA
Suidobashi
Kagurazaka
Okachi-machi
Kiyosubashi-dori Ave.
Kuramae-dori Ave.
Shin-Okubo
Okubo
Seibu-Shinjuku
Iidabashi
Ochanomizu
AKIHABARA
Ome-kaido Ave.
SHINJUKU
Jimbocho
JIMBOCHO
Akihabara
Asakusa-bashi
Akebonobashi
Yashukuni-dori Ave.
Shinjuku
Ichigaya
Kanda
ICHIBAN-CHO
Shinjuku-dori Ave.
Yoyogi
Shinjuku Gyoen Garden
Yotsuya
IMPERIAL PALACE
HAMA-CHO
Akasaka-mitsuke
Sendagaya
Shinanomachi
Akasaka Palace
Uchibori-dori Ave.
Tokyo
Nihombashi
NIHOMBASHI
River
Meiji Shrine Inner Garden
Meiji Shrine
1
2
3
4
5
6
12

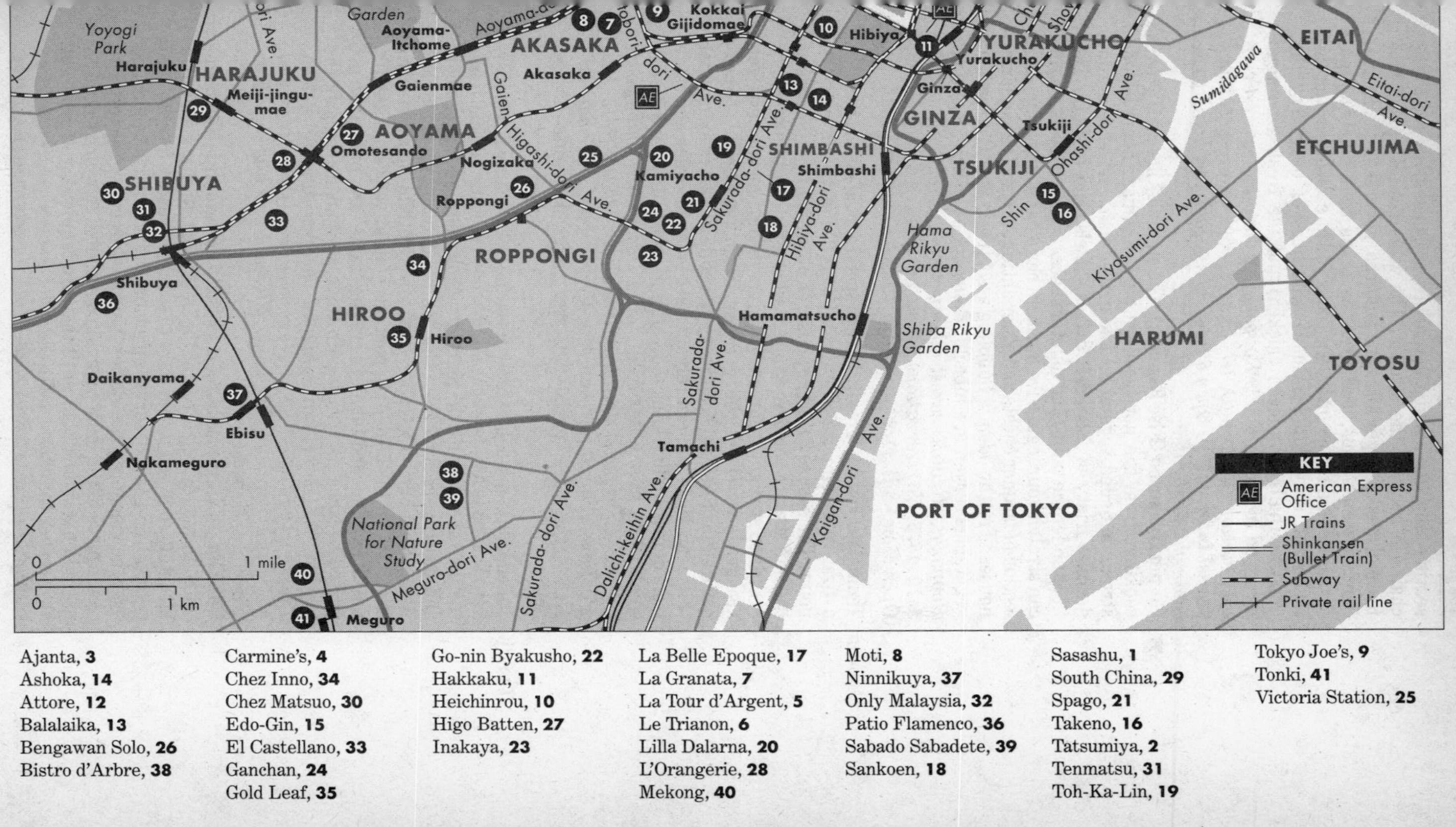
KEY
American Express Office
JR Trains
Shinkansen (Bullet Train)
Subway
Private rail line
0 1 mile
0 1 km
HARAJUKU
SHIBUYA
AOYAMA
AKASAKA
ROPPONGI
HIROO
SHIMBASHI
GINZA
YURAKUCHO
TSUKIJI
EITAI
ETCHUJIMA
HARUMI
TOYOSU
PORT OF TOKYO
Yoyogi Park
National Park for Nature Study
Hama Rikyu Garden
Shiba Rikyu Garden
Sumidagawa
Harajuku
Meiji-jingu-mae
Shibuya
Daikanyama
Nakameguro
Ebisu
Meguro
Omotesando
Gaienmae
Aoyama-Itchome
Nogizaka
Roppongi
Akasaka
Kokkai Gijidomae
Kamiyacho
Hiroo
Hibiya
Yurakucho
Ginza
Tsukiji
Shimbashi
Hamamatsucho
Tamachi
Gaien Higashi-dori Ave.
Sakurada-dori Ave.
Hibiya-dori Ave.
Dalichi-keihin Ave.
Meguro-dori Ave.
Kaigan-dori Ave.
Kiyosumi-dori Ave.
Shin Ohashi-dori Ave.
Eitai-dori Ave.
Ajanta, 3
Ashoka, 14
Attore, 12
Balalaika, 13
Bengawan Solo, 26
Bistro d'Arbre, 38
Carmine's, 4
Chez Inno, 34
Chez Matsuo, 30
Edo-Gin, 15
El Castellano, 33
Ganchan, 24
Gold Leaf, 35
Go-nin Byakusho, 22
Hakkaku, 11
Heichinrou, 10
Higo Batten, 27
Inakaya, 23
La Belle Epoque, 17
La Granata, 7
La Tour d'Argent, 5
Le Trianon, 6
Lilla Dalarna, 20
L'Orangerie, 28
Mekong, 40
Moti, 8
Ninnikuya, 37
Only Malaysia, 32
Patio Flamenco, 36
Sabado Sabadete, 39
Sankoen, 18
Sasashu, 1
South China, 29
Spago, 21
Takeno, 16
Tatsumiya, 2
Tenmatsu, 31
Toh-Ka-Lin, 19
Tokyo Joe's, 9
Tonki, 41
Victoria Station, 25

seating only, for about 15; you have to squeeze to get to the chairs in back by the kitchen. The walls are festooned with festival masks, paper kites and lanterns, gimcracks of all sorts, handwritten menus, and greeting cards from celebrity patrons. Behind the counter, the cooks yell at each other, fan the grill, and serve up enormous schooners of beer. Try the *tsukune* (balls of minced chicken) and the fresh asparagus wrapped in bacon. *6-8-23 Roppongi, Minato-ku (nearest subway station: Roppongi), tel. 03/3478–0092. No reservations. Dress: informal. V. Open 6 PM–2:30 AM, Sun. and holidays 6–midnight. Moderate.*

★ **Go-nin Byakusho (Five Farmers).** The specialty here is Tohoku cooking, from the northeastern part of Japan: hearty food, strong on boiled vegetables and grilled fish, served in a wonderful variety of folk-craft dishes, bowls, and baskets. The floor under the tables and counter spaces is on two levels, so you can stretch your legs. Five Farmers has a particularly fine collection of lacquer chests and other antiques from Tohoku farmhouses. Try the *oden*, a bubbling assortment of fish cakes and vegetables served in a hibachi. *Roppongi Sq. Bldg. 4F, 3-10-3 Roppongi, Minato (nearest subway station: Roppongi), tel. 03/3470–1675. No reservations. Dress: informal. AE, DC, MC, V. Open Mon.–Sat. 11:30–2, 5–9:15. Closed Sun. Moderate.*

Shibuya

Tenmatsu. You don't really have to spend a lot of money to enjoy a first-rate tempura restaurant, and Tenmatsu proves the point. The best seats in the house, as in any *tempura-ya*, are at the immaculate wooden counter, where your tidbits of choice are taken straight from the oil and served up immediately. You also get to watch the chef in action. Tenmatsu's brand of good-natured professional hospitality just adds to your enjoyment of the meal. Here you can rely on a set menu or order à la carte from delicacies like lotus root, shrimp, *unagi* (eel), and *kisu* (a small white freshwater fish). *1–6–1 Dogenzaka, Shibuya-ku (nearest JR/subway station: Shibuya), tel. 03/3462–2815. Reservations advised for counter seating. Dress: informal. DC, MC, V. Open 11–2 and 5–9. Closed Thurs. Moderate–Expensive.*

Tsukiji

Takeno. Just a stone's throw from the Tokyo central fish market, Takeno is a rough-cut neighborhood restaurant that tends to fill up at noon with the market's wholesalers and auctioneers and office personnel from the nearby Dentsu ad agency and Asahi Shimbun newspaper company. Nothing here but the freshest and the best—big portions of it, at very small tariffs. Sushi, sashimi, and tempura are the staple fare; prices are not posted because they vary with the costs that morning in the market. *6-21-2 Tsukiji, Chuo-ku (nearest subway station: Tsukiji), tel. 03/3541–8698. No reservations. Dress: informal. No credit cards. Open 11–9. Closed Sun. and holidays. Moderate–Expensive.*

Edo-Gin. In an area that teems with sushi bars, Edo-Gin maintains its reputation as one of the best. Portions have shrunk a bit lately, but you would have to visit once every few years to notice. Edo-Gin still serves up generous slabs of fish that drape over the vinegared rice rather than perch demurely on top. The centerpiece of the main room is a huge tank, in which the day's ingredients swim about until they are required; you can't get any fresher than that! *4-5-1 Tsukiji, Chuo-ku (nearest subway station: Tsukiji), tel. 03/3543–4401. No reservations. Dress:*

informal. AE, MC, V. Open 10–10. Closed Sun., every second Mon., and some national holidays. Moderate.

American

Akasaka-mitsuke **Tokyo Joe's.** The very first foreign branch of famed Miami Joe's was in Osaka, a city where volume-for-value really counts in the reputation of a restaurant. The Tokyo branch opened about five years ago and upholds its reputation the same way—by serving enormous quantities of stone crab, with melted butter and mustard mayonnaise. The turnover here is fierce; waiters in long red aprons scurry to keep up with it, but the service is remarkably smooth. The crabs are flown in fresh from the Florida Keys, their one and only habitat. There are other choices on the menu, but it's midnight madness to order anything else. Top it all off—if you have room—with Key lime pie. *Akasaka Eight-One Bldg. B1, 2-13-5 Nagata-cho, Chiyoda-ku (nearest subway station: Akasaka-mitsuke), tel. 03/3508–0325. Reservations advised. Dress: informal. AE, DC, MC, V. Open 11 AM–10:30 PM. Expensive.*

Roppongi **Spago.** So far, this is the only venture overseas by trendsetting Spago of Los Angeles. Owner-chef-celebrity Wolfgang Puck comes periodically to Tokyo to oversee the authenticity of his California cuisine: Will duck sausage pizza with boursin cheese and pearl onions ever be as American as apple pie? Maybe. Meanwhile, Spago is a clean, well-lighted place, painted pink and white and adorned with potted palms. The service is smooth, and the tables on the glassed-in veranda attract a fair sample of Tokyo's Gilded Youth. *5-7-8 Roppongi, Minato-ku (nearest subway station: Roppongi), tel. 03/3423–4025. Reservations advised. Dress: informal. AE, DC, MC, V. Open 5:30–10:30. Closed Dec. 31 and Jan. 1. Expensive–Very Expensive.*

Victoria Station. The basic elements of an American restaurant chain are instantly recognizable and infinitely exportable: a certain kind of packaging, a style of management, and a penchant for themes. Victoria Station's theme is the British railway system, executed with platform signs on the walls, railroad prints, old posters, brass fittings—and even a truncated caboose. The space is huge and is well laid out in "compartments," with a much-appreciated no-smoking section. The specialty of the house is roast prime rib; the salad bar is one of the best in town. *15-13 Akasaka 3 chome, Minato-ku (nearest subway station: Roppongi), tel. 03/3586–0711. No reservations. Dress: informal. AE, MC, V. Open 11 AM–midnight, Sun. and holidays 11 AM–10 PM. Moderate.*

Chinese

Harajuku **South China.** A Chinese restaurant for everybody—or at least for everybody you know, and most of their friends. South China occupies the three basement floors of a building near the main entrance to the Meiji Shrine; it can host a reception for a thousand people or a banquet for a hundred, and it boasts 13 smaller rooms for private parties. How many tons of red lacquer have gone into the decor is anybody's guess. The menu is on a commensurate scale—over 20 entries, about half of them Cantonese. South China's 35 cooks can also handle the fiery Szechuan cuisine, as well as the Peking and Shanghai styles. Specialties of the house include shark's fin with crab meat and Peking duck. *Co-op Olympia Bldg. B1-3, 6-35-3 Jingu-mae, Shibuya-ku (nearest JR station: Harajuku), tel. 03/3400–0031. No reservations. Dress: informal. AE, MC, V. Open 11:30–9:30. Moderate–Expensive.*

Toranomon

Toh-Ka-Lin. Year after year, the Hotel Okura is rated by business travelers as one of the three best hotels in the world. That judgment has relatively little to do with its architecture, which is rather understated. It has to do instead with its polish, its impeccable standards of service—and, to judge by the Toh-Ka-Lin, the quality of its restaurants. The style of the cuisine here is eclectic; two stellar examples are the Peking duck and the sautéed quail wrapped in lettuce leaf. Some people would find it a little bizarre to drink fine French wines with Chinese food, but in case you don't, the Toh-Ka-Lin also has one of the most extensive wine lists in town. *Hotel Okura, 2-04-4 Toranomon, Minato-ku (nearest subway stations: Kamiya-cho and Toranomon), tel. 03/3505–6068. Reservations recommended. Dress: informal. AE, DC, MC, V. Open 11:30–2:30 and 5:30–9:30. Expensive–Very Expensive.*

Uchisaiwai-cho ★

Heichinrou. A branch of one of the oldest and best restaurants in Yokohama's Chinatown. On the top floor of a prestigious office building about five minutes' walk from the Imperial Hotel, Heichinrou commands a spectacular view of Hibiya-Koen Park and the Imperial Palace grounds. Much of the clientele comes from the law offices, securities firms, and foreign banks on the floors below. The decor is rich but subdued; the lighting is soft; the linen is impeccable. Heichinrou boasts a banquet room that will seat a hundred, and a "VIP Room," with separate telephone service, for power lunches. The cuisine is Cantonese, and it's first-rate. *Fukoku Seimei Bldg. 28F, 2-2-2 Uchisaiwai-cho, Chiyoda-ku (nearest subway station: Uchisaiwai-cho), tel. 03/3508–0555. Reservations advised, especially for a table by the window. Jacket and tie required. AE, DC, MC, V. Open 11–9. Closed Sun. and holidays. Expensive.*

French

Akasaka-mitsuke

La Tour d'Argent. Pride of the New Otani Hotel since 1984, La Tour d'Argent is a worthy scion of its ritzy Parisian parent. This is a place of grand centerpieces. One of them is in the foyer, enclosed in a glass case—the entire table setting at the Café Anglais (forerunner of the original Tour d'Argent) on June 7, 1867, when Bismarck hosted a dinner for Czar Alexander II of Russia and Emperor William I of Prussia. The other, in the main dining room, is the enormous drapery-sculpted marble carving table, with its silver duck press. The specialty of the house, naturally, is *caneton:* as in Paris, you receive a card recording the number of the duck you were served. In 1921, when Crown Prince Hirohito dined at the Tour d'Argent in Paris, he had duck number 53,210; the numbers here in Tokyo began with 53,211 when the restaurant opened. *4-1 Kioi-cho, Chiyoda-ku (nearest subway station: Akasaka-mitsuke), tel. 03/3239–3111. Reservations required. Jacket and tie required. AE, DC, MC, V. Open 5:30–9. Very Expensive.*

Le Trianon. Chef Sadao Hotta came over in 1976 from the Tokyo branch of Maxim's to open Le Trianon in the old guest house of the Akasaka Prince Hotel. The house was built for the king of Korea in the style of a French country estate, with parquet floors, lofty wooden beams, and stained-glass windows. The restaurant, which takes up the whole second floor, has seven private dining rooms; the largest will hold a party of 12. Many of the regular clientele work in the nearby centers of power: the National Diet, the Liberal-Democratic party headquarters, and the Supreme Court. *1-2 Kioi-cho, Chiyoda-ku (nearest subway station: Akasaka-mitsuke), tel. 03/3234–1111. Reservations required. Jacket and tie required. AE, DC, MC, V. Open noon–3 and 5–9:30. Very Expensive.*

Kyobashi **Chez Inno.** Chef Noboru Inoue studied his craft at Maxim's in Paris and Les Frères Troisgros in Roanne; the result is a brilliant, innovative French food. The main dining room, with seating for 28, has velvet banquettes, white stucco walls, and stained-glass windows; there's also a smaller room for private parties. Across the street is the elegant Seiyo Hotel—making this block the locus of the very best Tokyo has to offer the upscale traveler. Try the fresh lamb in wine sauce with truffles and *fines herbes*, or the lobster with caviar. *3-2-11 Kyobashi (nearest subway station: Kyobashi), tel. 03/3274–2020. Reservations required. Dress: Jacket and tie suggested. AE, DC, V. Open noon–2 and 6–9. Sun. 6–9. Very Expensive.*

Omotesando **L'Orangerie.** This very fashion-minded restaurant is on the fifth floor of the Hanae Mori Building, just a minute's walk from the Omotesando subway station on Aoyama-dori. It's a joint venture of the original L'Orangerie in Paris and Mme. Mori's formidable empire in couture. A muted elegance marks the decor, with cream walls, deep brown carpets, and a few good paintings. Mirrors add depth to a room that actually seats only 40. The menu, an ambitious one to begin with, changes every two weeks; the salad of sautéed sweetbreads, when they have it, is excellent. The lunch and dinner menus are nouvelle and very pricey. L'Orangerie is best approached on a warm Sunday between 11 and 2:30, for the buffet brunch, when for ¥3,500 you can graze through to what's arguably the best dessert tray in town. *Hanae Mori Bldg. 5F, 3-6-1 Kita-Aoyama, Minato-ku (nearest subway station: Omotesando), tel. 03/3407–7461. Reservations required. Dress: informal, but jacket suggested. AE, DC, MC, V. Open 11:30–2:30 and 5:30–9:30, Sun. 11–2:30. Lunch: Moderate–Expensive. Dinner: Very Expensive.*

Shiroganedai **Bistro d'Arbre.** This tiny restaurant (seating for only 12), on what has become one of the more fashionable avenues among Tokyo's affluent young folks, depends on worth of mouth for its popularity; it doesn't get many foreign visitors—and more's the pity. Chef Takahiro Taniguchi trained briefly in France, but honed his skills mainly here on the job; his repertoire is not wide, but what he does, he does beautifully. Especially good are the smoked salmon crepes and the fillet of beef in bordelaise sauce. After dinner, climb the narrow, wrought-iron spiral staircase to the lounge on the second floor—an amiable clutter of leather armchairs and footrests made of old wine kegs, stacks of cordwood, antique lamps, and threadbare carpets—and settle in front of the huge, French country-style fireplace for coffee or a liqueur. There's nothing quite like this anywhere in town. *5-3-1 Shiroganedai, Minato-ku (nearest subway station: Hiroo), tel. 03/3446–4855. Reservations recommended. Dress: informal. AE, DC, MC, V. Open noon–2 and 6–10 (Sun. 6–9). Closed Mon. Expensive.*

Shoto **Chez Matsuo.** Shoto is the kind of area you don't expect Tokyo to have—at least not so close to Shibuya Station. It's a neighborhood of stately homes (the governor of Tokyo's, among them) with walls half a block long, a sort of sedate Beverly Hills. Chez Matsuo occupies the first floor of a lovely old two-story house in Western style. The two dining rooms look out on the garden, where you can dine by candlelight on summer evenings. Owner-chef Matsuo studied his craft in Paris, and in London as a sommelier. His food is nouvelle; the specialty of the house is Supreme of Duck. *1-23-15 Shoto, Shibuya-ku (nearest subway/JR station: Shibuya), tel. 03/3465–0610. Reservations advised. Dress: informal, but jacket suggested. AE, DC, MC, V. Open noon–2:30 (last order at 1) and 6–8. Closed Mon. Very Expensive.*

Toranomon **La Belle Epoque.** The flagship restaurant of the Hotel Okura, across the street from the American embassy, La Belle Epoque is a monument to the Japanese passion for art nouveau, curvilinear and graceful à la Aubrey Beardsley and Gustav Klimt, with panels of stained glass separating the tables into flowered alcoves. A chanson singer holds forth every evening to the strains of a harp and a piano. From the north dining room there's a fine view of the city, with the Eiffel-inspired Tokyo Tower in the foreground. The cuisine is French classique; chef Philippe Mouchel has three-star credentials, having trained at both the Restaurant Paul Bocuse near Lyons and the Moulin de Mougins on the French Riviera. *2-10-4 Toranomon, Minatoku (nearest subway station: Kamiyacho), tel. 03/3505–6073. Reservations required. Jacket and tie required. AE, DC, MC, V. Open 11:30–2:30 and 5:30–9:30. Very Expensive.*

Indian

Akasaka **Moti.** This is the second of three Motis, at last count; the first is in Akasaka-mitsuke, and the most recent is in Roppongi. They all serve the same good Indian cooking, but the Akasaka branch, right by the Chiyoda Line subway station, is the easiest to get into and the most comfortable. Moti has the inevitable Indian friezes, copper bowls, and white elephants, but the owners have not gone overboard on decor: the drawing card here is the food. They recruit their cooks in India through a member of the family who runs a restaurant in Delhi. The vegetarian dishes here, including lentils, eggplant, and cauliflower, are very good; so is the chicken *masala* style, cooked in butter and spices. *Kinpa Bldg. 3F, 2-14-31 Akasaka, Minato-ku (nearest subway station: Akasaka), tel. 03/3584–6640. Reservations advised. Dress: informal. AE, DC, V. Open 11:30–10. Inexpensive.*

Ginza **Ashoka.** The owners of the Ashoka set out to take the high ground—to provide a decor commensurate with its fashionable address. The room is hushed and spacious; incense perfumes the air; the lighting is recessed, and the carpets thick. Floor-to-ceiling windows overlook Chuo-dori, the main street of the Ginza. The waiters have spiffy uniforms; the *thali* (a selection of curries and other specialties of the house) is served up on a figured brass tray. All in all, a good show for the raj. The *khandari nan*, a flat bread with nuts and raisins, is excellent; so is the chicken tikka, boneless chunks marinated and cooked in the *tandoor* (clay oven). *Pearl Bldg. 2F, 7-9-18 Ginza, Chuo-ku (nearest subway station: Ginza), tel. 03/3572–2377. Reser-*

vations advised. Dress: informal. AE, DC, MC, V. Open 11:30–9:30, Sun. noon–8. Inexpensive–Moderate.

Nibancho **Ajanta.** The owner of Ajanta came to Tokyo to study electrical engineering, and he opened a small coffee shop near the Indian embassy. That was about 30 years ago. He used to cook a little for his friends; the coffee shop is now one of the oldest and best Indian restaurants in town. There's no decor to speak of; the emphasis instead is on the variety and intricacy of Indian cooking—and none of its dressier rivals can match Ajanta's menu for sheer depth. The curries are hot to begin with, but you can order them hotter. In one corner, there's a small boutique, where saris and imported Indian foodstuffs are for sale. *3-11 Nibancho, Chiyoda-ku, (nearest subway station: Kojimachi), tel. 03/3264–6955. Reservations advised. Dress: informal. Open 24 hrs. AE, DC, MC, V. Inexpensive–Moderate.*

Indochinese

Meguro **Mekong.** The owner of Mekong fled Cambodia and came to Japan almost two decades ago, and he went to work for a trading company. Later, with the help of some friends, he opened a hole-in-the-wall restaurant near Ebisu, with an eclectic menu of Cambodian, Thai, and Vietnamese cooking. Mekong prospered, and in 1987 it moved to larger quarters in Meguro—but it has remained very much a plastic-tablecloth operation. The selections are few, and the service can be a little disorganized, but at these prices, nobody complains. A menu in English attests to Mekong's popularity with the local foreign community. Try the fried spring rolls and the beef with mustard-leaf pickles. *Koyo Bldg. 2F, 2-16-4 Kamiosaki, Shinagawa-ku (nearest JR station: Meguro), tel. 03/3442–6664. Reservations advised weekends. Dress: informal. V. Open noon–1:30 and 5–11. Inexpensive.*

Indonesian/Malaysian

Roppongi **Bengawan Solo.** The Japanese, whose native aesthetic demands a separate dish and vessel for everything they eat, have to overcome a certain resistance to the idea of *rijsttafel*—a kind of Indonesian smorgasbord of curries, salad, and grilled tidbits that tends to get mixed up on a serving platter. Nevertheless, Bengawan Solo has maintained its popularity with Tokyo residents for about 30 years; this is one of the oldest and most durable restaurants in the city. The parent organization, in Jakarta, supplies the periodic infusion of new staff, as needed. The company also has a thriving import business in Indonesian foodstuffs. Bengawan Solo added a back room some years ago without appreciably reducing the amiable clutter of batik pictures, shadow puppets, carvings, and pennants that make up the decor. The eight-course rijsttafel is spicy-hot and ample; if it doesn't quite stretch for two, order an extra Gado-Gado salad with peanut sauce. *7-18-13 Roppongi, Minato-ku (nearest subway station: Roppongi), tel. 03/3408–5698. Reservations advised. Dress: informal. AE, DC, MC, V. Open Mon.–Sat. 11:30–2:30 and 5–9:45. Moderate.*

Shibuya **Only Malaysia.** Here's a restaurant with an official seal of approval: the Malaysian Ambassador to Japan hires only Malaysia to cater his parties. (Haji Raman, who runs the kitchen, was in fact the former ambassador's chef.) This is a small place (seating for only 45), and not easy to book for dinner—especially on weekends. Try the *ayam* (spicy chicken soup), or the *rendang* (chicken or beef with coriander and chili peppers). *Ikushin Bldg. 3F, 26-5 Udagawa-cho, Shibuya-ku (nearest subway/JR: Shibuya), tel. 03/3496–1177. Reservations recommended. Dress: informal. AE, MC, V. Open daily 11:30–2 and 5:30–9:30. Inexpensive–Moderate.*

International

Ebisu

Ninnikuya. In Japanese, *ninniku* means "garlic"—an ingredient conspicuously absent from the traditional local cuisine and one that the Japanese were once supposed to dislike. Not so nowadays, if you can believe the crowds that cheerfully line up for hours to eat at this cluttered little place in the Ebisu section. Owner-chef Eiyuki Endo discovered his own passion for the savory bulb in Italy in 1976. Since then, he has traveled the world for interesting garlic dishes. Endo's family owns the building, so he can give free rein to his artistry without charging a lot. There is no decor to speak of, and you may well have to share a table. Good fun. Ninnikuya is a little hard to find, but anybody you ask in the neighborhood can point the way. Try the littleneck clams Italian-style with garlic rice, or the Peruvian garlic chicken. *1-26-12 Ebisu, Shibuya-ku (nearest subway: Ebisu), tel. 03/3446–5887. No reservations. Dress: informal. No credit cards. Open Mon.–Sat. 6:15–10:30. Moderate.*

Italian

Akasaka

La Granata. Located on the basement level of the Tokyo Broadcasting Systems building, La Granata and its companion restaurant Granata Moderna are both very popular with the media crowd upstairs. Deservedly so: they offer some of the most accomplished, professional Italian food in town. La Granata is decked out in trattoria style, with brickwork arches and red checkered tablecloths; Granata Moderna has the same menu, but reaches for elegance with a polished rosewood bar, Art Deco mirrors, and stained glass. Specialties worth trying include the spaghetti with garlic and red pepper and the batter-fried zucchini flowers filled with mozzarella and asparagus. *TBS Kaikan B1, 5-3-3 Akasaka, Minato-ku (nearest subway: Akasaka), tel. 03/3582–5891. Reservations advised. Dress: informal. AE, MC, V. Open 11–9:30. Moderate–Expensive.*

Ichigaya

Carmine's. Everybody pitched in, so the story goes, when Carmine Cozzolino opened this unpretentious little neighborhood restaurant in 1987: Friends designed the logo and the interior, painted the walls (black and white), and hung the graphics, swapping their labor for meals. Good meals, too. For a real Italian gourmet five-course dinner, this could be the best deal in town. Specialties of the house include pasta twists with tomato and caper sauce, and veal scaloppine à la Marsala. Carmine's tiramisu is a serious dessert. Not easy to find, but well worth the effort. *1-19 Saiku-cho, Shinjuku-ku (nearest subway: Kagurazaka), tel. 03/3260–5066. Reservations recommended. Dress: informal. No credit cards. Open Mon.–Sat. noon–2 and 6–10. Lunch: Inexpensive; Dinner: Moderate.*

Kyobashi ★

Attore. The Italian restaurant of the elegant Seiyo Hotel, Attore is divided into two sections. The "casual" side, with seating for 60, has a bar counter, banquettes, and a see-through glass wall to the kitchen; the comfortable decor is achieved with track lighting, potted plants, marble floors, and Indian-looking print tablecloths. The "formal" side, with seating for 40, has mauve wall panels and carpets, armchairs, and soft, recessed lighting. On either side of the room, you get what is hands-down the best Italian cuisine in Tokyo. Chef Katsuyuki Muroi trained for six years in Tuscany and northern Italy and acquired a wonderful repertoire. Try the pâté of pheasant and porcini mushrooms with white truffle cheese sauce, or the walnut-smoked lamb chops with sun-dried tomatoes. *1-11-2 Ginza Chuo-ku (nearest subway: Ginza), tel. 03/3535-1111. Reservations advised. Jacket and tie suggested. AE, DC, MC, V. Open 11–10. Very Expensive.*

Korean

Azabu Ju-ban **Sankoen.** With the embassy of the Republic of Korea a few blocks away, Sankoen is in a neighborhood thick with barbecue joints; not much seems to distinguish one from another. About 10 years ago, however, Sankoen suddenly caught on, and people started coming in droves. Not just the neighborhood families showed up, but also customers who worked in the media industry. The Sankoen opened a branch, then moved the main operation across the street to new, two-story quarters. Korean barbecue is a smoky affair; you cook your own dinner—thin slices of beef and special cuts of meat—on a gas grill at your table. Sankoen also makes a great salad to go with its brisket. *1-8-7 Azabu Ju-ban, Minato-ku (nearest subway: Roppongi), tel. 03/3585-6306. No reservations. Dress: casual. AE, V. Open 11:30 AM–1:30 AM, Sun. 11:30 AM–Midnight. Closed Wed. Moderate–Expensive.*

Russian

Ginza **Balalaika.** With all the astonishing, radical changes taking place these days in what used to be the Soviet Union, someone may come up with a nouvelle version of Russian cooking. Until then, this is the place to go when you are truly seriously hungry. The Balalaika is by no means cheap, but it serves an excellent sort of ballast, if you have the room to stow it away. For example: *blinchiki*, small, sweet pancakes with garnishes of red and black caviar; *solyanka*, a savory broth with sausages and vegetables, which is just the thing to sop up with the Balalaika's excellent black bread; chicken Kiev; and *walenicki*, crescent-shaped pastries filled with cheese and topped with sour cream. What atmosphere there is here is provided by the Balalaika Trio, which holds forth every evening from 6 PM. Off the main dining room, simply furnished and softly lighted, are three small banquet rooms for private parties. *5-9-9 Ginza, Chuo-ku (nearest subway: Ginza), tel. 03/3572-8387. Reservations advised weekends. Dress: informal. AE, DC, MC. V. Open 11:30–2 and 5–10:30 (Sun. 5–9:30). Expensive.*

Spanish

Aoyama **El Castellano.** Owner Vicente, a native of Toledo who opened El Castellano in the late 1980s, doesn't advertise much; he relies instead on word of mouth. He runs a warm, friendly, cluttered place where Tokyo's Spanish residents come to eat. There's room here for perhaps 30 (elbow to elbow), and the word of mouth has gotten around well enough to pack it almost every night. No pretensions to elegance here: the once-whitewashed walls are covered with messages of appreciation scrawled with felt-tip pens, accented here and there with the inevitable bullfight posters, painted crockery, and photographs of Spanish soccer teams. Try the paella and a salad, with a jug of Spanish wine: a no-frills, satisfying meal. *Marusan Aoyama Bldg. 2F, 2-9-11 Shibuya, Shibuya-ku (nearest subway: Omotesando), tel. 03/3407-7197. Reservations advised. Dress: informal. No credit cards. Open 6–10. Closed Sun. and holidays. Moderate.*

Shibuya **Patio Flamenco.** This establishment rates less for its cuisine (good but not memorable) than for its dinner show. Owner Yoko Komatsubara, for many years Japan's leading professional flamenco dancer, travels regularly to Spain to find the talented singers, dancers, and guitarists who hold forth here nightly. A small room with seating for perhaps 30, the Patio Flamenco makes you feel as if you have the show to yourself. The specialty of the house is the paella Valenciana, with shrimp, squid, and mussels. Performances begin at 7:30, 9, and 10:15; expect a separate cover charge of ¥2,600 per person for the entertainment. *2-10-12 Dogenzaka, Shibuya-ku (nearest subway/JR station: Shibuya), tel. 03/3496-2753. Reservations advised. Dress: informal. AE, DC, MC, V. Open 5:30–10. Expensive.*

Shiroganedai **Sabado Sabadete.** Catalonia-born jewelry designer Mañuel Benito loves to cook. For a while, he indulged this passion by renting out a bar on Saturday nights and making an enormous *paella* for his friends; to keep them happy while they were waiting, he added a few *tapas* (Spanish-style hors d'oeuvres). Word got around: by 8 it was standing room only, and by 9 there wasn't room in the bar to lift a fork. Inspired by this success, Benito found a trendy location and opened his Sabado Sabadete full-time in 1991. The highlight of every evening is still the moment when the chef, in his bright-red Catalan cap, shouts out the Japanese equivalent of "soup's on!" and dishes out his bubbling-hot *paella.* Don't miss the *empañadas* (3-cornered pastries stuffed with minced beef and vegetables) or the *escalivada* (a Spanish ratatouille with red peppers, onions, and eggplant). *Genteel Shiroganedai Bldg. 2F, 5-3-2 Shiroganedai, Minato-ku (nearest subway: Hiroo), tel. 03/3445-9353. Reservations advised. No credit cards. Open 6–10. Closed Sun. and holidays. Moderate.*

Swedish

Azabu **Lilla Dalarna.** The original Dalarna, out in the suburbs of Tokyo, was the brainchild of Seiichi Okubo, who, when most of his adventurous contemporaries were wandering through France and Italy, somehow wound up in Sweden. He honed his craft for ten years in a series of Stockholm restaurants, then returned to Tokyo and opened a sort of country inn, with two long wooden tables where his customers could eat family-style. He did so well that he was able to open a branch a few minute's walk from the trendy Roppongi district. The effect here is cozy-cute, achieved mostly with plants, whitewash, and Scandinavian knicknacks. The food is basic and plentiful. Try the meatballs and potatoes, or the sausages with bell peppers. *5-9-19 Roppongi, Minato-ku (nearest subway: Roppongi), tel. 03/3478-4690. Reservations recommended. Dress: informal. AE, DC, MC, V. Open noon–3 and 6–9:30. Moderate.*

Thai

Hiroo ★ **Gold Leaf.** The hottest gastronomic fad in Tokyo now-a-days, literally and figuratively, is "ethnic"; in effect, that's meant a welcome profusion of good new Thai restaurants—among which the Gold Leaf (as the name implies) is probably the most elegant. Gleaming hardwood floors, black-laquered furniture, and fine linen complete the decor. The two chefs, trained in the cooking school of the famed Oriental Hotel in Bangkok, prepare a decidedly upscale version of this spicy yet subtle traditional cuisine. Try the prawn soup and the green curry with chicken. *Taisei-Koki Bldg. B1, 5-4-12 Hiroo, Shibuya-ku (nearest subway: Hiroo), tel. 03/3447-1212. Reservations advised. Dress: informal. AE, DC, MC, V. Open noon-2 and 5:30-9:45 (9:15 Sun.). Moderate-Expensive.*

Lodging

When you select a hotel in Tokyo, you should focus on three factors: the hotel's location, the size of its rooms, and the costliness of the capital city. Three factors of minimal concern are cleanliness, safety, and helpful service, because these attributes may be found at practically all Japanese hotels.

The general location of the hotel has a considerable effect on the price charged for a room. Real estate throughout Tokyo is horrendously expensive, and the more central the location, the more outrageous is the cost of a square yard. Consequently, hotel prices in the central Imperial Palace and Ginza districts (in Chiyoda-ku ward) reflect the area's super-expensive real estate. On a business trip to Tokyo it may make sense to select a hotel close to where one's business partners are located, but for the visitor, the hotel's location may be only marginally important. Bear in mind that, except for rush hour, Tokyo's subway and train system is comfortable and always rapid, inexpensive, safe, and efficient. The only drawback is that trains stop running at midnight.

As a working estimate, expect to pay about ¥350 for each square foot of your hotel guest room, with this price decreasing as you move away from central Tokyo. Because anything less than 65 square feet is small for a double room, expect around ¥23,000 for what one may consider an average room. Less expensive hotels offer fewer services and a more basic decor than do expensive hotels. This affects the cost of the guest room (on a square-foot basis) less than one might imagine. The larger hotels make more of their profits from the banquet and dining facilities than from the guest rooms. The cost of the extra services is not part of the room rate. Consequently, even though the deluxe hotels do charge a high price for the guest rooms, in one sense they give more for the yen than do the less expensive hotels. Of course, that's all very well, but one must be willing to pay ¥26,000 and more to enjoy the bargain!

In other words, rather than selecting an inexpensive hotel in a central location, consider a better hotel in one of the city subcenters: Roppongi, Shinjuku, Ikebukuro, Meguro, and Asakusa all offer quite acceptable choices.

In Tokyo, hotels may be divided into six categories: first-class (full-service) hotel, business hotel, ryokan, capsule hotel, youth hostel, and pink hotel.

First-class (full-service) **hotels** are exactly what you would expect; most of them tend also to be priced in the Expensive and Very Expensive categories. Virtually all of these full-service hotels have several restaurants offering different national cuisines, room service, direct-dial telephone and another phone in the bathroom, minibars, a *yakuta* (cotton bedroom kimono), concierge service, and porters. Most of the larger full-service hotels are now equipped with a business center and a physical fitness center. A few also have swimming pools. At least 90% of the guest rooms are Western style. Usually a few token Japanese rooms (tatami mats and futons) are available, and these are offered at a higher price than the other rooms.

Business hotels are found throughout Japan; Tokyo has an ample supply of them. Business hotels are designed primarily for the traveler who needs a room in which to leave his luggage, sleep, and take a quick shower or bath. Guest rooms are never large; some are tiny. A single traveler will often take a small double room rather than suffer claustrophobia in a single room. Each room has a telephone, a small writing desk, a television (sometimes the pay-as-you-watch variety), slippers, a yakuta, and a private bathroom. These bathrooms are small, plastic, prefabricated units with tub, shower, and washbasin; they are invariably scrupulously clean. The hotel's facilities are limited usually to one restaurant and a 24-hour receptionist, with no room service or porters. Since the definition of a business hotel is relative, the listing below has not separated them into a special category. However, most of those hotels listed in the Moderate price category could be classified as business hotels.

Ryokan have lost their strict meaning as a more personal hotel where guests are served dinner and breakfast in their rooms. Some are still like that, but often they mean any hostelry that offers rooms with tatami mats on the floors and futons. They may or may not serve meals in the room. Those listed in the Tokyo section do not. All are of the frugal variety, often family-run. Many of them have rooms with and without bath, and service stems from goodwill, not from professionalism. Because they have few rooms and the owners are usually on hand to answer their guests' questions, these small, relatively inexpensive ryokan are very hospitable places to stay.

Capsule hotels are literally plastic cubicles stacked on top of each other. They are used by very junior business travelers or commuters who have missed their last train home. Guests crawl into their capsule, which has a small bed, an intercom, and a radio. Washing and toilet facilities are shared. (Very rarely, a capsule hotel will have a separate floor for women; otherwise, women are not admitted.) One such place is **Green Plaza Shinjuku** (1-29-2 Kabukicho, Shinjuku-ku, tel. 03/3207–5411), two minutes from Shinjuku Station. It is the largest of its kind, with 660 sleeping slots. Checking out in the morning is pandemonium. A rush of bleary-eyed businessmen clamor to settle their accounts and scurry sheepishly to their offices. A night's stay in a capsule is about ¥4,100.

Pink hotels are "love" hotels, where rooms are rented by the hour. However, after the peak time (around 9 PM), one can sometimes rent (very inexpensively, about ¥4,000–¥5,000, depending on your negotiating skills) a room for the entire night. Be aware, though, that if you do not leave by the agreed-upon time in the morning, your extra time will be charged at the hourly rate! They are, by the way, spotlessly clean. These pink hotels are easily recognized by their garish facades and are usually located near the entertainment quarters—several may be found in Kabukicho (Shinjuku), Roppongi, and along the suburban highways. In Shinjuku, one such hotel, the **Hotel Perrier** (2-7-12 Kabukicho, Shinjuku-ku, tel. 03/3207–5921), has rooms with saunas and various scintillating decors—one room, the Galaxy Room, has lights that turn on and off with the sound of your voice.

Separate categories are provided in this section for (1) hotels near Narita Airport and (2) youth hostels and dormitory accommodations. All rooms at the hotels listed below have private baths, unless otherwise specified.

A 3% federal consumer tax is added to all hotel bills. Another 3% local tax is added to the bill if it exceeds ¥15,000. At most hotels, a 10%–15% service charge is added to the total bill. Tipping is not necessary.

The most highly recommended accommodations are indicated by a star ★.

Category	Cost*
Very Expensive	over ¥30,000
Expensive	¥21,000–¥30,000
Moderate	¥10,000–¥21,000
Inexpensive	under ¥10,000

**Cost is for a double room, without tax or service*

Very Expensive

Akasaka Prince Hotel. This 40-story building on top of a small hill has an eye-catching design. The architect is the well-known Kenzo Tange, who completed this ultramodern building in 1983. It may be considered either coldly sterile or classical in the simplicity of its half-moon shape; all the guest rooms (the higher up, the better) have wide, sweeping views of Tokyo. The decor of white and pastel grays in the guest rooms accentuates the light from the wide windows that run the length of the room. The result is a feeling of spaciousness, though the rooms are no larger in size than those in other deluxe hotels. A welcome feature is the dressing mirror and sink in an alcove before the bathroom. The marble and off-white reception areas on the ground floor are pristine. The hotel's whole atmosphere is crisp, but a little impersonal; it's ideal for the clusters of people at large weddings and convention parties. The Grand Ballroom can accommodate up to 2,500 guests. *1-2 Kioi-cho, Chiyoda-ku, Tokyo 102 (nearest subway: Akasaka-mitsuke), tel. 03/3234–1111, fax 03/3205–1956. 761 rooms, most Western style. Facilities: 12 restaurants, including the Blue Gardenia on the 40th floor, which serves Continental food; the Top of Akasaka for cocktails, with spectacular views of Tokyo's skyline; and a French restaurant, Le Trianon, in the old gatehouse to the side*

Tokyo Lodging
Mejiro
Mejiro-dori Ave.
Gokokuji
Koishikawa Botanical Gardens
Hongo-dori Ave.
Hakusan-dori Ave.
Myogadani
Uguisudani
UENO
Ueno Park
Showa-dori Ave.
ASAKUSA
Kappabashi-dori Ave.
Takadanobaba
Edogawabashi
Ueno
Asakusa-dori Ave.
Inaricho
Tawaramachi
Asakusa
Waseda
Waseda-dori Ave.
Korakuen
Korakuen Garden
Kasuga-dori Ave.
YUSHIMA
Hongo-sanchome
Okachi-machi
Kiyosubashi-dori Ave.
Kuramae-dori Ave.
Kagurazaka
Iidabashi
Suidobashi
Shin-Okubo
Okubo
Seibu-Shinjuku
Ochano-mizu
AKIHABARA
Akihabara
Asakusa-bashi
Ome-kaido Ave.
SHINJUKU
Jimbocho
JIMBOCHO
Shinjuku
Akebonobashi
Yashukuni-dori Ave.
Ichigaya
Kanda
ICHIBAN-CHO
Shinjuku-dori Ave.
Yotsuya
Yoyogi
Shinjuku Gyoen Garden
IMPERIAL PALACE
HAMA-CHO
Nihombashi
NIHOMBASHI
Tokyo
Sendagaya
Shinanomachi
Meiji Shrine Inner Garden
Meiji-dori Ave.
Meiji Shrine Outer Garden
Akasaka Palace
Uchibori-dori Ave.
Chuo-dori Ave.
Showa-dori Ave.
River
Sumidagawa
Akasaka-mitsuke
Sotobori-dori Ave.
Aoyama-dori Ave.
Aoyama-Itchome
AKASAKA
Hibiya
Hibiya Park
YURAKUCHO
Yurakucho
Ginza
EITAI
Eitai-dori
Yoyogi Park
Harajuku
HARAJUKU
Meiji-jingu-
Gaie
Akasaka
AE
1
2
3
4
5
6
7
8
9
10
11
12
13
14
15
16
17
18
19
20
21
22
23
24
25

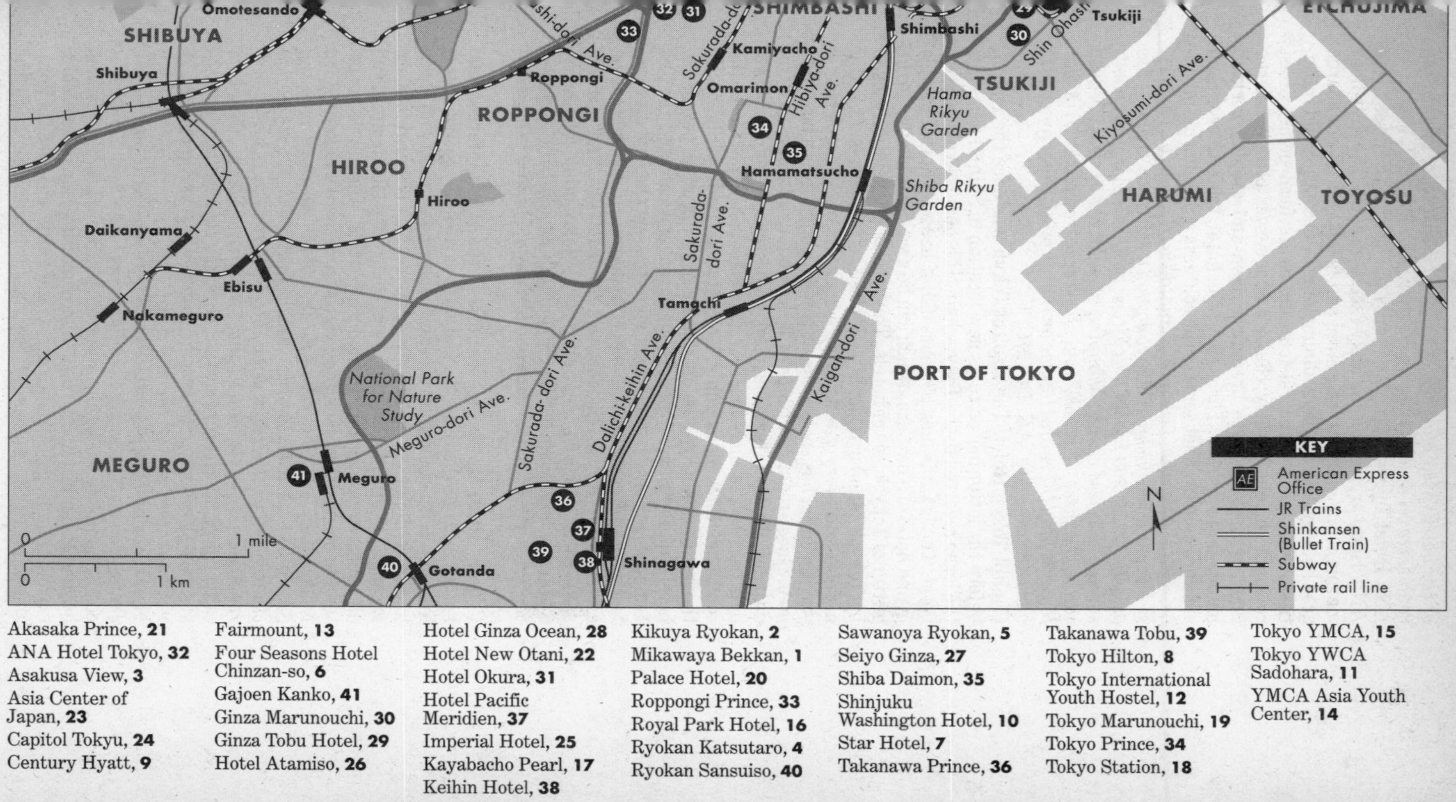

Akasaka Prince, **21**
ANA Hotel Tokyo, **32**
Asakusa View, **3**
Asia Center of Japan, **23**
Capitol Tokyu, **24**
Century Hyatt, **9**
Fairmount, **13**
Four Seasons Hotel Chinzan-so, **6**
Gajoen Kanko, **41**
Ginza Marunouchi, **30**
Ginza Tobu Hotel, **29**
Hotel Atamiso, **26**
Hotel Ginza Ocean, **28**
Hotel New Otani, **22**
Hotel Okura, **31**
Hotel Pacific Meridien, **37**
Imperial Hotel, **25**
Kayabacho Pearl, **17**
Keihin Hotel, **38**
Kikuya Ryokan, **2**
Mikawaya Bekkan, **1**
Palace Hotel, **20**
Roppongi Prince, **33**
Royal Park Hotel, **16**
Ryokan Katsutaro, **4**
Ryokan Sansuiso, **40**
Sawanoya Ryokan, **5**
Seiyo Ginza, **27**
Shiba Daimon, **35**
Shinjuku Washington Hotel, **10**
Star Hotel, **7**
Takanawa Prince, **36**
Takanawa Tobu, **39**
Tokyo Hilton, **8**
Tokyo International Youth Hostel, **12**
Tokyo Marunouchi, **19**
Tokyo Prince, **34**
Tokyo Station, **18**
Tokyo YMCA, **15**
Tokyo YWCA Sadohara, **11**
YMCA Asia Youth Center, **14**

of the hotel. Also massage service, dry cleaning, 30 meeting rooms, travel desk, banquet facilities. AE, DC, MC, V.

ANA Hotel Tokyo. In the proximity of the U.S. Embassy, the ANA Hotel arrived on the Tokyo scene in 1986. The first-floor marble lobby clamors for glitter and fashion; it covers a large area split by a coffee shop, dining lounge, escalator, and reception desks, with a central fountain as its focal point. Guest rooms are bright and airy; the 34th floor serves as the concierge floor, with a separate breakfast room and evening cocktail lounge for its guests. Throughout the hotel, tasteful vases and artwork help to offset some of the coldness of the marble interior. *12-33 Akasaka 1-chome, Minato-ku, Tokyo 107 (nearest subways: Kamiyacho and Toranomon), tel. 03/3505–1111, fax 03/3505–1155. 900 rooms. Facilities: gym, outdoor pool, men's sauna, business center, shopping arcade, travel desk, beauty salon, Chinese, French, and Japanese restaurants, 3 bar lounges, and the Astral lounge on the top (37th) floor for superb views over the city. AE, DC, MC, V.*

Capitol Tokyu Hotel. The Capitol Tokyu was once the Hilton, before the latter moved to its new location in Shinjuku in 1984; the lease reverted to the Tokyu chain. It is now Tokyu's flagship hotel. Though it is only 29 years old, it has a feeling of being a grand hotel of a past era, which can be a welcome change to the glitter of Tokyo's newer hotels. The hotel is also relatively small by Tokyo's standards, and, with close to two permanent staff members to every guest, service is excellent. Perhaps that is why the hotel has such a repeat trade among foreign businessmen. Guest-room furnishings (dark wood furniture) have a traditional Western feel, but the shoji screens add a warm lightness to the ambience. As an extra benefit, some of the rooms, no. 1039, for example, look onto the Hie Jinja Shrine. To the left of the lobby is a small garden with a pond; two of the hotel's dining rooms (the Origami breakfast café and the Tea Lounge) look onto it (a pleasant sight to start the day at breakfast). *10-3 Nagatacho 2-chome, Chiyoda-ku, Tokyo 100 (nearest subway: Kokkai-gijidomae), tel. 03/3581–4511, fax 03/3581–5822. 459 rooms. Facilities: 8 restaurants (including Chinese, Continental, French, and Japanese), bars, business center, steam bath, massage in one's room, outdoor pool, small shopping arcade. AE, DC.*

Century Hyatt Hotel. This member of the Hyatt international hotel chain has the trademark atrium-style lobby—seven stories high, with open-glass elevators soaring upward and three huge chandeliers suspended from above. The larger rooms are arranged to offer the semblance of a separate sitting area, and all rooms are decorated in modern pastels. The single rooms tend to be small and lack good views from their windows. *2-7-2 Nishi-Shinjuku, Shinjuku-ku, Tokyo 160 (nearest subway: Shinjuku), tel. 03/3349–0111, fax 03/3344–5575. 774 rooms, including a few luxurious Japanese-style rooms, 1- and 2-bedroom Western-style suites, and 2 concierge floors. Facilities: indoor pool, 12 restaurants and bars; the Hyatt places emphasis on its cuisine, with special gourmet weeks supervised by visiting international chefs. AE, DC, MC, V.*

★ **Four Seasons Hotel Chinzan-so.** Where else will you have a chance to sleep in a million-dollar room? That's about what it cost to complete each guest room at this Tokyo property, which opened in January 1992. Dark-wood furniture, plush carpeting, ceramic lamps, gold-frame prints, and yards and yards of floral chintz make these some of the classiest hotel rooms in the world. Not surprisingly they were decorated by Frank Nicholson, Inc., which also designed rooms for the Chicago Ritz-Carlton. Most of the furnishings are American, complemented by Japanese accessories (lamps, ashtrays, tea sets, and so on). The rooms are large by any standard and have bathrooms that are equally grand. These have cream-marble walls and floor, with gold-tone fixtures and a separate toilet room with an electronically controlled toilet/bidet. In the wainscotted lobby there's a green-marble floor from Italy covered by huge wool area rugs woven in Ireland. For some, the best part about the Four Seasons is its setting, in the beautiful Chinzan-so Gardens. The hotel makes it easy to get downtown by offering complimentary shuttle-bus service to the subway station and complimentary limousine service to Tokyo Station. *2-10-8 Sekiguchi, Bunkyo-ku, Tokyo 112, tel. 03/3943–2222 or 800/332–3442, fax 03/3943–2300. 284 rooms, 2 Japanese-style suites. Facilities: 4 restaurants, bar, lounge, Japanese baths, massage, Jacuzzi, indoor pool, gym, barbershop, salon, shops, ballroom and meeting rooms, Shinto and Christian chapels. AE, DC, MC, V.*

Ginza Tobu Hotel. This hotel's relatively reasonable prices, friendly service, and comfortably sized rooms make it worth considering as a deluxe hotel in the high-rent district of Ginza. The higher price of the concierge floors provides a much larger room; breakfast, afternoon tea, and complimentary cocktails in the concierge lounge; and extras, such as a terry-cloth bathrobe and hair dryers. Especially useful is the hotel's 24-hour coffeehouse restaurant. *6-13-10 Ginza, Chuo-ku, Tokyo 104 (nearest subway: Higashi-Ginza), tel. 03/3546–0111, fax 03/3546–8990. 206 rooms, all Western style. 2 concierge floors. Facilities: 24-hour coffeehouse, French restaurant, excellent Japanese restaurant (The Muraki), business center. AE, DC, MC, V.*

Hotel New Otani Tokyo and Tower. The New Otani is virtually a town in itself. When all the rooms (almost 2,100) are occupied and all the banquet facilities are in use, the traffic flow in and out of the restaurants, lounges, and shopping arcades is like rush hour at a busy railway station. The hotel's redeeming feature is its peaceful, 10-acre manicured garden. *4-1 Kioi-cho, Chiyoda-ku, Tokyo 102 (nearest subway: Akasaka-mitsuke), tel. 03/3265–1111, fax 03/3221–2619. 2,051 rooms, 30 on the 21st floor for women only. Facilities: outdoor pool, spa facilities (includes a sports and beauty complex), rooms for the physically handicapped, 24-hour child-care facilities, Christian chapel, shopping arcades, banking facilities, numerous restaurants (including Japan's first Trader Vic's and the revolving Sky Lounge, which completes one revolution every hour). AE, DC, MC, V.*

★ **Hotel Okura.** As one of the most prestigious of Tokyo hotels, the Okura is continually striving to maintain a position at the top. The Okura is understated in its sophistication, except for its vast lobby. Ever since it was completed just before the 1964 Olympics, the Okura has been a favorite of the diplomatic and knowledgeable business traveler. The atmosphere is traditional, even old-fashioned to some, and the emphasis is on exemplary service. The spacious guest rooms are tastefully furnished, including sliding frosted shoji screens in front of the windows, which permits a relaxing light to fill the room. Remote-control draperies, hair dryers, and terry-cloth bathrobes are but a few of the extras that come with the room. The odd-numbered rooms, 871–889 inclusive, look onto a small Japanese landscaped garden. On the hotel grounds is the Okura Art Museum, in a traditional Japanese building, with exhibits of antique porcelain, mother-of-pearl, and ceramics. A tea ceremony is held every day 11 AM–noon and 1 PM–5 PM. In recent years, the Okura has added the South Wing, which is slightly detached from most of the hotel's facilities; the main building is preferable. *10-4 Toranomon 2-chome, Minato-ku, Tokyo 105 (nearest subways: Kamiyacho and Toranomon), tel. 03/3582–0111, fax 03/3582–3707. 883 rooms (including 83 suites and 11 superb Japanese-style rooms). Facilities: gym, indoor (heated) and outdoor pools, steam bath, masseur, business center, 8 restaurants (French, Chinese, Japanese, etc.), extensive banquet facilities. AE, DC, MC, V.*

Imperial Hotel. The location of this prestigious establishment could not be better—in the heart of central Tokyo, between the Imperial Palace and Ginza. You can exit from the rear of the hotel and be in the center of the city's shopping and restaurant district. If you exit from the front of the hotel and walk five minutes, you can begin jogging around the grounds of the Imperial Palace. Guest rooms are newly furnished with the choicest rooms high up (on the 30th floor) in the New Tower; these afford views of the Imperial Palace. The lobby has a vast lounge area for watching Tokyo's beautiful people. The shopping arcade has prestigious boutiques, while the restaurants are some of Tokyo's finest and most sophisticated. A particularly memorable place to meet acquaintances before dinner is the Old Imperial Bar, with artifacts from the former Imperial building, designed by Frank Lloyd Wright. From its outset (the Imperial opened its doors in 1891), the hotel has been justly proud of its Western-style facilities and Japanese service. Now, with its new tower addition, the hotel is a vast complex, but it still retains its personalized service. *1-1 Uchisaiwaicho 1-chome, Chiyoda-ku, Tokyo 100 (nearest subways: Hibiya and Yurakucho), tel. 03/3504–1111, fax 03/3581–9146. 1,058 rooms, which range from standard twin size to suites that are larger than many homes. Facilities: indoor pool, fitness center, and masseur on the 20th floor; 64 boutiques in the shopping arcade; business center; limousine service; 21 restaurants and bars, though none stays open 24 hours a day. AE, DC, MC, V.*

★ **Palace Hotel.** This is a less expensive alternative to the Imperial Hotel for anyone wanting a deluxe hotel near the Imperial Palace. Service is extremely helpful and professional; half the staff has been with the hotel for more than 10 years. The location is as close to the Imperial Palace as one could be; only a water-filled moat separates the hotel from the palace grounds. On the other hand, it is a taxi or subway ride to the bright lights of Ginza, or anywhere else, for that matter. The sedate, calm atmosphere of the hotel reflects its over 50 years as a leading Tokyo accommodation. The guest rooms are reasonably spacious; those on the upper floors facing the Imperial Palace are definitely preferred. The hotel's public areas are rectangular and uninspiring. Nevertheless, location and good value make it particularly attractive to businessmen who want to be close to downtown. *1-1-1 Marunouchi, Chiyoda-ku, Tokyo 100 (nearest subway: Tokyo), tel. 03/3211–5211, fax 03/3211–6987. 405 rooms. Facilities: business center, shopping arcade, 7 restaurants (including French, Japanese, and Chinese), 3 bars, 2 lounges. AE, DC, MC, V.*

Seiyo Ginza. Location and personalized service are the two reasons to choose this shockingly expensive hotel. Right in the heart of Ginza, it is designed for those traveling on a generous expense account who want to be close to their Ginza appointments, as well as the shopping and nightlife of the area, and who need a personal secretary to take care of their every need (each room has a direct line to a secretary). Standard rooms and one-bedroom suites are smaller than what Americans might expect for this price, but the modern furnishings and quiet beige-and-peach decor make the rooms seem larger. Although the hotel is now five years old, and the hallway carpeting is beginning to show signs of wear, guest rooms have held up well. White-marble bathrooms are sparkling clean; those in the suites have steam showers. With only 79 rooms, the Seiyo Ginza is quiet and private, almost like a luxury apartment complex but with 220 courteous attendants aiming to make your stay just right. Double rooms start at ¥55,000. *1-11-2 Ginza, Chuo-ku, Tokyo 104, (nearest subway: Ginza), tel. 03/3535–1111, fax 03/3535–1110. 79 rooms. Facilities: 4 restaurants (including the Pastorale, which may rank as one of Tokyo's best and most expensive—dinner with wine, an easy ¥50,000 for 2), bar, lounge, banquet hall, cake shop, business services, 24-hour fitness center. AE, DC, MC, V.*

Tokyo Hilton Hotel. Built in 1984, this is the newest of the three deluxe Shinjuku skyscraper hotels and is the largest Hilton in Asia. The Hilton is frequented by Western businessmen. The atmosphere of its public areas is one of impersonal efficiency. However, the guest rooms offer good views of the other Shinjuku skyscrapers and benefit from using shoji screens instead of curtains. The Imari Room, with its displays of museum-quality traditional pottery, is one of Tokyo's more elegant places to dine. *6-2 Nishi-Shinjuku 6-chome, Shinjuku-ku, Tokyo 160 (nearest subway: Shinjuku), tel. 03/3344–5111, fax 03/3342–6094. 807 rooms, including the concierge floor. Facilities: sauna, indoor and outdoor pools, business center, small shopping arcade, beauty salon, 8 restaurants (including American, Mediterranean, Chinese, Continental, and Japanese), disco, nightclub cabaret. AE, DC, MC, V.*

Expensive

Asakusa View Hotel. If you want an elegant place to stay in the heart of Tokyo's old Asakusa area—actually resurrected after the World War II fire bombings—then this hotel is the only choice. A smart marble lobby features a harpist in the tea lounge, and expensive boutiques line the second floor. The standard pastel guest rooms are similar to what you find in all modern Tokyo hotels, but you also have access to communal *hinoki* (Japanese cypress) bathtubs that look onto a sixth-floor Japanese garden. *3-17-1 Nishi-Asakusa, Taito-ku, Tokyo 111 (nearest subway: Tawaramachi), tel. 03/3847–1111, fax 03/3845–0530. 350 rooms, mostly Western style. Concierge floor. Facilities: Chinese, French, Italian, and Japanese restaurants, coffee lounge, outdoor pool, a bar that keeps your personal bottle, gym and fitness center, banquet rooms. AE, DC, MC, V.*

★ **Fairmount Hotel.** Nostalgia buffs will love the Fairmount; here's a place that underwent a major renovation in 1988 and the water pipes are still exposed. Neatly wrapped and painted, of course, but exposed just the same. In relentlessly high-tech Tokyo, you'd have to look long for a hotel with pull-chain ventilators and real tile in the bathrooms. The Fairmount has all that and furniture (a little chipped) that Sears & Roebuck must have phased out of the catalog in 1955. The hotel isn't seedy, mind you, just old (it was built in 1951) and a bit set in its ways. The best thing about the seven-story Fairmount is its frontage on the park that runs along the east side of the Imperial Palace grounds; rooms facing the park have a wonderful view of the moat and Chidoriga-fuchi pond, where Tokyo couples take rented rowboats out on summer Sunday afternoons. *2-1-17 Kudan-Minami, Chiyoda-ku Tokyo 102 (nearest subway: Kudanshita), tel. 03/3262–1151, fax 03/3264–2476. 205 rooms, 3 suites. Facilities: restaurant, bar. AE, DC, MC, V.*

Ginza Marunouchi Hotel. This establishment opened in 1976 and immediately became popular with foreign visitors because of its price and its location to the side of Ginza's high-rent district. Recent redecorating has improved this small hotel. Guest rooms are small, compact, and clean. Except when a large tour group arrives, the lobby/lounge area invites a shared fellowship among the guests. *1-12 Tsukiji 4-chome, Chuo-ku, Tokyo 104 (nearest subway: Higashi-Ginza), tel. 03/3543–5431, fax 03/3543–6006. 114 rooms. Facilities: Western restaurant. AE, DC, MC, V.*

Hotel Pacific Meridien. Located on grounds that were once part of the imperial family's estate, the Pacific Meridien is across from the Shinagawa Station and glitters with glass and marble. The hotel markets itself to convention groups and to business travelers who wish to be in this area of Tokyo. Decor is pastel and lilac all the way to the Sky Lounge on the 30th floor, which has views over Tokyo Bay. The coffee lounge on the ground floor offers a tranquil view of the gardens. *3-13-3 Takanawa, Minato-ku, Tokyo 108 (nearest JR station: Shinagawa), tel. 03/3445–6711, fax 03/3445–5137. 954 rooms. Facilities: 9 restaurants and bars, outdoor pool, shopping arcade (good bookstore with English-language books), business center, banquet halls, parking garage, large Japanese garden. AE, DC, MC, V.*

Roppongi Prince Hotel. The most memorable feature of the Roppongi Prince is a swimming pool in its open central courtyard. A solar mirror directs sunshine into the courtyard, and the pool's surrounding decks have their floors heated. The sides of the pool are made of transparent Plexiglas. The swimmer, above and below water, becomes the visual entertainment for voyeurs sitting around the pool or in one of the two café/restaurants off to the side. The remaining facilities, including the rooms, are functional rather than memorable. However, for the price, the rooms are relatively spacious. In a good location, the hotel is in walking distance of either the IBM building (for business) or Roppongi (for partying). *2-7 Roppongi 3-chome, Minato-ku, Tokyo 106 (nearest subway: Roppongi), tel. 03/3587–1111, fax 03/3587–0770. 221 rooms. Facilities: Italian, Western, and Japanese restaurants; discounted tickets to Roppongi's discos; pool. AE, DC, MC, V.*

Royal Park Hotel. This hotel would recommend itself if only for the connecting passageway to the Tokyo City Air Terminal where you can complete all your check-in procedures before you climb on the bus for Narita Airport. There's no luxury—especially at the end of an intensive business trip—like being able to pack, ring for the bellhop, and not have to touch your baggage again until it comes off the conveyor belt back home. Built in 1989, the 20-story Royal Park is well-designed: The large, open lobby has perhaps a bit more marble than it needs, and the inevitable space-age chandelier, but this is offset by wood-paneled columns, brass trim, and lots of comfortable lounge space. Guest rooms, done in coordinated neutral grays and browns, have good proportions; deluxe twins have handsome writing tables instead of built-in desktops. Ask for a room on one of the Executive Floors (16F-18F) with a northeast view of the Sumida River; another good option would be a room lower down (6F-8F) on the opposite side, overlooking the hotel's delightful 5th-floor Japanese garden. *2-1-1 Nihombashi-Kakigaracho, Chuo-ku, Tokyo 103 (nearest subway: Suitengumae), tel.03/3667–1111, fax 03/3665–7212. 441 rooms, 9 suites. Facilities: 3 restaurants, shops. AE, DC, MC, V.*

Takanawa Prince Hotel. This hotel is separated from its big brother, the New Takanawa Prince, by a beautiful garden that is part Western and part Japanese. This Prince establishment is more geared to the individual traveler than to large groups, though the lobby's design is the large, open plan so favored by the Japanese. Guest rooms are fairly compact, and those overlooking the garden are the best. *13-1 Takanawa 3-chome, Minato-ku, Tokyo 108 (nearest JR station: Shinagawa), tel. 03/3447–1111, fax 03/3446–0849. 416 rooms, each with a balcony, and 18 tatami suites. Facilities: 2 pools, 6 restaurants and bars, shopping arcade. AE, DC, MC, V.*

Takanawa Tobu Hotel. Across the street from the monolithic New Takanawa Prince and a five-minute walk from the Shinagawa Station, the hotel offers good value. The guest rooms are on the small side, and no proper lobby sitting area is available, but the virtues are a welcoming staff (who speak modest English) and a friendly bar lounge. *7-6 Takanawa 4-chome, Minato-ku, Tokyo 108 (nearest JR station: Shinagawa), tel. 03/3447–0111, fax 03/3447–0117. 190 rooms. Facilities: bar; small Western restaurant, the Boulogne. AE, DC, MC, V.*

Tokyo Marunouchi Hotel. In business since 1924, the Tokyo Marunouchi has rooms that were last refurbished in 1987; these have seen a lot of traffic since then. This hotel is very popular with Westerners, and the staff have come to anticipate their needs. Within two blocks of Tokyo Station, three blocks from the Imperial Palace, and two subway stops from Ginza, the lodging is in the prime-rent district. The guest rooms tend to be a little drab but are (for Tokyo) of reasonable size; they have more individuality than the boxlike rooms in other modern Tokyo hotels. *1-6-3 Marunouchi, Chiyoda-ku, Tokyo 100 (nearest subway: Tokyo), tel. 03/3215–2151, fax 03/3215–8036. 210 rooms. Facilities: bar, coffeehouse, Western restaurant. AE, DC, MC, V.*

Tokyo Prince Hotel. This square, squat building, which overlooks the garden of Shiba-Koen Park and the famed Zojoji Temple, appears larger than it is, with a wide-open lobby and unappealing furniture that accentuates the hotel's lack of warmth and personality. You may want to leave this member of the Prince chain to the tour groups that tend to patronize the hotel. *3-1 Shiba-koen 3-chome, Minato-ku, Tokyo 105 (nearest subway: Onarimon), tel. 03/3432–1111, fax 03/3434–5551. 484 rooms. Facilities: pool; shopping arcade; French, Chinese, and Japanese restaurants; American snack-café; 4 cocktail lounges. AE, DC, MC, V.*

Tokyo Station Hotel. Above Tokyo Station, this building is part of Tokyo's heritage. It was saved in 1990 from the wrecker's ball by preservationists and recently completed an interior renovation, which included a fresh paint job, a fresh coat of varnish on the grand old wooden staircase from the lobby to the second floor, and new carpets for the corridors (which, incidentally, are wider than the rooms of many Tokyo hotels). For the moment, this hotel should only be recommended for an overnight stay between trains, though it can be a useful place for breakfast before setting out on a journey. *1-9-1 Marunouchi, Chiyodu-ku, Tokyo 100 (nearest subway: Tokyo), tel. 03/3231–2511, fax 03/3231–3513. 170 rooms, 56 with bath. AE, DC, MC, V.*

Moderate

Gajoen Kanko Hotel. After a major renovation in 1986, this pre–World War II hotel has made a comeback and offers good value in a residential area, away from the noise and bustle of Tokyo's traffic. The Gajoen Kanko is full of old prints, scrolls, and decor that is oriental rococo. The hotel has grown since its days as an occupation-era accommodation by the addition of an annex. This place may not appeal to all, but it is one of the very few Tokyo accommodations that have character and individuality. *1-8-1 Shimo-Meguro, Meguro-ku, Tokyo 153 (nearest JR station: Meguro), tel. 03/3491–0111, fax 03/3495–2450. 108 rooms. Facilities: Chinese and Western restaurants. AE, DC, MC, V.*

Hotel Atamiso. This hotel is not well known to many Westerners; its location, however, is convenient (near Ginza area), and the staff's friendliness (marginal English is spoken) makes this place a real find. Formerly a ryokan, the Atamiso was transformed into a Western hotel in 1984 but has kept its Japanese appreciation of hospitality. For the size of the rooms, the hotel is an extremely good value. The hotel is too small to computerize its guests' names, so the receptionist remembers names of guests instead of consulting a computer screen. *4-14-3 Ginza, Chuo-ku, Tokyo 104 (nearest subway: Higashi-Ginza), tel. 03/3541–3621, fax 03/3541–3263. 74 rooms (singles, doubles, and Japanese-style rooms). Facilities: Swiss and Japanese restaurants. AE, DC, MC, V.*

★ **Hotel Ginza Ocean.** This delightful small hotel is around the corner from the Kabuki-za Theater in the Ginza section. The rooms, though not large, are comfortable. Virtually no English is spoken here, but sign language serves to communicate basic needs. *7-18-15 Ginza, Chuo-ku, Tokyo 104 (nearest subway: Higashi-Ginza), tel. 03/3545–1221, fax 03/3545–1226. 32 Western-style rooms. Facilities: excellent Japanese restaurant, Matsuryu. AE, DC, V.*

Kayabacho Pearl Hotel. The rooms are strictly utilitarian, but the price is low, unless you sleep late; the staff adds a ¥3,000–¥4,000 charge for late check-out (after 10 AM). The hotel is located just across the bridge from Tokyo City Air Terminal, a five-minute walk from exit number 3 or 4 of Kayabacho Station on the Hibiya or Tozai Line. *1-2-5 Shinkawa, Chuo-ku, Tokyo 104 (nearest subway: Kayabacho), tel. 03/3553–2211, fax 03/3555–1849. 262 rooms, all with phone and television. Facilities: restaurant, open 7–midnight. AE, DC, MC, V.*

Keihin Hotel. Directly across the street from Shinagawa Station, the Keihin is best described as a business hotel. The building is small, as are the rooms, but the staff are personable, and the manager speaks English enthusiastically and enjoys having Westerners stay. For a modest hotel, the Keshin is a good value, given its convenient location. *4-10-20 Takanawa, Minato-ku, Tokyo 108 (nearest JR station: Shinagawa), tel. 03/3449–5711, fax 03/3441–7230. 52 Western-style rooms. Facilities: Japanese restaurant; many other cafés (Western and Japanese) nearby. AE, DC, MC, V.*

Mikawaya Bekkan. This small ryokan resembles a boarding house; its tiny tatami-mat rooms have noisy kerosene heaters during the winter and cranky air-conditioning units during the summer. The shared washing facilities are compact, and the communal bath has hot water between 4 and 8 PM. Doors to the inn close at 11 PM. The owners are not very helpful, so don't expect much in the way of hospitality. Still, the rooms are clean, the price is inexpensive for Tokyo, and the location—right by Asakusa's Sensoji Temple—is ideal for exploring the area. Japanese-style dinner is optional, though you are expected to take either a Western or Japanese breakfast. *1-31-11 Asakusa, Taito-ku, Tokyo 111 (nearest subway: Asakusa on the Ginza Line; walk to the Kaminarimon Gate and take a right up the stall-covered Nakamise toward the Sensoji Shrine. The inn will be down the 4th alley on the left), tel. 03/3843–2345, fax 03/3843–2348. 12 rooms. Facilities: restaurant for breakfast and dinner, air-conditioning. AE, MC, V.*

Shiba Daimon Hotel. For a moderately priced hotel that is popular with in-the-know Japanese, try this small establishment located close to the Zenoji Temple. The smart, clean rooms are no smaller than what you usually find in Tokyo hotels. Service is politely Japanese—speak a couple of words of the native tongue, and the staff is even friendly. Shiba Daimon does not cater to the foreign tourist, and there are no English-language brochures available, but the staff is willing to help when they can. A good restaurant situated on the ground floor serves breakfast and then Chinese cuisine in the evening. *2-3-6 Shiba-kōen, Minato-ku, Tokyo 105 (nearest subways: Daimon and Hamamatsu-cho), tel. 03/3431–3716, fax 03/3434–5177. 96 rooms. Facilities: restaurant. AE, DC, MC, V.*

Shinjuku Washington Hotel. This is truly a business hotel, where service is computerized as much as possible. On the third-floor lobby, automated check-in and check-out systems are available; you are assigned a room and provided with a plastic card that allows entry to your small room and access to the minibar. A few staff members in the lobby explain the process, but after that you are on your own. *3-2-9 Nishi-Shinjuku, Shinjuku-ku, Tokyo 160 (nearest subway: Shinjuku), tel. 03/3343–3111, fax 03/3342–2575. 1,650 rooms. Facilities: refrigerator, minibar, TV, in rooms. AE, DC, MC, V.*

★ **Star Hotel.** This small, friendly hotel has rates more reasonable than many in the area. The staff speak only Japanese but are sympathetic to sign language. The rooms are clean, though not spacious; a small, pleasant restaurant serves Japanese and Western food. The Star lacks the amenities of doormen, bellhops, telex machines, and the countless bars of the larger hotels, but the size of the hotel allows the front-desk manager to remember your name without the help of a computer. *7-10-5 Nishi-Shinjuku, Shinjuku-ku, Tokyo 160 (nearest subway: Shinjuku), tel. 03/3361–1111, fax 03/3369–4216. 80 Western-style rooms. Facilities: Japanese–Western restaurant. AE, DC, MC, V.*

Inexpensive

Asia Center of Japan. This hotel seems to host more foreign guests than many other establishments. It is popular for its central location, only a 15-minute walk to Roppongi for a cosmopolitan night of entertainment. The rooms are basic, clean, small, and not too well soundproofed, but you get a good value for what you pay. *10-32 Akasaka 2-chome, Minato-ku, Tokyo 107 (nearest subways: Roppongi and Aoyama Itchome; turn left out of the subway up Aoyama-dori and right at the Akasaka Post Office. The hotel is just down the first left-hand side street), tel. 03/3402–6111, fax 03/3402–0738. 172 Western-style rooms; some with private bath. Facilities: cafeteria-style dining room, bar, garden patio. No credit cards.*

Kikuya Ryokan. This small inn in the Asakusa district is a 10-minute walk from the Sensoji Temple. Be warned, the inn locks its doors at midnight, and everything here is midget-sized. *2-18-9 Nishi-Asakusa, Taito-ku, Tokyo 111 (nearest subway: Tawaramachi; then walk 2 blocks up Kokusai-dori Ave., take a left, and just before Kappabashi-dori Ave., the ryokan is on the left-hand side), tel. 03/3841–6404. 8 tatami rooms, 4 with private bath. Facilities: air-conditioning. AE, MC, V.*

Ryokan Katsutaro. This is a simple, economical Japanese hotel that is a five-minute walk from Ueno Park and a 10-minute walk from the National Museum. The lodging is small, with the quietest rooms in the back, away from the main street. *4-16-8 Ikenohata, Taito-ku, Tokyo 110 (nearest subway: Nezu; leave by the Ikenohata exit, cross the road, take the street running northeast, go right at the "T" junction, and the ryokan is 25 yards on the left-hand side of Dobutsu-en-Uramon-dori Ave.), tel. 03/3821–9808, fax 03/3891–4789. 7 rooms, 4 with private bath. Facilities: coin-operated TV. Continental breakfast. AE, DC, MC, V.*

Ryokan Sansuiso. If you're traveling on a tight budget and want to immerse yourself in Japanese culture, consider this basic ryokan near Gotanda Station on the Yamanote Line. The proprietor will greet you with a warm smile and a bow, and escort you to a small tatami room with a pay TV and a rather noisy heater/air-conditioner mounted in the wall. Some rooms are stuffy (you can't open a window), and only two have private baths, but the Sansuiso is clean, easy-to-find, and only 20 minutes on the subway from Tokyo Station and the Ginza. Although students and young travelers will be most comfortable here, the midnight curfew poses a problem for night owls. This hotel is a member of the Japanese Inn Group; the Japanese National Tourist Organization can help make reservations. *2-9-5, Higashi-Gotanda, Shinagawa-ku, Tokyo, tel. 03/3441–7475, fax 03/3449–1944. 2 rooms with bath, 7 rooms share bath. AE, V.*

★ **Sawanoya Ryokan.** Sawanoya is situated in a quiet area to the northwest of Ueno Park; the residential locale and the hospitality of the ryokan make you feel at home in traditional Tokyo. The owners truly welcome travelers; they help them plan trips and arrange future accommodations. No dinner is offered, but breakfast (Continental or Japanese) is available at an extra charge. Sawanoya has become very popular with low-budget travelers; a wise move would be to make a reservation by fax (03/3822–2252) well before you arrive. *2-3-11 Yanaka, Taito-ku, Tokyo 110 (nearest subway: Nezu; walk 275 yards north along Shinobazu-dori Ave., take the street on the right, and the*

Sawanoya is 165 yards on the right), tel. 03/3822–2251, fax 03/ 3822–2252. 12 rooms, only 2 with private bath. Facilities: breakfast, pay TV, air-conditioning. AE, MC, V.

Hostels and Dormitory Accommodations

Tokyo International Youth Hostel. All residents here are required off the premises 10 AM–3 PM. The hostel is very close to Iidabashi Station on the JR, Tozai, and Yurakucho lines. *18F Central Plaza Bldg., 1-1 Kagura-kashi, Shinjuku-ku, Tokyo, tel. 03/3235–1107. 138 bunk beds. Inexpensive.*

Tokyo YMCA. Rooms are with and without bath. Both men and women can stay at the hostel, which is a three-minute walk from Awajicho Station on the Marunouchi Line or seven minutes from Kanda Station on the Ginza Line. *7 Kanda-Mitoshirocho, Chiyoda-ku, Tokyo 101. 40 rooms, tel. 03/3293–1919, fax 03/3293–1926. Inexpensive.*

Tokyo YWCA Sadohara. Rooms are available here with bath; also rooms for married couples. The hostel is located close (3-min. walk) to the Ichigaya Station. *3-1-1 Ichigaya-Sadaharacho, Shinjuku-ku, Tokyo, tel. 03/3268–7313, fax 03/3268–4452. 16 rooms. Moderate.*

YMCA Asia Youth Center. Both men and women can stay here; all rooms have private baths. The hostel is an eight-minute walk from Suidobashi Station on the JR Mita Line. *5-5 Saragakucho 2-chome, Chiyoda-ku, Tokyo, tel. 03/3233–0611, fax 03/3233–0633. 55 rooms. Inexpensive.*

Near Narita Airport

Narita International Hotel. This accommodation resembles a resort hotel with spacious grounds. It is new and modern, but it has some greenery on its 72 acres of land. A shuttle bus runs between the hotel and the airport from noon to 4 PM on the hour, and every 30 minutes from 4:30 to 11; the trip takes about 15 minutes. *650-35 Nanaei, Tomisato-machi, Inba-gun, Chiba 288-02, tel. 0476/93–1234, fax 0476/93–4834. 500 rooms, with individually controlled air-conditioning. Facilities: outdoor pool (the largest in Narita), tennis courts, jogging trail, duty-free shop, Japanese and Western restaurants. AE, DC, MC, V. Very Expensive.*

ANA Hotel Narita. Opened in 1990, this hotel—like many in the ANA chain—aspires to architecture in the grand style; assume the cost of brass and marble to show up on your bill. The amenities measure up, and the proximity to the airport (about 15 min. by shuttle bus) make this a good choice for visitors in transit. *68 Horinouchi, Narita-shi, Chiba-ken 286-01, tel. 0476/33–1311, fax 0476/33–0244. 422 Rooms. Facilities: pool, Japanese and Western restaurants, shopping arcade, bar. AE, DC, MC, V. Expensive.*

Holiday Inn Tobu Narita. A 10-minute ride by shuttle bus from the airport, this establishment offers Western-style accommodations with a full range of amenities. *320-1 Tokko, Narita-shi, Chiba 286-01, tel. 0476/32–1234, fax 0476/32–0617. 500 soundproof rooms that can also be rented for daytime-only use (¥13,000 for 2 beds). Facilities: outdoor pool, steam bath, massage, barber and beauty salons. French, Chinese, Japanese, and steak restaurants, bar. AE, DC, MC, V. Expensive.*

Narita View Hotel. Boxy and uninspired, the Narita View offers no view of anything in particular, but can be reached by shuttle bus from the airport in about 15 minutes. Short on charm, it tends to rely on promotional discount "campaigns" to draw a clientele. *700 Kosuge, Narita-shi, Chiba-ken 286-01, tel. 0476/32–1111, fax 0476/32–1078. 504 rooms, that can also be rented for daytime use from 11 AM to 6 PM at 50% the normal rate. Facilities: massage, hairdresser, Japanese and Western restaurants. AE, DC, MC, V. Expensive.*

Narita Winds Hotel. A shuttle bus (at Terminal bus stop #3) is offered, which makes a regular 10-minute trip to the hotel. The modern and efficient Narita Winds is an all-purpose hotel, with banquet rooms and meeting facilities. *560 Tokko, Narita-shi, Chiba 286-01, tel. 0476/33–1111, fax 0476/33–1108. 321 soundproof rooms. Facilities: outdoor pool, sauna, tennis courts, shopping arcade, 5 restaurants. AE, DC, MC, V. Expensive.*

Narita Airport Rest House. A basic business-style hotel without much in the way of frills, the Rest House offers the closest accommodations to the airport itself, less than five minutes away by shuttle bus. *New Tokyo International Airport, Narita-shi, Chiba-ken 286-11, tel. 0476/32–1212, fax 0476/32–1209. 210 soundproofed rooms that can also be rented for daytime use from 10 AM to 5 PM (double: ¥10,000). Facilities: restaurant. AE, DC, MC, V. Moderate.*

The Arts

Few cities have as much to offer as Tokyo does in the performing arts. It has Japan's own great stage traditions: Kabuki, Noh, Bunraku puppet drama, music, and dance. It has an astonishing variety of music, classical and popular; Tokyo is a proving ground for local talent and a magnet for orchestras and concert soloists from all over the world. The Rolling Stones, Jean Pierre Rampal, the Berlin Philharmonic, Oscar Peterson: Whenever you visit, the headliners will be here. It has modern theater—in somewhat limited choices, to be sure, unless you can follow dialogue in Japanese, but Western repertory companies can always find receptive audiences here for plays in English. In recent years musicals have found enormous popularity here; it doesn't take long for a hit show in New York or London to open in Tokyo. Film, too, presents a much broader range of possibilities than it used to. The major commercial distributors bring in the movies they expect to draw the biggest receipts—horror films and Oscar nominees—but there are now dozens of small theaters in Tokyo catering to more sophisticated audiences. Japan has yet to develop any serious strength of its own in opera or ballet, but for that reason touring companies like the Metropolitan and the Bolshoi, Sadler's Wells, and the Bayerische Staatsoper find Tokyo a very compelling venue—as well they might, when ¥20,000 seats are sold out even before the box office opens.

Information and Tickets

The best comprehensive guide in English to performance schedules in Tokyo is the "Cityscope" insert in the monthly *Tokyo Journal* magazine. You can probably pick up the *Journal* at one of the newsstands at Narita Airport on your way into the city; if not, it's on sale in the bookstores at all the major international hotels. "Cityscope" has reviews and recommendations; in addition to films, plays, and concerts, it also covers museums and art galleries, television, festivals, and special events. Another source, rather less complete, is the *Tour Companion,* a tabloid visitor's guide published every two weeks that is available free of charge at hotels and at Japan National Tourist Organization offices. For a weekly update, the Monday edition of the English-language *Mainichi Daily News* also carries information on performances.

If your hotel cannot help you with bookings, two of the city's major ticket agencies have numbers to call for assistance in English: **Ticket Pia** (tel. 03/5237–9999) and **Ticket Saison** (tel. 03/3286–5482; closed Wed.). A third possibility is the **Playguide** agency, which has outlets in most of the department stores and in other locations all over the city; you can stop in at the main office (Playguide Bldg., 2-6-4 Ginza, Chuo-ku, tel. 03/3561–8821) and ask for the nearest counter. Note that agencies normally do not have tickets for same-day performances but only for advanced booking.

Traditional Theater

Kabuki emerged as a popular form of entertainment in the early 17th century; before long, it had been banned by the authorities as a threat to public order. Eventually it cleaned up its act, and by the latter half of the 18th century, it had become Everyman's Theater par excellence—especially among the townspeople of bustling, hustling Edo. Kabuki had music, dancing, and spectacle; it had acrobatics and sword fights; it had pathos and tragedy and historical romance and social satire. It didn't have beautiful girls—women have been banned from the Kabuki stage since 1629—but in recompense it developed a professional role for female impersonators, who train for years to project a seductive, dazzling femininity that few real women ever achieve. It had superstars and quick-change artists and legions of fans, who brought their lunch to the theater, stayed all day, and shouted out the names of their favorite actors at the stirring moments in their favorite plays. Edo is now Tokyo, but Kabuki is still here, just as it has been for centuries. The traditions are passed down from generation to generation in a small group of families; the roles and great stage names are hereditary. The Kabuki repertoire does not really grow or change, but stars like Ennosuke Ichikawa and Tamasaburo Bando have put exciting, personal stamps on their performances that continue to draw audiences young and old.

Certainly the best place to see Kabuki is at the **Kabuki-za** (4-12-15 Ginza, Chuo-ku, tel. 03/5565–6000; call by 6 PM the day preceding performance for reservations), built especially for this purpose in 1925, with its *hanamichi* (runway) passing diagonally through the audience to the revolving stage. The Kabuki-za was rebuilt after the war. The facade of the building recalls the castle architecture of the 16th century; the lanterns and banners and huge theater posters outside identify it unmistakably. Matinees usually begin at 11 AM and end at 3:30 PM; evening performances, at 4:30 PM, end around 9 PM. Reserved seats are expensive and hard to come by on short notice; for a mere ¥600 to ¥1,000, however, you can buy an unreserved ticket that allows you to see one act of a play from the topmost gallery. The gallery is cleared after each act, but there's nothing to prevent you from buying another ticket: the price is low for an hour or so of this fascinating spectacle. Bring binoculars: the gallery is *very* far from the stage. You might also want to rent an earphone set (¥600) to follow the play in English, but this is really more of an intrusion than a help—and you can't use the set in the upmost galleries, anyway.

Two other theaters in Tokyo specialize in traditional performances and offer Kabuki at various times during the year. The **Shimbashi Embujo** (6-18-2 Ginza, Chuo-ku, tel. 03/5565–6000, the same reservation office as the Kabuki-za), which dates back to 1925, was built originally for the geisha of the Shimbashi quarter to present their spring and autumn performances of traditional music and dance. It's a bigger house than the Kabuki-za, and it still presents a lot of traditional dance as well as conventional drama (in Japanese), but there is no gallery; reserved seats commonly run ¥3,000– ¥13,500. **The National Theater of Japan** (4-1 Hayabusa, Chiyoda-ku, tel. 03/3265–7411), mentioned in our exploring tour of the Imperial Palace area, plays host to Kabuki companies based elsewhere; it also has a training program for young people who may not have one of the hereditary family connections but want to break into this closely guarded profession. Debut performances, called *kaomise*, are worth watching to catch the stars of the next generation. *Admission: ¥1,400 to ¥8,200.*

Noh is a dramatic tradition far older than Kabuki; it reached a point of formal perfection in the 14th century and survives virtually unchanged from that period. Where Kabuki was Everyman's Theater, Noh developed for the most part under the patronage of the warrior class. It is dignified and solemn, ritualized and symbolic; many of the plays in the repertoire are drawn from classical literature or tales of the supernatural, and the texts are richly poetic. Where the Kabuki actor is usually in brightly colored makeup derived from the Chinese opera, the principal character in a Noh play wears a carved wooden mask. Such is the skill of the actor, and the mysterious effect of the play, that the mask seems to express a whole range of emotions. As in Kabuki, the various roles of the Noh repertoire all have specific costumes—robes of silk brocade with intricate patterns that are works of art in themselves. Noh is not a very *accessible* kind of theater: its language is archaic; its conventions are obscure; and its measured, stately pace can put even Japanese audiences to sleep. More than anything else you will see in Tokyo, however, Noh will provide an experience of Japan as an *ancient* culture.

Somewhat like Kabuki, Noh is divided into a number of schools, the traditions of which developed as the exclusive property of hereditary families. It is occasionally performed in public halls, like the **National Noh Theater** (4-18-1 Sendagaya, Shibuya-ku, tel. 03/3423–1331), but primarily in the theaters of these schools—which also teach their dance and recitation styles to amateurs. The most important of these are the **Kanze Noh-gakudo** (1-16-4 Shoto, Shibuya-ku, tel. 03/3469–5241), the **Kita Noh-gakudo** (4-6-9 Kami-Osaki, Shinagawa-ku, tel. 03/3491–7773), the **Hosho Noh-gakudo** (1-5-9 Hongo, Bunkyo-ku, tel. 03/3811–4843), and the **Umewaka Noh-gakuin** (2-6-14 Higashi-Nakano, Nakano-ku, tel. 03/3363–7748). The very best way to see Noh, however, is in the open air, at torchlight performances called Takigi Noh, held in the courtyards of temples. The setting and the aesthetics of the drama combine in an eerie theatrical experience. These performances are given at various times during the year; consult the "Cityscope" or *Tour Com-*

panion listings. Tickets are normally available only through the temples and are sold out very quickly.

The third major form of traditional Japanese drama is **Bunraku,** or puppet theater. Itinerant puppeteers were plying their trade in Japan as early as the 10th century; sometime in the late-16th century, a form of narrative ballad called *joruri,* performed to the accompaniment of a three-string banjolike instrument called the *shamisen,* was grafted onto their art, and Bunraku was born. The golden age of Bunraku came some 200 years later, when most of the great Bunraku plays were written and the puppets themselves evolved to their present form—so expressive and intricate in their movements that they require three people at one time to manipulate them. Puppeteers and narrators (who deliver their lines in a kind of high-pitch croak, deep in the throat) train for many years to master this difficult and unusual genre of popular entertainment.

The spiritual center of Bunraku today is Osaka, rather than Tokyo, but performances are given here with some frequency in the Small Hall of the National Theater. In recent years, it has also begun to enjoy a minor vogue with younger audiences, and Bunraku troupes will occasionally get booked into trendier locations. Consult the "Cityscope" listings, or check with one of the English-speaking ticket agencies.

Modern Theater

The **Shingeki** (Modern Theater) movement began in Japan at about the turn of the century. The first problem its earnest young actors and directors encountered was the fact that they had no native repertoire. The "conservative" faction at first tended to approach the problem with translations of Shakespeare; the "radicals," with Ibsen, Gorki, and Shaw. It wasn't until around 1915 that Japanese playwrights began writing for the Shingeki stage. Japan of the 1930s and 1940s, in any case, was none too hospitable an environment for modern drama; the movement did not develop any real vitality until after World War II.

The watershed years came around 1965, when experimental theater companies—unable to find commercial space—began taking their work to young audiences in various unusual ways: street plays and "happenings"; dramatic readings in underground malls and rented lofts; tents put up on vacant lots for unannounced performances (miraculously filled to capacity by word of mouth) and taken down the next day. It was in this period that surrealist playwright Kobo Abe found his stride, and director Tadashi Suzuki developed the unique system of training that now draws aspiring actors from all over the world to his "theater community" in the mountains of Toyama Prefecture. Japanese drama today is a lively art indeed; theaters small and large, in unexpected pockets all over Tokyo, attest to its vitality.

The great majority of these performances, however, are in Japanese, for Japanese audiences; you're unlikely to find one with program notes in English to help you follow it. Unless it's a play you already know well, and you're curious to see how it translates *(Fiddler on the Roof,* for example, has been running in Japanese for over 20 years), you might do well to think of some other way to spend your evenings out.

There is one exception: the **Takarazuka**—the wonderfully goofy all-girl review. The troupe was founded in the Osaka suburb of Takarazuka in 1913 and has been going strong ever since; today it has not one but five companies, one of them with a permanent home in Tokyo, right across the street from the Imperial Hotel (1-1-3 Yuraku-cho, Chiyoda-ku, tel. 03/3591–1711). A Takarazuka chorine never gives her parents a moment's anxiety about her chosen career; this is show business with a difference—a life chaste and chaperoned, where the yearning admirers waiting with roses by the stage door are mostly teenage girls. Everybody sings; everybody dances; the sets are breathtaking; the costumes are swell. Where else but at the Takarazuka could you see a musical version of *Gone With the Wind*, sung in Japanese, with a girl in a mustache and a frock coat playing Rhett Butler?

Music

The live music scene in Tokyo keeps getting better and better. Every year, a host of new promoters and booking agencies gets into the act; major corporations, anxious to polish their images as cultural institutions, are building concert halls and unusual performance spaces all over the city, adding to what was already an excellent roster of public auditoriums. It would be impossible to list them all; here are only a few of the most important:

The biggest acts from abroad in **rock** and **popular music** tend to appear at the 56,000-seat **Tokyo Dome sports arena,** which opened in 1988 on the site of the old Korakuen Stadium (1-3-61 Koraku, Bunkyo-Ku, tel. 03/3811–2111), and at **Nakano Sun Plaza** (4-1-1 Nakano, Nakano-ku, tel. 03/3388–1151). For **Western classical music,** including **opera,** the major venues are **NHK Hall,** home base for the Japan Broadcasting Corporation's NHK Symphony Orchestra (2-2-1 Jinnan, Shibuya-ku, tel. 03/3465–1111); **Tokyo Bunka Kaikan** (5-45 Ueno Koen, Taito-ku, tel. 03/3828–2111), which we've mentioned in our exploring tour of Ueno; and **Suntory Hall,** in the new Ark Hills complex (1-13-1 Akasaka, Minato-ku, tel. 03/3505–1001). To these should be added three fine places designed especially for **chamber music: Iino Hall** (2-1-1 Uchisaiwai-cho, Chiyoda-ku, tel. 03/3506–3251), **Ishibashi Memorial Hall** (4-24-12 Higashi Ueno, Taito-ku, tel. 03/3843–3043), and the very recent **Casals Hall** (1-6 Kanda Surugadai, Chiyoda-ku, tel. 03/3294–1229), designed by architect Arata Isozaki, who also did, among other things, the Museum of Contemporary Art in Los Angeles.

Dance

Traditional Japanese Dance, like flower arranging and the tea ceremony, is divided into dozens of styles, ancient of lineage and fiercely proud of their differences from each other. In fact, only the aficionado can really tell them apart. They survive, not so much as performing arts but as schools, offering dance as a cultured accomplishment to interested amateurs. At least once a year, teachers and their students in each of these schools will hold a recital, so that on any given evening there's very likely to be one somewhere in Tokyo. Truly professional performances are given, as we've mentioned, at the National Theater and the Shimbashi Embujo; the most important of the classical schools, however, developed as an aspect of Kabuki, and if you attend a play at the Kabuki-za you are almost guaranteed to see a representative example.

Ballet began to attract a Japanese following in 1920, when Anna Pavlova danced *The Dying Swan* at the old Imperial Theater. The well-known companies that come to Tokyo from abroad perform to full houses, usually at the Tokyo Bunka Kaikan in Ueno. There are now about 15 professional Japanese ballet companies, several of which have toured abroad, but this has yet to become an art form on which Japan has had much of an impact. **Modern Dance** is a different story—a story that begins with a visit in 1955 by the Martha Graham Dance Company. The decade that followed was one of great turmoil in Japan; it was a period of dissatisfaction—political, intellectual, artistic—with old forms and conventions. The work of pioneers like Graham inspired a great number of talented dancers and choreographers to explore new avenues of self-expression; one of the fruits of that exploration was **Butoh,** a movement that was at once uniquely Japanese and a major contribution to the world of modern dance.

The father of Butoh was the dancer Tatsumi Hijikata (1928–1986); the watershed work was his *Revolt of the Flesh,* which premiered in 1968. Others soon followed: Kazuo Ohno, Min Tanaka, Akaji Maro and the Dai Rakuda Kan troupe, Ushio Amagatsu and the Sankai Juku. To most Japanese, their work was inexplicably grotesque. Dancers performed with shaved heads, dressed in rags or with naked bodies painted completely white, their movements agonized and contorted. The images were dark and demonic, violent and explicitly sexual. Butoh was an exploration of the unconscious: its gods were the gods of the Japanese village and the gods of prehistory; its literary inspirations came from Mishima, Genet, Artaud. Like many other modern Japanese artists, the Butoh dancers and choreographers were largely ignored by the mainstream until they began to appear abroad—to thunderous critical acclaim. Now they are equally honored at home. Butoh does not lend itself to conventional spaces (a few years ago, for example, the Dai Rakuda Kan premiered one of its new works in a limestone cave in Gumma Prefecture), but if there's a performance in Tokyo, "Cityscope" will have the schedule. Don't miss it.

Film

One of the positive things about the business of foreign film distribution in Japan is that it is extremely profitable—so much so that the distributors can afford to add Japanese subtitles rather than dub their offerings, the way it's done so often elsewhere. The original soundtrack, of course, may not be all that helpful to you if the film is Polish or Italian, but the vast majority of first-run foreign films here are made in the United States. There are, however, other disincentives: the choices are limited; the good films take so long to open in Tokyo that you've probably seen them all already at home; and the tickets are expensive—around ¥1,700 for general admission, and ¥2,200–¥2,500 for a reserved seat, called a *shiteiseki.*

The native Japanese film industry has been in a slump for over 20 years, and it shows no signs of recovery. It yields, at best, one or two films a year worth seeing, and these are invariably by independent producer/directors. A very small number of theaters will offer one showing a week, with English subtitles, of films that seem to have some international appeal; "City-scope" will have the listings.

First-run theaters that feature new releases, both Japanese and foreign, are clustered for the most part in three areas: Shinjuku, Shibuya, and Yurakucho/Hibiya/Ginza. The most astonishing thing about them is how early they shut down; in most cases, the last showing of the evening starts at around 7. This is not the case, however, with the best news on the Tokyo film scene: the growing number of small theaters that take a special interest in classics, revivals, and serious imports. Many of them are in the "vertical boutique" buildings that represent the latest Japanese thinking in urban architecture and upscale marketing; somewhere on the premises will also be a chrome-and-marble coffee shop, a fashionable little bar, or even a decent restaurant. Most of them have a midnight show—at least on the weekends. One such is the **Cine Vivant** (Wave Building, 6-2-27 Roppongi, Minato-ku, tel. 03/3403–6061); another is the **Cine Saison Shibuya** (Prime Building, 2-29-5 Dogen-zaka, Shibuya-ku, tel. 03/3770–1721); still others are the **Haiyu-za Cinema Ten** (4-9-2 Roppongi, Minato-ku, tel. 03/3401–4073), and the **Hibiya Chanter Cinema** (1-2-2 Yuraku-cho, Chiyoda-ku, tel. 03/3591–1511). **Bunka-mura,** the showcase complex next door to the Tokyu Department Store in Shibuya (2-24-1 Dogenzaka, tel. 03/3447–9111) has two movie theaters, a concert hall, and a performance space; it is the principal venue for many of Tokyo's film festivals.

Nightlife

Tokyo has more entertainment choices and a greater diversity of nightlife than any other Japanese city. For the tourist to Japan, the structure of Japan's nightlife may be confusing. The neon lights of bars and clubs excite with their glitter, but these places are forbidding to enter for several reasons: an indication of the prices charged for a drink is rarely offered (the charge could be a mere ¥1,000 a drink, or a ¥20,000 cover and another ¥15,000 for a bottle of whiskey); it is often unclear whether the bar has hostesses, and, if it does, whether there is a hostess charge and whether she is there for conversation only; and, finally, one never knows whether foreigners will be welcome, let alone whether a word of English will be spoken.

In this section, the establishments listed make foreigners welcome; often, someone will be around who speaks a few words of English. Most of the bars listed are more of the international variety, rather than being bars with hostesses. Hostess bars become like personal clubs, and your appreciation of them depends on how well you enjoy the conversations of the particular hostesses. You are unlikely to appreciate them unless you speak Japanese, especially when the tab will be about ¥20,000 to ¥30,000 a person. At karaoke bars, patrons request a piece of music and accompany it by singing the song into a microphone while reading the words to the song from the bottom of the video screen.

There are five major districts in Tokyo that have an extensive nightlife. While each area offers similar entertainment, the areas have different characters and different price ranges:

Akasaka has an area of two main streets, Tamachi-dori and Hitotsugi-dori, with small alleys connecting them. Cabarets, wine bars, nightclubs, coffee shops, eating and drinking places, as well as a couple of expensive ryotei with geisha entertainment, are all here. It is a sophisticated neighborhood that is not quite as expensive as Ginza and not as trendy as Roppongi. Also, the area's compactness makes it a comfortable locale for the foreigner to test the waters of Japanese nightlife.

Ginza is probably the city's most well-known entertainment district; however, its heyday is over as an attractive place for foreign visitors to visit at night. The exorbitant price of Ginza's real estate has made its nightlife one of the most, if not the most, expensive in the world. Not even foreign businessmen on expense accounts take their Japanese clients here. Only Japanese corporate expense accounts can afford the prices. There are some affordable places to visit in the evening, but these are not nightclubs as such, but bars and eating and drinking places.

Roppongi, spreading out toward Shibuya, has become Tokyo's main entertainment area for the cosmopolitan, trendy, and fashionable. It is the district where Westerners feel most comfortable; the prices are considerably better here than in Ginza, or even in Akasaka. During the day Roppongi is a quiet, residential area, but after 9 PM it seems that every Tokyo reveler is here making the rounds. More discos and bars of the variety you usually find in any major world capital are located here than in anyplace else in Japan. While Akasaka and Ginza virtually close down by midnight, some of the Roppongi bars stay open until the subways start running in the morning, so, if you have the stamina, this is the area to come for an all-nighter.

Shibuya has recently developed a nightlife. Less expensive than Roppongi and not raunchy like Shinjuku, it attracts students and young professionals to its numerous *nomiya* (inexpensive bars). Not many of the establishments have English-speaking staff, but if you know a little Japanese, this is a pleasant and inexpensive area for a night's entertainment.

Shinjuku's Kabukicho is the wildest of areas in Tokyo for evening revelry, offering a wide range of places, from the sleazy to the respectable. Bars, nightclubs, cabarets, discos, restaurants, and love hotels are all here. Just stay clear of touts speaking English to lure you to their dive, and you'll be fine. We do, however, recommend that unescorted women stay out of Kabukicho after 9 PM, because by then there are bound to be a few drunken males who will make irritating advances.

Bars

Ari's Lamplight. An intimate, comfortable place popular with foreign businesspeople and journalists, Ari's serves some of the best hamburgers in town. A "traditional classic" atmosphere maintains; there's live music on Thursday nights and the piano tends to turn away the black vinyl crowd. *Odakyu Building, 7-8-1 Minami-Aoyama, Minato-ku, tel. 03/3499–1573. Drinks start at ¥800. Open 5:30 PM–2 AM. Closed Sun.*

Charleston. This has been for years the schmoozing-and-hunting bar for Tokyo's single (or putatively single) foreign community, and the young Japanese who want to meet them. Noisy and packed until the wee small hours. *3-8-11 Roppongi:*

minato-ku, tel. 03/3402–0372. Drinks are ¥850 and up. Open daily 6PM–4AM.

Den. Launched by the mammoth beer and whiskey maker Suntory, Den is partly an exercise in corporate image-making. Meant to express the company's eco-consciousness and its roots in traditional Japanese culture, the motif here is confected of stones, trees, and articles of folkcraft. Den draws a fashionable crowd from the TV production, PR, and design companies thick in this part of town. *DST Building 1F, 4-2-3 Akasaka, Minato-ku, tel. 03/3584–1899. Drinks start at ¥800. Open 6 PM–2 AM. Closed Sun.*

Garbus Cine Café. Young sophisticates, especially those with latent screen ambitions, come to this smart café for exotic coffees, as well as cocktails. The large plate-glass windows of the café overlook a small square, where palms of famous movie actors are imprinted in stone. The square also flickers with a digital clock flashing the time from under a water fountain. *Hibiya Chanter 1F, 1-2-2 Yurakucho, Chiyoda-ku, tel. 03/3501–3185. Coffees start at ¥600. Open daily 11–11.*

Giger Bar. Designed by—and named for—the German cyberpunk visionary who created the sets of *Alien*, the Giger Bar looks like something out of a Sigourney Weaver nightmare. A roulette table in the minicasino on the lower lever strikes an earthly note; otherwise, the surroundings here are . . . well, spaced out. If you're in that sort of mood, the Giger Bar is fun; if you're a gentleman alone, the management will provide you a winsome companion. Surroundings to the contrary, this service comprises nothing weird. *5-10-15 Shiroganedai, Minato-ku, tel. 03/3440–5751. Drinks start at ¥1,000. Open 7 PM–4 AM. Closed Sun.*

Hard Rock Cafe. Akin to the London establishment of the same name, the bar reopened a couple of years ago with a new decor, similar to that of an American midwestern saloon and offering the same kind of fare for snacks. The building is easy to spot, with a huge sculpted gorilla hanging from the outside wall. *5-4-20 Roppongi, Minato-ku, tel. 03/3408–7018. Drinks start at ¥900. No cover. Open weekdays 11 AM–2 AM, Fri. and Sat. 11:30 AM–4 AM, Sun. 11:30 AM–11:30 PM.*

Henry Africa. Both Japanese and expatriates frequent this Akasaka bar, where the decor is like a movie set used to film an African safari, including the elephant tusks. (There is a similar bar with the same name in Roppongi.) *Akasaka Ishida Bldg., 2F, 3-13-14 Akasaka, Minato-ku, tel. 03/3585–0149. Drinks begin at ¥600. Snacks are available. Open daily 11:30–11:30, Sat. 5:30–11:30.*

Highlander. Should you become tired of Japanese whiskey and want some real Scotch, the Highlander at the Hotel Okura has a selection of more than 200 brands from which to choose. This is a smart place to meet business acquaintances or to have a civilized drink. *Hotel Okura, 2-10-4 Toranomon, Minato-ku, tel. 03/3505–6077. Drinks are ¥1,100 and up. Open daily 11:30 AM–1 AM, Sun. 11:30 AM–midnight.*

The Old Imperial Bar. If you want a place to meet someone for evening drinks, this hotel bar has a comfortable old-world charm with mementos taken from the original Imperial Hotel designed by Frank Lloyd Wright. *Imperial Hotel, 1-1-1 Uchisaiwaicho, Chiyoda-ku, tel. 03/3504–1111. Drinks ¥1,000 and up. Open daily 11:30 AM–10 PM.*

Stonefield's. A small bar that really wanted to be born a Nashville saloon, Stonefield's surrounds you with down-home hospitality and takes pride in its collection of country-and-western tapes. Now and again, they'll book in a live band; drop by on one of those evenings and discover how surprisingly good Japanese pickers 'n fiddlers can be. *Sunlight Akasaka Building 4F, 3-21-4 Akasaka, Minato-ku, tel. 03/3583–5690. Drinks start at ¥500; a bottle of bourbon is ¥7,000. Open 7 PM–midnight. Closed Sun.*

Suishin. This is one of many sake bars that you can find under the railway trestles south of Yurakucho Subway Station and near the JNTO's Tourist Information Office. This particular sake bar is small, barren except for a counter and chairs, but it is reputed to have some of the best Hiroshima sake. To find it, go down the alley under the railway between Tokyu Kotsu Kaikan and the Seibu Department Store; the pub is on the west side of the alley. *7-2-15 Ginza, tel. 03/3214–8046. Sake begins at ¥500. Open 11:30 AM–2 PM and 4–11:30 PM, Sun. 4 PM–10 PM.*

Wine Bar. Similar to a European wine bar, the cellarlike atmosphere appeals to Japanese and foreigners alike. It is a good place to take a date before hopping on to the Roppongi discos. *3-21-3 Akasaka, Minato-ku, tel. 3586–7186. Drinks start at ¥380. Open Mon.–Sat. 5 PM–midnight, Sun. 4–11 PM.*

Yuraku Food Center (2-2 Nishi-Ginza, Chuo-ku). Inside this building and one floor up is a collection of places to eat and drink at reasonable prices. It is where the people who work in the neighborhood go after work. One popular place for drinks, as well as for snacks, is the **Americana** (tel. 03/3564–1971). Drinks start at ¥800. Farther along the hallway is the **Music Pub** (tel. 03/3563–3757), which has live bands playing swing jazz. The cover varies but is usually ¥2,800–¥4,400, and drinks start at ¥700. There are also restaurants in the food center that, along with the bars, start closing at 11 PM. Yuraku Food Center is situated to the east of Yurakucho Subway Station and is the next building east of the Kotsu Kaikan Building (where JNTO has its administrative offices). The Kotsu Kaikan Building can be recognized by the circular sky lounge on its rooftop.

Beer Halls

Kirin City. This beer hall is a newer entry and has less of the glass-thumping atmosphere of other brewery-sponsored drinking establishments. (There are also Kirin beer halls in Roppongi, just south of the Roppongi Crossing, tel. 03/3479–2573; and in Shinjuku, on the west side of the station and opposite the Yodobashi Camera store, tel. 03/3344–6234.) *Izumo Bldg., 8-8 Ginza, Chuo-ko, tel. 03/3571–9694. Beer is ¥450. Open 11:30 AM–11 PM.*

Levante Beer Hall. This is a favorite spot for the Japanese male to stop in and have some drinks and down a half dozen raw oysters. Over the years, this old-fashioned beer hall has become a well-known landmark and an anachronism in an area that is modern with its marble and flashing lights. Located in the Ginza district, Levante is behind the Imperial Hotel and opposite the Tokyu Kotsu Kakan store. *2-8-7 Yurakucho, Chiyoda-ku, tel. 03/3201–2661. Beer starts at ¥530. Open Mon.–Sat. 11:30 AM–2 PM and 5–10 PM.*

Sapporo Lion. For a casual evening spent drinking beer and eating snacks—anything from yakitori to spaghetti—the Sapporo Lion offers an inexpensive night out. The beer hall's entrance is off Chuo-dori Avenue, near the Matsuzakaya

Department Store. *6-10-12 Ginza, Chuo-ku, tel. 03/3571–2590. Beer starts at ¥480. Open daily 11:30–10:30 PM.*

Discos

The disco scene is alive in Tokyo, but less well than it was before the uptown crowd started to feel the pinch in its discretionary income. Discos have always been ephemeral ventures, anyhow; they disappear fairly regularly, to open again with stranger names and newer gimmicks: the money behind them is usually the same. Even the ones we've listed here come with no guarantee that they'll still be around when you arrive, but it can't hurt to investigate. Where else can you work out, survey the vinyl miniskirt brigades, and get a drink at 3 AM?

Lexington Queen. From the day it opened in 1980, the Lexington Queen has been patronized by celebrities—from sumo wrestlers to rock stars to media celebrities, such as Sylvester Stallone and Rod Stewart. And they still keep coming. Why? Because the owner is Bill Hersey, society writer for *Tokyo Weekender*, a biweekly local newspaper. A lot of attractive people show up here, from foreign models to those working in the movie industry. *Daisan Goto Bldg., B1, 3-13-14 Roppongi, Minato-ku, tel. 03/3401–1661. Cost: ¥4,000 men, ¥3,000 women, which includes a free drink; a meal ticket to be used at the sushi bar costs ¥1,000. Many waiters speak some English. Open nightly 6 PM–5 AM.*

Maharaja. Eclectic is the word here, from the plaster *Venus de Milo* in the display window outside to the quasi-Mogul motifs within. Maharaja survives by being all things to all clients: it's a member's club that doesn't really require a membership; it runs "college nights"; it draws the hip young foreigners from Hiroo and the spillover crowd from nearby Roppongi. It shuts down, however, unaccountably early. *TBC Azabu Building, 1-3-9 Azabu Ju-ban, Minato-ku, tel. 03/3582–7700. Cost: Mon.–Fri. ¥4,000 men, ¥3,500 women; Sat.–Sun. ¥4,500 men, ¥4,000 women. Open 6 PM–midnight.*

The Square Building Discos. (Roppongi Square Bldg., 3-10-3 Roppongi, Minato-ku). Ten floors of assorted nightlife ventures, karaoke clubs, and restaurants that manage, despite the current uncertainties of the trade, to provide a few discos. The most durable of the lot is **Giza,** with its Egyptian motif (tel. 03/3403–6538; cost: ¥4,000 for men, ¥3,000 for women; open 6 PM–4 AM); another that's been around for a while is **Buzz-zz,** which boasts the latest music videos from "Rock America" (tel. 03/3405–7900; cost ¥4,000 for men, ¥3,000 for women; open 6 PM–midnight).

Live Music

Blue Note Tokyo. Young entrepreneur Tosuke Ito acquired the Tokyo franchise for this famed New York night spot in 1988 and set about making it the premier jazz club in town. *5-13-3 Minami-Aoyama, Minato-ku, tel. 03/3407–5781. Cover charge varies from ¥7,000 for relative unknowns to as high as ¥17,000 for superstars. Two sets a night, at 7:30 and 10. AE, MC, V.*

Body and Soul. Owner Kyoko Seki has been a jazz fan and an impresario for more than 15 years. There's still nothing fancy about this place; just good, serious jazz. *Senme Bldg. 1F, 3-12-3 Kita-Aoyama, Minato-ku, tel. 03/5466–3525. Cover* *charge ¥3,000, drinks from ¥600. Open 6 PM–12:30 AM. Closed Sun. AE, MC, V.*

Club Quattro. More of a concert hall than a club, the Quattro does one show nightly, with the accent heavy on "ethnic" music—especially Latin and African—by both Japanese and foreign groups. Audiences tend to be young and enthusiastic. *Parco IV Building, 32-13 Utagawa-cho, Shibuya-ku, tel. 03/3477–8750. Cover charge from ¥2,500 to ¥6,000. Shows usually start at 7 PM.*

Pit Inn. The shows change nightly, but the emphasis is on Japanese and Western light jazz, attracting performers such as pianist Cecile Taylor. The atmosphere is friendly, with seating shaped in a half-moon facing the stage. It is by no means elegant, more like a well-worn theater than a nightclub. The audience is mostly in their early 20s. *3-16-4 Shinjuku, Shinjuku-ku, tel. 03/3354–2024. Cost: ¥3,000 (¥4,000 on occasion, for headliners), 1 drink included. Open 7:30–11 PM.*

Nightclubs and Cabarets

Cordon Bleu. A full-course meal is served in this dinner theater, with seats to accommodate about 150 people. However, it is more intimate than its size suggests and attracts well-known names. Muhammad Ali's name is in the guest book. There are three shows a night (7:30, 9:30, and 11), with singers and topless dancers bobbing up and down onstage. It is possible to just eat hors d'oeuvres and watch the show. *6-6-4 Akasaka, Minato-ku, tel. 03/3582–7800. Reservations advised. Cost: ¥19,800 or ¥16,500 for full-course dinner and 1 drink; ¥13,200 for hors d'oeuvres and 1 drink. Open nightly 6:30 PM–2:30 AM.*

Showboat. Downstairs at the Hilton is this small, cheerful club with international cabaret acts, which attract both hotel guests and nonresidents for their leg-kicking dancers and warbling singers. *Tokyo Hilton Hotel, 6-6-2 Nishi-Shinjuku, Shinjuku-ku, tel. 03/3344–0510. Cover charge ¥3,500; table charge ¥1,000. Drinks start at ¥1,000. Open nightly 6 PM–1 AM; showtimes 7:30, 9:15, and 11:45.*

Skyline Lounges

Pole Star Lounge. For a view of old and new Shinjuku flickering beneath you, this lounge bar on the penthouse floor of the Keio Plaza is hard to beat. *Keio Plaza Inter-Continental, 2-2-1 Nishi-Shinjuku, Shinjuku-ku, tel. 03/3344–0111. Drinks start at ¥1,450. Open weekdays 4–11 PM, weekends 3–11 PM.*

Top of Akasaka. On the 40th floor of the Akasaka Prince Hotel, you can enjoy some of the finest views of Tokyo. If you can time your visit for dusk, the price of one drink gets you two views—the daylight sprawl of buildings and the twinkling lights of evening. *Akasaka Prince, 1-2 Kioi-cho, Chiyoda-ku, tel. 03/3234–1111. Drinks start at ¥1,100. Table charge: ¥800 per person. Open 11 AM–2 AM.*

4 Tokyo Excursions

Nikko

By Jared Lubarsky

At Nikko, a few hours' journey to the north of Tokyo, is the monument to a warlord so splendid and powerful that he became a god. In the year 1600, Ieyasu Tokugawa won a battle at a place called Sekigahara, in the mountains of south-central Japan, that left him the undisputed ruler of the archipelago. He died in 1616, but the Tokugawa Shogunate would last about another 252 years, holding in its sway a peaceful, prosperous, and united country.

A fit resting place would have to be made for the founder of such a dynasty. Ieyasu had provided for one in his will: a mausoleum at Nikko, in a forest of tall cedars, where a religious center had been founded more than eight centuries earlier. The year after his death, in accordance with Buddhist custom, he was given a *kaimyo*—an honorific name to bear in the afterlife; thenceforth, he was Tosho-Daigongen: The Great Incarnation Who Illuminates the East. The Imperial Court at Kyoto declared him a god, and his remains were taken in a procession of great pomp and ceremony to be enshrined at Nikko.

The dynasty he left behind was enormously rich. Ieyasu's personal fief, on the Kanto Plain, was worth 2.5 million *koku* of rice; one koku, in monetary terms, was equivalent to the cost of keeping one retainer in the necessities of life for a year. The shogunate itself, however, was still an uncertainty; it had only recently taken control after more than a century of civil war. The founder's tomb had a political purpose: It was meant to inspire awe and to make manifest the wealth and power of the Tokugawas. It was Ieyasu's legacy, a statement of his family's right to rule.

Toshogu Shrine was built by his grandson, the third shogun, Iemitsu. (It was Iemitsu who established the policy of national isolation, which closed the doors of Japan to the outside world for more than 200 years.) The mausoleum and shrine required the labor of 15,000 people for two years (1634–1636); craftsmen and artists of the first rank were assembled from all over the country. Every surface was carved and painted and lacquered in the most intricate imaginable detail; Toshogu shimmers in the reflections from 2,489,000 sheets of gold leaf. Roof beams and rafter ends with dragon heads, lions, and elephants in bas-relief; friezes of phoenixes, wild ducks, and monkeys; inlaid pillars and red-lacquer corridors—the Toshogu is everything a 17th-century warlord would consider gorgeous, and the inspiration is very Chinese.

Foreign visitors have differed about the effect Iemitsu achieved. Victorian-era traveler Isabella Bird, who came to Nikko in 1878, was unrestrained in her enthusiasm: "To pass from court to court," she writes in her *Unbeaten Tracks in Japan*, "is to pass from splendour to splendour; one is almost glad to feel that this is the last, and that the strain on one's capacity for admiration is nearly over." Fosco Mariani, a more recent visitor, felt somewhat differently: "You are taken aback," he observes in his *Meeting with Japan* (1959). "You ask yourself whether it is a joke, or a nightmare, or a huge wedding cake, a masterpiece of sugar icing made for some extravagant prince with a perverse, rococo taste, who wished to alarm and entertain his guests." Clearly, it is impossible to feel indifferent about Toshogu; perhaps, in the end, that is all Ieyasu could ever really have expected.

Nikko (which means "sunlight") is not simply the site of the Tokugawa shrine, however; it is also a national park of great beauty, about which opinion has never been divided. From above Toshogu, the Irohazaka Driveway coils its way up through maple forests to the park plateau and Chuzenji, a deep lake some 13 miles (21 kilometers) around. To the north, there are hot springs; at the west end of the lake, the spectacular Kegon Falls tumble more than 300 feet to the Daiya River. Towering above this landscape, at 1,312 feet, is the extinct volcanic cone of Mt. Nantai. "Think nothing splendid," asserts an old Japanese proverb, "until you have seen Nikko." Whoever said it first may not even have been thinking of the mausoleum down below.

Arriving and Departing

It's possible, but unwise, to go by car from Tokyo to Nikko. The trip will take at least three hours; getting from central Tokyo to the Tohoku Expressway—an hour of the trip or more—is a nightmare. Coming back, especially on a Saturday or Sunday evening, is even worse. If you must drive, take the expressway north to exit 10 (marked in English), and follow the green toll-road signs from there into Nikko.

Far easier and more comfortable are the Limited Express trains of the Tobu Railway, with 10 direct connections every morning, starting at 7:20 AM (additional trains on weekends and holidays) from the Tobu Asakusa Station, a minute's walk from the last stop on the Ginza subway line in Tokyo. The one-way fare is ¥2,300. All seats are reserved. Bookings are not accepted over the phone; consult your hotel or a travel agent. From Asakusa to the Tobu Nikko Station is 1 hour and 40 minutes. If you are making a day trip, the last return trains are at 5:40 (direct express) and 7:38 PM (with a transfer at Shimo-Imaichi).

If you have a JR Rail Pass, we suggest you use JR service, which connects Tokyo and Nikko, from Ueno. Take the Tohoku Line limited express to Utsunomiya (about 1½ hours) to Utsunomiya and transfer to the train (45 minutes) for JR Nikko Station. The earliest departure from Ueno is at 6:51 AM; the last connection back leaves Nikko at 8:25 PM and brings you into Ueno at 10:45. More expensive but faster is the "yamabiko" train on the north extension of the Shinkansen. The first one leaves Tokyo Station at 6:00 AM (or Ueno at 6:06 AM) and takes about 45 minutes to Utsunomiya; change there to the train to Nikko Station. To return, take the 9:24 PM train from Nikko to Utsunomiya and catch the last "yamabiko" back at 10:40, arriving in Tokyo at 11:32.

Getting Around

In Nikko itself, you won't need much in the way of transportation but your own two feet; nothing is terribly far from anything else. Local buses leave the railway station for Lake Chuzenji, stopping just above the entrance to the Toshogu Shrine, approximately every 30 minutes from 6:35 AM. The fare to Chuzenji is ¥1,050 for adults, ¥530 for children under 12; the ride takes about 50 minutes. The last return bus from the lake leaves at 8:29 PM. Cabs are readily available; the one-way fare from the Tobu Nikko Station to Chuzenji is about ¥5,800.

Guided Tours

From Tokyo, two companies offer guided tours to Nikko. **Japan Amenity Travel** (tel. 03/5952–1500) operates a one-day motorcoach tour (lunch included) daily March 20–November 30. The tour includes the Toshogu Shrine and Lake Chuzenji. Pickup from major hotels begins at 8 AM. Cost: ¥19,000 adults, ¥14,300 children under 12 (lunch included).

Tobu Travel Co., Ltd. (tel. 03/3281–6622). All-Day Nikko Tour departs at 9 AM; it includes Lake Chuzenji and returns at 6:45 PM. Cost (breakfast and lunch included): ¥19,000 adults, ¥14,300 children under 12.

Exploring

Numbers in the margin correspond to points of interest on the Nikko Area map.

Toshogu Shrine Area

The town of Nikko is essentially one long avenue (Cryptomeria Avenue), extending for about a mile from the railway stations to Toshogu. This street is lined with tourist inns and shops, and if you have time, you might want to make this a leisurely walk. The antiques shops along the way may turn up interesting—but expensive— pieces (armor fittings, hibachi, pottery, dolls), and the souvenir shops will have ample selections of the local wood carvings. Alternatively, you can save yourself the hike up through town by taking the bus from either railway station (fare: ¥180) to Shinkyo (the Sacred Bridge).

Before the bridge, at the top of the hill, on the left, is the entrance to the **Kanaya Hotel**, owned and operated by the same family for over 100 years. The main building is a delightful, rambling Victorian survival that has played host to royalty and other important personages—as the guest book attests—from all over the world. The road curves to the left and crosses the Daiya River; on the left is the red-lacquer wood **Shinkyo**, a bridge built in 1636 for shoguns and imperial messengers on their visits to the shrine. It is still used for ceremonial occasions. (The original structure was destroyed in a flood; the present version dates to 1907.) Once, ordinary mortals were not permitted on the bridge. Now, you may pay ¥300 for the privilege of walking over it.

The main entrances to the Toshogu Shrine area are opposite the bridge, on the right, where there is also a **Monument to Masatane Matsudaira,** one of the two feudal lords charged with the actual construction of the Toshogu. Matsudaira's great contribution was the planting of the wonderful cryptomerias (Japanese cedars) around the shrine and along all the approaches to it. The project took over 20 years, from 1628 to 1651; the result was some 40 miles (64 kilometers) of cedar-lined avenues. Fire and attrition have taken their toll, but some 13,000 of these trees still stand—a setting of solemn majesty the buildings themselves could never have achieved.

Take either the ramp or the stone stairway to the grounds of the Toshogu Shrine (The buildings on the grounds are open Apr.–Oct., 8–5 [enter by 4:30]; Nov.–Mar., 8–4 [enter by

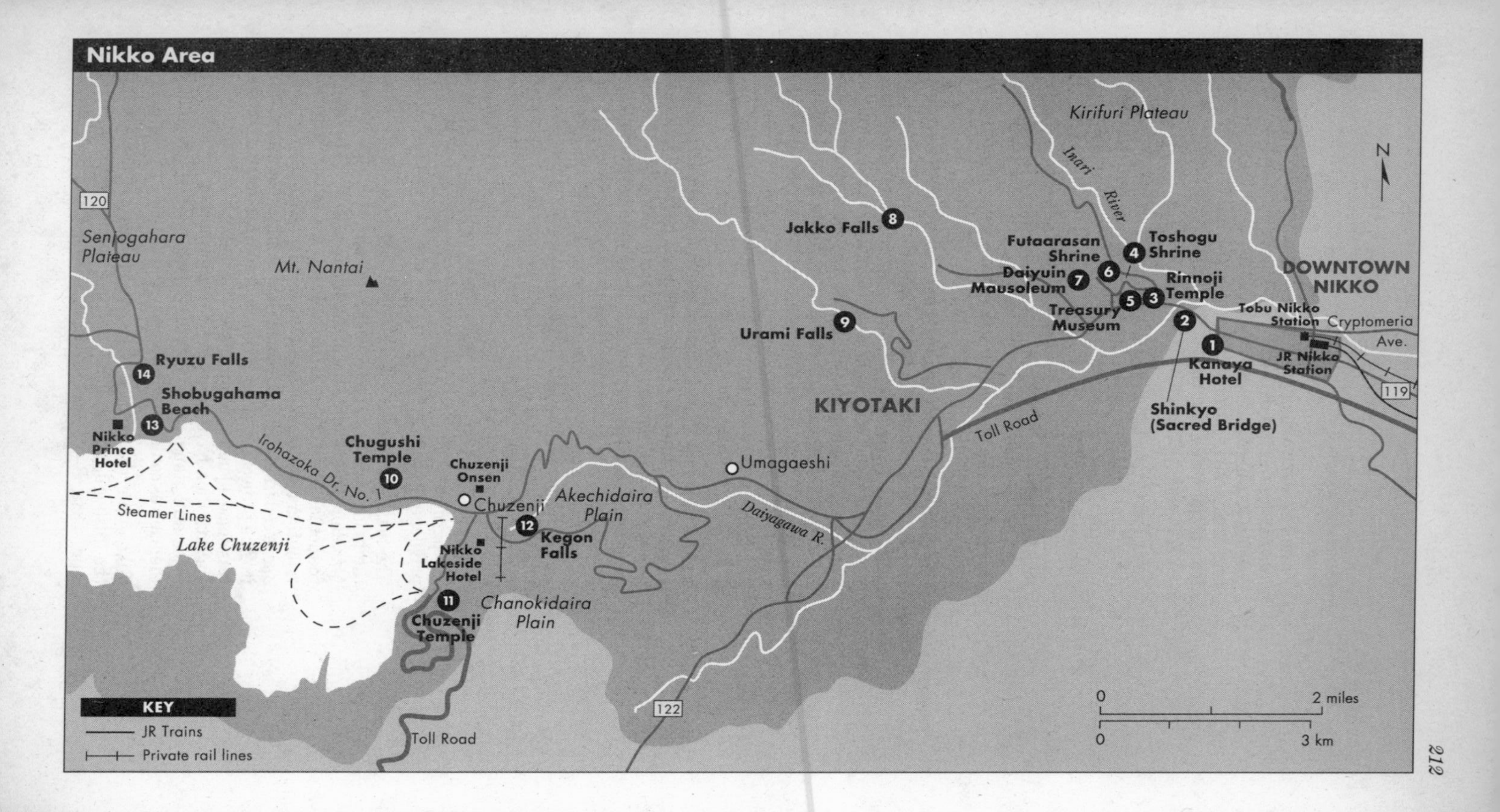

Nikko Area
Kirifuri Plateau
Inari River
Jakko Falls
Futaarasan Shrine
Toshogu Shrine
Daiyuin Mausoleum
Rinnoji Temple
DOWNTOWN NIKKO
Tobu Nikko Station
Cryptomeria Ave.
Treasury Museum
Urami Falls
Kanaya Hotel
JR Nikko Station
119
KIYOTAKI
Shinkyo (Sacred Bridge)
Toll Road
120
Senjogahara Plateau
Mt. Nantai
Ryuzu Falls
Shobugahama Beach
Nikko Prince Hotel
Chugushi Temple
Chuzenji Onsen
Irohazaka Dr. No. 1
Umagaeshi
Chuzenji
Akechidaira Plain
Steamer Lines
Daiyagawa R.
Kegon Falls
Lake Chuzenji
Nikko Lakeside Hotel
Chanokidaira Plain
Chuzenji Temple
KEY
JR Trains
Private rail lines
122
Toll Road
0
2 miles
0
3 km

3:30].) At the top of the stairway, in the corner of the car park, you can purchase a multiple entry ticket (¥1,250 adults, ¥400 children under 12) for the Rinnoji Temple, the Daiyuin (the mausoleum of the third shogun, Iemitsu Tokugawa), the Toshugu Shrine, and the Futaarasan Shrine; separate fees are charged for admission to other areas.

Turn left from the ticket area to enter the grounds of the ❸ **Rinnoji Temple** (open 8–4; enter by 3:30). The Rinnoji belongs to the Tendai sect of Buddhism, the head temple of which is Enryakuji, on Mt. Hiei near Kyoto. Behind the Hondo—the abbot's quarters—is an especially fine little Japanese garden, made in 1815, and a museum, which has a good collection of lacquer, paintings, and Buddhist sculpture. *Museum admission, including the gardens: ¥710 adults, ¥280 children under 12. Open 8–4.*

The main hall of the temple, called the **Sambutsudo,** is the largest single building at Toshogu; it enshrines an image of Amida Nyorai, the Buddha of the Western Paradise, flanked on the right by a Senju (Thousand-Armed) Kannon, the goddess of mercy, and on the left by a Bato-Kannon, regarded as the protector of animals. These three images are lacquered in gold and date from the early part of the 17th century. The original Sambutsudo is said to have been built in 848 by the priest Ennin (794–864), also known as Jikaku-Daishi; the present building dates from 1648. Opposite, on the north side of the compound, is the **Gohotendo,** a hall that enshrines three of the Seven Gods of Good Fortune. These three are Buddhist deities derived from Chinese folk mythology: Daikoku and Bishamon, who bring wealth and good harvests, and Benten, patroness of music and the arts.

Leave Rinnoji by the west gate, turn right, and walk up the ❹ cedar-lined avenue to the stone *torii* arch of the **Toshogu Shrine.** On the left is the five-story **Pagoda** of the shrine—a reconstruction dating to 1818 but lately repaired. The first story is decorated with the 12 signs of the zodiac; the black-lacquer doors above each bear the three hollyhock leaves of the Tokugawa family crest.

Walk up the stone steps, and enter the shrine through the Omotemon (Front Gate) or the Niomon—Gate of the Deva Kings—with its two red-painted guardian gods. From here the path turns to the left; in the first group of buildings you reach on the left is the **Stable,** decorated with carved panels of pine trees and monkeys. The second panel from the left is the famous group of three monkeys—"Hear no evil, see no evil, speak no evil"—that has become almost the symbol of Nikko, reproduced endlessly on plaques, bags, and souvenirs of every sort. The Stable houses a white horse; this animal, either real or represented in a painting or carving, is traditionally found in Shinto shrines. A few steps farther, where the path turns to the right, is a granite font where visitors purify themselves by washing their hands and rinsing their mouths before entering the shrine. Behind the font is the **Kyozo** (Sutra Library), which is a repository for some 7,000 Buddhist scriptures, kept in a huge revolving bookcase nearly 20 feet high. Unfortunately, the Kyozo is not open to the public.

As you pass under the second (bronze) torii arch and up the steps, you see on the right a belfry and a tall bronze candelabrum; on the left is a drum tower and a bronze revolving lantern. The two works in bronze were presented to the shrine by the Dutch government in the mid-17th century. Under the policy of national seclusion, only the Dutch retained trading privileges with Japan, and even they were confined to the tiny artificial island of Deshima, in the port of Nagasaki; they regularly sent tokens of their esteem to the shogunate to keep their precarious monopoly. Behind the drum tower is the **Yakushido,** which enshrines a manifestation of the Buddha (Yakushi Nyorai) as the healer of illnesses. The original 17th-century building was famous for a huge India-ink painting on the ceiling of the nave, *The Roaring Dragon,* by Yasunobu Kano (1607–1685). The work was so named because when visitors clapped their hands beneath it, the echoes made it seem as though the dragon had roared. The Yakushido was destroyed by fire in 1961, and rebuilt; the dragon on the ceiling is by Nampu Katayama.

At the top of the steps is the **Yomeimon,** the Gate of Sunlight, which is the centerpiece of the shrine and is designated a National Treasure. It is also called the Higurashimon (Twilight Gate), implying that one could spend all day until sunset looking at its richness of detail. Rich the gate certainly is; dazzling white and two stories (36 feet) high, it has 12 columns, beams, and roof brackets that are carved with dragons, lions, clouds, peonies, Chinese sages, and immortals. The gate has numerous carvings that are painted red, gold, blue, and green. On one of the central columns, there are two carved tigers; the natural grain of the wood is used to bring out the "fur." To the right and left of the Yomeimon as you enter are galleries running east and west for some 700 feet, their paneled fences also carved and painted with a profusion of motifs from nature: pine and plum branches, pheasants, cranes, and wild ducks.

Inside the gate to the left is the **Mikoshigura,** a storeroom where the portable shrines that appear in the annual Toshogu Festival on May 17–18 are kept. The paintings on the ceiling of *tennin* (Buddhist angels) playing harps are by Ryokaku Kano. To the right is the **Kaguraden,** a hall where ceremonial dances are performed to honor the gods. Directly ahead, across the courtyard, is the **Karamon** (Chinese Gate), the official entrance to the inner shrine—also a National Treasure, and, like the Yomeimon, carved and painted in elaborate detail with dragons and other auspicious figures. Extending right and left from the gate is a wall, which encloses the **Honden** (Main Hall) of the shrine.

The entrance is to the right; here you remove your shoes (lockers are provided) and pass into the outer part of the hall, called the **Haiden** (Oratory), with its lacquered pillars, carved friezes, and coffered ceilings painted with dragons. Over the lintels are paintings of the 36 great poets of the Heian period, by Mitsuoki Tosa (1617–1691), with their poems in the calligraphy of Emperor Gomizuno-o. The Haiden is divided into three chambers: At the back of the central chamber is the Sacred Mirror, believed to represent the spirit of the deity enshrined; the room on the right was reserved for visiting shoguns and members of the three principal branches of the Tokugawa family; and the room on the left for the chief abbot of Rinnoji—who was always a prince of the imperial line.

Beyond the Haiden is a passage called the Ishi-no-Ma (Stone Room). This connects in turn with the sanctum, which is divided into three parts: the Haiden (Sanctuary), the Naijin (Inner Chamber), and the Nai-Naijin (Innermost Chamber). No visitors come this far. Here, in the very heart of Toshogu, is the gold-lacquered shrine where the spirit (but not the body) of Ieyasu resides—along with two other deities, whom the Tokugawas later decided were fit companions. One was Hideyoshi Toyotomi, Ieyasu's mentor and liege lord in the long wars of unification at the end of the 16th century; the other was Yoritomo Minamoto, brilliant military tactician and founder of the earlier (12th century) Kamakura Shogunate. (Ieyasu, born Takechiyo Matsudaira, son of a lesser baron in what is today Aichi Prefecture, claimed Yoritomo for an ancestor.)

Return to the courtyard between the Karamon and Yomeimon gates, turn left, walk down the long passage painted in red cinnabar, and then left into an open corridor. Just above the gateway here is another famous symbol of the Toshogu, the **Sleeping Cat**—a small panel said to have been carved by the sculptor Jingoro Hidari. A separate admission charge (¥430 adults, ¥300 children under 12) is levied to go beyond this point to the **Sakashitamon** (The Gate at the Foot of the Hill) and to the flight of 200 stone steps, up through the cryptomeria trees to **Ieyasu's Tomb.** The climb is worth making, if only for the view of the Yomeimon and Karamon from above.

Retrace your steps (it's a lot easier coming down), return to the arch in front of the shrine, and turn right. A few minutes' walk will bring you to the **Treasury Museum,** on the left, which houses a collection of antiquities from the various shrines and temples. *Admission: ¥500 adults, ¥200 children under 12. Open Apr.–Oct. 8:30–5, Nov.–Mar. 8:30–4.*

At the end of the avenue, bear right for the **Futaarasan Shrine.** To the gods enshrined here, Ieyasu must seem but a callow newcomer: Futaarasan was founded in the 8th century to honor the Shinto deity Okuni-nushi-no-Mikoto (god of the rice fields, bestower of prosperity), his consort Tagorihime-no-Mikoto, and their son Ajisukitaka-hikone-no-Mikoto. The shrine is actually in three parts: the Honsha, or main shrine, at Toshogu; the Chugushi, or middle shrine, on Lake Chuzenji; and the Okumiya, or inner shrine, on top of Mt. Nantai.

Walk through the bronze torii arch to the Karamon (Chinese Gate) and the Honden (sanctum)—the present version of which dates to 1619. To the left, in the corner of the enclosure, is an antique bronze lantern, some 7 feet high, under a canopy. Legend has it that the lantern would assume the shape of a goblin at night; the deep nicks in the bronze were inflicted by swordsmen of the Edo period—on guard duty, perhaps, startled into action by a flickering shape in the dark. This proves, if not the existence of goblins, then the incredible cutting power of the Japanese blade. *Admission free. Open Apr.–Nov., 8–5; Dec.–Mar., 9–4.*

Retrace your steps and turn right. The first two buildings you come to, on the left, are the Jogyodo and Hokkedo (popularly called the Futatsudo, or **Twin Halls**) of the Rinnoji Temple, founded in 848. Between them, a path leads to the compound of the **Jigendo Hall,** built in honor of Tenkai (1536–1643), the first abbot of the Nikko temples. The Jigendo is at the north end of the compound, to the right. At the west end is the **Go-oden,** shrine to Prince Kitashirakawa (1847–1895), last of the imperial princes to serve as abbot; behind it is his tomb and the tombs of his 13 predecessors.

❼ Return to the Twin Halls and turn left for the **Daiyuin Mausoleum.** (Admission is included in multiple entry ticket to Toshogu Shrine area mentioned earlier. Open Apr.–Oct., 8–4:30; Nov.–Mar., 8–3:30.) Iemitsu (1603–1651), one suspects, had it in mind to upstage his illustrious grandfather; he marked the approach to his own tomb with no fewer than six different decorative gates. The first is another Niomon—a Gate of the Deva Kings—like the one at the Toshogu Shrine. The dragon painted on the ceiling is by Yasunobu Kano (1613–1685). A flight of stone steps leads from here to the second gate, the Nitenmon, a two-story structure protected front and back by carved and painted images of guardian gods. Beyond it, you climb two more flights of steps to the middle courtyard. There is a bell tower on the right and a drum tower on the left, and directly ahead is the third gate, the Yashamon, so named for the figures of Yasha (a demon) in the four niches. This structure is also called the Botanmon (Peony Gate) for the carvings that decorate it.

On the other side of the courtyard is the Karamon (Chinese Gate), gilded and elaborately carved; beyond it is the Haiden, the oratory of the shrine. The Haiden, too, is richly carved and decorated, with the ceiling covered with dragons; the Chinese lions on the panels at the rear are by two distinguished painters of the Kano school. Behind the Haiden is the Ai-no-Ma (anteroom or Connecting Chamber). From here you can see the sanctum (Honden). Designated a National Treasure, it houses a gilded and lacquered Buddhist altar some 9 feet high, decorated with paintings of animals, birds, and flowers, in which resides the object of all this veneration: a seated wooden figure of Iemitsu.

Return to the Karamon Gate, turn left and left again. At the far west end of the wall, on the right, is the fifth gate: the Kokamon, built in the Chinese style of the late Ming Dynasty. From here, another flight of stone steps leads to a small, white-painted oratory. There is one last climb, to the sixth and last gate—the bronze Inukimon—and Iemitsu's tomb.

If you return to the torii arch in front of the Futaarasan Shrine and take the path to the right (south) down Nishisando, you will soon come to an exit from the Toshogu Shrine area on the main road. At this point, you may have given Nikko all the time you had to spare. If so, turn left, and a short walk will bring you back to the Sacred Bridge. If not, turn right, and in a minute or so you will come to the Nishisando bus stop, where you can take the local bus to Lake Chuzenji.

To Lake Chuzenji

❽ About ½-mile from the shrines (Tamozawa bus stop) is a narrow road to the right that leads to the **Jakko Falls**—an uphill walk of some 2 miles (3 kilometers). The falls descend in a series of seven terraced stages, forming a sheet of water about 100 feet high. Another turn to the right off the Chuzenji road, by ❾ the Arasawa bus stop, leads to the **Urami Falls.** "The water," wrote the great 17th-century poet Basho, "seemed to take a flying leap and drop a hundred feet from the top of a cave into a green pool surrounded by a thousand rocks. One was supposed to inch one's way into the cave and enjoy the falls from behind." It's a steep climb to the cave; the falls and the gorge are striking, but only the visitor with good hiking shoes and a willingness to get wet should try this particular view.

The real climb to Chuzenji Lake begins at **Umagaeshi** (literally: Horse-Return), about 6 miles (10 kilometers) from the Tobu Station, 5 miles (8 kilometers) from Toshogu. Here, in the old days, the road became too rough for riding; the traveler on horseback had to alight and proceed on foot. The lake is 4,165 feet above sea level. From Umagaeshi, the bus climbs a new one-way toll road up the pass; the old road has been widened and is used for the traffic coming down. The two roads are full of steep hairpin turns, and on a clear day the view up and down the valley is magnificent—especially from the halfway point at **Akechidaira,** from which you can see the summit of **Mt. Nantai,** reaching 2,484 meters (8,149 ft.). From May 5 to October 15, you'll often see energetic climbers making the ascent in about four hours.

The bus trip ends at Chuzenji village, which was named after the temple established here in 784. The temple was renamed **Chugushi** in the 19th century and incorporated into the Futaarasan Shrine; it lies just outside the village, on the road along the north side of the lake. The treasure house (admission: ¥300 adults, ¥150 children under 12) has an interesting historical collection, including swords, lacquerware and medieval shrine palanquins. *Temple open Apr.–Oct., 8–5; Nov.–Mar., 8:40–3:30.*

Chugushi is not to be confused with the present-day **Chuzenji Temple** (Tashikikannon), which you reach by turning left as you leave the village and walking about a mile along the eastern shore of the lake. The temple is part of the Rinnoji, at Toshogu. The principal object of worship is a 17-foot-high statue of Kannon, the goddess of mercy, said to have been carved over 1,000 years ago by the priest Shodo from the living trunk of a single Judas tree. *Admission: ¥300 adults, ¥100 children under 18. Open Apr.–Oct., 8–5; Nov., 8–4; Dec.–Feb., 8:30–3:30; Mar., 8–4.*

In front of the temple was the Utagahama (Singing Beach), so named because an angel was said to have descended from heaven here to sing and dance for Shodo; unfortunately, the "beach" is now a parking lot and a pier.

Just by the bus stop at Chuzenji village is a gondola (round-trip fare: ¥820 adults, ¥410 children under 12) to Chanokidaira Hill; about 1,000 feet above the lake, it commands a wonderful view of the whole surrounding area. Just below the gondola, on the outskirts of the village, is the top of **Kegon Falls.** Farther on, as the road starts to descend into the valley, you'll find an elevator (fare: ¥520 adults, ¥310 children under 12) that will take you to an observation platform at the bottom of the gorge. The flow of water over the falls is carefully regulated, but it is especially impressive after a summer rain or a typhoon. In the winter, the falls do not freeze completely, but form a beautiful cascade of icicles.

If you have budgeted an extra day for Nikko, you might want to consider a walk around the lake. A paved road along the north shore extends for about 5 miles (8 kilometers, or ⅓ of the whole distance), as far as **Shobugahama Beach;** a "nature trail" parallels the road, but it's not very attractive, especially in summer when there are hordes of visitors. It is better to come this far by boat or bus. From here the road branches off, for Senjogahara Plain and Yunoko Lake. Just above the Nikko Prince Hotel at Shobugahama are the **Ryuzu** (Dragon's Head) **Falls.** To the left is a steep footpath that continues around the lake to Senjugahama, and thence to a campsite at Asegata. The path is well marked but can be rough going in places. From Asegata, it's less than an hour's walk back to Chuzenji Temple.

Dining

Nikko has no shortage of popular restaurants geared to the tourist trade, though there is nothing special to distinguish one from another. Because they all have display cases outside with price-tagged plastic models of the food they serve, you at least know what you're letting yourself in for. Noodle shops are always safe for lunch; the dishes called *soba* and *udon* are inexpensive, filling, and tasty. In recent years Nikko has also come in to its share of Western-style fast-food restaurants.

For a meal in somewhat more upscale surroundings, try the dining room at one of the hotels listed below. Lunch will cost about ¥3,500 per person. Lunch at the Kanaya, with its air of old-fashioned gentility, is especially pleasant; the Boat House, at the hotel's branch hotel on the shore of Chuzenji, often has fresh trout from the lake.

Lodging

Kanko (tourist) hotels everywhere in Japan do most of their business with tour groups and large private parties. In Nikko and Chuzenji, especially, hotels seem almost relentless in the way they organize their schedules to move these groups in and out. At 7 or 7:30 AM, someone will knock on your door, demanding to remove the bedding; by 8:30, in most cases, no more breakfast service is available. Nothing is leisurely about kanko hotels; they tend to be noisy and relatively expensive for what they provide.

Four Western-style hotels in the area provide a welcome alternative. They fall into two price categories, Very Expensive and Expensive. Be warned that these hotels may add a surcharge to the basic rate at various times: weekends, nights before local festivals, July–August, October—in other words, whenever you are likely to want a room. Call ahead, or check with your travel agent for the prevailing rate at the time.

A 3% federal consumer tax is added to all hotel bills. Another 3% local tax is added to the bill if it exceeds ¥15,000. At most hotels, a 10%–15% service charge is added to the total bill. Tipping is not necessary.

The most highly recommended accommodations are indicated by a star ★.

Category	Cost*
Very Expensive	over ¥25,000
Expensive	¥17,000–¥25,000

Moderate	¥10,000–¥17,000
Inexpensive	under ¥10,000

**Cost is for double room, without tax or service*

Nikko ★

Nikko Kanaya Hotel. A little worn around the edges after a century of operation, the Kanaya still has the best location in town—literally across the street from the Toshogu Shrine area. The hotel is very touristy—daytime visitors, especially Westerners, come to browse through the old building and its gift shops. The staff is very helpful and is better at giving information on the area than the city information office. Rooms vary a great deal, as do their prices—up to ¥25,000 per person on weekends. The more expensive are all spacious and comfortable, with wonderful high ceilings; in the annex, you fall asleep to the sound of the Daiya River murmuring below by the Sacred Bridge. *1300 KamiHatsuishi-cho, Nikko 321-14, tel. 0288/54–0001 or (Tokyo office) 03/3271–5215. 77 rooms, 62 with bath. Facilities: pool, nearby golf. AE, DC, MC, V. Expensive.*

Pension Turtle. This member of the Japanese Inn Group offers friendly, modest, and cost-conscious accommodations with or without private bath. Located 15 minutes by foot from the Shinkyo in the direction of Lake Chuzenji (take the Chuzenji bus from either railway station and get off at the Sogo Kaiken-mae bus stop), the inn is conveniently located near the Toshogu Shrine. *2-16 Takumi-cho, Nikko 321-14, tel. 0288/53–3168. 7 Western- and 5 Japanese-style rooms. Facilities: Japanese and Western breakfasts and dinners. AE, MC, V. Inexpensive.*

Chuzenji

Chuzenji Kanaya. On the road from the village to Shobugahama, this branch of the Nikko Kanaya has its own boat house and restaurant on the lake. The atmosphere here is something like that of a private club. The hotel recently reopened after extensive renovations, and is now a bit more posh than ever. *2482 Chugushi, Nikko 321-16, tel. 0288/55–0356. 60 rooms. Facilities: boating, fishing, waterskiing. AE, DC, MC, V. Very Expensive.*

Nikko Lakeside Hotel. This is a recently built hotel in the village of Chuzenji, at the foot of the lake. The accommodation has no particular character, but the views are good, and the transportation connections (to buses and excursion boats) are ideal. Prices vary considerably from weekday to weekend and season to season. Check ahead. *2482 Chugishi, Nikko 321-16, tel. 0288/55–0321. 100 rooms, all with bath. AE, DC, MC, V. Moderate–Very Expensive.*

Shobugahama

Nikko Prince Hotel. This is a new luxury hotel, within walking distance of the Ryuzu Falls. The Prince chain is one of Japan's largest and most successful leisure conglomerates, with hotels in most major cities and resorts. Minor differences in architecture aside, they are all pretty much the same experience: modern creature comforts and professionalism. *Shobugahama Chugushi, Nikko 321-16, tel. 0288/55–0661. 46 twin rooms and 14 split-level maisonettes, all with bath. Facilities: pool, 2 tennis courts, water sports. AE, DC, MC, V. Expensive–Very Expensive.*

Kamakura

By Nigel Fisher

Visitors are attracted to Kamakura by its cultural souvenirs of the 141-year period when the city was the seat of Japan's first shoguns. The attraction is even greater because, after the 14th century, the ravages of history occurred elsewhere, and Kamakura's glorious past was unsullied; its history became a romantic blend of fact and fiction. During the 12th century, the Taira and the Minamoto clans were at each other's throats battling for supremacy. The Taira family won a major battle that should have secured their absolute control over Japan, but they made a serious mistake. They killed the Minamoto chief but spared his son, Yoritomo, and sent him to live in a monastery. But Yoritomo Minamoto was not destined for a monk's life; instead he sought to avenge his father. Gathering support against the Taira clan, he chose Kamakura as his base of operations. Surrounded on three sides by hills and with the fourth side guarded by the sea, Kamakura was a natural location for defense against enemy attacks. The battle between the Minamoto and the Taira clans revived. By 1192, under the leadership of Yoritomo's skillful half-brother, Yoshitsune, the Minamoto were victorious, and the Kamakura era (1192–1333) began; Yoritomo established a shogunal government. The emperor was left as a figurehead in Kyoto, and, for the first time in Japan's history, the seat of power was structurally and geographically removed from the imperial capital. The little fishing village of Kamakura became Japan's power center.

Yoritomo kept his antagonists at bay during his lifetime, but his successors were less than successful. His first son was assassinated, even though he had abdicated his position as shogun to become a monk, and the second son had his head sliced off by a disgruntled nephew. Because neither of Yoritomo's two sons had children, the Minamoto dynasty ended. Yoritomo's wife, Masako, who had followed tradition by shaving her head and becoming a nun when her husband died, filled the power vacuum. Upon the murder of her second son, her family, the Hojos, took power. This family remained in control, often acting as regents for nominal child shoguns, for the next hundred years.

The demise of the Kamakura era began as the Hojo resources were drained in the support of armies warding off two invasions (1274 and 1281) by the Mongol armies of China's Yuan dynasty. Although the fortuitous typhoons—the *kamikaze* (divine wind)—may have saved the day against the Mongols, Kamakura still had to reward the various clans who fought alongside the Kamakura army and who had to remain on the alert for further invasions. Displeased with what they received, these clans grew dissatisfied with the Kamakura Shogunate. Emperor Godaigo saw his opportunity and rallied the discontented nobles to successfully defeat the shogunate. Thus ended the Kamakura era. The nation's authority, brought back to Kyoto, was shortly to be wrested away from Emperor Godaigo by the Ashikaga clan.

Kamakura reverted to a sleepy backwater on the edge of the sea. It remained an isolated temple town until the Yokosuka railway line was built in 1889, and not until after World War II did Kamakura develop rapidly as a wealthy residential district for commuters to Yokohama and Tokyo.

Arriving and Departing

By far the best way to reach Kamakura is by train. From Tokyo, trains run from Tokyo Station (and Shimbashi Station) every 10–15 minutes during the day. The trip takes 56 minutes to Kita-Kamakura (North Kamakura) and one hour to Kamakura. Take the JR Yokosuka Line from track no. 1 downstairs in Tokyo Station. (Track no. 1 upstairs is on a different line and does not go to Kamakura.) The cost is ¥760 to Kita-Kamakura, and ¥880 to Kamakura (or use your JR Rail Pass).

Guided Tours

Unfortunately, no English-speaking tours may be booked in Kamakura. However, you can take one of the Japanese-speaking tours, which depart from Kamakura Station eight times daily, starting at 9:20 AM. Purchase tickets at the bus office to the right of the station. Two itineraries are offered, one lasting about 2½ hours (¥2,400), the other about three hours (¥3,200). The last tours leave at 1:40 PM. Take with you the book *Exploring Kamakura: A Guide for the Curious Traveler*, written in English by Michael Cooper, and you'll have more information at your fingertips than your fellow Japanese tourists on the bus.

On Saturdays and Sundays, a free guide service is offered by the Kanagawa Student Guide Federation. Students show you the city in exchange for the chance to practice their English. Arrangements need to be made in advance through the Japan National Tourist Office in Tokyo (tel. 03/3502–1461). Be at Kamakura Station by 10 AM.

Tours from Tokyo are available every day, often combined with trips to Hakone. All major hotels in Tokyo can make the bookings, and, in most instances, a free pickup service is available from the major hotels. However, before you select a tour, make sure that it covers all of the Kamakura that you wish to see. Many do nothing much more than offer a fleeting glance of the Daibutsu (Great Buddha) in Hase. Our advice is to see Kamakura on your own. It is one of the easiest sightseeing trips to enjoy out of Tokyo.

Exploring

Numbers in the margin correspond to points of interest on the Kamakura map.

A tour of Kamakura is a walk through Japan's feudal era that brings back the personalities who lived and fought in the city's glorious age. The city has 65 Buddhist temples and 19 Shinto shrines. This chapter can include only a small percentage of them, but, hopefully, we can induce you to spend a little longer in Kamakura than the guided tours from Tokyo permit. Furthermore, Kamakura is accustomed to tourists, and most of the sights are either within walking distance of each other or a short hop on the bus or train.

For the purpose of seeing Kamakura's major temples and shrines, the following exploring section is divided into three separate areas. Traveling between each area is easily accomplished by short train rides. You could also walk everywhere, but there is certainly enough walking around the shrines and temples to satisfy most visitors.

The first tour explores the Tokyo side of Kamakura. Referred to as Kita-Kamakura (*kita* means north), it features the Engakuji Temple. The second tour covers Kamakura, one station stop south of Kita-Kamakura. This is downtown Kamakura, with a multitude of shops, restaurants, and Kamakura's venerated Tsurugaoka Hachimangu Shrine. The third tour visits Hase, to the southwest of Kamakura. It is reached by a 10-minute train ride on the Enoden Line. Hase's main attractions are the Daibutsu (Great Buddha) in Kotokuin Temple and the Hasedera Temple. These four sights (Engakuji, Tsurugaoka Hachimangu, Daibutsu, and Hasedera) are Kamakura's most important. It is easy to cover all four in a day and still leave time for lunch, shopping, and even a few more temples. However, a single day would be insufficient to cover all the places discussed in the following excursion, so judicious pruning may be required, and with only one day, you should not take the time to visit Enoshima Island, described at the end of this excursion.

Kita-Kamakura is the first train station to be reached from Tokyo on this excursion. For geographical simplicity, this excursion works its way south through Kamakura and Hase to Enoshima Island, a resort area along the coast. From there, rather than return through Kamakura, we take a train, using the Odakyu Line, back to Tokyo's Shinjuku. However, most visitors only have the time to go as far south as Hase before returning to Kamakura and Tokyo.

Kita-Kamakura

The first temple of major importance in Kita-Kamakura is ❶ **Engakuji Temple.** When you leave Kita-Kamakura Station, keep the train tracks on your right and walk five minutes to the south. On your left will be Engakuji Temple. This is the second most important of Kamakura's five Great Mountain Temples and once contained as many as 50 buildings. It has had more than its fair share of fires, and, though many of the buildings have been restored, Engakuji's former glory has long since passed. However, a simplicity of mood and a feeling of agelessness permeates this temple complex. One would expect it to be so: This Buddhist temple adheres to the Rinzai sect of Zen Buddhism.

Introduced into Japan from China at the beginning of the Kamakura period (1192–1333), Zen Buddhism was quickly accepted by the samurai class. The samurai caste evolved from the stewards and lesser retainers on imperial estates who led lives far from the ease and refinement of the Kyoto court; these new warrior clans were especially attracted to Zen Buddhism, particularly the Rinzai sect, with its asceticism and its spontaneous moments of enlightenment. Rinzai sees the path to enlightenment through the ability to get beyond the immediate reality by understanding, for example, what is meant by the sound of one hand clapping. To reach this understanding is to have reached a spiritual level where mortal feeling is transcended. Searching for the spiritual among the old Japanese cedars and stone-paved walkways of Engakuji seems natural.

Among the National Treasures within the temple complex is the Shariden (Hall of the Holy Relics of Buddha). It has survived the many fires that have raged through the complex these last seven centuries and is the only temple to have kept its orig-

Engakuji Temple, **1**
Ennoji Temple, **6**
Enoshima Island, **17**
Hasedera Temple, **15**
Hokokuji Temple, **10**
Jochiji Temple, **4**
Jomyoji Temple, **11**
Kamakura Museum, **9**
Kamakuragu Shrine, **13**
Kenchoji Temple, **5**
Kotokuin Temple (Daibutsu), **14**
Meigetsu-in Temple, **3**
Municipal Museum of Modern Art, **8**
Ryukoji Temple, **16**
Tokeiji Temple, **2**
Tsurugaoka Hachimangu Shrine, **7**
Yoritomo's Tomb, **12**

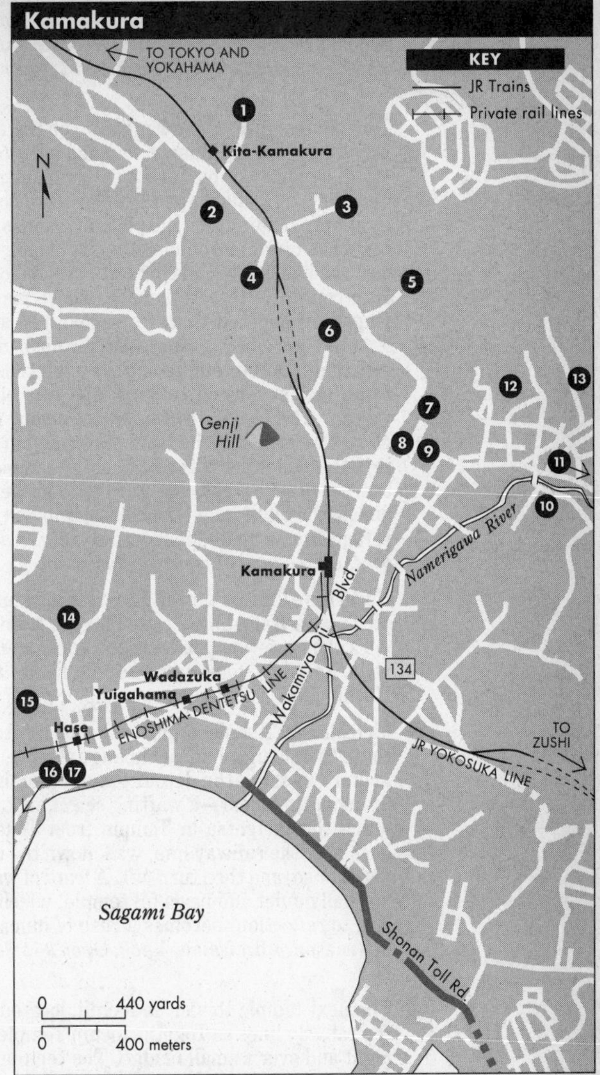

inal form since it was built, in 1282. You cannot go beyond its gate, but you can peer through the gate for a fairly good look. The other famous National Treasure at Engakuji is the great belfry standing on the hilltop. Cast in 1301, Kamakura's most celebrated bell stands eight feet tall. Only on rare occasions is it used, such as New Year's. If you are fortunate enough to hear its deep resonant tone, you will be one step closer to understanding the sound of one hand clapping. The two structures open to the public are Butsunichian, which has a long tearoom where visitors can enjoy the Japanese tea ceremony, and the Obai-in. The latter is the mausoleum of Hojo Tokimune, his son, and his grandson, the last three regents before Kamakura fell. Off to the side of the mausoleum is a quiet garden with apricot trees (they bloom in Feb.), where you can contemplate Kamakura's demise. *Admission: ¥200 adults, ¥100 children under 12. Open Nov.–Mar., 8–4; Apr.–Sept., 8–5; Oct., 8–4:30.*

2 Ten minutes away from Engakuji, on the other side of the railway line, is **Tokeiji Temple,** founded in 1285. Its fame, or notoriety, is indicated by its more common name, the "Divorce Temple." In feudal Japan, the husband could obtain a divorce by simply sending his wife packing. Not so for the wife; no matter what cruel and unusual punishments her husband meted out, she had no grounds for securing a divorce. However, in the 13th century, Hojo Tokimune (whose mausoleum you saw at Engakuji) decreed that if a woman ran away and made it to Tokeiji before being caught by her husband, she could receive sanctuary at the temple and stay there as a nun. After three years (later reduced to two), she was officially declared divorced. The temple remained a convent until the end of the Meiji Restoration. The last abbess died in 1902; her headstone is in the cemetery at the back of the temple. The cemetery has the peace of a Japanese garden. The headstones, scattered among the plum trees (they blossom in Feb.), are the symbols of refuge from a male-dominated society. *Admission: ¥50 (¥300 for the Treasury Museum). Open 8:30–5.*

If you have limited time in Kamakura, return from Tokeiji Temple to Kita-Kamakura Station for the train (one stop) to Kamakura. If, however, you have the energy and the time, you can walk to visit four temples en route to the Tsurugaoka Hachimangu Shrine, the next major place of interest.

3 **Meigetsu-in Temple** requires a small detour from the direct route to Tsurugaoka Hachimangu Shrine, but if you are in Kamakura in June, the detour may be worthwhile to see the hydrangeas in bloom—a wafting sea of pink, white, and blue. To reach the Meigetsu-in Temple from Tokeiji, you must cross back over the railway line, walk down the main road a hundred yards or so, and then turn left. A word of warning, though: This normally quiet and peaceful temple, which is usually so conducive to reflection, becomes a rush of humanity during hydrangea season. *Admission: ¥200. Open 9–4:30, hydrangea season 7–5.*

4 The next temple to visit is **Jochiji,** located on the same side of the railway lines as Tokeiji. Jochiji Temple's entrance is on the right and over a small bridge. The temple is at the top of a series of moss-covered steps. The buildings are new replacements (about 50 years old) for the originals, which, like so many other temples in Japan, were destroyed by fire. But rather than Jochiji's buildings, it is the garden that makes the temple complex so appealing—standing in the northern sector are statues of the Seven Gods of Fortune. *Admission: ¥100 adults, ¥50 children under 12. Open 9–5.*

5 The next temple on the way to Tsurugaoka Hachimangu Shrine is **Kenchoji,** the most important of Kamakura's five main temples. One has only an inkling of how magnificent this temple was when it was completed in 1253. Successive fires destroyed the buildings, and, though many of the buildings have been authentically reconstructed, the complex is half its original size. Near the Sanmon Gate is a bronze bell cast in 1255. It is the most revered treasure of the temple. The other key structures

are the Main Hall and its Ceremonial Gate, a huge structure held together by wood wedges, yet having a light and delicate appearance. Both Kenchoji and Engakuji (the temple we visited first) are still active temples of the Rinzai sect of Zen Buddhism, where novitiates are trained and laymen come to take sessions in zazen meditation. You will often see groups of laymen sitting on the grounds while the master, who carries a wooden staff, stands among them, ensuring that their concentration is not wandering. *Admission: ¥300 adults, ¥100 children under 14. Open 8:30–4:30.*

❻ Across the road from Kenchoji is **Ennoji Temple.** While it may not have great aesthetic value, this structure is a macabre change from the others. During the feudal period, a belief was held that souls en route to the afterlife would be judged by the Ten Kings of Heaven. Ennoji houses statues of these judges, and, far from looking compassionate, the judges display the most merciless countenances. To see them is enough to place you on your best behavior until their images fade from your memory. *Admission: ¥100 adults, ¥50 children under 12. Open 10–4.*

If you walk another 200 yards south from Ennoji Temple, you ❼ arrive at the **Tsurugaoka Hachimangu Shrine.** However, for the benefit of those who took the train from Kita-Kamakura to Kamakura, we will begin our visit to Tsurugaoka Hachimangu Shrine from the station.

Kamakura

From the east side of Kamakura Station, walk across the plaza and go left on the main broad avenue, Wakamiya Oji. You'll easily recognize it. The golden arch of McDonald's is on the left and straight ahead is the first of three torii arches leading to the Tsurugaoka Hachimangu Shrine (often abbreviated to "Hachiman Shrine"). This is Kamakura's most important Shinto shrine and the best place to remember the Minamoto family.

When Yoritomo Minamoto became a father-to-be, he decreed that a stately avenue should be built through the center of Kamakura from the sea to the shrine. Such an avenue was to be fitting for a young prince's procession to the shrine. The avenue was completed and a son, Yoriie, was born, and a magnificent procession advanced up the avenue to the shrine for the prince to be blessed. Yoriie's future, though, was limited. At the age of 18, he became shogun. Weak in popularity and unable to master intrigue, Yoriie soon abdicated to become a monk. A year later he was assassinated. Although Yoriie never completed great deeds, his memory lives on with Wakamiya Oji, which translates as "Young Prince Avenue."

At the far end of Wakamiya Oji and at the entrance to the shrine, a small steeply arched vermilion bridge (Drum Bridge) crosses over a small stream that links two lotus ponds. Yoritomo had requested the creation of these ponds, and his wife, Masako, suggested placing islands in each. In the large pond to the right, filled with white lotus flowers, she placed three islands to represent the Minamoto clan (the Genji Pond); in the smaller pond to the left, she had four islands symbolizing the defeated Taira clan (the Heike Pond). The symbolism is significant. Three is considered a lucky number; four is unlucky.

Once you go over the Drum Bridge, the first structure you see is the Maiden Hall. The hall is the setting for the story so often retold in Noh and Kabuki theater, and it bears telling here. Though Yoritomo was the political force in defeating the Taira and establishing the Kamakura Shogunate, it was his dashing half-brother, Yoshitsune, who actually defeated the Taira in battle. In so doing, he won the admiration of many, and Kyoto used this to promote rumors that Yoshitsune had plans to become shogun. Yoritomo started to believe these rumors, and despite Yoshitsune's declaration of allegiance, Yoritomo had him exiled and sent assassins to have him killed. Yoshitsune spent his life fleeing from one place to another until, in his 30th year, his enemies surrounded him and he was left with two options, suicide or capture. He chose the former.

Meanwhile his lover, Shizuka Gozen, a former dancer, was left behind in Kamakura. Yoritomo and his wife, Masako, commanded Shizuka to perform a dance, expecting her to do penitence. Instead, she danced to the joy of her love for Yoshitune and her concern for him in exile. Yoritomo was furious, and only Masako's influence kept him from ordering her death. However, when he found out that she was with child by his half brother, he ordered that, if it was a boy, the child was to be killed. Tension built up as Shizuka came closer to motherhood. A boy was born. Some historians tell how the child was brutally slaughtered down by the sea, while others say the child was placed in a cradle and cast adrift in the reeds, Moses-style. The tear-rendering drama is enacted once a year during the Spring Festival on the stage at Maiden Hall.

Behind the Maiden Hall is a flight of steps leading to the shrine's Main Hall. To the left of these steps is a ginkgo tree that was witness to a dastardly deed 700 years ago. From behind this tree, Priest Kugyo lurched out and lopped off the head of his uncle, the 26-year-old Minamoto-no-Sanetomo, the second and last son of Yoritomo. The priest was quickly apprehended, but the head of the second son was never found.

Like all Shinto shrines, the Main Hall is relatively bare and not particularly noteworthy. It was originally built in 1191, but the current version dates back to 1828. Within the shrine's precincts are two museums. The **Municipal Museum of Modern Art** (tel. 0467/22–5000) the ferro-concrete complex near the Heike Pond, contains Japanese oil and watercolor paintings, wood blocks, and sculptures. *Admission: ¥720 to ¥920, depending on the exhibition. Open 10–4:30. Closed Mon. and the day following national holidays.*

The other museum, the **Kamakura Museum** (tel. 0467/22–0753) exhibits a fine collection of objects pertaining to the Kamakura period and a display of ukiyo-e (wood-block prints). Of the two exhibitions, the latter is more interesting and has more relevance to Japan's early shogunate. *Admission: ¥150 adults, ¥70 children under 12. Open 9–4. Closed Mon. and national holidays.*

While crowds may gather at the Tsurugaoka Hachimangu Shrine, peace is often found at the **Hokokuji Temple,** a little Zen temple of the Rinzai sect that was built in 1334. Over the years, it fell into disrepair and neglect until, recently, an enterprising priest took over. He has since cleaned up the gardens and successfully promotes the temple for sessions in zazen and for calligraphy exhibitions. While some criticize the temple's commercial endeavors, on a quiet day the gardens offer rest and, at the back of the temple, a thick bamboo grove, with a small teahouse. Relaxing here an hour or so makes for a delightful interlude from the endless trail from statue to altar. To reach Hokokuji, take the street that leads off to the right from Tsurugaoka Hachimangu Shrine and Wakamiya Oji. After a mile, there will be a sign on the right-hand side, which leads you to Hokokuji. *Admission: ¥200. Open 9–4.*

⓫ Several other temples are in the vicinity of Hokokuji. **Jomyoji Temple,** which was founded in 1188, is across the street and 100 yards to the right. Some 300 yards back on the road to Kamakura and then up a street to the right is ⓬ **Yoritomo's Tomb.** It is surprisingly plain, but you may want to pay tribute to the man who placed Kamakura on the map. To the right of Yoritomo's Tomb (you must retrace your steps for 100 yards and make virtually a U-turn at the first street on the left) is the ⓭ **Kamakuragu Shrine.** This Shinto shrine was built after the Meiji Restoration as a tribute to Prince Morinaga and as propaganda for the revived imperial regime. Prince Morinaga was the third son of Godaigo. After Godaigo's successful defeat of the Kamakura Shogunate, the imperial family soon came under pressure from the Ashikaga clan. Morinaga was an effective champion of the imperial cause. Naturally, this did not suit the Ashikaga clan's plans for takeover, so they denounced Morinaga as a traitor to the throne of Godaigo. Morinaga was held captive in the cave behind the present site of the Kamakuragu Shrine, and, before the truth finally dawned on Godaigo, Morinaga was beheaded.

A bus to and from Kamakura Station (bus stop #5) travels the street on which all these temples have their access roads. We recommend walking out from Kamakura and returning by the bus, because it is easier to recognize the stop for downtown Kamakura than the stops for each of the shrines. Downtown Kamakura is a good place to stop for lunch and shop. Restaurants and shops selling locally made products abound on Wakamiya Oji Avenue, and its parallel street, Komachi-dori Avenue.

Hase

Hase is the next area to explore for reliving Kamakura's past. Here you'll find the ⓮ **Daibutsu** (Great Buddha) in the **Kotokuin Temple,** and also the Hasadera Temple. To reach Hase, take the train (the Enoden Line located on the western side of the JR Kamakura Station) three stops to Hase Station. Off to the left of the station is the main street, and this leads, after a 10-minute walk, to the Kotokuin Temple.

Kotokuin Temple is totally dominated by the 37-foot-tall bronze statue of the Great Buddha. Sitting cross-legged, robed with drapes flowing in the classical lines reminiscent of ancient Greece, the compassionate Amida Buddha serenely smiles down on its audience. The bronze statue was cast in 1292, three centuries before Europeans reached Japan; the concept of the classical Greek lines used in the Buddha's robe must have been transmitted down the Silk Route through China during the time of Alexander the Great. The Daibutsu was probably first conceived, though not completed, in 1180 by Yoritomo Minamoto, who wanted a statue to outshine the enormous Daibutsu in Nara. Until 1495, the statue was housed in a wooden temple, which was washed away in a great tidal wave. Since then, the loving Buddha has stood exposed, facing the cold winters and hot summers for the last five centuries.

To some of us, it seems sacrilegious to walk inside the Great Buddha and inspect the statue's innards. But not to the Japanese. For an extra ¥20, one can enter Buddha's right side into his stomach. Not particularly interesting, but it is something that is done by many visitors. *Admission to the Kotokuin Temple: ¥150 adults, ¥100 children under 12. Open 8–5.*

If you retrace your steps from Kotokuin for about three-quarters of the way along the main street (toward Hase Station) and then take a right turn, **Hasedera Temple** will be before you. Hasedera is one of the most enchanting, sad, and beautiful temples in Japan. First, as you enter, is the garden with a small pond formation that inspires serenity despite the many visitors. Then, as you climb the flights of steep stone steps up to the Amida and Kannon Hall, you are astonished by the innumerable small stone images of Jizobosatsu. Jizobosatsu is one manifestation of the bodhisattva who stands on the border of this life and the next to guide souls to salvation. In its Japanese version, Jizobosatsu has many representations. Here at Hasedera, the Jizobosatsu is the bodhisattva who guides the souls of stillborn children. Mothers who have experienced the misfortunes of losing their unborn children dedicate small images of this god to pray for their souls. (Included in the term "stillborn" are aborted children.) The sight of the stone statues is strangely touching and melancholic.

Walking farther up the steps, one reaches the temple's main building; visitors are allowed in the **Amida Hall** (Amida-do) and the **Kannon Hall** (Kannon-do). The Kannon Hall is Hasedera's main attraction. In the center of the hall is Juichimen (11-faced Kannon); standing 30 feet tall, it is the largest carved wood statue in Japan. The merciful Kannon has 10 smaller faces on top of her head, symbolizing her ability to see and search out in all directions those in need of help. No one knows for sure when Juichimen was carved. Certainly it was before the 12th century. According to the temple records, a monk, Tokudo Shonin, carved two images of the 11-faced Kannon from a huge laurel tree in 721. The image from the main trunk was installed in Hase, located in what is known today as the Nara Prefecture. The other image was thrown into the sea to go wherever the sea decided that there were sentient souls in need of the benevolence of Kannon. The statue washed up near Kamakura. (It was not until much later, in 1342, that the statue was covered with gold leaf by Takauji Ashikaga, the first of the 15 Ashikaga shoguns who followed the Kamakura era.)

Amida Hall, the other major building of Hasedera Temple, has the image of a seated Amida. Yoritomo Minamoto ordered the sculpting of this statue in an effort to ward off the dangers of reaching the ripe old age of 42. (This age was considered to be unlucky.) The statue did the trick. Yoritomo made it until he was 52, when he was thrown from a horse and died soon after. Hence, the popular name for this Buddha is the *yakuyoke* (good-luck) Amida, and many visitors take the opportunity to make a special prayer here, especially before graduation exams. To the left of Amida Hall is a small restaurant where you can buy good-luck candy and admire the view over Kamakura Beach and Sagami Bay. Hasedera is the only Kamakura temple looking onto the sea, and this view, accompanied by the benevolent spirit of Hasedera, makes an appropriate end to a day of Kamakura sightseeing. *Admission: ¥200 adults, ¥100 children under 12. Admission to the Homutsukan (Treasure Museum) is ¥100 adults, ¥50 children under 12. Open Mar.–Nov., daily 8–5; Dec.–Feb. 28, daily 8–4:30.*

Enoshima

The Kamakura story would not be complete without Nichiren, the monk who founded the only native Japanese sect of Buddhism. Nichiren spent several years advocating his beliefs and criticizing the Hojo regents, who held power after the Minamoto shoguns. Exasperated, the authorities sent him to exile on the Izu Peninsula, then allowed him to return. But Nichiren still kept on criticizing, and in 1271, the Hojo rulers condemned him to death. Execution was to take place on a hill to the south of Hase. As the executioner swung his sword, a lightening bolt struck the blade and snapped it in two. A little taken aback, the executioner sat down to collect his wits. Meanwhile, a messenger ran back to tell the Hojo regents of the event. On his way, he met another messenger, who was carrying a writ from the Hojo regents commuting Nichiren's sentence to exile on Sado Island.

16 Followers of Nichiren built a temple in 1337 to mark this event on the hill where he was to be executed. The temple is **Ryukoji** and is reached by continuing south on the Edoden Line from Hase. The train cuts through Kamakura's defensive hills to the shoreline en route to Enoshima. Get off the train at the last station, Koshigoe, and walk in the direction of Enoshima. The temple is on the right.

While there are other Nichiren temples closer to Kamakura, Myohonji and Ankokuronji, for example, Ryukoji not only has the typical Nichiren-style main hall with gold tassels hanging from its roof but also a beautiful pagoda (1904), built as if to embrace the surrounding trees.

The shoreline in this vicinity, by the way, has some of the beaches closest to Tokyo, and, during the hot, humid summer months, it seems that all of the city's teeming millions pour onto these beaches in search of a vacant patch of rather dirty gray sand. It is not a beach resort to be recommended.

17 A more enjoyable place to feel the sea breezes is to cross over the causeway from Enoshima Station to **Enoshima Island.** The island is only 2½ miles (4 kilometers) in circumference and peaks with a hill at its center. At the top of the hill is the shrine at which fishermen would pray for a bountiful catch—before it became a tourist attraction. It used to be quite a hike up to the shrine, but now there is a series of moving escalators to the top with an array of souvenir stalls. Spaced around the island are several cafés and restaurants. On a clear, warm day you can have lunch at one of these restaurants with a balcony facing the bay.

The way back to Tokyo from Enoshima is by train to Shinjuku on the Odakyu Railways. There are five afternoon trains between 2:20 and 8:20 (more in the summer); the express takes about 70 minutes to make the trip and costs ¥1,080. Alternatively, one can retrace one's steps to Kamakura and take the JR Yokosuka Line to Tokyo Station.

Dining

Kamakura has a multitude of restaurants from which to choose, with places to eat near every sightseeing area. One can literally drop into a restaurant whenever the appetite strikes or a rest is needed. However, should you be in the vicinity of those mentioned below and the urge for a good meal comes over you, they are recommended.

A 3% federal consumer tax is added to all restaurant bills. Another 3% local tax is added to the bill if it exceeds ¥7,500. At more expensive restaurants, a 10%–15% service charge is also added to the bill. Tipping is not necessary.

The most highly recommended restaurants are indicated by a star ★.

Category	Cost*
Very Expensive	over ¥8,000
Expensive	¥5,000–¥8,000
Moderate	¥2,000–¥5,000
Inexpensive	under ¥2,000

**Cost is per person without tax, service, or drinks*

Kaseiro. Located on the street that leads toward Daibutsu at the Kotokuin Temple, this establishment offers the best Chinese food in the city. The restaurant is located in an old Japanese house, where the dining room windows look onto a small, restful garden. *3-1-14 Hase Kamakura-shi, Kamakura, tel. 0467/22–0280. Reservations advised. Dress: informal. AE, DC, MC, V. Open 11–8. Expensive.*

★ **Tori-ichi.** This elegant restaurant serves traditional Japanese fare (*kaiseki*) in tranquil surroundings. In an old country-style building, kimono-dressed waitresses serve sumptuous multi-course meals, including one or more subtle-tasting soups, sushi, tempura, grilled fish, and other delicacies. *7-13 Onarimachi, Kamakura, tel. 0467/22–1818. Reservations advised. Dress: informal. No credit cards. Open noon–2 and 5–9. Closed Tues. Moderate–Expensive.*

Tonkatsu Komachi. This restaurant is a useful place for lunch when you are shopping on Komachi-dori Avenue or going to (and from) Tsurugaoka Hachimangu Shrine. A range of Japanese food is offered (visual menu in the window); however, the tasty *tonkatsu* (pork cutlet) is its specialty. *1-6-11 Komachi, Kamakura 248, tel. 0467/22–2025. No reservations. Dress: informal. No credit cards. Open 11:30–7:30. Closed Tues. Inexpensive–Moderate.*

Kado Restaurant. This is a small noodle shop on the right side of the main road leading into town from Tokeiji Temple. The owners don't speak English and the menu is in Japanese, but the large portions of noodles with vegetables, meat, and/or fish will supply the energy you'll need to finish touring Kamakura. *Kamakura-Kaido, no tel. No reservations. Dress: informal. No credit cards. Inexpensive.*

Yokohama

By Nigel Fisher

For more than 200 years, Japan closed its doors to virtually all foreign contact. Then, in 1853, a flotilla of American ships under Commodore Matthew Perry sailed into the bay of Tokyo (then Edo) and forced the reluctant Tokugawa Shogunate to open Japan to the West. Three years later, Townsend Harris became America's first diplomatic representative to Japan. Once the commercial treaty with the United States was signed, Harris lost no time in setting up his residence in the Hangakuji Temple in Kanagawa. However, Kanagawa was one of the 53 relay stations on the Tokaido Highway, and the presence of unclean, long-haired barbarians caused offense to the traditional Japanese. Moreover, many samurai wanted Japan to remain in isolation and would be willing to give their lives to rid Japan of the foreign pestilence. Unable to protect the foreigners in Kanagawa, the shogunate required that Harris and all foreigners move from Kanagawa and establish a foreign trading port at nearby Yokohama.

At the time, Yokohama was a small fishing village surrounded by ugly mud flats. Foreigners, diplomats, and traders were confined to a compound, guarded with checkpoints. Harris considered, probably correctly, that he and every other Westerner were being placed in isolation. But changes were happening very fast in Japan. Within 30 years, seven centuries of shogunate rule would come to an end, and the period known as the Meiji Restoration would begin, in which, under the authority of Emperor Meiji, Japan sought Western advice and ideas. By the early 1900s, Yokohama was to become one of the world's busiest ports and Japan's major export and import center.

Yokohama's growth has been as dramatic as the crippling blows it has suffered. As soon as it became a designated international port in 1869, it started to grow rapidly. Most of the foreign traders who came to Japan set up business in Yokohama; as the port grew, so did the international community. An especially large community of British citizens developed from whom the Japanese frequently sought advice, on the grounds that Great Britain was also an island nation. Reminders of their presence can still be seen in the occasional game of cricket at the Yokohama Country and Athletic Club, which, while now open to all nations, used to be the domain where British expatriates would drink their gin and enjoy their refined activities.

Then Yokohama came tumbling down. On September 1, 1923, the Great Kanto Earthquake struck both Tokyo and Yokohama and destroyed much of the latter. Some 60,000 homes made of wood and paper burned, and 20,000 lives were lost. After such devastation, Yokohama could not retain its preeminence as Japan's international city and chief trading port. During the six years that it took to restore the city, many foreign businesses took up quarters elsewhere, primarily in Kobe and Osaka, and did not return to Yokohama.

Nevertheless, over the next 20 years, Yokohama mushroomed once more; a large industrial zone was built along its shoreline. Then everything came tumbling down again. On May 29, 1945, in a span of four hours, 700 American B-29 bombers leveled 42% of the city. Destruction was more extensive than that caused by the earthquake. Even so, Yokohama rose once more from the debris, and, boosted by Japan's postwar economic miracle, extended its urban sprawl all the way to Tokyo to the north and to Kamakura in the south.

With the advent of air travel and increased competition from other ports (Nagoya and Kobe, for example), Yokohama's decline as Japan's seaport continued. The glamour of great liners docked at Yokohama's piers has become only a memory, kept alive by a museum ship and the occasional visit by a luxury liner on a Pacific cruise. The only regularly scheduled passenger services are by a Russian and a Chinese vessel. To replace its emphasis on being a port city, Yokahama has concentrated on its industries—shipbuilding, automobiles, and petrochemicals are three of its largest—and its service to Tokyo as a satellite city. Yokohama has always been politically and culturally overshadowed by Tokyo, and that is no more apparent than today, as commuters swarm into Tokyo every morning from their homes in Yokohama.

Is Yokohama worth a visit? Certainly, it should not get top priority. The city has perhaps more interest to the Japanese than to Westerners. Up to World War II, people from Tokyo would come to Yokohama to see the strange *gaijin* (foreigners), their alien ways, and their European-style buildings. That image still persists, despite the destruction of most of the city's late-19th- and early 20th-century buildings. After all, Yokohama had Japan's first bakery (in 1860), operated by an enterprising Japanese, Noda Hyogo, who catered to Westerners. It was also the first city to have public toilets—83 of them were built in 1871. A year later, Japan's first railway, linking Yokohama and Shimbashi in Tokyo, was completed. So Yokohama does have memories of Japan's first encounters with the West; a notable building in the center of the city is the Port Memorial Hall, which commemorates Yokohama's position as the front-runner in opening Japan to the West. Yet, as fun as this trivia may be, Yokohama has less to see than one would expect. Indeed, a visit to Yokohama should only be made if one has an extra day to spare while in Tokyo, or when returning to Tokyo from an excursion to Kamakura, 20 minutes on the train south of Yokohama.

Arriving and Departing

Between the Airport and Center City

From Narita Airport, a direct limousine-bus service departs two or three times an hour between 6:45 AM and 10:20 PM for Yokohama City Air Terminal (YCAT). The fare is ¥3,300. JR Narita Express trains going on from Tokyo to Yokohama leave the airport every hour from 8:13 AM to 9:43 PM. The fare is ¥4,100 (or ¥4,900 for the first-class "Green Car" coaches). Alternatively, you can take the limousine-bus service from Narita to Tokyo Station and continue on to Yokohama by train. With either method, the total journey will take more than two hours, more likely three if the traffic is heavy. YCAT is a five-minute taxi ride from Yokohama Station.

By Train

From Tokyo

JR trains from Tokyo Station leave approximately every 10 minutes, depending on the time of day. Take the Yokosuka, the Tokaido, or Keihin Tohoku lines to Yokohama Station. (The Yokosuka and Tokaido lines take 30 min., and the Keihin Tohoku Line takes 40 min.) From there, the Keihin Tohoku Line (platform 3) goes on to Kannai and Ishikawa-cho, Yokohama's business and downtown areas. If you are going directly to downtown Yokohama from Tokyo, the blue-colored commuter trains of the Keihin Tohoku Line are best. From Shibuya Station in Tokyo, the Tokyu Toyoko Line, a private line, connects directly with Yokohama Station and, hence, is an alternative if you leave from the western part of Tokyo.

From Nagoya and Points South The Shinkansen Kodama trains stop at Shin-Yokohama Station, 5 miles (8 kilometers) from the city center. It is then necessary to take the local train for the seven-minute ride into town.

Getting Around

By Train Yokohama Station is the city transport center, where all train lines link together and connect with the city's subway and bus service. However, Kannai and Ishikawa-cho are the two train stations for the downtown areas. Use the Keihin Tohoku Line from Yokohama Station to reach these areas. Trains leave every two to five minutes from Platform Three. Once you are at Kannai or Ishikawa-cho, most of Yokohama's points of interest are within easy walking distance of each other. The one notable exception is the Sankeien Garden, which requires a short train and bus ride from downtown.

By Taxi During the day, ample taxis are available. Taxi stands are outside the train stations, and cabs may also be flagged in the streets. However, often the congested traffic makes walking a faster means of traveling. The basic fare is ¥600 for the first 1¼ miles, then ¥90 for every additional 1,145 feet. Vacant taxis show a red light in the windshield.

By Subway One line connects Shin-Yokohama, Yokohama, and Totsuka.

By Bus Buses exist, but their routes confuse even the locals.

By Car Rental cars are available from Yokohama Station, but the congested traffic and lack of street signs make driving difficult.

Important Addresses and Numbers

Tourist Information The **Yokohama Tourist Office** (tel. 045/441–7300; open 10–6; closed Dec. 28–Jan. 3) is in the central passageway of the Yokohama Station. A similar office with the same closing times is located at Shin-Yokohama Station (tel. 045/473–2895). The head office of the **Yokohama International Tourist Association** (tel. 045/641–5824; open daily 9–5, closed national holidays) is on the first floor of the Silk Center Building, a 15-minute walk from Kannai Station.

Emergencies **Ambulance** or **Fire,** tel. 119; **Police,** tel. 110. The **Yokohama Police Station** has a Foreign Affairs Department (tel. 045/623–0110).

Doctors **Washinzaka Hospital** (169 Yamate-cho, Naka-ku, tel. 045/623–7688).

English-Language Bookstore **Maruzen** (2-34 Bentendori, Naka-ku, tel. 045/212–2031) has a good selection.

Guided Tours

Double-decker buses of the **Blue Line** depart every 30 minutes from the east exit of Yokohama Station, circle the major tourist route—Osanbashi Pier, Chinatown, Motomachi, Harbor View Park, Yamashita Pier, Osanbashi Pier, Bashamichi—and return to the station. These tours operate weekdays, weekends, and national holidays 9:30–7:30 (Dec.–Feb. 10:10–5:25). Fare: ¥270 adults, ¥140 children under 12.

The **Teiki Yuran Bus** is a seven-hour sightseeing bus tour that covers the major sights and includes lunch at a Chinese restaurant in Chinatown. The tour is in Japanese only, though pamphlets written in English are available at most sightseeing stops. Tickets are sold at the bus offices at Yokohama Station (east side) and at Kannai, and the tour departs daily at 10 AM from bus stop 14 on the east side of Yokohama Station. Cost: ¥6,520 adults, ¥4,320 children under 12.

A shuttle boat, the ***Sea Bass,*** connects Yokohama Station and Yamashita Park in 15 minutes. The boat leaves every 20 minutes 10–7 from the east side of Yokohama Station and offers another view of Yokohama.

The sightseeing boat ***Marine Shuttle*** (tel. 045/651–2697) makes 40-, 60-, and 90-minute tours of the harbor and bay for ¥750, ¥1,200, and ¥2,000, respectively. Boarding is at the pier at Yamashita Park; boat departures are 10:30, noon, 2, 4:40, and 6:30 PM. Another boat, the ***Marine Rouge,*** offers 90-minute tours departing at 11 AM, 1:30 PM, and 4 PM, and a special two-hour evening tour at 7 PM (¥2,500).

Home-Visit System

The Yokohama International Tourist Association arranges visits to the homes of English-speaking Japanese families. These visits are usually for a few hours and are designed to give foreigners a glimpse into the Japanese way of life. To arrange a visit or for more information, call the Yokohama International Tourist Association (tel. 045/641–5824).

Exploring

Numbers in the margin correspond to points of interest on the Yokohama map.

As large as Yokohama is, its central area is quite self-contained. Because Yokohama developed as a port city, much of its activity has always been around its waterfront (the Bund) on the west side of Tokyo Bay. Kannai (literally: "within the checkpoint") is downtown, where the international community was originally confined by the shogunate. Though downtown has expanded to include the waterfront and Ishikawa-cho, Kannai has always been Yokohama's heart.

Downtown may be viewed as consisting of two adjacent rectangular areas. One area is the old district of Kannai, bounded by Bashamichi Street to the north and Nippon-odori Avenue to the south, with Kannai Station on the western side and the waterfront on the eastern. This area contains the business offices of modern Yokohama. South of Nippon-odori is another main area. Its northern boundary is Nippon-odori, and the southern boundary runs along the Motomachi Shopping Street and the International Cemetery. This rectangle is flanked by the Ishikawa-cho Station to the west, and Yashamita-Koen Park and the waterfront to the east. The middle of this part of the city is dominated by Chinatown.

Notwithstanding the lure of Bashamichi's shops and its reconstructed 19th-century appearance, the southern area holds the most interest if you are short of time. That is where the following walking tour of Yokohama begins.

Whether one is coming from Tokyo, Nagoya, or Kamakura, the best place to begin a tour of Yokohama is from the **Ishikawa-cho Station.** Take the south exit from the station and head in the direction of the waterfront. Within a block of the station is the 1 beginning of the **Motomachi Shopping Street,** which follows the Nakamura River toward the harbor. This is where the Japanese set up shop 100 years ago to serve the strange foreigners living within Kannai. Now the same street is lined with smart boutiques, jewelry stores, and coffee shops, and it attracts a fashionable younger crowd.

At the far end of Motomachi and up to the right is a small hill. 2 Here is the **International Cemetery,** a Yokohama landmark as a preserve for foreigners and a reminder of the port city's heritage. The cemetery started in 1854 when an American sailor chose this spot for his final resting place. Since then the burial ground has been restricted to non-Japanese. About 4,000 graves are on this hillside, and the inscriptions on the crosses and headstones attest to some 40 different nationalities who lived and died in Yokohama.

3 Behind the cemetery is the **Yamate Shiryokan Museum,** which preserves mementoes of the late-19th-century lifestyle of Westerners who lived in Yokohama. It is perhaps more interesting to the Japanese than it is to foreigners. *247 Yamate, Naka-ku, tel. 045/622–1188. Admission: ¥200 adults, ¥150 children under 12. Open daily 11–4. Closed Dec. 30–Jan. 1.*

4 One hundred yards beyond the museum is **Minato-No-Mieru-Oka Park** (Harbor View Park). Once the barracks of the British forces in Yokohama, the hilltop park offers a fine view overlook- 5 ing **Yamashita-Koen Park** and the harbor beyond. Should you ever find yourself staying the night in Yokohama, come to this park for the splendid sight of the harbor lights and floodlit gardens of Yamashita below.

Yamashita-Koen Park, just down from Minoto-No-Mieru-Oka, parallels the waterfront. It is a park for strolling or a place to rest, if one can find an empty bench free of dating Japanese cou- 6 ples. Near the park is the **Yokohama Doll Museum,** which houses 4,000 dolls from Japan and the rest of the world. The fairy-tale quality of the museum is a pleasant diversion from Yokohama's rather mundane sights with or without a child in tow. *18 Yamashita-cho, Naka-ku, tel. 045/671–9361. Admission: ¥300 adults, ¥150 children under 15. Open 10–5, July–Aug. 10–7. Closed Mon. (Tues. after a national holiday), Dec. 29–Jan. 1.*

Yamashita-Koen Park is a green urban oasis. Its existence is perhaps the only redeeming factor of the Great Kanto Earthquake in 1923. The debris of collapsed buildings left by the earthquake were swept away, and the area was made into a 17-acre park with lawns, trees, and flowers. The park's fountain, by the way, is a statue of the Guardian of the Water, presented to Yokohama by San Diego, one of Yokohama's sister cities.

Chinatown, **12**
Hikawa-maru, **8**
International Cemetery, **2**
Iseyama Shrine, **14**
Kanagawa Prefectural Museum, **11**
Marine Tower, **7**
Minato-No-Mieru-Oka Park, **4**
Motomachi Shopping Street, **1**
Nippon Memorial Park, **15**
Sankeien Garden, **13**
Silk Museum, **9**
Sojiji Temple, **16**
Yamashita-Koen Park, **5**
Yamate Shiryokan Museum, **3**
Yokohama Archives of History, **10**
Yokohama Doll Museum, **6**

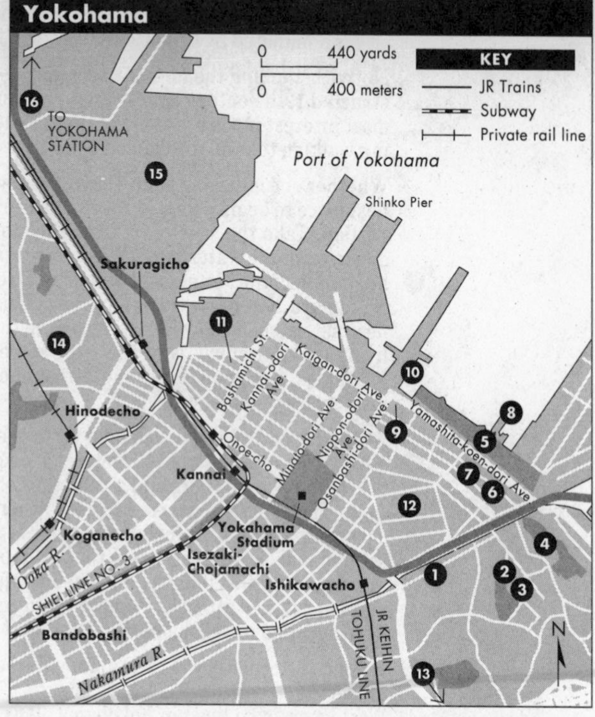

At the entrance to Yamashita-Koen Park is the rather ugly **Marine Tower** (tel. 045/641–7838), a decagonal building standing 348 feet high. It has a navigational beacon at the 338-foot mark and purports to be the tallest lighthouse in the world. At the 100-meter (328-foot) level, an observation gallery offers 360-degree views of the harbor and city. It is the best place to acquire an aerial appreciation of the area, and on clear days, preferably in the autumn, it is possible to see Mt. Fuji in the distance. Also contained within the Marine Tower is a bird museum (Birdpia) and the Yokohama Science Museum. *The Marine Tower Observation Room admission: ¥700 adults, ¥350 children 6–15, ¥250 children 3–6. Open 10–9, winter 10–6. (If sunny on winter holidays, open until 8:30.)*

On the waterfront and halfway down the park is where the ***Hikawa-maru*** is moored. For 30 years, the ship shuttled passengers between Yokohama and Seattle, making a total of 238 trips. It recalls the time when Yokohama was a great passenger port of oceangoing liners. It is not worth touring the ship, as brochures suggest, but the *Hikawa-maru* does have a public restaurant. A visit is best in the summer, when the ship's upper deck becomes a beer garden.

At the northern end of the park is the Silk Center Building; on its second floor is the **Silk Museum.** At the turn of the century, all of the Japanese silk for export was shipped out of Yokohama, and the museum pays tribute to those days. As well as a display of a variety of silk fabrics, the museum has an informative exhibit on the silk-making process. The attendants are very happy to answer questions. Also in the Silk Center Building, on the first floor, is the head office of the Yokohama International Tourist Association and the Kanagawa Prefecture Tourist Information Office. *1 Yamashita-cho, Naka-ku, tel. 045/641–0841. Admission: ¥300 adults, ¥100 children under 15. Open 9–4:30. Closed Mon., on the day after a national holiday, and Dec. 29–Jan. 1.*

10 Across the street from the Silk Building is the **Yokohama Archives of History.** The building was once the British Consulate and now houses some 140,000 items recording the history of Yokohama since the port's opening. On the other side of the street is the monument to the U.S.–Japanese Friendship Treaty. *3 Nihon Odori, Naka-ku, tel. 045/201–2100. Admission: ¥200 adults, ¥100 children under 15. Open 9:30–4:30. Closed Mon., on the day after a national holiday, and Dec. 29–Jan. 1.*

If one continues along the street running parallel to the waterfront, one reaches **Bashamichi,** the street that runs between Kannai Station and Shinko Pier. Literally, Bashamichi means "horse-carriage street," so named after it was widened to allow Westerners' carriages to pass. Now this redbrick road has become a nostalgic symbol of the city's 19th-century international past with antique-looking telephone booths and imitation gas
11 lamps. Halfway up the street is the **Kanagawa Prefectural Museum.** This Western-style structure with a domed roof was built in 1904 and is one of the few buildings in Yokohama to have survived both the Great Kanto Earthquake and World War II. The exhibits inside the museum—archaeological and natural-history artifacts from the region—have only marginal interest for the tourist. *Note:* The Museum will be closed for the whole of 1994 for renovations. *5-60 Minami Naka-dori, Naka-ku, tel. 045/201–0926. Admission: ¥200. Open 9–4. Closed Mon., the last Fri. of each month, and the day after national holidays.*

At the top end (away from the waterfront) of Bashamichi is
12 Kannai Station. One of Yokohama's unique neighborhoods, **Chinatown** is a 10-minute walk from there. From the station, just before you reach Yokohama Stadium, turn left to cut through Yokohama-Koen Park to reach the top of Nippon-odori Avenue. Then take a right, and you'll enter Chinatown through the North Gate leading to the 50-foot-high vermilion Hairomon Gate. If you have decided not to walk as far as Bashamichi, walk up Kaigan-dori from the Silk Building and turn left onto Nippon-odori, past the monument to the U.S.–Japanese Friendship Treaty, and then left, through the North Gate.

Yokohama's Chinatown is the largest settlement of Chinese in Japan. Not only are its small alleys full of shops selling Chinese goods, biscuits, and medicines, but also wonderful exotic aromas exude from the shops selling spices. The area offers a good opportunity to dine on authentic Chinese food and is the choice place for lunch in Yokohama. You'll find more than a hundred restaurants from which to choose. If you prefer a good Western meal, continue walking along the main street through Chinatown; you'll exit at the East Gate leading to Yamashita-Koen Park and the New Grand Hotel.

Additional Attractions

What has been left out of this walking tour through Yokohama are Sankeien Garden, Iseyama Shrine, Nippon Memorial Park, and Sojiji Temple. Let's first go to the Sankeien Garden, of which the *hamakko* (the name the locals give each other) are justly proud.

13 **Sankeien Garden** was once the garden of Tomitaro Hara, one of Yokohama's wealthiest men, who made his money as a silk merchant before becoming a patron of the arts. His garden was opened to the public in 1906. Amid its rolling hills, valleys, and ponds are traditional Japanese buildings, some of which have been transported from Kamakura and the Kansai area of Western Honshu. Especially noteworthy is the Rinshunkaku building, a villa built for the Tokugawa clan in 1649. There is also a tea-ceremony house, Choshukaku, built by the third Tokugawa shogun, Iemitsu Tokugawa. The other noteworthy buildings are the small temple transported from Kyoto's famed Daitokuji Temple and the farmhouse brought from the Gifu district in the Japan Alps.

Walks through Sankeien are especially rewarding for its flowering trees in the spring: plum blossoms in February, and cherry blossoms in early April. Then, in June, come the irises, followed by the water lilies. With the coming of autumn, the trees come back into their own with their tinted golden leaves. To reach Sankeien Garden, use the JR Keihin Tohoku Line to Negishi Station, where you can take a 10-minute bus ride to the garden. *293 Honmoku Sannotani, Naka-ku, tel. 045/621-0635. General admission: ¥300 adults, ¥60 children. The inner garden with the old traditional buildings has a separate admission of ¥300 adults, ¥120 children; it is open 9–4. The outer garden is open 9–4:30. Both gardens closed Dec. 29–31.*

14 **Iseyama Shrine,** a branch of the nation's revered Grand Shrines of Ise, is the most important shrine in Yokohama (admission free; open dawn–dusk). Its location requires a 10-minute walk from the Sakuragicho Station and is, for the tourist, perhaps only worth the time if one has seen most of everything else in 15 Yokohama. The **Nippon Memorial Park,** also 10 minutes by foot from the Sakuragicho Station but in the direction of the bay, is now the resting place of the ***Nippon-maru.*** This 1930 sailing vessel was used as a training ship and, in its time, made 46 voyages around the world. She was a beautiful sight under sail, but now she resides in permanent dry dock alongside the recently constructed (1989) maritime museum.

The last notable sight to visit before totally leaving Yokohama 16 is the **Sojiji Temple.** This is a worthwhile stop en route back to Tokyo. Take the JR Keihin Tohoku Line two stops to Tsurumi Station. Upon exiting the station, walk five minutes south (back toward Yokohama), passing Tsurumi University on your right. You'll soon reach the temple complex, which you may enter at the stone lanterns.

The Soto Buddhist sect, founded in 1321, was headquartered at Ishikawa on the Noto Peninsula (on the north coast of Japan, near Kanazawa). However, when the complex at Ishikawa was destroyed by fire in the 19th century, the sect erected its Yokohama temple complex. (Another Sojiji Temple is located at Eiheiji in Fukui Prefecture.) The Yokohama Sojiji is, therefore, relatively new, but it is a good example of Zen architecture; it is a very busy temple, with more than 200 monks and novitiates living in the complex. Visitors are not allowed to enter Emperor Godaigo's mausoleum (he was the emperor who defeated the Kamakura Shogunate), but one can visit the Buddha Hall and Main Hall. Both are large concrete structures. The Treasure House contains a wide variety of Buddhas. *Admission: ¥300. Open 10–4:30.*

Dining

Yokohama is a large, international city. The number and variety of restaurants are great, including more than 100 Chinese restaurants in Chinatown. The number of Japanese restaurants is uncountable; in the Mitsukoshi Department Store alone there are at least 32 tearooms and restaurants. The following are thus a small selection of what Yokohama offers and are restaurants familiar with the needs of foreign guests.

A 3% federal consumer tax is added to all restaurant bills. Another 3% local tax is added to the bill if it exceeds ¥7,500. At more expensive restaurants, a 10%–15% service charge is also added to the bill. Tipping is not necessary.

The most highly recommended restaurants are indicated by a star ★.

Category	Cost
Very Expensive	over ¥8,000
Expensive	¥5,000–¥8,000
Moderate	¥2,000–¥5,000
Inexpensive	under ¥2,000

**Cost is per person without tax, service, or drinks*

★ **Diane.** One of the most elegant restaurants in town, Diane is on the top floor of a seven-story banquet facility called Excellent Coast, between the Motomachi and Chinatown districts. The facade of the building evokes the Paris Opera House; Diane itself is impeccably done in brocaded chairs and draped alcoves, hand-painted bone china and Italian silver. The food (French classic) is superb; the service is spot-on. *105 Yamashita-cho, Naka-ku, tel. 045/211–2251. Reservations recommended, especially on weekdays. Jacket and tie suggested. AE, DC, MC, V. Open Tues.–Sun. 11:30–2:30 and 5:30–9:30. Very Expensive.*

Scandia. Known for its smorgasbord, Scandia is located near the Silk Center and the business district. It is popular for business lunches as well as for dinner. It also stays open later (midnight) than many other restaurants. *1-1 Kaigan-dori, Naka-ku, Yokohama 231, tel. 045/201–2262. Reservations advised. Dress: informal. No credit cards. Open 11 AM–midnight; Sun. 5–midnight. Very Expensive.*

Rinka-en. If you visit the Sankeien Garden, drop in at this traditional country restaurant serving kaiseki-style cuisine. The owner, by the way, is the granddaughter of Mr. Hara, the founder of the Sankeien Garden. *Honmoku Sannotani, Naka-ku, tel. 045/621–0318. Reservations recommended. Jacket and tie suggested. No credit cards. Open noon–5. Closed Wed. and midsummer. Expensive–Very Expensive.*

Kaseiro. A smart Chinese restaurant with red carpets and gold-tone walls, Kaseiro serves Beijing cuisine and is the best of its kind in the city. *164 Yamashita-cho, Naka-ku, tel. 045/661–0661. Reservations recommended. Jacket and tie suggested in the evening. AE, DC, V. Open 11:30–9:30. Expensive.*

Seryna. This establishment is famous for its Ishiyaki steak, which is fried on a hot stone, as well as for its shabu-shabu. *Shin-Kannai Bldg., 1 floor down, Sumiyoshi-cho, Naka-ku, tel. 045/681–2727. Reservations advised. Dress: informal. AE, DC, MC, V. Open 11:30–9. Expensive.*

Chongking. This is the city's best restaurant for Szechuan cooking. Although there has been a recent refurbishing, the focus of attention here is purely on the food. *164 Yamashita-cho, Naka-ku, tel. 045/641–8288. Reservations unnecessary. Dress: informal. AE, DC, MC, V. Open noon–9. Moderate–Expensive.*

★ **Aichiya.** Should you wish to try fugu (blowfish), the only chef in Yokohama licensed to prepare this delicacy is at this seafood restaurant. The crabs here—as expensive as the fugu—are also a treat. *7-156-1 Sezaki-cho, Naka-ku, tel. 045/251–4163. Reservations required. Jacket and tie suggested. No credit cards. Open 3–9. Closed Mon. Moderate.*

Rome Station. Located between Chinatown and Yamashita-Koen Park (just down from the Holiday Inn), this restaurant is popular for Italian food. *26 Yamashita-cho, Naka-ku, tel. 045/681–1818. Reservations suggested. Dress: informal. No credit cards. Open 11:30–10, holidays noon–9. Moderate.*

★ **Sparta.** This is Yokohama's best Greek restaurant, a relaxed and funky taverna where you can wander back to the kitchen to see what looks good. Sailors off the Greek ships in port bring the owners feta cheese, spices, the latest pop music, and sirtaki dancing tapes from Athens. Serious moussaka. *4-45 Akebono-cho, Naka-ku, tel. 045/261–3491. Reservations unnecessary. Dress: informal. AE, D, MC, V. Open 5 PM–midnight. Moderate.*

Fuji-Hakone-Izu National Park

By Nigel Fisher

The Fuji-Hakone-Izu National Park is one of Japan's most popular resort areas. The park's proximity to Tokyo has encouraged several tour operators to promote the region to foreign visitors. However, while the area offers certain pleasures, perhaps other excursions from Tokyo, for example to Nikko and Kamakura, should take precedence for those with limited time in Japan.

The park's chief attraction is, of course, Mt. Fuji. This dormant volcano (last erupted in 1707) is undoubtedly beautiful and, in changing light and from different perspectives, spellbinding. Mt. Fuji rises to an altitude of 12,388 feet, and its perfect symmetry and supreme majesty have been immortalized by poets and artists alike. Some have even assigned spiritual qualities to the mountain. Unfortunately, during spring and summer, Mt. Fuji often hides behind a blanket of clouds, to the disappointment of the crowds of tourists who travel to Hakone or the Fuji Five Lakes for a glimpse of Japan's most revered mountain.

Aside from Mt. Fuji, the Fuji-Hakone-Izu National Park offers an escape from the urban pace and congestion of Tokyo. Each of the three areas of the park—the Izu Peninsula, Hakone, and the Fuji Five Lakes—has its own special attractions. The Izu Peninsula has a craggy coastline with beaches and numerous hot-spring resorts, both along the shore and among the mountains. The Hakone region has aerial cable cars traversing the mountains, boiling hot springs, and lake cruises. The Fuji Five Lakes is a recreational area with some of the best views of Mt. Fuji's cone. In each of these areas are monuments to Japan's past.

Though it is possible to make a grand tour of all three areas at one time, most travelers make each of them a separate excursion from Tokyo. For those interested in climbing Mt. Fuji, a popular activity in July and August, *see* Mt. Fuji section, *below*.

Routes to reach the different areas of the national park are given at the beginning of each section. Because these are tourist attractions accustomed to foreign visitors, there is always someone to help out in English should you want to explore off the beaten track.

Guided Tours

Several different tours from Tokyo cover Hakone and the Fuji Five Lakes, either as separate tours or combined with other destinations. For example, **Japan Amenity Travel's** (tel. 03/3573–1417 direct) Imperial Coachman Tour is a full-day excursion: first to the Fuji Lakes district, then to Hakone with a ride on the gondola over Owakudani Valley, a cruise on Lake Ashino to Hakone-machi and the Hakone Barrier, and then the Shinkansen back to Tokyo. (Offered daily Mar.–Nov.; Cost: ¥19,000 with lunch; ¥16,800 children under 12.)

Another option is to combine Kamakura and Hakone in one day. **Sunrise Tours,** a division of the **Japan Travel Bureau** (tel. 03/3276–7777), offers a tour that does short shrift to Kamakura, with a quick stop at Daibutsu (the Great Buddha), before going to Hakone, crossing Lake Ashino on the cruise boat, and traveling the gondola over Owakudani Valley. (Cost: ¥19,000 adults, ¥14,300 children 6–11, including return to Tokyo station from Odawara by Shinkansen.) The Sunrise Tours depart daily (Mon.–Fri., Mar. 22–Nov. 26) from the Hamamatsucho Bus Terminal.

You may also consider including Hakone on a tour that continues on to Kyoto. For example, through Japan Amenity Travel, you may take a three-day tour that includes the Fuji Lakes area, Hakone, Kyoto, and Nara. For two nights and no meals, the cost is ¥72,000, including most meals it is ¥97,100. However, read the print carefully. This tour, billed as three days, is only 2½ days, and it ends back at Tokyo Station.

There are no tours of the Izu Peninsula, though the Japan Travel Bureau can make arrangements for all your hotel and travel needs.

Izu Peninsula

South of Mt. Fuji, the Izu Peninsula projects out into the Pacific. The central part consists of the Amagi Highlands, a continuation of the Hakone Mountains. The shores are a combination of rugged headlands and beautiful bays. The whole area is covered with woods and some 2,300 hot springs (*izu* means "springs"). In fact, the Izu Peninsula has ⅕ of all the hot-spring baths in Japan, and, with its mild climate, the region is a favorite resort area for the Japanese, especially for honeymooners.

Arriving and Departing

By Train

The best way to start a tour of the Izu Peninsula is to take the Kodama Shinkansen from Tokyo to Atami (48 min.), then travel by local train to Ito (25 min.) and on to Shimoda (another hour). Atami is also served by the JR Odoriko Super Express (not the Shinkansen), which continues beyond Atami to Ito and on to Shimoda. The Odoriko from Tokyo to Ito takes one hour, 52 minutes. South of Atami, the railroad tracks are privately owned by Izu Railways. Hence, the JR Rail Pass is not valid after Atami. The journey between Tokyo and Shimoda by the Odoriko takes 2 hours, 44 minutes.

To continue around the Izu Peninsula from Shimoda or up through its center, one must use buses, which run frequently during the day. However, you should always check the time of the last bus to make sure that you are not left stranded.

Shuzenji, the spa resort in the northern central part of the Izu Peninsula, can be reached from Tokyo via Mishima on the Izu-Hakone Railway Line. Mishima is on the JR Tokaido Line, with direct train service to Tokyo. The train ride between Shuzenji and Tokyo takes approximately two hours, 20 minutes.

By Car

It is approximately a four-hour drive from Tokyo to Atami on the express highway. It will take a further three hours to drive down the east coast of the Izu Peninsula to Shimoda. It takes some effort—but exploring the peninsula *is* a lot easier by car than by public transportation. The best solution is to call either the Nissan or Toyota rental agencies in Tokyo and book a car to be picked up at their Shimoda branch, and go to Shimoda by train. To get to Shuzenji from Shimoda, drive back up the coast to Kawazu (35 min.), on to Yugashima (1 hr.), and then to the hot-spring resort (30 min.).

Exploring

Numbers in the margin correspond to points of interest on the Fuji-Hakone-Izu National Park map.

❶ The gateway to the Izu Peninsula is **Atami.** Often, honeymooners make it no farther into the peninsula, so Atami has numerous hotels, ryokan, and souvenir shops. When you arrive, collect a map from the Atami Tourist Information Office (tel. 0557/81–6002) located at the train station.

The most worthwhile attraction in the area is the **MOA Art Museum,** named after its founder, Mokichi Okada. While establishing one of Japan's new religions, the Church of Messianity, Okada was able to collect more than 3,000 works of art, dating from the Asuka period (6th and 7th centuries) to the present day, including a most notable exhibit of *ukiyo-e* (wood-block prints) and ceramics. Located on a hill above the station and set in a garden full of old plum trees and azaleas, the museum also offers a sweeping view over Atami and the bay. *To find out about special exhibitions, call 0557/84–2511. Admission: ¥1,500 adults, ¥500 children under 15. Open 9:30–4:30. Closed Thurs.*

Fifteen minutes by bus from Atami, or an eight-minute walk from Kinomiya Station (the next stop south of Atami and serviced only by local trains), is **Atami Baien Plum Garden.** The time to visit here is in late January or early February, when the 850 trees come into bloom. At other times, it is simply a pleasant, relaxed garden. If you do come here, also stop by the small

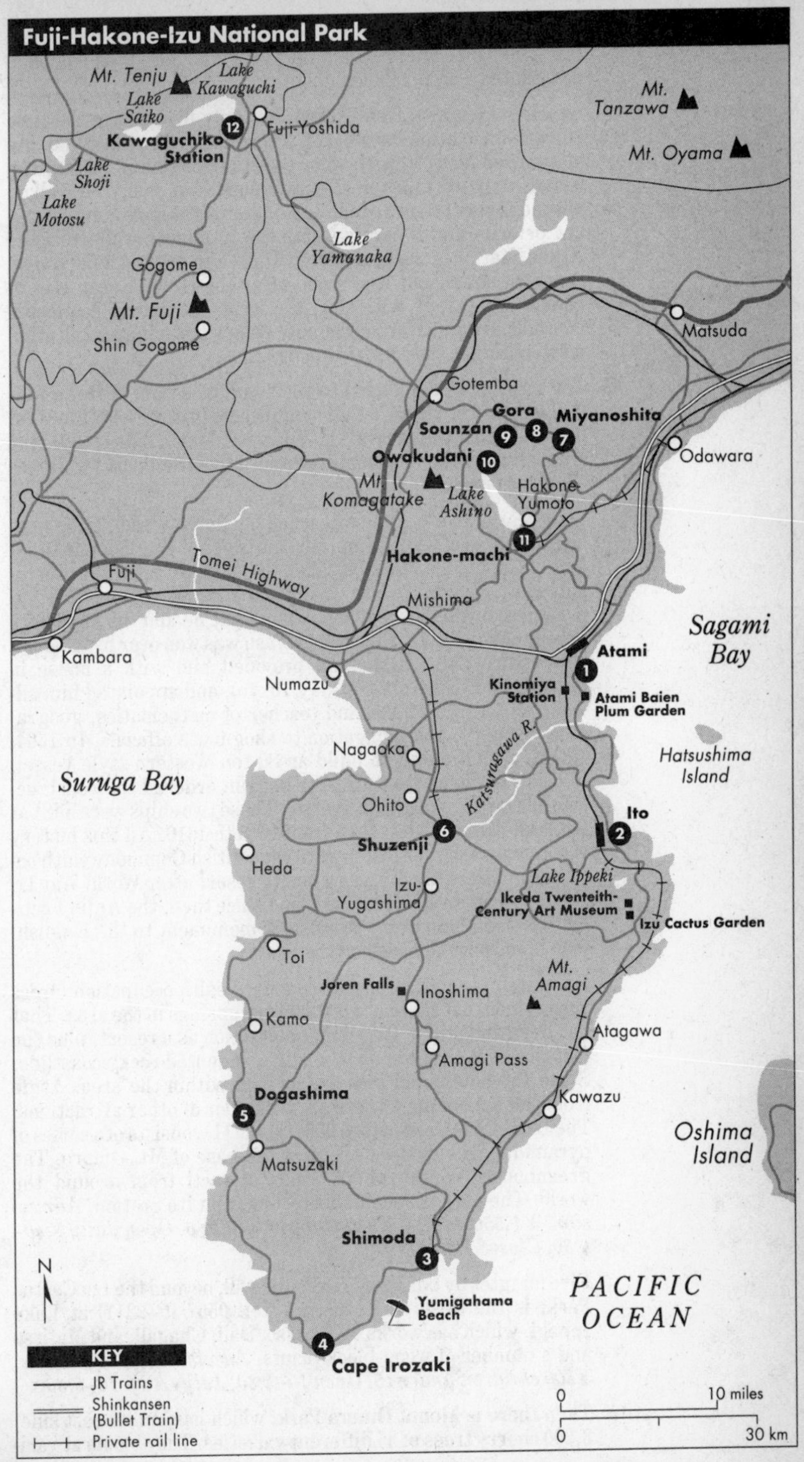
Fuji-Hakone-Izu National Park
Mt. Tenju
Lake Kawaguchi
Lake Saiko
Fuji-Yoshida
Kawaguchiko Station
Lake Shoji
Lake Motosu
Mt. Tanzawa
Mt. Oyama
Lake Yamanaka
Gogome
Mt. Fuji
Shin Gogome
Matsuda
Gotemba
Gora
Miyanoshita
Sounzan
Owakudani
Odawara
Mt. Komagatake
Lake Ashino
Hakone-Yumoto
Hakone-machi
Fuji
Tomei Highway
Mishima
Kambara
Sagami Bay
Atami
Numazu
Kinomiya Station
Atami Baien Plum Garden
Katsuragawa R.
Nagaoka
Hatsushima Island
Suruga Bay
Ohito
Ito
Shuzenji
Heda
Lake Ippeki
Izu-Yugashima
Ikeda Twenteith-Century Art Museum
Izu Cactus Garden
Toi
Mt. Amagi
Joren Falls
Inoshima
Kamo
Atagawa
Amagi Pass
Dogashima
Kawazu
Oshima Island
Matsuzaki
Shimoda
N
PACIFIC OCEAN
Yumigahama Beach
KEY
Cape Irozaki
JR Trains
Shinkansen (Bullet Train)
Private rail line
0
10 miles
0
30 km

shrine, dedicated to the God of Temperance, to see the huge and ancient camphor tree on its grounds. The tree has been designated a national monument.

Another excursion from Atami, but only if you have the time and the inclination for a beach picnic, is to take the 40-minute high-speed ferry from the pier over to **Hatsushima Island.** The island, only 2½ miles in circumference, can easily be walked around in less than two hours. Another sight in Atami that has low priority and is barely worth the 15-minute walk from the Atami Station is the **Oya Geyser.** It used to gush at a fixed time every 24 hours, but it stopped after the Great Kanto Earthquake. Not happy with this, the local chamber of commerce now makes it gush for four minutes every five minutes and gives it top billing in the tourist brochures.

❷ Ten miles (16 kilometers) to the south of Atami is **Ito,** a full-fledged spa resort town that can trace its history with the West to 1604, with the arrival of William Adams (1564–1620), the Englishman whose adventures served as the basis for James Clavell's novel *Shogun.*

Four years earlier, Adams beached his Dutch vessel, *De Liefde,* on the shores of Kyushu and became the first Englishman to set foot on Japan. He was first taken to Osakajo Castle for interrogation by Shogun Ieyasu Tokugawa and was temporarily imprisoned on the basis of the rumor that he and his men were Portuguese pirates. However, Ieyasu was won over by Adams's personality and, as shogun, provided him with a house in Nihombashi, Edo (present-day Tokyo), and appointed him adviser on foreign affairs and teacher of mathematics, geography, gunnery, and navigation to shogunate officials. In 1604, Adams was ordered to build an 80-ton Western-style vessel. Pleased with this venture, the shogun ordered the construction of a larger oceangoing vessel. These two ships were built at Ito, and Adams lived there from 1605 to 1610. All this history was temporarily forgotten until the British Commonwealth occupation forces used Ito as a health resort after World War II. Adams's memory was revived, and since then, the Anjin Festival has been held every August. A monument to the Englishman stands at the mouth of the river.

One reason that the British Commonwealth occupation forces chose Ito is that there are 800 thermal springs in the area. That has been and still is Ito's major attraction as a resort, plus the fact that it is situated on a beautiful indented rocky coastline. Some 150 hotels and inns are located within the area. Aside from the hot springs, there are a number of other attractions. The **Izu Cactus Garden** (tel. 0557/51–1111) consists of a series of pyramidal greenhouses set up at the base of Mt. Omuro. The greenhouses contain 5,000 kinds of cacti from around the world. The park is 20 minutes by bus from Ito Station. *Admission: ¥1,550 adults, ¥310 children under 6. Open daily 8:40–4:30. Closed Dec. 28–30.*

Five minutes by bus, or a 15-minute walk beyond the Izu Cactus Park, is the **Ikeda Art Museum** (tel. 0557/45–2211) at Lake Ippeki, which has works by Picasso, Dali, Chagall, and Matisse and a number of wood-block prints. *Admission: ¥800 adults, ¥400 children under 15. Open 10–4:30; July–Aug. 10–5:30.*

Then there is **Mount Omura Park,** which has, on its east side, 3,000 cherry trees of 35 different varieties. They bloom at various times throughout the year. The park is reached by a 20-minute bus ride from Ito Station. *Admission free.*

South of Ito, the coastal scenery is more of the same—each sweep around a headland gives another picturesque sight of a rocky indented shoreline. There are several spa towns en route to Shimoda. Higashi-Izu is a collection of hot-spring towns, of which **Atagawa** is the most fashionable. Farther south is **Kawazu,** which offers quiet solitude, with pools in the forested mountainside and waterfalls plunging through lush greenery. However, for history, none of these resort towns has the distinction of **Shimoda.**

❸

Shimoda's meeting with the West occurred when Commodore Perry anchored his ships off the coast in 1854. To commemorate the event, the Kurofune Matsuri (Black Ship Festival) is held annually May 16–18. It was here, too, that the first American Consulate was located before being transferred to Yokohama in 1857. Townsend Harris was the consul, and Tojin Okichi was his consort. There are several versions about the Harris-Okichi relationship. With the Japanese penchant for sad romance, the heroine is Okichi. One version has Okichi being ordered by the authorities to leave her lover and comfort Harris so that he may feel at home. Another version suggests that Harris picked Okichi out of a line of prostitutes. In either case, when Harris returned to America, he abandoned her. (Harris's version is that he forthrightly declined her advances.) Whatever is the truth, apparently when Harris left poor Okichi, she tried for a reconciliation with her former lover, Tsurumatsu. When that failed, she opened a restaurant, took to drink, and eventually took a final plunge into the river.

The easiest itinerary in English to follow is the one given by the **Shimoda Tourist Office** (tel. 0558/22–1531), located in front of the station. The 1½-mile itinerary covers most of the major sites, and all of those concerning Okichi. Also, on request, the tourist office will find travelers accommodations in Shimoda.

The **Hofukuji Temple** was the family temple of Tojin Okichi and serves as her memorial museum. The adjoining annex displays a life-size image of the woman. Just behind the temple is her grave; you'll notice that incense is still kept burning in her memory. (The grave of her lover, Tsurumatsu, is at the Todenji Temple, about mid-way between Hofukuji and the station.) *Admission: ¥300 adults, children under 13 free. Open 8–5.*

The major site on this Shimoda walk is **Ryosenji,** the temple at which the talks were concluded on the Japan–U.S. Friendship Treaty that forced the Tokugawa Shogunate to open Japan to the West. The temple's treasury hall also contains personal artifacts of Tojin Okichi. In the adjoining temple, **Chorakuji,** the U.S.–Japan treaty was actually signed, as was the trade agreement with the Russians. *Admission: Ryosenji, ¥500 adults, ¥150 children; open 8:30–5. Chorakuji ¥200 adults, children free. Open 9–5.*

Slightly farther down the road is a monument to Perry and to Harris, built to celebrate the establishment of U.S.–Japanese relations. Still farther along, overlooking Shimoda Harbor, is another monument to Perry. Finally, one comes across the Sushikane Restaurant. It is said to be the same restaurant as the one opened by Tojin Okichi a few years before she committed suicide. Part of the restaurant's display are Okichi's belongings.

Shimoda is not quite at the southernmost point of the Izu Peninsula. That point is **Cape Irozaki,** reached either by bus from Shimoda Station or by a sightseeing boat from Shimoda. If you visit Cape Irozaki in January, you are in for a special treat: a blanket of yellow daffodils to greet you. To reach the cape, whatever the season, the best plan is to take the boat one way and the bus the other. Both take about 40 minutes. The bus travels past Yumigahama Beach, one of the best sandy beaches on the whole peninsula, and then continues on to Cape Irozaki, the last stop on the route. From where the bus stops, there is a walk past the **Irozaki Jungle Park** (tel. 0558/65-0050), with huge hothouses containing 3,000 varied and colorful tropical plants, to the lighthouse at the edge of the cliff facing the breadth of the Pacific Ocean. *Park admission: ¥700 adults, ¥350 children. Open 8–5.*

Just as Shimoda is the end of the line for the trains, so it is for visitors. Most take the two-hour, 45-minute express train ride back to Tokyo.

However, for the more adventurous, a bus from Shimoda continues around the Izu Peninsula to the seaside town of **Dogashima.** There is little to do here but walk the sandy beaches and watch the fishermen at work. The tourist office (tel. 05585/2-1268) is in the small building behind the bus station and near the pier.

Dogashima is famous for its sedimentary rock formations jutting out from the coast into the sea. The best way to see them is on the sightseeing boat that leaves from the pier. Erosion has shaped the rocks into different forms. If you understand Japanese you'll hear the names of the rocks being called out from the loudspeaker on the cruise boat, which makes 20-minute runs to see the rock formations (cost: ¥850 adults, ¥425 children). If you don't understand Japanese, close your ears to the incessant loudspeaker and take the boat anyway. It is the best (and virtually only) way to appreciate the varied shapes of these rocks.

From Dogashima, another bus travels up the coast as far as Heda and then turns inland to **Shuzenji,** a traditional spa town in the center of the peninsula. A more relaxing return trip is to take the boat from Dogashima to Numazu and catch the train back to Tokyo from there.

An alternative, and easier, way of reaching Shuzenji is to take one of the five daily buses from Shimoda and go by way of the Amagi Mountains. The scenery is attractive and the trip only takes about two hours (cost: ¥1,510 adults, ¥750 children). However, you may wish to stretch your legs at **Inoshishi-mura,** where trained boars and badgers put on a show. The show is not particularly worthwhile, but there is a pleasant 15-minute walk to **Joren-no-taki Waterfall,** from which you can rejoin the bus. By the way, the specialty dish at the local ryokan is roasted boar meat.

Shuzenji is a lavish inland spa town along the valley of the Katsuragawa River. Don't judge the town by the area around the station. Most of the hotels and springs are a mile to the west of the station. Though Shuzenji has the notoriety of being the place where the second Kamakura shogun was assassinated (though he had abdicated his office) early in the 13th century, there is little to interest the foreign visitor. However, we recommend making this return trip through the center of the Izu Peninsula, because it offers a mountainous contrast to the route along the coast. There are numerous hotels in Shuzenji, and 15 miles farther north is **Izu-Nagaoka,** with several deluxe ryokan.

From Shuzenji, you can catch the private railway line (cost: ¥470) to Mishima and change for the Shinkansen to Tokyo or Kyoto. There are also frequent buses that leave from Mishima Station to make the 40-minute ride to Hakone–machi (cost: ¥900).

Hakone

Hakone is a popular day trip from Tokyo and a good place for a close-up view of Mt. Fuji. A word of caution, though, before you dash off to Hakone with plans to see Mt. Fuji: It is often cloud covered, especially during the summer months. Also, the excursion to Hakone has become so popular that sometimes it seems that all of Tokyo has come with you. You can expect to stand in line at the cable cars and be stuck in traffic on the roads.

Arriving and Departing

By Train

The privately owned Odakyu Line has trains departing from Tokyo's Shinjuku Station to Odawara. Odakyu's commuter trains leave every half hour. However, Odakyu also has a special train, the "Romance Car," which offers comfortable seating and large viewing windows. These Romance Cars go one stop beyond Odawara to Hakone-Yumoto. Reservations on the Romance Car are required, and tickets can be purchased from any Odakyu railway station or Odakyu Travel Service agency (cost: ¥1,820). Beyond Odawara and Hakone-Yumoto, travel is on the privately owned Hakone Tozan Tetsudo Line or by bus.

If you are using a JR Rail Pass, it is more economical to take the Kodama Shinkansen from Tokyo Station to Odawara. (The faster Hikari does not stop at Odawara.) From Odawara, change to the private railway.

The most economical way of traveling to and within Hakone is to purchase the Hakone Free Pass. Sold by the Odakyu Railways, this coupon ticket allows you to use any mode of transportation in the Hakone area, such as the Hakone Tozan Railway, the Hakone Tozan Bus, the Hakone Ropeway, the Hakone Cruise Boat, the Sounzan Cable Car, and so on (cost: ¥4,850 from Shinjuku, with an additional surcharge of ¥800 to travel on the Romance Car). If you hold a JR Rail Pass, then purchase the Hakone Free Pass just for the travel within the Hakone region and use JR Railways to reach Odawara (cost: ¥3,500). The coupon is valid for four days and is sold at any station serving the Odakyu Railways. With the exception of a detour up the east side of Lake Ashino to the Prince Hotel, all of the itinerary described below is covered by the Hakone Free Pass. On this itinerary, the savings from the Hakone Free Pass amount to ¥1,070 from Shinjuku. With a JR Pass and the coupon bought in Odawara, the savings are ¥300.

Getting Around

Hakone has a network of public transportation from cable cars to buses and from railways to cruise boats. Because traffic on the narrow mountain roads is a slow-moving jam, rental cars are not advised. Indeed, part of the pleasure of exploring Hakone is traveling one way on the cruise boats and aerial gondolas, which you would miss when driving your own car.

Exploring The following itinerary covers the best of Hakone in a one-day trip out of Tokyo. If you want to enjoy the curative powers of the thermal waters or do some hiking, then an overnight stay will be necessary. The two areas we recommend are around Miyanoshita, an old-fashioned spa town, and the new Prince Hotel resort area, on the slopes of Mt. Komagatake facing Lake Ashino.

Though the itinerary described below sounds complex, it is not. In fact, though many companies offer guided tours of the region, this is one excursion from Tokyo that is so well defined that there is no risk of becoming lost. Indeed, except in the coldest winter months, thousands of Japanese visitors take this same itinerary. The route is a procession of tourists. However, if you wish to take a guided tour, see the beginning of this chapter.

From Odawara or Hakone-Yumoto, you will travel to Togendai on the shore of Lake Ashino. The way we recommend is over the mountains (described below). However, the easiest way is simply to catch a bus from Odawara Station. Doing so, though, one misses half the reason for coming to Hakone in the first place. Still, if any members of your group cannot stand heights, we recommend putting them on the bus at Odawara, Hakone-Yumoto, or Miyanoshita for Togendai and joining them on the pier at Togendai in about 2½ hours. The bus is scheduled to do the journey in 60 minutes, though traffic usually increases travel time to 90 minutes. Your trip over the mountains will take about two hours.

To go over the mountains, either from Odawara or Hakone-Yumato, take the Hakone Tozan Tetsudo Line for Gora. The train may be accused and excused for being possibly the slowest train you've ever taken. It takes 50 minutes to travel the 10 miles (16 kilometers) from Odawara to Gora (35 min. from Hakone-Yumoto). How the train climbs the mountain is a wonder. But, by using three switchbacks, it steps up the cliff side, and the views become grander as the plunges down the mountain grow steeper.

The train makes several stops on the way. The first of note is ❼ **Miyanoshita.** True, Hakone-Yumoto is a bigger resort center, with some 60 inns, but Miyanoshita has a more sophisticated air and elegant approach. There is one old Western-style hotel, the **Fujiya,** that is full of 19th-century charm. But, if you're not staying there, drop in for a morning coffee on the first floor overlooking the garden and, on the way out, take a peek at the library for its vintage collection of old books and magazines. (*See* Lodging, *below.*)

The next stop of note is **Chokoku-no-mori.** Within a minute's walk of the station is the **Hakone Open-Air Museum.** This is one of Japan's more attractive museums, in which the building is designed to work with the environment. Outside are displayed numerous statues by such masters as Rodin and Moore; inside, there are works by Picasso, Leger, and Kotaro Takamura, among others. Perhaps the collection of art exhibits may have more novelty interest to the Japanese, but the setting of the sculpture gardens set into the cliff side has universal appeal. *To* *find out about special exhibitions, call 0460/2-1161. Admission: ¥1,500 adults, ¥800 children under 15. Open daily 9–5 (9–4 in winter).*

8 The final stop on the line is **Gora.** Gora is a small town that services both the visitor who has chosen the village as a base for hiking and exploring, and those passing through on their way up to Sounzan. Shops and small restaurants abound. However, if you can be first out of the train, forget the souvenir stands and make a dash for the cable car located in the same building as the train station. If you let the rest of the passengers arrive there before you, and perhaps a tour bus or two, you may stand 45 minutes in line.

9 The cable car travels up to **Sounzan.** It departs every 20 minutes and takes nine minutes to make the journey to the top (cost: ¥290; free with the Hakone Free Pass). There are four stops en route, and one may get off and reboard the cable car if one has purchased the full fare up to the top. The one stop in particular where you may consider disembarking is **Koen-kami,** the second stop up, to visit the **Hakone Art Museum** for its collection of porcelain and ceramics from China, Korea, and Japan. *Tel. 0460/2-2623. Admission: ¥800 adults, ¥300 children under 15. Open 9–4. Closed Thurs.*

At Sounzan, the gondola begins a 28-minute journey down to **Togendai.** The gondola is in the same building as the cable-car terminus. With your ticket (cost: ¥1,300) or your Hakone Free Pass, stand in line to get a boarding-pass number. This will determine when you can stand in the line for clambering into a car. The gondola seats about eight adults and departs every minute.

Less than 10 minutes out of Sounzan, the gondola swings over a ridge and crosses over **Owakudani Valley.** Suspended hundreds of feet above the "boiling valley," you may observe volcanic activity on the ground below, with sulfurous steam escaping through holes from some inferno deep within the earth.

10 Having swung safely over the valley, at the top of the far ridge you'll reach **Owakudani,** one of the two stations on the gondola route. If you disembark here, however, keep in mind that you—and the others in front of you—must wait for someone to disembark before you can board again. It can be at least a 15-minute wait.

Below Owakudani Station is a restaurant. The reputation for its food is terrible, but, on a clear day, the view of Mt. Fuji is perfect, and that view should tempt you to suffer the food. Next to the station is the **Owakudani Natural Science Museum,** which has exhibits relating to the ecosystems and volcanic history of the area. *Tel. 0460/4-9149. Admission: ¥400 adults, ¥250 children under 12. Open daily 9–4:30.*

There is also a ½-mile-long walking course which passes by some "hellholes" with steam pouring out. You may see someone who boils eggs in the holes and sells them at exorbitant prices.

From Owakudani, the descent to Togendai on the shore of **Lake Ashino** takes 25 minutes. There is no reason to linger at Togendai. It is an arrival and departure point. Buses leave from here back to Hakone-Yumoto and Odawara, as well as the resort villages in the northern area of Hakone. For us, it is the

11 departure point for the cruise boat to **Hakone-machi.** The boat

is free with your Hakone Free Pass; otherwise you must purchase your ticket (cost: ¥950) at the office in the terminus. The pier is 100 yards away, and, if the boat is in, you'll recognize it by its gaudy design. (One boat is made to look like a 17th-century warship.) Boats depart every 30 minutes, and the cruise to Hakone-machi takes about 30 minutes, giving you the opportunity to appreciate the bow-shape Lake Ashino. Because the mountains plunge to the lake, one of the attractions of the boat ride is the reflection of the mountains in the lake's waters.

The key sight in Hakone-machi is **Hakone Sekisho** (Hakone Barrier), located a few minutes' walk from the pier in the direction of Moto-Hakone, if you keep as close to the lakeshore as is possible. Hakone was on the main Tokaido Highway between the imperial capital of Kyoto and the administrative center of the shogunate at Edo (present-day Tokyo). Because of the steep mountains, travelers could scarcely avoid passing through Hakone. It was, thus, a strategic checkpoint where travelers to and from Edo could be stopped. The Tokugawa Shogunate erected a barrier in 1618 and required travelers to be rigorously searched. Especially important for the security of the shogunate was the examination of each *daimyo* (feudal lord) and his retainers, making their required visit to Edo. Every procession was checked for its number of warriors and their weaponry.

To fully understand the significance of the Hakone Sekisho, remember that the Tokugawa Shogunate required that each daimyo make a visit to Edo once every two years. This served two purposes. It reaffirmed the shogun's authority and diminished the authority of the daimyo, who had to be absent from his lands for a considerable time in order to make the trip. Second, because the daimyo had to travel with a large number of retainers, the expense to the daimyo was great and kept him poor. The less trustworthy daimyo were given lands far from Edo, so their expenses and their time away from their power base were even more crippling. One other method to control the obeisance of the daimyo was used: The wives of the daimyo were required to live in Edo all the time. They were, in fact, hostages; if a daimyo stepped out of line, he did so at the risk of his wife's head. The Hakone Sekisho was, therefore, also a barrier to prevent wives from returning to their husbands.

For two and a half centuries, travelers were stopped at the Hakone Barrier. Then, in 1869, with the Meiji Restoration, it was demolished. However, for the delight of tourists, an exact replica, including an exhibition hall displaying costumes and arms used during Japan's feudal period, was rebuilt in 1965. *Admission: ¥200 adults, ¥100 children under 12. Open 9–4:30.*

From Hakone-machi and the Hakone Sekisho, buses run every 15–30 minutes to Hakone-Yumoto (40 min.) and Odawara (1 hr.) for either the Romance Car back to Shinjuku Station or the JR Shinkansen to Tokyo Station. The fare is ¥840 to Yumoto, ¥1,050 to Odawara—or free with the Hakone Free Pass.

Fuji Five Lakes

Whereas Hakone is the region south of Mt. Fuji, Fuji-Goko (literally, "Fuji-five-lakes") is the area to the north of Mt. Fuji.

Needless to say, the star attractions of this area are the view of the mountain and the base from which one can climb to its summit. However, the area also has five lakes that add to the scenic beauty and offer the chance to see Mt. Fuji reflected in the waters. The Fuji Lakes are a popular resort for families and business seminars. Numerous outdoor activities, ranging from skating and fishing in the winter to boating and hiking in the summer, are organized to accommodate the increasing numbers who visit here each year.

Of the five lakes, Lake Kawaguchi and Lake Yamanaka are the two most developed resort areas. Lake Yamanaka, to the east of Lake Kawaguchi, is the largest lake, but Lake Kawaguchi is considered the focus of Fuji-Goko. The area can be visited in a day trip from Tokyo, but because the main reason for coming to this region is relaxation, more than one day is really necessary unless you want to spend most of the day on buses or trains. Though there are plenty of others who would disagree with us, for the foreign visitor we rank this region as the third most interesting in this chapter, unless you plan to climb Mt. Fuji.

Arriving and Departing

The transportation hub, as well as being one of the major resort areas in Fuji-Goko, is Kawaguchiko. Getting there from Tokyo requires a change of trains at Otsuki. The JR Chuo Line "Kaiji" and "Azusa" express trains depart from Shinjuku Station to Otsuki on the half-hour throughout the morning (less frequently in the afternoon) and take approximately one hour. At Otsuki, change to the private Fujikyuko Line for Kawaguchiko, which takes another 50 minutes. The total traveling time is about two hours, and one can use one's JR Pass as far as Otsuki. The fare from Otsuki to Kawaguchiko is ¥1,110. Because there are about seven trains a day (more in the summer) from Shinjuku that make convenient connections at Otsuki, we suggest you arrange a schedule with Japan Travel Bureau or the JR information office the day before you leave Tokyo. There are also one or two trains on Sundays and national holidays (Mar.–Nov.) that operate directly between Shinjuku and Kawaguchiko Station. On weekends (Mar.–June 28), an express train departs from Shinjuku early in the morning and arrives at Kawaguchiko about 1½ hours later; a train making the return trip departs Kawaguchiko in the late afternoon and arrives at Shinjuku in the early evening. (Times should be verified before your departure; only coaches 1, 2, and 3 make the through run.)

There is also a direct bus service from Shinjuku to Kawaguchiko that operates hourly between 8:30 AM and 6 PM (cost: ¥1,520).

For a different route back to Tokyo, you may want to consider taking the bus from Kawaguchiko to Mishima. It is a two-hour bus ride, with approximately six buses a day (cost: ¥2,010), and it skirts the western lakes and circles Mt. Fuji before descending the mountains to Mishima. At Mishima, transfer to the JR Shinkansen Line for Tokyo or Kyoto. A shorter bus ride (70 min., cost: ¥1,390) is from Kawaguchiko to Gotemba with a transfer to the JR local line.

Should one want to go to Hakone rather than Tokyo from Fuji-Goko, take the bus from Kawaguchiko first to Gotemba, then change to another bus to Sengoku. From Sengoku, there are frequent buses to Hakone-Yumoto, Togendai, and elsewhere in the

Hakone region. If you want to go to the Izu Peninsula, then take the bus to Mishima and, from there, go by train either to Shuzenji or Atami.

Buses depart from Kawaguchiko Station to all parts of the area and to all five lakes. On a single day's visit, you will probably only have the time to visit Lake Kawaguchi and, if you don't rest up, possibly one other lake.

Exploring (12)

Arriving from Tokyo at **Kawaguchiko Station,** you'll have a five- to 10-minute walk to the lakeshore. If you take a left along the shore, another five minutes will bring you to the gondola for a quick ride up to **Mt. Tenjo.** At the top of Mt. Tenjo (3,622 feet), there is an observatory from which you can get a look at the lay of the land. Lake Kawaguchi is before you, and beyond the lake is a classic view of Mt. Fuji. Back down the gondola and across the road is the pier for the Kawaguchi's cruise boat. The boat offers 30-minute tours of the lake. The promise, not always fulfilled, is to have two views of Mt. Fuji: one in its natural form, and another inverted in the reflection from the water.

On the north shore of the lake next to the Fuji Lake Hotel is **Fuji-Hakubutsukan** (Fuji Museum; tel. 0555/73–2266), where on the first floor there are displays related to the geology and history of the area. The kids view these academic exhibits while adults (only those aged 18 and older are permitted) visit the second floor. Here are exhibits of erotic paraphernalia used, apparently, by Japanese families until relatively recently. *Admission: ¥350 adults, ¥20 children under 12. Open 8:30–4.*

Kawaguchi is the most developed of the five lakes; all around its shores are villas owned by companies and universities, where weekend retreats are held. There are also a number of recreational facilities, the largest of which is the **Fuji-kyu Highland.** It is not particularly recommended for the day visitor, but it does have everything to amuse children, from a scream-engendering loop-the-loop to a more genteel carousel. The amusement park stays open all year and in the winter offers superb skating, with Mt. Fuji for its backdrop. To reach Fuji-kyu Highland, take the train back (in the direction of Odawara) one stop, or walk the 15 minutes from Lake Kawaguchi.

Buses from Kawaguchiko Station go to all the other lakes. The lake that is the farthest away is **Motosu.** It takes about 50 minutes to reach the lake by bus. Motosu is the deepest lake of the Fuji-Goko and has the clearest waters. **Shoji** is the smallest of the lakes and is regarded by many to be the prettiest. It has the added pleasure of not being built up with vacation homes. The Shoji Trail leads from the lake to Mt. Fuji through Aokigahara (Sea of Trees), a forest under which is a magnetic lava field that makes compasses go haywire. For that reason, people planning to climb Mt. Fuji are advised to take this route with a guide.

Between Shoji and Kawaguchi is **Saiko,** the third largest lake of the region and only modestly developed. From its western side, there is a good view of Mt. Fuji. The largest of the five lakes is **Yamanaka,** 35 minutes by bus to the east of Kawaguchi. Lake Yamanaka has a 30-minute cruise-boat ride circling the lake and several hotels on its shore. Because this lake is the closest to the popular trail up Mt. Fuji that starts at Gogome, many climbers use this lake resort for their base.

Mt. Fuji

There are six possible routes to the summit of Mt. Fuji, but two are recommended: Gogome (fifth station) on the north side, and Shin Gogome (new fifth station) on the south side. From Gogome, it is a five-hour climb to the summit, and a three-hour descent if you return the same way. From Shin Gogome, the ascent to the summit is slightly longer and stonier than from Gogome, but the descent is faster. Hence, we recommend climbing Mt. Fuji from Gogome and descending to the Shin Gogome, via the Sunabashiri—more about that in a moment.

Arriving and Departing Buses take about one hour from Kawaguchiko Station to Gogome, and there are three to 15 runs a day, depending on the season (cost: ¥1,620). There are also three buses from Tokyo (Hamamatsucho or Shinjuku stations) that go directly to Gogome, departing from Hamamatsucho at 8:15 AM and 7 PM, and from Shinjuku at 7:45 AM, 8:45 AM, and 7:30 PM. The last bus allows sufficient time for the tireless to make it to Mt. Fuji's summit before sunrise. The journey takes about three hours from Hamamatsucho and two hours, 30 minutes from Shinjuku (cost: ¥2,340 from Hamamatsucho, ¥2,160 from Shinjuku). Reservations are required, through the Fuji Kyuko Railway (tel. 03/3374–2221), the Japan Travel Bureau (tel. 03/3284–7026), or other major travel agents.

To return from Shin Gogome, there is a bus that takes 70 minutes to Gotemba (cost: ¥1,420). Then take the JR Tokaido and Gotemba lines to Tokyo Station, or the JR Line to Matsuda and change to the Odakyu Line for Shinjuku (cost: ¥1,120).

The Climb It has become increasingly popular to make the climb at night in order to reach the summit just before sunrise. Sunrises, wherever you are, are beautiful, but the sunrise from the top of Mt. Fuji is exceptional. *Goraiko*, as the sunrise is named, takes on a mystical quality as the reflection of the light shimmers across the sky just before the sun itself appears over the horizon. Mind you, there is no guarantee of seeing it: Mt. Fuji attracts clouds, especially in the early morning.

The climb is taxing, but not as arduous as one would imagine it is climbing to Japan's highest mountain, 12,388 feet above sea level. However, it is humiliating to struggle to find the oxygen for another step ahead when 83-year-old grandmothers stride past you; on occasion, they do. Have no fear in getting off the trail on either of the two main routes. Some 196,000 people make the climb during the official season, July 1–August 31, and en route there are vendors selling food and drinks. (Consider taking your own nourishment and some water rather than paying their high prices.) In all, there are 10 stations to the top—you start at the fifth. However, the stations are located at unequal distances. Also, along the route at each station are huts where, dormitory-style, you can catch some sleep. A popular one is at the Hachigome (eighth station), from which it is about a 90-minute climb to the top. However, these huts are often overcrowded and are none too clean, so more and more people leave Gogome (the fifth station) at midnight and plan to be at the summit 4½ hours later for sunrise. The mountain huts are open July 1–Aug. 31. Lodging costs approximately ¥4,800 with two meals, ¥3,800 without food. Camping on the mountain is prohibited.

Coming back down is easy. Instead of returning to Gogome, descend to Shin Gogome, using the volcanic sand slide called Sunabashiri—you take a giant step and slide. It's fun, but not so much fun that you will want to climb Mt. Fuji again.

Be prepared for fickle weather around and up Mt. Fuji. Summer days can be warm (very hot when climbing), and nights can be freezing cold. Wear strong hiking shoes. The sun really burns at high altitude, so take protective clothing and a hat. Gloves are a good idea; they protect the hands while climbing and when sliding down the volcanic sand during the descent. Use a backpack so that your hands are free.

Lodging

Because the region covered in this chapter is a resort area, most hotels quote prices on a per-person basis with two meals, exclusive of service and tax. If you do not want dinner at your hotel, it is usually possible to renegotiate the price. Stipulate, too, whether you wish to have Japanese or Western breakfasts, if any. For the purposes here, the categories assigned to all hotels reflect the cost of a double room with private bath and no meals. However, if you make reservations at any of the noncity hotels, you will be expected to take breakfast and dinner at the hotel—that will be the rate quoted to you, unless you specify otherwise. During the peak season, July 15–August 31, prices can increase by 40%.

A 3% federal consumer tax is added to all hotel bills. Another 3% local tax is added to the bill if it exceeds ¥15,000. At most hotels, a 10%–15% service charge is added to the total bill. Tipping is not necessary.

The most highly recommended accommodations are indicated by a star ★.

Category	Cost*
Very Expensive	over ¥25,000
Expensive	¥17,000–¥25,000
Moderate	¥10,000–¥17,000
Inexpensive	under ¥10,000

**Cost is for double room, without tax or service*

Izu Peninsula
Atami
★ **Taikanso Ryokan.** A Japanese inn of the old style with beautiful furnishings and individualized service, the villa was once owned by the Japanese artist, Taikan. The views over the sea must have been his inspiration. *7-1 Hayashigaokacho, Atami, Shizuoka 413, tel. 0557/81–8137. A 10-minute walk from the station. 44 Japanese-style rooms. Breakfast and dinner served in your room. AE, DC, V. Very Expensive.*

New Fujiya Hotel. A modern resort hotel with large public areas, this is a useful hotel to use simply as a base for sightseeing. It is located inland, and only the top rooms have a view of the sea. The impersonal, but professional, service only gets flustered when a group arrives. *1-16 Ginzacho, Atami, Shizuoka 413, tel. 0557/81–0111. Five minutes by taxi from the station. 316 rooms, half are Western-style. Facilities: indoor pool, hot-*

spring baths, sauna, Japanese and Western restaurants. AE, DC, MC, V. Expensive.

Dogashima **Ginsuiso.** This is the smartest luxury resort on Izu's west coast. Service is first class, despite its popularity with tour groups. The location along the top of the cliff, with every room overlooking the sea, is superb. *2977-1 Nishina, Nishi-Izucho, Dogashima, tel. 05585/2-1211. 90 Japanese-style rooms. Facilities: outdoor pool, nightclub with cabaret, shops. AE, DC, MC, V. Very Expensive.*

Ito ★ **Ryokan Nagoya.** This small, very personable establishment with understated elegance and sophistication is furnished with antiques, placed around the inn with simplicity and harmony. English is not spoken, but smiles and a few words in Japanese seem to go a long way. *1-1-18 Sakuragaoka, Ito, Shizuoka, tel. 0557/37-4316. 14 rooms. Breakfast and dinner served in your room. No credit cards. Very Expensive.*

Izu-Nagaoka ★ **Ryokan Sanyoso.** Elegant and beautiful, the Sanyoso is decorated with antiques and luxurious furniture, as one would expect from the former villa of the Iwasaki family of the Mitsubishi conglomerate. Meals cannot be excluded from the room fee. *270 Domanoue, Izu-Nagaoka, Tagata-gun, Shizuoka 410, tel. 05594/8-0123. Five minutes by taxi from the station. 21 rooms. AE, DC, MC, V. Very Expensive.*

★ **Izu Hotel.** Actually a small Japanese inn, the Izu has a classic Japanese garden upon which to gaze from your tatami room. Not as elegant as the Ryokan Sanyoso (*see above*), but also not quite as expensive. *1356 Nagoaka, Izu-Nagaoka-cho, Tagata-gun, Shizuoka 410-22, tel. 05594/8-0678. 9 Japanese rooms. Facilities: outdoor pool. AE, DC, V. Expensive.*

★ **Matsushiro-kan.** This small ryokan is nothing fancy, yet because it is a family operation, it feels like a friendly home. Some English is spoken. Japanese meals are served in a common dining room. Room-only reservations (no meals) are accepted only on weekdays. *55 Kona, Izu-Nagaoka, Tagata-gun, Shizuoka 410-22, tel. 05594/8-0072. Five minutes by bus or taxi from the station. 16 rooms. AE, V. Moderate.*

Shimoda **Shimoda Prince Hotel.** This V-shape modern resort hotel faces the Pacific, only steps away from a white sandy beach. The building and rooms are more functional than aesthetic in design and are geared to those seeking a holiday by the sea. However, the broad expanse of picture windows from the dining room, offering a panorama of the Pacific Ocean, does make this establishment the best in town. *1547-1 Shirahama, Shimoda, Shizuoka 415, tel. 05582/2-7575. Located just out of Shimoda, 10 min. by taxi from the station. 134 rooms, mostly Western-style. Facilities: Continental main dining room, Japanese restaurant, terrace lounge, bar, nightclub, outdoor pool, sauna, tennis courts. AE, DC, MC, V. Expensive–Very Expensive.*

Shimoda Tokyu Hotel. Perched just above the bay, the Shimoda Tokyu has impressive views of the Pacific from one side (where the rooms cost about 10% more) and mountains from the other. The public areas are large and lack character and warmth, but that is typical of Japanese resort hotels. Prices run significantly higher in the mid-summer months. *5-12-1 Shimoda, Shimoda, Shizuoka 415, tel. 05582/2-2411. 117 rooms, mostly Western-style. Facilities: outdoor pool, hot-spring baths, Western dining room, Japanese restaurant, sushi bar, summer* *garden restaurant, tennis courts, shops. AE, DC, MC, V. Expensive–Very Expensive.*

Hakone *Lake Ashino* ★ **Hakone Prince Hotel.** This is a completely self-contained resort complex on the edge of the lake at Hakone-en. The hotel attracts tours, the individual traveler, and business meetings. The location is superb, with the lake on one side and Mt. Komagatake on the other. One can escape the largeness of the hotel by staying in one of two Japanese-style annexes. Request the *ryuguden*, which overlooks the lake and has its own hot-spring bath; it is absolutely superb, despite having the most expensive rooms in the hotel. *144 Moto-Hakone, Hakone-machi, Ashigarashimo-gun, Kanagawa 250-05, tel. 0460/3-7111. 455 rooms; the main building has 96 rooms; the chalet has 12 rooms; the lakeside lodge has 77 rooms; the 2 annexes have a total of 73 rooms. Facilities: formal Western dining room, steak and seafood restaurant, Chinese restaurant, Japanese restaurants, coffeehouse, bar/lounge, tennis courts, outdoor pools, shops. AE, DC, MC, V. Expensive–Very Expensive.*

Miyanoshita ★ **Fujiya Hotel.** Though the Western building is showing signs of age (built in 1878, but with modern additions), that simply increases the hotel's charm, which is especially felt in the library, with its stacks of old books. In the delightful gardens in the back is an old imperial villa used for dining. With the exceptional service and hospitality of a fine Japanese inn, this is the best traditional Western hotel in town. *359 Miyanoshita, Hakone-machi, Kanagawa 250-04, tel. 0460/2-2211. 149 Western-style rooms. Facilities: Western and Japanese restaurants, indoor and outdoor pools, thermal pool, golf. AE, DC, MC, V. Very Expensive.*

★ **Ryokan Naraya.** A traditional inn, the Naraya retains a simple, even mystical, understated elegance and an exquisite formal hospitality. The same family has owned the inn for generations and has earned the right to choose their guests. The main building has more atmosphere than does the annex. *162 Miyanoshita, Hakone-machi, Kanagawa 250-04, tel. 0460/2-2411. 19 rooms, not all with private bath. You are expected to have breakfast and dinner, which are served in your room. AE, DC, MC, V. Very Expensive.*

Hotel Kowakien. This hotel attracts busloads of tourists. It's far from ideal, but its prices are reasonable for the fair-size rooms. Thus, the hotel is worth knowing about, and one can usually get a reservation. (The hotel also owns the adjacent **Hakone Kowakien,** which is equally large and with little character, but has Japanese-style rooms.) *1297 Ninotaira, Hakone-machi, Kanagawa 250-04, tel. 0460/2-4111. 237 Western-style rooms. Facilities: Western and Japanese restaurants, indoor and outdoor pools, thermal pool, sauna, golf, tennis, gym. AE, DC, MC, V. Expensive.*

Sengoku **Fuji-Hakone Guest House.** A small, family-run Japanese inn, this guest house has simple tatami rooms with the bare essentials. Since July '91 the family has also operated the nearby Moto-Hakone Guest House (103 Moto-Hakone, Kanagawa 250-05; tel. 0460/3-7880), which has five Japanese-style rooms, none with private bath. The owners, Mr. and Mrs. Takahashi, speak English and are a great help in planning off-the-beaten-path excursions. *912 Sengokuhara, Hakone, Kanagawa 250-06, tel. 0460/4-6577. Located between Odawara Stn. and Togendai. Take bus at Odawara St. terminal (Bus Lane 4), get* *off at the Senkyoro-mae bus stop, and walk back 1 block. 12 Japanese-style rooms, none with private bath. Facilities: hot spring. AE, MC, V. Inexpensive.*

Fuji Five Lakes
Lake Kawaguchi

Fuji View Hotel. Conveniently located on Lake Kawaguchi, the Fuji View is a little threadbare, but it does provide comfort. Its terraced lounge offers fine views of the lake and of Mt. Fuji beyond. The staff also speak English and are helpful in planning your excursions. Rates are significantly higher on weekends and in August. *511 Katsuyama-mura, Minami-Tsuru-gun, Yamanashi 401-04, tel. 05558/3-2211. 78 rooms, mostly Western-style (twins only; no doubles). Facilities: Western restaurant; hotel will arrange golf, boating, tennis. AE, DC, MC, V. Expensive–Very Expensive.*

Hotel Ashiwada. This new Japanese-style hotel on Lake Kawaguchi has been designed as a utilitarian base for those interested in seeking the recreational facilities in the area rather than sitting around the hotel. The staff are helpful and, though Japanese food is served in the small dining room, they will make English breakfasts. *395 Nagahama, Ashiwada-mura, Minami-Isuru-gun, Yamanashi 401-04, tel. 05558/2-2321. 40 Japanese-style and 4 Western-style rooms, not all with private bath. Facilities: Japanese dining room, laundry room. AE, DC, MC, V. Moderate–Expensive.*

Lake Yamanaka

Hotel Mount Fuji. The best resort hotel on Lake Yamanaka, the Mount Fuji offers all the facilities needed for a recreational holiday, and its guest rooms are larger than those at the other hotels on the lake. The lounges are spacious, rather like waiting rooms, but they do offer fine views of the lake and mountain. Rates are about 20% higher on weekends. *Yamanaka, Yamanakako-mura, Yamanashi 401-05, tel. 0555/62-2111. 88 Western-style rooms, 4 Japanese-style. Facilities: Western and Japanese restaurants, outdoor pool, tennis, golf, skating. AE, DC, MC, V. Expensive–Very Expensive.*

New Yamanakako Hotel. This is a less expensive accommodation on the lake. Though the rooms are slightly smaller than those at Hotel Mount Fuji, the New Yamanakako has its own thermal pool, especially pleasant after summer hiking or winter skating. Rates go up dramatically on weekends and in August. *Yamanaka, Yamanakako-mura, Yamanashi 40105, tel. 05556/2-2311. 63 rooms, mostly Western-style. Facilities: Western and Japanese restaurants, thermal pool, tennis. AE, DC, V. Moderate–Expensive.*

5 Nagoya, Ise-Shima, and the Kii Peninsula

By Nigel Fisher

Gazing out the window of the Shinkansen as it speeds out of Tokyo, you will see one continuous strip of factories and concrete office blocks. This is the industrial quarter of Honshu, which stretches to Hiroshima; to some, an economic miracle. The sight is most likely to make travelers want to stay on the train in the vain hope of reaching the greenery of travel-brochure Japan. But there are reasons to disembark: Kyoto, Japan's capital for more than 10 centuries, is located along this route, and to the north and south of this corridor lie lush countryside and small towns still rich in traditional culture. Consider stopping first in Nagoya, the fourth-largest industrial center of Japan, to explore areas to the city's north and southwest.

Nagoya has only a few major national treasures. The two most important are the Nagoyajo Castle and the Atsuta Jingu Shrine. The city is not among Japan's most attractive, but it is a convenient base from which to set out into the countryside. After visiting the major sights of Nagoya, the first recommended excursion takes you on a trip of one or two days to the north of the city to see cormorant fishing, sword making, fertility shrines, and much more. Heading south from Nagoya, the second and longer excursion covers the Grand Shrines of Ise, the Shima Peninsula and its pearl industry, and proceeds to the Kii Peninsula, including Mt. Koya and Yoshino. This second excursion ends at Nara.

Nagoya

A visit to Nagoya today gives little indication of the city's role in the Tokugawa period (1603–1868). Then, Nagoya was an important stop between Kyoto and Edo (Tokyo). In 1612, Ieyasu Tokugawa established Nagoya town by permitting his ninth son to build a castle. In the shadow of this magnificent castle industry and merchant houses sprang up, as did pleasure quarters for the samurai. A town was born, and because of its location between Kyoto and Edo, the seat of the shogunate, it quickly grew in strategic importance. Supported by taxing the rich harvests of the vast surrounding Nobi plain, the Tokugawa family used the castle as its power center for the next 250 years. By the early 1800s, Nagoya's population had grown to around 100,000. Although it was smaller than Edo, where the million-plus population surpassed even Paris, Nagoya had become as large as the more established cities of Kanazawa and Sendai.

Only with the Meiji Restoration in 1868, however, when Japan embraced Western ideas and technology, did Nagoya develop as a port city. Once its harbor was open to international shipping (1907), Nagoya's industrial growth accelerated, so that by the 1930s it was supporting Japanese expansionism in China with munitions and aircraft. That choice of industry caused Nagoya's ruin. American bombers virtually razed the city to the ground during World War II. Very little was left standing (and nothing belonging to the Tokugawa period) by the time the Japanese surrendered unconditionally, on August 14, 1945.

Nagoya has been born again as an industrial metropolis. Except for the fact that every building is of recent vintage, there is no evidence of its war-blitzed past. Now the fourth largest city in Japan, Nagoya bustles with 2.2 million people living in its 126.5-square-mile area. Industry is booming, with shipbuilding, food processing, and the manufacturing of ceramics, railway rolling stock, automobiles, textiles, machine tools, and even aircraft. Nagoya has become prosperous: a comfortable cosmopolitan town for its 36,000 foreign residents, but with only a few sites to interest the visitor.

In rebuilding this city, urban planners created the new Nagoya on the grid system, with wide avenues intersecting at right angles. Hisaya-odori, a broad avenue with a park in its meridian, is 328 feet wide and bisects the town. At its center is Nagoya's symbol of modernity, an imposing 590-foot-high television tower; it is ugly to look at but useful for visitors to establish their bearings. To the north of the tower is Nagoyajo Castle, to the west are the botanical gardens and zoo, to the south is Atsuta Jingu Shrine, and to the east is the Japan Railways (JR) station. The main downtown commercial area (subway stop: Sakae) is located east of Hisaya-odori Avenue, and a secondary commercial area has developed next to the JR station.

Arriving and Departing

By Plane There are direct overseas flights to Nagoya on Japan Airlines (JAL) from Honolulu, Hong Kong, and Seoul. The major airlines that have routes to Japan have offices in downtown Nagoya. For domestic travel, All Nippon Airways (ANA) and Japan Air System offer flights between Nagoya and most major Japanese cities.

Between the Airport and Center City The Meitetsu bus makes the 50-minute run between the airport and the Meitetsu Bus Center, near the Nagoya Railway Station.

By Train Nagoya is on the Shinkansen Line, with frequent bullet trains between Nagoya and Tokyo (1 hr., 52 min. on the fast Hikari; 2½ hrs. on the slower Kodama); Nagoya and Kyoto (43 mins.); and Nagoya and Shin-Osaka (1 hr.). You can also take the less expensive Limited Express trains. In addition limited Express trains proceed from Nagoya into and across the Japan Alps (to Takayama and Toyama, and to Matsumoto and Nagano).

By Bus Buses connect Nagoya with Tokyo and Kyoto. The bus fare is half that of the Shinkansen trains, but the journey by bus takes three times as long.

By Car The journey on the expressway to Nagoya from Tokyo takes about five hours; from Kyoto, allow two hours.

Getting Around

By Subway Several main subway lines run under the major avenues. The Higashiyama Line runs from the north down to the JR station and then due east, cutting through the city center at Sakae. The Meijo Line runs north–south, passing through the city center at downtown Sakae. The Tsurumai Line also runs north–south through the city, but between the JR station and Sakae, at the city center. A fourth subway line, the Sakura-dori, opened in 1990, cuts through the city center from the JR Station, paralleling the east–west section of the Higashiyama Line. The basic fare, good for three stops, is ¥180. A one-day pass, good for Nagoya's buses and subways, is ¥820.

By Bus Buses crisscross the city, running either in a north to south or an east to west direction. The basic fare is ¥200.

By Taxi Metered taxis are plentiful, with an initial fare of ¥520.

Important Addresses and Numbers

Tourist Information **Nagoya International Center** (3rd floor, Nagoya Kokusai Center Bldg., 1–47 Nakono, 1-chome, Nakamura-ku, Nagoya, tel. 052/581–5618) is quite possibly the best-equipped information center in Japan for assisting foreign visitors and residents. Not only is there an information desk to provide answers to your questions, but there are also audiovisual presentations and an extensive library of English-language newspapers (both Japanese and foreign), magazines, and books. The center also provides an English language telephone hot-line service (tel. 052/581–0100) manned from 9–8:30. **City Tourist Information Office** (1-4 Meieki 1-chome, Nakamura-ku, Nagoya, tel. 052/541–4301) will give you city maps and make your hotel reservations. A branch of the Tourist Office is also in the center of the Nagoya Railway Station (tel. 052/541–4301, open 9–5).

Japan Travel-Phone This toll-free service will answer travel-related questions and help with communication, daily 9–5. Dial 0120/444–800 for information on western Japan.

Travel Agencies **Japan Travel Bureau** (tel. 0521/563–1501) has several locations, including the JR station and in the Matsuzakaya Department Store downtown. The major domestic airlines (JAL, tel. 052/563–4141; JAS, tel. 052/201–8111; and ANA, tel. 052/962–6211) have offices in Nagoya, as do major international carriers.

Emergencies **Police,** tel. 110; **Ambulance,** tel. 119. **National Nagoya Hospital,**
Doctors tel. 0521/951–1111; **Kokusai Central Clinic,** Nagoya International Center Building, tel. 0521/201–5311.

English-Language Bookstore **Maruzen** (tel. 0521/261–2251) is located downtown behind the International Hotel Nagoya. 3-23-3 Nishiki, Naka-ku, Nagoya.

Guided Tours

Five different sightseeing bus tours of the city are operated daily by the **Nagoya Yuran Bus Company** (tel. 052/561–4036). The three-hour "panoramic course" tour (¥2,250) includes Nagoyajo Castle and Atsuta Jingu Shrine and has scheduled morning and afternoon departures. A full-day tour (¥5,250) takes travelers out of Nagoya to visit the Meiji Village and the Tagata Shrine.

Exploring

Numbers in the margin correspond to points of interest on the Nagoya map.

With its rectangular layout, Nagoya is simple to navigate. JR (1) trains arrive at the **Nagoya Railway Station,** where this tour of the city begins. First, stop at the Visitor's Information Office in the middle of the station's central mall, identified by a big red question mark. Even if the tourist section, with its English-speaking attendant, is closed, you can collect an English-language map from the other officials behind the counter. In Japanese or sign language, they will also give directions and obtain hotel reservations for you.

Four subway lines run under the city's main avenues. To get to the first attraction on this tour, the Nagoyajo Castle, take the

Atsuta Jingu Shrine, **9**
Gohyaku Rakan Hall, **7**
Kenchuji Temple, **8**
Nagoyajo Castle, **3**
Nagoya Railway Station, **1**
Ninomaru Gardens, **4**
Nittaiji Temple, **6**
Noritake China Factory, **10**
Tokugawa Museum, **5**
TV tower, **2**

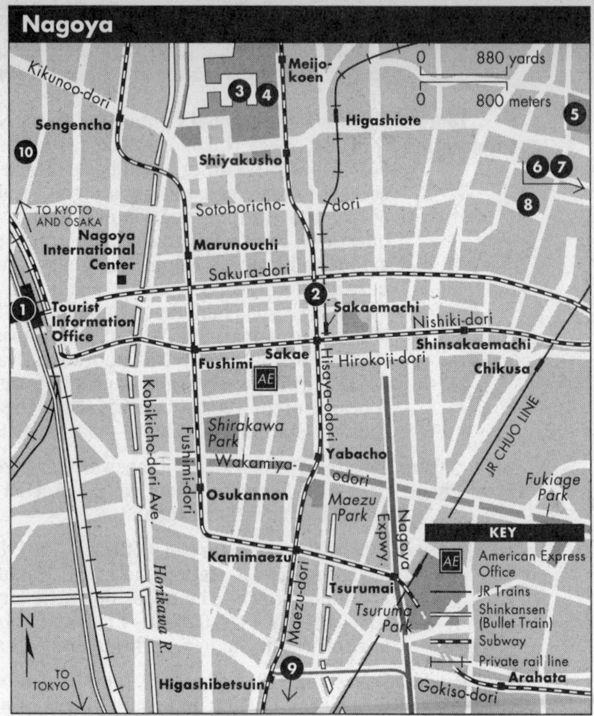

Higashiyama subway, located in front of the railway station, to the center of town (walking takes about 15 minutes) or take bus #8 directly to Nagoyajo. The subway is easy to take, because all subway signs are written in both Japanese and English. Get off at Sakae, the second stop, where you can either change for the Meijo subway line and ride one stop to the Shiyakusho Station, or exit in the middle of downtown Nagoya and walk up Hisaya-odori Avenue past the 590-foot-tall **TV tower** to Nagoyajo Castle. **2**

Your Nagoya tourist brochure will suggest taking the elevator up the TV tower to its observation platform for the view. Certainly, if there is no smog, haze, or clouds, you will get a wide panorama that reaches the Japan Alps to the north and Ise Bay to the south. However, what one mostly sees is the city, and, if you have seen urban sprawls before, the view will simply add to that tiresome list. *Admission: ¥600. Open Mon.–Fri. 10–5:20, Sat. and Sun. 10–8.*

Continuing up Hisaya-odori Avenue, past the Prefectural Government Office and Shiyakusho subway station, one catches a first glimpse of **Nagoyajo Castle**, standing as a memory of times long past. The castle was originally built in 1612, severely damaged in 1945, and rebuilt with ferro-concrete in 1959. It is famous for its impressive size and the pair of golden dolphins, male and female, mounted on the roof of the *donjon* (stronghold). The donjon and the dolphins are replicas, but they are faithful to their originals. In contrast to the castle's exterior, however, the interior makes no attempt to replicate the original residential quarters of the Tokugawa family. Instead, you'll **3** find a museum containing artifacts—toys, armor, swords and so forth—from the original castle. Completely incongruous to this re-created 17th-century castle is an elevator that takes visitors between floors; yet without it, one perhaps would miss the fourth floor of the castle. Here is a collection of paper dolls representing the people who take part in the city's Chrysanthemum Exhibition, held in October—the best time to appreciate Nagoyajo Castle.

To the east of the castle, but within the castle complex, are the ❹ **Ninomaru Gardens.** The refined simplicity of these gardens makes them a place to restore one's inner harmony, which Nagoya's traffic does its best to undermine. However, during the October festival, the display of chrysanthemum bushes can be disconcerting. Each bush is shaped so that its flowers form faces and hands. Then, the bush is dressed in costumes and arranged to represent a legend or historic event. The effect is extremely surrealistic, resembling a fantasy filled with flower children. *Admission to the castle and gardens: ¥400. Open 9:30–4:30. Closed Dec. 29–Jan. 1.*

After the castle, the next Nagoya attraction worth visiting is ❺ the **Tokugawa Museum.** Walk back to Shiyakusho Station and take the Meitetsu Seto train line two stops to Ozone Station, or take bus #16 from "Stop 6" (near Shiyakusho Station) to Shindekamachi. Because the museum is on a back street, you may need to ask directions; in Japanese it's called Tokugawa Bijutsukan.

Some 7,000 historical treasures are stored in Tokugawa Museum, but only a fraction of the collection is displayed at any one time. All that you can be sure of seeing are ancient armor, swords, paintings, and assorted artifacts from the Tokugawa family. For many, the main reason for visiting the museum is the various picture scrolls, including one illustrating the *Tale of Genji.* If you'd like to see the scrolls, ask your hotel to telephone the museum to make sure they are on display. *Tel. 052/935–6262. Admission: ¥1,000. Open 10–4:30. Closed Mon.*

From the Tokugawa Museum, take a 15-minute brisk walk east along Chayagasaka-dori Avenue. After passing the Nagoya Women's College, take a right down Tenma-dori Avenue. This ❻ will lead to the **Nittaiji Temple,** which was given to Japan by the king of Siam in 1904. Supposedly, its function is to serve as a repository for Buddha's ashes, but all you can see is a magnificent gilded Buddha. In fact, the actual temple is less notewor- ❼ thy than the nearby **Gohyaku Rakan Hall** (Hall of the 500 Rakan), with rows of Buddha's 500 disciples carved in wood, each statue in a slightly different pose from the others. Slightly closer to the Tokugawa Museum (in a southwest direction) is ❽ **Kenchuji Temple,** which is famous for its original two-story gate (1651), one of the few Nagoya structures to survive the bombing of World War II.

If the Nagoyajo Castle is the number one tourist attraction in ❾ Nagoya, the **Atsuta Jingu Shrine,** in the southern part of the city, is number two. To get there from either the Tokugawa Museum or the castle and downtown, take the Meijo subway line south to Jingunishi Station. Take a right as you leave the station and walk down the main avenue to reach the shrine.

For 1,700 years, a shrine has been at the site of the Atsuta Jingu. The current one is, like Nagoyajo Castle, a concrete replica of the one destroyed in World War II. That diminishes neither its importance nor the reverence in which it is held by the Japanese. The Atsuta Jingu Shrine remains one of the three most important shrines in the country and has the distinction of serving as the repository of one of the emperor's three imperial regalia, the Kusanagi-no-Tsurugi (Grass Mowing Sword). The shrine is located on thickly wooded grounds, with a 15th-century bridge (Nijugo-cho-bashi). The attraction is an oasis of tradition in the midst of bustling, modern industrialism. When you witness Shinto priests blessing newborn children held in the arms of their kimono-clad mothers, you will easily recognize the reverence with which the Atsuta Jingu Shrine is still accorded. *Admission free. Open sunrise–sunset.*

A little farther to the south of the shrine is **Nagoyako Port,** now Japan's third largest port, outranked only by Kobe and Tokyo. From here, Honda, whose factories are in Nagoya's suburbs, ships its automobiles around the world.

10 The last place of major interest in Nagoya is the **Noritake China Factory,** a 15-minute walk north of Nagoya Railway Station or five minutes from the Kamajima subway station (one stop north of Nagoya station on the Higashiyama line). Noritake is the world's largest manufacturer of porcelain. A free, one-hour tour of the factory is offered, with an English-speaking guide and a short film. *Tel. 052/562–5072. Admission free. Open weekdays 10–4. 1-hr. factory tours at 10 and 1. Reservations for the tour are required.*

Rather than making purchases at the factory, you may want to browse through the downtown shops. To return downtown, get on the Higashiyama subway at Kamajima station, traveling toward Nagoya station and on to Sakae (the third stop). Sakae is not only Nagoya's shopping center but also the entertainment center, with hundreds of bars and small restaurants. Many of these restaurants display their dishes with prices in the windows, so you may decide what you want and how much it will cost before you enter. Furthermore, because Nagoya prides itself on being an international city, Westerners are usually welcomed without the fluster of embarrassment that sometimes greets them in less cosmopolitan areas.

Excursions from Nagoya

While Nagoya is modern Japan hurtling into the 21st century, traditional Japan is still visible to the north and south of the city. The two excursions described below take in most of these sights. The first covers a circular route to the north of Nagoya. The second goes southwest to the Shima Peninsula, from which you can either return to Nagoya or, better yet, continue on to Nara and Kyoto—either directly or, as we have done in this excursion, via the Kii Peninsula.

Gifu and North of Nagoya

Numbers in the margin correspond to points of interest on the Nagoya Excursions map.

To the north of Nagoya, and not more than an hour or so by train, are several places of interest whose origins for the most part are centuries old. The general area is the southern part of the Gifu Prefecture, an area that also includes the mountains of the Japan Alps around Takayama. However, this tour does not go that far north and instead keeps within the foothills of the mountains.

❶ Begin this excursion at **Gifu** and work your way back down to Nagoya. Gifu is a half-hour's journey on a JR train from Nagoya and can easily be visited in a day. During the summer, however, if you want to watch the evening event of cormorant fishing in the rivers, it's a good idea to make this an overnight excursion.

Bombing during World War II destroyed the attractiveness of Gifu, but the city still attracts visitors for several reasons, although you may wish to skip it and go straight to Inuyama. Gifu is famous for making paper lanterns and umbrellas, for ukai fishing, and for its bathhouses, which have been described as "sex spas." The latter may not interest most foreigners, but they do seem to raise the local hotel prices. Gifu is also a major manufacturer of apparel, and you'll see some 2,000 wholesale shops crammed on a couple of city blocks as you leave the station. A **city tourist office** is located at the train station (tel. 0582/62–4415).

Umbrellas are made by certain families in small shops. Though these umbrellas are available in Gifu's downtown stores, there are one or two umbrella-making shops a 15-minute walk to the southeast of the JR station. If you speak a little Japanese, the shop owner may invite you back to watch the process. The easiest store to visit is **Sakaida's** (tel. 0582/63–0111).

Lantern making is easier to see. The major factory, **Ozeki** (tel. 0582/63–0111), welcomes visitors. To reach Ozeki, take the tram toward downtown Gifu and disembark at the Daigaku Byoin-mae stop, the fifth from Gifu Station. It's at the junction of the main road, which leads to the Kinkazan Tunnel. The factory is up this road on the left. Visitors are led through the process of winding bamboo or wire around several pieces of wood to give the lantern shape. The tour then progresses to where the paper is pasted onto the bamboo. Once the paste has dried, the pieces of wood that have given the lantern its shape are removed from one end of the lantern. The actual design on the lantern may either be stenciled on the paper at the beginning of the process or painted on by hand after the lantern has been made. To arrange to see the lantern-making process, consult the information desk at your hotel.

Ukai fishing is the major summer (May 11–Oct. 15) evening event for locals and visitors. It is an organized spectator attraction and an occasion for partying while watching a centuries-old way of catching fish. Fishermen, dressed in the traditional costume of reed skirts, glide down the river in their boats. Suspended in front of each boat is a wood brazier burning bright to attract *ayu* (river smelt or sweet fish) to the surface. Ukai (cormorants), several to a boat, are slipped overboard on leashes to snap up the fish. Because of a small ring around each of the birds' necks, the fish never quite reach the cormorants' stomachs. Instead, their long necks expand to hold five wiggling fish. When a bird can't take in another fish, the fisherman hauls the bird back to the boat, where it is made to regurgitate its neckful. The actual fishing lasts less than a half-hour, but the partying takes much longer.

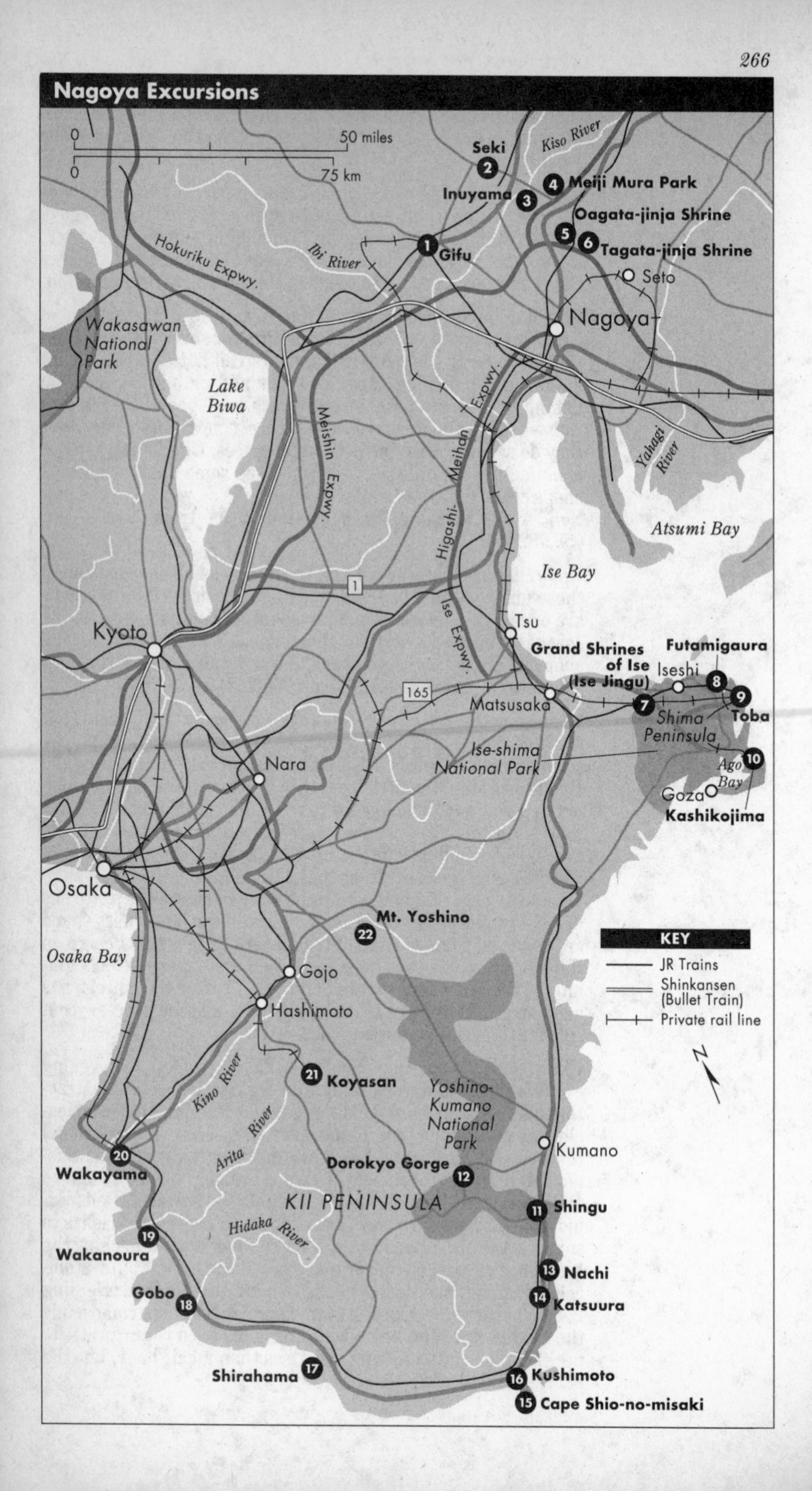

Nagoya Excursions
0
50 miles
0
75 km
Seki
Kiso River
Meiji Mura Park
Inuyama
Oagata-jinja Shrine
Gifu
Tagata-jinja Shrine
Ibi River
Hokuriku Expwy.
Seto
Nagoya
Wakasawan National Park
Lake Biwa
Meishin Expwy.
Higashi-Meihan Expwy.
Yahagi River
Atsumi Bay
Ise Bay
1
Tsu
Ise Expwy.
Kyoto
Grand Shrines of Ise (Ise Jingu)
Futamigaura
Iseshi
165
Matsusaka
Shima Peninsula
Toba
Ise-shima National Park
Ago Bay
Nara
Goza
Kashikojima
Osaka
Mt. Yoshino
Osaka Bay
KEY
JR Trains
Shinkansen (Bullet Train)
Private rail line
Gojo
Hashimoto
Kino River
Koyasan
Yoshino-Kumano National Park
Arita River
Kumano
Wakayama
Dorokyo Gorge
KII PENINSULA
Shingu
Hidaka River
Wakanoura
Nachi
Gobo
Katsuura
Shirahama
Kushimoto
Cape Shio-no-misaki

Approximately 130 boats, carrying 10 to 30 spectators in each, heave-to in the Nagara River about two hours before the fishing commences. This is party time, consumed by eating and drinking. A boat, full of singing and dancing maidens dressed as geisha, drifts through the spectator boats. Other boats ply the river, selling food and drink. Since the ayu are attracted by the light from a boat's wood-burning braziers, no fishing occurs when the river is muddy from heavy rains or on nights when there is a full moon. Tickets for the spectator boats are sold in most of Gifu's hotels and also at the main ticket office downstream from the Nagarabashi Bridge. *Cost: about ¥2,600 without food or drink. The ticket office opens at 6, but you may make advance reservations through the Gifu City Spectators Office, tel. 0582/62–0104, or at the Gifu City Tourist Agency at the station, tel. 0582/62–4415.*

Architectural sights in Gifu are worth visiting only if you have the spare time to wander around waiting for the ukai fishing. An unusual statue of Buddha (45 feet tall), with a 6-foot-long ear as a symbol of omnipotent wisdom, is housed in an orange-and-white building, **Shoji.** This building is easy to recognize from the street as you ride the bus from the train station into downtown Gifu and toward the river. It is about a five-minute walk from its entrance to the cable car that takes you to Mt. Kinka. The statue, one of the three largest Buddhas in Japan, was completed in 1747 after 38 years of pasting together 2,000 pounds of paper *sutra* (prayers); this was then coated with clay and stucco before being lacquered and gilded.

The other major feature of Gifu is the **Gifujo Castle** which houses a museum and stands before Mt. Kinka (Gold). The castle serves as a picturesque backdrop to the city. It is relatively new (1951), replacing a 16th-century structure that was destroyed by an earthquake in 1891. You can either climb up the mountainside or take the aerial gondola (called ropeway in Japan), but the castle really looks its best at night from down below, when it is all lit up. *Admission: ¥310. Open spring and fall, 9–6; summer, 9–7; winter, 9–4:30.*

❷ **Seki,** which is north of Gifu, is an easy excursion of 9 miles (15 kilometers) on a tramcar/train. It is one of the most famous traditional centers of sword production. Seki is a must to visit, but only if you can time your trip to coincide with a demonstration showing the traditional method of sword production. This show will help you understand the artistry and mystique of the traditional Japanese sword, which may cost around ¥6 million. *The demonstration occurs at the Sangyo Shinko Center (Industry Promotion Center), tel. 05752/2–3131. Admission free. The show is given 5 times a day on the 1st Sun. of the month; in Oct. it's held on the 2nd Sun.; in Jan. it is held on Jan. 2.*

❸ The next stop is **Inuyama.** Though the JR line can be used from Gifu, the privately operated Meitetsu Line is more convenient. If you want to make use of a JR Rail Pass, take the JR train to Unuma and change to the Meitetsu Line for a three-minute ride to Inuyama. If you are coming straight from Seki, the JR line goes to Inuyama. Coming to Inuyama directly from Nagoya, take the Meitetsu Line, which continues on to Gifu.

Inuyama is known for having Japan's oldest existing castle, **Inuyamajo,** built in 1440. It is not a grand structure, but it is a pleasant change to see the real thing rather than another concrete replica. The top floor of this quaint four-story castle is a lookout room that offers a commanding view of the river below. *Admission: ¥300. Open 9–5. Closed Dec. 29–Jan. 1.*

Even better is Inuyamajo's location on a cliff above the **Kiso River,** which makes the castle romantically picturesque. This part of the Kiso River is attractive; it has been dubbed "Nihon Rhine" (the Japanese Rhine); with its mysterious rock that looms up out of the water, it's a fine place for water nymphs to congregate. A pleasant way to see the river is by raft (completely safe). To take this 8-mile river trip, take the train on the Meitetsu Hirome Line from Inuyama to Nihon-Rhine-Imawatri. Once there, check out several companies before selecting the type of boat you prefer. The trip downstream takes about one hour and costs ¥2,700.

Inuyama also offers another opportunity to watch cormorant fishing, and, as in Gifu, tickets are available from the major hotels. Because there is no difference between cormorant fishing in Gifu and Inuyama, the choice is best decided by where you will be at nightfall.

In the Urakuen Garden of the Meitetsu Inuyama Hotel and 350 yards from the castle is the **Jo-an Teahouse.** Registered as a national treasure, the building was constructed by Grand Master Urakusai Oda during the early development of the tea-making ceremony and moved to its present site only recently. *Admission: ¥800 for teahouse and gardens; additional ¥500 for tea. Open daily 9–5.*

A short distance to the east and south of Inuyama on the 4 Meitetsu-Komaki Line is **Meiji Mura Park.** (Get off at the Meiji-mura-guchi Station and take a bus for 3 mi to the park.) More than 50 buildings from the Meiji Restoration (1868–1912) have been transplanted here. Emperor Meiji, who regained his imperial power from the Tokugawa Shogun dynasty, opened the doors of Japan to the west and began Japan's rapid transformation into a modern economy. This transformation is illustrated by Meiji Mura's exhibits. Traditional buildings, such as a Kabuki theater and a bathhouse, exist alongside Christian places of worship and Western-style mansions. The 19th-century buildings and Western architecture make this park more appealing to the Japanese than to Westerners. An exception may be the lobby taken from the old Imperial Hotel, which was designed by Frank Lloyd Wright. *Admission: ¥1,550. Open 10–5 Mar.–Oct., 10–4 Nov.–Feb. To reach Meiji Mura Park directly from Nagoya, take the 1-hour bus journey (fare: ¥1,120) from the Meitetsu Bus center, a 5-min. walk from JR Nagoya Station.*

More fascinating for the foreign tourist are two of Japan's most 5 accessible fertility shrines, **Oagata-jinja Shrine** (the first stop 6 southeast of Meiji Mura) and **Tagata-jinja Shrine** (two stops southeast of Meiji Mura). Both stops are on the Komaki Line. Oagata-jinja is the female shrine. It attracts women who are about to marry and wives who want children. Most of the objects in the shrine are symbols to that end, such as a cleft rock resembling female genitalia. Tagata-jinja is the male shrine, with a bewildering collection of phalluses, ranging in size from a few inches to 6 feet, left as offerings by thankful mothers.

The big event at Tagata-jinja is on March 15. Every year at this time, a splendid festival is held; sake flows liberally from morning to night. The festival's focal point is a 9-foot phallus, carried by a woman who is accompanied by a Shinto priest (with an elongated nose) and by several other women carrying more modest-size male accoutrements. The procession, which starts from a minor shrine on the other side of town, makes frequent stops to imbibe from sake casks set up at the side of the road. The participants become progressively drunker; when they finally reach Tagata-jinja in the late afternoon, the entire village is seeing double.

Time Out If you have to wait for a train, drop into **Terukumni** (tel. 0508/77–9647), a small *nomiya* (informal bar) located on the main street not far from the station. There is sushi if you are hungry, but you can also order just a beer.

From Tagata-jinja, one can hop on board a train at the Tagata Station and be back in Nagoya in 30 minutes, but you will need to transfer to the Miejo subway at Kamijida. It may be easier to return to Inuyama and take the direct train to Nagoya.

Ise-Shima National Park and the Kii Peninsula

Southwest of Nagoya are the Shima and Kii Peninsulas. On the Shima Peninsula are the most venerated shrines in Japan, the Grand Shrines of Ise. The shrines are part of Ise-Shima National Park, which extends from Ise-shi to Toba, the center of the pearl industry, and south to Kashikojima, with its indented coastline studded with pine-clad islands. The Kii Peninsula, southwest of the Shima Peninsula, boasts magnificent marine scenery, coastal fishing villages and resorts, and Yoshino-Kumano National Park. The latter features pristine gorges, holy mountains, and two large, ancient Buddhist community complexes, one of which, Mt. Yoshino, has perhaps the finest display of cherry blossoms in Japan.

A traveler may visit the Grand Shrines of Ise in a day or all of the Shima Peninsula in two. To cover both the Shima Peninsula and the Kii Peninsula requires a minimum of five days. One has the option of returning to Nagoya from anywhere on these peninsulas or heading directly for Nara, Kyoto, and Osaka.

7 The **Grand Shrines of Ise** (also called the Ise Jingu Shrines) in Ise-shi are the first recommended attractions to visit outside Nagoya. You may travel to the shrines from Nagoya on a JR train, but the trip requires a train change, usually at Taki, and each train is a local. The fastest and most direct route is the privately owned Kintetsu Line. Fare: ¥1,950 (taking the Kintetsu train all the way to Kashikojima costs ¥3,100). Even if you have a JR Rail Pass, the time saved on the Kintetsu may be worth the extra cost.

The journey out of Nagoya takes you through depressing industrial suburbs, but don't despair. Thirty minutes before Ise-shi, the polluting factories end and the farmlands begin. Ise-shi is a small town whose major business comes from the pilgrims who pay respects to the Outer Shrine and the Inner Shrine. From either the Kintetsu or the JR train station it is only a 10-minute walk through town to the Outer Shrine. A frequent shuttle bus makes the 4-mile trip between the Outer and Inner Shrines; a bus also goes directly from the Inner Shrine to Ise-shi Station. The most crowded times to visit the shrines are during the Grand Festival held October 15–17 every year, when thousands come to see the pageantry, and on New Year's Eve and Day when Shinto believers pray for a good new year.

Astounding as it may be, the main halls at both the Outer and Inner Shrines are, in accord with Shinto tradition, torn down every 20 years. New constructions are then built, as exact replicas of the previous halls, using the same centuries-old method, on adjacent sites. The main halls you see now were completed in 1993 at a cost estimated to be over ¥4.5 billion.

The Outer Shrine (Geku) is dedicated to Toyouke-Omikami, goddess of grain and agriculture. Its buildings are all in a traditional style, predating the surge of Chinese influence that swept through the country in the 6th century. Located deep in a park full of ancient cedars, Geku dates from AD 478. Its plain design makes it seem part of the magnificent grounds; it is made from unpainted *hinoki* (cypress) wood, with a fine, closely shaven thatch roof. Unfortunately, the visitor can see very little of the exterior of the Geku and none of its interior. Four fences surround the shrine, and only the imperial family and its envoys may enter it.

The same is true for the other even more venerated shrine, the Inner Shrine (Naiku), located to the southwest of Geku. Naiku is where the Yata-no-Kagami (Sacred Mirror) is kept, one of the three sacred treasures of the imperial regalia. This shrine is also the home to Amaterasu, the sun goddess and the highest deity in the Shinto pantheon. (The name "Japan" in Japanese is *Nihon,* meaning "the origin of the sun.") Amaterasu, born of the left eye of Izanagi (in Japanese mythology, the first god to inhabit earth), was the great-great-grandmother of the first mortal emperor of Japan, Jimmu Tenno. Seventy generations later, Hirohito, who led Japan through World War II and into prosperous peacetime, became the 123rd divine emperor. Hirohito, however, renounced his divine relationship at the insistence of the U.S. occupation forces.

The Grand Shrines both have more of a natural harmony with nature than the more controlled, even contrived, buildings in later Japanese architecture. The Inner Shrine's architecture is simple. If one did not know its origin, one would term it classically modern. Again, the use of unpainted cedar causes the shrine to blend into the ancient forest that circles it and covers the grounds of the 63-acre park. As with Geku, the visitor can see very little through the wooden fences surrounding the shrine. Although the sightseeing is limited at the Grand Shrines, one's reward is in feeling the sanctity surrounding both sights. This experience is totally Japanese, one that Westerners can only begin to understand. *Admission to grounds of both shrines free. Grounds open sunrise–sunset.*

Two routes may be followed onward to Toba, the resort town made famous by Mikimoto pearls. You can take a 45-minute bus ride from near the Inner Shrine for ¥910. There is one bus every hour, with the last bus at 3:56 PM. The bus goes along the **Ise-Shima Skyline Drive,** which offers fine mountainous and wooded scenery. The other alternative, and perhaps the more memorable, is to take the JR train (it follows the coast road) from Ise-shi to Toba (fare: ¥ 560) with a stop at **Futamigaura,** a popular spot for Japanese lovers. Two rocks, one said to be male and the other female, rise out of the water. Because they are of the opposite sex, the Japanese married them, linking the two together with a straw rope (replaced every Jan. 5 as part of a cheerful festival). These rocks, known as the **Meoto-Iwa** (wedded rocks), represent Izanagi and Izanami, Japan's Adam and Eve. Imagine the striking view with the sun rising behind them.

9 Back on the train, it is less than 10 minutes to **Toba,** where the cultivation of pearls was perfected. Before Kokichi Mikimoto completed his technique for harvesting pearl-bearing oysters at the turn of the century, pearls were a rare freak of nature. *Ama* (women divers—women because it was believed they had bigger lungs) could dive all day long; even after bringing up a thousand oysters, they might not find one with a valuable pearl. Thanks to Mikimoto, the odds have changed. Nevertheless, even after the considerable effort of injecting an irritating substance—muscarine, from Iowa—into two-year-old oysters, only one in two bears pearls, and no more than 5% are of gem quality. Because the two-year-old oyster takes three more years to secrete layer after layer of nacre over his irritating implant to form the pearl, these gems remain expensive.

On **Pearl Island,** 500 yards from Toba Station, **Mikimoto's Museum** (he died in 1954) gives a fascinating, if a little long-winded, account of pearl cultivation. A demonstration is also given by female pearl divers. *Admission: ¥850. Open 8:30–5 (9–4 in winter).*

Before pearl-oyster farming, women dove for pearls with more frequency than now. Such a hit-or-miss operation can no longer support them in face of the larger quantities (and cheaper prices) possible through Mikimoto's research and farming. However, on the outlying islands, women do still dive for abalone, octopus, and edible seaweed. These women are not lithe, scantily clad nymphs of the water, but mature ladies who wear diving suits and make peculiar whistling sounds.

Toba is a resort town with resort hotels and activities. An aquarium displays native and exotic marine life, such as rare Alaskan sea otters and Baikal seals (admission: ¥1,200; open 8–5). The ship ***Brazil Maru,*** which transported many Japanese rice farmers to Brazil, is now a floating entertainment center with restaurants and souvenir shops (admission: ¥1,050; open daily 8:30–4:30). Cruise boats make 50-minute tours of Toba Bay (cost: ¥1,350), and ferries go to the outer islands. Because the town has a couple of reasonable hotels (Toba International offers the best views; *see* Dining and Lodging, *below*), Toba makes a possible overnight stop. Alternatively, Kashikojima is 40 minutes away by rail.

10 The Kintetsu Line continues from Toba to **Kashikojima** (fare: about ¥900), in the center of Ago Bay, but the tracks cut inland. (There are also two buses a day at 9:40 and 2:25; fare is ¥1,300.) To appreciate the spectacular coastline, disembark the train at Ugata and take the bus to Nakiri. Then change buses for the one going along the headland to Goza, a small fishing village that faces Kashikojima from across Ago Bay. From Goza, frequent ferries navigate past hundreds of rafts, from which pearl-bearing oysters are suspended, to Kashikojima. Ago Bay has a wonderfully indented coastline and is a fitting climax to the Ise Peninsula. The town of Kashikojima is now the pearl center and has a few reasonable hotels for an overnight stay; the most sophisticated is the Shima Kanko Hotel (*see* Din-

ing and Lodging, *below*). Consider however, one of the smaller guest houses, such as the Asanaro, where you will have the opportunity to explore and meet the local community. Be sure to visit Daio, the fishing village tucked behind a promontory. Standing above the village is a grand lighthouse (admission ¥80; open daily 9–5). To reach this towering structure, walk up the narrow street lined with fish stalls at the back of the harbor. From this lighthouse, you can see Anori, the third oldest lighthouse in Japan, 7 miles (11 kilometers) to the east. Between the two lighthouses on the curving bay are small fishing villages, coffee shops, and restaurants. And there are three golf courses, of which Hamajima Country Club (Hamajima 517–04, tel. 05995/2–1141; greens fees ¥8,000 weekdays, ¥18,000 weekends, caddy ¥3,500) has especially fine views of Ago Bay, dotted with numerous small islands and oyster beds.

It is possible to follow the coast from Kashikojima to the Kii Peninsula, but there is no train and in many places the road cuts inland, making the journey long and tedious. You are far better off taking the Kintetsu train back from Kashikojima to Iseshi, where you must change to the JR Sangu Line and travel to Taki, at which point you must change to another JR train, heading south to the peninsula. If you prefer to skip the Kii Peninsula, you can take the Kintetsu Line directly to Nagoya or to Matsusaka, where connections to Nara and Kyoto may be made.

To go to the Kii Peninsula, transfer at Taki to the JR Kisei main line for Shingu and Kushimoto. Take your nap at the beginning of the train ride, for within hours the scenery becomes more and more picturesque as the train runs along the coastline. The first major town is Kumano, not a particularly attractive place, but often used by hikers as a gateway to the Yoshino-Kumano National Park.

If you have limited time it is better to continue on the train to (11) **Shingu.** This town is home to an important shrine, Kumano-Hayatama Taisha, but the thrill for the adventurous is to take a four-hour trip (fare: ¥4,500) up the Kumano River on flat-bottom, air propeller-driven boats to (12) **Dorokyo Gorge.** The trip up the valley is gently attractive, with hills rising on either side of emerald-green water. In late-May–early June, with azaleas and rhododendrons lining the banks, the valley is a beautiful introduction to the gorge that lies farther upstream. Dorokyo is considered by many to be Japan's finest gorge. Sheer, 150-foot cliffs tower above the Kumano River, which alternates between gushing rapids and calm waters. You may also travel up through the valley by taking a 45-minute bus ride from Shingu Station (fare: ¥1,250) or a 30-minute bus ride from Kumano Hongu (fare: ¥960).

The boat trip ends at **Doro-hatcho,** the first of the three gorges and rapids that extend for several miles upstream and may also be explored by boat. Long, fiberglass boats continue up the gorge for a two-hour round-trip (cost is ¥3,280). A less expensive alternative is a bus up to Kitayamakyo, where there are good glimpses of the Doro-hatcho Gorge.

From Doro-hatcho, you can take a bus back to Shingu. If you do not want to continue around the Kii Peninsula, an alternative is to backtrack by bus as far as Shiko and pick up the Shingu-Nara bus. The bus takes seven hours from Shingu (6 hrs. from Shiko) to reach Nara and passes through the heart of Yoshino-Kumano National Park. (The bus stops at Gojo, where you can make your way to Mt. Koya and Yoshino.)

Back in Shingu, if you have the time, take a quick look at Kumano-Hayatama Taisha Shrine, one of the three main shrines of Kii Peninsula. Though it is a bright and cheerful place, it is not worth missing your train, unless you are there on October 15 for its festival. The other two main shrines are at Hongu, near Doro-hatcho, and at Nachi, the next stop around the Kii Peninsula.

13 To get to **Nachi,** take the local JR train 9 miles (14 kilometers) south. A 20-minute bus ride from the Nachi train station will bring you to the next major attraction, **Nachi-no-taki,** the highest waterfall in Japan, with a drop of 430 feet. At the bus stop near the falls, you'll see a torii at the top of several stone steps, which lead down to a paved clearing near the foot of the falls. For a view from the top, climb up the path from the bus stop to **Nachi-Taisha,** which, aside from being one of the three great shrines of the Kii area (founded in the 4th century), offers a close-up view above the waterfall. Next to the shrine is the Buddhist Seigantoji Temple, a popular stop for pilgrims.

A couple of miles farther down the coast from Nachi, and the halfway point (6 hrs. either way by rail) between Osaka and 14 Nagoya, is **Katsuura,** located on a pleasant bay surrounding pine-covered islands. Sightseeing boats cruise the bay (cost: ¥ 1,550), promoting it as Kii-no-Matsushima. The bay is named after one of the three big scenic draws in Japan, Matsushima Bay near Sendai, and if you've seen that, taking the cruise is not worth the money.

Another 30 miles (48 kilometers) down the coast at the bottom 15 of the Kii Peninsula is **Cape Shio-no-misaki,** Honshu's most southerly point, marked by a white lighthouse high above its 16 rocky cliffs. Nearby is the resort town of **Kushimoto,** which, with its direct flights to Nagoya and Osaka, has become popular with residents from those cities. Stretching out to sea toward Oshima (the island a mile offshore) is a notable and odd formation of 30 large rocks, spaced evenly as they jut out to sea. They resemble what their name suggests, Hashi-kui-iwa (rock pillars), though more imaginative authors describe them as a procession of hooded monks trying to reach Oshima.

Rounding the peninsula, 34 miles (54 kilometers) to the north, 17 is **Shirahama,** rated (by the Japanese) as one of the three best hot-spring resorts in the country. (The other two are Beppu on Kyushu and Atami on the Izu Peninsula. We would add Noboribetsu Onsen in Hokkaido to these.) Unfortunately, the Japanese have a penchant for building mammoth, drab hotels around their spa waters, and this town fits that mold. But it does have some attractive coastal scenery, so Shirahama can be a pleasant place for an overnight stay. Be warned, though, that the town itself is a 17-minute bus ride from the train station.

Between Shirahama and Wakanoura is the famous **Dojoji Temple in Gobo.** 18 According to legend, Kiyohime, a farmer's daughter, became enamored of a young priest, Anchin, who often passed by her house. One day she blurted out her feelings to him. He, in turn, promised to return that night and take advantage of her feelings. However, during the course of the day, the priest had second thoughts and returned to the Dojoji Temple.

Spurned, Kiyohime became enraged. She turned herself into a dragon and set in pursuit of Anchin, who, scared out of his wits, hid under the temple bell that had not yet been suspended. Kiyohime sensed his presence and wrapped her dragon body around the bell. Her fiery breath heated the bell until it became red-hot. The next morning, only the charred remains of Anchin's body were found under the bell.

Equally as good as Shirahama for an overnight stay is (19) **Wakanoura,** 30 miles (48 kilometers) farther north. It is another resort, one that makes the rather ambitious claim of having the most beautiful coastal scenery in Japan. A few miles north (20) of Wakanoura is **Wakayama.** This is the largest town one reaches since leaving Nagoya. Ferries (from Wakayama-ko Port) depart for Ko matsushima on the island of Shikoku. As a city, Wakayama has little of interest for the visitor other than its being a source for replenishing camera film, yen, and other needs before traveling inland to visit sacred Koyasan (Mt. Koya) and Mt. Yoshino before ending this itinerary in Nara.

To get to Koyasan, take the JR line to Hashimoto and change onto the Nankai Line for the final 12 miles (19 kilometers) to Gokuraku-bashi Station. From there, a cable car runs up to the top of sacred Mt. Koya. (If one has cut across the Yoshino-Kumano National Park by bus from Shingu or Hongu on Rte. 168, instead of circling the Kii Peninsula, get off the bus at Gojo and backtrack one station on the JR line to Hashimoto for the Nankai Line.)

To reach Koyasan directly from Tokyo or Kyoto, go first to Osaka and take the private Nankai Line that departs for Koyasan every 30 minutes from Namba Station. (To reach Namba Station from Shin-Osaka Shinkansen Station, use the Midosuji subway.) The Osaka-Koyasan journey takes just under two hours, including the five-minute cable car ride up to the Koyasan Station, and costs around ¥2,000 including reservations.

(21) On a mesa amid the mountains is **Koyasan,** a great complex of 120 temples, monasteries, schools, and graves. It is the seat of the Shingon sect of Buddhism founded by Kobo Daishi in 816. Every year about a million visitors pass through the Daimon Gate, a huge wooden structure typical of many entrances to Japanese temples.

The cable car will deposit you at Koyasan Station, at the top of 3,000-foot Mt. Koya, where you can pick up a map. You will need to take a bus to the main attractions, which are 1.4 miles from the station and 3.4 miles from each other, on opposite sides of town.

There are two buses that leave the station every 20 or 30 minutes, when the cable car arrives. One goes to Okunoin Cemetery, on the eastern side of the main road, and the other goes to Daimon Gate, on the west side of town. Both buses start out following the same route to the center of town, to a "T" junction, where the tourist office is located (600 Koyasan, Koya-cho, Itogun, Wakayama-ken, tel. 07365/6–2616). The bus fare is ¥300 to the tourist office. En route from the station, you will pass the mausoleums of the first and second Tokugawa shoguns. You may want to walk back and visit these two gilded structures later (open 9–5).

If your time is limited, head for Okunoin Cemetery first. Take the bus to the Ukunoin-mae bus stop, where you can pick up a path that provides a shortcut to the Lantern Hall (you can take the long route out). Many of your fellow visitors will be Japanese, who are making pilgrimages to the mausoleum of Kobo Daishi or paying their respects to their ancestors buried here. The pilgrims often travel in groups; they dress in white and carry wooden staffs. Make sure you arrive very early in the morning, before the groups take over.

Entering this cemetery is like entering Alice's Wonderland. Magnificent 300-year-old cedar trees stretch skyward, some of their dark textured trunks forming columns 12-feet around. This old-growth forest is a rarity in most places, including Japan. And among these towering cedars are the graves of some of the country's most illustrious families, graves marked by moss-covered pagodas and red- and white-robed buddhas carved from black stone. You will feel small here, but contemplative; the holiness of Koyasan is strongly sensed.

The path from Okunoin-mae leads into the main avenue of mausoleums, a cobblestone lane that ends at the Lantern Hall, named after its 11,000 lanterns. Two fires burn in this hall: One has been alight since 1016, the other since 1088. Behind the hall is the mausoleum of Kobo Daishi (774–835). *Lantern Hall admission free. Open Apr.–Oct., 8–5; Nov.–Mar., 8:30–4:30.*

You may be tempted to spend the day wandering through the cemetery, but be careful, it is easy to get lost if you stray from the main avenue. Some people prefer to visit the cemetery at dusk, when the cobbled lane is lit by lanterns, setting an erie mood. In any case, you should exit Okunoin by way of the 1.3-mile main avenue, lined with tombs, monuments, and statues. More than 100,000 historical figures are honored here. The lane exits the cemetery at Ichinohashi-guchi; follow the main street straight ahead to return to the center of town (a 20-min. walk) or wait for the bus that is headed for Kongobuji Temple.

Located on the southwestern side of Mt. Koya, **Kongobuji Temple** (Temple of the Diamond Seat) is the chief temple of Shingon Buddhism, a sect that is closest to that practiced in Tibet. Kongobuji was built in 1592 as the family temple of Hideyoshi Toyotomi, but it was rebuilt in 1861 and is now the main temple of the Koyasan community. *Admission: ¥350. Open 8–5; in winter, 8–4:30.*

Walk down the main stairs of the temple and take the road to the right of the parking lot in front of you; in less than five minutes you will reach **Danjogaran,** a complex consisting of many halls as well as the **Daito** (Great Central Pagoda). This red pagoda, with its interior of brilliantly colored beams, is home to five sacred images of Buddha. Built in 1937, the two-story structure stands out in part because of its unusual style, but also because of its rich vermilion color. It's worth taking a look inside. *Admission to buildings: ¥100 each. Open Apr.–Oct., 8–5; Nov.–Mar., 8:30–4:30.*

South and across a small path from the Danjogaran is the **Reihokan Museum,** with a total of 5,000 art treasures. The exhibits are continually changing, but at least some of the 180 pieces that have been designated as national treasures are always on display. *Admission: ¥500. Open 9–5 (9–4 in winter).*

Although you can easily visit Koyasan's major sites in a day trip from Kyoto or Osaka, it is best to spend the night in a buddhist temple here (*see* Dining and Lodging, *below*).

22 The next and final stop before Nara is **Mt. Yoshino,** the other major religious and historical site of the region. To get to Yoshino from Koyasan, rejoin the train at Hashimoto for Yoshino-guchi, and change to the Kintetsu Line for Yoshino. (This Kintetsu Line is the Osaka–Yoshino route, which departs from Abeno-bashi Station in Osaka. Yoshino may also be reached directly from Kashikojima on the Kintetsu Line.)

Though the community of temples at Mt. Yoshino is less impressive than that of Koyasan, Mt. Yoshino is one of the most beautiful places in Japan to visit during cherry-blossom season. The Cherry Blossom Festival, which attracts thousands of visitors each year, is April 11–12. Because of its 100,000 trees in four groves that are staggered down the mountainside, and because of the differing temperatures, the wafting sea of pink petals lasts at least two weeks. When you look upon this vision of color, thank En-no-Ozunu, the 7th-century Buddhist priest who planted the trees and put a curse on anyone who tampered with them.

In the middle of the cherry groves is **Kimpusenji Temple,** the main temple of the area. Make a point of seeing the main hall, Zaodo, which is not only the second largest wooden structure in Japan, but also has two superb sculptures of Deva kings at the main gate. The other important temple is **Nyoirinji,** founded in the 10th century and located just to the south of Kimpusenji. Here the last remaining 143 warriors prayed before going into their final battle for the imperial cause in the 14th century. Behind the temple is the mausoleum of Emperor Godaigo (1288–1339), who brought down the Kamakura Shogunate. *Admission: ¥300. Open 9–5.*

Built into the surrounding mountains, Yoshino is a quaint town where the shops—and there are many to serve the thousands of visitors—are on the third floor of the house, the first and second floors being below the road. All around Yoshino are superb mountain vistas and isolated temples. For the hiker (and pilgrim) Mt. Sanjo is considered the holiest mountain, with two temples at the summit, one of which is dedicated to En-no-Ozunu, the cherry-tree priest. Lodgings are available at both temples May 8–September 27. The **tourist office** (Yoshinoyama, Yoshino-machi, Yoshino-gun, Nara ken, tel. 07463/2–3014) can arrange accommodations at local minshukus. From Yoshino, **Nara** is an hour away (on the Kintetsu Line, with a change either at Kashihara-jingu Station or to the JR line at Yoshino-guchi), and **Kyoto** is 50 minutes farther north.

Dining and Lodging

Dining

Nagoya is known for only a few special dishes: **Kishimen,** white, flat noodles of the *udon* variety, with a velvety smoothness against the palate; **Miso Nikomi Udon,** a thick noodle boiled with chicken and Welsh onion; **Moriguchi-zuke** (Japanese pickle), made from a special radish, pickled either with or without sweet sake; and **Uiro,** a sweet cake made of rice powder and sugar, most often eaten during the tea ceremony. The most highly prized food product is the **Nagoya-tori,** a type of chicken similar to the famous French *poulet Bresse*. These chickens are given special feed just before their execution, said to improve the texture and taste of their white meat.

Other than these items, Nagoya's cuisine is mostly Kyoto-style (*see* Dining in Chapter 7), but every type of Japanese and international food may be found in this cosmopolitan city. For Western cuisine, the best choices in the city are the French restaurants at Hotel Nagoya Castle, the Nagoya Kanko Hotel, and the International Hotel Nagoya. The one good Western restaurant outside the hotels is the Okura Restaurant.

On the Ise Peninsula, the **lobster** is especially fine. On the Kii Peninsula, farmers raise cattle for **Matsuzaka beef** (the town of Matsuzaka is 90 minutes by train from Nagoya). However, the best beef is typically shipped to Tokyo, Kyoto, and Osaka.

Outside Nagoya, if you want to eat Western food, you should go to the dining rooms of the larger hotels. However, we strongly recommend that you eat out at local Japanese restaurants. Most reasonably priced restaurants have a visual display of their menu in the window. On this basis, you can decide what you want before you enter. If you cannot order in Japanese, and no English is spoken, after securing a table, lead the waiter to the window display and point.

Unless the establishment is a *ryotei* (high-class, traditional Japanese restaurant) or a formal restaurant at a hotel or a ryokan, reservations are usually not required. Whenever reservations are recommended or required at any of the restaurants listed, this is indicated.

A 3% federal consumer tax is added to all restaurant bills. Another 3% is added to the bill if it exceeds ¥7,500. At more expensive restaurants, a 10%–15% service charge is also added to the bill. Tipping is not the custom.

Category	Cost*
Very Expensive	over ¥6,000
Expensive	¥4,000–¥6,000
Moderate	¥2,000–¥4,000
Inexpensive	under ¥2,000

**Cost is per person without tax, service, or drinks*

Lodging

The cosmopolitan city of Nagoya offers a range of lodging, from clean, efficient business hotels offering the basics to large luxury hotels with additional amenities. Nagoya has three major areas in which to stay: the district around the Nagoya JR Station, the downtown area, and Nagoya Castle area. Though ryokan are listed below, international-style hotels are often more convenient for the Nagoya visitor who wants flexible dining hours.

Outside Nagoya, most hotels quote prices on a per-person basis with two meals, exclusive of service and tax. If you do not want dinner at your hotel, it is usually possible to renegotiate the price. Stipulate, too, whether you wish to have Japanese or Western breakfast, if any. The categories assigned to all hotels below reflect the cost of a double room with private bath but no meals. However, if you make reservations at any of the noncity hotels, you will be expected to take breakfast and dinner at the hotel; the rate quoted to you will include these meals unless you specify otherwise.

A 3% federal consumer tax is added to all hotel bills. Another 3% is added to the bill if it exceeds ¥15,000. At most hotels, a 10%–15% service charge is added to the total bill. Tipping is not the custom.

Category	Cost*
Very Expensive	over ¥20,000
Expensive	¥15,000–¥20,000
Moderate	¥10,000–¥15,000
Inexpensive	under ¥10,000

**Cost is for double room, without tax or service*

The most highly recommended restaurants and accommodations for each city or area are indicated by a star ★.

Nagoya

Dining

★ **Koraku.** One of the most exclusive restaurants in Nagoya, Koraku serves some of the best chicken dishes in all of Japan. The restaurant is in an old samurai mansion, with formal service by women dressed in beautiful kimonos. The setting is traditional and refined; guests feel as if they are stepping back into Japan's more noble past. *3-3 Chikara-machi, Higashi-ku, Nagoya, tel. 052/931–3472. Reservations essential, preferably with an introduction. Dress: formal. AE. No lunch. Very Expensive.*

Kamone. The innovative Japanese menu here adds Chinese and/or French touches to the dishes, and as if to enhance the foreign culinary influences on the Japanese dishes, the decor is more Western than Japanese—window drapes instead of shoji screens, for example. Since the restaurant is on the 15th floor of the Meiji Seimei Building, try for a table by the window in order to enjoy the view. *1-1 Shin-Sakaemachi, Naka-ku, Nagoya (located across from the Sakaecho subway station exit), tel. 052/951–7787. Reservations advised. Jacket and tie required. DC, MC, V. Open noon–3 and 5–9. Closed Mon. Expensive.*

★ **Okura Restaurant.** The Okura has the best French cuisine in Nagoya, outside of the hotels. This is the place where Western businessmen often entertain their Japanese partners. Some recommended dishes include the veal slices with mushrooms in madeira sauce and the steamed salmon. Another good choice is Matsuzaka beef (a Nagoya specialty) served with béarnaise sauce. *Tokyo Kaijo Bldg., 23rd floor, Naka-ku, Nagoya, tel. 052/201–3201. Reservations required. Dress: formal. AE, DC, V. Expensive.*

Torikyu. This traditionally decorated restaurant in a Meiji-period building specializes in chicken dishes—raw, grilled, in a casserole, or as a very formal meal. The restaurant is next to a river, and in the old days, patrons used to arrive by boat. *1-15*

Naiyacho, Nakamura-ku, Nagoya, tel. 052/541–1888. Reservations advised. Jacket and tie required. AE. Open 11–9:30. Closed Sun. Expensive.

★ **Yaegaki.** This is the best tempura restaurant in town; the fish and vegetables are cooked before you, and you eat them immediately after the chef decides they're done to perfection. The restaurant building is one of the few wood structures among a sea of concrete, and it has its own small garden. An English-language menu is offered. *3-7 Nishiki, Naka-ku, Nagoya, tel. 052/951–3250. Reservations advised. Jacket and tie required. AE, V. Open noon–9. Closed Sun. Expensive.*

Kani Doraku. The specialty here is crab, either boiled or steamed, elegantly served by waitresses dressed in kimonos. The restaurant, which is located opposite the Nagoya Tokyu Hotel's entrance, may be identified by its small sign of a crab. *4-chome, Sakae, Naka-ku, Nagoya, tel. 052/242–1234. Reservations advised. Jacket and tie required. AE, V. Moderate.*

Kisoji. Located not far from the International Hotel Nagoya, Kisoji has a reasonably priced (¥4,000) *shabu-shabu* beef dinner, but if you take the shabu-shabu special with tempura and sashimi, the price jumps up. The decor is rustic, but the kimono-clad waitresses give it a touch of tradition and smartness. *Nishiki 3-chome, Naka-ku, Nagoya, tel. 052/951–3755. Reservations not required. Dress: informal. Open 11–10. V. Moderate.*

Usquebaugh. This bar/restaurant with a polished wood decor takes its name from the Gaelic word for "water of life"—whiskey. Nautical paintings and gear hang on the walls, and there are some impressive glass-enclosed wine racks. Modern *kaiseki* cuisine is served at reasonable prices; you can also have a light meal at the bar. The restaurant is located on Hirokuji-dori Avenue, one block east of the Rich Hotel. *2-4-1 Sakae, Naka-ku, Nagoya, tel. 052/201–5811. No reservations. Jacket and tie required. AE, DC, MC, V. Moderate.*

Yamamotoya. For Nagoya's local dish, *misonikomi* (noodles in broth), you can't beat this no-frills eatery, which serves a steaming bowl of *udon* for ¥1,500. The superb misonikomi is especially welcome during the colder months. The restaurant is located one block east of the Rich Hotel. *2-4-5 Sakae, Naka-ku, Nagoya, tel. 052/471–5547. No reservations. Dress: casual. No credit cards. Inexpensive.*

Lodging

★ **Nagoya Hilton.** The newest of the city's leading hotels, this 28-story building delivers all the modern creature comforts of an international deluxe accommodation. Rooms on the upper floors have a panoramic view of Nagoya. The light-pastel furnishings and the *shoji* window screens add to the bright, airy feel of the rooms. The plastic polyurethane covering on the tables and chairs should be eliminated, but the king-size beds are a pleasure. Single travelers do especially well because the hotel has none of the closet-size rooms found in most Japanese hotels. You'll appreciate the attentive, enthusiastic staff. Be sure to browse the designer boutiques in the Hilton Plaza. The collection of high-price and -status merchandise exemplifies Japan's new-found riches and the importance attached to image. *1-3-3 Sakae, Naka-ku, Nagoya 460, tel. 052/212–1111, fax 052/204–2389. 453 rooms, including 26 suites, and 2 concierge floors. Facilities: 3 specialty restaurants (Chinese, Continental, and Japanese), coffee shop, Clark Hatch fitness center, sauna, indoor pool, massage service in room, tennis court, business cen-*

ter, wedding and conference facilities, and shopping plaza. AE, DC, MC, V. Very Expensive.

★ **Nagoya Castle Hotel.** Its location next to Nagoyajo Castle makes this the choice hotel in Nagoya. A room with a view onto the castle shows Nagoya at its best—especially at night, when the castle is floodlit. The bedrooms are spacious and attractively furnished, including original oil paintings. Even the lobby is attractively and hospitably decorated, with plenty of wood paneling. The establishment is efficiently run, with a range of restaurants and bars; at the Rosen Bar, Western and Japanese businessmen meet for a drink after work. The hotel has a new, vast annex of 6,400 square feet of convention halls. *3-19 Hinokuchi-cho, Nishi-ku, Nagoya 451 (Castle Area), tel. 052/521–2121, fax 052/531–3313. 274 rooms, including 5 suites. Facilities: Western, Chinese, and Japanese restaurants, indoor pool, health club, business center, shops, beauty salon, and an hourly shuttle bus to the JR station. AE, DC, MC, V. Expensive–Very Expensive.*

International Hotel Nagoya. With the best location in the city, the International Hotel has been a longtime favorite with business travelers. It is not the newest accommodation in town, but it maintains a high standard. The lobby resembles that of a European hotel, with gold and dark-brown tones and antique furnishings. Some of the rooms are small for the price, but they are comfortably furnished. *3-23-3 Nishiki, Naka-ku, Nagoya 460 (downtown), tel. 052/961–3111, fax 052/962–5937. 265 Western-style rooms. Facilities: Western, Chinese, and Japanese restaurants, penthouse bar with live music, business center. AE, DC, MC, V. Expensive.*

Ryokan Suihoen. A large concrete city, Nagoya is not the ideal setting for old-style ryokan, but this one is the most traditional, luxurious, and expensive of its kind in Nagoya. The tatami rooms are furnished with good reproductions of traditional furniture. Meals may be served in your room. *1-19-20 Sakae, Naka-ku, Nagoya 460 (downtown), tel. and fax 052/241–3521. 25 rooms, most with bath. AE. Expensive.*

Castle Plaza Hotel. A five-minute walk from the main railway station, the Castle Plaza is an efficient and top-notch business person's hotel, with more amenities than most. The few Japanese rooms are larger in size than the others. *4-3-25 Meieki, Nakamura-ku, Nagoya 450, tel. 052/582–2121, fax 052/582–8666. 258 Western-style rooms, 4 Japanese-style rooms. Facilities: gym, indoor pool, sauna, Western and Japanese restaurant. AE, V. Moderate.*

Nagoya Terminal Hotel. Since its recent redecoration, this has become the best choice for a less-expensive hotel close to the station. Of course, the rooms are small, as one must expect in Japan, but they are not as depressing as most. Even the public rooms are pleasant. At the Kurumaya restaurant the creative chef imports French ideas for his Japanese cooking. The Playmates lounge bar offers a 20th-floor panorama view, and the Bagpiper is a friendly bar. *1–2 Mei-Eki 1-chome, Nakamura-ku, Nagoya 450, tel. 052/561–3751, fax 052/581–3236. 246 rooms. Facilities: Japanese/French restaurant, coffee shop, bar, banquet facilities. AE, DC, MC, V. Moderate.*

Fitness Hotel. This new business hotel, two blocks from the JR Station in the direction of downtown, is considerably smarter than neighboring business-category hotels. Rooms, albeit typically small, are done in gay, cheerful fabrics, and there's the ubiquitous wooden cabinet to serve as desk and table top for the

TV. The fitness center is high tech, and the business center has a computer work station. A friendly, intimate café and bar is on the ground level next to the lobby. The welcoming staff is good with gesturing, if your Japanese fails you. The hotel is five minutes' walk from JR Nagoya Station. *1-2-7, Sakae, Nakamura, Nagoya 450, tel. 052/562–0330, fax 052/562–0331. 120 Western rooms. Facilities: Japanese restaurant, café/bar, fitness center, business center. AE, DC, MC, V. Inexpensive–Moderate.*

Oyone Ryokan. In a small wood building, Oyone is a friendly inn resembling a B&B with its small, sparsely furnished rooms. *2-2-12 Aoi, Higashi-ku, Nagoya (downtown—take the Higashiyama subway line, exit at Chikusa, 2 stops after Sakae), tel. 052/936–8788, fax 052/936–8883. 18 rooms, all without bath, but with air-conditioning. AE, MC, V. Inexpensive.*

Ryokan Meiryu. This inn, consisting of a four-story concrete building and a two-story annex, has no particular charm except its low price for a small tatami room, which has nothing more than a table and a futon. Meals (optional) are served in a small dining room. *2-24-21 Kamimaezu, Naka-ku, Nagoya 460 (downtown—the hotel is located opposite the YMCA, close to Kamimaezu Station, 2 stops south of Sakae on the Meijo subway), tel. 052/331–8686, fax 052/321–6119. 23 rooms, all without bath. AE, V. Inexpensive.*

Outside Nagoya

Futaminoura
Lodging

Ryokan Futamikan. This traditional Japanese inn is located on the coast near the wedded rocks off the Ise Peninsula, about 10 miles (16 kilometers) north of Toba. *569-1 Futamimachi, Mie Prefecture (3-min. taxi ride away from Futaminoura Station), tel. 05964/3–2003. 43 rooms. AE. Expensive.*

Gifu
Lodging

Ryokan Sugiyama. Close to the Nagara River, Sugiyama is Gifu's best Japanese inn. The presence of the river adds to the mood of peace and quiet. Very good food, including *ayu* (river smelt), is usually served in the rooms. *73-1 Nagara, Gifu 502, tel. 0582/31–0161, fax 0582/33–5250. 49 Japanese-style rooms. AE. Expensive.*

Gifu Grand Hotel. This large resort hotel is efficiently run and slightly impersonal, but it is popular with the Japanese who come for its thermal baths. *648 Nagara, Gifu 502, tel. 0582/33–1111, fax 0582/33–1122. 147 rooms, about half Western-style. Facilities: pool, hot springs, sauna, Western and Japanese restaurants. AE, V. Moderate.*

Inuyama
Lodging

Mietetsu Inuyama Hotel. This resort hotel's location on the Kiso River makes it a good base for shooting the rapids. *107 Kita-Koken, Inuyama, Aichi Prefecture 484, tel. 0568/61–2211, fax 0568/67–5750. 99 rooms, mostly Western-style, but Japanese-style rooms in the annex. Facilities: Western and Japanese restaurants, outdoor pool. AE, V. Moderate.*

Ise-shi
Lodging

Hoshide Ryokan. A small Japanese inn in a traditional-style wood building, the Hoshide is bare and simple, but it has clean tatami rooms and congenial hosts. The food served follows a macrobiotic diet, though instant coffee is available at breakfast! *2-15-2 Kawasaki, Ise-shi, Mie Prefecture 516 (a 7-min. walk from the Kintetsu Station or the Ise Outer Shrine), tel. 0596/28–2377, fax 059/627–2830. 13 Japanese-style rooms,* *without private bath. Facilities: laundry room, Japanese bath. AE, MC, V. Inexpensive.*

Kashikojima
Lodging

★ **Shima Kanko Hotel.** This large and established resort hotel has grand views over Ago Bay, especially at sunset. Certainly for its location, it's a choice hotel. The staff are friendly and efficient, willing to help advise you in your travel and touring, even willing to make arrangements for golf. Some English is spoken. The hotel's smart French restaurant offers the best Western cuisine on the Shima Peninsula, creatively using the delicious local lobster to its best advantage. Guest rooms are spacious and smartly furnished, though in a rather dreary pale yellow/beige color. All rooms have views of the bay. *731 Shimmei Ago-cho, Shima-gun, Mie Prefecture 517 (a shuttle bus runs to and from Kashikojima Station), tel. 05994/3–1211, fax 05994/3–3538. 147 Western-style rooms, 51 Japanese-style rooms. Facilities: pool, arrangements for golf, boating, and fishing, beauty parlors, shops, French and Japanese restaurants. AE, DC, V. Moderate–Expensive.*

★ **Asanaro Minshuku.** Owner Yuzoo Matsmura is boisterously friendly. In broken English, he welcomes his guests with enthusiastic abandon. The inn is located in a small fishing village facing the Pacific between Daio and Anori lighthouses. Rooms are large, spotlessly clean, and come with air-conditioning and heating. Bathrooms, also spotless, are just down the hall. Breakfast and dinner are served in your room. Dinner is absolutely superb—fresh broiled lobsters, sashimi, fried oysters, fish cooked in soy sauce or grilled, and fresh fruit. Matsmura-san will insist you use his bicycles to explore and will take you in his car to all the places you missed. He also owns a snack bar (pub), similarly called Asanaro (tel. 05994/3–4197) in Ugata, where he will no doubt take you after dinner. *3578 Kooka Ago-chiyo, Shima Gun, Mie 517–05, tel. 05994/5–3963. 8 rooms. 2 meals included. Owner will meet guests at Ugata Station; telephone on arrival. No credit cards. Inexpensive.*

★ **Ryokan Ishiyama-So.** On tiny Yokoyama-jima Island in Ago Bay, this small concrete inn is just a two-minute ferry ride from Kashikojima. Phone ahead, and your hosts will meet you at the quay. The inn is nothing fancy, but it has warmth and hospitality. The meals are good, too, but don't let the hosts try pleasing you with Western-style food. *Yokoyama-jima, Kashikojima, Ago-cho, Shima-gun, Mie Prefecture 517-05, tel. 05995/2–1527, fax 059/952–1240. 12 Japanese-style rooms, 3 with private bath. AE, MC, V. Inexpensive.*

Koyasan (Mt. Koya)
Lodging

Mt. Koya has no actual hotels. Fifty-three of the temples offer Japanese-style accommodations—tatami floors and futon mattresses—although only a handful accept foreign guests. The temples do not have private baths, and the two meals served are vegetarian, the same as those eaten by the priests. The price is either side of ¥10,000 per person, including the two meals. These prices are higher than those at other temples in Japan. This may be because this is the only Buddhist sect in which wealth is necessary for advancement in the religious hierarchy. If possible, reservations should be made in advance through **Koya-san Kanko Kyokai,** Koya-san, Koya-machi, Itsu-gun, Wakayama Prefecture, tel. 07365/6–2616. Reservations can also be booked through the Nankai Railway Company office in Osaka, and the Japan Travel Bureau in most Japanese cities. One especially lovely temple that is open to foreigners is **Rengejoin Temple** (tel. 07365/6–2231). Both the head priest and his mother speak English. Be sure to ask where the morning service takes place and rise before 6 to see and hear it.

Matsuzaka
Dining
★

Restaurant Wadakin. This establishment claims to be the originator of Matsuzaka beef; it raises cattle with loving care on its farm. Sukiyaki or the chef's steak dinner will satisfy both your taste buds and any craving for red meat. *1878 Nakamachi, Matsuzaka 515, Mie Prefecture (located 10 min. on foot directly away from the railway station, opposite a parking garage), tel. 0598/21–3291. Reservations suggested. Jacket and tie required. Open 10:30–9. Closed 4th Tues. of each month. No credit cards. Expensive.*

Shirahama
Lodging

Shirasso Grand Hotel. This resort-spa hotel seems to be more appealing to the Japanese than to Westerners. Though it has little architectural merit as a modern, rectangular cement block structure, it does have thermal baths for adults. *Shirahama, Wakayama Prefecture 649, tel. 0739/42–2566, fax 073/942–2438. 125 Japanese-style rooms with bath. Facilities: shopping arcade, electronic games for children, thermal baths, Western and Japanese restaurants. AE, DC, V. Expensive.*

Toba
Lodging

Toba International Hotel. Toba's chief resort hotel sits up on a bluff overlooking the town and bay. Take a room facing the sea, and be sure to be up for the marvelous sunrises. The hotel has amenities for the entire family. *1-23-1 Toba, Mie Prefecture 517, tel. 0599/25–3121, fax 0599/25–3139. 147 rooms, mostly Western, but Japanese-style rooms in the annex. Facilities: golf, fishing, pool, boating. AE, DC, V. Moderate.*

6 The Japan Alps

By Nigel Fisher

Although 80% of all of Japan is categorized as mountainous, it took a Briton, the Reverend Walter Weston, to call the north–south mountain ranges of Honshu's central region the Japan Alps. Through his writings, the Reverend Weston helped to change the Japanese attitudes to the mountains from one of reverence and superstition—a place where gods alight from the heavens—to one of physical appreciation. Mountain climbing is now a popular national sport, and the Japan Alps are a training ground for the Japanese. Another Englishman, Archdeacon A. C. Shaw, who served as his church's prelate in Tokyo, gave prestige to the mountains by building his summer villa on the lower slopes of Mt. Asama to escape the muggy summers of the capital. Since then, and over the course of the past hundred years, the Japan Alps have been "discovered" by the Japanese, not only for their grandeur but also for the rural traditional culture, architecture, and folkcraft, which have been bulldozed away by the industrial progress sweeping the coastal plains. Of all the regions of Japan, the Alps have perhaps the most to offer the first-time visitor: forested mountains, snowy peaks, rushing rivers, fortified castles, temples, folklore, festivals, and food.

In the winter, the Japan Alps attract skiers to their northern slopes, where the snow is deepest. The southern slopes, those facing the Pacific, get very little snow. In spring, the trees start blossoming, and, by summer, the alpine flowers are out. The temperatures are warm and crisp compared with the hot humidity of the lowland areas of the Chubu region (middle or central part). In autumn, the changing colors of the trees turn the Japan Alps into a kaleidoscope of hues. Then winter comes again, with the sweetest shrimps to be plucked from the cold waters of the Sea of Japan. In other words, the Japan Alps offer particular seasonal delights, but it is in the summer that they are the most crowded with both Japanese and foreign tourists.

The Japan Alps are only the ranges within the Chubu region of Honshu. Chubu is the relatively fat section of Japan's main island, bracketed by Tokyo and Niigata to the north and east and Kyoto and Fukui on the south and west. This chapter focuses on the mountains of Chubu, the so-called Japan Alps, and includes the north coast of Chubu, along with Japan's fifth largest island, Sado, which is situated in the Sea of Japan slightly north of Niigata.

Essential Information

Arriving and Departing

Several major access routes are available into the Japan Alps, and which one you take depends on where you are coming from and which places you want to visit. Below are several routes into the Japan Alps by train, arranged by destination. For Kanazawa, flight information is also given.

By Train

Kanazawa. From Osaka, the JR Hokuriku to Kanazawa takes just under three hours; the same train from Kyoto takes two hours and 20 minutes. From Niigata, the JR Hokuriku takes four hours. From Tokyo, take the Tokaido Shinkansen to Maibara, then the Hokuriku Honsen Express to Kanazawa for a journey that takes four hours and 40 minutes.

Karuizawa. From Tokyo's Ueno Station on the JR Shinetsu Line, the train to Karuizawa takes two hours. From Niigata, use the Shinkansen to Takasaki and change to the JR Shinetsu Line to Karuizawa. The total traveling time is approximately two hours.

Matsumoto. From Tokyo's Shinjuku Station on the JR Chuo Line, the journey to Matsumoto takes three hours. From Nagoya, the JR Chuo Line takes two hours and 40 minutes.

Nagano. From Tokyo's Ueno Station on the JR Shinetsu Line, the same train that goes to Karuizawa continues on to Nagano. The total journey takes just under three hours. From Nagoya, the JR Chuo Line to Nagano takes just over three hours. It is the same train that stops in Matsumoto.

Niigata. From Tokyo's Ueno Station the Joetsu Shinkansen to Niigata makes the journey in two hours, seven minutes.

Takayama. From Nagoya, the JR Takayama Line takes a little over two hours. From Toyama, the JR Takayama Line takes just under two hours. There are eight trains a day.

Toyama. From Nagoya via Takayama, the JR Takayama takes approximately four hours; there are four trains a day in each direction. From Nagoya via Kanazawa, the journey takes just under four hours; there are seven trains a day in each direction. Numerous daily trains run from Osaka and Kyoto; the journey takes three and a half and three hours, respectively.

By Plane

Kanazawa. From Tokyo's Haneda to Komatsu Airport is a one-hour flight on Japan Airlines (JAL) or All Nippon Airlines (ANA), plus 55 minutes for the airport bus connection to downtown Kanazawa.

Getting Around

Roads and railways that travel through the Japan Alps follow the valleys. All major stations have someone who speaks sufficient English to plan your schedule. Each major town described in the following excursion section has a tourist office at the railway station that will supply free maps and, if necessary, find you accommodations. Remember that the last train or bus in the evening can be quite early.

Rental cars are available at the major stations, but it is best to make arrangements to collect the car before you leave Tokyo, Nagoya, or Kyoto. The Nippon-Hertz company has the greatest number of locations in this region.

During the winter months, certain roads through the central Japan Alps are closed. In particular, the direct route between Matsumoto and Takayama via Kamikochi cannot be taken between November and April.

Important Addresses and Numbers

Tourist Information

JR Travel Information Centers and Japan Travel Bureau are available at all the train stations at the major cities and towns.

Kanazawa

Kanazawa Tourist Information Service is in front of the JR station (tel. 0762/31–6311).

Karuizawa

Karuizawa Station Tourist Office is at the JR station (tel. 0267/42–2491).

Kiso Valley **The Magome Tourist Information Office** (tel. 0264/59-2336). Open 8:30-5; closed Sunday December-March. Reservations at the local inns are made from here. **Tsumago Tourist Information Office** (tel. 0264/57-3123). Open 9-5; closed January 1-3. Reservations at the local inns are made from here.

Matsumoto **Matsumoto City Tourist Information Office** is on the street level at the front of the JR station (tel. 0263/32-2814).

Niigata **Niigata City Tourist Information Center** is in front of the JR station (tel. 0252/41-7914).

Takayama **Hida Tourist Information Office** is in front of the JR station (tel. 0577/32-5328). Open April-October, 8:30-6:30; November 1-March, 8:30-5.

Japan Travel-Phone The nationwide service for English language assistance or travel information is available 9-5 daily. Dial toll-free 0120/444-800 for information on western Japan. When using a yellow, blue, or green public phone (do not use the red phones), insert a ¥10 coin, which will be returned.

Emergencies **Police,** dial 110; **ambulance,** dial 119.

Guided Tours

The Japan Travel Bureau has offices at every JR station in each major city and town and can assist in local tours, hotel reservations, and travel ticketing. Though you should not assume that any English will be spoken, you can usually find someone whose knowledge is sufficient for your basic needs. Most of the traveling through this region is very straightforward, using public transport. On the two occasions where public transportation is infrequent—the Noto Peninsula and Sado Island—local tours are available, though the guides speak only Japanese.

Noto Peninsula We recommend using the tours to the Noto Peninsula from Kanazawa. The Hokuriku-Tetsudo Co. (tel. 0762/37-8111), for example, has a tour that in 6½ hours covers much of the peninsula for ¥5,500. It operates year-round and departs from Kanazawa Station.

Sado Island A tour of Sado Island is useful only because it covers the Skyline Drive, which public buses do not travel. The price for this tour, which departs from Ryotsu, May-November, is ¥3,600. Contact the Niigata Kotsu Information Center at the Ryotsu Bus Terminal (tel. 0259/27-3141).

Regional Tour The Japan Travel Bureau operates a five-day tour from Tokyo departing every Tuesday, April 1-October 26. The tour goes via Lake Shirakaba to Matsumoto (overnight), to Tsumago and Takayama (overnight), to Kanazawa (overnight), to Awara Spa (overnight), and ends in Kyoto. Cost: ¥150,000, including four breakfasts and two dinners.

Exploring

Although several routes, by train and road, are available into the Japan Alps from either the Sea of Japan or the Pacific coastal regions, this chapter begins its itinerary from Tokyo and enters the eastern edge of the Japan Alps at Karuizawa. From there it stays up in the mountains to work its way first to Nagano, then west to Matsumoto. A tour has been included from Matsumoto that visits the old post towns, Tsumago and Magome, along the Kiso Valley, where the trunk road between Kyoto and Tokyo used to pass during the Edo period (1603–1868). (This excursion may also be managed from Nagoya.) From Matsumoto the itinerary crosses over the mountains via Kamikochi to one of Japan's most attractive and preserved towns, Takayama. Then the tour descends to the Sea of Japan to Kanazawa and the Noto Peninsula. Many travelers may want to end their journey through this part of Japan and take the train from Kanazawa to Kyoto. However, we make the final leg of our journey north along the Sea of Japan to Niigata, where we take a short ferry ride to Japan's fifth largest island, Sado.

To cover and enjoy the whole itinerary would take a week, or five days if you did not go up to Niigata and over to Sado Island. However, there is no need to cover all the destinations in the itinerary. For example, if you were returning to Kyoto from Tokyo, you could go up to Kanazawa and cross the Japan Alps via Takayama en route to Nagoya, where you could catch the Shinkansen for Tokyo. Such a trip could easily be managed in 48 hours.

Karuizawa

Numbers in the margin correspond to points of interest on the Japan Alps map.

1 **Karuizawa,** two hours on the JR Shinetsu Line from Tokyo's Ueno Station, is a fashionable entrance to the Japan Alps from Tokyo. The best way to travel around Karuizawa is by bicycle, plenty of which are available for hire (about ¥500 an hr., ¥1,500 a day) at the Karuizawa train station, a mile south of the main town.

Karuizawa's popularity began when Archdeacon A. C. Shaw, an English prelate, built his summer villa here in 1888. His example was soon followed by other foreigners living in Tokyo, and Karuizawa's popularity continues today among affluent Tokyoites, who transfer their urban lifestyle in the summer to this small town located 3,000 feet above sea level. The camp followers come as well; every summer, branches of more than 500 trendy boutiques open their doors here to sell the same goods as their main stores in Tokyo. Karuizawa becomes a little Ginza.

Nature, though, still prevails over Karuizawa. **Mt. Asama,** a triple-cratered active volcano, soars 8,399 feet above and to the northwest of town. Lately, Mt. Asama has been making grumbling sounds, possibly threatening to erupt; these noises certainly provide a sufficient reason to prohibit climbing up to the volcano's crater. For the time being, one must be satisfied with a panoramic view of Mt. Asama and its neighbor, **Mt. Myogi,** as well as the whole **Yatsugatake Mountain Range,** from the observation platform at **Usui Pass.** The view justifies the 90-minute uphill walk from Nite Bridge, located at the end of Karuizawa Ginza, the boutique-filled street.

Outside Karuizawa are the **Shiraito Falls,** whose height is only about 10 feet, but whose width is 220 feet. The falls is at its best in the autumn, when the maples are crimson and the sun glints in the streaks of white water that tumble over the rocks. It can be reached by a 30-minute bus ride from Karuizawa Station.

However, you can also take the 25-minute bus ride to Mine-no-chaya (mountain-top teahouse) and then hike for an hour down through the forests of birch and larch to the falls. You can then return to Karuizawa by bus or continue the walk, via more falls, at **Ryugaeshi,** and return through the small spa village of **Kose Onsen** to the old **Mikasa Hotel,** the oldest wood Western-style hotel in Japan. From the Mikasa it is a 30-minute walk back to Karuizawa. The total course from Mine-no-chaya to town is about 7 miles (11 kilometers) and takes 4½ hours.

Karuizawa has other amusements, such as archery in summer, skating rinks, tennis, and horseback riding, all of which can be arranged through your hotel. Also, a short distance by bus from Karuizawa and close to **Hoshino Onsen,** a spa, is the **Wild Bird Wood Sanctuary,** where about 120 species of birds have taken up residence. Along the 1½-mile forestal course are two observation huts from which the birds' habitat may be observed.

The same JR train climbs steeply from Karuizawa through the mountains to a plateau before making a quick descent into Nagano. This is the easiest route to take, but an alternative is ❷ through the mountains by road (bus or car) via **Kusatsu,** one of Japan's best-known spa resorts. More than 130 ryokan cluster around the *yuba* (hot spring field) which supplies the gushing, boiling, sulfur-laden water. Netsunoyu is the main public bath; its water is unbearably hot, even for some Japanese.

The Shiga-Kusatsu-kogen Ridge Highway (a toll road, closed in winter), continues across the Kusatsu Pass and at times climbs as high as 6,550 feet to Yudanaka, the base from which skiers ❸ set out to the **Shiga Heights Ski Resort.** This is Nagano's largest ski area, with 22 ski grounds and a combination of 81 lifts, gondolas, and ropeways. Nearby **Yudanaka Onsen,** by the way, is a hot-spring resort made famous by photographs of monkeys covered with snow sitting in open-air pools to keep warm. From here, both the road and train line descend for the 15-mile (24 kilometers) run to Nagano.

Nagano

❹ In spring 1991 **Nagano** (pop. 300,000) was chosen to be the host city of the 1998 Winter Olympic Games. Construction and preparations for this major event are already underway: Hotels and athletic structures are being built, and there are rumors of plans for several golf courses and an amusement park. A Shinkansen line direct from Tokyo is also being constructed and will be ready in time for the Olympics. It will cut travel time from Tokyo considerably, making Nagano as closely connected to the capital as it is to its surrounding mountains.

In the meantime, Nagano's only major attraction is **Zenkoji Temple,** which draws thousands of pilgrims each year. Founded in the 7th century by Yoshimitsu Honda, this temple is unique to Japan for two reasons: it belongs to no particular Buddhist sect, and it has never closed its doors to women. Zenkoji's most venerated statue, a bronze dating from 552, is displayed only once every seven years—the next time will be in spring 1994.

You can pick up a free map at the City Tourist Office (tel. 0262/26–5626) to the left of the station entrance before hopping on one of the frequent buses that makes the 10-minute journey

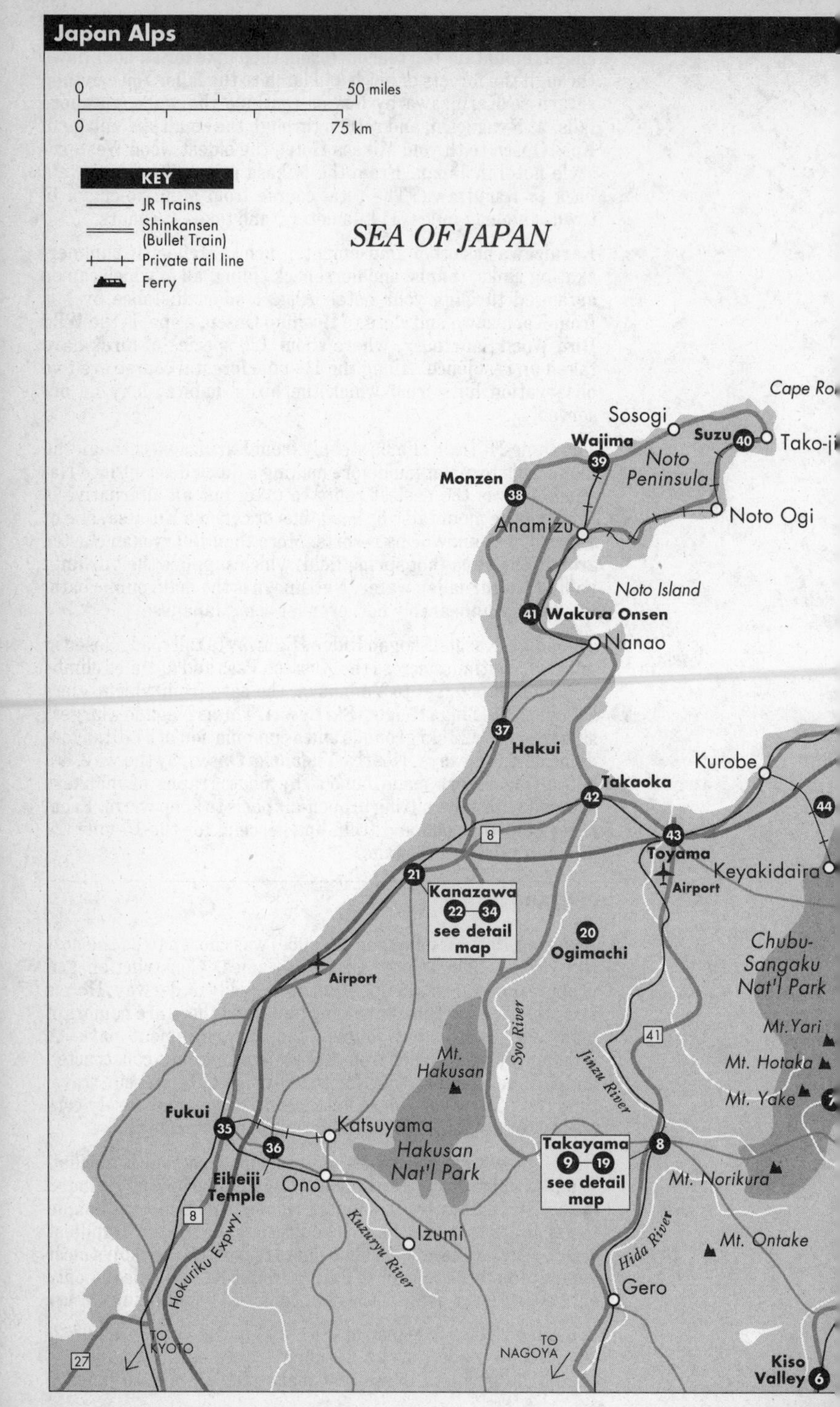
Japan Alps
0
50 miles
0
75 km
KEY
JR Trains
Shinkansen (Bullet Train)
Private rail line
Ferry
SEA OF JAPAN
Cape Ro
Sosogi
Wajima
Suzu
Tako-ji
Noto Peninsula
Monzen
Anamizu
Noto Ogi
Noto Island
Wakura Onsen
Nanao
Hakui
Kurobe
Takaoka
Toyama
Airport
Keyakidaira
Kanazawa
see detail map
Ogimachi
Chubu-Sangaku Nat'l Park
Airport
Mt. Yari
Mt. Hotaka
Mt. Yake
Syo River
Jinzu River
Mt. Hakusan
Fukui
Katsuyama
Hakusan Nat'l Park
Takayama
see detail map
Eiheiji Temple
Ono
Mt. Norikura
Kuzuryu River
Izumi
Mt. Ontake
Hokuriku Expwy.
Hida River
Gero
TO KYOTO
TO NAGOYA
Kiso Valley

Kiso Valley

❻ Another trip from Matsumoto is to the **Kiso Valley,** located halfway between Matsumoto and Nagoya. Called Kisoji by the Japanese, this deep valley, formed by the Kiso River, is surrounded by the Central Alps to the east and the North Alps to the west. It was through this valley that the old Nakasendo Highway connected Kyoto and Edo (present-day Tokyo) between 1603 and 1867. For 250 years, daimyos (lords) and their retinue used this highway when they made their annual trip to Edo to pay their respects to the Shogunate. This part of the highway was the most difficult section for travelers. The valley's thick forests and steep slopes required three days to pass through, while today the new road allows the same trip to be done in a few hours.

With the building of the new Tokaido route from Kyoto to Tokyo along the Pacific coast and the Chuo train line from Nagoya to Niigata, the 11 old post villages where travelers had stopped to refresh themselves became deserted backwaters (sometimes referred to as Minami-Kiso). Two of the villages, **Tsumago** and **Magome,** are easy to reach. Take the JR train from Matsumoto to Nagiso, about 60 minutes away, and then take a 10-minute bus ride (fare: ¥240) from the Nagiso JR station to Tsumago. Buses from the JR station leave every hour for the 30-minute trip. From Tsumago you can take either the footpath to Magome or another bus. Still another bus travels from Magome to Nakatsugawa on the JR line. Then, it is back to Matsumoto or on to Nagoya by train, or over the mountains to Takayama. This trip to Kiso Valley could be accomplished with equal ease as a day trip from Nagoya.

Both Tsumago and Magome have retained much of their old character. Indeed, more than in most places in Japan, walking along the main street of Tsumago is like stepping back in time to the shogun era (except for the souvenir shops). If you have time, it's a pleasant three-hour walk along the old post trail between Tsumago and Magome. (Be sure to go from Tsumago to Magome, since walking in the other direction is almost completely uphill.) Both are served by buses from Nakatsugawa and Nagiso stations, so you can bus to one village and return from the other. There are ryokan and minshukus throughout the valley should you wish to stay overnight, and both Tsumago and Magome have tourist information offices that will help find accommodations and provide free maps.

Takayama

There There are two routes to **Takayama** from Matsumoto. One is by JR trains all the way, but this requires descending to the coastal plain and changing trains at Nagoya for the two-hour run up the Hida River Valley to Takayama. This is the least interesting route and can take up to four hours' traveling time, but it is the only way in the winter. If you wish to go straight from Kiso Valley to Takayama, take a one-hour, 50-minute bus ride from Magome to Gero and transfer to the JR train for a 45-minute run to Takayama. Buses leave three times daily (7:21 AM and 12:05 with a change at Sakashita, and a direct bus at 4 PM; cost: ¥1,950).

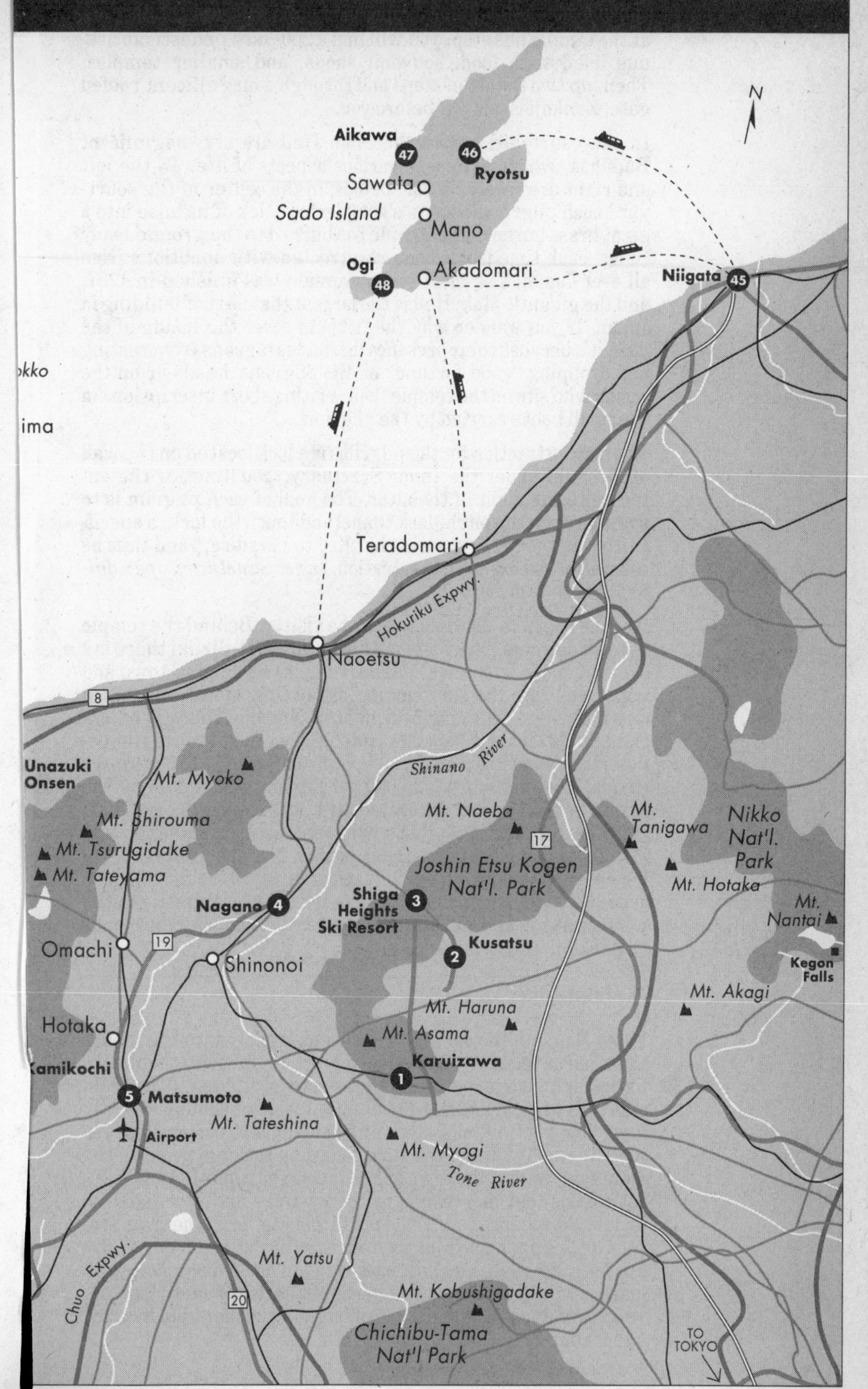

through the center of Nagano to the temple. After getting off at the temple bus stop, you will find a 200-yard pedestrian avenue lined with food, souvenir shops, and smaller temples. Then, up two flights of steps and through a magnificent roofed gate, Zenkoji is laid out before you.

In the courtyard before the Main Hall are six magnificent Buddhas, which represent various aspects of life. To the left and right are several small shrines; in the center of the courtyard each pilgrim deposits a smoldering stick of incense into a giant brass burner. The temple has burned to the ground many times; each time it has been resurrected with donations from all over Japan. The most recent version was finished in 1707, and the gigantic Main Hall is the largest thatch-roof building in Japan. If you wonder why the fishnets cover the inside of the roof, it's because their presence dissuades pigeons from resting and dropping "good fortune" on the pilgrims' heads or on the scribe who sits on the temple floor writing short inscriptions in the small books carried by the pilgrims.

The main attraction for the pilgrims is a lock located on the wall of a tunnel under the Inner Sanctuary. You'll notice the entrance to the right of the alter. The goal of each pilgrim is to walk through the pitch-dark tunnel and touch the lock, a specific stone in the wall known as the "Key to Paradise," and thus be assured of an easy path to salvation. *Inner Sanctuary open daily 5:30 AM–4:30 PM.*

Nagano has little else to interest the visitor. Behind the temple is an amusement park for small kids, and at Mt. Jizuki there is a zoo, but, aside from that, Nagano remains a pilgrims' town and a gateway into the surrounding mountains. However, should one find oneself staying overnight in Nagano, there is an ancient traditional ryokan, the Hotel Fujiya, just before the pedestrian avenue to Zenkoji. The ryokan's pride is its *daimyo* (feudal lord) suite; for ¥20,000 per person, one can enjoy the suite's several rooms decorated with ancient scrolls and look into a garden that is magnetic in its contrasting complexity and simplicity (*see* Nagano Lodging, *below*). Nagano prefecture, of which Nagano is the capital, is famous in Japan for its delicious *soba* (buckwheat noodles). You can see soba being made in the window at a couple of restaurants near the walkway that leads to Zenkoji.

Matsumoto

From Nagano, the JR Shinonoi climbs steeply into the mountains and at the town of Shinonoi it begins to follow switchbacks to the high plateau on which **Matsumoto** is situated. (The train ride takes two hours and 40 minutes if you are coming directly from Tokyo's Shinjuku station; from Nagano, the train takes just over an hr.) In a basin surrounded by the high peaks of the mountain ranges, the town of Matsumoto has one of Japan's finest castles, set in grounds of cherry trees and open spaces, about a 20-minute walk to the north and east from the train station (pick up a map from the tourist office at the front of the station). En route you will pass through the old section, with many stone Kura houses, typical of the early Meiji period, which are unusual in their use of irregular stones held in place by mortar.

Known as **Karasujo** (Crow Castle) f
tive walls, the castle was built in 15
civil wars. The surrounding moats
imposing five-tier, six-story *donjo*
ing donjon in Japan. While it is an
and walk through all six stories, th
what life as a samurai was like dur
from the sixth story of the donjon
panorama of the surrounding alpi
popular attraction; be there whe
whelming crowds. You will have t
while walking through the castle.

In front of Karasujo Castle is t
whose 70,000 artifacts display the
day life of preshogun days and of
¥500, covering castle and museu
8:30–4:30. Closed Dec. 29–Jan. 3

The other points of interest in t
with the castle. Directly across t
tion is the **Matsumoto Folkcraft**
600 local home utensils of wood
there, either take a taxi or a 15-
the Shimoganai Mingeikan Guch
Open 9–5. Closed Mon. and Dec.

More worthwhile is the **Japan U**
station. Unfortunately it is too f
so one must invest in a ¥1,250 t
Kamikochi train from Matsum
from which it is a 10-minute wal
to the **Japan Judicature Museu**
Japanese palatial court building
seum every month rotates its
wood-block prints from the E
some of Japan's finest prints an
world. *Admission: ¥750. Open*

One stop from Matsumoto Stat
From the station, it is a 10-minu
seum. Rokuzan Ogiwara, who
ter sculptor and is often ref
Orient." His works are displaye
Rokuzan's works, the gallery i
ery against a backdrop of th
¥500. Open 9–5 (9–4 Nov.–
following national holidays.

Also near Hotaka is the **Gohod**
(Japanese horseradish) farm
must rent a bike or take a 40-m
train station. (The station att
Wasabi is cultivated in the cle
curving valley. The Gohoden
Surrounded by rows of acacia
ments, the fields of fresh gree
flowers in the late spring. B
unique foods, which range fro
green wasabi ice cream.

The other route is straight over the mountains through Chubu-Sangaku National Park via **Kamikochi.** This is one of the most scenic routes through the Japan Alps and should not be missed. You should even consider spending the night at Kamikochi to fully enjoy the scenery. It does require a bus/train combination, but it is straightforward and poses no problem. However, it can only be accomplished in the summer (May–Oct.), because winter snows close the road.

First, take the Matsumoto Electric Railway from Matsumoto Station to Shin-Shimashima. The journey takes 30 minutes (fare: ¥650). Do not make the mistake of getting off the train at Shimojima, three stops before Shin-Shimashima. Once off the train, cross over the road at Shin-Shimashima Station for the bus going to Nakanoyu and Kamikochi. The total bus journey takes about one hour and 20 minutes (fare: ¥1,950). The most scenic part is the 20 minutes from Nakanoyu to Kamikochi, and you'll quickly understand why the road is closed by the winter snows (mid-Nov.–mid-April). Just before reaching Kamikochi, the valley opens onto a plain with a backdrop of mountains. **Mt. Oku-Hotaka** is the highest at 10,466 feet. To the left is **Mt. Mae-Hotaka,** 10,138 feet, and to the right is the smaller **Mt. Nishi-Hotaka,** 9,544 feet. Through the narrow basin flow the icy waters of the Azusagawa River to form a small lake, **Taisho Pond,** at the entrance to the basin, where lodges and inns are located. The bus terminal is a few hundred yards beyond.

There are trails in and around Kamikochi to please every level of hiker and climber. One easy three-hour walk is along the river past the rock sculpture of the Reverend Walter Weston, the Briton who was the first to explore and climb these mountains. Then comes the Kappabashi Bridge, a small suspension bridge over the crystal-clear waters of the Azusagawa. Continuing on the south side of the river, the trail cuts through the pasture to rejoin the river at Myoshin Bridge. The Hodaka Shrine is on the other side at the edge of Myoshin Pond. Here is another bridge that leads to the trail back on the opposite side of the river to the Kappabashi Bridge.

From Kamikochi, buses (six a day, only between early May and early Nov.) take an hour and 15 minutes to **Hirayu Onsen** (fare: ¥1,510), where one must change to another bus (operates all year) for the 70-minute ride to Takayama (fare: ¥1,360).

Coming from either Tokyo or Kyoto take the Shinkansen to Nagoya and change for the JR Limited Express to Takayama. The train leaves every hour during the day and takes two hours and 20 minutes.

Exploring 8

One of the most attractive towns in the Japan Alps, **Takayama,** is often left off foreign tourists' itineraries; it is their loss. In the heart of the Hida Mountains, this tranquil town has retained its old-fashioned charm. No wonder so many artists have made their homes here. The city is laid out in a grid pattern; it's compact and easy to explore on foot or by rented bicycle. A rental shop is to the right of the station building (cost: ¥300 per hour). An exotic option is a 30-minute ricksha tour of the old town for ¥1,000 per person. You'll find the rickshas based in San-machi Suji. If you just want to pose in one for a photograph, be ready to hand over ¥200.

Make a point of collecting maps and information from the tourist office just in front of the JR station. Also, throughout

Takayama you can get help at businesses that are designated as Travel Information Desks (look for the "?" sign in the window). In most cases, the person at the cash register in these establishments will speak English or will find someone who speaks English to assist you. Although sightseeing bus tours are available, they are unnecessary and expensive (about ¥3,100 for 3 hours). *Open 8:30–6:30 (8:30–5 Nov.–Mar.)*

Numbers in the margin correspond to points of interest on the Takayama map.

Walking (or riding) down Hirokoji-dori Street for a few blocks, one reaches the old section of town with its small shops, houses, and tearooms. Before the bridge, which crosses the small Miyagawa River, go right, past another bridge, and the

9 **Takayama Jinya** will be on your right. Though perhaps not worth the admission charge to enter, this imposing structure was the manor house of the governor, with samurai barracks and a garden behind the house. In front of the manor house, 7 AM–noon each morning, the Jinya-mae Morning Market sells vegetables, fruits, and local handicrafts. *Admission to house: ¥310. Open daily 8:45–4:30.*

Across the river from the market area and up the hill, a small

10 street leads to Shiroyama Park and **Shorenji Temple.** The Main Hall of this temple was built in 1504 and was moved in 1961 from its original site in Shirakawago before the area was flooded by the Miboro Dam. Now, positioned on the hill looking down on Takayama, the sweep of its curved roof, its superb drum tower, and the surrounding gardens give an earthy tranquillity that symbolizes the atmosphere of all of Takayama. *Admission: ¥ 200. Open daily 8–4:30. (Shiroyama Park is always open; no admission charge.)*

Down from Shiroyama Park, the main street leads to Sanmachi

11 Street. To the right is the **Tenshoji Temple** and youth hostel. This is a magnificent building and a delightful place for a youth hostel, though the rooms are sure to be bitterly cold in the winter. On Sanmachi Street, just across from the road leading from Shiroyama Park, is the folk toy museum and the

12 **Takayama-shi Kyodo-kan** (History Museum), which exhibits various antiques and folklore materials of the Hida people. *Admission: ¥300. Open 8:30–5. Closed Mon. and Dec. 29–31.*

Still on Sanmachi Street, to the left of the toy museum and to-

13 ward the Miyagawa River is the **Hida Minzoku Koko-kan** (Archaeology Museum), in an old house that once belonged to a physician who served the local lord. The unique structure of the mansion, with its hanging ceilings, secret windows, and hidden passages, hints of spies, so prevalent in the Edo period. Now the house displays wall hangings, weaving machines, and sundry items, both archaeological and folkloric, collected from the Hida region. *Admission: ¥300. Open daily 7–7 (8–5 Dec.–Feb.).*

14 North of the Archaeology Museum you enter the **Sanmachi-Suji** section, which includes Ichinomachi, Ninomachi, and Sannomachi streets, all parallel to the Miyagawa River. This was the merchant area during the feudal days. Most of the old teahouses, inns, dye houses, and sake breweries with latticed windows and doors are preserved in their original state, making Sanmachi-Suji a rare vestige of old Japan before the Meiji Res-

Hida Minzoku Koko-kan, **13**
Hida Minzoku-mura, **19**
Kokubunji Temple, **18**
Kusakabe Mingeikan Folkcraft Museum, **15**
Sanmachi-Suji, **14**
Shorenji Temple, **10**
Takayama Jinya, **9**
Takayama-shi Kyodo-kan, **12**
Takayama Yatai Kaikan Hall, **17**
Tenshoji Temple, **11**
Yoshijima-ke Family House, **16**

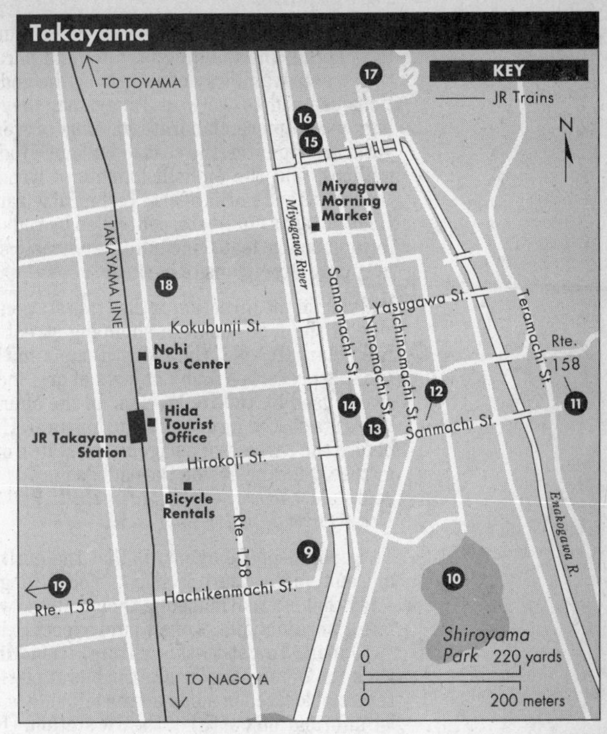

toration. Down along the river is the Miyagawa Morning Market, where flowers and vegetables are sold until noon each day.

15 Across a small tributary of the Miyagawa and on the left side of Ninomachi Street is the **Kusakabe Mingeikan Folkcraft Museum.** The building is the old Kusakabe (wealthy merchant) family home of the 1880s. Inside, the heavy beams of polished wood emphasize the refined taste of that period, and it is an appropriate setting for a display of Hida folkcrafts. *Admission: ¥500. Open daily 9–5 (9–4:30 and closed Fri. Dec.–Feb.). Closed Dec. 27–Jan. 4.*

16 On the next corner is another elegant merchant house, the **Yoshijima-ke Family House.** It was rebuilt in 1908, but it retains the distinctive characteristics of the Hida architectural style. *Admission: ¥300. Open daily 9–5 (9–4:30 and closed Tues. Dec.–Feb.). Closed Dec. 28–Jan. 1.*

17 Up the street to the right of the Yoshijima House and next to the Hachiman Shrine is the **Takayama Yatai Kaikan Hall,** which displays four of the 11 Takayama festival floats *(yatai),* which are used in Takayama's famous Spring Sanno Matsuri (Apr. 14–15) and Autumn Yahata Matsuri (Oct. 9–10) festivals. (Some 160,000 visitors come each year for the festivals, nearly tripling Takayama's population of 68,000. Hotels are booked solid, so if you plan to visit during this time, make your reservation months in advance.) These floats have many figurines representing people in the parade, as well as elaborately carved wooden lion heads used for dances in the parade. *Admission: ¥600. Open 8:30–5 (9–4:30 Dec.–Feb.).*

More than two centuries ago, when the country was ravaged by the plague, the building of yatai and parading them through the streets was a way of appeasing the gods. Because these actions seemed to work in Takayama, they continued building bigger and more elaborate yatai as preventive medicine. The yatai are gigantic (the cost to build one today would exceed ¥1 million), and the embellishments of wood-carved panels and tapestries are works of art. Technical wizardry is also involved. Each yatai has puppets, controlled by rods and wires, that perform amazing feats, including gymnastics that you would expect only Olympians to perform.

Walking in the direction of the train station, just off to the right side of the main modern shopping street (Kokubunji-dori) is

18 **Kokubunji Temple,** the oldest temple in the city. Founded in 1588, it preserves many objects of art, including the precious sword used by the Heike clan. In the Main Hall (built in 1615) there is a seated figure of Yakushinyorai (Healing Buddha), and before the three-story pagoda is a statue of Kannon. The ginkgo tree standing beside the pagoda is said to be more than 1,200 years old. *Admission to Main Hall: ¥200. Open 9–4. Closed Dec. 31 and Jan. 1.*

The delight of Takayama is that the entire town resembles a museum piece; there is also a "Folk Village" less than 2 miles away that is a real museum, though it's so well done that it looks like a working village one would expect to have found in medie-

19 val Japan. To get to this village, **Hida Minzoku-mura,** either walk the 20 minutes or take the bus at platform #2 from the bus terminal located in a bay on the left side (same side as the tourist information booth) of the JR station. (If you walk, go right from JR Takayama Station and take a right over the first bridge onto Highway 158. Continue walking straight for 20 min.)

Set against a mountain backdrop, Hida Minzoku-mura (Hida Folk Village) is a collection of traditional farmhouses moved to a park from several areas within the Hida region. Since the traditional Hida farmhouse is held together by ropes rather than nails, the dismantling and reassembling of the buildings posed few problems. Many of them have high-pitch thatch roofs, called *gassho-zukuri* (hands in prayer); others are shingle-roofed. Twelve of the houses are "private houses" that display such folk materials as tableware and spinning and weaving tools. Another five houses are folkcraft workshops, with demonstrations of ichii ittobori wood carving, Hidanuri lacquering, and other traditional arts of the region. *Admission: ¥700. Open daily 8:30–5 (8:30–4:30 Nov.–Mar.). Closed Dec. 30–Jan. 2.*

Numbers in the margin correspond to points of interest on the Japan Alps map.

From Takayama there are frequent trains out of the mountains to Toyama and on to Kanazawa (an absolute must to visit) and the Noto Peninsula. Kanazawa, with a change of trains at Toyama is about a two-hour trip from Takayama, but consider tak-

20 ing a side trip to **Ogimachi,** a traditional town in Shirakawago Valley.

Surrounded by mountains and dotted with terraced rice fields and gardens, Ogimachi is one of the most beautiful old-style towns in Japan. The majority of the residents in this quiet little

Hida Minzoku Koko-kan, **13**
Hida Minzoku-mura, **19**
Kokubunji Temple, **18**
Kusakabe Mingeikan Folkcraft Museum, **15**
Sanmachi-Suji, **14**
Shorenji Temple, **10**
Takayama Jinya, **9**
Takayama-shi Kyodo-kan, **12**
Takayama Yatai Kaikan Hall, **17**
Tenshoji Temple, **11**
Yoshijima-ke Family House, **16**

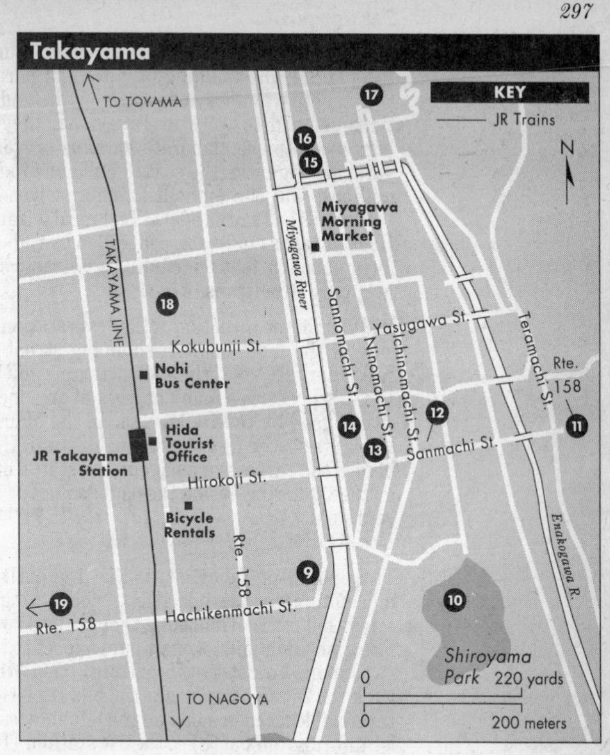

toration. Down along the river is the Miyagawa Morning Market, where flowers and vegetables are sold until noon each day.

15 Across a small tributary of the Miyagawa and on the left side of Ninomachi Street is the **Kusakabe Mingeikan Folkcraft Museum.** The building is the old Kusakabe (wealthy merchant) family home of the 1880s. Inside, the heavy beams of polished wood emphasize the refined taste of that period, and it is an appropriate setting for a display of Hida folkcrafts. *Admission: ¥500. Open daily 9–5 (9–4:30 and closed Fri. Dec.–Feb.). Closed Dec. 27–Jan. 4.*

16 On the next corner is another elegant merchant house, the **Yoshijima-ke Family House.** It was rebuilt in 1908, but it retains the distinctive characteristics of the Hida architectural style. *Admission: ¥300. Open daily 9–5 (9–4:30 and closed Tues. Dec.–Feb.). Closed Dec. 28–Jan. 1.*

17 Up the street to the right of the Yoshijima House and next to the Hachiman Shrine is the **Takayama Yatai Kaikan Hall,** which displays four of the 11 Takayama festival floats *(yatai)*, which are used in Takayama's famous Spring Sanno Matsuri (Apr. 14–15) and Autumn Yahata Matsuri (Oct. 9–10) festivals. (Some 160,000 visitors come each year for the festivals, nearly tripling Takayama's population of 68,000. Hotels are booked solid, so if you plan to visit during this time, make your reservation months in advance.) These floats have many figurines representing people in the parade, as well as elaborately carved wooden lion heads used for dances in the parade. *Admission: ¥600. Open 8:30–5 (9–4:30 Dec.–Feb.).*

More than two centuries ago, when the country was ravaged by the plague, the building of yatai and parading them through the streets was a way of appeasing the gods. Because these actions seemed to work in Takayama, they continued building bigger and more elaborate yatai as preventive medicine. The yatai are gigantic (the cost to build one today would exceed ¥1 million), and the embellishments of wood-carved panels and tapestries are works of art. Technical wizardry is also involved. Each yatai has puppets, controlled by rods and wires, that perform amazing feats, including gymnastics that you would expect only Olympians to perform.

Walking in the direction of the train station, just off to the right side of the main modern shopping street (Kokubunji-dori) is 18 **Kokubunji Temple,** the oldest temple in the city. Founded in 1588, it preserves many objects of art, including the precious sword used by the Heike clan. In the Main Hall (built in 1615) there is a seated figure of Yakushinyorai (Healing Buddha), and before the three-story pagoda is a statue of Kannon. The ginkgo tree standing beside the pagoda is said to be more than 1,200 years old. *Admission to Main Hall: ¥200. Open 9–4. Closed Dec. 31 and Jan. 1.*

The delight of Takayama is that the entire town resembles a museum piece; there is also a "Folk Village" less than 2 miles away that is a real museum, though it's so well done that it looks like a working village one would expect to have found in medieval Japan. To get to this village, 19 **Hida Minzoku-mura,** either walk the 20 minutes or take the bus at platform #2 from the bus terminal located in a bay on the left side (same side as the tourist information booth) of the JR station. (If you walk, go right from JR Takayama Station and take a right over the first bridge onto Highway 158. Continue walking straight for 20 min.)

Set against a mountain backdrop, Hida Minzoku-mura (Hida Folk Village) is a collection of traditional farmhouses moved to a park from several areas within the Hida region. Since the traditional Hida farmhouse is held together by ropes rather than nails, the dismantling and reassembling of the buildings posed few problems. Many of them have high-pitch thatch roofs, called *gassho-zukuri* (hands in prayer); others are shingle-roofed. Twelve of the houses are "private houses" that display such folk materials as tableware and spinning and weaving tools. Another five houses are folkcraft workshops, with demonstrations of ichii ittobori wood carving, Hidanuri lacquering, and other traditional arts of the region. *Admission: ¥700. Open daily 8:30–5 (8:30–4:30 Nov.–Mar.). Closed Dec. 30–Jan. 2.*

Numbers in the margin correspond to points of interest on the Japan Alps map.

From Takayama there are frequent trains out of the mountains to Toyama and on to Kanazawa (an absolute must to visit) and the Noto Peninsula. Kanazawa, with a change of trains at Toyama is about a two-hour trip from Takayama, but consider taking a side trip to 20 **Ogimachi,** a traditional town in Shirakawago Valley.

Surrounded by mountains and dotted with terraced rice fields and gardens, Ogimachi is one of the most beautiful old-style towns in Japan. The majority of the residents in this quiet little

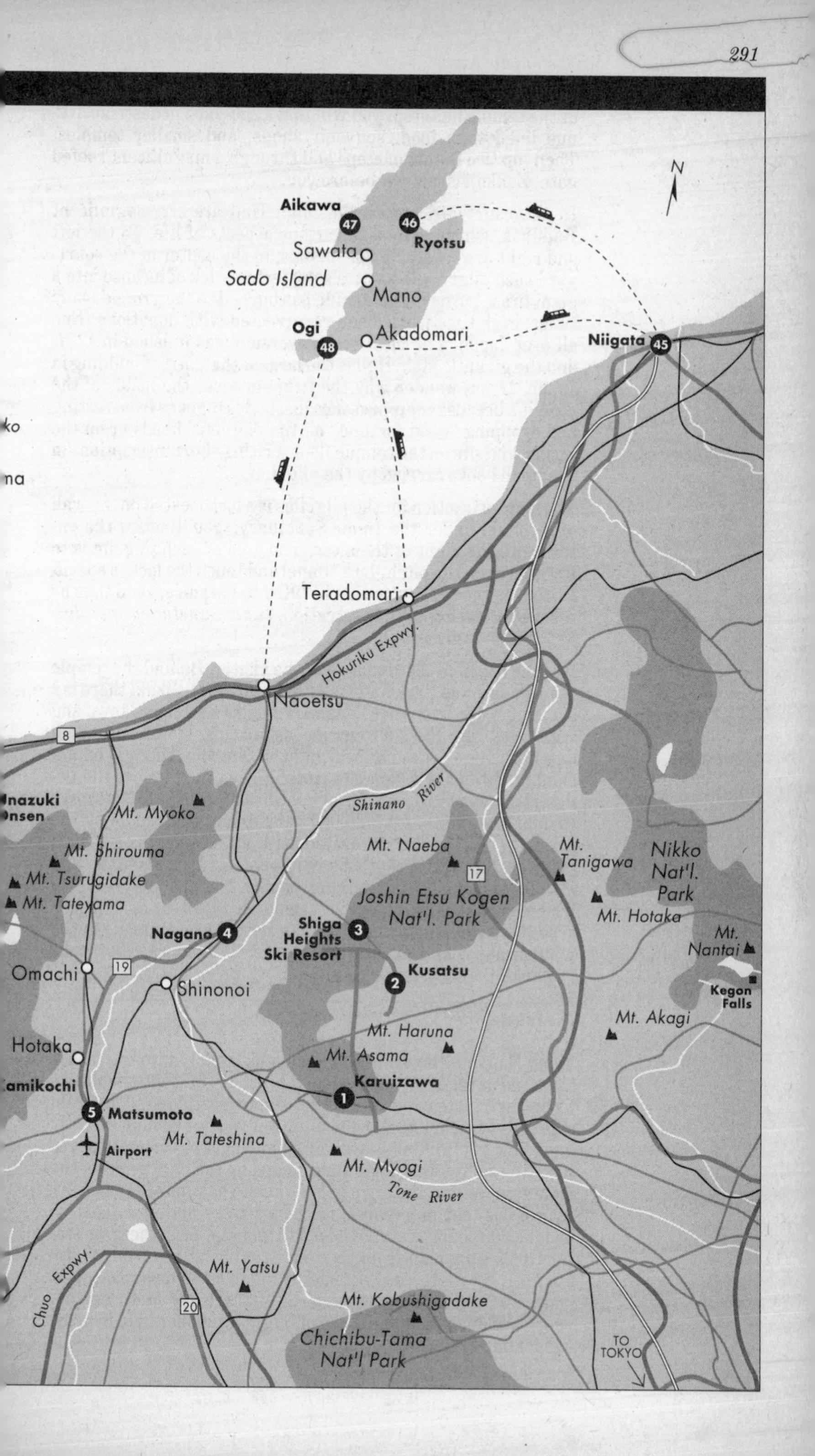

N
Aikawa
47
46
Ryotsu
Sawata
Sado Island
Mano
Ogi
48
Akadomari
Niigata
45
Teradomari
Hokuriku Expwy.
Naoetsu
8
Shinano River
Mt. Myoko
Mt. Shirouma
Mt. Tsurugidake
Mt. Tateyama
Mt. Naeba
17
Mt. Tanigawa
Nikko Nat'l. Park
Joshin Etsu Kogen Nat'l. Park
Mt. Hotaka
Shiga Heights Ski Resort
3
Nagano
4
Mt. Nantai
Omachi
19
Kusatsu
2
Kegon Falls
Shinonoi
Mt. Akagi
Mt. Haruna
Hotaka
Mt. Asama
Karuizawa
1
5
Matsumoto
Mt. Tateshina
Airport
Mt. Myogi
Tone River
Chuo Expwy.
Mt. Yatsu
20
Mt. Kobushigadake
Chichibu-Tama Nat'l Park
TO TOKYO

through the center of Nagano to the temple. After getting off at the temple bus stop, you will find a 200-yard pedestrian avenue lined with food, souvenir shops, and smaller temples. Then, up two flights of steps and through a magnificent roofed gate, Zenkoji is laid out before you.

In the courtyard before the Main Hall are six magnificent Buddhas, which represent various aspects of life. To the left and right are several small shrines; in the center of the courtyard each pilgrim deposits a smoldering stick of incense into a giant brass burner. The temple has burned to the ground many times; each time it has been resurrected with donations from all over Japan. The most recent version was finished in 1707, and the gigantic Main Hall is the largest thatch-roof building in Japan. If you wonder why the fishnets cover the inside of the roof, it's because their presence dissuades pigeons from resting and dropping "good fortune" on the pilgrims' heads or on the scribe who sits on the temple floor writing short inscriptions in the small books carried by the pilgrims.

The main attraction for the pilgrims is a lock located on the wall of a tunnel under the Inner Sanctuary. You'll notice the entrance to the right of the alter. The goal of each pilgrim is to walk through the pitch-dark tunnel and touch the lock, a specific stone in the wall known as the "Key to Paradise," and thus be assured of an easy path to salvation. *Inner Sanctuary open daily 5:30 AM–4:30 PM.*

Nagano has little else to interest the visitor. Behind the temple is an amusement park for small kids, and at Mt. Jizuki there is a zoo, but, aside from that, Nagano remains a pilgrims' town and a gateway into the surrounding mountains. However, should one find oneself staying overnight in Nagano, there is an ancient traditional ryokan, the Hotel Fujiya, just before the pedestrian avenue to Zenkoji. The ryokan's pride is its *daimyo* (feudal lord) suite; for ¥20,000 per person, one can enjoy the suite's several rooms decorated with ancient scrolls and look into a garden that is magnetic in its contrasting complexity and simplicity (*see* Nagano Lodging, *below*). Nagano prefecture, of which Nagano is the capital, is famous in Japan for its delicious *soba* (buckwheat noodles). You can see soba being made in the window at a couple of restaurants near the walkway that leads to Zenkoji.

Matsumoto

From Nagano, the JR Shinonoi climbs steeply into the mountains and at the town of Shinonoi it begins to follow switchbacks (5) to the high plateau on which **Matsumoto** is situated. (The train ride takes two hours and 40 minutes if you are coming directly from Tokyo's Shinjuku station; from Nagano, the train takes just over an hr.) In a basin surrounded by the high peaks of the mountain ranges, the town of Matsumoto has one of Japan's finest castles, set in grounds of cherry trees and open spaces, about a 20-minute walk to the north and east from the train station (pick up a map from the tourist office at the front of the station). En route you will pass through the old section, with many stone Kura houses, typical of the early Meiji period, which are unusual in their use of irregular stones held in place by mortar.

Known as **Karasujo** (Crow Castle) for its unusual black protective walls, the castle was built in 1504, during the turbulence of civil wars. The surrounding moats and walls remain, and the imposing five-tier, six-story *donjon* (keep) is the oldest surviving donjon in Japan. While it is an exercise in agility to climb and walk through all six stories, the effort adds to the feeling of what life as a samurai was like during feudal Japan. The views from the sixth story of the donjon are inspiring, with a broad panorama of the surrounding alpine peaks. Karasuju is a very popular attraction; be there when it opens to avoid the overwhelming crowds. You will have to wear the slippers provided while walking through the castle.

In front of Karasujo Castle is the **Japan Folklore Museum**, whose 70,000 artifacts display the folklore, history, and everyday life of preshogun days and of the Edo period. *Admission: ¥500, covering castle and museum. Castle and museum open 8:30–4:30. Closed Dec. 29–Jan. 3.*

The other points of interest in town are minor in comparison with the castle. Directly across town to the east of the JR station is the **Matsumoto Folkcraft Museum**, which displays some 600 local home utensils of wood, bamboo, and glass. To get there, either take a taxi or a 15-minute bus ride and get out at the Shimoganai Mingeikan Guchi bus stop. *Admission: ¥200. Open 9–5. Closed Mon. and Dec. 29–Jan. 3.*

More worthwhile is the **Japan Ukiyo-e Museum**, west of the JR station. Unfortunately it is too far to walk, and there is no bus, so one must invest in a ¥1,250 taxi ride. (You can also take the Kamikochi train from Matsumoto Station to Oniwa Station, from which it is a 10-minute walk to the museum.) Located next to the **Japan Judicature Museum** (admission: ¥500), the oldest Japanese palatial court building still existing, the Ukiyo-e Museum every month rotates its collection of 100,000 ukiyo-e wood-block prints from the Edo period. The collection has some of Japan's finest prints and is the largest of its kind in the world. *Admission: ¥750. Open 10–4:30. Closed Mon.*

One stop from Matsumoto Station on the Oito Line is **Hotaka**. From the station, it is a 10-minute walk to the **Rokuzan Art Museum.** Rokuzan Ogiwara, who died at the age of 32, was a master sculptor and is often referred to as the "Rodin of the Orient." His works are displayed here. Aside from the appeal of Rokuzan's works, the gallery is in a beautiful setting of greenery against a backdrop of the Northern Alps. *Admission: ¥500. Open 9–5 (9–4 Nov.–Mar.). Closed Mon. and days following national holidays.*

Also near Hotaka is the **Gohoden Wasabi-en**, the largest *wasabi* (Japanese horseradish) farm in the country. To reach it you must rent a bike or take a 40-minute walk along a path from the train station. (The station attendant will give you directions.) Wasabi is cultivated in the clean water beds built in a shallow, curving valley. The Gohoden farm scenery is pastoral Japan. Surrounded by rows of acacia and poplar trees on the embankments, the fields of fresh green wasabi leaves bloom with white flowers in the late spring. Be sure to try some of the farm's unique foods, which range from wasabi cheese and chocolate to green wasabi ice cream.

Kiso Valley

❻ Another trip from Matsumoto is to the **Kiso Valley,** located halfway between Matsumoto and Nagoya. Called Kisoji by the Japanese, this deep valley, formed by the Kiso River, is surrounded by the Central Alps to the east and the North Alps to the west. It was through this valley that the old Nakasendo Highway connected Kyoto and Edo (present-day Tokyo) between 1603 and 1867. For 250 years, daimyos (lords) and their retinue used this highway when they made their annual trip to Edo to pay their respects to the Shogunate. This part of the highway was the most difficult section for travelers. The valley's thick forests and steep slopes required three days to pass through, while today the new road allows the same trip to be done in a few hours.

With the building of the new Tokaido route from Kyoto to Tokyo along the Pacific coast and the Chuo train line from Nagoya to Niigata, the 11 old post villages where travelers had stopped to refresh themselves became deserted backwaters (sometimes referred to as Minami-Kiso). Two of the villages, **Tsumago** and **Magome,** are easy to reach. Take the JR train from Matsumoto to Nagiso, about 60 minutes away, and then take a 10-minute bus ride (fare: ¥240) from the Nagiso JR station to Tsumago. Buses from the JR station leave every hour for the 30-minute trip. From Tsumago you can take either the footpath to Magome or another bus. Still another bus travels from Magome to Nakatsugawa on the JR line. Then, it is back to Matsumoto or on to Nagoya by train, or over the mountains to Takayama. This trip to Kiso Valley could be accomplished with equal ease as a day trip from Nagoya.

Both Tsumago and Magome have retained much of their old character. Indeed, more than in most places in Japan, walking along the main street of Tsumago is like stepping back in time to the shogun era (except for the souvenir shops). If you have time, it's a pleasant three-hour walk along the old post trail between Tsumago and Magome. (Be sure to go from Tsumago to Magome, since walking in the other direction is almost completely uphill.) Both are served by buses from Nakatsugawa and Nagiso stations, so you can bus to one village and return from the other. There are ryokan and minshukus throughout the valley should you wish to stay overnight, and both Tsumago and Magome have tourist information offices that will help find accommodations and provide free maps.

Takayama

Getting There

There are two routes to **Takayama** from Matsumoto. One is by JR trains all the way, but this requires descending to the coastal plain and changing trains at Nagoya for the two-hour run up the Hida River Valley to Takayama. This is the least interesting route and can take up to four hours' traveling time, but it is the only way in the winter. If you wish to go straight from Kiso Valley to Takayama, take a one-hour, 50-minute bus ride from Magome to Gero and transfer to the JR train for a 45-minute run to Takayama. Buses leave three times daily (7:21 AM and 12:05 with a change at Sakashita, and a direct bus at 4 PM; cost: ¥1,950).

The other route is straight over the mountains through Chubu-Sangaku National Park via **Kamikochi.** This is one of the most scenic routes through the Japan Alps and should not be missed. You should even consider spending the night at Kamikochi to fully enjoy the scenery. It does require a bus/train combination, but it is straightforward and poses no problem. However, it can only be accomplished in the summer (May–Oct.), because winter snows close the road.

First, take the Matsumoto Electric Railway from Matsumoto Station to Shin-Shimashima. The journey takes 30 minutes (fare: ¥650). Do not make the mistake of getting off the train at Shimojima, three stops before Shin-Shimashima. Once off the train, cross over the road at Shin-Shimashima Station for the bus going to Nakanoyu and Kamikochi. The total bus journey takes about one hour and 20 minutes (fare: ¥1,950). The most scenic part is the 20 minutes from Nakanoyu to Kamikochi, and you'll quickly understand why the road is closed by the winter snows (mid-Nov.–mid-April). Just before reaching Kamikochi, the valley opens onto a plain with a backdrop of mountains. **Mt. Oku-Hotaka** is the highest at 10,466 feet. To the left is **Mt. Mae-Hotaka,** 10,138 feet, and to the right is the smaller **Mt. Nishi-Hotaka,** 9,544 feet. Through the narrow basin flow the icy waters of the Azusagawa River to form a small lake, **Taisho Pond,** at the entrance to the basin, where lodges and inns are located. The bus terminal is a few hundred yards beyond.

There are trails in and around Kamikochi to please every level of hiker and climber. One easy three-hour walk is along the river past the rock sculpture of the Reverend Walter Weston, the Briton who was the first to explore and climb these mountains. Then comes the Kappabashi Bridge, a small suspension bridge over the crystal-clear waters of the Azusagawa. Continuing on the south side of the river, the trail cuts through the pasture to rejoin the river at Myoshin Bridge. The Hodaka Shrine is on the other side at the edge of Myoshin Pond. Here is another bridge that leads to the trail back on the opposite side of the river to the Kappabashi Bridge.

From Kamikochi, buses (six a day, only between early May and early Nov.) take an hour and 15 minutes to **Hirayu Onsen** (fare: ¥1,510), where one must change to another bus (operates all year) for the 70-minute ride to Takayama (fare: ¥1,360).

Coming from either Tokyo or Kyoto take the Shinkansen to Nagoya and change for the JR Limited Express to Takayama. The train leaves every hour during the day and takes two hours and 20 minutes.

Exploring 8

One of the most attractive towns in the Japan Alps, **Takayama,** is often left off foreign tourists' itineraries; it is their loss. In the heart of the Hida Mountains, this tranquil town has retained its old-fashioned charm. No wonder so many artists have made their homes here. The city is laid out in a grid pattern; it's compact and easy to explore on foot or by rented bicycle. A rental shop is to the right of the station building (cost: ¥300 per hour). An exotic option is a 30-minute ricksha tour of the old town for ¥1,000 per person. You'll find the rickshas based in San-machi Suji. If you just want to pose in one for a photograph, be ready to hand over ¥200.

Make a point of collecting maps and information from the tourist office just in front of the JR station. Also, throughout

Takayama you can get help at businesses that are designated as Travel Information Desks (look for the "?" sign in the window). In most cases, the person at the cash register in these establishments will speak English or will find someone who speaks English to assist you. Although sightseeing bus tours are available, they are unnecessary and expensive (about ¥3,100 for 3 hours). *Open 8:30–6:30 (8:30–5 Nov.–Mar.)*

Numbers in the margin correspond to points of interest on the Takayama map.

Walking (or riding) down Hirokoji-dori Street for a few blocks, one reaches the old section of town with its small shops, houses, and tearooms. Before the bridge, which crosses the small Miyagawa River, go right, past another bridge, and the

9 **Takayama Jinya** will be on your right. Though perhaps not worth the admission charge to enter, this imposing structure was the manor house of the governor, with samurai barracks and a garden behind the house. In front of the manor house, 7 AM–noon each morning, the Jinya-mae Morning Market sells vegetables, fruits, and local handicrafts. *Admission to house: ¥310. Open daily 8:45–4:30.*

Across the river from the market area and up the hill, a small

10 street leads to Shiroyama Park and **Shorenji Temple.** The Main Hall of this temple was built in 1504 and was moved in 1961 from its original site in Shirakawago before the area was flooded by the Miboro Dam. Now, positioned on the hill looking down on Takayama, the sweep of its curved roof, its superb drum tower, and the surrounding gardens give an earthy tranquillity that symbolizes the atmosphere of all of Takayama. *Admission: ¥ 200. Open daily 8–4:30. (Shiroyama Park is always open; no admission charge.)*

Down from Shiroyama Park, the main street leads to Sanmachi

11 Street. To the right is the **Tenshoji Temple** and youth hostel. This is a magnificent building and a delightful place for a youth hostel, though the rooms are sure to be bitterly cold in the winter. On Sanmachi Street, just across from the road leading from Shiroyama Park, is the folk toy museum and the

12 **Takayama-shi Kyodo-kan** (History Museum), which exhibits various antiques and folklore materials of the Hida people. *Admission: ¥300. Open 8:30–5. Closed Mon. and Dec. 29–31.*

Still on Sanmachi Street, to the left of the toy museum and to-

13 ward the Miyagawa River is the **Hida Minzoku Koko-kan** (Archaeology Museum), in an old house that once belonged to a physician who served the local lord. The unique structure of the mansion, with its hanging ceilings, secret windows, and hidden passages, hints of spies, so prevalent in the Edo period. Now the house displays wall hangings, weaving machines, and sundry items, both archaeological and folkloric, collected from the Hida region. *Admission: ¥300. Open daily 7–7 (8–5 Dec.–Feb.).*

14 North of the Archaeology Museum you enter the **Sanmachi-Suji** section, which includes Ichinomachi, Ninomachi, and Sannomachi streets, all parallel to the Miyagawa River. This was the merchant area during the feudal days. Most of the old teahouses, inns, dye houses, and sake breweries with latticed windows and doors are preserved in their original state, making Sanmachi-Suji a rare vestige of old Japan before the Meiji Res-

village still live in *gassho-zukuri*–style farmhouses, many of which serve as minshukus. *Gassho-zukuri* means "hands held in prayer" and refers to the thatched roofs of the structures. Inside, cooking is still done over an *irori*, or open hearth, with guests seated around the fire as the smoke rises and escapes through the thatched roof. Among the local specialties served are mountain vegetables cooked in dark miso over a small burner. Reservations can be made through the Ogimachi tourist office (tel. 0576/96–1751). It's best to ask a Japanese-speaking person to do this for you before you arrive, but stop at the tourist office in the square at the center of town for a map. Most of the buildings here look pretty much the same and none of the minshukus have signs, so get someone to circle the location of your minshuku on your map. Once you've checked in, go out and stroll, and make sure you have a camera. Find your way to the hill that looks out over the town. In the evening, try to locate the local bar, which from the outside looks like all the other structures; the noise of people partying will give it away.

Opposite Ogimachi, on the banks of the Showkawa River is **Shirakawa Gassho-mura,** a restored village where you can learn how the farmers of the Japan Alps region used to live. The gassho-zukuri–style houses here were actually transplanted from four villages that fell prey to progress—the building of the Miboro Dam 20 years ago. There are demonstrations of local craftmaking in some of the 25 buildings. *Admission: ¥500. Village open daily 8:30–5; Dec.–Mar. 9–4.*

To reach the village from Takayama, take the Nohi bus to Makido for an hour and 35 minutes and then the JR bus to Ogimachi for one hour. There are only six buses a day (four a day Dec.–Mar.) from Takayama, so before leaving Takayama, plan your schedule with the help of the tourist office in front of Takayama Station.

From Shirakawago, instead of returning to Takayama, you

21 may want to take a bus that leaves Ogimachi for **Kanazawa;** the trip takes just under three hours (departs Ogimachi 2:40 PM; arrives Kanazawa 5:27 PM). On this route you will see more of the Hida Mountains than you can from the JR train out of Takayama, which passes through many tunnels and narrow valleys.

It you are not arriving from Takayama, Kanazawa can easily be reached by JR limited express trains from Kyoto (2 hrs., 30 min.) and Nagoya (3 hrs.). A new city and prefecture Tourist Office in the JR Station dispenses maps and can help you find accommodations. The terminal for buses to downtown is at the front of the station.

Kanazawa

Numbers in the margin correspond to points of interest on the Kanazawa map.

Many sizable Japanese cities were destroyed by the bombs of World War II; Kanazawa is an exception. Many of its old neighborhoods have remained intact for the past two or three centuries, despite modern Japan's tendency to bulldoze the old and

22 replace it with concrete. **Kanazawajo Castle,** though, has fallen

23 victim to seven fires in all, and only the **Ishikawa Gate** remains intact (rebuilt in 1788). Note the gate's lead tiles: The *daimyos*

Gyokusenen Garden, **26**
Higashi-no-Kurawa (Eastern Pleasure Quarter), **34**
Honda Museum, **28**
Ishikawa Gate, **23**
Ishikawa Prefectural Art Museum, **27**
Kanazawajo Castle, **22**
Kenrokuen Garden, **24**
Kosen Kutani Pottery Kiln, **32**
Myoryuji Temple, **31**
Nagamachi Samurai District, **30**
Nishi-no-Kurawa (Western Pleasure Quarter), **33**
Oyama Jinja Shrine, **29**
Seisonkaku Villa, **25**

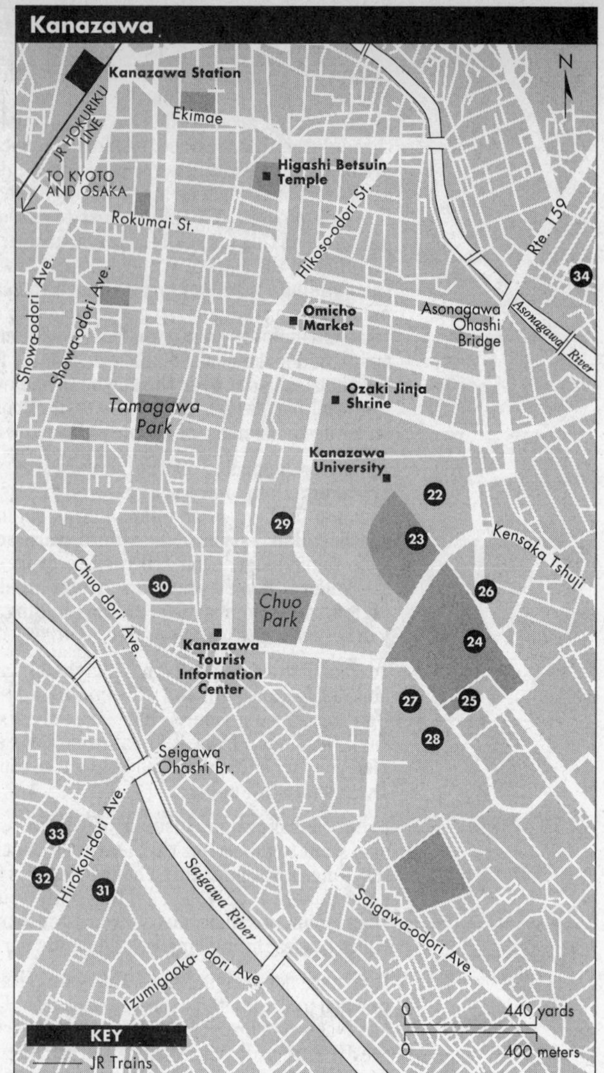

(feudal lords) never knew when they might be under siege and require more munitions, which could be made from the tiles.

Because Kanazawa was a fortress town centered on its castle, this is the best point from which to start appreciating Kanazawa and its past. To reach the castle from the train station, take any bus (fare: ¥160) from gate 11 at the bus terminal outside the JR station. You can also purchase, for ¥650, an intracity "Free Pass" from the Hokutetsu Bus Ticket Office, in front of the JR station. The pass permits unlimited day travel on the city's buses. Beneath the recently rebuilt Kanazawa JR station there are arcades with numerous restaurants and shops. A station branch of the Kanazawa Information Office (tel. 0762/31–

6311, open Mon.–Sat., 9–5) is adjacent to the JR Reserved Seat Ticketing office.

Should you want to go directly downtown, to Oyama Jinja Shrine, the New Grand or Tokyu hotels, or the City Information Center (tel. 0762/22–1500; open 10–6; closed Wed.) on the ground floor of the Kohrinbo 190 Building, take bus #30, #31, or #32 from gate 8, or bus #20 or #21 from gate 9.

During the Tokugawa period (1603–1868), the fertile region around Kanazawa (Kaga region) was dominated by the Maeda daimyo. Their wealth was tremendous, based on the 1 million koku rice harvests of the region. With this wealth came power and distrust. They distrusted the shogun in Edo, and the shogun distrusted them. The manifestation of this distrust was a mighty castle that had not only the protection of high walls and moats but also the intentionally winding, narrow town streets around the castle, which made attacks more difficult. Two other security measures were taken. A Buddhist temple complex was set up on the road to Edo as a delaying tactic; it also supplied an underground escape route back to the castle. Then, at another two approaches to the city, entertainment quarters were established so that invaders might be waylaid by amorous pursuits rather than by fighting.

These security measures appear to have been successful. Kanazawa maintained its independence and prospered for three centuries. Moreover, throughout its dynasty, the Maeda clan encouraged education and cultural pursuits. It seems fitting, therefore, that the castle grounds are now the site of Kanazawa University.

24 The best-known tourist attraction in Kanazawa is **Kenrokuen Garden,** across from Kanazawajo Castle's Ishikawa Gate. For many Japanese, Kenrokuen is one of the three finest landscaped gardens in Japan. (The other two are Mito's Kairakuen and Okayama's Korakuen.) Kenrokuen began as the outer garden of Kanazawajo in 1676 under the fifth daimyo. Two hundred years and eight generations of daimyos later, Kenrokuen reached its final form. It received its name because it possessed the six superior qualities required for the perfect garden: extensiveness, factitiousness, antiquity, abundant water, wide prospect, and quiet seclusion. Today, the last quality seems in question. The gardens are near bedlam in the holiday season, with Japanese tourists being told the names of the trees through their group leader's megaphone. Either arrive at the garden first thing in the morning or risk losing its intended solemnity. *Admission: ¥500. Open daily 6:30–6 (Oct. 16–Mar. 15, 8–4:30).*

25 In the southeast of Kenrokuen is the **Seisonkaku Villa,** a two-story residence built in 1863 by one of the Maeda lords for his mother's retirement. Now it houses the family heirlooms and a collection of art objects that have been handed down through the generations of the Maeda clan. *Admission: ¥500. Open 8:30–4:30. Closed Wed.*

A much quieter garden, and one preferred by those who desire 26 tranquillity, is **Gyokusenen Garden.** (Admission: ¥400. Open daily 9–4; closed mid-Dec.–mid-Mar.) This garden has an intimacy created by an owner (a wealthy merchant) seeking calm and contemplative peace rather than grand accolades for his green thumb. The moss, maple trees, and small steppingstones by the pond are more serene than the bold strokes of Kenrokuen. The garden is located to the northeast of Kenrokuen Garden and before the **Kanko Bussankan,** a building that demonstrates Yuzan dyeing, pottery, and lacquerware production.

27 Walking southwest for five minutes takes you to the **Ishikawa Prefectural Art Museum,** which displays the best permanent collection of Kutani pottery, dyed fabrics, old Japanese paintings, and various other art objects. *Admission: ¥350. Open 9:30–4:30.*

28 A narrow path at the back of the art museum leads to the **Honda Museum.** The Honda family members were the key political advisers to the Maeda daimyos, and the museum contains 700 art objects, armor, and household utensils used by the Honda family during its tenure. Don't miss the uniforms of the Honda family's personal firefighters and the trousseau of the Maeda brides marrying into the Honda family. *Admission: ¥500. Open 9–5. Closed Thurs. Nov.–Feb. and Dec. 29–Jan. 1.*

29 Retracing your steps and keeping south of Kanazawajo, you find the **Oyama Jinja Shrine.** Built in 1599, the shrine is dedicated to Lord Toshiie Maeda, the founder of the Maeda clan. However, architecturally, the shrine is noted for its three-story Shimmon Gate, designed in 1875 with the assistance of two Dutch instructors. At the top of the gate's squared arch is a stained-glass window that originally beamed a light to guide ships in from the Sea of Japan to the Kanaiwa port, 4 miles to the northwest. *Admission free.*

30 A few blocks southwest of the Oyama Jinja is the **Nagamachi Samurai District,** where the Maeda clan's samurai lived. Narrow, crooked streets are lined with tile-roof mud walls designed to protect the quarters from curious eyes. One of the houses has been carefully restored and turned into a museum, Buke Yaskiki. Another old house is now the **Saihitsuan Yuzen Silk Center,** which demonstrates the art of painting intricate designs on yuzen silk used for kimonos. *Admission: ¥500. Open 9–12 and 1–4:30. Closed Thurs. and Dec. 28–Jan. 4.*

Time Out While in this area of samurai houses, you can take green tea and Japanese cookies at **Nikore** (tel. 0762/61–0056). Mrs. Mori and her son converted a samurai house in order to serve tea on a veranda facing a small garden. To find Nikore, walk straight ahead from Saihitsuan Yuzen Silk Center and cross the street. It's on your right, marked by three Japanese *Kanji* characters in yellow. Open 10–5.

After your green tea, go left from Nikore to the corner and take another left. On the next corner across the street is the **Nomura House.** Though most of the samurai houses were demolished with the Meiji Restoration, this abode was rebuilt by an industrialist at the turn of the century and furnished in that period's traditional style. Visit the Jyodan-no-ma drawing room made of cypress wood, with elaborate designs in rosewood and ebony. Each of the sliding (paper) doors has a great landscape drawn by Sasaki Senkai of the Kano school. Facing the living room is a small garden with a winding stream and a bridge made of cherry granite. *Tel. 0762/21–3553. Admission: ¥400. Open 10–5.*

Crossing over to the south side of the Saigawa River and a five-minute walk beyond is the **Myoryuji Temple,** famous for its complicated structure. Its popular name, the **Ninjadera** (Temple of the Ninja—ninja are warriors and experts in the art of concealment), tells all. The innocent-looking temple is a complex of labyrinthine corridors, trapdoors, hidden chambers, secret tunnels, and 29 staircases to 22 of its 23 rooms. An exaggerated case of paranoia, perhaps, but it was designed to hold off invaders until the daimyo could make good his escape. In high tourist season, there is a line of visitors waiting for a tour. Reservations are essential, though late in the afternoon one may be able to slip in with a small group. *Tel. 0762/41–2877. Admission: ¥500. Open 9–4:30 (Dec.–Feb., 9–4).*

The small housed *jizo* figure (representations of bodhisattva, an altruist Buddhist deity) in the temple grounds is not on the tour, but he does have a story to tell. His facial features are almost rubbed away. In days before penicillin, syphilitics would rub the little jizo's nose in the hope that their disease would go away. Today Japanese come to ritually scrub him with a nail brush and take photographs of themselves with the little figure. Why the little jizo is here at the temple is a mystery, but its presence may be related to the belief that the daimyo used the secret passages of the Ninjadera as a way of reaching the Western Pleasure Quarter undetected. There's no fee to rub the jizo although donations are accepted.

One street over and one block to the south from the Myoryuji is the **Kosen Kutani Pottery Kiln,** where you can watch the entire process of making local Kutani pottery. *Admission free. Open 8:30–12 and 1–5. Closed Sun. afternoon.*

From the Kosen Kutani Pottery Kiln you can catch a bus or make a brisk walk back along Hirokoji-dori Avenue and over the Seigawa Ohashi Bridge to the downtown shopping center and Kanazawajo. If you are walking, pass through **Nishi-no-Kurawa (Western Pleasure Quarter)** en route. The geishas are no longer walled in, but the checkpoint that kept the ladies from escaping has been preserved. The area lacks the bustle of intrigue that existed 200 years ago; however, in the maze of narrow, crooked streets, perhaps you'll see a geisha or two. They are said to be younger and more beautiful in this quarter than those in **Higashi-no-Kurawa (Eastern Pleasure Quarter),** on the other side of town and across the Asanogawa, Kanazawa's other river.

The Eastern Pleasure Quarter was set aside as a high-class area of entertainment. Now, the pleasures of visiting here are the old buildings with wood-slat facades in the narrow, winding streets. Most of the old geisha houses have been turned into tearooms or minshukus, but occasionally one sees a scurrying geisha traveling to her appointment. One elegant former geisha house, **Shima-ke,** is open to the public and gives us a chance to see the inside and its relaxing garden. *Admission: ¥200. Open 8:30–4:30. Closed Mon.*

The easiest way to reach the Eastern Pleasure Quarter is to take the JR bus from the JR station using a Japan Rail Pass (¥160 without the pass). The bus stops at Hachira-cho, just before the Asonagawa Ohashi Bridge. You can also take this bus to get to the **Omicho Market,** and, if you don't mind a 10-minute walk, you can take it to the site of Kanazawa's Castle and the Kenrokuen Gardens.

Only Kanazawa's major sights have been touched upon here. It is a city full of little surprises, such as a small temple that does an amazing business reading *sutra* (Buddhist precepts) and dispensing herbs to cure hemorrhoids. Anyone staying for more than a day should obtain a copy of Ruth Stevens's detailed English-language guide, *Kanazawa*. It's a book written with a love for the city and leads the visitor to all the discoveries Ms. Stevens has made during her 10 years of living there. The book can be purchased in English-language bookstores in Tokyo; sometimes it is available in the lobby book stand of the Holiday Inn Hotel across from the Kanazawa JR station and at the Kanazawa Information Office at the station.

Numbers in the margin correspond to points of interest on the Japan Alps map.

35 From Kanazawa you can take a train west to **Fukui.** The town is not very interesting, but 12 miles (19 kilometers) southeast of 36 Fukui is **Eiheiji Temple,** one of the two main temples of the Soto sect of Zen Buddhism. Founded in 1244, the complex of 70 temple buildings is built on a hillside surrounded by trees, some of which are as old as the original temple buildings. The temple is still very active, and there are 200 novitiates in training at any given time. Visitors are welcome, and an English pamphlet is given at the gate to mark out the key buildings, once visitors have had a long-winded introductory lesson to the Soto sect. Foreigners are also welcome to stay at the temple, though arrangements should be made by writing in advance. *Admission: ¥300. Open 5–5.*

Eiheiji Temple is most easily reached by train from Fukui. If you do not want to return to Fukui and reboard the train for Kyoto and Osaka, there is a bus that runs down to the JR line that allows you to travel up to Ono and the two gorges, Kuzuryu and Managawa, both noted for their scenic beauty.

There are several hotels in Fukui, but consider spending the night at **Awara Onsen,** just northwest of Fukui. To get there, get off at JR Awara Onsen and take a bus from gate 2 to the Awaracho Onsen. The area is close to the rocky shore of the Sea of Japan, and off the beaten track for foreigners. It is, however, a popular resort for Japanese families. There are attractive and expensive ryokan as well as less expensive minshukus (*see* Lodging, *below*).

Noto Peninsula

The **Noto Peninsula** is rolling countryside with paddies, divided by steep hills, and a coastline that is mild and peaceful. On the eastern side, the inner (*uchi*) shore, there are many indentations and sea-bathing opportunities, while the western outer (*soto*) coast is rugged and rock-strewn. It's best to work your way around the peninsula by car or, because it is relatively flat, by bicycle; however, the peninsula can be explored through a combination of train and bus. There are also daylong bus tours of the area that set out every day from Kanazawa (*see* Guided Tours, *above*).

Wajima is the terminal for the JR line from Kanazawa and is reached in a two-hour, 15-minute train ride; however, the line turns inland and misses some of Noto Peninsula's best sights. Hence, the best itinerary is to take the 40-minute train ride 37 from Kanazawa as far as **Hakui.** The Chirihama beach is a 20-minute walk from the station. This stretch of coast is good for taking in the summer sun and for swimming, as well as being one of the noted scenic spots along the Noto coast. The Japanese like this area because they can drive their cars along the sand and bring *bento* picnic lunches.

A few miles north by bus from Hakui (buses leave outside the train station) is the 17th-century **Myojoji Temple,** a five-story pagoda that stands out from the surrounding plain. It was originally built in the 13th century, though the present structure dates to the 1600s.

Although it's a longer journey, rather than take the inland bus route north to Monzen, take the bus that runs along the coast to Monzen, which includes the 8-mile (13-kilometer) stretch of coastline known as Noto-Kongo. The coastline is noted for its oceanic beauty, marked by fantastic formations of eroded rock. 38 The journey will take about 70 minutes. **Monzen** is where the Zen temple **Sojiji** stands. Sojiji was once the headquarters of the Soto sect, but a fire destroyed most of the buildings in 1818 and the sect moved its headquarters to Yokohama. (The Eiheiji Temple near Fukui, mentioned earlier in this chapter, is, in fact, as important to the Soto sect as is the one in Yokohama.)

The next stop on the bus, only 10 miles (16 kilometers) up the 39 road, is **Wajima,** a fishing town that is known not for its fish but for its lacquerware. Every shop in town seems to sell this craft, though before you buy, first visit the **Wajima Shikki Kaikan** (Lacquerware Hall). It's easy to find; ask the ticket-booth conductor at the bus station for directions. Here the patient process of its creativity is shown: It involves about 18 different steps, from wood preparation to coating of numerous layers of lacquer, with careful polishing in between each coat. *Admission: ¥300. Open 8:30–5:30.*

Once familiar with the product, walk to the *asaichi* (morning market), held every day between 8 and 11:30, except the 10th and 25th of each month. Here, among the fruit, vegetables, and seafood, the local crafts and lacquerware are sold to tourists. There is also *yuichi* (evening market), a smaller version of asaichi, which starts around 3:30 PM.

From Wajima, a bus travels 20 minutes farther north up to Sosogi, a small village, passing terraced rice fields that descend from the hills to the edge of the sea. At Sosogi the road forks inland. Soon after the fork (five minutes) are two traditional farm manor houses. The **Shimo-Tokikuni House** is more than 300 years old and is furnished with antiques. Rent the tape recorder at the entrance for an English explanation of each room. Close by is **Kami-Tokikuni House,** which took 28 years to rebuild in the last century and remains in near-perfect condition. Each room has a special purpose, and, by following the English leaflet, one becomes very conscious of the strict adherence to the class ranking system of medieval Japan. *Both houses charge a small admission. Open 9–4:30.*

40 The same bus route (hourly service) continues to **Suzu,** on the *uchi* coast (inner, or eastern, shore), serviced by the Noto Railway Line. It is, in fact, possible to travel around the northern tip of the Noto Peninsula by bus (continue on from Sosogi to

Cape Rokko and down to the northern terminus of the Noto Railway Line at Tako-jima), but the views and scenery do not justify the infrequency of public transport.

From Suzu, take the train line south to **Tsukumo-wan** (Noto Ogi Station). Tsukumo-wan means "a bay with 99 indentations." To help appreciate this part of the rocky coastline, there are glass-bottom boats that circle the bay. Farther south and (41) on the train line is **Wakura Onsen.** This is the Noto Peninsula's smart resort town, with many hotels and ryokan. It is especially popular among Japanese families, who take their children across the bridge to Notojima Island, where there is an elaborate new marine park. Wakura Onsen is on the train line linked directly with Kanazawa, approximately a two-hour ride away. However, one can take a bus south and east along the coastal (42) road (Rte. 160) to the city of **Takaoka.**

Takaoka is the southern gateway to the Noto Peninsula and is not worth lingering in, but if there is time, the city does claim to have Japan's third largest *Daibutsu* (statue of Buddha), after those at Nara and Kamakura. It is made of bronze and stands 53 feet high. There is also the **Zuiryuji Temple,** a 10-minute walk from the station, which is a delightful Zen temple of the Soto sect and doubles as the local youth hostel. However, the city is mostly known for its craft traditions of copper, lacquerware, and ironware, especially its cast-iron bells.

(43) Southeast of Takaoka is **Toyama,** a busy industrial center. Its only redeeming virtue is the Toyamajoshi (castle park), which is a spread of greenery with a reconstructed version of the original (1532) castle in the center of town. Forty minutes to Toyama's northeast, one stop after Kurobe on the Toyama Chiho (44) Tesudo Line, is **Unazuki Onsen,** located at the mouth of a mountain valley. There is a tramcarlike train (the Kurobe Kyokoku Railway—operates May–mid-Nov.) that runs through this valley for 12 picturesque miles (19 kilometers), past gushing springs and plunging waterfalls and through the Kurobe Gorge to Keyakidaira (cost: ¥1,260).

From Toyama (or Kurobe, if you have visited Unazuki Onsen), (45) this itinerary takes the express train up to **Niigata** to board the ferry to Sado Island. Niigata is Japan's major port and industrial city on the Japan Sea coast and is linked to Tokyo's Ueno Station by a two-hour trip on the Joetsu Shinkansen. Niigata is a good place for replenishing supplies and changing money; however, the city has limited attractions for the sightseer. The tourist information office to the left of the station can help you find a hotel as well as supply city maps and ferry schedules for Sado Island.

Sado Island

Sado has always been a melancholy island. Its role in history has been as a place where antigovernment intellectuals, such as the Buddhist monk Nichiren, were banished to endure the harshest exile. Then, when gold was discovered during the Edo period (1603–1868), the homeless, especially those from Edo (now Tokyo), were sent to Sado to work as forced laborers in the gold mines. This heritage of hardship has left behind a tradition of soulful ballads and folk dances. Even the bamboo grown on the island is said to be the best for making *takohochi,* the plaintive flutes that accompany the ballads.

May through September is the best time to visit Sado. During the other months the weather can prevent sea and air crossings, and in January and February Sado is also bitterly cold. Though the island is Japan's fifth largest, it is comparatively small (331 sq mi). Two parallel mountain chains, running along the north and south coasts, are split by an extensive plain containing small rice farms and the island's principal cities. Despite the fact that more than a million tourists visit the island each year (more than 10 times the number of island inhabitants), the pace of life is slow, even preindustrial. That is Sado's attraction.

Getting There

By Boat. There are two main ferry routes across to Sado Island with each route having both a regular ferry and a hydrofoil service. The bus from bay #6 at the terminal in front of the Niigata JR station takes 15 minutes to reach the dock for the Sado Kinsen ferries (tel. 025/245–1234) sailing to Ryotsu. The same company has ferries going to Ogi, leaving from Naoetsu (tel. 0225/43–3791), south of Niigata. From Niigata to Ryotsu the ferry crossing takes 2½ hours, with six or seven crossings a day (cost: ¥1,780 for ordinary second class, ¥2,600 for a seat reservation, ¥3,560 for first class, and ¥5,340 for special class). The hydrofoil takes one hour, with seven to 10 crossings in the summer, two in the winter, and anywhere between three and eight at other seasons depending on the weather. In February, the hydrofoil service is down to one crossing per day (cost: ¥5,460 one way, ¥10,590 round trip). To Ogi from Naoetsu the hydrofoil cost is the same as the Niigata–Ryotsu crossing, while the regular ferry is ¥1,960 for ordinary second class, ¥2,780 for a seat reservation, ¥3,930 for first class, and ¥5,890 for special class). The ferry terminal is a ¥130 bus ride or ¥660 taxi ride from the Naoetsu JR station.

There is also one ferry a day from Niigata to Akadomari in winter; two more are added in summer. The route takes two hours (cost: ¥1,550). Depending on the season, one to three ferries sail between Teradomari (near Okutsu on Honshu) and Akadomari, taking two hours (cost: ¥1,220 for second class and ¥2,450 for first class).

By Plane. The small plane takes 25 minutes from Niigata; there are six flights a day in the summer and three in the winter (tel. 025/275–4352; cost: ¥7,360).

Getting Around

Frequent bus service is available between the major towns, making travel around the island simple. There are also four- and eight-hour tours of the island that depart from both Ryotsu and Ogi (not available Dec.–Apr.). However, these tour buses do tend to patronize the souvenir shops. The best combination is to use the tour bus for the mountain skyline drive (¥3,700) or the two-day Skyline and Historic Site combined tour (¥5,150) and then rent a bike to explore on one's own.

Exploring

46

Sado's usual port of entry is **Ryotsu**, the island's largest township. The center of town is the strip of land that runs between Lake Kamo and the Sea of Japan, with most of the hotels and ryokan on the shore of the lake. Lake Kamo is actually connected to the Sea of Japan by a small inlet running through the middle of town. The Ebisu quarter has the island's concentration of restaurants and bars. Every evening (8:30–9:30) April–early November, the Ryotsu Kaikan Hall stages a performance of *Okesa,* melancholic folk dances and songs performed by women, and the *Ondeko*, a lion dance to drum beats. Admission: ¥600 (¥100 discount if the ticket is bought at any ryokan in Ryotsu). Similar performances during the summer season are given elsewhere on Sado: the Sado Kaikan in Aikowa; the Niigata Kotsu, 2nd floor, in Ogi; and the Sado Chuo Kaikan in Sawata.

47 The simplest way to begin exploring Sado is to take the bus from Ryotsu to **Aikawa.** Buses leave every 30 minutes and take about 90 minutes to make the trip (fare: ¥630). Once Aikawa was a small town of 10,000 people. Then, in 1601, gold was discovered, and the rush was on. The population swelled to 100,000 until the ore was exhausted. Now it is back to 10,000 inhabitants, and the tourists coming to see the old gold mine are a major source of the town's income.

Though some 10,000 tons of silver and gold ore are still mined annually, Aikawa's **Sado Kinzan Mine** is more of a tourist attraction than anything else. There are some 250 miles (400 kilometers) of underground tunnels, some running as deep as 1,969 feet beneath sea level, and some of this extensive digging is open to the public. Instead of the slave labor that was used throughout the Edo period, there are now robots serving in its place. These robots are, in fact, quite lifelike, and they demonstrate the appalling conditions that were endured by the miners. Sound effects of shovels and pick axes add to the sobering reality. *Admission: ¥600. Open 8–5:30 (until sunset in autumn and winter).*

To reach the mine from the bus terminus, it is a tough 40-minute uphill walk or a five-minute taxi ride (about ¥800). On the way back from Sado Kinzan, walking is easier.

North of Aikawa is **Senkakuwan** (Senkaku Bay), the most dramatic stretch of coastline and a must-see on Sado Island. To reach the bay, take a 15-minute bus ride from Aikawa to Tassha and then the 40-minute sightseeing cruise boat (Apr.–Oct.) to see rugged beauty accented by fantastic, sea-eroded rock formations and cliffs rising 60 feet out of the water. The boat disembarks at the Senkakuwan Yuen, a park where one can picnic, stroll, and gaze upon the varied rock formations offshore. From the park, you can return by bus to Aikawa. *One-way cruise-boat fare: ¥600; includes admission to the park.*

The most scenic drive on Sado is the **Osado Skyline.** However, no public buses take this route. You must either take a tour bus from Ryotsu or a taxi from Aikawa across the skyline drive to Chikuse (cost: ¥3,700), where one connects with a public bus either to Ryotsu or back to Aikawa.

To reach the southwestern tip of Sado, first make your way on a bus to Sawata either from Aikawa or Ryotsu, then transfer to the bus for Ogi. En route you may want to stop at **Mano,** where the emperor Juntoku (1197–1242) is buried. There is a sadness to this mausoleum built for a man who at 24 was exiled for life to Sado by the Kamakura shogunate for his unsuccessful attempt to regain power. The mausoleum and the museum that exhibits some of the emperor's personal effects are in **Toki-no-Sato Park.** *Admission: ¥500. Open Apr.–mid-Nov., daily.*

At Mano, incidentally, the *tsuburosashi* dance is given nightly at the Sado New Hotel. The unique dance is performed by a man holding a *tsuburo* (phallic symbol) with the goddesses

Shagri and Zeni Daiko. The trip from Sawata to Ogi takes 50 minutes, with the journey's highlight being the beautiful Benteniwa rock formations, just past Tazawaki. Be sure to take a window seat on the right-hand side of the bus.

48 **Ogi** can be used as a port for returning to Honshu by the ferry, which takes 2½ hours to reach Naoetsu, or on the jetfoil, which takes an hour. Other than that, Ogi's chief attraction is the *taraibune,* round, tublike boats used in the past for fishing. They are now available to tourists for rent (¥450 for a 30-min. paddle). They accommodate up to three people, and with a single oar you wend your way around the harbor. The taraibune can also be rented at Shukunegi; it's a more attractive town on the Sawasaki Coast, where the water is dotted with rocky islets and the shore is covered with rock lilies in summer. It has become a sleepy backwater since it stopped building small wood ships to ply the waters between Sado and Honshu, and has retained its traditional atmosphere and buildings. One can reach Shukunegi from Ogi by a sightseeing boat or by bus; both take about 20 minutes, so consider using the boat one way to have the view of the cliffs, which were created by an earthquake 250 years ago.

Rather than return to Ryotsu for the ferry to Niigata, it's nice to take the bus along the coast from Ogi to Akadomari and catch the ferry for Niigata from there.

Dining and Lodging

Dining

Virtually all regions in Japan have their own way of cooking, and none more so than the regions within the Japan Alps and the coastal areas of the Sea of Japan. In the area called Hokuriku, which consists of the Ishikawa, Fukui, and Toyama prefectures, fish from the cold, salty waters of the Sea of Japan is superb.

Toyama has **beni-zuwaigani,** a long-leg red crab that is a special delicacy during the November–March season. **Amaebi,** a sweet prawn that, when eaten raw with **wasabi** (Japanese horseradish) literally melts in the mouth, is available from Toyama Bay. Another local treat is **masu-zushi,** salmon trout pressed onto shallow, round cakes of vinegared rice.

In Ishikawa, the cuisine is called **Kaga,** in which the harvest from the sea is prepared with Kyoto-style elegance. **Tai** (bream), cooked in a style called **karamushi,** is certainly one dish to try. The **kaga-ryori** is a kind of cooking in which the mountain vegetables of mushrooms and ferns are used. Fish and shellfish are frequently included in regional dishes. **Miso soup,** for example, often contains tiny clams still in their shells; sweet crab legs are a mouth-watering delicacy.

In Fukui, the **echizen-gani** crabs stretch 28 inches on the average. These crabs are pure heaven when boiled with a little salt and eaten with the fingers after being dipped in a little rice vinegar. **Wakasa-karei** is a fresh sole that is dried briefly before being lightly grilled. In both Fukui and Ishikawa, there is **echizen-soba,** buckwheat noodles, handmade and served with mountain vegetables. Echizen-soba is also served with dips of sesame oil and bean paste, a reflection of the Buddhist vegetarian tradition.

In the Niigata Prefecture, try **noppei,** a hot or cold soup with **sato imo** (a kind of sweet potato) as its base, and mushrooms, salmon, and other local ingredients. It goes with hot rice and grilled fish. **Wappameshi** is a hot dish of steamed rice garnished with local ingredients. In the autumn, try **kiku-noohitashi,** a side dish of chrysanthemum petals marinated in vinegar. Like other prefectures on the Sea of Japan coast, Niigata has outstanding fish in winter—yellowtail, flatfish, sole, oysters, abalone, and shrimp. A local specialty is **nanban ebi,** raw shrimp dipped in soy sauce and wasabi. It is especially sweet and butter-tender on Sado Island. Also on Sado Island, take advantage of the excellent *wakame* (seaweed) dishes and *sazae-no-tsuboyaki* (wreath shellfish) broiled in their shells with soy or miso sauce.

In the landlocked Hida Prefecture around Takayama, the cuisine looks to the mountains and rivers for its produce. The typical cuisine of the district is called **san-sai,** in which mountain vegetables, such as edible ferns and wild plants, are cooked with the rich local miso or bean paste. **San-sai ryori** includes fresh river fish, such as the **ayu,** which are grilled with salt or soy sauce. The local specialty is **hoba-miso,** where miso, mixed with vegetables, is roasted on a magnolia leaf. Other local foods are **mitarashi-dango,** grilled rice balls flavored with soy sauce, and **shio-senbei,** salty rice crackers.

The Nagano Prefecture is famous for its handmade buckwheat noodles; more esoteric dishes in the area include raw horse-meat and sweet-boiled baby bees. Matsumoto is known for its wasabi.

A 3% federal consumer tax is added to all restaurant bills. Another 3% local tax is added to the bill if it exceeds ¥7,500. At more expensive restaurants, a 10%–15% service charge is also added to the bill. Tipping is not the custom.

Category	Cost*
Very Expensive	over ¥6,000
Expensive	¥4,000–¥6,000
Moderate	¥2,000–¥4,000
Inexpensive	under ¥2,000

**Cost is per person without tax, service, or drinks*

Lodging

Accommodations cover the wide spectrum from Japanese-style inns to modern, large resort hotels that have little character but offer all the facilities of an international hotel. All of the large city and resort hotels offer Western and Japanese dining. During the summer season, hotel reservations are advised.

Youth hostels have not been listed. However, there are youth hostels in all the major areas. Their names and addresses can easily be obtained by requesting the Japan National Tourist Organization's free booklet *Youth Hostels in Japan*.

Outside the cities or major towns, most hotels quote prices on a per-person basis with two meals, exclusive of service and tax. If you do not want dinner at your hotel, it is usually possible to renegotiate the price. Stipulate, too, whether you wish to have Japanese or Western breakfasts, if any. The categories assigned below to all hotels reflect the cost of a double room with private bath and no meals. However, if you make reservations at any of the noncity hotels, you will be expected to take breakfast and dinner at the hotel—that will be the rate quoted to you unless you specify otherwise.

A 3% federal consumer tax is added to all hotel bills. Another 3% local tax is added to the bill if it exceeds ¥15,000. At most hotels, a 10%–15% service charge is added to the total bill. Tipping is not the custom.

Category	Cost*
Very Expensive	over ¥20,000
Expensive	¥15,000–¥20,000
Moderate	¥10,000–¥15,000
Inexpensive	under ¥10,000

**Cost is for double room, without tax or service*

The most highly recommended restaurants and accommodations in each city or area are indicated by a star ★.

Awaracho-onsen

Lodging **Minshuku Kimuraya.** This quiet minshuku, located in the center of the spa town, is a welcome alternative to staying in a plain hotel in Fukui. A few words of Japanese help here, but the family that runs the place will do their best to understand your sign language. The rooms are large—eight or ten tatami mats—and heated by kerosene stoves. A table with a blanket heater is the sole furnishing. The home-style Japanese fare for breakfast and dinner is average. Awara-onsen is close to the Japan Sea coast and west of Fukui. To reach the minshuku from the JR station take a bus from gate 2 (fare ¥270) to the Awarayunomachi bus stop in Awaracho-onsen. The minshuku is a five-minute walk from the bus-stop. *Awaracho-onsen 910-41, tel. 0776/77-2229. 10 rooms. No credit cards. Inexpensive.*

Fukui

Lodging **Hotel Akebono Bekkan.** This small two-story wooden building is a simple and convenient Japanese inn for those who want to stay in Fukui. The owners can arrange training sessions in Zen meditation and classes in pottery and papermaking. All the small tatami rooms share the communal bath. Both Japanese and Western breakfasts are offered, but only Japanese dinners are available. The inn is located 10 minutes by foot from the JR Fukui Station and next to the Sakura Bridge. *3-9-26, Chuo, Fukui City, 910 Fukui, tel. 0776/22-0506, fax 0776/22-8023. 10 Japanese-style rooms, all without bath. Facilities: restaurant. AE, V. Inexpensive.*

Kamikochi

All hotels and ryokan close down mid-November–late April.

Lodging

★ **Imperial Hotel.** This is the best place to stay in Kamikochi. It may have no particular charm, but it's modern and well maintained. It is owned by Tokyo's Imperial Hotel, whose staff, on a monthly rotating basis, operates this establishment in the summer. You'll see the hotel right near the bus terminal. *Kamikochi, Azumimura, tel. 0263/95–2006. 75 rooms. Facilities: Western and Japanese cuisine. AE, V. Expensive–Very Expensive.*

Gosenjuku Ryokan. A standard Japanese inn that is reasonably priced and located just beyond the bus terminal en route to the Kappabashi Bridge. *4468 Kamikochi, Azumimura, tel. 0263/95–2131. 31 Japanese-style rooms. AE, V. Moderate.*

Kanazawa

Dining

Goriya. The specialty here is river fish, including *gori*. One of Kanazawa's oldest restaurants (over 200 years old), Goriya is justly famous, with its lovely garden on the banks of the Asano River. The dining areas consist of several small rooms, and the setting is unusual, even if the cooking may not be Kanazawa's finest. *60 Tokiwa-cho, tel. 0762/52–5596. Reservations advised. Jacket and tie required. AE, V, MC. Open 11–9:30. Very Expensive.*

★ **Tsubajin.** One of Kanazawa's best restaurants for Kaga cooking, Tsubajin is actually part of a small, traditional, and expensive ryokan. Try the crab, and also the house specialty, a chicken stew called *jibuni*. Be forewarned that dinner for two will exceed ¥20,000. *5-1-8 Teramachi, tel. 0762/41–2181. Reservations required. Dress: formal. AE. Open 11–9. Lunch is less elaborate and less expensive than dinner. Very Expensive.*

★ **Kincharyo.** This restaurant, associated with the famous Kincharyo ryokan, recently moved to the Tokyu Hotel and is now that establishment's showpiece. The private dining room's Gotenyo ceiling is an impressive piece of delicate craftsmanship. Equally compelling is the lacquered, curved countertop of the sushi bar. The main dining room's decor is less noteworthy but the chef's culinary skill is superb. The menu here features seasonal specialties. In the spring, for example, your seven or eight dishes may include *hotaru-ika* (baby squid that by law may be taken from Toyama Bay only in the spring) and *i-doko* (baby octopus) no larger than a thumbnail. *3F, Kanazawa Tokyu Hotel, 1-1 Korimbo, 2-chome, tel. 0762/31–2411. Reservations advised. Jacket and tie required. AE, DC, MC, V. Open 11–2 and 5–10. Expensive.*

★ **Miyoshian.** Excellent *bento* (box lunches) and fish and vegetable dinners have been served here for about 100 years in the renowned Kenrokuen Garden. *11-Kenroku-cho, tel. 0762/21–0127. Reservations advised. Jacket and tie required at dinner. AE, V. Open 11:30–9:30. Closed Tues. Moderate.*

Sennin. For a restaurant near the station, the Sennin is a lively, friendly izakaya with counter service or tatami-mat seating (you sit on the floor, but there is a well for your feet). An array of Kaga cooking is offered from succulent sweet shrimp to *kani* (crab) and vegetables served in steaming broth. The restaurant is located beyond the right side of Miyako Hotel in the basement of the Live One building—look for a plaque above the stairs reading "Kirin," because the restaurant's name is written in kanji. *2-13-4 Katamachi, tel. 0762/21–1700. No reservations. Dress: casual. No credit cards. Open noon–2:30 and 5–10. Moderate.*

Lodging

★ **Ryokan Asadaya.** This new, small, luxury ryokan is designed in a grand style that combines the luxury of modernity with classical simplicity. The antique furnishings and the carefully positioned scrolls and paintings establish a pleasing harmony. There is no ferro-concrete or plastic here. *23 Jukken-machi, Kanazawa, Ishikawa 920, tel. 0762/32–2228. 5 rooms. Facilities: superb regional cuisine served in the room or in the restaurant. AE. Very Expensive.*

★ **Ryokan Kincharyo.** This small picture-postcard Japanese inn with six small houses on an incline overlooks the Saigawa River. Prime ministers and princes have slept here, and guests need references in order to stay here. The Kaga cooking is superb, featuring regional fresh fish and vegetables. *1 Teramachi, Kanazawa, Ishikawa 920, tel. 0762/43–2121. AE. Very Expensive.*

ANA Kanazawa. After opening in early summer 1990, this new member of the ANA chain has established itself as the swankest and most expensive hotel in the proximity of JR Kanazawa Station. The building has a moon-shaped tower, an expansive lobby with waterfall and pond, and the hotel has more than its share of marble glitter. It is within a block of the JR station and a 10-minute taxi ride from Kanazawa's center. Guest rooms are remarkably soothing. Soft beige wallpaper, fabrics, and furnishings give a restful ambience and the L-shape rooms are a pleasant change from the usual box-like shape of most Japanese hotel rooms. The staff, most of whom speak English, go out of their way to help foreign guests. Of the several restaurants, the penthouse Teppanyaki offers succulent grills with a panoramic view of the city, while the Unkai restaurant offers kaiseki dinners with excellent sashimi and a view of a miniature version of Kanazawa's renowned Kenrokuen garden. *16-3, Showa-cho, Kanazawa, Ishikawa 920, tel. 0762/24–6111, fax 0762/24–6100. 255 rooms. Facilities: Chinese, Japanese, and Western restaurants; coffee shop, shopping arcade, fitness center, parking. AE, DC, MC, V. Expensive–Very Expensive.*

Holiday Inn Kanazawa. Standing in the shadow of the ANA hotel on the other side of the station plaza, this modern redbrick facility lacks the character of the city, as do most of the contemporary hotels. On the other hand, it has a fresh, smart lobby with a book stand, and the guest rooms have good-size American beds, a rare find, especially in single rooms. As an added benefit, coffee refills are free in the coffee lounge, instead of the usual ¥400 plus per cup. Many of the staff speak some English. *1-10 Horikawacho, Kanazawa, Ishikawa 920, tel. 0762/23–1111, fax 0792/23–1110. 169 Western-style rooms. Facilities: shops, coffee shop, Japanese and Western restaurant, lounge on 12th floor. AE, DC, MC, V. Expensive.*

★ **Kanazawa New Grand Hotel.** English is spoken at this large, established international hotel in the center of the city. The service is excellent, and its location across from the Oyama Shrine is another plus. Watching the sunset is especially pleasant from the hotel's sky lounge or from the adjacent Sky Restaurant Roi, which features French nouvelle cuisine, possibly the best of its kind in Kanazawa. Guest rooms are done in soft colors and are reasonably spacious. *1-50, Takaokamachi, Kanazawa, Ishika-*

wa 920, tel. 0762/33–1311, fax 0762/33–1591. 109 rooms, mostly Western style. Facilities: Continental, Japanese, and Chinese restaurants; coffee shop, sky lounge shops. AE, DC, MC, V. Expensive.

Kanazawa Tokyu Hotel. Conveniently located in the heart of town, this modern hotel has a spacious lobby on the second floor and a pleasant coffee shop. Guest rooms are standard and efficient, with pale cream walls. Kincharyo is a superb Japanese restaurant. The Schloss Restaurant on the 16th floor serves French cuisine and offers a skyline view. *1-1 Korimbo 2-chome, Kanazawa, Ishikawa 920, tel. 0762/31–2411, fax 0762/63–0154. 120 rooms. Facilities: 3 restaurants, shops, meeting rooms. AE, DC, MC, V. Expensive.*

Ryokan Miyabo. The rooms at this traditional Japanese inn open onto beautiful gardens. Once the teahouse of Kanazawa's first mayor, the ryokan is peaceful, authentic, and charming, though it could use a slight sprucing up. *3 Shimo-Kakinokibatake, Kanazawa, Ishikawa 920, tel. 0762/31–4228, fax 0762/32–0608. 39 Japanese-style rooms. Meals usually included. AE, V. Expensive.*

Garden Hotel Kanazawa. Across from the station, this is a good alternative business hotel to the Kanazawa Station Hotel. Recently spruced up, and with a cheerful, polite staff, the hotel is equally good, though with higher prices (¥5,800 for a single and ¥10,000 for a small double). The hotel also has a small, but comfortable and friendly lounge for breakfast or light snacks. *2–16–16, Hon-machi, Kanazawa, Ishikawa 920, tel. 0762/63–3333, fax 0762/63–7761. 54 rooms. Facilities: restaurant, coffee shop. AE, V. Inexpensive–Moderate.*

Kanazawa Station Hotel. The rooms are not as coffin-like as they often are at inexpensive business hotels; hence, we rate it Kanazawa's best in this category. A three-minute walk from the station and across from the Holiday Inn, it is also convenient for the bus stop to downtown. There is a small comfortable lounge for tea, coffee, and drinks, and a room for breakfast. *18-8 Horikawacho, Kanazawa, Ishikawa 920, tel. 0762/23–2600, fax 0762/23–2607. 62 rooms. Facilities: Japanese restaurant, coffee lounge. AE, DC, MC, V. Inexpensive.*

Minshuku Toyo. This very small private house is just across the wooden pedestrian bridge, Ume-no-hashi, in the Eastern Pleasure Quarter (Higashiyama). Rooms are small, but the price is only ¥3,800 for a single and ¥4,800 for a double, and guests are not required to take their meals at the inn. There is a small restaurant next door and an excellent traditional Japanese restaurant, the Seifuso, across the street, but a kaiseki dinner there will exceed ¥10,000 per person. *1–18–19, Higashiyama, Kanazawa, Ishikawa 920, tel. 0762/52–9020. 5 rooms, none with private bath. Take the JR bus from the station to Higashi-hashi Bridge. No credit cards. Inexpensive.*

Yogetsu. This small minshuku is in a 100-year-old geisha house in the Eastern Pleasure Quarter. With aged wood and beams, it's a delightful home. The guest rooms are small, but owner Temeko Ishitata is a welcoming hostess and offers rooms with out meals (¥4,500), with breakfast (¥5,000), and with breakfast and dinner (¥6,000). *1-13-22 Higashiyama, Kanazawa, Ishikawa 920, tel. 0762/52–0497. 5 rooms. Facilities: Japanese breakfast and dinner usually included. Inexpensive.*

Karuizawa

Lodging **Hotel Kayu Kajima-no-Mori.** An exclusive resort, this hotel is tastefully furnished with Japanese handicrafts and antiques. The buildings are surrounded by forest, which heightens the mood of tranquillity. *Hanareyama, Karuizawa-machi, Nagano Prefecture 389–01, tel. 0267/42–3535. 50 rooms. Facilities: golf course, tennis courts, Western/Japanese restaurant. AE, DC, V. Very Expensive.*

★ **Karuizawa Prince Hotel.** Though the Prince is a large resort hotel, it is quiet and relaxing. Because of its popularity, reservations need to be made well in advance for the summer season. In winter, the neighboring mountain serves as a modest ski-slope for the hotel. *Karuizawa, Karuizawa-machi, Kitasaku-gun, Nagano Prefecture 389–01, tel. 0267/42–8111, fax 0267/42–7139. 240 rooms, mostly Western style. Facilities: golf, pool, horseback riding. Western and Japanese restaurants. AE, MC, V. Expensive; Very Expensive during July and Aug.*

Pensione Grasshopper. Among the guest houses in the area, the Grasshopper has friendly hospitality, Western beds (great views of Mount Asama from room 208), and a mix of Japanese and Western fare. The owner, Mrs. Kayo Iwasaki, speaks English. The house is in the suburbs, and the management will transport you to and from the station. *5410 Karyada, Karuizawa, Kitasaku-gun, Nagano 389-01, tel. 0267/46–1333. 10 rooms, none with private bath. Facilities: dining room. MC, V. Inexpensive.*

Kiso Valley

Lodging Many small Japanese inns are located in the area, though reservations are strongly advised, especially during weekends. The **Magome Tourist Information Office** (tel. 0264/59–2336) and the **Tsumago Tourist Information Office** (tel. 0264/57–3123) will make these reservations for you. Telephone between 9 and 5. Magome's office is closed Sundays December–March; Tsumago's office closes January 1–3.

One particularly good minshuku is the **Onyado Daikichi,** Tsumago, Minamo Kisomachi (Kiso-gun 399–54, tel. 0264/57–2595, fax 0274/57–2209; ¥6,500 per person). All six tatami rooms face the valley, the wood bath is shared, the dinners, making good use of the local exotic specialties (horse sashimi, fried grasshoppers, and mountain vegetables), are excellent, and Nobaka-san (the lady of the house) in her limited English makes foreigners feel very welcome. For surroundings and service that match Tsumago's traditional atmosphere, check in at **Matsushiro Ryokan** (Tsumago, Nagiso-machi, Kiso-gun, Nagano-ken, tel. 0264/57–3022; ¥9,000–¥12,000 per person), which has been operating as a guest house for 140 years. Ten large tatami rooms share a single bath and four pit toilets that are immaculately clean. Dinner is a delicious feast served in your room. The Japanese breakfast is also satisfying. No one speaks English here, but the tourist office will make you a reservation.

Matsumoto

Dining **Kura.** For an informal evening dining on feathery tempura or sushi from the sea of Japan, Kura is well priced. In an old moated house—the moat smells a bit—in the center of town, husband and wife run the cashier's desk while the two waitresses bring trays of food from the kitchen to a high ceilinged, tavernlike dining room. There are tables and counter service and shabu shabu for those who like to cook their food. *Ko Kudesai (behind the Parco department store), tel. 0263/33-6444. No reservations. Dress: casual. No credit cards. Moderate.*

Hachimen. Named after a local resistance hero of the Shogunate era, this bar is for the young or young at heart. Diners sit on stools at three counter areas, eating, talking, and drinking. Most of the Japanese food is grilled, but noodles and a hotpot are offered as well. It is in the central shopping area, down a small alley that has a Mister Donut on the corner. *Ise-machi-dori, tel. 0263/35-3832. No reservations. Dress: casual. No credit cards. Inexpensive.*

Lodging

Hotel Buena Vista. Matsumoto's newest and most expensive hotel opened in 1992. It has a large Spartan marble lobby; a coffee lounge; and Chinese, sushi, kaiseki, and teranaki restaurants as well as a French restaurant with a sky lounge bar. The rooms are decorated in pastels. Singles snugly fit a small double bed; standard double and twin-bedded rooms have enough space for a table and easy chairs. Corner rooms are the choice at ¥20,000. *1-2-1, Honjyo, Matsumoto 390, tel. 0263/37-0111, fax 0263/37-0666. 127 Western-style rooms. Facilities: 5 restaurants, coffee lounge, business center, disco, banquet and meeting rooms, parking. AE, DC, MC, V. Expensive.*

Matsumoto Tokyu. The convenience of this hotel across from the JR train station makes it a good choice as a functional base in Matsumoto. The rooms are not much larger than those of a typical business hotel, so you may want to upgrade yours. But beware, while the small doubles fall in the moderate price range, the deluxe twin-bed rooms with a separate mirror and sink outside the bathroom climb to the Very Expensive category. *1-2-37 Fukashi, Matsumoto 390, tel. 0263/36-0109, fax 0263/36-0883. 99 Western-style rooms. Facilities: dining rooms serving Japanese and Western food. AE, V. Moderate–Expensive.*

Hotel New Station. Like all business-class hotels, the single rooms are tiny, but the furniture that can fit into the rooms is worn wood rather than plastic. The hotel offers good value and has at least some character. The smallest singles are ¥5,000; the deluxe twin for ¥12,000 is actually a full-sized room. The staff is friendly and cheerful. The location is a minute from the station in the direction of the castle and close to many restaurants, but you should be sure to have one meal in the hotel. In the rock pool just inside the door are iwana, a freshwater fish special to the region with a taste akin to smoked salmon, which quicky become sashimi or are grilled or boiled in sake. (If this hotel is fully booked, the Mount Hotel is an adequate, slightly more expensive hotel at the back of the JR station, tel. 0263/35-6480.) *1-1-11 Chuo, Matsumoto 390, tel. 0263/35-3850, fax 02361/83-6301. 103 rooms. Facilities: Japanese restaurant, conference rooms. AE, V. Inexpensive–Moderate.*

Enjyo Bekkan. This small, concrete inn is just outside Matsumoto in the spa village of Utsukushigahara Onsen, reached by a 20-minute bus ride from the Matsumoto JR station to the Utsukushigahara bus terminal. The tatami rooms don't leave much room after your futon is laid out, but the inn is neat and clean. Some English is spoken. Only a few rooms have private bath. *110 Utsukushigahara Onsen, Satoyamabe-ku, Matsumoto City, Nagano 390–02, tel. 0263/33–7233, fax 0263/36–2084. 19 rooms (8 with bath). Facilities: a small dining room serving only Japanese food. AE, MC, V. Inexpensive.*

Nagano

Lodging ★

Hotel Fujiya. This establishment appears the same today as it was 300 years ago. The age-darkened wood and creaking floors transport guests back to the day when feudal lords stayed here while making pilgrimages to Zenkoji. The tatami guest rooms vary from small (¥15,000 for two, including meals) to large. Consider the royal suite (¥30,000 for two, including meals); it has three rooms with sliding doors onto an old, slightly overgrown garden. The furnishings are priceless antiques and scrolls. The hotel also has a deep, indulgent Japanese bath. This inn is not smart or sophisticated, but it is wonderfully old-fashioned. No English is spoken, but the management loves its inn and will respect foreigners who show their appreciation. *Central Avenue, Nagano City 380, tel. 0262/32–1241, fax 0262/32–1243. 30 rooms. AE. Moderate–Very Expensive.*

Nagano Royal Hotel. Across from the JR station, this new hotel sparkles with crisp efficiency. Guests enter the marble lobby at street level and take the escalator up to the first floor reception area and tea lounge. On the 10th floor, the Sky Bar offers seats with a view out to the city below. A similar view is enjoyed by the Lambert restaurant, which serves Continental French fare. A Japanese restaurant is on the second floor. A coffee table and two easy chairs are squeezed into the compact neat guest rooms, which are decorated with subdued colors. *1-28-3 Minami Chitose, Nagano 380, tel. 0262/28–2222, fax 0262/28–2244. 114 rooms. Facilities: Japanese and French restaurants, coffee shop, bar. AE, DC, MC, V. Moderate.*

Niigata

Dining

Ishihawa. Located only two blocks from the station (on the left just before the second traffic light as you head downtown), this restaurant is run by a charming lady, who will guide you through the menu in her best English. You can settle for tempura or try the more interesting local dishes, such as *wappaneshi* (steamed rice with fish and vegetables), or fresh fish caught in the Sea of Japan. Seating is either at the counter or in a raised alcove on tatami matting. Ishihawa is one flight down from the street—look for the several signs for a barber shop, which is also in the building's basement. *1B, 4-19 Kawabata-cho, tel. 0252/45–2602. No reservations. Dress: casual. DC, V. Inexpensive–Moderate.*

Lodging ★

Onaya Ryokan. This is a classic ryokan, a joy to stay in, with excellent food and service. The guest rooms look over a tranquil Japanese garden. All rooms have a private toilet, but the Japanese bath is separate and prepared for guests individually. Recent refurbishings have made this the most fashionable ryokan in the city. No English is spoken, and guests should know a few words of Japanese. *981 Furamachi-dori, Niigata 951, tel. 0252/29–2951. 24 Japanese-style rooms. AE. Very Expensive.*

Okura Hotel Niigata. A modern, sparkling hotel on the Shinano River, across the bridge from the station, the Okura is the newest addition to Niigata's international hotels. The service is first-class, and the rooms are tastefully decorated, with rich-colored bedspreads contrasting with the pastel walls. For those who like to read or work at the hotel, the Okura is one of few places that has ample lighting in its rooms. Because of the view, rooms overlooking the Shinano River are the best. The formal French restaurant in the penthouse looks down on the city lights, and over the Japan Sea to Sado Island. The Japanese restaurant has superb kaiseki dinners, while the Chinese restaurant is nothing special. Breakfast and lighter meals are served in the Grill Room. (If you cannot get reservations here, the next choice is the Hotel Niigata, tel. 0252/45–3331, a 15-min. walk from the station.) *6-53 Kawabata-cho, Niigata 951, tel. 0252/24–6111, fax 025/225–7060. 300 rooms, mostly Western style. Facilities: 4 restaurants (2 European, 1 Japanese, 1 Chinese), business center, shopping arcade. AE, DC, MC, V. Moderate–Expensive.*

Niigata Toei Hotel. For an inexpensive business hotel conveniently located a block and a half from the station, this ranks the best. The 9th floor has two restaurants and a bar for evening entertainment. *1-6, 2 Benten, Niigata 950, tel. 025/244–7101, fax 025/241–8485. 90 rooms. Facilities: 2 restaurants, banquet/conference rooms. AE, D, MC, V. Moderate.*

Sado Island

Lodging Hotel reservations can be made at the information counters of Sado Kisen ship company at Niigata Port or Ryotsu Port.

Sado Royal Hotel Mancho. This is the best hotel on Sado's west coast. The establishment caters mostly to Japanese tourists, but the staff makes the few Westerners who come by feel welcome; however, English is not spoken. *58 Shimoto, Aikawa, tel. 0259/74–3221. 87 rooms. Facilities: Japanese dining, but a few Western dishes are offered. DC, V. Expensive.*

★ **Sado Seaside Hotel.** Located 20 minutes by foot from the Ryotsu Port, this is more a friendly inn than a hotel. If you telephone before you catch the ferry from Niigata, the owner will meet you at the dock. He'll be carrying a green Seaside Hotel flag. *80 Sumiyoshi, Ryotsu City, Niigata 952, tel. 0259/27–7211. 14 Japanese-style rooms, not all with private bath. Facilities: Japanese meals available, laundry room, Japanese baths. AE. Inexpensive.*

Takayama

Dining ★ **Suzaki.** This is Takayama's number one restaurant for *kaiseki* cuisine served in traditional style with kimono-clad waitresses. Make a point of trying a meal prepared with wild plants from the Hida mountains and salted river fish. Each dish is exquisitively presented on delicate chinaware. *4-14 Sinmei, tel. 0577/32–0023. Reservations advised. Jacket and tie required. AE, V. Open lunch and dinner. Expensive.*

★ **Kakusho.** The most established restaurant for Takayama's well-known *shojin-ryori*, a vegetarian meal that consists of various mountain plants, Kakusho is located on the far side of the Miyagawa River from the railway station and near the Tenshoji Temple. There is no restaurant sign in English; look for a small building with a courtyard patio diagonally across from a car park. Meals here are both nourishing and tasty—

often a local bean paste is used in the cooking to add extra flavor. If the freshwater fish *ayu* is on the menu, be sure to try it. Owner Sumitake-san will happily help you with the menu; her English is delightful. *2 Babacho Rd., tel. 0577/32-0174. Reservations advised. Jacket and tie required. AE, V. Open lunch and dinner. Moderate–Expensive.*

Susuya. Across Kokobunji-dori from the Sogo Palace hotel is this delightful small Japanese restaurant in a traditional Hida-style house. Owned by the same family for generations, the timbered restaurant is small and intimate. The traditional specialty is *sansai-ryori,* with mountain plants and freshly caught river fish, such as ayu, grilled with soy sauce. It's superb. *24 Hanakawa, tel. 0577/32-2484. Reservations advised. Dress: casual. AE, V. Open lunch and dinner. Moderate.*

Lodging The **Hida Tourist Information Office** (tel. 0577/32-5328), just in front of the train station, will help you find accommodations, both in town and in the surrounding mountains. This is one of the most helpful information offices in Japan.

★ **Ryokan Kinkikan.** This splendid traditional Japanese inn is Takayama's top place to stay. It is also very small, and reservations are essential. Antique Hida furniture is used throughout the inn and makes classic Japan come alive. *48 Asahicho, Takayama 506 (located in the center of town, left off Kokobunji-dori and 2 blocks from the river), tel. 0577/32-3131. 9 Japanese-style rooms. AE. Very Expensive.*

★ **Ryokan Hishuya.** For the genuine atmosphere of a Japanese inn, with delicately served meals and refined furnishings, stay at this ryokan. Quiet and contemplative, it is away from Takayama and close to Hida-no-sato Village. *2581 Kami-Okamotocho, Takayama 506, tel. 0577/33-4001. 16 Japanese-style rooms. AE, MC. Expensive.*

★ **Hida Plaza Hotel.** This is the best international-style hotel in town. Although its newer, modern wing is not attractive, the rooms in that part of the hotel are larger. In terms of value, all the rooms are a cut above most Japanese hotels. In the older structure, the traditional Hida ambience is present, particularly in the old, exposed beams and wide-plank floors of the Japanese restaurant. The Hida plaza is a three-minute walk from the train station and a 10-minute walk from downtown. *2-60 Hanaokacho, Takayama 506, tel. 0577/33-4600. Fax 0577/33-4602. 152 Western-style rooms. Facilities: Japanese and Continental restaurants, coffee shop, disco, karaoke bar, indoor pool, health center, sauna, mineral baths, shopping arcade. AE, DC, MC, V. Moderate–Expensive.*

Honjin Hiranoya. There are two parts to this hotel, Honkan (old) Hiranoya and Shinkan (new) Hiranoya, in two buildings on the same street, across from one another. Though both have the same name and ownership, they were built three centuries apart. Years ago the old structure was a samurai house; now it is a friendly ryokan with lots of aged charm, though short on elegance. The rooms vary from Western-style to tatami-style. The Shinkan Hiranoya has modern tatami rooms and a superb multiperson bath on the seventh floor with huge windows overlooking the Hida Mountains. Meals are included. *1-chome, Honmachi, Takayama 506, tel. 0577/34-1234. 19 rooms in the old building, 27 rooms in the new. Facilities: restaurant. AE, DC, MC, V. Moderate.*

Sogo Palace. Conveniently located in the center of Takayama, this is a fairly modern Japanese inn. It may not have the charm of the older, traditional inns, but it caters to and understands the international traveler. Service is extremely friendly and helpful, which adds to the pleasure of this hotel. *54 Suehirocho, Takayama 506, tel. 0577/33-5000. 20 Japanese-style and 7 Western-style rooms. V. Moderate.*

★ **Yamaku.** This inn offers one of the best values in town. Though listed as a minshuku, Yanaku is more like a small, privately run Japanese-style hotel. The building is old, and cozy nooks in the lobby with chairs and coffee tables serve as small lounges. The tatami guest rooms are typically small, but the ample closets help add space. Room #33 is the quietest. The public baths are large and are given the kind of social importance found in an onsen—in the men's bath, a water wheel slowly turns to hypnotize you as you soak. Dinner hours are more flexible than those at the typical minshuku: The food is good, though not extraordinary. The inn is on the other side of town from the Takayama JR station (a 20-min. walk). *58, Tenshojimachi, Takayama 506, tel. 0577/32-3756. 22 rooms, none with private bath. Facilities: Japanese meals served in dining room, souvenir shop. Inexpensive–Moderate.*

Minshuku Sosuke. Although this concrete building is a private home, it feels more like a boarding house for travelers, both Japanese and Western. Mama-san rules with a firm hand and speaks essential English. Only after dinner has been served does she loosen up for a chat. Rooms are small, either four tatami or six tatami mats, and have electric (rather than kerosene) heaters. The shared toilets are kept spotless. The food here is average, but since meals are taken at long tables (tatami seating), guests have the opportunity to meet each other. Although this minshuku is located 15 minutes from the town's center, the room rate makes it a good value. To get there, turn right from JR Takayama station, then right at the first bridge, and walk seven minutes. The minshuku is opposite the huge and ugly Green Hotel. *1-64, Okamoto-cho, Takayama 506, tel. 0577/32-0818. 14 rooms (none with private bath). Meals included. Facilities: dining room. AE, V. Inexpensive.*

Yudanaka Onsen

Lodging **Uotoshi Ryokan.** This small Japanese inn has only eight tatami rooms, which share a delightful *hinoki* (Japanese bath tub made from cypress) filled with hot thermal spring waters to ease your weary traveler muscles. Western food is not served, but don't miss the dinners: They are a treat of mountain vegetables and fresh seafood from the Japan Sea. The owners can arrange for you to try Japanese archery. To reach Yudanaka Onsen, take the 40-minute train ride on the Nagano Dentetsu Railway from Nagano. The inn is a seven-minute walk from Yudanaka Station. The owners will also collect you, for a fee, from the JR Nagano Station. *2563, Sano, Yamanouchi-machi, Shimo-Takai-gun, 381-04 Nagano, tel. 0269/33-1215, fax 0269/33-0074. 8 Japanese-style rooms. Facilities: Restaurant. AE, V. Inexpensive.*

7 Kyoto

By Nigel Fisher

Kyoto's history is full of contradictions: famine and prosperity, war and peace, calamity and tranquillity. Although the city was Japan's capital for more than 10 centuries, the real center of political power was often somewhere else, such as in Kamakura (1192–1333) and in Edo (1603–1868). Such was Kyoto's decline in the 17th and 18th centuries that, when the power of the government was returned from the shoguns to the emperor, he moved his capital and imperial court to Edo, renaming it Tokyo. Though that move may have pained the Kyoto residents, it actually saved the city from destruction. While most major cities in Japan were flattened by World War II bombs, Kyoto survived; it is now the sixth largest city in Japan.

Until 710, Japan's capital was moved to a new location with the succession of each new emperor. This continuous movement started to become rather expensive as the size of the court and the number of administrators grew, so Nara was chosen as the permanent capital. It did not last long as the capital. Buddhists rallied for, and achieved, tremendous political power. In the effort to thwart them, Emperor Kammu moved the capital in 784 to Nagaoka; the Buddhists were left behind in their elaborate temples. Within 10 years, however, Kammu decided that Kyoto (then called Uda) was better suited for his capital. Poets were asked to compose verse about Uda and invariably they included the phrase Heian-kyo, meaning "Capital of Peace," which no doubt reflected the hope and desire of the time.

For 1,074 years, Kyoto remained the capital, though at times only in name. From 794 to the end of the 12th century, the city flourished under imperial rule. One might say that this was the time when Japan's culture started to become independent of Chinese influences and began to develop its unique characteristics. Unfortunately, the use of wood for construction, coupled with Japan's two primordial enemies, fire and earthquakes, have destroyed all the buildings from this era, except the Byodoin Temple in Uji. The short life span of a building in the 11th century is exemplified by the Imperial Palace, which burned down 14 times in a 122-year period. As if natural disasters were not enough, imperial power waned in the 12th century. Then came a period of rule by the shoguns, but each shogun's rule was tenuous; by the 15th century, civil wars tore the country apart. Many of Kyoto's buildings were destroyed or looted, especially during the Onin Civil War.

The decade of the Onin Civil War (1467–1477) was a dispute between two feudal lords, Yamana and Hosokawa, over who should be the shogun's successor. The dispute was devastating for Kyoto. Yamana camped in the western part of the city with 90,000 troops, and Hosokawa settled in the eastern part with 100,000 troops; central Kyoto was the battlefield.

Not until the end of the 16th century, when Japan was welded by the might of Nobunaga Oda and Hideyoshi Toyotomi, did Japan settle down. This period was soon followed by the usurpation of power by Ieyasu Tokugawa, who began the dynasty of the Tokugawa Shogunate that lasted for the next 264 years, during which time the government's power was in Edo. However, Kyoto did remain the imperial capital, and the first three Tokugawa shoguns paid homage to it. Old temples were restored, and new villas were built. Much of what one sees in Kyoto was built or rebuilt at this time (the first half of the 17th century) to legitimize the rule of the Tokugawa Shogunate.

Steeped in history and tradition, Kyoto has in many ways been the cradle of Japanese culture, especially with its courtly aesthetic pastimes, such as moon-viewing parties, and tea ceremonies. A stroll through Kyoto today is a walk through 11 centuries of Japanese history. Yet this city has been swept into the modern industrialized world with the rest of Japan. Glass-plate windows, held in place by girders and ferroconcrete, dominate central Kyoto. Elderly women, however, continue to wear kimonos as they make their way slowly along the canal walkways. Geishas still entertain, albeit at prices out of reach for most of us. Sixteen hundred temples and several hundred shrines surround central Kyoto. Rather a lot to see, to say the least. Our exploration of Kyoto will be selective. Even so, the exploration will be expensive. With attractions charging ¥400 to ¥500 for admission, in three days of visiting temples and museums you can easily part with $100 per person.

Essential Information

Festivals and Seasonal Events

Many of the special celebrations of Kyoto are associated with the changing of the seasons. Most are free of charge and attract thousands of visitors as well as locals. Double-check with your hotel concierge or the Kyoto Tourist Information Center for current dates and times. For the big three festivals of Kyoto, the Gion, Jidai, and Aoi festivals, hotel bookings should be made well in advance.

May 15. The **Aoi Festival,** also known as the Hollyhock Festival, is the first of Kyoto's three most popular celebrations. Dating back to the 6th century, an "imperial" procession of 300 courtiers starts from the Imperial Palace and makes its way to Shimogamo Shrine to pray for the prosperity of the city. Today's participants are local Kyotoites.

July 16–17. The **Gion Festival,** which dates back to the 9th century, is perhaps Kyoto's most popular festival. Twenty-nine huge floats sail along downtown streets and make their way to the Yasaka Jinja Shrine to thank the gods for protection from a pestilence that once ravaged the city.

Aug. 16. Daimonji Gozan Okuribi features huge bonfires that form Chinese characters on five of the mountains that surround Kyoto. The most famous is the "Dai," meaning big, on the side of Mt. Daimonji in the eastern district of Kyoto. Dress in a cool yukata (cotton robe) and walk down to the banks of the Kamogawa River to view this spectacular summer sight, or catch all five fires from the rooftop of your hotel downtown.

Oct. 22. Jidai Festival, the Festival of Eras, features a colorful costume procession of fashions from the 8th through 19th centuries. The procession begins at the Imperial Palace and winds up at Heian Jingu Shrine. More than 2,000 Kyotoites voluntarily participate in this festival, which dates back to 1895.

Oct. 22. For the **Kurama Fire Festival** at the Kurama Shrine, a roaring bonfire and rowdy portable shrine procession makes its way through the narrow streets of the small village in the northern suburbs of Kyoto. If you catch a spark, it is believed to bring good luck.

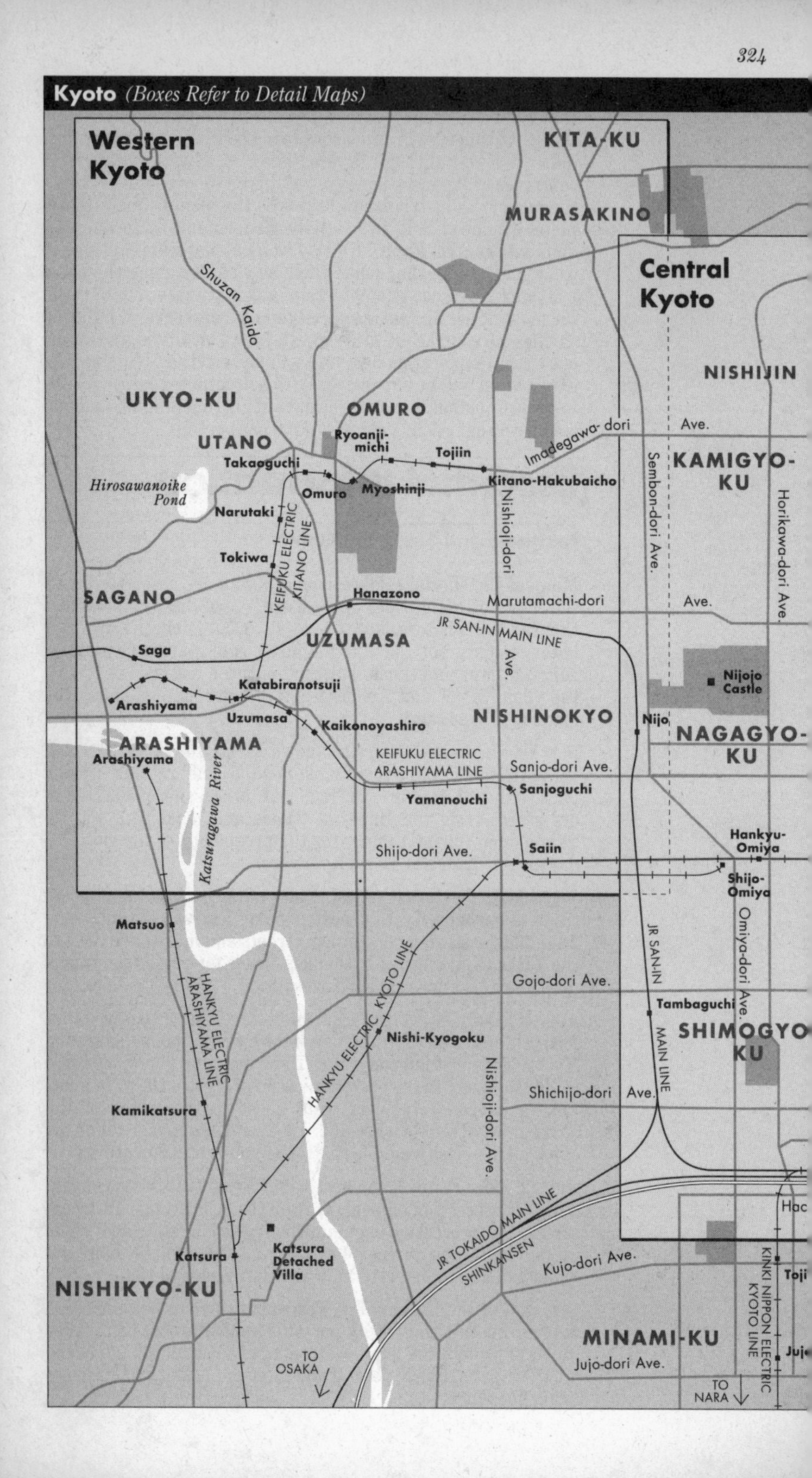
Kyoto (Boxes Refer to Detail Maps)
Western Kyoto
Central Kyoto
KITA-KU
MURASAKINO
NISHIJIN
UKYO-KU
OMURO
UTANO
KAMIGYO-KU
SAGANO
UZUMASA
NISHINOKYO
NAGAGYO-KU
ARASHIYAMA
SHIMOGYO KU
NISHIKYO-KU
MINAMI-KU
Shuzan Kaido
Hirosawanoike Pond
Ryoanji-michi
Takaoguchi
Tojiin
Omuro
Myoshinji
Kitano-Hakubaicho
Narutaki
Tokiwa
Hanazono
Saga
Katabiranotsuji
Arashiyama
Uzumasa
Kaikonoyashiro
Nijo
Nijojo Castle
Yamanouchi
Sanjoguchi
Saiin
Hankyu-Omiya
Shijo-Omiya
Matsuo
Tambaguchi
Nishi-Kyogoku
Kamikatsura
Katsura
Katsura Detached Villa
Toji
Imadegawa-dori Ave.
Sembon-dori Ave.
Horikawa-dori Ave.
Nishioji-dori Ave.
Marutamachi-dori Ave.
Sanjo-dori Ave.
Shijo-dori Ave.
Gojo-dori Ave.
Shichijo-dori Ave.
Omiya-dori Ave.
Kujo-dori Ave.
Jujo-dori Ave.
KEIFUKU ELECTRIC KITANO LINE
JR SAN-IN MAIN LINE
KEIFUKU ELECTRIC ARASHIYAMA LINE
Katsuragawa River
HANKYU ELECTRIC ARASHIYAMA LINE
HANKYU ELECTRIC KYOTO LINE
JR TOKAIDO MAIN LINE
SHINKANSEN
KINKI NIPPON ELECTRIC KYOTO LINE
TO OSAKA
TO NARA

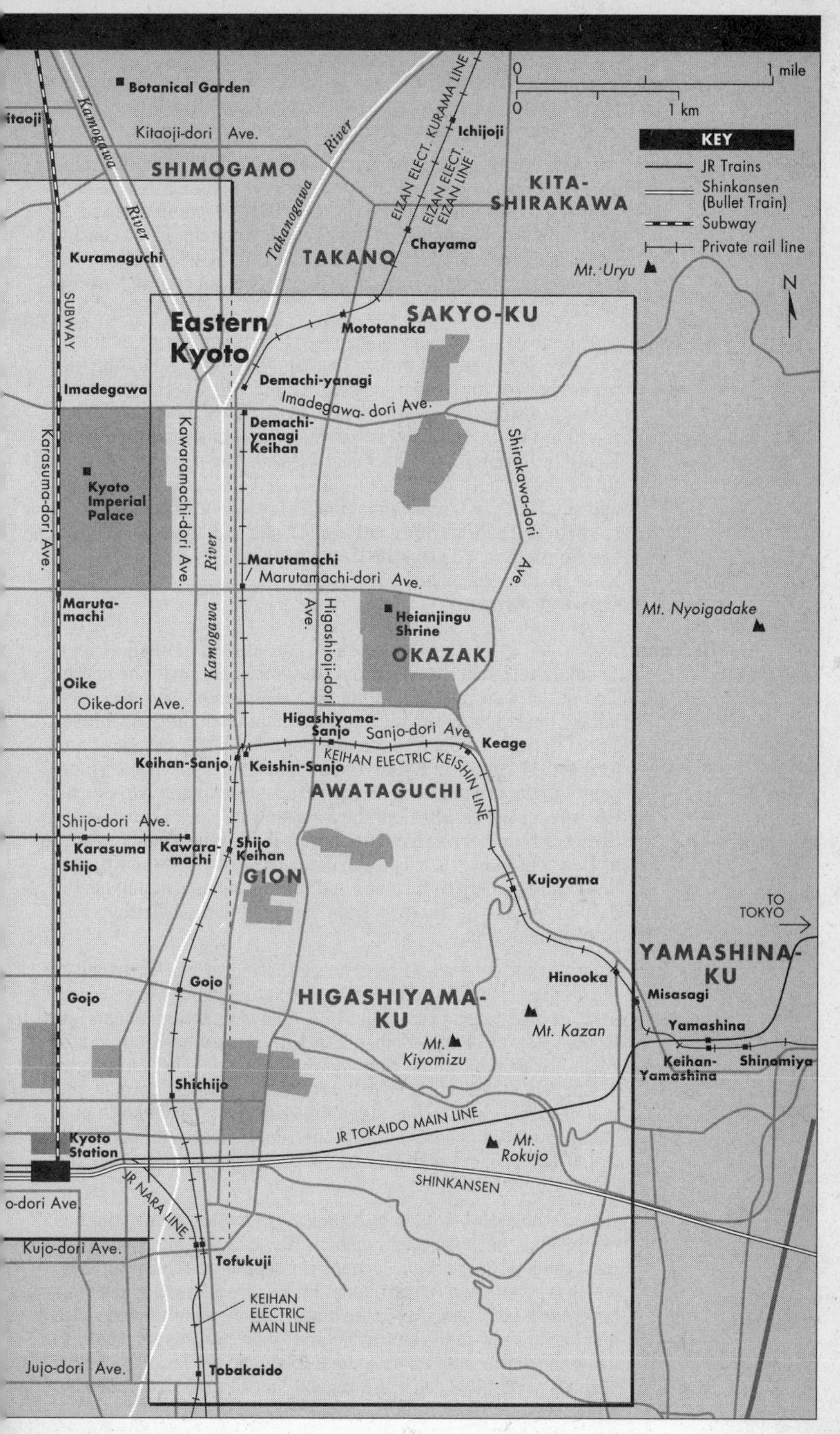

Eastern Kyoto
KEY
JR Trains
Shinkansen (Bullet Train)
Subway
Private rail line
0 1 mile
0 1 km
N
Botanical Garden
Kitaoji
Kitaoji-dori Ave.
Kamogawa River
SHIMOGAMO
Takanogawa River
EIZAN ELECT. KURAMA LINE
EIZAN ELECT. EIZAN LINE
Ichijoji
KITA-SHIRAKAWA
Chayama
TAKANO
Kuramaguchi
Mt. Uryu
SUBWAY
SAKYO-KU
Mototanaka
Demachi-yanagi
Imadegawa
Imadegawa-dori Ave.
Demachi-yanagi Keihan
Shirakawa-dori Ave.
Karasuma-dori Ave.
Kawaramachi-dori Ave.
Kyoto Imperial Palace
Marutamachi
Marutamachi-dori Ave.
Maruta-machi
Higashioji-dori Ave.
Heianjingu Shrine
Mt. Nyoigadake
OKAZAKI
Oike
Oike-dori Ave.
Higashiyama-Sanjo
Sanjo-dori Ave.
Keage
Keihan-Sanjo
Keishin-Sanjo
KEIHAN ELECTRIC KEISHIN LINE
AWATAGUCHI
Shijo-dori Ave.
Karasuma
Shijo
Kawara-machi
Shijo Keihan
GION
Kujoyama
TO TOKYO
YAMASHINA-KU
Hinooka
Misasagi
Gojo
HIGASHIYAMA-KU
Mt. Kazan
Yamashina
Mt. Kiyomizu
Keihan-Yamashina
Shinomiya
Shichijo
JR TOKAIDO MAIN LINE
Kyoto Station
Mt. Rokujo
SHINKANSEN
JR NARA LINE
o-dori Ave.
Kujo-dori Ave.
Tofukuji
KEIHAN ELECTRIC MAIN LINE
Jujo-dori Ave.
Tobakaido

Arriving and Departing

By Plane The closest airport to Kyoto is the Osaka International Airport, about an hour away by bus from Kyoto Station. Flights from Tokyo to Osaka are frequent and take 70 minutes.

Between the Airport and Center City Airport buses depart for Kyoto approximately every 20 minutes, 7:45 AM–9:30 PM, and drop passengers at nine hotels, as well as at Kyoto Station. The bus trip takes 55 to 90 minutes and costs ¥890 or ¥950, depending on the Kyoto destination. If you consider the distance involved and the high cost, it does not make sense to take a taxi from the airport to Kyoto as it can run well over ¥ 10,000.

By Train Frequent daily Shinkansen express trains run between Tokyo and Kyoto (2 hrs., 40 min.). The one-way fare, including express charges for a reserved seat, is ¥12,970. JR train service between Osaka and Kyoto (30 min.) costs ¥530, one way. From the Shin-Osaka Station, you can take the Shinkansen and be in Kyoto in 15 minutes; tickets cost ¥2,250. You may use a Japan Rail Pass on both these trains. Two private lines, the Keihan and the Hankyu trains (40 min. each), are less expensive than the JR. The one-way fare between Osaka and Kyoto is ¥360 on the Keihan and ¥350 on the Hankyu train.

Getting Around

By Train Kyoto has a thirteen-station subway line that runs between Takeda Station in the south and Kitayama Station in the north. The entire run takes 20 minutes. Tickets must be purchased before boarding at the station's automatic vending machines. Fares depend on destination and begin at ¥180. Service runs 5:30 AM–11:30 PM. In Kyoto, the Keihan train from Osaka is now partly underground (from Shichijo to Demachi) and extends all the way up the east bank of the Kamogawa River to Imadegawa Street. From there a passage connects it with the Eizan Railway at Demachi-Yanagi station. The Eizan has two lines, the Kurama line running north to Kurama, and the Eizan line running northeast to Yase. The Hankyu train connects with the subway at Karasuma Station.

By Bus Kyoto has a network of bus routes that cover the entire city. Most of the city buses operate 7 AM–9 PM daily, but a few start as early as 5:30 AM and run until 11 PM. The main bus terminals are Kyoto Station, Sanjo-Keihan Station, Karasuma-Kitaoji, and Shijo-Karasuma Intersection. Many city buses do not have signs in English, so you will need to know the bus number. Because you will probably ride the bus at least once in Kyoto, try to pick up a bus map early in your stay from the Tourist Information Center (tel. 075/371–5649) at the Kyoto Tower Building, across from the JR Kyoto Station.

At each bus stop, a guidepost indicates the stop name, the bus route, and the bus-route number. Because the information at most guideposts is only in Japanese (except for the route number, which is given as an Arabic numeral), you are advised to ask your hotel clerk beforehand to write down your destination and route number to show to the bus driver and fellow passengers; this will allow the driver and others to help you if you get lost. You might also ask your hotel clerk beforehand how many stops your ride will take.

Within the city, the standard fare is ¥200, which you pay before leaving the bus; outside the city limits, the fare varies according to distance. Special one-day passes are available that are valid for unlimited rides on the subway, city buses, and private Kyoto bus lines, with restrictions on some routes. The passes cost ¥1,050 for adults and ¥530 for children under 12. Two-day passes for adults are ¥2,000, for children ¥1,050.

There is one local JR bus on which you can use a JR Rail Pass.

By Taxi Taxis are readily available in Kyoto. Fares for smaller-size cabs start at ¥530 for the first 2 km, with a cost of ¥90 for each additional 540 meters. Medium-size cabs have room for one more person and start at ¥540. The fare from Kyoto Station to various hotels is ¥1,000–¥1,500.

Important Addresses and Numbers

Tourist Information The Japan National Tourist Organization (JNTO) **Tourist Information Center** (TIC) is located in the Kyoto Tower Building, in front of the JR Kyoto Station (take the Karusama exit, on the opposite side from the Shinkansen tracks). *Karasuma-dori Higashi-Shiokojicho, Shimogyo-ku, tel. 075/371–5649. Open 9–5 weekdays; 9–noon Sat. Closed Sun. and national holidays.*

The JNTO Teletourist Service (tel. 075/361–2911) offers taped information on events in and around the city.

The **Kyoto City Government** operates a tourist information office. *Kyoto Kaikan, Okazaki, Sakyo-ku, tel. 075/752–0215. Open 8:30–5 weekdays, 8:30–noon Sat. Closed 2nd and 4th Sat. of the month, Sun. and national holidays.*

The Japan Travel-Phone, a nationwide telephone information system in English for visitors, is available 9–5 daily, year-round. It is run out of the same office as the TIC (*see above*). In Kyoto, tel. 075/371–5649. The call costs ¥10 for three minutes.

Consulates The nearest U.S., Canadian, and British consulates are located in Osaka (*see* Chapter 9).

Emergencies **Police,** tel. 110; **Ambulance,** tel. 119.

Doctors **Japan Baptist Hospital,** Kitashirakawa, Yamanomoto-cho, Sakyo-ku, tel. 075/781–5191.

Daini Sekijuji Byoin (2nd Red Cross Hospital) at Kamanza-dori, Marutamachi-agaru, Kamigyo-ku, tel. 075/231–5171; and **Daiichi Sekijuji** (Red Cross Hospital) at Higashiyama Hommachi, Higashiyama-ku, tel. 075/561–1121.

Sakabe Clinic (435 Yamamoto-cho, Gokomachi, Nijo Sagaru, Nakagyo-ku, tel. 075/231–1624) has 24-hour emergency facilities.

English-Language Bookstores **Maruzen Kyoto** is temporarily located at Gokomachi Nishiki Agaru Nakagyo-ku (tel. 075/241–2169), but by mid-1994, it should move back to the building at 296 Kawaramachi-dori, Nakagko-ku.

Izumiya Book Center (Avanti Bldg., 6F, south of Kyoto Station, Minami-ku, tel. 075/682–5031).

Kyoto Shoin (3F Kawaramachi, north of Shijo, Nakagyo-ku, tel. 075/221–1062).

Travel Agencies **Japan Travel Bureau** (Kyoto Eki-mae, Shiokoji Karasuma Higashi-iru, Shimogyo-ku, tel. 075/361–7241).

Japan Amenity Travel (International Hotel Kyoto lobby, tel. 075/222–0121).

Kintetsu Gray Line Tours Reservation Center (New Miyako Hotel, Minami-ku, tel. 075/691–0903).

Joe Okada Travel Service (Masugata Bldg., Teramachi-agaru Imadegawa, Kamigyo-ku, tel. 075/241–3716).

Guided Tours

Orientation Tours Half-day morning and afternoon deluxe motor-coach tours featuring different city highlights are offered daily by the **Japan Travel Bureau** (Kyoto Eki-mae, Shiokoji Karasuma Higashi-iru, Shimogyo-ku, tel. 075/361–7241). Tours are also given daily March–November by **Kintetsu Gray Line Tours** (New Miyako Hotel, Minami-ku, tel. 075/691–0903) and **Japan Amenity Travel** (International Hotel Kyoto lobby, tel. 075/222–0121, or the Kyoto Grand Hotel lobby, tel. 075/343–2304). Pickup service is provided at major hotels, and reservations can be made through travel agents or by calling the numbers above. A morning tour costs ¥5,000, and a full-day tour including lunch costs ¥10,600. An evening tour with dinner runs about ¥10,000.

Special-Interest Tours **Joe Okada Travel Service's** (3F Masugata Bldg., Teramachi-agaru Imadegawa, Kamigyo-ku, tel. 075/241–3716) samurai Joe Okada conducts special tours of Kyoto and arranges home visits for individuals and groups. Call Joe and he will tailor your tour to fit your interests and budget. Private tours are more expensive, so it's best to get together a group. Home visits also are arranged by the **Tourist Section, Department of Cultural Affairs and Tourism** (Kyoto City Government, Kyoto Kaikan, Okazaki, Sakyo-ku, Kyoto, tel. 075/752–0215).

Walking Tours The Japan National Tourist Organization publishes suggested walking routes, which offer maps and brief descriptions for five tours (ranging in length from about 40 min. to 80 min.). The walking-tour brochures are available from the JNTO's Tourist Information Center office at the Kyoto Tower Building in front of the Kyoto Station (tel. 075/371–5649). For its guests, the Kyoto Grand Hotel suggests three jogging and walking courses around the famous temples near that hotel.

Excursions Full- and half-day tours to Nara are offered by **Japan Travel Bureau** (tel. 075/361–7241), **Fujita Travel Service** (tel. 075/222–0121), and **Kintetsu Gray Line Tours** (tel. 075/691–0903). Pickup service is available at principal hotels. An afternoon tour to Nara costs about ¥6,500.

Personal Guides Contact **Japan Amenity Travel** (tel. 075/222–1111), **Joe Okada Travel Service** (tel. 075/241–3716), and **Inter Kyoto** (tel. 075/256–3685). **Volunteer Guides** are available free of charge through the Tourist Information Center (TIC), but arrangements must be made by visiting the TIC in person one day in advance (*see* Important Addresses and Numbers, *above*).

Exploring

Most of what interests the visitor is on the north side of Kyoto Railway Station. Let's think of this northern sector as three rectangular areas abutting each other, with their short south sides running along the north side of the railway tracks. The middle rectangular area fronts the exit of Kyoto Railway Station. This is central Kyoto. Here are the hotels, the business district, the Pontocho geisha district, and the Kiyamachi entertainment district. Central Kyoto also contains one of the oldest city temples (Toji Temple), the rebuilt Imperial Palace, and Nijojo Castle, former Kyoto abode of the Tokugawa shoguns.

The rectangular area to the east of central Kyoto is appropriately named the eastern district (Higashiyama). This area includes Gion, which serves as a traditional shopping neighborhood by day and a geisha entertainment locale by night. Many of Kyoto's renowned tourist attractions are to be found in the eastern district; it can easily take two full days to cover them. Some of the famous sights here are the Ginkakuji Temple (Silver Pavilion), the Heian Jingu Shrine, and the Kiyomizudera Temple.

The rectangular area to the west of central Kyoto is the western district. Here are more reflections of Kyoto's past, including the Ryoanji Temple and the Kinkakuji Temple (Golden Pavilion).

An exploration of these three areas will take up most of a three-day visit to Kyoto. However, two other areas have major sights to see and experience. Farther to the west of the western district is Arashiyama, which is home to Tenryuji Temple. To the north of central Kyoto is the northern district of Mt. Hiei and Kyoto's suburb, Ohara, where the poignant story of Kenreimon-in takes place at Jakko-in Temple.

Kyoto's attractions do cover a wide area. However, many of the sights are clustered together, so you may walk from one to another. Where the sights are not near each other, you can use Kyoto's bus system, which works on a grid pattern, and is easy to follow. Maps of the bus routes are supplied by the JNTO office. The following exploring sections keep to the divisions described above so as to allow walking from one sight to another. However, notwithstanding the traffic, if armed with a bus-route map, you could cross and recross Kyoto with not too much difficulty should you wish to choose sights to suit your special interests.

Our exploration begins in the eastern district (Higashiyama); if you have time to visit only one district, this is the one we would recommend. This area has a lot to see, more than you could cover comfortably in one day, so you may want to judiciously prune some of the following itinerary according to your interests.

Eastern Kyoto (Higashiyama)

Numbers in the margin correspond to points of interest on the Eastern Kyoto map.

Let's start at the northernmost landmark in eastern Kyoto, 1 **Ginkakuji Temple.** One of Kyoto's most famous sights, it is a wonderful villa turned temple. To reach Ginkakuji, take the #5 bus from Kyoto Station to Ginkakuji-michi bus stop. Walk on the street along the canal, going east. Just after the street crosses another canal flowing north–south, there will be the **Hakusasonso Garden,** the quiet villa of the late painter Hashimoto Kansetsu, with an exquisite garden and tea house open to the public. *Admission: ¥700; with tea and sweets, an extra ¥500. Open 10–5 (enter by 4:30).*

Chion-in Temple, **24**
Chishaku-in Temple, **17**
Chorakuji Temple, **23**
Eikando Temple, **4**
Ginkakuji Temple, **1**
Gion Kaburenjo Theater, **28**
Heian Jingu Shrine, **14**
Honen-in Temple, **3**
Kawai Kanjiro Memorial House, **19**
Kiyomizudera Temple, **20**
Kodaiji Temple, **21**
Konchi-in Temple, **7**
Kyoto Craft Center, **27**
Kyoto Handicraft Center, **15**
Kyoto International Community House, **8**
Kyoto Museum of Traditional Industry, **13**
Kyoto National Museum, **18**
Kyoto Zoo, **10**
Maruyama-Koen Park, **22**
Municipal Art Museum, **11**
Murin-an Garden, **9**
Nanzenji Temple, **6**
National Museum of Modern Art, **12**
Nomura Art Museum, **5**
Path of Philosophy, **2**
Pontocho Kaburenjo Theater, **29**
Sanjusangendo Hall, **16**
Shoren-in Temple, **25**
Yasaka Jinja Shrine, **26**

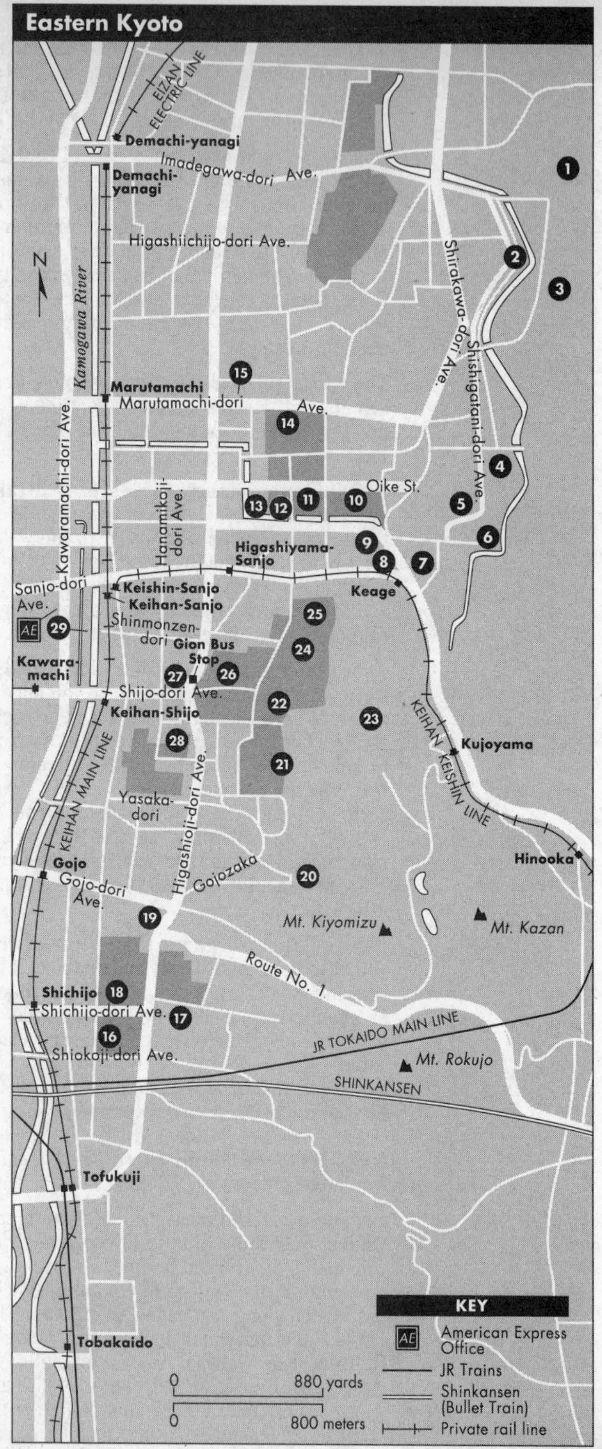

Ginkakuji means Silver Pavilion, but it's not silver. It was only intended to be. Shogun Yoshimasa Ashikaga (1435–1490) had this villa built for his retirement. He started building it as early as the 1460s, but it was not until 1474 that, disillusioned with politics, he gave his full attention to the construction of his villa and to the aesthetic arts of women, moon gazing, and the tea ceremony, which he helped develop into a high art. Though he never had time to complete the coating of the pavilion with silver foil, he had constructed a dozen or so buildings. Many of them were designed for cultural pursuits such as incense sniffing and tea tasting. On his death, the villa was converted into a Buddhist temple, as was often the custom during the feudal era. However, with the decline of the Ashikaga family, Ginkakuji fell into decline, and many buildings were destroyed.

What we see today are the two remaining original buildings, **Togudo** (East Request Hall) and **Ginkakuji,** or the **Silver Pavilion.** The four other structures on the grounds were built in the 17th and 19th centuries. The front room of Togudo is where Yoshimasa is thought to have lived, and the statue of the priest is probably of Yoshimasa himself. The back room is called Dojinsai (Comradely Abstinence); it is noteworthy because it became the prototype for the traditional tea-ceremony room that is still used today.

Ginkakuji is a simple and unadorned two-story building. On the upper floor, it contains a gilt image of Kannon (the Goddess of Mercy) said to have been carved by Unkei, a famous Kamakura-period sculptor, though it is not ordinarily open to public view. Mostly it is the exterior shape of the structure that is so appealing and restful, as it combines Chinese elements with the developing Japanese Muromachi (1333–1568) architecture. Ginkakuji overlooks the complex gardens attributed to architect and artist Soami. They are in two sections and serve to contrast each other to establish a balance. Adjacent to the pavilion is the pond, with a composition of rocks and plants designed to offer different perspectives from each viewpoint; the other garden has two sculptured mounds of sand, with the higher one perhaps symbolizing Mt. Fuji. The garden sparkles in the moonlight and has been aptly named "Sea of Silver Sand." *Ginkakuji-machi, Sakyo-ku. Admission: ¥400 adults, ¥200 children 6–15. Open Mar. 15–Nov. 30, 8:30–5; winter, 9–4:30.*

If you can tear yourself away from Ginkakuji, retrace your steps on the entrance road until you reach, on your left, the

❷ **Path of Philosophy** or, as the Japanese say, "Tetsugaku-no-michi." This walkway along the canal is lined with cherry trees and has been a place for contemplative strolls since a famous scholar, Ikutaro Nishida, took his constitutional along the shaded paths. Now professors and students have to push their way through tourists who take the same stroll and whose interest lies mainly with the path's specialty shops.

Time Out The Path of Philosophy has several coffee shops and small restaurants at which to stop and relax along the way. **Omen** restaurant, one block west of the Path of Philosophy, is an inexpensive, popular place, known for its homemade white noodles. If you are desperate for Western food, you can try **Bobby Soxer** for pizza.

At the fourth bridge (larger than the first three) off the path, ❸ cross over the canal and take the road east to **Honen-in Temple,** a modest structure with a thatched roof. Not too many people come here, and the walk through the trees leading to the temple is mercifully quiet and comforting. The temple was built in 1680, on a site that in the 13th century simply consisted of an open-air Amida statue. Honen-in honors a man, Priest Honen (1133–1212), who brought Buddhism down from its lofty peak to the common folk. He made the radical claim that all were equal in the eyes of Buddha. Honen focused on faith in the Amida Buddha; he believed that *nembutsu* ("Namu Amida Butsu," the invocation of Amida Buddha), which he is said to have repeated up to 60,000 times a day, and reliance on Amida, the All-Merciful, were the path of salvation. Because his ideas threatened other sects, especially the Tendai sect, Honen's teachings of "Jodo-shu, the the Pure Land Sect," were accused of advocating that the masses seduce the ladies of noble classes. At the insistence of the established Buddhist powers, Emperor Gotoba had several of Honen's followers executed and Honen sent to exile. Eventually, in 1211, Honen was pardoned and permitted to return to Kyoto, where a year later, at Chion-in Temple, he fasted to death at the age of 79. *Admission free. Open 7–4.*

From Honen-in Temple, walk back to the Path of Philosophy and continue in a southerly direction. In 15 minutes or so you'll ❹ reach **Eikando Temple** on your left.

Eikando is the temple's popular name. Officially it is Zenrinji Temple, founded in 856 by Priest Shinsho, but it honors the memory of an 11th-century priest, Priest Eikan, which explains the popular name. He was a man of the people and would lead them in a dance in celebration of Amida Buddha. On one such occasion, the Amida statue came to life and stepped down from his pedastal to join the dancers. Taken aback, Eikan slowed his dancing feet. Amida looked back over his shoulder to reprimand Eikan for slowing his pace. This is the legend that explains why the unusal statue in the Amidado Hall has its face turned to the side, as if glancing backward. For the energetic, a climb to the top of the pagoda offers superb views of the grounds below and Kyoto beyond. In autumn, the grounds are especially magnificent with the turning leaves of the maple trees. The buildings are 16th-century reconstructions made after the originals were destroyed in the Onin War (1467–1477). *Admission: ¥400. Open 9–5 (enter by 4:30).*

If you cross the street from Eikando Temple, and continue ❺ south, you'll see the **Nomura Art Museum** on the right. Instead of bequeathing their villas to Buddhist sects, the modern wealthy Japanese tend to donate their art collections to museums. Such is the case here. Founder of the Daiwa Bank and a host of other companies, Tokushichi Nomura gave his collection of scrolls, paintings, tea-ceremony utensils, ceramics, and other art objects to establish his namesake museum. *61 Shimogawara-cho, Nanzen-ji, Sakyo-ku, tel. 075/751–0374. Admission: ¥600. Open (enter by 4) 10–4:30 late-Mar.–mid-June and mid-Sept.–early Dec. Closed Mon. (when national holidays fall on Mon., the museum is open and will close the following day).*

(If the day is close to an end, walk from the Nomura Art Museum to the Heian Jingu Shrine, and the Kyoto Handicraft Center on Marutamachi-dori behind it. If not, continue this tour, which will come back shortly to the Heian Jingu Shrine.)

Next, walk south from the Nomura Art Museum and follow the 6 main path; on your left you'll reach **Nanzenji Temple,** which is another one of those retirement villas turned into a temple on the death of its owner. This donor was Emperor Kameyama (1249–1305). The Onin Civil War (1467–1477) demolished the buildings, but some were resurrected during the 16th century, and Nanzenji has become one of Kyoto's most important temples, in part because it is the headquarters of the Rinzai sect of Zen Buddhism. As you enter the temple, you'll pass through the **Sanmon** (Triple Gate), built in 1628. This is the classic "gateless" gate of Zen Buddhism serving as a symbol of entrance into the most sacred part of the temple precincts. From the top floor of the gate there is a view of Kyoto spread out below. The steps are pretty steep, and you might decide to forgo the pleasure, but give a moment to Goemon Ishikawa, a Robin Hood–style outlaw of Japan who hid in this gate until his eventual capture.

On through the gate is the **Hojo Hall,** a National Treasure. Inside, the chambers are divided by screens with impressive 16th-century paintings. These wall panels of the *Twenty-four Paragons of Filial Piety and Hermits* are by Eitoku Kano (1543–1590) of the Kano school (really the Kano family, because the school consists of eight generations—Eitoku being from the fifth—of one bloodline). The Zen-style garden attached to the Hojo Hall has stones amid the sculpted trees and sand. This garden has been assigned several names, but the one that stands out is "Leaping Tiger Garden."

Within Nanzenji's 27 pine tree–covered acres are several other temples, known more for their gardens than for their buildings. Two are worth visiting if you have time. The first is **Nanzen-in Temple,** once the temporary abode of the Kameyama (1249–1305), who founded the temple. Nanzen-in holds a mausoleum and has a garden that dates to the 14th century; a small creek passes through it. Only recently open to the public, Nanzen-in is not as famous as other temples, making it a peaceful place to visit. *Admission: ¥350. Open Nov.–Mar., 8:30–4:30 and Apr.–Oct., 8:20–5.*

The other temple worth visiting is outside the main gate of Nanzenji but still part of it. As you leave Nanzenji, take the 7 side street to the left and you will come to **Konchi-in Temple,** with its pair of gardens, one with a pond in the shape of the Chinese character *kokoro,* or heart, and the other a dry garden with a "sea of sand" and a backdrop of greenery borrowed from the mountains behind. The garden was designed by the famous tea master and landscape designer, Kobori Enshu, in 1632. The two rock groupings in front of a plant-filled mound are in the crane-and-tortoise style. Since ancient times these creatures have been associated with longevity, beauty, and eternal youth. In the feudal eras, the symbolism of the crane and the tortoise became very popular with the samurai class, whose profession often left them with only the hope of immortality. *86 Fukuchi- cho, Nanzenji, Sakyo-ku. Admission: ¥400 adults, ¥300 high school students, ¥200 for children under 12. Open 8:30–5 (8:30–4:30 in winter).*

(8) At the intersection at the foot of the road to Nanzenji, you'll see the expansive grounds of the **Kyoto International Community House** across the street to the left. The center offers library and information facilities and rental halls for public performances. The bulletin board by the entry way is full of tips on housing, study, and events in Kyoto. The KICH also offers weekly lessons in tea ceremony, koto, calligraphy, and Japanese language at reasonable prices. The book *Easy Living in Kyoto* (available free) gives helpful information for a lengthy stay. *2-1 Awata-guchi, Torii-cho, Sakyo-ku, tel. 075/752–3010. Admission free. Open 9 AM–9 PM. Closed Mon. (when Mon. is a national holiday, the House closes the following day instead).*

(9) Walk back to the main road to Nanzenji and turn left. Cross at the traffic light to **Murin-an Garden,** whose entrance is on a side road half a block east. The property was once part of Nanzenji Temple, but it was sold to Prince Yamagata, a former prime minister and advocate of the reforms which followed the Meiji Restoration (1868). The garden incorporates new ideas into Japanese thinking, just as the Meiji Restoration did. There is more freedom of movement in this garden than in the rigid, perfected harmony of more traditional gardens. *Admission: ¥200. Open 9–4:30. Closed Dec. 29–Jan. 3.*

(10) Walk back toward the canal and turn left. If you were to cross the canal at the first right, you would be at the **Kyoto Zoo.** There is no pressing reason to visit it, unless you have children in tow. The zoo has a Children's Corner, where your youngsters can feed the farm animals. *Hoshoji-cho, Okazaki, Sakyo-ku, tel. 075/771–0210. Admission: ¥400 adults, free for elementary-school children and younger. Open 9–5, Dec.–Feb. 9–4:30. Closed Mon. (When Mon. is a national holiday, it closes the following day instead.)*

Unless you turn off for the zoo, continue to the next right and cross the bridge over the canal. You'll see an immense vermilion *torii* gate, because this is the road that leads to the Heian Jingu  Shrine. Immediately after the torii gate, the **Municipal Art** (12) **Museum** will be on your right, and the **National Museum of Modern Art** will be on your left.

The Municipal Art Museum is primarily an exhibition hall for traveling shows and those of local art societies. It owns a collection of Japanese paintings of the Kyoto school, a selection of which goes on exhibit once a year. *Enshoji-cho, Okazaki, Sakyo-ku, tel. 075/771–4107. Admission: depends on exhibition, but usually around ¥600. Open 9–5 (enter by 4:30). Closed Mon.*

The National Museum of Modern Art, established in 1903, reopened in 1986 in a new building designed by Fumihiko Maki, one of the top contemporary architects in Japan. The museum is known for its collection of 20th-century Japanese paintings, as well as for its ceramic treasures by Kanjiro Kawai, Rosanji Kitaoji, Shoji Hamada, and others. *Enshoji-cho, Okazaki, Sakyo-ku, tel. 075/761–4111. Admission: ¥400 (more for special exhibitions). Open 9:30–5. Closed Mon.*

(13) The **Kyoto Museum of Traditional Industry** (Dento Sangyo Kaikan) houses a wide array of traditional Kyoto crafts. It has been closed for renovations for two years but is scheduled to reopen in 1994. *9-2 Seishoji-cho, Okazaki, Sakyo-ku, tel. 075/*

761–3421. Admission free. Open 9–5 (enter by 4:30). Closed Mon.

14 The street between the Municipal Art Museum and the National Museum of Modern Art leads directly to the **Heian Jingu Shrine.** This shrine is one of Kyoto's newest historical sites. It was built in 1895 to mark the 1,100th anniversary of the founding of Kyoto. The shrine is dedicated to two emperors: Kammu (737–806), who founded the city in 794, and Komei (1831–1866), the last emperor to live out his reign in Kyoto. The new buildings are for the most part replicas of the old Imperial Palace, but only two-thirds the original size. In fact, because the original palace (rebuilt many times) was finally destroyed in 1227, and only scattered pieces of information are available relating to its construction, the Heian Jingu Shrine should be taken as a Meiji interpretation of the old palace. Still, the dignity and the relative spacing of the **East Honden, West Honden** (Main Halls), and the **Daigokuden** (Great Hall of State), where the Heian emperor would issue decrees, conjure up an image of the magnificence that the Heian court must have presented.

During New Year, the imposing gravel forecourt leading to Daigokuden is trampled by kimono-clad and gray-suited Japanese who come to pay homage; the most wonderful time to visit is in the spring, during cherry-blossom time. The gardens are also a modern interpretation of a Heian garden, but they follow the Heian aesthetic of focusing on a large pond whose shores are gracefully linked by the arched Taibei-kaku Chinese-style bridge. An even better time to visit the shrine is during Jidai Festival, held on October 22. The festival celebrates the founding of Kyoto. The pageant features a procession of 2,000 people, attired in costumes from every period of Kyoto history. It winds its way from the original site of the Imperial Palace and ends at the Heian Jingu Shrine. *Okazakinishi Tenno-cho, Sakyo-ku. Admission to the garden: ¥500 adults, ¥400 teenagers 15–18, ¥250 children 6–14, children under 6 free. Open Mar. 15–Aug. 31, 8:30–5:30; Sept.–Oct. and Mar. 1–Mar. 14, 8:30–5; Nov.–Feb., 8:30–4:30.*

Another choice time to be at the shrine is on June 1–2 for Takigi-noh performances. This form of Noh is so-called because it is performed at night in the open air and the lighting is provided by burning firewood *(takigi);* the performances are presented on a stage built before the shrine's Daigokuden Hall. Admission for Takigi-noh ¥3,000 at the gate; ¥2,000 in advance. Call the TIC for advance ticket outlets (*see* Important Addresses and Numbers, *above*).

15 If the urge comes on to do some shopping, on the north side of the Heian Jingu Shrine and slightly to the left, across Marutamachi-dori Avenue, is the **Kyoto Handicraft Center,** where there are seven floors of everything Japanese, from dolls to cassette recorders. The center caters to tourists. *(See* Shopping, *below.) Kumano Jinja Higashi, Sakyo-ku, tel. 075/761–5080. Open 9:30–6 (9:30–5:30 in winter). Closed Dec. 31–Jan. 3.*

At the crossroads of Marutamachi-dori Avenue and Higashioji-dori Avenue (west of the Kyoto Handicraft Center) is the Kumano Jinjya-mae bus stop. If you've had enough sightseeing for one day, just five stops south on Higashioji-dori Avenue, using Bus 202 or 206, is the Gion bus stop; here, the world of restaurants and bars is at your disposal. Gion will be discussed later. If you are going to continue sightseeing, stay on Bus 202 for five more stops (Higashiyama-Shichijo) to explore the southern part of Higashiyama. If you have taken Bus 206, stay on it for one more stop (it makes a right turn onto Shichijo-dori Ave. and heads for the station) and get off at the Sanjusangendo-mae bus stop. You may want to join this tour here tomorrow. If that is the case, you may also reach Sanjusangendo-mae bus stop by taking Bus 206 or 208 from Kyoto Station.

If you disembarked from the bus at Sanjusangendo-mae bus stop, Sanjusangendo Hall will be to the south, just beyond the Kyoto Park Hotel. If you disembarked from Bus 202 at Higashiyama-Shichijo bus stop, you need to walk down Shichijo-dori Avenue and take the first major street to the left. However, you may want to visit Chishaku-in Temple first; that will allow you to avoid doubling back.

⑯ **Sanjusangendo Hall** is the popular name for Rengeo-in Temple. Sanjusan means "33"; that is the number of spaces between the 35 pillars that lead down the narrow, 394-foot-long hall. Enthroned in the middle of the hall is the 6-foot-tall, 1,000-handed Kannon (National Treasure), carved by Tankei, a sculptor of the Kamakura period (1192–1333). Surrounding the statue are 1,000 smaller statues of Kannon, and in the corridor behind are 28 guardian deities who are protectors of the Buddhist universe. Notice the frivolous-faced Garuda, a bird that feeds on dragons. If you are wondering about the 33 spaces mentioned earlier, Kannon can assume 33 different shapes on her missions of mercy. Because there are 1,001 statues of Kannon in the hall, 33,033 shapes are possible. People come to the hall to see if they can find the likeness of a loved one (a deceased relative) among the 1,001 statues. *657 Sanjusangendo-Mawari-cho, Higashiyama-ku. Admission: ¥400 adults, ¥300 high-school and junior-high-school students, ¥200 grade-school children. Open 8–4:30 (9–3:30 in winter).*

From Sanjusangendo, you need to retrace your steps back to Shichijo-dori Avenue and take a right. Chishaku-in Temple will be facing you on the other side of Higashioji-dori Avenue.

⑰ The major reason for visiting **Chishaku-in Temple** is for its famous paintings. They were executed by Tohaku Hasegawa and his son Kyuzo (known as the Hasegawa school, rivals of the Kano school) and are some of the best examples of Momoyama art. These paintings were originally created for the sliding screens at Shoun-in Temple, a temple built in 1591 on the same site but no longer in existence. Shoun-in was commissioned by Hideyoshi Toyotomi. When his concubine, Yodogimi, bore him an heir in 1589, Hideyoshi named his son Tsurumatsu (Crane-pine), two symbols of longevity. Ironically, the child died when he was two, and Shoun-in was built for Tsurumatsu's enshrinement. The Hasegawas were then commissioned to do the paintings. Saved from the fires that destroyed Shoun-in, the paintings are now on display in the Exhibition Hall of Chishaku-in. These paintings, rich in detail and using strong colors on a gold ground, splendidly display the seasons by using the symbols of cherry, maple, pine, and plum trees and autumn grasses.

You may also want to take a few moments in the pond-viewing garden. It is only a vestige of its former glory, but from the

temple's veranda, you'll have a pleasing vie
garden. *Admission: ¥350. Open 9–4:30.*

18 Back across Higashioji-dori Avenue is the
National Museum. It has a collection of more
of art housed in two buildings. Exhibitior
changing, but you can count on an excellent display of paintings, sculpture, textiles, calligraphy, ceramics, lacquerware, metalwork, and archaeological artifacts from its permanent collection. *Yamato-oji-dori, Higashiyama-ku, tel. 075/541–1151. Admission: ¥400 (more for special exhibitions). Open 9–4:30. Closed Mon.*

19 Just north, less than a five-minute walk along Higashioji-dori Avenue from the Kyoto National Museum, is **Kawai Kanjiro Memorial House.** Now a museum, this was the home and studio of one of Japan's most renowned potters. The house was designed by Kanjiro Kawai, who took for his inspiration a traditional rural Japanese cottage. He was one of the leaders of the *Mingei* (Folk Art) Movement, which sought to promote a revival of interest in traditional folk arts during the 1920s and '30s, when all things Western were in vogue in Japan. On display are some of the artist's personal memorabilia and, of more interest, some of his exquisite works. An admirer of Western, Chinese, and Korean ceramic techniques, Kawai won many awards, including the Grand Prix at the 1937 Paris World Exposition. *Gojozaka, Higashiyama, tel. 075/561–3585. Admission: ¥700 adults, ¥500 college and high school students, ¥300 junior high students and younger. Open 10–5. Closed Mon., Aug. 10–20, Dec. 24–Jan. 7. (When Mon. is a national holiday, museum closes following day instead.)*

20 The next place to visit is a very special temple, **Kiyomizudera Temple,** which may be reached by crossing the major avenue Gojo-dori and walking up Higashioji-dori Avenue. The street to the right, Gojozaka, leads into Kiyomizuzaka, which is the street you take to the temple.

Kiyomizuzaka is lined with shops selling souvenirs, religious articles, and ceramics. There are also tea shops where you can sample *yatsuhashi,* a doughy triangular sweet filled with cinnamon-flavored bean paste—a Kyoto specialty. Because of the immense popularity of the temple above it on the hill, this narrow slope is often crowded with sightseers and bus tour groups, but the magnificent temple is worth the struggle.

Kiyomizudera Temple is a 1633 reconstruction of the temple that was built here in 798, four years after Kyoto was founded. It is a unique temple in more ways than one. It does not belong to one of the local Kyoto Buddhist sects but rather to the Hosso sect that developed in Nara. Kiyomizudera is one of the most visited temples in Kyoto and is closely associated with the city's skyline. In the past, people would come here to escape the open political intrigue of Kyoto and to scheme in secrecy. Visually, Kiyomizudera is unique because it is built on a steep hillside. Part of its Main Hall is held up by 139 giant pillars. Finally, it is one of the few temples where you can walk around the veranda without taking your shoes off.

The temple's location is marvelous. Indeed, one reason for coming here is the view. From the wood veranda you have both a fine view of the city and a breathtaking look at the valley below. "Have you the courage to jump from the veranda of Kiyomizu?"

is a saying asked when someone sets out on a daring new venture.

The temple is dedicated to the popular 11-faced Kannon (Goddess of Mercy), who can bring about easy childbirth. Over time, Kiyomizudera has become "everyone's temple"; you'll see evidence of this throughout the grounds, from the little *jizo bosatsu* statues (representing the god of travel and children) stacked in rows to the many *koma-inu* (mythical guard dogs) marking the pathways, which have been given by the temple's grateful patrons. *Kiyomizu, 1-chome, Higashiyama-ku. Admission: ¥300 adults, ¥200 junior high school students and younger. Open: 8–6.*

If you take a right halfway down the road leading from Kiyomizudera, you can walk along the Sannenzaka and Ninenzaka slopes. These two lovely winding streets are an example of old Kyoto with their cobbled paths and delightful wooden buildings. This area is one of four historic preservation districts in Kyoto, and the shops along the way offer local crafts such as *Kiyomizu-yaki* (Kiyomizu-style pottery), Kyoto dolls, bamboo basketry, rice crackers, and antiques.

Take a left after Ninenzaka Slope and then an immediate right, as you keep going in a northerly direction. After walking another five minutes, you will see, on the right, (21) **Kodaiji Temple,** a quiet nunnery established in the early 17th century and only recently opened to the public. The temple was built as a memorial to Hideyoshi Toyotomi by his wife Kita no Mandokoro, who lived out her remaining days in the nunnery there. Kodaiji has gardens designed by Kobori Enshu, and the Kaisando (Founder's Hall) has ceilings decorated in raised lacquer and paintings by artists of the Tosa school. The teahouse above on the hill was designed by tea master Sen no Rikyu. It has a unique umbrella-shape bamboo ceiling and a thatched roof. *Admission: ¥500. Open 9–4:30 (9–4 in winter).*

Continuing northward: by doing a right–left zigzag at the Maruyama Music Hall, you reach (22) **Maruyama-Koen Park.** The road to the right (east) leads to (23) **Chorakuji Temple,** which is behind Higashi-Otani. Chorakuji Temple is famous today for the stone lanterns that lead to it. Although it's a pleasant temple, it may not be worth the hard climb up the mountainside.

Proceed north through Maruyama-Koen Park and you'll find (24) **Chion-in Temple,** headquarters of the Jodo sect of Buddhism, the second largest Buddhist sect in Japan. The entrance here is through a 79-foot, two-story Sanmon Gate. In many people's minds, this is the most daunting temple gate in all of Japan, and it leads to one of Japan's largest temples. On the site of Chion-in, Honen, the founder of the Jodo sect, fasted and died in 1212. The temple was built in 1234; because of fires and earthquakes, the oldest standing buildings are the Main Hall (1633) and the Daihojo Hall (1639). The temple's belfry houses the largest bell in Japan, which was cast in 1633 and requires 17 monks to ring. The corridor behind the Main Hall, which leads to the Assembly Hall, is called *uguisu bari* (nightingale floor). It was constructed to "sing" at every footstep to warn the monks of intruders. Walk underneath the corridor to examine the way the boards and nails are placed to create this inventive burglar alarm. *400 Hayashishita-cho, 3-chome, Yamato Oji, Higashi-Hairu, Shinbashi-dori, Higashiyama-ku. Admission: ¥300* *adults, ¥200 junior-high-school students and younger. Open 9–4:30 (9–4 in winter). Not all buildings are open to the public.*

25 More paintings by the Kano school are on view at the **Shoren-in Temple,** a five-minute walk to the north of Chion-in. Though the temple's present building dates only from 1895, the sliding screens of the Main Hall have the works of Motonobu Kano, second-generation Kano, and Mitsunobu Kano of the sixth generation. The gardens of this temple are pleasant—with an immense camphor tree at the entrance gate and azaleas surrounding a balanced grouping of rocks and plants. It was no doubt more grandiose when Soami designed it in the 16th century, but with the addition of paths through the garden, it invites a stroll. Another garden on the east side of the temple is sometimes attributed, probably incorrectly, to Kobori Enshu. Occasionally, koto concerts are held in the evening in the Soami garden. (Check with a Japan Travel Bureau office for concert schedules.) *Admission: ¥400. Open 9–5. Closed one day in Oct. or Nov. for a special Buddhist ceremony (no specific date is set).*

Should you have missed visiting the Heian Jingu Shrine, the National Museum of Modern Art, and the Municipal Museum of Art described earlier, these are just 10 minutes by foot north of Shoren-in, on the other side of Sanjo-dori Avenue. If you take a right (east) from Shoren-in on Sanjo-dori Avenue, you'll eventually reach the Miyako Hotel; left (west) on Sanjo-dori Avenue leads across Higashioji-dori Avenue to the downtown area and covered mall. If you turn left on Higashioji-dori Avenue, you will reach Shijo-dori Avenue and the Gion district.

At the Gion bus stop, Shijo-dori Avenue goes off to the right (west). Before going down this street, consider taking a short
26 walk east (into Maruyama-Koen Park) to **Yasaka Jinja Shrine.** Because its location is close to the shopping districts, worshipers drop by for some quick salvation. This is a good shrine to come to if you have business or health problems; you'll want to come here to leave a message for the God of Prosperity and Good Health, to whom the shrine is dedicated. Especially at New Year, Kyoto residents flock here to ask for good fortune for the coming year. *625 Gion-machi, Kitagawa, Higashiyama-ku. Admission free. Open 24 hours.*

Walk back from Yasaka Jinja, cross Higashioji-dori Avenue, and you are in Kyoto's Gion district. This is Shijo-dori Avenue.
27 On the right-hand corner is the **Kyoto Craft Center,** where Kyoto residents shop for fine contemporary and traditional crafts—ceramics, lacquerware, prints, and textiles. You can also find moderately priced souvenirs, such as dolls, coasters, bookmarks, and paper products. *Higashi-Kitagawa, Hanamikoji, Gion-Shijo-dori, Higashiyama-ku, tel. 075/561–9660. Open 10–6. Closed Wed.*

Parallel to Shijo-dori Avenue and to the north is Shinmonzen Street. This street is famous for its antiques shops and art galleries. Here you'll find collectors' items—at collectors' prices, too—but there is no harm in just browsing. The shops on Shijo-dori Avenue have slightly more affordable products, from handcrafted hair ornaments to incense to parasols—all articles that are part of the geisha world.

Off Shijo-dori Avenue, halfway between Higashioji-dori and the Kamogawa, is Hanamikoji-dori Avenue. The section of this street that runs south of Shijo-dori (on the right, if you are walking back from the river) will bring you into the heart of the Gion district. Here is where the top geisha live and work; they can be seen scurrying in the evening en route to their assignments, trailed by young apprentice geisha (*maiko*), who can be distinguished from their mistresses by the longer sleeve lengths of their kimonos. Because Westerners have little opportunity to enjoy a geisha's performance in a private party setting, a popular entertainment during the month of April is

28 the Miyako-Odori (Cherry Blossom Dance) held at the **Gion Kaburenjo Theater** (Gion Hanamikoji, Higashiyama-ku, tel. 075/561–1115). Miyako-Odori features musical presentations by geisha, who are dressed in their elaborate traditional kimonos and makeup. Next door to the theater is **Gion Corner,** where demonstrations of traditional performing arts are held nightly from March through November (*see* The Arts and Nightlife, *below*).

If you continue east along Shijo-dori Avenue, you'll cross over the Kamogawa River; on your right will be Pontocho-dori Avenue. Like Gion, this area is known for its nightlife and geisha entertainment. At the top (north) end of Pontocho-dori Ave-

29 nue, the **Pontocho Kaburenjo Theater** presents geisha song-and-dance performances in the spring (May 1–May 24) and autumn (Oct. 15–Nov. 7). *Pontocho, Sanjo Sagaru, Nakagyo-ku, tel. 075/221–2025.*

Western Kyoto

Numbers in the margin correspond to points of interest on the Western Kyoto map.

This exploration starts at the northern part of western Kyoto, where the major attractions are located. Then, if you become tired or run out of time, you can cut short the tour and return to your hotel. We have chosen to begin this exploration at the Kitano Temmangu Shrine because it is a Kyoto landmark, but if you are short of time, you may want to begin at Daitokuji Temple.

To reach the Kitano Temmangu Shrine from downtown, take either Bus 50 or 52 from downtown Kyoto and Kyoto Station.

1 The rides take a little more than ½ hour. The **Kitano Temmangu Shrine** made history in about 942 when Michizane Sugawara was enshrined here. Previously the shrine had been dedicated to Tenjin, the god of thunder. Michizane had been a noted poet and politician, but when Emperor Godaigo ascended to the throne, Michizane was accused of treason and sent to exile on Kyushu, where he died. For decades afterward, Kyoto suffered inexplicable calamities. Then the answer came in a dream. The problem was Michizane's spirit; he would not rest until he had been pardoned. Because the dream identified Michizane with the god of thunder, Kitano Temmangu Shrine was dedicated to him. Furthermore, Michizane's rank as minister of the right was posthumously restored. When that was not enough, he was promoted to the higher position of minister of the left, and later to prime minister. The shrine was also the place where Hideyoshi Toyotomi held an elaborate tea party, inviting the whole of Kyoto to join him. Apart from unifying the warring clans of Japan and attempting to conquer Korea, Toyotomi is remembered in Kyoto as the man responsible for

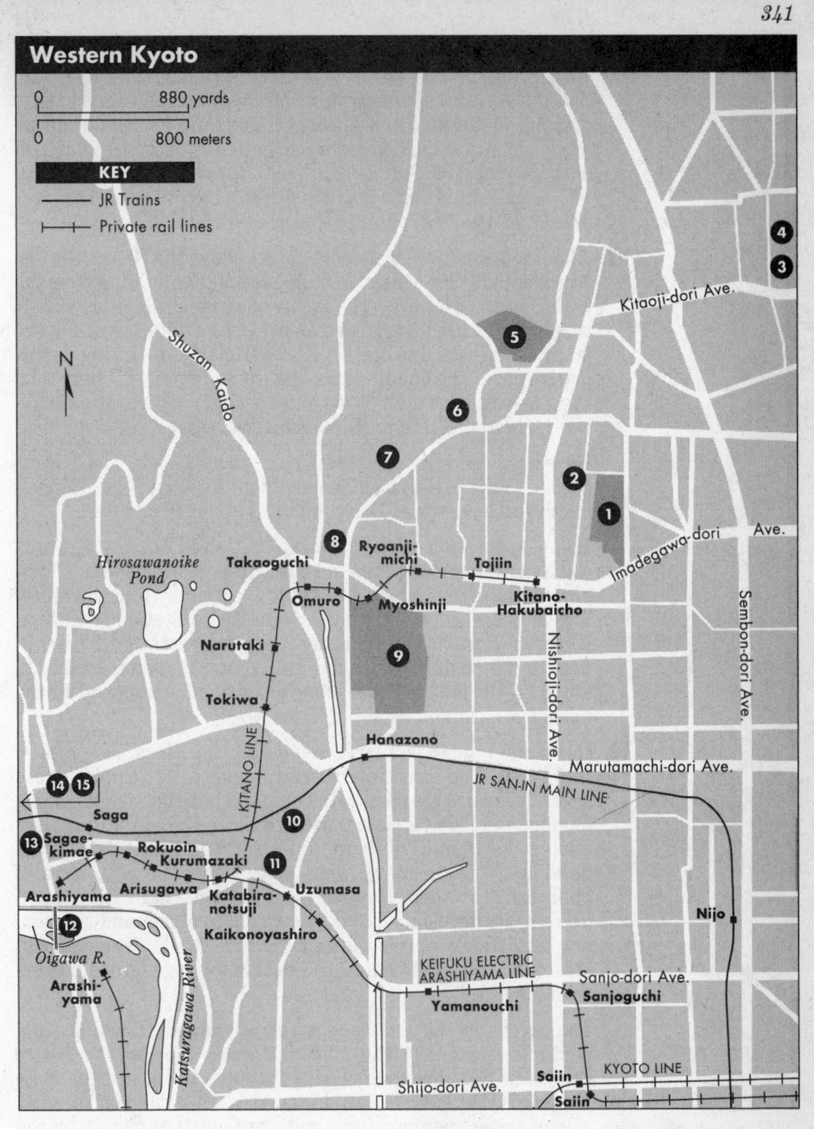

Bamboo forest, **14**
Daisen-in, **4**
Daitokuji Temple, **3**
Hirano Shrine, **2**
Kinkakuji Temple, **5**
Kitano Temmangu Shrine, **1**
Koryuji Temple, **11**
Kyoto Municipal Domoto Insho Art Museum, **6**
Myoshinji Temple, **9**
Ninnaji Temple, **8**
Okochi Sanso Villa, **15**
Ryoanji Temple, **7**
Tenryuji Temple **13**
Togetsukyo Bridge, **12**
Uzumasa Eigamura Movie Village, **10**

restoring many of the city's temples and shrines during the late 16th century. The shrine's present structure, by the way, dates from 1607. A large flea market is held on the shrine's grounds on the 25th of each month; there are food stalls and an array of antiques, old kimonos, and other collectibles. *Bakuro-cho, Kamigyo-ku. Admission free. The plum garden is open in Feb. and Mar. Admission: ¥400 (includes green tea). Shrine open 5:30 AM–6 PM; plum garden open 10 AM–4 PM.*

2 About a five-minute walk north of Kitano is the **Hirano Shrine,** which actually consists of four shrine buildings dating from the 17th century. However, the shrine has a much older history. It was brought from Nagaoka (the previous capital) as one of the many shrines used to protect Kyoto (Heian-kyo) during its formative days. The buildings are less the reason to visit here than the gardens, with their 80 varieties of cherry trees. *Miyamoto-cho 1, Hirano, Kita-ku. Admission free. Open 6 AM–5 PM.*

Now head for Daitokuji Temple. If you go east from Hirano Shrine to the bus stop on Sembon-dori Avenue, Bus 206 going north will have you at Daitokuji in less than 10 minutes.

If you do not want to start the exploration of Western Kyoto at the Kitano Temmangu Shrine but instead with Daitokuji Temple, you have several ways to get to the temple from downtown Kyoto. Take the subway north from Kyoto Station to Kitaoji-Eki-mae Station, and take any bus going west along Kitaoji-dori to the Daitokuji-mae bus stop. You can also take Bus 12 north up Horikawa-dori Avenue and disembark soon after the bus makes a left on Kitaoji-dori Avenue.

3 **Daitokuji Temple** is a large temple of the Rinzai sect of Zen Buddhism. The name refers to a complex of 24 temples in all, several of which are open to the public. The original temple was founded in 1319 by Priest Daito Kokushi (1282–1337), but fires during the Onin Civil Wars destroyed it in 1468. Most of the buildings you see today were built under the patronage of Hideyoshi Toyotomi. However, it is thought that Priest Ikkyu oversaw its development. Ikkyu was both a poet and a priest, and he certainly caused a few tongues to wag. He is reported to have said, "Brothels are more suitable settings for meditation than temples."

The layout of the temple is straightforward. Running from north to south are the Chokushi-mon, the Sanmon Gate, Butsuden (Buddha Hall), Hatto (Lecture Hall), and the Hojo (Abbots' Quarters). The 23 subtemples are located on the west side of these main buildings and were donated mainly by the wealthy vassals of Toyotomi.

The **Chokushi-mon** (Gate of Imperial Messengers) originally served as the south gate of Kyoto's Imperial Palace when it was constructed in 1590. Then, Empress Meisho in the mid-17th century bequeathed it to the Daitokuji. It is appreciated today for its curved-gable style, typical of the Momoyama period. The Sanmon triple gate is noteworthy for the addition of its third story, designed by tea master Sen-no-Rikyu (1521–1591), who is, by the way, buried in the temple grounds. *Daitokuji-cho, Murasakino, Kita-ku, Kyoto. Admission to different temples averages ¥500. Temple hours vary between 9 and 4.*

4 Of all the subtemples at this complex, **Daisen-in** is perhaps the most well known, especially for its excellent landscape paint-

ings by the renowned Soami (1465–1523) and for its *karesansui* (dry-style) garden that some attribute to Soami and others to Kogaku Soko (1465–1548). The sand and stone represent the eternal aspects of nature, while the streams suggest the course of life. The single rock, once owned by Shogun Yoshimasa Ashikaga, may be seen as a ship. Be aware, though, that Daisen-in has become commercialized. *Admission: ¥400 adults, ¥270 junior-high students and younger. Open 9–5 (9–4:30 in winter).*

Another subtemple open to the public is **Koto-in,** famous for its long, maple tree–lined approach and the single stone lantern that is central to the main garden. Not as popular as Daisen-in, it is often quiet and peaceful, as is **Ryogen-in,** still another subtemple. Ryogen-in has five small gardens of moss and stone, one of which (on the north side) is the oldest in the Daitoku-ji. *Admission to each: ¥300. Open 9–4:30 (enter by 4).*

❺ The best way to our next stop, **Kinkakuji Temple,** is to hop on Bus 12 going west on Kitaoji-dori Avenue for a 10-minute ride to the Kinkakuji-mae bus stop.

For a retirement home, Kinkakuji Temple (Golden Pavilion) is pretty magnificent. Shogun Yoshimitsu Ashikaga (1358–1409) had it constructed in 1393 for the time when he quit politics (in 1394) to manage the affairs of state through the new shogun, his 10-year-old son. On Yoshimitsu's death, his son followed his father's wishes and converted the villa into a temple named Rokuonji. The structure is positioned, following the Shinden style of the Heian period, at the edge of the lake. The three-story pavilion is supported on pillars, extends over the pond, and is reflected in the calm waters. It is a beautiful sight, but it also was designed to convey its existence somewhere between heaven and earth. The pavilion was the shogun's political statement of his prestige and power. To underscore that statement, he had the ceiling of the third floor of the pavilion covered in gold leaf. Hence, not only the harmony and balance of the pavilion and its reflection, but also the richness of color shimmering in the light and in the water make Kinkakuji one of Kyoto's most powerful visions.

In 1950, a student-monk with metaphysical aspirations torched Kinkakuji and razed it to the ground. It was rebuilt in 1955 following the original design, except that all three stories were covered with gold leaf (as had been the shogun's intention) instead of only the third-floor ceiling. Marveling at this pavilion, one finds it difficult to imagine the historical perspective of the time when Shogun Yoshimitsu Ashikaga lived out his golden years. The country was in turmoil, and Kyoto residents suffered severe famines and plagues that sometimes reached death tolls of 1,000 souls a day. *1-Kinkakuji-cho, Kita-ku. Admission: ¥300 adults and older students, ¥200 junior-high school students and younger. Open 9–5:30 (9–5, Oct.–Mar.).*

From Kinkakuji, walk back to the Kinkakuji-mae bus stop and take Bus 12 or 59 south for 10 minutes to the Ritsumeikan-❻ Daigaku-mae bus stop for the **Kyoto Municipal Domoto Insho Art Museum,** which exhibits paintings and sculpture by Insho Domoto, the 20th-century abstract artist. *Kami-yanagi-cho, Hirano, Kita-ku, tel. 075/463–1348. Admission: ¥500 adults, ¥400 college and high-school students, ¥200 junior-high and* *younger students. Open 10–5. Closed Mon. and Dec. 28–Jan. 4.*

7 When you leave the Domoto Art Museum, either hop on Bus 12 or 59, or walk for about 10 minutes going south; the **Ryoanji Temple** will be on your right.

The garden at Ryoanji, rather than the temple, attracts visitors from all over the world. Knowing that the temple belongs to the Rinzai sect of Zen Buddhism helps one to appreciate the austere aesthetics of the garden. It is a dry (*kare sansui*) garden: just 15 rocks arranged in three groupings of seven, five, and three in gravel. From the temple's veranda, the proper viewing place, only 14 rocks can be seen at one time. Move slightly and another rock appears and one of the original 14 disappears. That's significant. In the Buddhist world, 15 is a number which denotes completeness. You must have a total view of the garden to make it a whole and meaningful experience.

Ideally, one would make a special trip out to Ryoanji in the morning before the crowds come, disturbing the contemplative scene. If you do need a moment or two to yourself, there is a small restaurant on the temple grounds near an ancient pond, where you can rest awhile with an expensive beer. *13 Goryoshita-machi, Ryoanji, Ukyo-ku. Admission: ¥350 adults, ¥200 junior high school students. Open 8–5 (8:30–4:30 Dec.–Feb.)*

8 From Ryoanji, it is about a mile farther south on Bus 26 to Myoshinji Temple. En route there will be the **Ninnaji Temple** on the right. The temple was once the palace of Emperor Omuro, who started the building's construction in 896. Needless to say, nothing of that remains. The complex of buildings that stands today was rebuilt in the 17th century. There is an attractive five-story pagoda (built 1637), and the Main Hall, which was moved from the Imperial Palace, is also worth noting as a National Treasure, with its focus of worship, the Amida Buddha. *Admission: ¥350. Open 9–5.*

At Ninnaji, take the street veering to the left (southwest direction); within ½ mile you'll reach Myoshinji. Another option from Ryoanji is to take Bus 12 or 59 three stops south to Ninnaji and then change to Bus 8 or 10.

9 Should you wish to see Japan's oldest bell (cast in 698), it hangs in the belfry near the South Gate of **Myoshinji Temple.** The temple complex is large; in all, it has some 40 structures, though only four are open to the public. Myoshinji was founded in the 14th century. When Emperor Hanazono died, his villa was converted into a temple and the work required so many laborers that a complex of buildings was built to house them. Beware of the dragon on the ceiling of Myoshinji's Hatto (Lecture Hall). Known as the "Dragon Glaring in Eight Directions," it will be looking at you wherever you stand. *Admission: ¥400. Open 9–4.*

The other temple to visit is **Taizoin,** which was built in 1404; like the rest of the Myoshinji Temple complex, it suffered in the Onin War and had to be rebuilt. Taizoin has a famous painting by Sanraku Kano called *Four Sages of Mt. Shang,* recalling the four wise men who lived in isolation on a mountain to avoid the reign of destruction. The garden of Taizoin is gentle and quiet—a good place to rest. *Admission: ¥400. Open 9–5.*

Leave the temple complex by the south side and you can pick up Bus 61 or 62; both go southwest to the Uzumasa Eigamura Movie Village. If, however, you have no interest in stopping off here—a visit will take at least two or three hours—continue on the bus to Koryuji Temple.

⑩ **Uzumasa Eigamura Movie Village** is Japan's equivalent of the United States' Hollywood. Had Kyoto been severely damaged in World War II, this would have been the place to see old Japan. Traditional country villages, ancient temples, and old-fashioned houses make up the stage sets, and if you are lucky, a couple of actors dressed as samurai will be snarling at each other, ready to draw their swords. It is a fine place to bring children. For adults, whether it is worth the time touring the facilities and visiting the museum depends on your interest in Japanese movies. *10 Higashi-Hachigaoka-cho, Uzumasa, tel. 075/881–7716. Admission: ¥1,800. Open 9–5 (9:30–4 in winter). Closed Dec. 21–Jan. 1.*

⑪ **Koryuji Temple** is a short walk south of Uzumasa Eigamura Movie Village. One of Kyoto's oldest temples, it was founded in 622 by Kawakatsu Hata in memory of Prince Shotoku (572–621). Shotoku, known for issuing the Seventeen-Article Constitution, was the first powerful advocate of Buddhism after it was introduced to Japan in 552. In the Hatto (Lecture) Hall of the main temple stand three statues, each a National Treasure. The center of worship is the seated figure of Buddha, flanked by the figures of the Thousand-Handed Kannon and Fukukenjaku-Kannon. In the rear hall (Taishido) is a wood statue of Prince Shotoku, which is thought to have been carved by him personally. Another statue of Shotoku in this hall was probably made when he was 16 years old.

In the temple's Treasure House (Reihoden), you'll find numerous works of art, many of which are National Treasures, including the most famous of all, the Miroku-Bosatsu. The statue has been declared Japan's number one National Treasure. This image of Buddha is the epitome of serene calmness, and of all the Buddhas that you see in Kyoto, this is likely to be the one that will most captivate your heart. No one knows when it was made, but it is thought to be from the 6th or 7th century, perhaps even carved by Shotoku himself. *Hachigaoka-cho, Uzumasa, Ukyo-ku. Admission: ¥500. Open Mar.–Nov., 9–5; Dec.–Feb., 9–4:30.*

From Koryuji, it is easy to head back into downtown Kyoto. Either take the bus (60–64) back past the Movie Village to Hanazono JR Station, where the JR San-in Line will take you into Kyoto Station, or take the privately owned railway, the Keifuku Electric Railway Arashiyama Line, and go east to its last stop at Shijo Omiya. This stop is on Shijo-dori Avenue, where Buses 201 or 203 will take you to Gion, or Bus 26 will take you to Kyoto Station.

However, because we are so close to the area known as Arashiyama, we are going to take the Keifuku Electric Railway Arashiyama Line going west to Tenryuji Temple and the bamboo forests just to the north. This visit is a pleasant end to the day. You may get the chance to watch some cormorant fishing. If you decide to postpone this excursion until tomorrow, use the JR San-in Line from Kyoto Station to Saga Station, or use the Keifuku Electric Railway Arashiyama Station.

Arashiyama

The pleasure of Arashiyama, the westernmost part of Kyoto, is the same as it was a millennium ago. The gentle foothills of the mountains, covered with cherry and maple trees, are splendid, but it is the bamboo forests that really create the atmosphere of untroubled peace. It is no wonder that the aristocracy of feudal Japan liked to come here and leave behind the famine, riots, and political intrigue that plagued Kyoto with the decline of the Ashikaga Shogunate.

To the south of Arashiyama Station is the Oigawa River and the ⓬ **Togetsukyo Bridge.** During the evening in July and August you can watch *ukai* (cormorant) fishing from this bridge. Fishermen use cormorants to scoop up small sweetfish, which are attracted to the light from the flaming torches hung over the fisherman's boats. The cormorants would love to swallow the fish, but small rings around their necks prevent their appetites from being assuaged. After about five fish, the cormorant has more than his gullet can hold. Then the fisherman pulls the bird back on a string, makes the bird regurgitate his catch, and sends him back for more. The best way to watch this spectacle is to join one of the charter passenger boats. *Cost: ¥1,500 adults, ¥750 children. Reservations: Arashiyama Tsusen, 14-4 Nakao-shita-cho, Arashiyama, Nishikyo-ku, tel. 075/861–0223 or 861–0302. You may also contact the Japan Travel Bureau (075/361–7241) or your hotel information desk.*

The temple to head for is Tenryuji. If you have arrived at Arashiyama Station, walk north; if you have arrived on the JR line at Saga Station, walk west.

⓭ **Tenryuji Temple** is for good reason known as the Temple of the Heavenly Dragon. Emperor Godaigo, who had successfully brought an end to the Kamakura Shogunate, was unable to hold on to his power. He was forced from his throne by Takauji Ashikaga. After Godaigo died, Takauji had twinges of conscience. That is when Priest Muso Kokushi had a dream in which a golden dragon rose from the nearby Oigawa River. He told the shogun about his dream and interpreted it to mean the spirit of Godaigo was not at peace. Worried that this was an ill omen, Takauji built Tenryuji in 1339 on the same spot where Godaigo had his favorite villa. Apparently that appeased the spirit of the late emperor. In the Hatto (Lecture) Hall, where today's monks meditate, a huge "Cloud Dragon" is painted on the ceiling. Now for the bad news. The temple was often ravaged by fire, and the current buildings are as recent as 1900; the painting of the dragon was rendered by 20th-century artist Shonen Suzuki. The garden of Tenryuji dates to the 14th century. It is noted for the arrangement of vertical stones in the large pond and for being one of the first to use "borrowed scenery," incorporating the mountains in the distance into the design of the garden. *68 Susukino-Baba-cho, Saga-Tenryu-ji, Ukyo-ku. Garden admission: ¥500 adults, ¥300 junior-high-school students and younger. (An additional ¥100 is required to enter the temple building). Open Apr.–Oct., 8:30–5:30; Nov.–Mar., 8:30–5.*

One of the best ways to enjoy some contemplative peace is to walk the estate grounds of one of Japan's new elite—Denjiro Okochi, a renowned silent movie actor of samurai films. To reach his estate, you must either walk through the temple gar-